Later Auden

Also by Edward Mendelson

Early Auden

Later Auden

EDWARD MENDELSON

faber and faber

First published in Great Britain
by Faber and Faber Limited
3 Queen Square London WC1N 3AU

Printed in England by Clays Ltd, St Ives plc

A CIP record for this book
is available from the British Library

ISBN 0-571-19784-1

For Cheryl

Contents

Preface and Acknowledgments   ix

Introduction   xiii

PART ONE

Vision and After

1939–1947

    I   Demon or Gift   3

   II   The Vision Enters   31

  III   Against the Devourer   61

  IV   Investigating the Crime   89

    V   It Without Image   122

  VI   Imaginary Saints   148

 VII   The Absconded Vision   175

VIII   The Murderous Birth   205

  IX   Asking for Neighborhood   242

PART TWO

The Flesh We Are

1948–1957

  X   The Murmurs of the Body   277

 XI   Waiting for a City   306

XII   The Great Quell   332

XIII   Number or Face   360

XIV   The Altering Storm   389

PART THREE
Territorial
1958–1973

XV   Poet of the Encirclement   417

XVI   The Air Changes   440

XVII   This Time Final   462

XVIII   The Concluding Carnival   493

Notes   523

Index   561

Preface and Acknowledgments

This book is a history and an interpretation of W. H. Auden's work from the time he moved from England to the United States in 1939 until his death in 1973. It finishes the story begun in a book called *Early Auden*, although each of the two books was also written to be a narrative complete in itself.

The most rapid and drastic changes in Auden's life occurred during a period of about a dozen years starting around 1936. In *Early Auden* I devoted almost as much space to 1936–38 as to the nine preceding years; in this book I devote as much space to 1939–47 as to the next quarter century. But in both books, I argue that the poems Auden wrote before and after this period of psychological and historical crises were as memorable as those he wrote during it; here, I argue further that much of his most profound and personal work was written in the last fifteen years of his life.

Auden divided his 1966 *Collected Shorter Poems* into four sections, each representing what he described in his foreword as a "chapter in my life." The last two sections, dated 1939–47, when he was living in the United States all year round, and 1948–57, when he wintered in Italy, correspond to the first two parts of this book; the third part covers the work of his last years, when he wintered in Austria.

Auden frequently revised the poems he had written from the late 1920s to the early 1940s, and dropped some famous ones from his canon. The poems discussed in this volume were first published in book form in *Another Time* (1940), *The Double Man* (1941; British title *New Year*

Letter), *For the Time Being* (1944), *The Collected Poetry of W. H. Auden* (1945; similar to the British *Collected Shorter Poems 1930–1944*, 1950), *The Age of Anxiety* (1948), *Nones* (1951), *The Shield of Achilles* (1955), *Homage to Clio* (1960), *About the House* (1965), *City Without Walls* (1969), *Epistle to a Godson* (1972), and the posthumous and uncompleted *Thank You, Fog* (1974). Almost all are available, in texts based on Auden's final revisions, in his *Collected Poems* (second edition, 1991). I usually quote from the original editions, although when referring to poems from Auden's earlier years that first appeared without titles, I have sometimes used the titles Auden added later. In quoting Auden's letters and other unpublished work I have corrected spellings where necessary but have left punctuation mostly unchanged.

═══

Nicholas Jenkins and Katherine Bucknell helped me to think about every aspect of Auden's career and to improve every page of this book. I am indebted to them for the subtlety of their understanding, the resourcefulness of their scholarship, and the steadfastness of their friendship.

Richard Davenport-Hines read a draft of the manuscript with a generous and critical eye and suggested one of the central strands of the narrative of the finished book; his biography *Auden* (1995) was an indispensable source and companion. John Fuller has for years given me the benefit of his encyclopedic knowledge of Auden's poetry and everyone else's, and did so again in the margins of the draft; my debt to his *W. H. Auden: A Commentary* (1998) will be obvious. Jane Lincoln Taylor brought her careful intelligence to the final typescript and proofs. Humphrey Carpenter, in his *W. H. Auden: A Biography* (1981) and a hundred other ways, helped me understand the shape and details of Auden's career. Stan Smith's two books entitled *W. H. Auden* (one in the Rereading Literature series, 1985, the other in the Writers and Their Work series, 1997) are highly illuminating and sympathetic, and their author has been a faithful friend through transatlantic mail, although we have never met. Other friends whose writings and conversation have been invaluable to me throughout this work include B. C. Bloomfield, David Bromwich, Caroline Walker Bynum, John Hollander, Samuel Hynes, Arthur Kirsch, Lucy McDiarmid, Wayne Proudfoot, Robert Somerville, Monroe K. Spears, Rosanna Warren, and John Whitehead. I owe a special debt for kindness and much else to Sheila Auden, Dr. Rita Auden, and Anita Money.

Auden's friends and family continued to be generous with biographical information. Among those to whom I am most indebted are many who are not alive to find their names here: above all, Chester Kallman, Dr. John B. Auden, Christopher Isherwood, Lincoln Kirstein, Charles Monteith, Ursula Niebuhr, Sir Stephen Spender, James Stern, and Tania Kurella Stern; also James Luther Adams, Hannah Arendt, Owen Barfield, Sir Isaiah Berlin, Benjamin Britten, Robert Fitzgerald, Orlan Fox, Geoffrey Gorer, Wendell Stacy Johnson, Golo Mann, Charles Miller, Sonia Brownell Orwell, Sir Peter Pears, Mary Valentine, and Amos Wilder. I am grateful for many important details to Alan Ansen, John Bridgen, Thekla Clark, Robert Craft, John Deedy, Valerie Eliot, Dorothy Farnan, James Fenton, Timothy Foote, Wallace Fowlie, Margaret Gardiner, Hans Werner Henze, J. Chester Johnson, R.W.B. Lewis, David Luke, Paul Mariani, Donald Mitchell, Janet Montefiore, Rosalie Moore, Adrian Poole, Selden Rodman, Tony Schwartz, Lady Spender, Anne and Irving Weiss, and Michael and Marny Yates.

I have relied, as always, on the intelligence and friendship of Laurence Dreyfus, Barbara Fields, and Michael Seidel. The book could not have been finished without the generous efforts of John Bodley, Glenn Horowitz, and Robert A. Wilson. Among others who gave scholarly and critical help, I want especially to thank Meryl Altman, Francesco Binni, Harold Bloom, Marcellus Blount, George Bradley, the Rev. George W. Brandt, James Buzard, Angus Cochran, Maria DiBattista, Gavin Ewart, John Gross, Jack Kroll, Suzanne Laizik, J. D. McClatchy, Mary McLeod, Nathan Neel, Jacek Niecko, Professor Dennis Nineham, Martin and Mary Price, Edward Said, Peter Schilling, Harold Stahmer, Michael Sullivan, Rachel Wetzsteon, John Willett, and Elliot R. Wolfson.

Writers whose books and articles have taught me much about Auden include Pascal Aquien, Bernard Bergonzi, John R. Boly, Edward Callan, John Carey, Peter Firchow, Herbert Greenberg, Anthony Hecht, Daniel Hoffman, Clive James, Richard A. Johnson, Bernard Knox, John Lanchester, Lachlan Mackinnon, Peter Porter, Peter Walker, and George T. Wright. Jahan Ramazani's deep and wide-ranging study, *The Poetry of Mourning* (1994), was especially valuable. Throughout this book I have tried to answer the questions asked by Michael Wood in his review of Auden's *Collected Poems* in *Parnassus* (Spring–Summer 1977).

Auden's publishers, Random House, Faber & Faber, and Princeton University Press, kindly gave permission to quote from his printed work. The chart in Chapter VIII was expertly prepared for the press by Ann

Obringer/BTD. A fellowship from the John Simon Guggenheim Foundation gave me time to write when I most needed it.

Librarians and curators have consistently been patient with my requests and importunities. Stephen Crook, Francis O. Mattson, Philip Milito, Rodney Phillips, and Lola Szladits at the Henry W. and Albert A. Berg Collection of the New York Public Library were especially generous, and I am deeply indebted also to curators and staff members at the Columbia University Library, the Harry Ransom Humanities Research Center at the University of Texas at Austin, the Bodleian Library, the British Library, Harvard College Library, the University of Michigan Library, Princeton University Library, Radcliffe College Library, Swarthmore College Library, Yale University Library, and, among many others, the libraries at Bennington College, Dartmouth College, the New School for Social Research, Olivet College, Smith College, Tulsa University, the University of California at Berkeley, and the University of North Carolina at Chapel Hill. I received many courtesies from archivists at the Kurt Weill Foundation for Music, the British Broadcasting Corporation, the Columbia Broadcasting System, the National Broadcasting Company, *The New York Review of Books*, *The New York Times*, *The New Yorker*, and *Time*. I am also grateful to the New York and London offices of Auden's agents, Curtis Brown Ltd., for free access to their files.

I want to offer belated but heartfelt thanks to Ross Borden, Altie Karper, and Jennifer Snodgrass for help with *Early Auden* that came too late to be acknowledged in the book itself.

James Mendelson helped me understand many of the themes of this book and brought delight to all the places in which it was written.

A critic ought to write for readers whose learning, wisdom, and charity are greater than his. The readers I had in mind while writing this book were the ones who taught me most of what I needed to know in order to finish it: Elisabeth Sifton, Sir Frank Kermode, and the reader to whom it is dedicated.

Introduction

In 1939, soon after he made his final decision to remain in the United States instead of returning to his native England, Auden wrote a series of poems and essays in which, at the age of thirty-two, he reinterpreted his childhood. Two themes recur in these works. One was his early "conviction (though I am unaware of ever having held any supernatural beliefs) that life is ruled by mysterious forces." The other was his sense that what mattered most in life were the lonely choices of love and attention that one made without any external compulsion, as in the "passionate love affairs" he had from the age of four to thirteen "with pictures of, to me, particularly attractive water-turbines, winding-engines, roller-crushers," and other obsolete mining machines, and the even more passionate love he felt for the rusting and abandoned machines themselves when he visited the lead mines of northern England at the age of twelve.

These two beliefs debated with each other in different forms throughout his career. He alluded to the first when he expressed the hope, in a love poem, that his beloved would be sustained "by the involuntary powers," and to the second when he gave thanks, in another poem, that he had been given "your voluntary love." The first belief informed the political poems in which he imagined an inevitable future state brought about by "history, that never sleeps or dies, / And, held one moment, burns the hand." The second informed the poems in which he understood history as the realm of human time, in which "We live in freedom by necessity," uncontrolled by historical forces or recurring cycles:

"Abruptly mounting her ramshackle wheel, / Fortune has pedalled furiously away."

"For a poet like myself," Auden wrote late in life to his short-story-writing friend James Stern, "an autobiography is redundant since anything of importance that happens to one is immediately incorporated, however obscurely, in a poem." Even when he wrote a commissioned or occasional poem for an academic ceremony or a niece's wedding, he incorporated the significant events of his life. But he confronted each time a new variation on his inner debate: whether those events were better understood as the product of involuntary necessity or of free choice. The body, left to itself, belonged to the world of necessity, joining "plants in their chaster peace which is more / To its real taste," while the mind, until recalled by the senses to a world it has only limited freedom to alter, imagines itself "Unhindered, unrebuked, unwatched, / Self-known, self-praising, self-attached." The same person, Auden wrote, could be the author of two unrecognizably different autobiographies; in one, the writer would appear passive, "lacking in a capacity for affection, easily bored and smaller than life-size," in the other active, "a passionate Knight forever serenading Faith or Beauty, humorless and over-life-size."

The "new problems of Form and Content" he faced in each new poem extended from the technical details of verse to the largest questions of meaning. Traditional forms and regular metres were among the means by which he evoked an order that existed prior to any personal intervention: physical laws, bodily instincts, social conventions, beliefs and habits inherited from a family or a culture. Irregular metres, newly invented or modified forms, prose poetry, and forms and metres that had not yet been naturalized into English verse—all these were used in his work to evoke voluntary, unpredictable acts, newly found accommodations between, on one hand, the world of nature and the instinctive body and, on the other, the world of history and the individual face. But the metrical form of Auden's poems typically presented only one side of his poems' arguments with themselves. The most conventional-seeming form, such as the eighteenth-century couplets of "New Year Letter," could mask the most unstable and innovatory content; the most unconventional form, such as the extravagantly varied prose of Caliban's impersonations in "The Sea and the Mirror," could contain uncompromising statements of psychological and ethical necessity.

Through all his changes in form, style, and content, Auden faced the issue of two opposing ways to write or read a poem: whether to treat the poem as a *myth*, a statement or imitation of some overarching necessity that no one can evade or control, or as a *parable*, a statement or imitation of acts and feelings that both writer and reader are free to choose or renounce, free to treat as an example or a warning. Auden gave different names at different times to these two views of poetry and their implications for the role and status of the poet: nature and history, number and face, poet and historian, the Ariel-dominated poet and the Prospero-dominated poet. Their exponents, he said, were the Grecian urn that says "Beauty is Truth, Truth Beauty," and Samuel Johnson, who said, "The only end of writing is to enable the readers better to enjoy life, or better to endure it."

The category of myth, as Auden treated it, ranged from traditional beliefs in which individual lives are in the hands of an inexorable god or fate, to modern beliefs, like those derived from Marx, in which history moves inevitably toward the dictatorship of the proletariat, or those derived from Freud, in which the forces of superego and id are locked in struggle to rule over the ego. Myth also comprised all statistical and official versions of reality, all quasi-magical beliefs that the forces that ultimately shape the world are the impersonal powers of social restraint or the grammatical structures of language.

The characteristic myths of twentieth-century writing were those decreed by the writers themselves. The great modernist poets and prose writers of the generation preceding Auden's were justifiably proud of their command of myth. W. B. Yeats devoted half a lifetime to the task of organizing the events of his time and the personalities of his friends into a system built on the phases of the moon and the oppositions of malleable face and controlling mask. T. S. Eliot, in his 1923 essay "*Ulysses*, Order, and Myth," described Joyce's method of "a continuous parallel between contemporaneity and antiquity" (a method also used, although Eliot did not say so, in *The Waste Land*) as having "the importance of a scientific discovery," and as something as inescapable as a physical law: "Mr. Joyce is pursuing a method which others must pursue after him." This method, "already adumbrated by Mr. Yeats," was, Eliot explained, "a way of controlling, of ordering, of giving a shape and a significance to the immense panorama of futility and anarchy which is contemporary history."

Auden was as intent as Eliot was to give shape and significance to his work, but he wanted more to discover the shapes and meanings of history than to impose his own, and he was less certain that the disasters of his time were the product of futile anarchic disorder rather than of effective purposive evil. He grew up in a household in which the scientific inquiries of his father maintained an uneasy truce with the ritualized religion of his mother. George Augustus Auden was a physician in York when his third son, Wystan Hugh, was born in 1907; he became the school medical officer in Birmingham the following year, and later was also Professor of Public Health at Birmingham University. He was one of the first public health officials in England to make use of psychoanalytic theory and technique, and the young Wystan Auden impressed his schoolmates with Freudian secrets discovered in his father's library. Auden's father was also deeply learned in classical and Northern literature and archaeology, and published scholarly essays on fields as varied as madness in Greek tragedy, Norse antiquities, mathematical prodigies, and the psychology of juvenile delinquency. He transmitted to his son a lifelong love for Norse sagas, folktales, and myths.

Constance Rosalie Bicknell Auden, whose family had grand London connections that the prosperous Midlands Auden family did not, was among the first generation of women to receive a university degree in Britain—she won a gold medal in French—and when she met her husband she was training to become a missionary nurse. She and George Auden were both Anglo-Catholic; insistently proper and devout, she conducted daily prayers at home and took charge of the family's religious life. She reserved her fiercest anger for the Low Church Bishop Barnes of Birmingham, a mathematician and scientist who tried to suppress the High Church ceremonies she favored. "My first religious memories," Auden wrote later, "are of exciting magical rites."

Auden began writing poetry at fifteen—he discovered shortly afterward that he had lost his religious faith—and, after four or five years of adolescent imitations of Wordsworth, Hardy, and other poets of rural life, suddenly began writing about an imaginative world of his own invention, half-archaic, half-modern, in which the metres of Old English poetry evoked the industrial landscape of northern England and the conflicts analyzed by modern psychology. This was a largely mythical world in which any individual attempt to find love is baffled by hatreds inherited from past generations. Auden later alluded to the language of these poems as "magical lyrical phrases which seem to rise involuntarily to the consciousness." But in his mid-twenties he began to think about poetry as a dialogue with its readers, as a means of breaking the limits of personal isolation. Deliberately turning away from the incantations of his earlier style ("Obscurity is a bad fault," he told a friend who had objected to it in a review she wrote about his first published book, in 1930), he experimented with the vocabulary and rhythms of popular songs, adapted the public and accessible styles of Burns and Byron, and explored the problems of public poetry in a book-length poem in prose and verse, *The Orators*.

In the mid-1930s he wrote: "There must always be two kinds of art, escape-art, for man needs escape as he needs food and deep sleep, and parable-art, that art which shall teach man to unlearn hatred and learn love." Escape-art was in the same realm of necessity as involuntary powers, parable-art in the same realm of freedom as voluntary love, but when Auden wrote this formulation, at twenty-seven, he hoped that art could serve persuasion as well as freedom by guiding its readers into making the right free choice instead of the wrong one. He believed his verse could serve social causes, and to that end wrote parabolic plays in collaboration with his friend Christopher Isherwood, *The Dog Beneath the Skin*, *The Ascent of F6*, and *On the Frontier*, which, with varying degrees of irony and ambiguity, recommended left-wing political action.

Similar hopes impelled him to visit Spain early in 1937 with the intention of serving and witnessing the struggle of the socialist government in its civil war against the nationalist forces led by Franco and supported by Mussolini and Hitler. He returned after a few weeks, disturbed by the injustices committed by his own side and justified or concealed by propaganda. But because he was certain that the opposing side was worse, and that a victory for the Spanish nationalists would be a triumph for Fascist Italy and Nazi Germany, he said nothing about what he had seen beyond privately observing to friends that political expedience was no justification for lies. In 1938 he wrote:

> The primary function of poetry, as of all the arts, is to make us more aware of ourselves and the world around us. I do not know if such increased awareness makes us more moral or more efficient: I hope not.
>
> I think it makes us more human, and I am quite certain it makes us more difficult to deceive, which is why, perhaps, all totalitarian theories of the State, from Plato's downwards, have deeply mistrusted the arts. They notice and say too much, and the neighbours start talking.

In the same mood, he gave a broadcast talk, "In Defence of Gossip," praising the untidy and unintimidated personal voice that countered all collective impersonal official ones. By now he was celebrated as the leading political poet of his time—London papers reported his departure for Spain in the news pages, not the gossip columns—but he found this position false and constricting and wanted to escape it. Yet at the same time he felt a moral obligation to act in practical, rather than symbolic, ways against the ever more threatening and victorious evil of Fascism.

Auden insisted repeatedly in the later 1930s, as if arguing against an imaginary opponent, that one could not change one's life by going to some distant place, that any hope of finding another life in another climate was futile and delusory. "The promise is only a promise, the fabulous / Country impartially far," he wrote after traveling to Iceland, the source of his distant ancestors, in 1936. "The journey is false; the false journey really an illness," he wrote during a six-month voyage with Isherwood to report on the Sino-Japanese War in 1938. Then, on their way back from China, he and Isherwood traveled across "absolutely free America," as Auden called it in a poem a few months later, visited New York for two weeks, and decided to return for an indefinite stay. During the rest of 1938 Auden spent most of his time in Brussels, returning to England as little as possible and, when he was there, devoting much of his energy to political causes. ("I get very depressed running all over the place chatting about China," he wrote to a friend. "Does it do any good?")

After he sailed from Southampton to New York on 19 January 1939 he dropped his argument about the futility of changing one's climate, because he found that the journey was real, the fabulous country close enough to settle into. From 1939 until his death in 1973 he moved his home four times from one country to another. Each move coincided with fundamental changes in his work and outlook, and brought him to the landscape he thought most suitable to the kind of poetry he wanted to write. He left England partly to sever his involuntary, inherited relations with his family and country and his oratorical relations with an audience that admired him for his politics. After he arrived in the United States, which he saw as the loneliest and most isolating society on earth, he began experimenting with styles and metres that allowed him a new inwardness and depth of emotion while avoiding much of what he now regarded as preaching and heartiness in his earlier work. Within a few months he returned, tentatively at first, to the Anglican communion, but his beliefs took the form of a lonely existentialist Protestantism quite unlike the communal rituals of the Anglo-Catholicism he had abandoned at fifteen.

His next move to a different climate occurred in 1948, when he visited Italy for the first time and began spending his summers in a fishing village on the resort island of Ischia. His poetry almost immediately found a new conversational tone of voice and a new theme of civil comforts and obligations. Although he remained a member of the Anglican Church, his beliefs turned in the direction of a shared, corporate Catholicism that focused as much on the Communion service and the involuntary works of the flesh as his earlier beliefs had focused on the leap of faith and the voluntary commitments of the spirit.

In 1958—after an experience he described in terms of a dark night of the soul, when he thought himself impelled to defend his work and faith against faceless avengers—he moved his summer home to the Austrian village of Kirchstetten, an hour from Vienna by train. The poems he wrote there celebrated his privacy behind the walls of the only house he ever owned, and from this place of security and safety he explored metres and styles taken from a half-dozen distant cultures and classical languages. These poems also explored the bleakly modern religion he found expressed in the letters written by Dietrich Bonhoeffer from a German prison camp before his execution in 1945, letters that affirmed Christian belief in a world where no divine authority held back the violence and evil inflicted by the Nazis—whose strongest supporters, Auden observed, had been among Auden's Austrian neighbors.

In 1972, three years after he had first expressed a wish to do so, Auden gave up his winter home in New York and moved to the Oxford college where he had been an undergraduate forty-five years earlier. He was deliberately leaving behind the world of the present in the hope of returning to a world that existed partly in his memories of the past. His poems now increasingly addressed the dead instead of the living, and his religion took the form of timeless rituals in a dead language: before he left New York, when the local Anglican church adopted a modernized English text for the liturgy, he attended a Russian Orthodox church and joined in services conducted in Old Church Slavonic.

The poems in each stage of his career criticized those of the preceding stage, not so much for being wrong as for letting a parable harden into a myth. Verse techniques, historical interpretations, psychological insights, and ethical imperatives that he had labored to devise in response to earlier personal and public crises had gradually settled, he thought, into mere habits and conventions. He generally began each new stage with a vehement renunciation of past errors, overstating his objections in order to rouse himself to find something new.

The poems Auden wrote after 1939 are too various for broad generalizations, but a characteristic pattern can be found in many, perhaps most, of them. The reader is presented with two different kinds of experience in sequence. The first offers the aesthetic, formal, ritualized pleasures of a world of myth. A heightened style in the opening lines of the poem signals that this world is marked off from the ordinary world of prose, but is not so extreme that the poem claims the solemn status of an inspired or hermetic text. Openings of this kind may take the form of rapid and unexpected juxtapositions:

> Jumbled in the common box
> Of their dark stupidity,
> Orchid, swan, and Caesar lie . . .

Or a formulaic flight into song:

> Sing first that green remote Cockaigne
> Where whiskey-rivers run . . .

Or a statement of interest in art rather than life:

> Sylvan meant savage in those primal woods
> Piero di Cosimo so loved to draw . . .

The poem shows itself at this point to be a source of the aesthetic pleasure that is the first, and often the only, reason to spend one's time with a work of art. "A poem is a rite," Auden said in a lecture, and "the form of a rite must be beautiful, exhibiting, for example, balance, closure and aptness to that which it is the form of." Its form, he wrote elsewhere, is like those found in the involuntary realm of nature: "Considered as a verbal system, the poem is a natural not a historical object. The laws of prosody and syntax are to it what the laws of physics and chemistry are to the physical universe." The mythical world remains within its frame; it asks nothing of us beyond our attention. Auden found the clearest statement of the nature and rewards of this world of myth in Virginia Woolf's evocation of the experience of a concert of music:

> There is a square [Rhoda says in *The Waves*]; there is an oblong. The players take the square and place it along the oblong. They place it very accurately; they make a perfect dwelling-place. Very little is left outside. The structure is now visible; what is inchoate is here stated; we are not so various or so mean; we have made oblongs and stood them upon squares. This is our triumph; this is our consolation.

Auden quoted this passage repeatedly in the 1940s and later, and he used "Squares and Oblongs" as the title for two separate essays.

The second experience is subtly but unmistakably different. Near the end of the poem, the language becomes simpler, more straightforward, and makes a personal, not a ritual, statement about the poet's condition and ours:

> Once too often you and I
> Did what we should not have done.

Or:

> Because our sound committeeman
> Has murder in his heart.

Or:

> Our great society is going smash;
> They cannot fool us with how fast they go.

The mythical world has been disenchanted, and transformed into parable. Typically the poem returns to its heightened ritual style in its closing lines, but its brief descent into a darker tone has altered its mood. History, the realm in which acts cannot be reversed or undone, intrudes on nature's repetitive cycles and art's static calm. A year after Auden first quoted Woolf on the consolations of squares and oblongs, he wrote, as if in response, that the effect of the formal beauty of a work of art "is evil to the degree that . . . the pleasure of beauty [is] taken for the joy of Paradise, and the conclusion drawn that, since all is well in the work of art, all is well in history. But all is not well there." The sequence of myth, followed by parable, followed by a partial restoration of myth matches the structure Auden described in the typical detective story, in which the ritualized aesthetic world of the vicarage garden, "an innocent society in a state of grace," is suddenly transformed by the act of murder into a world of guilt where "the law becomes a reality and for a time all must live in its shadow."

Two questions, Auden wrote, interested him most when reading a poem:

The first is technical: "Here is a verbal contraption. How does it work?" The second is, in the broadest sense, moral: "What kind of guy inhabits this poem? What is his notion of the good life or the good place? His notion of the Evil One? What does he conceal from the reader? What does he conceal even from himself?"

An aesthetically tolerant reader who wants to defer the second question while enjoying the pleasurable difficulties of the first is made uncomfortable by the moral intelligence of the poems, by their transformation from a beautiful picture into an unflattering mirror. A morally censorious reader who prefers to skip over the first question is scandalized by the poems' self-delight in their bravura elegance of language and form. But to the reader willing to ask both questions, Auden's poems offer responses that combine the consoling triumph of form with the disturbing uncertainties of freedom.

PART ONE

Vision and After

1939–1947

CHAPTER ONE

Demon or Gift

In his first days in New York Auden felt a new sense of liberation and power. He arrived in the harbor with Christopher Isherwood on 26 January 1939, in the dead of winter, while a light snow disfigured the public statues. During their voyage, he and Isherwood had spoken aloud for the first time of their disaffection with the mass political movements they had hoped to serve with their poetry and plays. Three days after their arrival, the news came that W. B. Yeats had died at seventy-three. Auden, who was not yet thirty-two, had left England with the half-formed resolution that he would begin his career anew in a new country. He now wrote a memorable and audacious poem on the death of Yeats in which he proclaimed the rebirth of poetry and foresaw in the heroic labors of a living poet the renewal of the world.

Two ideas of poetry contend against each other in "In Memory of W. B. Yeats." The opening section, with its solemn, meditative, unrhymed verse paragraphs, acknowledges that the most a poet can achieve in the world is to be remembered by his admirers. The closing section, with its drumbeat stanzas and soaring visionary rhetoric, celebrates poetic language as a force more powerful than time or death, and glorifies the poet as a source of sustenance, healing, and rejoicing. The closing argument wins this debate, but the ironies and doubts insinuated by the opening one remain unanswered.

The first published version of the poem drew an absolute contrast between the dying impotence of the poet and the reviving power of verse. This version—it appeared in *The New Republic*, 8 March 1939—

was not yet the poem familiar from Auden's books: the opening and closing sections had almost reached their final form, but the quietly discursive middle section, where "poetry makes nothing happen" and "Ireland has her madness and her weather still," had not yet been written.

The opening section transforms traditional elegy into a bleak new mode:

> He disappeared in the dead of winter:
> The brooks were frozen, the air-ports almost deserted,
> And snow disfigured the public statues;
> The mercury sank in the mouth of the dying day.

The metaphors point to a world where facts may be counted or measured or reported in news bulletins, where neither poetry nor metaphor is any use. In English elegies, until Auden wrote this one, nature itself mourned the dead while an exclamatory "O" announced the personal grief of the elegist. In Milton's "Lycidas," for example:

> O the heavy change, now thou art gone,
> Now thou art gone, and never must return!
> Thee shepherd, thee the woods and desert caves,
> With wild thyme and the gadding vine o'ergrown,
> And all their echoes mourn . . .

In Auden's elegy, nature takes no interest in Yeats's death; the day is dark and cold merely by coincidence; and the poet, with conscious irony, exclaims over the weather report:

> O all the instruments agree
> The day of his death was a dark cold day.

(Intent on getting his prosaic facts right, Auden wrote to his own publishers to ask for the exact time of Yeats's death. They didn't know the answer, so he asked elsewhere until he learned that Yeats had died during "his last afternoon as himself.")

Yeats's readers, Auden among them, are almost as indifferent to his death as nature is. The poem treats him as the subject of ingenious public metaphors rather than as a person. "The provinces of his body revolted, / The squares of his mind were empty, / Silence invaded the suburbs, / The current of his feeling failed . . ." The city that was Yeats is conquered by his living readers. "By mourning tongues / The death of the poet was kept from his poems," but the tongues that recite the dead man's poems also swallow them: "The words of a dead man / Are modified in the guts of the living." Yeats "became his admirers." Soon his death will become an interesting event in their private memories and "A few thousand will think of this day / As one thinks of a day when one did something slightly unusual."

The transforming miracles at the end of traditional elegies occur also at the end of Auden's poem, but while the dead poet traditionally participated in those miracles, Yeats is excluded from them. Poetry, not Yeats, lives on in triumph. Language, worshipped by time, ascends beyond the mere mortality of poets and their mistaken politics, their cowardice and conceit. Elegies always looked away from the dead and turned toward tomorrow, to fresh woods and pastures new; but they usually were decorous enough to put off their departure until the final lines. Yeats is buried in the middle of Auden's elegy and forgotten long before the end. Like "the expensive delicate ship that must have seen / Something amazing, a boy falling out of the sky," in "Musée des Beaux Arts," written a few weeks earlier, Auden, and the rest of Yeats's indifferent admirers, "Had somewhere to get to and sailed calmly on."

Nothing that matters has been changed by Yeats's death. The opening section expects nothing better than

> the importance and noise of tomorrow
> When the brokers are roaring like beasts on the floor of the Bourse,
> And the poor have the sufferings to which they are fairly accustomed,
> And each in the cell of himself is almost convinced of his freedom.

But in the closing section the poem transforms itself. The irregular verse of the opening is replaced by rhymed, rhythmical stanzas, and the familiar world is illuminated by myth. Yeats is sent forth amid ritual and allegory:

> Earth, receive an honoured guest;
> William Yeats is laid to rest:
> Let the Irish vessel lie
> Emptied of its poetry.

No ceremony can end the chaos and imprisonment described in the opening section, but they are perceived now in subtly different ways:

> In the nightmare of the dark
> All the dogs of Europe bark,
> And the living nations wait,
> Each sequestered in its hate;
>
> Intellectual disgrace
> Stares from every human face,
> And the seas of pity lie
> Locked and frozen in each eye.

A nightmare implies waking; frozen seas can melt; eyes can meet. Instruments have been replaced by human faces, and the poem immediately calls forth their knight of deliverance, an unnamed mythical "poet" composed from the virtues of pilgrim, farmer, healer, singer, and teacher, an Orphic and messianic hero who can descend into the realms of death and release the waters of life. Yeats will remain earth's guest until the end of time, but the living poet can follow and return:

> Follow, poet, follow right
> To the bottom of the night,
> With your unconstraining voice
> Still persuade us to rejoice;
>
> With the farming of a verse
> Make a vineyard of the curse,
> Sing of human unsuccess
> In a rapture of distress.

The poem prays to the poet for miracles of transfiguration and cure. His power alone can teach the barking dogs of Europe and the staring intellectual disgrace, despite themselves, to sing:

> In the deserts of the heart
> Let the healing fountain start,
> In the prison of his days
> Teach the free man how to praise.

"Praise," in Auden's work in 1938 and 1939, was an explicit echo of Rilke's *dennoch preisen*. Auden used the word with the same troubled ambivalence he felt about Rilke, who stood for the kind of poetic vocation Auden simultaneously treasured and mistrusted. He honored Rilke's ecstatic visionary freedom while he recognized its indifference to suffering and injustice. Two months before Auden wrote "In Memory of W. B. Yeats," he had, in effect, written an anticipatory reply to the words with which he closed his elegy. "Certainly praise" began one of the sonnets he had written for "In Time of War": "let the song mount again and again." Then, after three lines, the sonnet changed its tone: "But hear the morning's injured weeping, and know why: / Cities and men have fallen; the will of the Unjust / Has never lost its power." The elegy for Yeats urges the living poet to sing rapturously of human un-success. But, as the sonnet knew, "History opposes its grief to our buoyant song."

In Auden's triumphant mood in his first days in New York, the doubts that had concluded his sonnet were pushed back to the first section of his elegy, and the poet of the closing section marched over the grave of more than one dead master. His elegy for Yeats was the first (and, for another quarter century, only) poem in which he responded to Milton; in it he made larger claims for poetry than Milton had dared to make in "Lycidas," and he did so by adopting as his own the vastly ambitious claims Milton had made in *Paradise Lost*. As Auden wrote in an essay ten years later, Milton was

> the first poet in English literature whose attitude toward his art is neither professional like that of Ben Jonson and Dryden nor amateur like that of Wyatt, but priestly or prophetic. Poetry to him was neither an amusing activity nor the job for which he happened to be qualified, but the most sacred of all human activities. To become a great poet was to become not only superior to other poets but superior to all other men.

Auden's elegy commandeers Milton's baroque manner and metaphors and makes them speak for the conflicting interests of romantic aspiration and modern irony. It omits the shepherds of Milton's pastoral elegy but retains the wolf that was the shepherds' bane: in 1939 "The wolves ran on through the evergreen forests," where in 1637, among the evergreen ivy "never sere," ran "The grim wolf with privy paws." Auden's iconography is medical and scientific—"The mercury sank in the mouth of the dying day"—but his descent of Mercury imitates the descent of the sun in "Lycidas": "So sinks the day-star in the ocean bed." Auden's poet descends "To the bottom of the night" in the same way Milton's poet visits "the bottom of the monstrous world." But the two rise again with the help of different powers. The poet of "Lycidas" is lifted up by "The dear might of him that walked the wave," and the singing of the saints wipes the tears from his eyes. Auden's poet ascends on his own, and the tears frozen in the eyes of others are released by his song.

About a year before Auden left England, he wrote a ballad, "As I walked out one evening," in which Time is a destroyer as undiscriminating and implacable as death. "You cannot conquer Time," an unheeding lover is warned by the clocks of the city. "Time breaks the threaded dances / And the diver's brilliant bow." Now, in the closing section of Auden's elegy, Time makes an exception, and acknowledges a greater power:

> Time that is intolerant
> Of the brave and innocent
> And indifferent in a week
> To a beautiful physique,
>
> Worships language and forgives
> Everyone by whom it lives;
> Pardons cowardice, conceit,
> Lays its honors at their feet.

The power by which the poet conquers time has a deceptively simple name: it is his *gift*. Auden began using "gift" in the special sense of an artist's power only in the last weeks of 1938, when he was preparing to leave for the United States and was beginning his conscious revolt from political causes. In the name of his gift, he rebelled briefly and sharply against every form of group and collective identity—political movements, his family, England—because he could imagine no other way to escape from false and constraining loyalties. As he had written in 1936 about the psychological prison of a schoolroom, "The bars of love are so strong."

The gift was the special form taken by larger and more mysterious powers when they made themselves incarnate in an artist. These daemonic, unnameable powers had made shadowy appearances in Auden's work since the early 1930s, but until he broke away from England he never imagined them to be in his own keeping. The knowing and ironic surface of his earlier poems kept his belief in their existence largely hidden from his readers, and perhaps partly hidden from himself. His belief broke through intermittently, however, sometimes disguised as allegorical figures of power and law, sometimes concealed within deterministic ideas about historical change. In 1932 he had addressed a verse prayer to the "Lords of Limit," mythical powers who maintain the boundaries of all things and secure the individual from disintegrating into chaos; a few months afterward, in "O Love, the interest itself in thoughtless Heaven," he had imagined a transforming force uncurling out of the future toward "the virgin roadsteads of our hearts" as the civilizing magician Merlin, "tamer of horses," once sailed toward a virgin England. Later the same year he had written a poem evoking "The Witnesses," figures of the same power, now armed with apocalyptic force to derange minds and destroy cities. In June 1933, as he wrote later, "a power which, though I consented to it, was irresistible and certainly not mine," induced the experience he called a vision of Agape, when, briefly and for the first time, he loved his neighbor as himself. But he did not speak explicitly of these powers until, a few months after his elegy for Yeats, he wrote a partly autobiographical book in prose, *The Prolific and the Devourer*, in which he described his "conviction . . . that life is ruled by mysterious forces." But he left the book unfinished, and never stated his conviction in print.

Auden recognized in himself and others that a belief in mysterious forces almost always accompanied a belief that a hero could be found who embodied them. In 1931, when he was twenty-four, Auden simultaneously indulged and renounced the temptations of hero worship in his book *The Orators*; then, amid the worsening social disorders of the time, he tried briefly to imagine Lawrence of Arabia and Lenin as embodiments of the future. His own sudden fame tempted him to imagine that he himself might become an agent of historical change. In 1933 he wrote a poem, "Friend, of the civil space by human love," in which he exhorted an unnamed friend to write the lines that would save his generation, and then proceeded, in the same poem, to write those lines himself. Auden never published it, and he kept his fantasy of himself as a leader and redeemer so well hidden that its only trace in his published work was his furious renunciation of it in 1936 in *The Ascent of F6*, a play in which the Lawrence-like hero, Michael Ransom, destroys himself and his friends in pursuit of his redemptive ambition. The hero of the play dies on a mountain that local legend says is haunted by a demon; in a final dream vision at the summit, the inner demon that haunts the hero is identified as a projection of his will to power, and when the veil covering its features falls it is revealed as the mother who had refused him the love she gave his brother.

The demon was another name for the mysterious forces Auden had invoked in earlier years. He wrote a compressed five-hundred-year history of them in a sonnet of 1936: they were the inner disorders that had once been projected outward as the imaginary shapes of giants and dragons perceived by superstition and legend. Then Baconian science banished them, or so it seemed:

> The vanquished powers were glad
> To be invisible and free; without remorse
> Struck down the son, indifferent to the mother's curse,
> And ravished the daughters, and drove the fathers mad.

In the first days of 1937, as a four-year love affair was coming to an end, Auden invoked the mysterious forces on behalf of his lover. May "noons of dryness see you fed / By the involuntary powers," he wrote in "Lay your sleeping head, my love." During his next two, mostly loveless, years, demons and powers disappeared from his work, although he tried, for what seemed compelling political reasons, to believe in a socialist future that private acts and errors could postpone but not prevent. When he began to write about the artist's gift, in late 1938, he imagined it as something separate from the world of history. His sonnet "The Novelist" portrays a quasi-allegorical figure (an idealized Isherwood) who "Must struggle out of his boyish gift" into adult sympathy with his characters. "The Composer," based loosely on Benjamin Britten, praises the one kind of artist who can only forgive, never accuse, for music has no negative: "Only your song is an absolute gift." Then, in his first heady days after moving to "absolutely free America," when the rebellion that had brought him there had succeeded, the gift suddenly became a world-transforming force.

In the original two-part version of "In Memory of W. B. Yeats" the gift's power is abrupt and complete. The closing verse paragraphs of the first part portray in falling cadences the roaring brokers and suffering poor; then the few thousand who remember Yeats's death as an incident in their lives, not his; then Yeats himself, who is dismissed in a few words: "He was silly like us: His gift survived it all." Then the first part ends by repeating the exclamation made earlier in the poem: "O all the instruments agree / The day of his death was a dark cold day." The last part of the poem, "Earth, receive an honored guest," follows immediately, with its triumphant metrical celebration of the surviving gift.

Throughout 1939 Auden named the gift as the liberating source of identity and power. D. H. Lawrence, he wrote in a review, "owes his influence for good or evil to his gift." In *The Prolific and the Devourer* he answered the challenge made by politically minded critics to "ivory-tower" artists by insisting that the way to escape the ivory tower is not to abandon one's gift but to embrace it. The poets of the 1890s, he wrote, can justly be accused of ivory-towerism because they failed to accept their gift completely: "the portion of life which they saw as poets was such a tiny fragment. Politics and science, indeed, they saw as average men of their social position, education, and income." But, he continued, the only way to perceive the whole is to perceive from one's own special perspective: "first discover what manner of person you are, and then see everything through the lens of your gift. One destroys one's ivory tower only when one has learnt to see the whole universe as an artist, or as a scientist, or as a politician." *The Prolific and the Devourer* was composed in the form of pensées, and Auden paid tribute to the master of the pensée in his 1939 poem "Pascal":

> Yet like a lucky orphan he had been discovered
> And instantly adopted by a Gift;
> And she became the sensible protector
> Who found a passage through the caves of accusation,
> And even in the canyon of distress was able
> To use the echo of his weakness as a proof
> That joy was probable, and took the place
> Of the poor lust and hunger he had never known.

When Auden reviewed a book about Shakespeare in October 1939, though he did not use the word "gift," he made the same point he had made about Pascal: "In the truest sense of the word 'pure,' [Shakespeare] is the purest poet who ever lived; that is to say, he explored all life through a single medium, that of language." Auden entitled this review "The Dyer's Hand" after Sonnet 111: "my nature is subdued / To what it works in like the dyer's hand." Many years later, when he had stopped defending the gift itself, he still saw the world through its lens, and again used the title "The Dyer's Hand" for a series of broadcasts about poetry in 1955 and a book of essays and lectures in 1962.

The gift survived personal death and public chaos, and could be destroyed only by a poet's rejection of it. In "Matthew Arnold," a poem Auden wrote shortly after "In Memory of W. B. Yeats," the gift willingly forgives Arnold's faults:

> His gift knew what he was—a dark disordered city . . .
> —Yet would have gladly lived in him and learned his ways . . .
> And [would have] found in the disorder a whole world to praise.

But Arnold, obedient to his father's memory, chose to write essays of "clear denunciation" instead of poems of praise, and "thrust his gift in prison till it died." Auden insisted that the gift survived the poet, yet, in the end, the poet held the gift's life or death in his own power.

═══

A few weeks after he wrote the two-part version of "In Memory of W. B. Yeats," Auden had second thoughts. He was now living in a hotel room in Manhattan with Isherwood, and had begun to settle into the life of a young literary celebrity, welcomed by patronesses in Park Avenue salons and offered more pay for reviews and lectures than he had ever hoped for in England. The daily temptations and struggles of his gift seemed less like the starkly heroic quest he had imagined when he stepped off the boat. In February or March he added a middle section between the two original sections of his poem. (This new version appeared in *The London Mercury* in April 1939 and in his next book of poems, *Another Time*, in 1940.) Here he addressed Yeats directly for the first time. The first line of the new section had originally been part of the opening section; Auden changed it from third person to second person when he reused it:

> You were silly like us: your gift survived it all;
> The parish of rich women, physical decay,
> Yourself . . .

Poetry's survival was now its persistence as itself, its quiet refusal of temptations, rather than any heroic ascent from death to transfiguration as in the closing section of the poem:

> For poetry makes nothing happen: it survives
> In the valley of its saying where executives
> Would never want to tamper; it flows south
> From ranches of isolation and the busy griefs,
> Raw towns that we believe and die in; it survives,
> A way of happening, a mouth.

Poetry, which flows here like the river Alpheus in "Lycidas," flows through these lines from its *source* (mad Ireland hurt you into poetry)* through upstream ranches and past downstream towns to issue, as all rivers do, at a *mouth*. Milton's "blind mouths" are in the background. The river seems as American as the Mississippi, flowing south past ranches and raw towns, in the country Auden had chosen partly because few of its citizens suffered from the delusion that poetry was something worth tampering with.

In the revised elegy, poetry remakes itself in two gradual steps instead of one abrupt leap from the unstructured verse at the start to the rhythmic assertions at the end. The dark cold day of the opening section recurs as Ireland's perennial weather in the middle section; and the middle section's flat statement that poetry *makes* nothing happen prepares for the final section's summons to poetry's unconstraining voice. The new section reads like a quiet transition between the original two, but it also casts doubt on the final claims of triumph by proposing a less theatrical idea of success. In the middle section, poetry seeks nothing but autonomous survival in the valley of its saying (which Auden later revised to "the valley of its making," or *poesis*), and the statement that "poetry makes nothing happen" simply means it has no effect on private or public acts. The closing section agrees that poetry has no power to *enforce*, but claims it has far greater powers to heal, soothe, teach, liberate, and triumph.

These two radically different visions of the power of art had surreptitiously opposed each other in Auden's work from the start. In the 1930s he had typically written a poem that argued one side of the question, then a second poem in which he answered the first. The public exhortations of "Spain," for example, were quietly refuted a few weeks later by the hermetic questionings of "Orpheus." Now the debate became explicit, and Auden repeatedly argued both sides in a single poem.

Arrayed on one side were his conscious wish for social justice, his didactic ethos, and all the deliberate choices of a poet's reflective will. On the other side were the irrational apolitical powers in every psyche,

---

* A few weeks earlier, in December 1938, Auden had written in similar terms in a brief essay on Byron for an Oxford University Press school anthology titled *Fifteen Poets*: "The source of the poetic gift is a mystery: it is possible that, had Byron's foot been cured by modern surgery, or had his parents got on with each other, he would never have written a line. On the other hand, there are plenty of cripples and children of unhappy parents who write bad poetry or none. The study of a poet's biography or psychology or social status cannot explain why he writes well, but it can help us to understand why his poetry is of a particular kind."

and the power special to those with a vocation—their gift. Auden's argument with himself is generally interpreted as a political one, a dispute over whether poetry ought to serve public causes. But he recognized that this inner political debate was a special case of a deeper and more sustained argument between the logic of day and the impulse of night. In a later poem, "Under Which Lyre," he named these antagonists Apollo and Hermes. When he let one side of the argument dominate in a poem, the result was usually a dry or bombastic failure and he sooner or later dropped it from his collected works. His poems succeeded when they took their energy from the struggle between these inner antagonists, each with its allies in the world outside.

Almost every poem Auden wrote in the weeks before and after his arrival in New York portrayed the *agon* of an artist in combat with his gift. Among the sonnets composed just before he sailed were two miniature biographies with diametrically opposed endings. In "Rimbaud," the gift is defeated and the poet fails, as Rimbaud, estranged "from lyre and weakness," dreams of "a new self . . . an engineer."* (Auden glossed this a year later when he reviewed a biography of Rimbaud: "as a man of action he was a self-tortured failure, for no one can live by will alone.") In "Edward Lear," the poet succeeds when the gift triumphs. Lear wept when his "Terrible Demon arose / Over his shoulder," but he was "guided by tears" away from the world of will to an innocent paradise where "Words pushed him to the piano to sing comic songs" and "the demon's false nose made the table laugh." Then, after Auden settled in New York, he wrote about Yeats, whose gift survived it all; about Herman Melville, on whom, once he renounced the "intricate and false" world of willed novels like *Moby-Dick* for the simplicity of *Billy Budd*, "the words descended like the calm of mountains"; and about Matthew Arnold, who, unlike Melville, refused and imprisoned his gift.

But the most instructive and rebuking example was the subject of "Voltaire at Ferney," a poet who denied even the existence of the gift. In Auden's cool discursive verse portrait, written a few days or weeks after his elegy for Yeats, Voltaire acknowledges no power but his own; among the enlightened he has "only himself to count upon"; among the murderous and evil, "Only his verses / Perhaps could stop them." But if your goal, like Voltaire's, is to stop the "horrible nurses / Itching to boil their children," you have faint prospects of achieving it by writing verse, especially if you write it in a spirit of rational analytic pride. Poetry

---

* Rimbaud had in fact dreamed of a son as an engineer, but the detail is elided for effect.

ought to be written, the poem implies in its closing lines, in an unconstraining voice that protests and promises nothing, in an idiom of pure
praise beyond mere human powers: "Overhead / The uncomplaining
stars composed their lucid song." In a review written around the same
time, Auden portrayed Voltaire as a writer who indeed made something
happen—not through his poetry, which the review entirely ignored, but
through his work in prose and his practical attempt to create at Ferney
"a community of which the members would feel happy enough to allow
the spirit of democracy to flower." Voltaire was "not only one of the
greatest Europeans of all time, but, though he might be surprised to hear
it, one of the greatest fighters for democracy, and one who should be as
much a hero for us as Socrates or Jefferson"—neither of whom furthered
democracy by writing verses.

Auden did not yet seriously doubt the political principles he had been
declaring in his prose for the past few years. He maintained his engaged
commitment to the democratic cause threatened by Fascism, though
he did not deceive himself into imagining that Fascism's enemies had
achieved a fully realized democracy. Nineteenth-century liberal democracy had failed and deserved to fail; its hypocritical tolerance for social
injustice had "created the most impersonal, the most mechanical and the
most unequal civilization the world has ever seen . . . a civilization torn
apart by the opposing emotions born of economic injustice, the just envy
of the poor and the selfish terror of the rich." He continued to believe
that socialist democracy must replace liberal democracy. Before his elegy
for Yeats soared above politics in its final stanzas, Auden took the trouble
to score partisan points against the right-wing views of Rudyard Kipling,
Paul Claudel, and Yeats himself, views that needed to be pardoned by
time; his own left-wing views, implicitly, needed to be pardoned by no
one. But he increasingly doubted that he served justice, rather than pub-
licity, when his poems preached a partisan cause to a choir of the politically converted, and he began to believe that the answer to political
failure must be found in personal beliefs, not in a further round of partisan politics. "For democracy is not a political system or party but an
attitude of mind," he wrote in his review about Voltaire. "There is no
such thing as the perfect democratic state, good for all time. What political form is most democratic at any given period depends on geography, economic development, educational level, and the like. But in any
particular issue it is always possible to say where a democrat should stand,
and to recognize one, whatever party label he may bear."

Auden questioned his own political poetry not because he disapproved of its politics but because he was unsure of its value as poetry. Like Voltaire's verse, he thought, it was the work of his will more than of his gift. Guiltily aware of his isolated literary vocation and upper-middle-class security, he was pressing his gift to serve causes in which it took no interest. Yet precisely because his gift was indifferent to fatal public disasters, he was not convinced that its autonomy deserved to be defended. Almost everything he wrote in 1939 was an attempt to clarify his mixed feelings about the rival claims of private gift and public good. When he set these two claims against each other in a poem, the gift generally had the advantage, for it was defending itself on its own ground; when he argued them in a prose essay or review, the gift sank under a lowering cloud of rebuke and often withdrew in shame.

"You are blind like us. Your hurt no man designed." This line opened a sonnet, "To Germany," written by Charles Hamilton Sorley at the start of the 1914–18 war, and Auden adopted its rhythm and diction for the opening line of his apostrophe to Yeats, and "hurt" for "mad Ireland hurt you into poetry" two lines later. Sorley's sonnet looked forward to a time when today's enemies could grasp hands and laugh at old pain. Auden's elegy also looked forward to a future of forgiveness, but he doubted whether public forgiveness could be achieved by a poet's private acts. The dogs of Europe would not be silenced quite so easily. To debate the question on the fairest possible terms, Auden now devised a work that was something between a prose poem and an essay: a quietly unsettling dialogue in which the conflicting claims of both sides have an almost equal chance to prevail.

"The Public v. the Late Mr. W. B. Yeats" was written for *Partisan Review*, a quarterly in which advocacy for modernist writing maintained a détente with socialist politics. He sent in the manuscript on 18 March 1939, perhaps only a few days after adding the middle section to "In Memory of W. B. Yeats." In form it is a pair of speeches by a public prosecutor and a counsel for the defense; each argues his side of the case to a jury implicitly consisting of the individual reader.* No verdict is announced, and the dialogue leaves the final judgment open. But the unspoken point is that it is not Yeats who is being weighed in the balance of justice but the jury.

For the jury to reach a just decision in the case against Yeats—and thereby vindicate itself—it must take notice of details that neither pros-

---

* Auden perhaps got the idea of two summations from the closing chapters of Dostoevsky's *The Brothers Karamazov*, a book he cited extensively later the same year.

ecution nor defense bothers to mention. The name of the case—The Public v. the Late Mr. W. B. Yeats—is subtly different from the names of cases tried in English-speaking courts. Yeats is being accused not by the Crown or the People but by a category for which Auden never in his life had a good word, the *Public*, not a community or a nation or a society or even a crowd, all of which comprise individuals with human faces, however distorted. The public is an abstract chimera that exists in a void. (The "public statues" in the elegy for Yeats are "disfigured," deprived of *figura* or human form.) As Auden wrote later, "A man has a distinctive personal scent . . . A crowd has a generalized stink. The public is odorless." And in "The Chimeras," a 1950 poem, he defined the public by its absences:

> Absence of heart—as in public buildings—
> Absence of mind—as in public speeches—
> Absence of worth—as in goods intended for the public . . .

The Public Prosecutor points to the damning evidence of Yeats's airs, affectations, feudal fantasies, and his "deplorable" *Oxford Book of Modern Verse*. Auden shared the Prosecutor's distaste for these things, but the Prosecutor cares little about such trivial though valid charges. He uses them only to convince a gullible juror of the truth of his most important accusations—which a shrewd juror will recognize as lies.

The Prosecutor freely admits that Yeats was talented; he can hardly do otherwise. What he denies is "that he was a *great* poet, the greatest of his century writing in English." To deserve the epithet "great," he argues, a poet "is commonly required to convince us of three things. The first is a gift of a very high order for memorable language." He is on firm ground with this echo of Auden's statement in 1935 that the best definition of poetry is "memorable speech," but he stumbles when he challenges the jurors to ask themselves how many of Yeats's lines they remember; as the representative of a passive and indifferent public, he cannot imagine that readers who care enough to read a dialogue about Yeats also care enough to know his poems by heart.

The Prosecutor's second requirement for a great poet is, in Auden's view, only partly right: a great poet, he says, must have "a profound understanding of the age in which he lives." Auden wrote in 1940 that Yeats's "utter lack of effort to relate his aesthetic Weltanschauung with that of science, a hostile neglect which was due, in part at least, to the age in which he was born when science was avidly mechanistic, was per-

haps the reason why he never succeeded in writing a long poem." Yet,
as Auden knew, there are many ways to understand one's era, and he
even brought himself to argue that the fairies and heroes of Yeats's early
work were attempts, however misguided, to cure an atomized society
through folk traditions. Furthermore, any deliberate attempt to understand one's age is likely to fail. Shortly before Auden composed his dialogue, his father had written him from England to express the hope that
through his poetry he might act as the mouthpiece for his age—apparently suggesting that in his recent work he had been turning away from
that role. Auden replied: "If he wishes to be the mouthpiece of his age,
as every writer does, it must be the last thing he thinks about. Tennyson
for example *was* the Victorian mouthpiece in *In Memoriam* when he was
thinking about Hallam and his grief. When he decided to be the Victorian Bard and wrote the *Idylls of the King*, he ceased to be a poet."

The Prosecutor's third requirement is wholly wrong. To be accounted
great, he says, a poet must have "a working knowledge of and sympathetic attitude towards the most progressive thought of his time." Auden
shared the Prosecutor's mockery of Yeats's belief—or pretense of belief
—in fairies in 1900 and "the mumbo-jumbo of magic and the nonsense
of India" in 1930, but he was not endorsing the Prosecutor's sly implication that because Yeats's social and scientific views were nonsense, the
opposing views must be accepted as true. The Defence Counsel sees
through this trick:

> Take away the frills, and the argument of the prosecution is reduced to this:
> "A great poet must give the right answers to the problems which perplex his
> generation. The deceased gave the wrong answers. Therefore the deceased is
> not a great poet." Poetry in such a view is the filling up of a social quiz; to
> pass with honors the poet must score not less than 75%.

We really do have problems we want solved, the Defence Counsel
continues, so "we are inclined to expect everyone, politicians, scientists,
poets, clergymen, to give us the answer, and to blame them indiscrimi-
nately when they do not. But who reads the poetry of the past in this
way?" Art and society are intertwined—"The relation between the two
is just as intimate and important as the prosecution asserts"—but the
Prosecutor has the relation backward: "Art is a product of history, not
a cause." Like everyone, poets are "from time to time excited emotionally and intellectually" by their social and material environment. In poets
"this excitement produces verbal structures which we call poems; if such

a verbal structure creates an excitement in the reader, we call it a good poem. Poetic talent, in fact, is the power to make personal excitement socially available."

Auden thought of poetry as a great teacher, not because it gives answers, but because it makes its questions urgent and memorable. The Prosecutor, proffering the reward of greatness to any poet willing to make a pact with the public, is a Mephistophelean tempter. His method is to make poets destroy themselves by choosing tasks they cannot even begin to accomplish. He talks of "social justice and reason" but cannot cite any just or reasonable acts, and the impersonal public for whom he speaks cannot, by its nature, perform any. Yet the Prosecutor claims the authority of "the most progressive thought of his time" and expects the jury to take him at his word. The Defence Counsel does not challenge this idea of progress, although when he points out that the liberal ideal of equality has led to "the most unequal civilization the world has ever seen," he makes the point that ideals of justice are not enough to create a just society.

Auden had been tempted for years by the Prosecutor's arguments, and was still not entirely immune to them. The same belief in mysterious forces that had led him into private fantasies of inspiration and hero worship also seemed consistent with public ideologies that were current during his adolescence and early adulthood. Since the late eighteenth century a conviction had gradually developed in European thought that individual lives, properly understood, were determined invisibly by vast social and instinctive energies. Unlike the older idea of Providence, which derived from a personal God, these impersonal powers—whether called *élan vital*, the life force, history, social class, psychological archetype, or the shaping power of language and myth—denied the reality of individual conscious choice. For Hegel or Nietzsche or Freud, exceptional persons could wrest individuality from the unconscious powers and direct them toward conscious goals; for Marx and his followers, the Communist Party was the means by which history's great forces shaped their own ends. In an age when theories of natural selection and random mutation had exploded kinder teleologies, it was almost impossible *not* to wish that the unconscious irrational energies of nature and history could be shown to have an inherent tropism toward rationality, that they might be taught by a gardener's care to flower into the knowledge, progress, and justice that they would inevitably, but more slowly, attain by themselves. This wish survived repeated disappointments and disillusionments. The 1920s, when Auden began writing, saw perhaps the fullest and most optimistic expressions of this hope in the very different prophetic certainties of Bergson, Shaw, and Lenin. All three inadvertently revealed how much had to be ignored and suppressed—and, in the political world, how many had to be murdered—in order to sustain it.

Auden never believed that the Soviet Union had achieved justice, but he more than once convinced himself that socialist justice might be achieved in the enlightened West. Justice required the destruction of his own privileged class, he reasoned, and he saw in the neurotic unhappiness of himself and his contemporaries an early sign of its imminent and inescapable end. When he wrote in 1935 that "All sway forward on the dangerous flood / Of history," he was using "history" in the same deterministic, purposive sense in which Marxist theoreticians of the time used it. Yet a year later, in a verse letter from Iceland to his socialist friend Richard Crossman, he condemned this idea of "history, hostile, Time the destroyer" as "our vulgar error," and renounced three variations of it: a perception of individual lives as mere "symbols of an end," meaningful only as visible signs of an invisible historical process; a conviction that a larger fate, a "maladjustment in the circling stars," rather than personal evil, has made things wrong; and a belief that goodness is not an attribute of personal acts but "just an abstract principle / Which by hypothesis some men must have / For whom we spend our idle lives in looking, / And are so lazy that we quickly find them." He did not mention a further variation of the same idea of purposive history in his fantasy, renounced the same year, of himself as a redemptive poet-hero.

Ten days after he wrote his verse letter from Iceland, civil war began in Spain. The struggle between history's forward impulse and Fascism's retrograde grasp seemed suddenly and dangerously real. Early in 1937 Auden volunteered to drive an ambulance for the socialist government in Spain—which instead set him to work broadcasting propaganda—and when he returned he published his poem "Spain" in a sixpenny pamphlet with a red cover that declared its political loyalty. Its closing lines warned that "History to the defeated / May say Alas but cannot help nor pardon." But the Moscow show trials of 1936 had destroyed the last possibility of hope in Soviet justice, and Auden, during his weeks in Spain, discovered that those who served history by resisting the manifest injustice of Franco found themselves implicated in the hidden injustice of Stalin's agents. The muddling European democracies, both before and after their concessions to Hitler at the Munich Conference of 1938, had proved unwilling and unable to act against any injustice at all.

Now, in a world tense with anticipation of war, with "the living nations . . . Sequestered in their hate," when all collective action seemed doomed to futility or injustice, Auden argued to himself that the only just acts open to him were private ones of teaching and praise. In his elegy for Yeats he portrayed these acts as the work of an exceptional individual who braved the realm of death and transformed the irrational powers; they were acts achieved through the mysterious power of a poet's gift, and were unconstraining acts that might teach a justice they would never impose.

This argument, as Auden knew, left large openings for vanity and evasion, and when the Defence Counsel makes his claim for Yeats's greatness, he relies on a doubtful parallel between questionable political values and equally questionable literary ones. "The social virtues of a real democracy," he tells the jury, "are brotherhood and intelligence, and the parallel linguistic virtues are strength and clarity, virtues which appear ever more clearly through successive volumes of the deceased." Yeats's later diction is therefore "the diction of a just man." Auden probably did not himself accept this smooth equation—he certainly did not accept it later—and never believed that strength was in itself an ethical virtue. Every merit praised by the Defence Counsel is an example of inherent virtue, the kind of *virtù* that belongs to impersonal powers, not a virtue of relationship, which concerns the merits of one's response to something outside oneself—as in a poet's love of language. Inherent virtue has more to do with force than with morals. The Defence Counsel, for all his good intentions, sounds uncomfortably like the Prosecutor. As Auden wrote in a later poem about two misguided aspects of himself, "both are worshippers of force." If the jury sees through the Prosecutor's lies and finds for the defense, the Prosecutor is none the less the victor.

Auden mistrusted Yeats as an ally even when he defended him, and knew that in both life and art the gift was not enough. The gift loves vivid particulars and has no interest in ethics or abstractions. Like an instinct, it wants its satisfactions now, not later. "All poets adore explosions, thunderstorms, tornadoes, conflagrations, ruins, scenes of spectacular carnage," he observed straight-facedly in 1947 in the first of the essays he entitled "Squares and Oblongs." "The poetic imagination is therefore not at all a desirable quality in a chief of state."

As Auden wrote in his sonnet on Matthew Arnold, the gift finds something to praise in the gravest disorder. But in a book review on Arnold written only a few days or weeks later, he sounded less sympathetic with the gift's insistence on praising. With Arnold as with Voltaire, Auden's prose and poetry took opposing views on the same question. The sonnet

mourned Arnold's anarchic celebratory gift; the review contrasted Arnold
with Walt Whitman, to whom Auden attributed the same impulses that
in the sonnet he had seen in Arnold's gift—and made clear that although
Whitman was the greater poet, Arnold, by suppressing his gift, had made
himself the better guide in matters of justice. Whitman—whom Auden
brought into the review largely because he now seized any chance to
write about an American subject when nominally writing about something else—"was so busy accepting everything that he forgot to notice
that one thing differs from another." Whitman praised "the dirt . . . the
everyday people," but "the anarchist-capitalist liberal democracy of
which Whitman was the spokesman, which accepted everyone and everything as perfectly free and perfectly equal and perfectly good, failed
to realize concretely the abstract virtues of Truth, Freedom, and Justice.
The dirt is getting tired of being just dirt." Arnold, Auden continued,
"may have been a prig, but he knew there is a difference between right
and wrong, and if democracy is not to be overwhelmed by an authori-
tarianism under which poetry will be impossible, it must listen not only
to Whitman's congratulations but also to Arnold's cold accusing voice."

Arnold and Whitman both interested Auden at this time because each
was a partial poet—the kind of poet he had left England to avoid becoming. "They represent approaches to life which are eternally hostile,
but both necessary, the way of the particularizing senses as against the
way of the generalizing intellect." Each partial approach has its own self-
deceptions. "The affectation of being a-theoretical and practical, the
homespun wit of Whitman or Will Rogers, and the fastidious highbrow
aloofness of Arnold or Woodrow Wilson, are both forms of conceit,
which is another word for cowardice." The equation of cowardice with
conceit was a public statement of Auden's private warnings to himself.
Conceit, he thought, encourages a writer to continue writing in the safe
familiar manner he has become conceited about, and the resulting cowardice traps him in his partial state. Although in Auden's elegy for Yeats
time "Pardons cowardice, conceit," it does not justify them. Yeats imagined heroic moments when "a man . . . completes his partial mind."
Auden imagined only that a writer could become less partial by adopting
"humility and courage," which are the opposites of conceit and cowardice. He named those better qualities in a review of a book of criticism
later in 1939. For a critic, he wrote, "the apparently easy approach of
simple appreciation is really the most difficult; it requires both humility
and courage, the humility to read the text without preconceived ideas of

what is to be found and the courage to speak without caring whether one is being clever or original."

Auden in his poetry hoped that the way of humility and courage had been opened to him by his gift—whatever different opinions he held in his prose. Herman Melville, in a gentle free-verse portrait Auden sketched in March 1939, had learned acceptance at last and "sailed into an extraordinary mildness." Auden's own poetic mildness at this time, his relaxations of diction, rhyme, and metre, were a form of acceptance, a conscious choice to listen to language instead of marching it across a parade-ground.* In earlier poems he had worked to concentrate human variety into dense allegorical abstractions. Now, in his poems about poets, from "Rimbaud" to "Herman Melville" (the first poems he wrote whose titles were the names of real historical figures), he attended to the particularities of named persons, and his private gift praised the gifts of others—who, unlike the private selves of his earlier poems, were neither idealized heroes like T. E. Lawrence nor helpless victims like Miss Gee.

———

In the poems and plays Auden had written in England in the 1920s and 1930s, the instinctive powers had often acted as murderous agents of family and state. In the poems he wrote during his first two months in New York, with England and his family an ocean away, the only mysterious power that remains is the healing, generous gift. As in the sonnet Auden had written in 1936, "The vanquished powers were glad / To be invisible and free." Then, without warning, they emerged in their shocking fury.

"Where do They come from?" is the opening question of a turbulent and ecstatic poem written in April 1939 that Auden first entitled "Crisis" but later renamed "They" in tribute to the unnameable powers it described. They are "Those whom we so much dread," who chill our landscape with their crooked wing, who "have purpose and knowledge / And towards us their hate is directed." Auden's poem is a rare modern instance of authentic mythological poetry: the powers it acknowledges

———

* "The looseness was deliberate," he wrote to his father, probably in February 1939, in response to his father's objections to the poem "Epitaph on a Tyrant," which he had written in January, just before he left England; "for what I was trying to do, a neatly chiselled epigram on the classical model would have been wrong" (Bodleian Library).

were not found in books or self-consciously invented (Yeats used both
methods in his poems about political and imaginative crisis) but imma-
nent beings in whose existence Auden now almost literally believed.
Nothing like it had been written in English since Blake populated his
prophetic books with mythical beings of his own creation, and Auden
wrote the poem at the start of a period of a year and a half in which he
repeatedly praised the poet he portrayed in "New Year Letter" as

> Self-educated *William Blake*
> Who threw his spectre in the lake,
> Broke off relations in a curse
> With the Newtonian Universe,
> But even as a child would pet
> The tigers Voltaire never met,
> Took walks with them through Lambeth, and
> Spoke to Isaiah in the Strand,
> And heard inside each mortal thing
> Its holy emanation sing.

Auden's relation with the creatures of myth was less confident than he
imagined Blake's had been. At the same time he was reminding himself
of the need for humility and courage, he was also experimenting with a
newly exalted fantasy of his own powers, and he was terrified by the
anarchic angers he glimpsed behind the smile of welcome offered by the
gift. Critics never write about "Where do They come from?" It is one
of the few poems of Auden's later years whose meanings are too idiosyncratic and private for readers to translate into their own meanings. Its
lurid mythography fits awkwardly into the standard portraits of the poet
as psychological analyst or Horatian sage. The Horatian stanzas in which
it is cast, learned from the example of mad Hölderlin, strain to hold
together its uncharacteristically broken syntax, where verbs of action do
their work without being motivated by nouns.

   In the moments of ecstasy and crisis when the creatures of myth appeared in Auden's work, they disrupted his attempts to believe in his
own freedom, and refuted his arguments for the efficacy of political
choice. In his vision of Agape in 1933, as he recorded it in "A Summer
Night," he had sat passively, "Enchanted as the flowers," while an irresistible power compelled him to love. But later in the same poem, he
also foresaw the doom of his privileged class in the "crumpling flood"
of social revolution. Now, in "Where do They come from?" the conquering and transforming powers were again instinctive and erotic, but

their driving force was the just anger felt by social and psychological outcasts.

In itself, this jagged and overheated poem scarcely justifies the effort needed to puzzle out its private myth. But the effort is worth making because versions of this myth pervade the greater poems that Auden wrote at around the same time, and because the myth's extravagant complexity was a mask for simpler feelings that he found too painful to bring to the surface of his verse. To its opening question the poem gives a detailed but riddling answer. *They* cannot be defined by language, and they have no language of their own. They are the chthonic powers that our intellectual pride has banished from ourselves, and they exist, paradoxically, because we banished them. Evolutionary and erotic instincts were inseparable from the whole being of a lower animal; they took on separate existence only when we human beings divided ourselves into proletarian Matter and aristocratic Idea, and excluded from both the instincts that had once informed the whole. Now, in the arid climate of our thought and culture, we indulge in Rousseauistic fantasies of a new golden age when the instincts will return from exile and give back to us "the extravagant joy of life." But they arrive instead in forms we never imagined. They manifest themselves in our moments of dreadful self-revelation, when we sense the violent impulse hidden within our ambition for praise or knowledge. To both self-absorbed Narcissus and knowledge-seeking Adam the powers are

> Terrible presences that the ponds reflect
> Back at the famous, and when the blond boy
>   Bites eagerly into the shining
>   Apple, emerge in their shocking fury.

It is too late to recover lost unity by reconciling matter and mind, because our divisions are social as well as psychological, and the exiled powers erupt in the violence of our politics. "The dirt is tired of being just dirt," Auden wrote in his review of Matthew Arnold; the instincts in the poem turn on us with "the resentment of outcasts" and "anarchist vivid abandon." They "reply to terror with terror." In the stark logic of the myth, they return because we ourselves, in our nostalgic wish, begged them to come back. "O we conjured them here like a lying map . . . We lured with a mirage of orchards."

We were convinced they were too naïve or forgiving to remember who had banished them, "Ready to see a charm in our childish fib / Pleased to find nothing but stones and / Able at once to create a garden." But exile changed them. Forced outside, they learned to envy our life of thought whose barren dryness taught us to envy them.

> Our money sang like streams on the aloof peaks
> Of our thinking that beckoned them on like girls;
> Our culture like a West of wonder
> Shone a solemn promise in their faces.

Repressed by a father's rage, perverted by "a mother's distorting mirror," they "come equipped / To reply to terror with terror."

When Auden's English confidante A. E. Dodds* asked him to explain the first title of the poem, "Crisis," he sent an answer that characterized the poem as an essay on public themes. "The Crisis," he told her, "is just the spiritual crisis of our time, i.e. the division between the reason and the heart, the individual and the collective, the liberal ineffective highbrow and the brutal practical demagogue like Hitler and Huey Long." This said nothing about the poem's private emotional meanings, but Auden hinted at them when, at the request of the editor of *The Atlantic*, the dignified New England monthly that first published the poem, he added an epigraph. He chose the lines Dante had written for the terrace of the envious in *Purgatorio*: "Of my sowing such straw I reap. O human folk, why set the heart there where exclusion of partnership is necessary?" Envy—like its counterpart in the mirror, narcissism —is a failure of a love; as narcissism imagines there is nothing it needs outside itself, envy imagines that *everything* it needs is outside itself. Auden was haunted at this time by the failure of his erotic life—his envious desire for the other world of the unformed and instinctive and relatively unlettered, and his narcissistic denial of shared humanity with those he desired. In "Where do They come from?" beneath the exfoliating images of political and spiritual crisis, he was also exploring a more private crisis.

Near the end of the poem, the gothic atmosphere turns extravagantly sexual. Our wish for the banished powers' return takes the explicit form of erotic longing, an involuntary desire to overcome the barrenness of thought. Our longing will be fulfilled, despite the invaders' anger—and

---

* Annie Edwards Dodds had been a lecturer in English at the University of Birmingham and was married to Professor E. R. Dodds, a longtime friend of Auden's family whose book *The Greeks and the Irrational* in 1951 was a meditation on the same themes as Auden's poem. She did much of the work of putting Auden's *Oxford Book of Light Verse* through the press in 1938.

despite our fear that the issue of our sexual union shall supplant us when a new spring melts the winter of ourselves:

> For a future of marriage nevertheless
> The bed is prepared; though all our whiteness shrinks
> From the hairy and clumsy bridegroom
> We conceive in the shuddering instant.

> For the barren must wish to bear though the Spring
> Punish; and the crooked that dreads to be straight
> Cannot alter its prayer but summons
> Out of the dark a horrible rector.

The poem follows D. H. Lawrence in assigning the feminine gender to our barren culture, and echoes Isaiah in prophesying that the crooked shall be made straight. But in his poems and letters Auden had repeatedly used "crooked" to refer to his homosexuality. At the start of his career, in 1928, he had briefly hoped to be made straight through psychoanalysis; now, at the start of his American career, he knew enough about himself not to entertain the same hope, but he used the same vocabulary. The change he wanted to achieve through the energies of instinct was a change not in the sexual object of his love but in its depth and permanence. In the weeks before he left England he had complained to a friend about a loss of feeling. In 1937 he had told a departing beloved to "Lay your sleeping head . . . on my faithless arm." Now for a "future of marriage" the bed was prepared.

As in Homer, where even Zeus is subject to the greater rule of mysterious impersonal fate, so in Auden's poem the instinctive powers are subject to a destiny larger and better than their own. The violent marriage of culture and instinct will produce peaceful offspring. During his first American year Auden again tried to teach himself a lesson he had derived from Marx, that history on the largest scale moved inescapably toward the "unity of mankind and a recognition of the common humanity of all men." Progress was inevitable, he told a lecture audience early in April 1939: "You cannot stop it; you can only limit its rate of progression." But in the past few weeks, Hitler had absorbed the last of Czechoslovakia, Franco had overrun the Spanish Loyalists, and Britain and France had pledged support to Poland in the event of aggression. Auden cautiously said nothing in his published prose about his faith in progress, although he had no hesitation in expressing it from the lecture podium and referred to it elliptically in his poems. He ended "Where do

They come from?" by affirming that our division—all that defines the
way we live now—will end in a future of peace we cannot yet imagine.

A few years earlier, Auden had denied that evolution had anything to
do with progress, and he cited the evidence of psychology and anthropology against "the nineteenth-century evolutionary doctrine of man
moving 'upward, working out the beast, / And let the ape and tiger
die.' " Now he affirmed that doctrine, and endorsed it in the same metaphors from Tennyson that he had earlier used to refute it. The ape and
the tiger will die because "we have / Failed as their pupils." The instinctive evolutionary Eros that brought them into being continues to direct
us forward. It is "a love we have never outgrown." Our tears, our cities,
even our armies all point, despite themselves, to an inevitable destiny
unlike everything they know:

> O the striped and vigorous tiger can move
> With style through the borough of murder; the ape
>   Is really at home in the parish
>   Of grimacing and licking; but we have
>
> Failed as their pupils. Our tears well from a love
> We have never outgrown; our cities predict
>   More than we hope; even our armies
>   Have to express our need of forgiveness.

A month later, in May 1939, Auden restated this myth in a stark, ambiguous way. In his elegy for the émigré German playwright Ernst Toller
(some of whose songs Auden had translated) he attributed to the mysterious powers full control over love and death. Against all his earlier
affirmations of consciousness and freedom, he now wrote that our sense
of ourselves as free agents is an illusion. Toller died by his own hand,
but it was the mysterious powers, not he, who chose his dying. In 1929
Auden had read in Freud's *The Ego and the Id* this paraphrase of the
teachings of Georg Groddeck: "The conduct through life of what we
call our ego is essentially passive . . . we are 'lived' by unknown and
uncontrollable forces." Now he wrote simply:

> We are lived by powers we pretend to understand.
> They arrange our loves; it is they who direct at the end
> The enemy bullet, the sickness, or even our hand.

It is their tomorrow hangs over the earth of the living
And all that we wish for our friends; but existence is believing
We know for whom we mourn and who is grieving.

The poem is radically skeptical about human autonomy—about the very
existence of any individual person—and at the same time morally certain
that persons exist through their insistence on doing so. Existence is active: it occurs in the act of valuing other persons enough to grieve for
them, in the act of believing we know who grieves and who is mourned.
To define the word "person" using nouns like "self" or "personality"
is to deceive oneself. To define it through verbs like "believing,"
"mourning," and "grieving," so that a person is that which thinks,
speaks, and acts in the first-person singular, is to come near to
truth.

Auden made the same argument in an elaborate joke at the end of a
poem he wrote a few weeks earlier as a gift for the manager of the un-
pretentious George Washington Hotel, where he and Isherwood stayed
during their first months in New York. The poem, titled simply "Ode,"
has the same stanza form used by Winthrop Mackworth Praed for light
social satire, but Auden preferred to make his most serious points in a
tone that refused to claim seriousness:

But now let me add in conclusion
    Just one little personal remark;
Though I know that the Self's an illusion,
    And that words leave us all in the dark,
That we're serious mental cases
    If we think that we think that we know,
Yet I've stayed in hotels in most places
    Where my passport permits me to go
(Excluding the British Dominions
    And Turkey and U.S.S.R.)
And this one, in my humble opinion's
    The nicest I've been in so far.

Fragile as acts of personal belief and "humble opinion" are, no impersonal power can overwhelm them. "In Memory of Ernst Toller" is a
poem of private mourning, in deliberate contrast to the public rhetorical

mourning of "In Memory of W. B. Yeats." Auden could now mourn someone who had died, because when he wrote his elegy for Toller he had suddenly discovered—thanks to the same instinctive powers whose appearance he had once dreaded—that he could love someone who was living.

CHAPTER TWO

The Vision Enters

The invisible powers had gathered into a single human form. In May 1939, about a month after Auden met Chester Kallman at a reading in New York, he had an experience that he later described—without saying it was his own—as a "Vision of Eros . . . a revelation of creaturely glory . . . the glory of a single human being." Conscious sexual desire is present in such a vision, "but physical desire is always, and without any effort of will, subordinate to the feeling of awe and reverence in the presence of a sacred being: however great his desire, the lover feels unworthy of the beloved's notice." This was more than the ordinary upheaval of falling in love. It was the same tumult of voices and visions that Dante experienced when he first saw Beatrice. Three years after his vision, Auden told a friend that he planned to write "a sort of modern *Vita Nuova*."

His second adult vision recapitulated the pattern of his vision of Agape in June 1933. Each was heralded by partial, distorted prefigurings. In May 1933, in his sestina "Hearing of harvests rotting in the valleys," he had hoped for the renewing waters that arrived in full flood in "A Summer Night"; around the same time, in his prose satire "Sermon by an Armament Manufacturer" (later the Vicar's sermon in *The Dog Beneath the Skin*), he condemned an egoistic perversion of the kind of religious experience he was about to receive. In April 1939, he had written in "Where do They come from?" about irresistible erotic powers driven by resentment and disorder, and had imagined in fascinated dread the destruction of barriers of class and personality that he was about to find in his relation with Kallman.

In both instances, he felt himself subject to an external power that compelled him to give the kind of love he had convinced himself he was unable to feel. During his vision of Agape he had felt love for friends and colleagues at the school where he was teaching, but he had no sexual interest in them. Sexual satisfaction occurred elsewhere. In "A Summer Night," written in the vision's afterglow, he was grateful to find next to him when he woke "one / Who has not gone away"—but this was someone with whom he was not in love. Then, during the next few weeks, he apparently began to experience a kind of erotic love he had not known before and wrote a love poem in which the beloved was recognizably a unique person, not an anonymous replaceable object of desire. "The fruit in which your parents hid you, boy" was the first of a series addressed during the next four years to an adolescent youth whom he had met in 1932 (not the older, more casual partner in "A Summer Night" who had not gone away).* Soon after writing it, Auden asked to review for *The Criterion* Violet Clifton's *The Book of Talbot*, a widow's biography of her husband. He used the review as a platform from which to proclaim that "the first criterion of success in any human activity, the necessary preliminary, whether to scientific discovery or to artistic vision, is intensity of attention or, less pompously, love." But his attention, he knew to his regret, was transient. His subsequent love poems alternated between awed praise for the beloved's beauty and troubled knowledge of mutual betrayal. "Dear, though the night is gone" is haunted by a dream in which the beloved, "unabashed, / Did what I never wished, / Confessed another love." "Lay your sleeping head, my love" predicts the lover's faithlessness when "Certainty, fidelity, / On the stroke of midnight pass." In 1937 this series of poems—the ones that used masculine pronouns for the beloved were disguised as cabaret songs for the voice of Benjamin Britten's favorite soprano, Hedli Anderson—came to an end with "Johnny," a valedictory song to a beloved who "frowned like thunder" and went away, and "Funeral Blues," a dirge for a dead beloved.

In 1933 Auden had loved someone too young to be his emotional equal. Although Chester Kallman was fourteen years younger than Auden, he was, at eighteen, in 1939, close to adulthood, and intellectually

---

* In *Early Auden* I identified a different poem as the first love poem Auden wrote after his vision of Agape. I was wrong.

reflective and quick. Now Auden was illuminated not by his love for *others*, an illumination insufficient to sustain permanent relations with any one person, but by his love for *another*. A quarter century later, in 1963, in a long essay on mystical experiences, he divided them into categories: the vision of nature, exemplified by Wordsworth and not uncommon in childhood and adolescence; the vision of Eros; the vision of Agape; and the vision of God. This sequence was less a Platonic ladder than the record of an increasing understanding of the value of unique persons— one person in the vision of Eros, then many persons in the vision of Agape, finally the unique God of whom everyone is the unique image. This sequence also traces a passage from childhood to maturity, though in Auden's private history the order of events had been different: his vision of Eros had been delayed and almost prevented by his conviction that he had been exiled from personal love by his sexuality and intellect.

In the twentieth century, any report of visionary experience prompts a knowing psychoanalytic nod, but Auden was unabashed.

> Half the literature, highbrow and popular, produced in the West during the past four hundred years has been based on the false assumption that what is an exceptional experience is or ought to be a universal one. Under its influence so many millions of persons have persuaded themselves they were "in love" when their experience could be fully and accurately described by the more brutal four-letter words, that one is sometimes tempted to doubt if the experience is ever genuine, even when, or especially when, it seems to have happened to oneself. However, it is impossible to read some of the documents, *La Vita Nuova*, for example, many of Shakespeare's sonnets or the *Symposium* and dismiss them as fakes.

But Dante's account of the vision is thoroughly different from Plato's. Dante, Auden wrote, is always aware of Beatrice as a person, not an allegory of something greater than herself, much less a way station on an ascent to it. Auden was baffled, he said, by Diotima's speech in the *Symposium*, because Plato "seems unaware of what we mean by a person" and can therefore encourage us to ascend from the love of physical beauty to the love of fair conduct and fair principles and finally to the love of beauty itself. Auden found himself arguing with Plato's ghost that "It is quite true, as you say, that a fair principle does not get bald and fat or run away with somebody else. On the other hand, a fair principle cannot give me a smile of welcome when I come into the room." He wrote elsewhere: "The natural human, or at least masculine, tendency, both in love and in friendship, is to be attracted by qualities rather than persons. We like people not for what they are in themselves but because they are beautiful or rich or amusing, so that if they lose their looks or their money or their wit, we lose our interest." Plato took our romantic interest in qualities as unalterable, and showed that "if qualities, not persons, are what we want, then the proper place to look for them is in Heaven, among the Universals."

Before he left England for the United States, Auden had devised an elaborate theory of love in which he tried to make sense of his faithless isolation while finding no means of escaping it. In a book review early in 1938 he had written about two apparently irreconcilable realms:

> Heaven and Hell. Reason and Instinct. Conscious Mind and Unconscious. Is their hostility a temporary and curable neurosis, due to our particular pattern of culture, or intrinsic in the nature of these faculties? . . . Does Life only offer two alternatives: "You shall be happy, healthy, attractive, a good mixer, a good lover and parent, but on condition that you are not overcurious about life. On the other hand you shall be attentive and sensitive, conscious of what is happening round you, but in that case you must not expect to be happy, or successful in love, or at home in any company. There are two worlds and you cannot belong to them both."

He had generalized his personal history into a universal condition:

> If you belong to the second of these worlds you will be unhappy because you will always be in love with the first while at the same time you will despise it. The first world on the other hand will not return your love because it is in its nature to love only itself. Socrates will always fall in love with Alcibiades; Alcibiades will only be a little flattered and rather puzzled.*

This presupposes that love is a hunger for something one lacks, a need prompted by inadequacy—therefore always unequal, always divided against itself. In his twenties, as he told friends later, Auden had typically fallen in love with someone from his own social class who was mild and strong, and puzzled by Auden's world of anxious thought. He had enjoyed uncomplicated sexual friendships with others whose intellect resembled his—after his adolescent infatuation with the older and more self-possessed Isherwood, their relations had settled into this kind of friendship—and he had experienced uncomplicated sexual desire for

---

* This refers less to Plato than to Hölderlin's poem "Sokrates und Alcibiades" (often quoted by Auden in the 1930s), which ends: "The wise bow to the beautiful."

those outside his class, such as the face "seen compressed / Over a lathe, refusing answer," in a poem written in 1929. In 1938 he still imagined he could desire and love only those with beauty, youth, and power—because he thought he lacked all three—and he therefore imagined his love was doomed to faithlessness, because "Beauty, midnight, vision dies." The word "person" was not yet part of his moral vocabulary, and it had not occurred to him that he could learn to love anything but qualities. Yet he ended his meditation on "the two worlds" with a guess that they might somehow be reconciled. "Perhaps the Socialist State will marry them; perhaps it won't . . . Perhaps again the only thing which can bring them together is the exercise of what Christians call charity."

His vision of Eros in 1939 demolished this whole theoretical structure of division and need. "I've spent years believing that I could only love the world of the Alter Ego," he told Mrs. Dodds, "but I was very foolish, because W. of the A.E. doesn't respond. Now I realize that I wanted someone rather like myself." This realization became possible only when he abandoned the idea that he lacked some essential quality he could find in someone else, a quality that no one else would ever seek in him. He wanted someone *rather* like himself, not an image of Narcissus. "All sexual desire," he wrote later, "presupposes that the loved one is in some way 'other' than the lover: the eternal and, probably, insoluble problem for the homosexual is finding a substitute for the natural differences, anatomical and psychic, between a man and a woman." In October 1939, in a nonchalantly joyous poem to which he gave the understated title "Heavy Date,"* he recanted old errors:

> I believed for years that
> Love was the conjunction
> Of two oppositions;
>   That was all untrue;
> Every young man fears that
> He is not worth loving:
> Bless you, darling, I have
> Found myself in you.

Chester Kallman was born into a bohemian, lower-middle-class, Jewish American family; his father was a dentist who had three sons by three different women (only two of whom he married), and his family's culture

---

* The title, a common Americanism apparently unknown in Britain, means an important assignation with a potential lover.

preserved its Romanian and Latvian sources. Everything about him seemed at odds with Auden's professional, university-trained, upper-middle-class, Anglo-Catholic background. But he shared Auden's knowledgeable love of literature and music, wrote competent and copious verse in Audenesque style, and delighted Auden with hilarious storytelling, extravagant mimicry, and sharp allusive puns. Auden inevitably took the role of teacher in his love affairs, but he felt isolated by it, and became Kallman's enthusiastic pupil in the field of opera. A few months after meeting Kallman, he wrote his first libretto, *Paul Bunyan*, and within a year, after attending matinee performances of the *Ring* and other works by Wagner at the Metropolitan Opera in New York, he was describing Wagner as "the greatest and the most typical modern artist, the forerunner, and in many ways the creator, of both the high-brow and the low-brow tastes of our time." Socrates and Alcibiades had more in common than they thought.

═════

The inner history of Auden's vision began about two months before the vision itself, when he made his first political speech since his arrival in the United States. In England he had been notably ineffective as a public orator. At one mass rally, trying to read aloud from an account of Spanish Civil War refugees, he was too affected by it to continue. At the first night of one of his and Isherwood's plays, after stepping before the curtain to appeal for aid for Spanish children, he never recovered from the fumble of his opening sentence: "As you know, worse things have been happening in the audience tonight than on the stage." Now, when he spoke on 16 March 1939 at a meeting of the Foreign Correspondents' Dinner Forum, a group set up to help Spanish refugees, he found himself wielding the rhetorical powers of the hero-poet in his elegy for Yeats and was astonished at his own success.

When Auden made his speech, the Spanish Republic was already doomed; Britain and France had recognized Franco's government; Republican Madrid was on the point of surrender. Fascism had won its first European war, and Hitler, earlier that same day, had completed his annihilation of independent Czechoslovakia. Auden began in a somber post-mortem tone. The Weimar Republic in Germany and the first liberal government in Spain had failed, he said, because their leaders "lacked the kind of character which alone makes a democratic form of government possible to run," and, he continued, the same failure was now threatening Britain and the United States. Democracy was a hard discipline. It could be won only by truth-telling and by an undogmatic and unsentimental attention to the reality of ordinary men and women.* If we want to save democracy, "we must first make it more worth saving; and to do this, we must first see to it that we personally behave like democrats in our private as [in our] public lives; and when I look at my own, I wish I had a clearer conscience."

All this was plausible enough—until his tone suddenly changed in his closing sentence. If the democracies do not live up to their promises, Auden concluded, "it will not be Germany, it will not be Italy, but our own people who will say 'To hell with talk, to hell with truth, to hell with freedom,' will rise up and sweep us away, and by God, ladies and gentlemen, we shall deserve it." This soapbox peroration, entirely unlike Auden's usual public manner, produced the opposite effect from the sobering one required by the words themselves, and the effect was intentional. As Auden described it in a letter to Mrs. Dodds five months later, when he was no longer too ashamed to talk about it: "I suddenly found I could really do it, that I could make a fighting demagogic speech and have the audience roaring." The members of such an audience scarcely notice they are roaring for an attack on themselves. They are flattered by the reminder of their high places that others dream of toppling, and roused by the vague bright prospect of self-improvement. As Auden imagined them saying in "September 1, 1939," "I *will* be true to the wife, / I'll concentrate more on my work."

The cheers of an audience unaware of what it is cheering about speak badly for the audience and the orator. "It is so exciting," Auden told Mrs. Dodds, "but so absolutely degrading; I felt just covered with dirt afterwards"—a charged phrase that suggests the intensity of his revulsion. Having made a speech that, in his eyes, did exactly what it pretended to renounce, that proclaimed exactly the false appeal to justice which it insisted should be replaced by true ones, he felt defiled by his own words. Having insisted that nations were listening to dictators only because the democracies had broken their promises of truth and justice, he heard in the roars of his audience a loud empty promise that did more to serve Hitler than to hinder him. In the autumn of 1938, when Auden had rushed around England giving speeches about the Sino-Japanese

---

* "Refugee Blues," a poem written around the same time, makes a similar appeal to public and private conscience by directing most of its satire against the democracies for their unfeeling exclusion of Jewish refugees (*Collected Poems*, p. 265).

War, he had no confidence that he was doing any good, but he had never imagined he was doing harm. Now he felt he had violated both his audience and himself.

"Never, *never* again will I speak at a political meeting," he told Mrs. Dodds in another letter. "Of all the ivory towers it is the most secluded." He stopped making public statements on politics, even as he worked actively through refugee groups and private contacts to find jobs and fund medical aid for those exiled from Germany. (After the war broke out he tried to organize German exiles and others to produce anti-Nazi propaganda, but the results, he said, were too statistical or too bitter to publish.) Meanwhile, he did not hesitate to use his newly discovered powers as a speaker when reading his poems at public gatherings. William Carlos Williams, one of the American poets who shared the podium with him at a 1940 reading in New York attended by perhaps a thousand people, recalled that "Auden's success before the audience as contrasted with the rest of us was the feature of the evening."

In March 1939, probably soon after his speech, Auden wrote "The Unknown Citizen," a poem that appears to be a neat uncomplicated satire on the corporate state in which freedom and happiness are equated with conformity. In Auden's elegy for Yeats, "all the instruments" of meteorology agreed that the day of the poet's death was dark and cold, but they knew nothing about the inner world of his dying. All the instruments of the state are equally ignorant of the unknown citizen's inner world:

> all the reports on his conduct agree
> That, in the modern sense of an old-fashioned word, he was a saint
> For in everything he did he served the Greater Community.

(The idea that there might be *saints*, although dismissed by the corporate voice of the poem, is implicitly endorsed by the voice of the poet.)

But, as no reader at the time could have noticed, the poem was also a concealed satire on its author, rebuking the corporate voice Auden had adopted in an essay written around November 1938 for a collection by American and European authors entitled *I Believe: The Personal Philosophies of Certain Eminent Men and Women of Our Time*. There he had introduced the premise that "people are happy and good who have found their vocation: what vocations there are will depend upon the society within which they are practiced." Personal good and evil were products of social good and evil: "bad environment is the chief cause of

badness in individuals." Ignoring the inner torment and division explored in his lyric poems, he wrote as if persons were indistinguishable
from functions and unhappiness was a social artifact that could be undone by social means. In the society imagined in his essay, personal
conflicts—for example, the personal conflict of someone like Auden who
pursued a celebrated political life while enduring private misery—would
remain incomprehensible and unknown:

> Was he free? Was he happy? The question is absurd:
> Had anything been wrong, we should certainly have heard.

And in April 1939, drawing a moral from Cyril Connolly's *Enemies of
Promise* (the last book he reviewed until the end of August), he empha-
sized exactly what his essay had denied—the value of unique personality.
"The individual who desires maturity must go on alone."

Before 1939 Auden's politics, like his love, had been driven by his desire
for "the world of the Alter Ego." In both public and private life he had
loved and envied a world he could not share. A few months after his
speech, in an autobiographical sketch that purported to be a review of a
memoir by Alvah Bessie of the Spanish Civil War, Auden described his
political development:

> I left school an anarchist individualist, but after a few years became dissatisfied
> with this attitude and adopted, though more in theory than in practice, a view
> of Mr. Bessie's: "It was necessary . . . to work in a large body of men, to
> submerge myself in that mass, seeking neither distinction nor preferment and
> in this way to achieve self-discipline, patience and unselfishness."

He had convinced himself that because he was shut away in the darkness
of private life, he had nothing to offer anyone else, that without some
radical upheaval, he could never be worth loving and would never
be loved (as he had said of himself in 1938, in the episodes Isherwood
called "these extraordinary scenes—Wystan in tears"). He now accused
himself of having chosen a political life in the hope that it could break
the isolation of a personal life in which he had always been the self-
conscious, ironic, and superior partner. And he recognized that his political success had only increased his distance from his audience; it locked
him more securely than before in the lonely eminence of a conscious
ironic power guiding an unthinking inarticulate mass. As he wrote of the

instinctual forces a few weeks later in "Where do They come from?":
"O we conjured them here like a lying map."

"You cannot give unless you also receive," he wrote in *The Prolific
and the Devourer* that summer. "What is it that you hope to receive from
politics? excitement? experience? Be honest." He answered his own question a few pages later:

> Whoever you are, artist, scientist, or politician, there remains the problem of
> how you are to live. Personal salvation, whatever you do or pretend, that is
> what you are really after, not the salvation of others. That you may occasionally
> be permitted to do, but only by the way. As a conscious goal, it is nothing but
> the conceit of the tyrant.

In his review of Bessie's memoir—a review in which he used Bessie's
words to reveal the unconscious psychological motives for acts that Bessie
explained as consciously political—Auden recalled that when he had
sought (in Bessie's words) self-discipline, patience, and unselfishness by
submerging himself in a mass political movement, "I lost what little
discipline, patience and unselfishness I possessed." Having taken up left-
wing politics partly out of loneliness, he now endorsed Bessie's observation that "the intellectual is likely to find his greatest satisfaction
(perverted as it is) in long periods of solitude when he can justify his
loneliness by looking down upon his fellow man." When Auden was
forced at school to live a group life for which he was unsuited, his reaction was "precisely that justificatory 'looking-down' that Mr. Bessie
can rightly call perverse, a reaction which, since my fellow man [at
school] was always a member of my own class, was a not unimportant
factor in my adoption of left political views." The middle-class intellectual who justifies his loneliness by disdaining others in his class easily
infers that the class he does not belong to is superior to his own. Auden
added a parenthetical sting: "*Mein Kampf* provides interesting corrobo-
rative evidence of the same occurrence in the working-class." The emotionally isolated working-class author of that book rejected his own class
and joined the political right in the same way the emotionally isolated
middle-class young man joined the left.

Four years later, in an essay entitled "Purely Subjective," Auden wrote
even more severely, although more elliptically, about his early politics.
This was the longest essay he ever wrote without much hope of being
paid for it—he gave it to *The Chimera*, a little magazine published by
Princeton students—and the motive behind its abstract religious specu-

lations was evidently an irresistible impulse toward self-analysis. Using the Kierkegaardian vocabulary he adopted in the early 1940s, he described the aesthetic and ethical stages without saying that they had been the main stages in his own life. In the aesthetic stage the "subject" says: "Over against me is a world of other individual-subjects who are responsible, not for my existence, but for my anxiety about it. When I have learnt how to persuade them to love me and serve me, I shall no longer be anxious." (This is the fantasy that destroys Michael Ransom in *The Ascent of F6*.) When the subject gives up the aesthetic solution for the ethical one, he no longer wishes to be loved as a personality but hopes to serve some objective and external reality:

> I [the unspecific *I* of the essay] proceed to identify subjectivity with ignorance, and to assume that all true requiredness is objective, that my weakness and conflicts are caused by my subjectivity. My new God, Scientific Truth, the Dialectic, the Absolute or whatever I may call him, cannot be accused of being like a human being, because He cannot conceivably be thought of as a subject. That does not however make him any the less anthropomorphic. He is the image of my subjective idea of myself as a pure epistemological I, without parts or passions.

That is, my new God knows the world without taking the slightest interest in it.

Both solutions are attempts to escape loneliness: the aesthetic one by glorifying personality, the ethical one by suppressing it—as Auden had done when he subordinated personality to the utopian powers of Marxist history. The roaring cheers for his political speech in March 1939 confirmed once and for all the futility of the aesthetic solution; he had been skeptical from the start about the ethical one.

On 4 April 1939, in a lecture at the University of North Carolina, Auden defined what he called the only two philosophies of life, one false and one true. Dualism was the false philosophy: both the romantic dualism of Rousseau and Hitler that calls feeling good and intellect bad (as in Auden's own earlier self-hatreds) and the Platonic dualism that calls the soul good and the passions evil (as in the wish to submerge one's personality in the dispassionate will of history). Monism, or "organized common sense," was the true philosophy that recognized no sharp division between body and soul. Blake, Voltaire, and Goethe were exponents of the true philosophy in culture. In politics the exponent was Marx (evidently for his analyses more than for his prophecies; when talking with students afterward, as one recalled, Auden "made no secret of his disillusionment with Communism, even though, he said, he still liked some Communists"). In the realm of general human conduct, Auden added without comment, the exponent of the true philosophy was Jesus.

======

Once Auden stopped trying to cure his personal life through politics, his personal life seemed to cure itself. Two days after his lecture in North Carolina, he, Isherwood, and Louis MacNeice (who was on a long visit to the United States) gave a reading in New York under the left-wing sponsorship of the League of American Writers. They read their own poems and prose, interspersed with the work of other writers. Auden's political glamour assured a large turnout, and to much of the audience (as reported by Selden Rodman, a young poet who co-edited the left-wing monthly *Common Sense*, to which Auden contributed poems and reviews) his apolitical opening remarks came as a "bombshell":

> Two hundred years from now nobody will care much about our politics. But if we were truly moved by the things that happened to us, they may read our poems. In his time Dante was a reactionary. It is also deplorable that Yeats's last poem calls for war. But because Yeats was one of those most rare writers who continued to be moved by what happened to him right up to the day he died, his work will always have that authentic ring we recognize as poetry.*

At most events organized by the League of American Writers, the Party line proclaimed in Moscow was echoed with fervent strictness. Auden, Isherwood, and MacNeice were studiedly casual. Each came to the podium to recite and talk about a poem or fragment of prose, then sat down until, after a pause, another of the three stood up to take a turn. Auden "jolted everybody," MacNeice remembered, by reading Kipling's "The Gods of the Copybook Headings" with obvious pleasure; later he read two of Rimbaud's "Illuminations," Rilke's "Archaic Torso of Apollo," Yeats's "The Second Coming," Hilaire Belloc's "Lord Lundy," and, from memory, his own elegy for Yeats. Afterward some students

---

* Everyone in the room had read exactly the same argument in the poem Auden had printed in *The New Republic* a few weeks earlier: "Time that with this strange excuse / Pardoned Kipling and his views, / And will pardon Paul Claudel, / Pardons him for writing well." But Auden's political reputation was so strong that apparently no one took him seriously when he said it in verse.

from Brooklyn College spoke briefly with Auden and chatted at length with Isherwood, who invited one of them to the apartment he and Auden shared in the Yorkville district of Manhattan, having moved a few days earlier from the hotel where they had stayed since they arrived. Two days later Chester Kallman appeared at the door. As Auden told Mrs. Dodds, "Nothing could have been less propitious than the first occasion, for he had come to see Christopher and not me, and I thought he was going to be someone else, and was very cross." Auden was too discreet to tell her they had gone to bed together that day, but he later referred to 8 April as their "anniversary."

Auden and Kallman saw each other often that month, with the blessing of Kallman's father, who had long since stopped trying to convince his son to turn heterosexual. Auden had accepted an invitation to teach for four weeks at St. Mark's School, near Boston, and when he left New York in early May, at around the same time Isherwood left for California, he and Kallman were established lovers. But Auden's feelings were still shadowed by the same fears of inadequacy and need that had afflicted all his earlier loves:

> what reason have you to love me,
> Who have neither the prettiness and moisture of youth, the appeal of the baby,
> The fencing wit of the old successful life,
>   Nor brutality's fascination?

He wrote these lines, in a poem titled "Love Letter," in the first days of his month at St. Mark's.

> O but I was mad to come here, even for money:
> To have put myself at the mercy of the postman and the daydream.
> That incorrigible nightmare in which you lie weeping or ill,
>   Or drowned in the arms of another.

The poem, one of the worst (and most straightforwardly self-revealing) he ever published,* yokes together, in the manner of "Where do They come from?" the form of Horace's sober and ironic stanzas with a tone of discordant extravagance: "in the net of the ribs / The heart flails like a salmon." "Why this self-abasement," Kallman replied in a letter on

---

* The only audience that saw it at the time was the limited readership of the Kenyon College undergraduate literary magazine, *Hika*. Auden did not include it in his new book of poems later in the year, *Another Time*, and never reprinted it.

13 May. "Can you be assured? I love you." Auden was perhaps ready to accept assurance. As in his other markedly bad poems, the faults of the verse indicate that he no longer believed what the poem was trying to say. This was the last time he thought it made sense to ask "What reason have you to love me," and the first time he hoped for fidelity:

> O never leave me,
> Never. Only the closest attention of your mouth
> Can make me worthy of loving.

The "attention of your mouth" was the sexual expression of the same interest he defined shortly after his vision of Agape in 1933 as "intensity of attention or, less pompously, love." Until now he had never imagined it focused upon himself.

Within a few days, Auden's agitation suddenly ended and his mood turned calm. When he later compiled for a friend a dated list of the poems in "the published record of l'affaire C," the first two, both dated May 1939, were "Not as that dream Napoleon" and "The Prophets." "L'affaire C" was something more than the affair with Chester. It began with an inner illumination, not at a public reading. Critics who have tried to puzzle out these two poems as addresses to God were not entirely wrong. The poems address a person through whom, unknown to the person himself, divine mercy and power have been revealed. Auden told Kallman in a letter in poetic prose on Christmas Day, 1941, "Because it is through you that God has chosen to show me my beatitude, / As this morning I think of the Godhead I think of you."

When the beatific vision occurs in the course of a sexual relation, it seems to occur because the beloved, as a real quotidian person, cannot carry the full burden of love that the lover bestows. Only a transfigured image of the beloved can accept so great a burden, and can do so because it is the image of a divinity whose power to give and receive love is infinite. Some of Auden's acquaintances amused themselves by debating whether he overvalued Kallman's fallen-angel style of physical attractiveness. They failed to notice that Auden's poems, after ten years of praise for the physical beauty of the beloved, had lost interest in "qualities rather than persons." It was the gift of love that mattered, not its wrappings.

The visionary love poems Auden wrote in the spring and summer of 1939 resembled no other love poems in recent literature. The poetic tradition he had inherited on the death of Yeats had for centuries been largely Protestant or secular, more adept at expressing the loss of vision than at expressing the vision itself. The only modern parallels to the ecstatic seventeenth-century rhetoric of Richard Crashaw, Henry Vaughan, or Thomas Traherne were the gnarled, tormented rhetoric of Gerard Manley Hopkins and the visionary-with-a-wink rhetoric of Yeats; Auden once remarked in conversation that while T. S. Eliot had mystical experiences of which he never spoke, Yeats had never had them but talked about them all the time. Auden revered Blake, but, after the experiment of "Where do They come from?" had no wish to populate a new Blakean world of myth. Instead, his solution to the difficulty of writing visionary poetry in English was a hesitant rhetoric of wonder. He wrote poems in which the early lines make a tentative approach to a truth that emerges in triumph only at the end, a style that owes something to Eliot's *Ash-Wednesday* but with a very different tone of gratification and delight.

The beloved of Auden's visionary poems—which he wrote mostly in Kallman's absence—is a figure more of mercy than of power. For the first time, he could imagine a beloved who, like Beatrice in the *Commedia*, willingly answers the lover's need and, as Beatrice does when she meets Dante on the heights of Purgatory, both rebukes and heals the lover's weakness. When Auden was a child his mother had tried and failed to stop his compulsive nail-biting, and John Maynard Keynes, after dining with Auden in Cambridge in 1938, had remarked that Auden's fingernails, bitten to the quick, were a sign of something unsatisfactory in his work. Kallman, in a letter he wrote to Auden in May 1939, commanded: "Do cease your nail-biting." At the end of May, Auden told Mrs. Dodds, "I always said that if this ever happened I would give up biting my nails. I have."

Auden began his first visionary poem of May 1939 by discarding all his false earlier images of the way love might come into his life. The beloved should arrive

> Not as that dream Napoleon, rumor's dread and center . . .
> Not as that general favorite and breezy visitor . . .
> Nor as any of those who will always be welcome,
> As luck or history or fun.*

---

* This echoes the Anglican hymn on the presentation of the infant Christ in the temple: "Hail to the Lord Who comes / . . . / Not with His Angel host, / Not in His Kingly state."

Fantasy had presented love as a conqueror, as a casual arrival, as an incident that becomes an event in one's history, as a mere amusement. "Do not enter like these: all these depart." (The sexual metaphors of the dream-Napoleon's advent are mildly startling: he is the one "Before whose riding all the crowds divide, / Who dedicates a column and withdraws.") Even if the arriving beloved were to bring the mild virtues of "politeness and freedom," these too would be transient in their "moderate success; / They exist in the vanishing hour." Moderation was as faithless and uncommitted as passion. All Auden's old metaphors of the beloved as a conquering arriving force—"on the arm / A fresh hand with fresh power"—were wrong. The true image of fidelity was a figure not of the beloved's power but of the lover's own weakness and desolation, to which the beloved can respond with love. It does not arrive as rumor's dread and center, but is "somewhere always, nowhere particularly unusual, / Almost anywhere in the landscape of water and houses." It was a figure that does not conquer but weeps:

> His crying competing unsuccessfully with the cry
> Of the traffic or the birds, is always standing
> The one who needs you, that terrified
> Imaginative child who only knows you
> As what the uncles call a lie,
> But knows he has to be the future and that only
> The meek inherit the earth, and is neither
> Charming, successful, nor a crowd;
> Alone among the noise and policies of summer
> His weeping climbs towards your life like a vocation.

Weakness triumphs, while strength makes too rapid an exit for anyone, including itself, to notice that it fails. The weeping child is always present in both the adult lover and the adult beloved, and its cries make a promise of transformation and purpose that no dream-Napoleon cares about. This is a "vocation" utterly different from those Auden had in mind when he wrote in 1938 about vocations that "depend upon the society within which they are practiced."

"Like a Vocation" was Auden's later title for "Not as that dream Napoleon," and in the years after he wrote it, the relation that seemed to him most like a vocation was marriage. He wore a wedding ring during his early months with Kallman. In June he wrote to his brother John, "This time, my dear, I really believe it's marriage. We are going on our honeymoon in ten days to Taos in New Mexico." He told Mrs. Dodds,

"For some years now I've known that the one thing I really needed was marriage, and I think I have enough experience to know that this relationship is going to be marriage with all its boredoms, troubles, and rewards." Later in 1939 he referred in a book review to the "marriage" of Rimbaud and Verlaine. His polemical use of the word was strengthened by the offhand manner with which he pretended there was nothing polemical about it. Marriage, as he regarded it in 1939, was any sexual relation governed by vows; it was an ethical and symbolic relation, not a legal and economic one, and was indifferent to the sexuality of the persons joined by it. Almost every allusion Auden had made earlier to his sexuality showed traces of defiant or despairing guilt. Now he wrote as if he had been freed from guilty isolation by the ordinariness of married life.

"For a future of marriage nevertheless / The bed is prepared," he had written apocalyptically in April in "Where do They come from?" In May, while revising his drafts of "Like a Vocation," he found that this sensual bed mattered less than he had thought. In an early version, he typed these lines:

> O but for life
> Politeness and freedom are not enough; they lead
> To a luxurious death-bed . . .

Then he turned over the page and began typing the revised version that, with only trivial changes, he sent off for publication:

> But politeness and freedom are never enough,
> Not for a life. They lead
> Up to a bed that only looks like marriage . . .

The vocation in the poem's final word—"His weeping climbs towards your life like a vocation"—is not the bed that "only looks like marriage" but marriage itself.

Auden in this poem returned to a landscape he had last visited in "Musée des Beaux Arts," written just before he left Europe. Death in the earlier poem occurred in "some untidy spot"; the weeping that "climbs towards your life" in the later one occurs in the same kind of place, "nowhere particularly unusual," unnoticed by traffic or birds. But all the relations in the earlier poem are now reversed. The plowman in "Musée des Beaux Arts" may have heard a forsaken cry, "But for him it was not an important failure"; in the typescript draft of "Like a Vocation," if the beloved chooses to be confident and charming, "The farmer [shall] go on ploughing while you watch." Into an indifferent landscape of the earlier poem a boy falls "out of the sky" with a "forsaken cry"; from an indifferent landscape in the later one, a child's weeping ascends. In the earlier poem, "everything turns away / Quite leisurely from the disaster," but now the forsaken child knows he has to be the future, that the meek shall inherit the earth.

This transformation of abandonment into love now became the central plot of Auden's poems. He told the story in two basic ways, one abstract and schematic, the other autobiographical and detailed. In the first, the pain of judgment is itself a promise of mercy; the more exact the judgment, the greater its implicit consolation: we are judged only by a power that takes an interest in us and will not abandon us to meaningless chaos. The poem "Kairos and Logos," written early in 1941, makes a compressed statement of the theme: "O blessing of reproach. O proof that silence / And condemnation presuppose our lives." Writing to his brother John on his "marriage," Auden said "I was really getting in despair," and added, "De profundus exclamavi." This is the opening phrase of the great prayer in Psalm 130—Out of the depths have I cried unto thee—which ends in a secure faith that iniquity will be redeemed by forgiveness.

Auden never explicitly named the second version of this plot, but its inner logic is clear from his poems: someone desolate and unworthy is rewarded with the gift of love because, in his presexual childhood many years earlier, with no thought of reward, he had himself given love to the desolate and unworthy. This is the plot of countless fairy tales and quest romances, a plot so familiar that every would-be hero knows to "look out for a stranded fish to be kind to," as Auden was to write in his sonnet sequence, "The Quest," in 1940. The fish, after all, may prove to be an enchanted prince (as in the Grimms' tale "The Fisherman and His Wife"). But as Auden had learned when he looked out for a political cause he could support with poems and speeches, the prince never lets himself be discovered by those who go looking for him.

A stranded fish doesn't smell like one to the hero who is truly kind to it. The objects of Auden's childhood love had been machines in the abandoned mines he explored in Wales and northern England whose rust and dereliction made them valueless in the eyes of the world, though in his they were entirely beautiful. In his 1963 essay on the four kinds of vision, he described this childhood experience without claiming it as his own, as a Wordsworthian "vision of Dame Kind," or nature, a vision not of persons but of nonhuman objects. "The basic experience is an overwhelming conviction that the objects confronting him [the visionary] have a numinous significance and importance, that the existence he is aware of is holy.* And the basic emotion is one of innocent joy, though this joy can include, of course, a reverent dread."

This childhood love was, as he now interpreted it in his poems, prophetic of the love he could both give and receive at thirty-two. He had learned as a child that the desolate and abandoned were not excluded from love. He had to wait for adulthood's vision of Eros to learn that the guilty and despairing were also not excluded.

"The Prophets" was Auden's later title for the poem in which he first gave thanks to a mercy that does not abandon, and first interpreted his childhood love as a sign of his adult vision. The weeping child in his previous poem, "Like a Vocation," has been comforted into a mood of quiet exhilaration:

> For now I have the answer from the face
> That never will go back into a book
> But asks for all my life, and is the Place
> Where all I touch is moved to an embrace
> And there is no such thing as a vain look.

He discovered that place because he had been there before. As early as 1933, in "A Summer Night," he had looked toward a revolutionary fulfillment that might occur in the future. Now, in "The Prophets," he looks back from a moment of emotional fulfillment to the past that prophesied it. The first of the prophets were the books in which he had found pictures of mining machinery that he had adored as only a child could do. Almost three decades later, he understands their silence:

* In the spring of 1939 Auden began quoting the last words of Blake's *The Marriage of Heaven and Hell*: "every thing that lives is Holy." Around this time he apparently read the proofs of the essay he had written for the collective volume *I Believe* and added Blake's phrase as an epigraph, although the phrase had nothing whatever to do with the thin-lipped functionalism of the essay itself. During the summer he used Blake's phrase again in *The Prolific and the Devourer* and then, in his poem "Pascal," gave the phrase a philosophical twist by using it to describe Pascal's conversion: "Everything that could exist was holy." Early in 1940 he included the phrase as a line in a draft of "New Year Letter" but dropped it before publication.

> Perhaps I always knew what they were saying:
> Even the early messengers who walked
> Into my life from books where they were staying,
> Those beautiful machines that never talked
> But let the small boy worship them . . .
> Love was the word they never said aloud
> As something that a picture can't return.

When he visited the machines themselves, their silence, like the silence of their pictures, praised his love for them:

> when I hunted the Good Place,
> Abandoned lead-mines let themselves be caught . . .
> The rusty winding-engine never taught
> One obviously too apt, to say Too Late:
> Their lack of shyness was a way of praising
> Just what I didn't know, why I was gazing,
> While all their lack of answer whispered "Wait,"
> And taught me gradually without coercion . . .

He remembers himself guiltily "too apt" even in childhood to believe he was already barred from any hope of love. But the silence with which the prophetic machines accepted his love was a promise that, because his adoration for them proved that mercy existed, he would someday receive what he gave:

> And all the landscape round them pointed to
> The calm with which they took complete desertion
> As proof that you existed.

And the calm with which this poem accepts happiness is the calm of rediscovery. The prophecy had never been forgotten, and all that needed to be said about its outcome was this poem's simple phrase: "It was true."

When Auden later wrote his account of the vision of Eros, he ended by retelling the story of Dante's loss and recovery of Beatrice. Dante can join Beatrice in Paradise because he has already had a vision of her on earth; yet he needs Beatrice's mercy in his second vision because he strayed from the revelation he was granted in the first. Dante "does not tell us exactly what the sins and errors were which brought him near to perdition nor, when they meet again, does Beatrice, but both of them speak of acts of infidelity to her . . . Though unfaithful to her image, he has, however, never completely forgotten it . . . and it is this memory, the fact that he has never completely ceased to love her, which makes it possible for Beatrice to intervene from Heaven to save his soul." (The Platonic ladder, in contrast, "makes the forgetting of a lower rung a moral duty.")

In 1936, in "Letter to Lord Byron," Auden remembered his childhood love as nothing more than an absorbing fad: "better far than any kings or queens / I liked to see and know about machines; / And from my sixth until my sixteenth year / I thought myself a mining engineer." In 1939, in a vocabulary learned from *La vita nuova*, he remembered each machine as if it had been Beatrice. He now considered the years between his childhood vision of a machine, which asked for nothing, and his adult vision of a beloved, who asked for all his life, as years of faithlessness to the early image. No one has ever betrayed a machine or a landscape, but everyone betrays some vision of glory. Auden accused himself of a double betrayal: he had turned away from visionary beauty to pursue the physical attractions and public charms of "the young for whom all wish to care," and, in his first adult poems, he had transformed his sacred country into a territory of murder. In *Paid on Both Sides*, the spy who sets in motion the cycle of revenge had opened with the line "My area is Rookhope" —the region with deserted mines in County Durham that, Auden said many years later, he had imagined as an Eden when he was twelve. In all the poems he wrote in his early twenties, the landscape of abandoned mines is one of hopeless isolation, a mirror of sexual guilt, a place where both language and love are stifled, and "the dead howl / Under the headlands in their windy dwelling."

Now, as he looked back from the perspective of 1939, he thought he had turned away from a solitary vision of love to a false belief that solitude was a form of hatred that must be overcome, and had turned to a political life in which, as he wrote in his review of Alvah Bessie, "my character did not become better; it became worse." But now, he was convinced, the true alternative to the group or political life in which he had hoped to submerge his solitude was not his lonely childhood vision; it was the personal love it had prophesied.

His first love had been personal in the sense that no one else could have shared it; his new love was personal in a more complex sense. "The beloved," he wrote about the vision of Eros, "possesses some degree of that beauty which is Nature's gift," but although the lover is aware of that beauty, "what seems to him infinitely more important is his awareness of the beloved as a person." What he now loved was a beauty conferred by the beholding eye:

> When I was a child, I
> Loved a pumping-engine,
> Thought it every bit as
> Beautiful as you.

On one of his return visits to New York from St. Mark's in May, he wrote a cabaret song for Britten to set for the voice of Hedli Anderson. "Calypso" praised "the one that I love to look on, / The acme of kindness and perfection," and concluded that "love's more important and powerful than / Even a priest or a politician." Except for a few lines written at Britten's request in 1940, this was the last time Auden wrote lines in which Hedli Anderson sang his feelings for him; from now on, he spoke in his own person when he wrote love poems. In 1938, in an earlier song written for Anderson, he had asked, "Will it alter my life altogether? / O tell me the truth about love." In 1939, answering his own question, he inscribed for Kallman a copy of his book *On This Island:* "To Chester / who told me the truth / (I was quite right; It did)."

In 1931 Auden had written a poem in which he imagined a voice telling him at the end of a journey, "This is your country and the hour of love." The poem depicted the journey as a quest that arrives at true certainties by abandoning false ones—by refusing a settled job, by ignoring a map that warns against dangerous impulsive woods. In 1939 he found his country and his hour of love, exactly as he had expected, in a place that offered no certainties. From America, in June, he wrote to an English friend:

> I am very glad indeed that I came here, which I did with considerable misgivings, as the distance from Europe has allowed one at last a little peace to consider what one really thinks. America has many faults, one of the worst being that Americans always want answers to everything, and when you tell them there aren't any, are very upset. But when they are in a tough spot they do look forward, unlike the English who the worse things get, the more passionately do they cling to the past. I have almost definitely decided now to become an American citizen.

He had no illusion that the United States had achieved a classless society—he told Mrs. Dodds that St. Mark's School "set out to be the American Eton and no Jews are admitted," adding that he hoped to teach next in a slum school—but because it was a country where the means existed to satisfy everyone's physical needs, it seemed to offer the most plausible hope for justice and freedom.

During the next few years he wrote repeatedly about the England of his childhood, but he wrote without nostalgia, because he had found in America the answer to his childhood wishes. His nostalgia for a lost past was discharged—for the moment—by fulfillments that let it be seen clearly for the first time. Auden, who now believed he had arrived at the lasting fulfillment of marriage, devoted much of the rest of 1939 and early 1940 to writing autobiographical recollections in a tone of gratitude he had never used before. He gave thanks in "The Prophets" for something he had loved as a child. He gave thanks in *The Prolific and the Devourer* for his release from political beliefs that had harmed him and those they were intended to serve. And he gave thanks to both his poetic father and his familial one. In an essay on Thomas Hardy, he wrote, "I cannot write objectively about Thomas Hardy because I was once in love with him . . . To begin with, he looked like my father: that broad unpampered moustache, bald forehead and deeply-lined face belonged to that other world of feeling and sensation (for I, like my mother, was a thinking-intuitive)." But, grateful as he remained to that other world of the Alter Ego, he no longer asked it to give him the strengths he lacked. "Hardy was my poetical father and if I seldom read him now, it is, perhaps, because our relationship is so assured as no longer to need being made conscious."

In June 1939, after leaving St. Mark's and returning to New York and Kallman, Auden began a systematic, but never explicit, program to refute his own earlier works or replace them with new ones on the same themes. He began by looking back to a poem he had written in 1937, a riddling essay on man that began, "Under the fronds of life, beside / The flower's soundless hunger." The opening phrase alludes, perhaps ironically, to the anonymous poem "All under the leaves and the leaves of life," about seven virgins "seeking for sweet Jesus Christ."* Auden's stanzas present a rapid allegorical portrait of "the expressive lover . . . the deliberate man," in his relation to the inhuman nature that surrounds him in space

---

* Auden apparently found the poem in Walter de la Mare's anthology *Come Hither!* (1923), the book he had "had the extraordinarily good fortune" to be given soon after he began writing verse (as he recalled in "Making, Knowing and Judging," reprinted in *The Dyer's Hand*).

and the past and future that surround him in time. The lonely representative "he" of the poem lives in a state of error and unknowing, "ruled by dead men never met, / By pious guess deluded." In his love "grandiose" and "faithless," he finds consolation in a deceiving nostalgic "dream of vaguer ages, / Hunter and victim reconciled." Tricked out of his birthright by his "legal father," abandoned daily by "a fresh deserter," he can expect only "further griefs and greater, / And the defeat of grief"—an ambiguous closing phrase that can signify either triumph or death.

Thus 1937. Auden now composed a reply to his own poem, using virtually the same stanza form and opening line ("Underneath the leaves of life" instead of "Under the fronds of life"), in which nature again frames a portrait of humanity. But the portrait has changed. Where the earlier poem saw loneliness and envy, the new one sees marriage. In the place where "Stands the deliberate man" in 1937, in 1939 "Stand the fallen man and wife." And the end of grief no longer is deferred to an ambiguous future but occurs repeatedly, here and now. Where in 1937 fresh deserters rode away from the deliberate man who was "able at times to cry," now, in 1939,

> Lovers running each to each
> Feel such timid dreams catch fire
>   Blazing as they touch,
> Learn what love alone can teach:
> Happy on a tousled bed
> Praise Blake's acumen who said:
> "One thing only we require
> Of each other; we must see
> In another's lineaments
>   Gratified desire";*
> That is our humanity;
>   Nothing else contents.

---

* One of Kallman's letters to Auden, at the end of May, replied to a letter in which Auden had written, as Kallman reminded him, "that you saw the 'lineaments of gratified desire' on May 25, 1939, at 11:30 p.m." Kallman noted that 25 May was a Thursday, a day on which Auden had not yet returned to New York from St. Mark's to visit him for the weekend, "and so I believe that some sort of explanation is forthcoming—Eh? I trust it will be good." (Auden had first alluded to Blake's lines on gratified desire in the verse commentary to the sonnet sequence "In Time of War" late in 1938.)

A few months later, when Auden collected his poems of the past several years for his book *Another Time*, he placed the first of these two poems at the start of the opening section and the second at its end. (He changed the opening phrase of the first from "Under the fronds of life" to "Wrapped in a yielding air"; his allusion to the leaves of life—and the virgins seeking Jesus—now occurred only in the unequivocal affirmations of the second poem.) This section of the book, the largest, contained thirty-one poems, and Auden used the first and last to emphasize a change in himself, as he had done with the first and last poems of his earlier books. He had begun his 1930 *Poems* with the hopeless ironies of "Will you turn a deaf ear" and closed it with the hopeful prayer of "Sir, no man's enemy." *On This Island* in 1936 began with the hopeful "Prologue" ("O Love, the interest itself in thoughtless heaven") and closed with the disillusioned "Epilogue" ("Certainly our city, with its byres of poverty"). Now he began *Another Time* with an ambiguous hope for either death or fulfillment and closed the main sequence with thanks for a future that had already arrived.

"Underneath the leaves of life" is dense with discoveries and hopes, although Auden's circumspection, at this early stage of his marriage, makes it impossible to unfold them without help from clues he planted in other works. His later title for this poem was "The Riddle." One discovery hidden in the poem was that he could receive the smile of mercy only when he accepted its apparent opposite, the desolation of judgment. This prompted these riddling lines:

> But the Judgment and the Smile,
>   Though these two-in-one
> See creation as they must,
>   None shall reconcile.

None shall reconcile these two-in-one because they must remain two, and the smile can never banish judgment:

> Soldiers who will judge
> Wind towards the little bridge.

This image had secret implications that Auden never explained in print, although he described them to a lecture audience in 1971, when he recalled from his early twenties a painting I saw of Christ's Agony in the Garden. In the foreground was the kneeling figure of Christ; nearby, on the ground, the disciples asleep. In the background some soldiers were crossing a little bridge. Visually they look quite harmless and there is nothing to show whither they are going. It is only because one has read the Gospel story that one knows that, in fact, they are coming to arrest Jesus.*

In 1932 this painting, he continued, had prompted him to write his ballad "O what is that sound that so thrills the ear," with its terrifying image of "the soldiers coming":

It occurred to me then, but not before, that I and I fancy nearly everybody have had a nightmare in which one is pursued by some malignant power, and that since this was a general experience, not private to myself, a poem might be based [on] it. In my own case, the pursuer used to be a steam-roller. That obviously might not be felt by readers as hostile. I have never dreamed of being pursued by soldiers, and I don't know whether others have, but since soldiers are by profession aggressive, it seemed to me that they could function for all readers as a symbol.

In the 1932 poem the image of pursuing soldiers had dominated a nightmare of sexual betrayal. In the 1939 poem the same image yielded to a waking reality of marriage and fulfillment.†

Most of the discoveries hidden in the poem are Auden's recent revelations about love. In *The Prolific and the Devourer* he took this lesson from the Gospels:

"Thou shalt love thy neighbor as thyself."
Again Jesus bases love on the most primitive instinct of all, self-preservation. Those who hate themselves will hate their neighbors or endow them with romantic perfections. The Neo-Romantics like Nietzsche and D. H. Lawrence have misread this text as "Thou shalt love thy neighbor *more* than thyself," and base their attack on Christianity upon this misreading . . . Jesus never said this, only the churches.

---

* The painting was probably the one by Bellini in the National Gallery in London, where a stone ridge in the background looks like a small bridge.
† In a similar transformation a few months later, Auden turned his private nightmare image into a comic prop. In "Heavy Date," as the poet awaits his beloved, he lets "the life that has been / Lightly buried in my / Personal Unconscious / Rise up from the dead . . . / As at lantern-lectures / Image follows image; / Here comes a steam-roller / Through an orange grove."

On the contrary, at the last supper, he took eating, the most elementary and solitary act of all, the primary act of self-love, the only thing that . . . all living creatures must do, irrespective of species, sex, race, or belief—and made it the symbol of universal love.*

This was a generalization from Auden's discovery that, as he put it to Mrs. Dodds, he had been foolish to believe he could love only the world of the Alter Ego, that he really wanted someone like himself. Self-love was paradoxically an escape from narcissism and its insistence on the irreconcilable differences between the self and others. To Auden, Kallman's Jewishness was less a source of difference between them than a prophecy of their identity. Auden had been "a Gentile inheriting an O-so-genteel anti-semitism" (as he told Kallman in his 1941 Christmas letter in poetic prose) who now found happiness with a Jew. Around the time he settled into his relation with Kallman, he began to imagine in his prose and verse a "true democracy" of free responsible persons, indifferent to distinctions of class or nation or church. For that democracy to exist in modern industrial society, he thought, the condition of the Jews would need to be recognized as everyone's. As he wrote in a review in 1941, observing that Kafka was "the artist who comes nearest to bearing the same kind of relation to our age that Dante, Shakespeare and Goethe bore to theirs":

It was fit and proper that Kafka should have been a Jew, for the Jews have for a long time been placed in the position in which we are now all to be, of having no home . . . What the contemporary anti-Semite sees in the Jew is the image of his own destiny, of which he is terrified; accordingly he tries to run to the same refuge [that still seems available to the Jew], race.

But the refuge of race is an illusion. In Kallman, Auden had seen a revelation of the personal uniqueness that such categories as race and nation conceal, and he came to think of Kallman's exile as a Jew as a symbol of everyone's uniqueness. In his poem "Diaspora," written in 1940, the representative "he," who stands for all Jewish exiles, draws to himself the angry terrors of a collective "they" who cannot imagine a homeless life without "their dogmas or their land,"

* Love and eating had a quite different relation in "Love Letter," the poem Auden wrote just before his vision of Eros, where love is described as having "a puritanical loathing of art and / Food."

Till there was no place left where they could still pursue him
Except that exile which he called his Race.*
But envying even that, they plunged right through him

Into a land of mirrors without time or space,
And all they had to strike now was the human face.

In *The Prolific and the Devourer* in 1939 Auden drew another moral from his new understanding of self-love and the unique value of the human face, this time from a more recent authority than the Gospels: "In its emphasis on the economic motives for human action, Marxism reveals not the selfishness of man, but the real basis of human love, which is not blood-kinship nor moral goodness or badness, but mutual need. We can love our neighbor as ourself because our need of each other is equal." Auden versified this thought later in the year in "Heavy Date," where love is possible between any things or persons, "Given one condition, / The one sine qua non / Being mutual need." Through love we discover "An essential secret / Called by some Salvation / And by some Success"—the secret that where there is mutual need, there is equal power to give, and so we love precisely what we ourselves are able to give. "We can only love what- / -ever we possess."

"Underneath the leaves of life" compresses this logic into its final stanza:

Nowhere else could I have known,
Than, beloved, in your eyes
    What we have to learn,
That we love ourselves alone:
All our terrors burned away
We can learn at last to say:
"All our knowledge comes to this,
That existence is enough,
That in savage solitude
    Or the play of love
Every living creature is
    Woman, Man and Child."

---

* "Race," as Auden's precise phrasing implies, is the word used by both sides to refer to the distinction between a group that excludes and a group that is excluded; it has no meaning except in a context of fear and hatred.

In the poem's final image, the "fallen man and wife" of the opening
stanza find their future in a child.

All our terrors burned away. This purgatorial triumph recurred in Auden's love poems throughout 1939. In October he sounded the same
note in the lyric "Warm are the still and lucky miles":

> Restored! Returned! The lost are borne
> On seas of shipwreck home at last:
> See! In a fire of praising burns
>   The dry dumb past, and we
> The life-day long shall part no more.

The exclamation points—which he used almost nowhere else—take the
place of the swelling music to which this poem evidently wishes to be
set. The song ends by looking forward, not to the life-long day, but to
the life-day that extends until death us do part.* The dry dumb past had
suddenly, miraculously, turned musical and fertile. In "Heavy Date" Auden addressed Kallman:

> I should love to go on
> Telling how I love you,
> Thanking you for happy
>   Changes in my life . . .

And a few weeks later, in *Paul Bunyan*, the libretto he wrote for music
by Britten, the rare and implausible blue moon, herald of Paul Bunyan's
birth, prompted Auden to celebrate his private vision in the rhythms of
popular song:

> But once in a while the odd thing happens,
>   Once in a while the dream comes true,
> And the whole pattern of life is altered,
>   Once in a while the Moon turns Blue.

The blue moon that foretells a hero's birth is a mythical event. Auden's
vision, as he acknowledged later, had blinded him to the reality of himself
and Kallman as persons, and he had chosen to remain blinded by it.
Having decided that he wanted and needed marriage, he had also de-

* The uncommon form "life-day long" may have been suggested by "The live-day long" in
Burns's "A Mother's Lament," a poem whose elegiac tone Auden transfigured into the exaltation of his own.

cided that Kallman unknowingly wanted and needed the same thing. Auden had convinced himself that his vision of Eros, unlike Dante's or Shakespeare's or anyone else's, had initiated a marriage and all the mundane mutuality it required. But this was a marriage in which only one partner wore a ring.

CHAPTER THREE

Against the Devourer

After his private experience of visionary love, Auden tried to find its public counterpart in a secular political faith based on the same pattern of prophecy and fulfillment. During the summer and autumn of 1939 he worked—explicitly in his prose, implicitly in his poems—to interpret the Gospels as rational, enlightened analyses of ethical imperatives and historical change. As he had done repeatedly in the 1930s, he tried to translate his emotional life into political theory, while omitting the intensity and ambivalence of his emotions. He deliberately excluded the visionary elements of his love and its promise of sacramental meaning, apparently doubting that his special revelation could be made accessible to anyone else. He quoted and explicated the teachings of Jesus—he avoided the honorific "Christ"—in order to demonstrate their superiority to all other historical and social teachings, but attributed no inspiration or divinity to him. Jesus, as Auden wrote about him in 1939, was the historian who first understood the evolution of modern industrial society, the scientist who first applied to human affairs the method of arguing from the particular to the general, the economist who first recognized that mutual need was the only possible basis for a working social order. Jesus had prophesied for the public world the love that Auden had now accepted in the private world. During these months before and after the outbreak of world war, Auden hoped to find the formulae that might demonstrate his personal fulfillment to be a microcosm and pledge of an inevitable political one. But formulae of that kind have never been found, and 1939 was an inauspicious year in which to look for them.

Auden used the summer as a working holiday in which he wrote no book reviews, lectures, or anything else on commission. He devoted most of his time to the prose pensées and dialogues that became *The Prolific and the Devourer*; the two nouns in the title are synonyms for "the artist" and "the politician." In the four chapters he completed before he abandoned this book, he analyzed and renounced his earlier political life and justified his new attempt to face the political present without a protective partisan mask. Late in June he and Kallman left New York for the summer journey he called their honeymoon. During the first week, when they traveled by bus to New Orleans, Kallman's roving eyes and hands did little to promote the harmony foreseen by Auden's theories (Auden wrote in a postcard to a friend that Kallman "needs to be kept on a chain"), but when they stayed two days with Katherine Anne Porter she noted Auden's "faith that mankind is good" (as she described it in a letter to their friend James Stern). From New Orleans they went to Taos, New Mexico, where they rented a cottage for the month of July from Mabel Dodge Luhan while Auden worked on his book and studiously ignored the local cult of D. H. Lawrence. One of the models he chose for his book, in addition to Pascal's *Pensées*, was Augustine's *Confessions*, and Auden set to work renouncing his political errors in the same way Augustine renounced his philosophical and erotic ones.

The Prolific and the Devourer are the names Blake devised in *The Marriage of Heaven and Hell* for the opposing principles of existence:

> The Giants who formed this world into its sensual existence, and now seem to live in it in chains, are in truth the causes of its life & the sources of all activity; but the chains are the cunning of weak and tame minds which have power to resist energy . . .
>
> Thus one portion of being is the Prolific, the other, the Devouring: to the Devourer it seems as if the producer was in his chains, but it is not so; he only takes portions of existence and fancies that the whole.
>
> But the Prolific would cease to be Prolific unless the Devourer as a sea received the excess of his delights . . .
>
> These two classes of men are always upon earth, & they should be enemies; whoever tries to reconcile them seeks to destroy existence.

Or, as Auden rewrote Blake:

> The Prolific and the Devourer: the Artist and the Politician. Let them realize that they are enemies, i.e. that each has a vision of the world which must remain

incomprehensible to the other. But let them also realize that they are both necessary and complementary, and further, that there are good and bad politicians, good and bad artists, and that the good must learn to recognize and to respect the good.

Five years earlier, in an essay on psychology and literature, Auden had remarked in a parenthesis that "the whole of Freud's teaching" about instinctual conflicts "may be found in *The Marriage of Heaven and Hell.*" But he began using the archetypes of the Prolific and the Devourer only when he found them again in the work of C. G. Jung, whose archetypal and mythologizing language now abruptly entered Auden's vocabulary and did not disappear for almost a decade. In *Psychological Types* (1923) Jung had made a connection between, on one hand, the opposition of introvert and extrovert and, on the other, Blake's opposition of prolific and devourer: "Blake's intuition did not err when he described the two forms as the 'prolific' and the 'devouring' . . . both forms are current and successful after their kind." But Jung equated the prolific with the extrovert, the devourer with the introvert, while Auden did the reverse, treating the introvert as the creative prolific and the extrovert as the devouring politician, "condemned to destroy or distribute the work of your betters." Except for this reversal of terms, Auden wholly took over Jung's account of introverts and extroverts. "I have yet to meet a poetry-lover under thirty who was not an introvert," he wrote in an essay on Hardy, "or an introvert who was not unhappy in adolescence." Jung's mythicizing optimism and his conviction that impersonal archetypes shape personal identities encouraged Auden to retain Marxist determinism while discarding Marxist anger. For the next few years, he peopled his poetic landscape with Jungian figures like the anima and animus, and incorporated phrases from Jung's latest writings into his verse. But he found his new Jungian vocabulary less serviceable in the discursive world of prose than in the symbolic world of poetry, and he dropped it from his essays some years earlier than from his poems.

In the figure of the introverted artist in *The Prolific and the Devourer* Auden presented an explicit allegory of his discovery of himself. Writing to an English friend later in the year, he described "America" as "The most decisive experience of my life so far. It has taught me the kind of writer I am, i.e. an introvert who can only develop by obeying his introversion. All Americans are introverts. I adore New York as it is the only city in which I find I can work and live quietly." Return to the noisier

literary life of England was inconceivable. "No, God willing, I never wish
to see England again. All I wish is, when this [war] is over, for all of you
to come here."

The Artist, throughout *The Prolific and the Devourer*, stands for all
the prolifics, whether or not they create works of art, and Auden was
uncharacteristically militant in his defense. "The Farmer—the Skilled
Worker—the Scientist—the Cook—the Innkeeper—the Doctor—the
Teacher—the Athlete—the Artist. Are there really any other occupa-
tions fit for human beings?" (Even innkeepers* and cooks are introverts,
for they do not try to reform their guests; so are authentic doctors
and teachers, who have no wish for helpless disciples.) The devouring
Politician—who makes nothing, but manages or destroys that which is
made by the Prolific—belongs almost to a different species, one of that
menagerie of creatures with exotic, incomprehensible sex lives. A few
months later, in "Heavy Date," Auden wondered:

> When a politician
> Dreams about his sweetheart,
> Does he multiply her
>   Face into a crowd,
> Are her fond responses
> All-or-none reactions,
> Does he try to buy her,
>   Is the kissing loud?

The best he had to say of this odd life form was a couplet in "The
Riddle": "Even politicians speak / Truths of value to the weak." His
tone was angrier in *The Prolific and the Devourer*, where he was driven
by fury against himself for having served the Devourer with his poems.
"The Enemy," he wrote, "was and still is the politician, i.e. the person
who wants to organize the lives of others and make them toe the line. I
can recognize him instantly in any disguise, whether as a civil servant, a
bishop, a schoolmaster, or a member of a political party, and I cannot
meet him however casually without a feeling of fear and hatred and a
longing to see him . . . publicly humiliated."

When Auden was planning *The Prolific and the Devourer*, in May, he
described it in a letter to E. R. Dodds as "a new Marriage of Heaven

---

* The innkeeper in Auden's list is a tribute to the hotel manager to whom Auden wrote the
ode quoted on p. 29.

and Hell that I am doing." After studying Pascal during the summer he called the book "my pensées." But the book's most striking feature has no model in Blake or Pascal or anyone else: it is the aphoristic auto-biography that Auden devised for the opening section, in which events from his personal history illustrate, and are explained by, the generalizing aphorisms interspersed among them. With this form he could write of himself as a unique personality, as one of a generation of artists who shared in the same mistakes, and also as one of the larger class of the Prolific, "Man the Maker" as opposed to "Man the Politician."

The book names a dozen motives for Auden's political engagement, some more worthy than others, none conducive to political or artistic success. One was a simple hunger for aesthetic thrills: "Few of the artists who round about 1931 began to take up politics as an exciting new subject to write about, had the faintest idea of what they were letting themselves in for." Another was a sense of ethical obligation: "He who undertakes anything, thinking he is doing it out of a sense of duty, is deceiving himself and will ruin everything he touches." A subtler motive was the fantasy that by immersing oneself in something alien to oneself, one can gain the power to destroy it: "I have never yet met a Left-Wing intel-lectual for whom the real appeal of Communism did not lie in its ro-mantic promise that with the triumph of Communism the State shall wither away." Auden was willing to give himself and others credit for honorable, "even if short-sighted," motives like a "desire for fresh ex-periences" and "humanitarian indignation at injustice and cruelty." But mixed with these was "a larger element of old-fashioned social climbing than we care to admit"; in the 1930s it became stylish for the first time to be further left than thou. Most destructive of all was the lure of ambition, "the voice of the Tempter" who says "Unless you take part in the class struggle, you cannot become a major writer"—precisely what the Public Prosecutor had said in many more words in "The Public v. the Late Mr. W. B. Yeats."

When Auden turned away from politics, he implied insistently, he did so to serve justice, not to escape into art. Everything in the book that defends artists is based on a conviction that the acts of Man the Maker —"cultivator, herdsman, engineer, artist"—do not merely cultivate his own garden but build the just city. Everything in the book that rebukes politicians expresses a conviction that the acts of Man the Politician ob-struct the just society he claims to build. But the artist stops serving the just city as soon as he imagines he knows how to build it. "One of the best reasons I have for knowing that Fascism is bogus is that it is too much like the kinds of Utopias artists plan over café tables very late at night."*

Auden still wanted to believe that history moved in a determined, purposive way toward a just future. During the past two years he had not stated this belief explicitly, and the hesitations and contradictions in his poems of that time were a sign of his inner revolt against the Marxist argument that history's purposes are served by revolutionary violence and necessary murder. In 1939 he could no longer tolerate his own silence, briefly convinced himself that the Prolific must not be a combatant in any war, and turned the Marxist argument against itself by proclaiming that history was indeed determined, but that its purposes were served only by the Prolific's love:

> Socialism is correct in saying that the world will inevitably become socialist, and that the actions of an individual can only either accelerate or retard that development, but in accepting the use of violence and hatred now . . . [socialists] are doing the opposite of what they imagine: they are ranging themselves on the side of the retarders.

Auden's historical faith was buttressed by his heightened sense of daemonic involuntary powers. The forces that rule our future, he wrote— "It is their tomorrow hangs over the earth of the living"—will impose on us a better world already promised by prophecy. "Our cities predict / More than we hope." At the most hopeless moment in Auden's personal history he had found the happiness that, he believed, had been prophesied when he was a child. At the most hopeless moment in world history, he predicted that the just future foretold in the Gospels would inevitably arrive.

The authority Auden cited for his faith was no longer the revolutionary hatred of Marx but the charitable sympathy of Jesus. Marx had illuminated the past by emphasizing Man the Maker as "the prime cause of historical change," the Prolific who creates wealth, which the devouring Man the Politician can only "destroy or distribute." Marx followed the economic teachings of Jesus, Auden wrote, but Jesus was the better historian, scientist, and prophet. Through his emphasis on the mutual love

---

* This was a recasting of an already famous aphorism in which Auden named a different model of the Fascist enemy: "The best reason I have for opposing Fascism," he wrote in an essay in *The Old School*, a collection put together by Graham Greene in 1934, "is that at school I lived in a Fascist state."

of individuals, whatever their class or nation, Jesus "forecast our historical evolution correctly." He had predicted the industrial world in which (as Auden wrote to E. R. Dodds early in 1940), "tradition, community roots and what have you are gone for ever," where the machine had destroyed the relations among neighbors and the associations of people to places, leaving instead "personal relations of choice united only by the automobile and the telephone." The historical authority of Jesus was based not on faith but on the evidence of things seen:

> Jesus convinces me that he was right because what he taught has become consistently more and more the necessary and natural attitude for man as society has developed the way it has . . . If we reject the Gospels, then we must reject modern life. Industrialism is only workable if we accept Jesus' view of life, and conversely his view of life is more workable under industrialism than under any previous form of civilization. Neither the heathen philosophers, nor Buddha, nor Confucius, nor Mohammed showed his historical insight.

Auden had never endorsed any other thinker in these terms, and when he had last written about the social and historical views of Jesus, in 1935, he had adopted a more neutral tone that praised Jesus' view of ethics while criticizing his view of history. The essay Auden contributed then to *Christianity and the Social Revolution*, a book that mapped the common ground of religion and Communism, emphasized that Jesus "indicated that the term neighbor admits of no distinction or qualification whatever. Every individual is of equal value"; to the beliefs of Jesus, he had written, "politics can have no meaning." But Jesus' ethical beliefs, he had continued in 1935, were linked in Jesus' mind to his mistaken historical belief that the Parousia—the Second Coming that will end the familiar world order—"was imminent, an event to take place within the disciples' lifetime," and that the Kingdom of God "will come suddenly and not by a slow evolution." Now, in *The Prolific and the Devourer*, the imminence of the Parousia was no longer a mistaken idea held by Jesus himself but a misinterpretation by the disciples of Jesus' teaching that the Kingdom of Heaven can be attained within themselves. Auden now interpreted Jesus' teaching as referring to a distant future in which it would be proved true, although sufficiently remote to leave openings for doubt. "The unequivocally apocalyptic nature of the teaching of Jesus has at once been Satan's [as in 1935 it had been Auden's] greatest hope of proving him wrong, and his greatest dread lest History should prove to mankind beyond a shadow of doubt that he was right."

Satan entered Auden's vocabulary in *The Prolific and the Devourer* not quite as a being with his own existence but as an embodiment of the ordinary human dread that Jesus may have been right in his prophecies and his commands. Under the name of Satan, this fear sought to corrupt Jesus through the Three Temptations; under other names, it devised the argument for the efficacy of political force "found in many books, *The Republic, The Prince, Leviathan, Mein Kampf,* but nowhere perhaps more completely and cogently expressed than by the Grand Inquisitor in Dostoyevsky's *The Brothers Karamazov.*" Jesus does not reply to the Inquisitor, Auden added, "any more than he answered Satan or Pilate, because he does not need to: their own experience answers for them and they know very well what they do, and that they have failed, so that, tormented by the knowledge of failure and of the hate they have aroused, they cry: 'Why dost thou come to hinder us?' " Jesus drives Satan's allies into torment and despair, not because he is God, but because they know he is right.

Satan is a name human beings give to denial and dread, and God is the name they give to truth and hope. Auden wrote in a book review a few weeks after *The Prolific and the Devourer*:

> Man is aware that his actions do not express his real nature, God is a term for what he imagines that nature to be. Thus man is always making God in his own image. In so far as Jesus was the first person to make the image correspond to the fact, he revealed God to man. "My father worketh and I work," refers to man only . . . "My father" is the real nature of man; "I," his conscious aware-ness of that nature. Again, in so far as, in Jesus, this awareness was complete, "I" and "my Father" are one. "None cometh to the Father, save through me."

In *The Prolific and the Devourer* Auden wrote about "divine laws" that are manifested in the workings of history. The word "divine" was a mere convention: "There are laws which govern human life . . . call them for convenience divine laws." These are mutable, not eternal, and they cooperate with human progress. "As a society changes, the divine laws change too." Political formulations of the laws become coercive and false when political change increases the urgency of breaking away from obsolete laws. As a society grows more complex, so do the laws it must obey if it hopes to survive, and as individual lives become "more and more unique, the application of the divine laws becomes more and more a special application for each individual." The increasing uniqueness of individual lives, in an apparent paradox, makes clear their common humanity, for their uniqueness does not depend on class or culture. But while the application of divine laws differs for each individual, the laws themselves are the same, and the same self-imposed punishments of anxiety and unhappiness afflict all who break them. "Happiness is what we feel when we are living according to those laws, and unhappiness what we feel when we are not."

Divine laws are not coercive on the local scale of personal life, and "for the most part we do not live according to those laws," but they ultimately rule in the larger scale of historical time. History moves in an unalterable "general direction,"* first identified by Jesus. "If Jesus was right," then

(A) The general direction of history must have been and be towards
  (1) The unity of mankind and a recognition of the common humanity of all men
  (2) The equality of men, through a recognition that all men are subject to the same divine law and
(B) (1) The Way of love and understanding, which must by its very nature intend this direction, must always have assisted events to so move,
  (2) The Way of hate and coercion, whether it intended Unity and Equality or their opposites, must have always hindered events from so moving, but also must have always failed finally to prevent them.

In this clipped, didactic style—a relic of his five years as a schoolmaster in the early 1930s—Auden claimed for the artist the prophetic and progressive power that Marx had attributed to the Communist Party. The workings of divine law had been hindered by politicians and served by artists. "Man the Maker," by attending to the uniqueness of things and

---

* The subject of an adult-education course Auden taught that autumn for the League of American Writers was "the relations between poetry and the general ideas of its time and between the personal experience of a poet and his work." The phrase "general ideas," which in Auden's usage approximates the later historical term *mentalité*, was a less polemical equivalent of "divine laws." Auden's description of a course entitled "Poetry and Culture" at the New School for Social Research the following spring similarly referred to the "medieval world picture" and the "romantic world picture." (The only earlier use of "world picture"—a phrase apparently based on *Weltanschauung*—recorded in the *Oxford English Dictionary* occurs in Lord Dufferin's *Letters from High Latitudes*, a book Auden wrote about in *Letters from Iceland*; E.M.W. Tillyard's *The Elizabethan World Picture* was not published until 1943.)

the density of relations between them, "has always followed the way of love." Thus Auden argued to himself as he wrote in the solitude of his cottage in New Mexico.

He made his argument public in a defense of Rilke composed in August, at the end of his working holiday. His review of a new translation of Rilke's poems looked shockingly detached from the realities of the world when it appeared in *The New Republic* in the first week of September—the European war broke out between the time he wrote it and the time it was printed—but he meant exactly what he said. He pointed to Rilke's growing influence on English poetry, an influence prompted by public events. "It is, I believe, no accident* that as the international crisis becomes more and more acute, the poet to whom writers are increasingly drawn should be the one who felt that it was pride and presumption to interfere with the lives of others (for each is unique and the apparent misfortunes of each may be his very way of salvation)." Rilke "occupied himself consistently and exclusively with his own inner life," but his practice

> implies not a denial of the importance of political action, but rather the realization that if the writer is not to harm both others and himself, he must consider, and very much more humbly and patiently than he has been doing, what kind of person he is, and what may be his real function. When the ship catches fire, it seems only natural to rush importantly to the pumps, but perhaps one is only adding to the general confusion and panic: to sit still and pray seems selfish and unheroic, but it may be the wisest and most helpful course.

Compared with the swelling praise for the poet-healer in "In Memory of W. B. Yeats," this tentative endorsement of passivity sounds sober and modest, but it makes an even loftier claim. Artists in Auden's poems a few months earlier struggled with their daemonic gift; now they were an army of unalterable law, agents of inevitable progress toward divine love and justice, and Auden invoked them in a vocabulary suitable for angels. In an "Epithalamion" he wrote in September for the marriage of Elisabeth Mann (his sister-in-law: he had married Erika Mann to provide her with a British passport after her German citizenship had been revoked by the Nazis), he summoned the wedding guests to offer their prayers to an empyrean reserved for artists:

---

* *It is no accident* was a standard rhetorical device in Marxist writings on history, deliberately used here as a rebuke to Marxist politics.

> Vowing to redeem the State,
> Now let every girl and boy
> To the heaven of the Great
> All their prayers and praises lift.

Among the Great he named Mozart, Blake, Tolstoy, Hölderlin, and "Goethe innocent of sin." (In 1940, when this hopeful fantasy had passed, he crossed out "innocent" in friends' copies and replaced it with "ignorant.") The conventional-sounding praise for marriage in this poem and its improbable tone of hearty affirmation lightly disguise the claims Auden made more explicitly in *The Prolific and the Devourer* for the shaping progressive powers of art and attention. The way of love, pursued as much by the solitary artist as by the bride and groom, will fulfill the vow that all of them make to redeem the State:

> Happier savants may decide
> That this quiet wedding of
> A Borgese and a Mann
> Planted human unity;
> Hostile kingdoms of the truth,
> Fighting fragments of content,
> Here were reconciled by love,
> Modern policy begun
>   On this day.

This was a long way from his springtime agonies, four months before, in "Love Letter," where "Love is a destroyer of cities." Now love was the figure whom Auden was to call (in his elegy for Freud, a few weeks later) "Eros, builder of cities."

The simple fact of Auden's happiness seemed to him all the proof he needed for these arguments. The fruits of the way of love and understanding included his own prolific writings. "I have never written nor read so much," he told an English friend late in 1939. "For the first time I am leading a life which remotely approximates to the way I think I ought to live." And he found further confirmation in science. Biologists, he wrote in *The Prolific and the Devourer*, have confirmed that "intelligence only functions when the animal is unafraid. An atmosphere of love and confidence is essential . . . Man is the most intelligent animal because he is the most affectionate." Hatred, in contrast, is "lethal to intelligence, and so, for an intelligent animal, to survival." The theories he proposed now that he was happily in love were, he believed, because of the nature of divine law, the theories most likely to be true.

Auden never found it difficult to write splendid and memorable poems about beliefs he later discarded or outgrew—as he did with most of the beliefs he held passionately in the late 1930s and early 1940s—but he found it hard to write well about beliefs he merely wanted or felt obliged to hold. He repeatedly tested the ideas in his prose by writing them into the more complex medium of poetry. When he tested the theories in *The Prolific and the Devourer* in this fashion, he seemed less sure of them than he had hoped. In August, while he and Kallman were visiting Isherwood in California, he composed "Pascal," a heavy, humorless verse meditation on the thinker he had described as, "of all the dualists . . . incomparably the noblest and most seductive." When Auden was at school and university, he wrote later, Pascal was "the only theological writer I knew of at that time whom I found readable and disturbing to my complacency," and although when he wrote about him again in 1955 he found "a certain element of fake in his writings, a kind of romantic indulgence in unhappiness, not so far removed from *The Sorrows of the Young Werther*, which may well have been what attracted me at that time," at least Pascal had "prevented me from banishing the thought of God from my mind when I should very much have preferred to do so."

The poem uses Pascal as a mask to disguise a parabolic autobiography, and the knotty stiffness of the verse—at once clumsy and complacent—was a sign that Auden could not convince himself of his own parable. It focuses on two circumstances in Pascal's life: the curse of childhood isolation and the saving blessing of an adult vision. The first half retells the story in which Pascal was bewitched in the womb and "born deserted / And lonelier than any adult." Like the adolescent Auden among abandoned machines that accepted his silent praise, Pascal prayed in solitude,

> Submitting to a night that promised nothing,
> Not even punishment, but let him pray.

The second half describes Pascal's rescue from the curse. After many years when he was nurtured by the gift that adopted him at birth, "in the night the Unexpected came," in the form of his vision of God in the person of Christ. Although the vision ended by morning—and Pascal, "His faculties for sin restored completely," continued to write "The lucid and unfair"—it promised a future in which the "crooked custom" of history proceeded inexorably in "Its move towards the just." That promise persists, in the emptily uplifting closing lines, "Wherever there are children, doubt and deserts, / Or cities that exist for mercy and for judgement."

Had Auden believed this prophecy as much as he wished he did, he would have written a better poem. But "Pascal" has the same evasiveness found in other complacent prophecies that he later abandoned, like "Spain" and "September 1, 1939." In "Pascal" as in "Spain" the future will come right because an impersonal force wills it to do so. In "Spain" that power bore the name history; in "Pascal" it was an unnamed power that brought "the Unexpected." But a just future that arrived whether we built it or not was no more plausible when it had no Marxist theory behind it than when it did.

Auden's faith in inevitable justice was shaken both by inner doubts and by the facts of the terrible present. In a review apparently written in August he claimed, "Progress is probable but not certain. The probability can be increased, but only by conscious human action." This was a much lesser claim for the future than the certainties expressed in *The Prolific and the Devourer*. Conscious human action, moreover, had other ends in view. Hitler was concluding his pact with Stalin; Germany took the first steps toward its seizure of Danzig; Britain made a formal alliance with Poland. On the train from California to New York on 28 August, Auden wrote to Mrs. Dodds: "There is a radio in this coach so that every hour or so, one has a violent pain in one's stomach as the news comes on."

His clever hopes expired four days later. In the typescript of "September 1, 1939," a poem that begins in a drumbeat catalogue of despair and ends by soaring into affirmation, he first wrote "The last mad hopes expire / Of a low dishonest decade," but he quickly recognized that those hopes were willful errors committed by intelligent and clever people, not involuntary errors of the mad. Before the poem was printed he revised it:

> I sit in one of the dives
> On Fifty-Second Street
> Uncertain and afraid
> As the clever hopes expire
> Of a low dishonest decade.

It was a bad moment for cleverness. "Waves of anger and fear / Circulate over the bright / And darkened lands of the earth." Auden per-

ceived the disaster in psychological and religious terms, and borrowed a
metaphor from a sentence in Jung's *Psychology and Religion* (1938): "Our
world is permeated by waves of restlessness and fear." (Jung also provided "the huge imago" that had been projected by Hitler onto "a
psychopathic god.") He opened the poem by naming the unique space
and time occupied by one person: on the first night of the war, in a bar
where New Yorkers listened to the new swing jazz. (This popular art
was, in the poem, a defense against reality, not a means of apprehending
it: "The lights must never go out, / The music must always play.") The
individual life was helpless against the public world. Waves of anger and
fear were "Obsessing our private lives." ("Obsessing" has its archaic
literal sense: waves of anger and fear *haunt* our lives as a demon might
haunt them, and as, in a later stanza, they obsess our "haunted wood.")

In *The Prolific and the Devourer*, Auden had found in the Marxist
emphasis on Man the Maker an "antidote to the pessimism which the
study of political history from Thucydides and Tacitus onward must always induce." Now, when he considered the evils that "Exiled Thucydides knew / . . . / The enlightenment driven away, / The habit-forming
pain, / Mismanagement and grief," he acknowledged simply: "We must
suffer them all again." The way of love and understanding was blocked
everywhere:

> What mad Nijinsky wrote
> About Diaghilev
> Is true of the normal heart;
> For the error bred in the bone
> Of each woman and each man
> Craves what it cannot have,
> Not universal love
> But to be loved alone.

What Nijinsky wrote in his diary was: "Some politicians are hypocrites
like Diaghilev, who does not want universal love, but to be loved alone."
Auden rewrote this to make everyone a politician.

Nonetheless, when he first typed out "September 1, 1939," in the early
days of September, he still wanted to affirm his faith in a just, inevitable
future. When he revised the poem for publication (in *The New Republic*
of 18 October 1939), he realized that even clever hopes had been supplanted by more subtly delusive ones, and he discarded all the poem's
statements of faith. As in his more political work a few years before, he

could almost deceive himself in prose about his own beliefs; in verse the untruth was painfully visible. So in the typescript of the poem that he gave to *The New Republic*, he crossed out a stanza in which he tried

> To testify my faith
> That reason's roman path
> And the trek of punishment
> Lead both to a single goal.

Whether or not we *know* it to be our goal ultimately does not matter in this stanza: nothing, not even ourselves, can prevent our arrival. The omitted stanza continues:

> Individual death,
> Each pert philosopher's
> Concupiscence or, worse,
> Practical wisdom, all
> Our public impatience can
> Delay but cannot prevent
> The education of man.

But when Auden wrote this he had already acknowledged in prose that "Progress is probable but not certain."

Even with this stanza removed, the poem still affirmed that the way of love was the inescapable road to the future. Love could not be refused because, as Auden had insisted in earlier poems, it was an instinctive need that must be satisfied in the same way that hunger must be satisfied. Like all instinctive drives and impersonal forces, "Hunger allows no choice / . . . / We must love one another or die." These are lines in which "no choice" and "must" mean exactly what they say, not some vague idea that love is better than any alternative.

Auden later recoiled from this view of love as involuntary mutual need rather than as voluntary mutual forgiveness. He also repudiated most of the other assumptions behind the poem. One, invisible to the readers of *The New Republic* but central to Auden's thought at the time, held that the artist as maker had the historical power to hasten the education of man. The dense commuters and the helpless devourer-governors could never escape the isolating necessity of their roles, yet escape and communication were what they needed most:

Who can release them now?
Who can reach the deaf,
Who can speak for the dumb?

Auden's answer to these questions points toward one prolific artist in
particular. Who can speak for the dumb? "All I have is a voice." Who
can release them now? "A voice / To undo the folded lie." Who can
reach the deaf? Another stanza that Auden struck from the typescript
suggests the answer: one who knows what need not be spoken because
the deaf, like everyone else, already know it:

What can I do but recall
What everyone knows in his heart,
One Law applies to us all . . .

"People have different functions," Auden told Selden Rodman in mid-
September. "Mine is not to fight; so far as I know what mine is, I think
it is to see clearly, to warn of excesses and crimes against humanity whoever commits them." Yet he doubted his own powers in the same way
he doubted the powers of inevitable justice. In the stirring final stanza
of the poem, where he saw points of light dotted everywhere and hoped,
like them, to "Show an affirming flame," he had originally typed "The
little points of light / Flash out wherever the Just / Exchange their
messages." In a handwritten revision he changed "The little points" to
"Ironic points." In an earlier stanza, the poem had already made a sad
ironic comment on the wish to keep the affirming flame burning and the
fantasy of one's own goodness and justice intact:

Faces along the bar
Cling to their average day:
The lights must never go out,
The music must always play,
All the conventions conspire
To make this fort assume
The furniture of home;
Lest we should see where we are,
Lost in a haunted wood,
Children afraid of the night
Who have never been happy or good.

Six months later, in "New Year Letter," the signals of the ironic but affirming points of light of "September 1, 1939" looked very different:

> Whichever way I look, I mark
> Importunate among the dark
> Horizon of immediacies
> The flares of desperation rise
> From signalers who justly plead
> Their cause is piteous indeed.

In September, in the first days of the war, they pretended their cause was triumphant.

═══════

Auden's private response to the advent of war was entirely unlike the public bravado of the final stanza of "September 1, 1939," and so different from anything he had experienced before that he did not know how to put it into verse. "The other day I burst into tears on hearing the news bulletin," he wrote at the end of his letter to Mrs. Dodds on 28 August, in the last week of nominal peace. He took the trouble to report this partly because of its surprising novelty, partly because it gave him an opportunity to violate the taboo against tears, and the confession of tears, among upper-middle-class Englishmen. He went out of his way to violate the taboo in public a few weeks later, in a digression from his review of Alvah Bessie's memoir of the Spanish Civil War:

> Again let me tell a story about myself. In the Munich crisis [of September 1938] I listened to the radio with a happy excitement, secretly hoping there would be a war, a hope for which I found excellent political reasons. This September, whenever I listened to the radio I started to cry. My attitude had changed because the personal problem which in 1938 was still unsolved and which in despair I was looking to world events to solve for me, was solved this year.

Because he could exult in the private world, he could weep over the public one. He was still engaged enough in left-wing politics to become a member of the League of American Writers in November—he was then teaching his course for the league on "the relations between poetry and the general ideas of its time"—but he insisted on responding to the murderous reality of public events instead of finding expedient rhetoric with which to conceal it. A few days after joining the league, he wrote to its secretary to express "profound disquiet" over the recommendation in the league's *Bulletin* that members refrain from criticizing the Nazi-Soviet Pact.*

Before this, the only change he could imagine was one imposed from without, either by a daemonic gift or by war—"the extraordinary compulsion of the deluge and the earthquake." War's excitement promised to force an end to his anxious loneliness. In a poem he wrote in 1940 he described this delusive promise:

> That last attempt to eliminate the Strange
> By uniting us all in a terror
> Of something known . . .

But his anxiety—his fear of that which was *not* known—was now, he thought, resolved, and he had no need to seek unity in terror because he believed he had found it in marriage.

He thought he could weep for others because the way of love had taught him to understand their suffering. "What weeps is the love that hears," he wrote in the same poem in 1940. That first unexpected moment of weeping in August 1939 echoed through all his later work. In "Homage to Clio," observing the impersonal natural world where a cock could crow though all his sons had been castrated and eaten, he wrote: "I was glad I could be unhappy." In "The Shield of Achilles" he portrayed a ragged urchin, aimless and alone, who had never heard of any world "where one could weep because another wept." One of the many falsehoods he rejected when he later discarded "September 1, 1939" was the poem's implicit claim that, in the midst of disaster, he could show an affirming flame without also weeping.

Whenever Auden wrote a poem he recognized as grand, emphatic, and false, he immediately followed it with one that was quiet, tentative, and truthful. The same moral propositions inform both "September 1, 1939" and "Law Like Love," but they are interpreted in drastically different

---

* He continued: "Political collaboration between Liberals and Communists is no longer possible" after the pact, so the league should confine itself to "literary problems and the economic status of the writer in this country." Any attempt by its Communist-controlled executive body "to impose a common policy where none exists will end in a disaster in which the Liberals will finally be forced into joining the [anti-Communist] witch-hunt which is already in full cry, a prospect which I, for one, find unappetizing." He abandoned the league after being denounced at a meeting for publishing in the "Trotskyite" *Partisan Review*.

ways. In a rejected stanza of "September 1, 1939," the one law that "applies to us all" operates at a level of generality that ignores individual persons; the only persons in the poem are the defeated commuters and governors, and the free but unimaginable just. In "Law Like Love" everything is different: the acts and velleities of individual persons, not of large historical movements, are the true analogues of events that occur on a universal scale.

In "September 1, 1939," Auden was an orator speaking in grandiose Yeatsian stanzas. In "Law Like Love" he chose irregular rhymes and a hesitant manner, variously comic, timid, and assertive, that imitated the give-and-take of conversation. Like most of Auden's serious poems, "Law Like Love" translates the abstract speculations of his prose into personal terms—perhaps back into the personal terms in which his speculations began. Like *The Prolific and the Devourer*, the poem affirms a connection between personal love and divine law. In prose, Auden had stated this theme as an argument based on systemic evidence drawn from biology and history. In verse, he was content to state it as a matter of belief. The poem begins as a mild satire on those who say that law is this or is that: gardeners say law is the sun, the old their wisdom, the young their senses, the judge his precedents ("as I've told you before"), all imagining law as a private image of justice that serves their own ends. Then the poem reveals itself to be a love poem, less a public statement about law than an address to a unique person: "If we, dear, know we know no more / Than they about the law . . ." And precisely because this is a love poem, its emotional and moral instruments let it guess at what it cannot know. If the poem cannot say *Law is* in a solitary voice of authority, it can replace the verb of identity "is" with the adjective of mutuality, "like." Instead of laying down the law, it speaks in the self-refuting manner of a boast: "We shall boast anyway: / Like love I say." This affirmation by a unique "I" can claim the fullest understanding of the law because the law, like love, is concerned (so Auden believed) with personal uniqueness, not with political generalization. Unique persons fulfill the law by loving—which can be done by unique persons only—and they fail to understand the law when they fail to love:

> Like love we don't know where or why
> Like love we can't compel or fly
> Like love we often weep
> Like love we seldom keep.

At a moment of international evil, the unkept law of the final line, and the grief of the line before, point to public failures and public guilts that correspond to everyone's private ones.

A few weeks after finishing "Law Like Love" Auden wrote an expository pendant to its final line, a poem he later entitled "The Hidden Law." He composed this poem in the precise artificiality of a *rondeau*, a French form notable for its artful repetition of key phrases and generally used for erotic trifles. Auden adapted it as a meditation on the infinite. The Law performs no miracles: it "does not deny / Our laws of probability." It does not rebuke: it "answers nothing when we lie." As political formulations falsified divine law in *The Prolific and the Devourer*, now "Legal definitions mar / The Hidden Law." We seldom keep the law, but now it has an interest in compelling us to a future in which we will keep it whether we want to or not:

> Its utter patience will not try
> To stop us if we want to die;
> When we escape it in a car,
> When we forget it in a bar,
> These are the ways we're punished by
>   The Hidden Law.

Everything Auden had written about the past and present in *The Prolific and the Devourer* still seemed true, but everything about the future was all too clearly false. He stopped work on the book when the war began, and told Selden Rodman in late September he probably would not publish it. He kept silent about his rejection of the book's argument and told Kallman merely that he had come to dislike its mandarin tone. At the same time, he was trying to find a different voice to undo the affirmations of "September 1, 1939," and he withdrew into dry, gnomic obscurity in three brief lyrics: "Hell is neither here nor there," "The hour-glass whispers to the lion's paw," and "For us like any other fugitive." These poems had nothing to say about the war, but they made a point of renouncing utopian or nostalgic efforts to deny the present. There is nothing egregiously wrong with them, but they have the lifeless quality that afflicted Auden's work when, instead of arguing both sides of an issue, he ignored one side and tried to generate interest by treating the other side as more complicated than it was. Two years later, in "Atlantis," he warned himself to "honor the fate you are, / Travelling and tormented, / Dialectic and bizarre." These poems suppressed the dialectic and the torment: they made misery sound easy to avoid and pretended there was no good reason to weep.

In almost every poem Auden wrote at this time, he remembered and corrected the content and tone of poems he had written earlier. These new lyrics recapitulate the dry riddling manner he had used in 1929 in "From scars where kestrels hover," "The strings' excitement," and other poems in which heroes die for no one's sake on futile journeys across a border. The fatal fantasy in 1929 had been that life was livable only in some other place. The fatal fantasy now was nostalgia for some other time, some imaginary uncomplicated reign of nation, property, and privilege. In "For us like any other fugitive":

> So many try to say Not Now,
> So many have forgotten how
> To say I Am, and would be
> Lost if they could in history.

The two stanzas that follow this relatively clear one are so tangled in their own riddling that an explication may be quarantined in a footnote:

> Bowing, for instance, with such old-world grace
> To a proper flag in a proper place,
> Muttering like ancients as they stump upstairs
> Of Mine and His or Ours or Theirs.

> Just as if time were what they used to will
> When it was gifted with possession still,
> Just as if they were wrong
> In no more wishing to belong.*

---

* Those who mutter about Mine and His act as if they themselves had willed the lost historical conditions in which possession and property thrived. But the present era, as foreseen by Jesus (according to *The Prolific and the Devourer*), rewards reciprocity and shared resources. And the mutterers are, ironically, correct in not wanting to belong to the present, because the present is no longer a time in which *belonging* (to a nation with a proper flag, for example) is possible. But the mutterers prefer to be wrong (in renouncing any desire to belong to the present), because otherwise they would have to acknowledge that there is a world that can be belonged to, and this would impose on them the intolerable imperative of moral obligation.

The poem touches on grief only in its final lines. If so many try to live outside the present,

> No wonder then so many die of grief,
> So many are so lonely as they die;
> No one has yet believed or liked a lie,
> Another time has other lives to live.

So many die of grief because they cannot believe the lie they try to live by. So many are lonely because the past they tried to live in was interested only in those who truly lived in it. (The phrase "has other lives to live" is an echo of Auden's earlier paraphrase of Groddeck: "We are lived by powers we pretend to understand.") Those who refuse to live by the powers of their own time must die through their refusal.

Shortly after writing this poem, Auden compiled into one volume the verse he had written during the past three years. He gave the book a title that assigned it to an earlier era of his life, a time of utopian hope and private despair, as if he were claiming that its contents had nothing to do with the present: they were the alien poems of *Another Time*. His earlier books, as the 1936 title *On This Island* suggested, contained poems about his failed effort to find the place of love, and many titles referred to real places: Iceland, Spain, Dover, Oxford, Macao, Hong Kong, China, Brussels. For some years after the decisive changes he experienced early in 1939, he abandoned place names in favor of time-conscious titles: "September 1, 1939," "Another Time," "Time With Us" (a manuscript title of "The hour-glass whispers"), "New Year Letter," "Spring in Wartime," "Autumn 1940," "No Time," "For the Time Being."

To resist living in one's own time, to try to live in an imaginary past, is human in the same way that being neurotic is human. Because the laws that govern human life evolve (as Auden argued in *The Prolific and the Devourer* and assumed in "For us like any other fugitive"), because we can never live by or formulate them, our unhappy knowledge of time is our eternal condition. In "The hour-glass whispers," clocks, which measure historical and human time, tell unheeding nature that it is wrong to be "always right"—to live by static natural laws. In the world of plants and animals there is no experience of past or future; but "Time with us was always popular" because we, who "judge a problem by its awkwardness," respond to the stimuli of choice and change. If we could ever know how to live by the laws of our historical moment, we would, like nature, have no wish; but in our world of history, we inevitably keep running in order to stand still:

> When have we not preferred some going round
> To going straight to where we are?

Each line in the poem has ten syllables except the last, which has eight, perhaps because the two missing syllables would have been a needless going round, whereas eight take the poem straight to where it wants to be. The private meaning behind the abstract plural language of these last lines is perhaps that by learning to love someone rather like himself, Auden had gone straight to where he was, and that by accepting his sexuality he had discovered it to be in the deepest sense not crooked but straight. Yet the poem's neutral tone excludes any sense of triumph, and its private meanings point to a discovery he could imagine making rather than one he claims to have made.

In *The Prolific and the Devourer* Auden had predicted "the unity of mankind and a recognition of the common humanity of all men" and had argued that the opposite condition—the state of "pure evil" that denied all relations—was "not possible even to electrons." Now he emphasized that although that condition does not exist, it inflicts real and unbearable grief on those who seek it. Auden named it in the first word of another of his riddling poems, "Hell is neither here nor there." Hell is "not anywhere" because it cannot exist, but it is nonetheless "hard to bear." Ordinary human perversity prefers a hard problem whether or not it is worth solving: those who try to live in different times imagined by nostalgia or utopianism deliberately seek the hellish grief of disconnectedness from the time in which they already are:

> It is so hard to dream posterity
> Or haunt a ruined century
> And so much easier to be.

In ordinary life, the most common excuse for one's self-destructive choices is that they are a sign of superiority to the placid herd. The excuse is partly true. Self-destruction is a challenging task, and it is "Only the challenge to our will / Our pride in learning any skill" that makes us prefer the difficulty of going round to the ease of going straight to where we are. The same pride that "Sustains our effort to be ill" sustains our perverse "hope, if we persist, / That one day Hell might actually exist."

We can never create a hell that is not possible even for electrons, but by
convincing ourselves that we have done so, we can produce a state that
is indistinguishable from it:

> In time, pretending to be blind
> And universally unkind
> Might really send us out of our mind.

Then, in the final stanza, Auden tried to allay his fears that we could
choose this hellish state, and inadvertently confirmed them. The stanza
argues—in a muted echo of the apocalyptic optimism of his *pensées*—
that we are not really so lost as we imagine:

> If we were really wretched and asleep
> It would be easy then to weep,
> It would be natural to lie,
> There'd be no living left to die.

The second line of this stanza trips over itself. It extends the general
assertion of the poem—that because we are not in hell, where unhappiness would be our natural state, it takes a deliberate effort to be
unhappy—but denies the state of unhappiness that was exactly Auden's
new experience of the public world: when war was imminent, he had
found it all too easy to weep. He sacrificed the logic of his poem because he insisted on writing about weeping while denying he had
done anything of the sort. Twenty-five years later, when he revised his
shorter poems for a collected edition, he rewrote this line as: "It would
then be *de trop* to weep"—which restored the truth by reversing the
meaning. The new version acknowledged—as the rest of the poem already did—that unhappiness was a sign not of hell but of our refusal to
live there.*

For two months Auden had been keeping his sorrow secret from his
work. He also kept it secret from his acquaintances. When the young
poet Robert Fitzgerald met him in September, Auden told him, "I'm
very hopeful," because, Fitzgerald noted in his diary, he felt that the
victories of Fascism and Communism were convincing people that a mil-

---

* Also among these gnomic poems written in September and October 1939 was the dedicatory
poem to *Another Time*: "Every eye must weep alone / Till I Will be overthrown." It foresees
a time when the overthrow of "I Will"—an overthrow effected by "I Know"—makes possible
"I Love." Auden never reprinted this riot of grammatical personifications.

lennium (in the biblical sense of the millennial reign of Christ) cannot be built overnight but must be won through gradual change. This left unacknowledged and unexplained his weeping at the news bulletins, his recognition that inevitable progress would not occur and that the triumph of love and understanding had been indefinitely deferred. But he was still unwilling to renounce publicly and explicitly the hopes that his poems and prose had repeatedly affirmed.

When he finally brought himself to renounce them, a short time afterward, he wrote one of his greatest poems, in which he buried his hopes while making a funeral oration for someone else. "When there are so many [whom] we shall have to mourn, / When grief has been made so public," he asked rhetorically, "Of whom shall we speak?" Sigmund Freud had died on 23 September 1939. Four weeks later Auden was working on an elegy for him, which he finished in November. He had written his elegies for Yeats and Toller almost as soon as he learned of their deaths, but "In Memory of Sigmund Freud" took longer to conceive and complete. This was the first of his poems in which he acknowledged a sorrow worth weeping about, and the first in which he used the syllabic metre that he almost invariably chose in his later years when writing the poems he valued most.

The innovation in content was inseparable from the innovation in form: both were rejections of assertive power. In syllabic metre each line has a fixed number of syllables, but no recurring pattern of stressed and unstressed syllables, as is found in the accentual verse of almost all English poetry of the previous six centuries. As Auden later told a lecture audience, he had become "interested in the possibilities of syllabic metre as one way of achieving a balance between freedom and order . . . I wanted to get away from a conventional pattern of iambics and trochees, and, at the same time, not to lose the sense of pattern." The verse forms favored by a poet indicate the kinds of coherence and order he sees, or wants to see, in the world outside, and the kind of relation he wants to have with poetic language. "There are some poets, Kipling, for example, whose relation to language reminds one of a drill sergeant," Auden wrote. "There are others, Swinburne, for example, who remind one more of Svengali."

In accentual metre, in Auden's seriously playful statement of the case, the poet imposes one fixed order on language; in syllabic metre, the poet listens to the many rhythms of language itself. But English is inherently accentual, like all Germanic languages, and Auden's syllabic verse was the product of more complex and difficult negotiations than he implied between the rhythms of the language and the order in his poems. Around 1929 he had read Robert Bridges's experiments in syllabic verse, but he found them too self-consciously classicizing to excite his interest. When in 1935 he discovered Marianne Moore's thoroughly modern syllabics, her verse "seemed so strange to the foolish undisciplined young man," as he told her in a letter written around the time he was finishing his elegy for Freud. "More and more, though," he continued, "I have come to appreciate its depth and integrity . . . Like Rilke, you really do 'Praise.' " Later, he described "the endless musical and structural possibilities of Miss Moore's invention" as a treasure from which he had "already stolen a great deal." Her syllabic verse "allows and encourages an unbroken run-on from line to line, stanza to stanza," a technique he exploited in the flowing unassertive sentences of his elegy for Freud. But Auden, who always delighted Moore with the courtliness of his manner to her, was too polite to say he had no interest in her eccentric home-grown stanza forms. Instead, he molded her innovative syllabic metre into traditional-looking shapes like the Horatian stanzas of his elegy. These stanzas looked the same on the page as those in "Where do They come from?" but those earlier stanzas were as metrically irregular as they sounded, while the stanzas of his Freud elegy conformed to a strict regimen of counted syllables while sounding conversational, irregular, and unconstraining. Through the example of this and later poems that combined the dignity of regular forms with the intimacy of a personal voice, Auden transformed syllabic verse into one of the great permanent resources of English poetry.

Rhymed accentual verse was a fitting medium in which to praise the nameless time-conquering poet in Auden's elegy for Yeats. Unrhymed syllabics were better suited to Freud, "this doctor" whose generous wish was "to think about our life," and who in death "quietly surrounds our habits of growth." The portrait of Freud in Auden's poem is drawn with shrewd precision, but the face in the picture bears a curious resemblance to that of the portraitist. Freud appears as a man who exemplifies Auden's theories while expounding somewhat different ones. Psychoanalysis, as the poem describes it, is a means of living in one's own time instead of dreaming of another time. Unlike the expired hopes of the 1930s, Freud "wasn't clever at all." He merely told

> The unhappy Present to recite the Past
> Like a poetry lesson till sooner
> Or later it faltered at the line where

Long ago the accusations had begun,
And suddenly knew by whom it had been judged.

Freud, that is, made the same discovery Auden made in *The Prolific and the Devourer* when he wrote: "To be forgiven means to realize that one has never been judged except by oneself." Just as Auden now imagined that his childhood love had prefigured his adult love, so Freud too restored the coherence of past and present. "While they lie in the grass of our neglect"—like abandoned mining machinery—"So many long-forgotten objects / Revealed by his undiscouraged shining / Are returned to us and made precious again." Freud also resolved the crisis of our struggle with the exiled powers of instinct. In "Where do They come from?" those powers had violent designs on us; now, thanks to Freud's understanding of them, they have a home in "the household of Impulse," and have grown into the "delectable creatures" of the night who need our guiding love and "long for the future / That lies in our power." Their imploring relation to us is the same as that in "Like a Vocation" between the weeping child (who stood in for Auden) and the visionary beloved; but Auden, having learned to receive a love he needed, can now imagine giving it to those who need it from him.

Yet the words of praise in this poem were also words of mourning. Against all the hope Freud promised, the poem balances the brutal fact that "every day they die / Among us, those who were doing us some good, / And knew it was never enough but / Hoped to improve a little by living." In these lines, Auden returned to the tone and content of a poem of mourning he had written in 1936, the "Epilogue" to *On This Island*: "Where now are They / Who . . . towards the really better / World had turned their face," that poem had asked. "Are They dead here?" The poem answered itself: "Yes. / And the wish to wound has the power." Now again, in 1939, when the wish to wound had even more vehement power, Auden ended his elegy for Freud in a tone entirely unlike the triumphs of his elegy for Yeats:

One rational voice is dumb: over a grave
The household of Impulse mourns one deeply loved.
    Sad is Eros, builder of cities,
    And weeping anarchic Aphrodite.

This mythological tableau is not quite appropriate to Freud, who had different ideas about Eros and Aphrodite. But Auden was not mourning

Freud so much as the whole body of hope that his poem described under Freud's name. When Auden had publicly affirmed these hopes in the closing stanzas of "September 1, 1939," he could not bring himself to admit that he had stopped believing them. Now he restated them more truthfully. In "September 1, 1939," all he had was a voice to undo the folded lie, and the Just used their voices to exchange their messages. Now one rational voice was dumb. In the earlier poem, because we must love one another or die, love could conquer death. Now, over the grave of her dead beloved, Aphrodite, goddess of love, stood weeping.

CHAPTER FOUR

Investigating the Crime

E arly in December 1939, Auden went to a German-language cinema in New York to see a newsreel that chronicled the Nazi conquest of Poland as a racial and national triumph. He heard the audience respond with murderous applause. About thirty years later he recalled to an interviewer that "quite ordinary, supposedly harmless Germans in the audience were shouting 'Kill the Poles,'" and he wrote to his Oxford tutor Nevill Coghill, around the same time, "What was remarkable about the film was its lack of hypocrisy. Every value I had been brought up on, and assumed everybody held, was flatly denied." And he spoke to other friends of (as Stephen Spender paraphrased him) "the brutal honesty of its assumption that might is right." He had tried to convince himself that the multitudes chose dictatorship only because democracy had failed to deliver the justice they instinctively desired. But the "quite ordinary, supposedly harmless" multitudes had chosen dictatorship because they worshiped injustice and force. Hatred was not the doomed preliminary stage of an irreversible ascent to love; it was an end in itself. The instinctual powers—described in his elegy for Freud as eager for enlightenment—were content with a future of murder. And, to the extent that Auden's poems were, as he imagined, the works of his daemonic gift, they too were driven by uncontrollable furies.

Auden sought out the German newsreel in a deliberate but apparently not quite conscious wish to be shocked into facing what he already knew. The film was showing in Yorkville, a Manhattan district heavily populated by Germans. Auden had lived there—a few streets away from the cinema—in the spring, but was now, after his honeymoon trip, living in an apartment five miles away, in Brooklyn Heights. (Kallman visited every afternoon at four, but continued to live with his father in Manhattan.) Evidently Auden read about the film in a review on 4 December by Archer Winsten in *The New York Post*, at that time the city's most intelligent liberal paper, with a large Jewish readership. Winsten devoted two brief paragraphs to the trivial German comedy *Das Ekel* (*The Pain in the Neck*), which was his ostensible subject, then turned to the newsreel:

> At last there was a picture of Hitler reviewing his troops. As the solid blocks of soldiers marched past, goose-stepping almost off the ground and making an enormously effective picture of mechanized drill, the 86th Street Garden Theatre burst into sudden and violent applause. My only point is that it is instructive to hear something like that. The contrast makes you think. It seems as though, given the proper conditioning, a human being can believe anything, cheer for death or fear a mouse. This does not apply merely to the Garden Theatre's audience among current phenomena.*

Auden probably went to Yorkville to see the audience as much as the film.

In the time of the "phony war"—the relatively quiet period after Germany and the Soviet Union divided Poland between them in September—Britain and France were officially at war with Germany, but the only hostilities occurred in occasional battles between ships at sea. The widely feared German air raids over England had not begun, and the French and British armies had not fired a shot. The next few years seemed to promise a slow, indecisive war without mass mobilization or mass destruction. Italy was officially neutral; Japan was at war only with China. In the United States, two years before the Japanese attack on Pearl Harbor, wartime anxieties could be assuaged by the vastness of two isolating oceans.

Auden's beliefs had been unsettled by the outbreak of war, but he had not understood how deeply they had been shaken until he witnessed national and racial hatred at first hand. A distant political event, no matter

---

* The name of the film and Winsten's review were discovered by Nicholas Jenkins. Auden made clear in interviews and conversations that he had sought out the film: "I went up to Yorkville to see a German film about the invasion of Poland" ("Interview with W. H. Auden," *Concern*, Winter 1971). The newsreel was not named in advertisements, and the only plausible way he could have learned of it was the review. (When he recalled the incident in his letter to Coghill he misremembered the date as November 1939 and identified the film as *Sieg in Poland* [for *Polen*].)

how terrifying, seldom has an immediate profound effect on poets and novelists (although critics tend to insist it should); the deepest reaction comes later, when the writer witnesses the effect of the event at home, like Wordsworth finding himself silent in the church where everyone else prayed loudly for an English victory against France, or when the writer witnesses small-scale events at the scene of war itself, like Wordsworth's sudden sympathy with a hungry servant girl in Paris or Auden's unexpected distress at the sight of boarded-up churches in Republican Spain.

Auden never wrote explicitly about an unsettling event at the time it occurred, but waited sometimes ten or more years until he thought he understood the effect it had had on him. His immediate responses were intense but indirect, usually taking the form of book reviews written in an exalted visionary tone that broke unexpectedly through the calmer manner of the rest of his prose. The first such instance, after his vision of Agape in 1933, was the paean to love disguised as a review of *The Book of Talbot.* The second was "Jacob and the Angel," a lurid archetypal parable of the daemon, which he wrote probably within days of his visit to the cinema in Yorkville and which was published in *The New Republic.* It was disguised, thinly, as a review of Walter de la Mare's anthology *Behold, This Dreamer!*

Auden evidently asked to review this book, three months after it had been widely reviewed elsewhere, because it gave him an excuse to write about the realm of impulse and dream. So intent on visionary matters that he did not transcribe the title accurately (he omitted the comma and exclamation point), he quoted de la Mare's introductory defense of the dream against "the prig, the prude and the precious" only, he said, "to extend and qualify it." Auden's vision of the dream world was now more dangerous than anything de la Mare had seen there.

The struggle between the worlds of night and day, instinct and reason, he wrote, was no longer one in which the night world needed to be restored to its rights and powers that materialistic rationalism had repressed—which is how he had viewed the matter in his elegy for Freud. We are confronted, he wrote, "by an ecstatic and morbid abdication of the free-willing and individual before the collective and the daemonic. We have become obscene night-worshipers who, having discovered that we cannot live exactly as we will, deny the possibility of willing anything and are content masochistically *to be lived*, a denial that betrays not only us but our daemon itself." In the years since the Great War, he went on, as people realized that rational liberalism could not guarantee material happiness, the public world had been transformed by a surge in "political

Romanticism"—the name he gave to the idea of a general will as the basis for collective action, as in theories that justified Fascism. But the private world had also been transformed in ways that he had not imagined until he heard the shouts in the Yorkville cinema. The Protestant epoch in which the worlds of day and night had been segregated from each other was ending:

> For that very day [i.e., day world] of work and money which is essentially the domain of conscious and willed acts, has, with the growth of centralization, specialization and mechanization, taken on more and more, for the vast majority, the arbitrary determined aspect of the night and the dream, and not a pleasant dream either. For how many millions is their free individual life now thrown back into a Personal Unconscious, to issue only at night or in popular entertainment as dreams, the mechanical properties of which betray their all too private origin, dreams that are in no sense visions.

The revelations of vision had been driven out by falsifying dreams whose only source was the self's resentful darkness.

The multitudes had ceased to believe in the humane reason recommended in "the professionally 'sunny' utterances of their governments," and now "follow voices whose hypnotic tones seem more consonant with life."

> For how should they know that the new song to which they listen with such rapture as the call of "Instinct" is nothing of the kind, but only the wailing of an egotistic "Reason" crippled by inaction? How should they know that the smug hypocrites were right in what they said, but did not act upon—that the daemonic powers are helpless by themselves, since it is the day life that must not only find the means to the ends they desire, but even discover the ends themselves?

This passage is a renunciation of everything Auden had written eight months earlier about our inevitable marriage with powers we pretend to understand. Instinctive destiny will do nothing to save us. We must, he continued, escape from "this society in which the positions of Anima and Animus are inverted—in which it is reason that more and more leads an underground 'imaginative' life, while politics becomes more and more 'surrealist.' " Our means of escape is indicated by the thought of "Darwin, Hegel, Marx, Freud, Jung, whatever modifications we shall have to make in their theories, and they will be many," for all these evolutionary and archetypal thinkers agree on one fundamental truth "beneath all their local and timely errors." They reveal "the line . . . along which the day can be reconciled with the night, Freedom with Destiny," the same line always followed by poetry "except when it has degenerated into academicism or nonsense."

In his closing paragraph, Auden tried to rescue his earlier beliefs about the guiding daemon, but his rescue has the air of a desperate rhetorical trick. "Yes," he wrote, "the Liberal *Aufklärung* was wrong: in the last analysis we *are* lived." But he retreated from this statement in the act of making it:

> for the night brings forth the day, the unconscious It fashions the conscious fore-brain; the historical epoch grows the idea, the subject matter creates the technique—but it does so precisely in order that it may itself escape the bonds of the determined and the natural. The daemon creates Jacob the prudent Ego, not for the latter to lead, in self-isolation and contempt, a frozen attic life of its own, but to be a loving and reverent antagonist; for it is only through that wrestling bout of which the sex act and the mystical union are the typical symbols that the future is born, that Jacob acquires the power and the will to live, and the daemon is transformed into an angel.

When the ecstatic metaphors are disentangled, this means that consciousness is the bootstrap created by the unconscious in order to lift itself up.

Auden's review was his first attempt to respond to the shouts of hatred he had heard in the Yorkville cinema. He seemed persuaded by his response when he wrote it in prose, using the same vocabulary of determinism and myth that he had used earlier to persuade himself of the inevitable triumph of love. He seemed less persuaded in verse. A brief poem on the same theme opened with "The reverent fury of couples on the wedding night, / Jacob wrestling with a river demon at the ford," and closed with the moment in the struggle when "Our powers flow back to us and our courage is restored / In the battle-embrace of our loving antagonist, / That terrible enemy who wishes to be our friend." Auden abandoned these verses of hollow uplift soon after writing them.

At the time he wrote "Jacob and the Angel," in December 1939, he had been working for two months on *Paul Bunyan*, an opera libretto in which the gigantic logger was treated not as a legendary American hero but as an archetypal myth. Auden had seized on the idea of a musical work about Paul Bunyan during the summer, when he wrote to Benjamin Britten, recently arrived in the United States, that he had an idea to discuss with him. Britten's American publisher had already urged him to compose an opera suitable for schools, and readily commissioned the work when Britten and Auden proposed it. The last opera with a libretto by a major English poet and composer had been Dryden and Purcell's *King Arthur*. Auden, who had occasionally quoted from *King Arthur*, found in Paul Bunyan the American equivalent of the legendary nation-builder Dryden had portrayed, and borrowed from Dryden such details as talking trees and national prophecies. No longer wishing to make himself into a poet loyal to one political line, he found in Dryden an example of a great public poet whose political loyalties were notoriously inconstant.

The original Bunyan legends were faux-naïf urban inventions, not genuine folktales; Auden studied, then largely ignored, the versions he found in the New York Public Library. Bunyan, as Auden reinvented him, is the American daemon, the disembodied bass voice of a figure too vast to be portrayed on stage. In the earliest layers of Auden's text, Bunyan personifies the collective impulse to tame unpeopled nature and build a civilized community. A prologue (dropped from the finished version) defines him in language borrowed from the vaguest reaches of Jung: "To begin with / Paul Bunyan is an American myth. / A myth is a collective dream . . . / Dream[s] are the meeting place / Of memory and intention / [Where] We and our fate come face to face."

Bunyan never dreams in earlier versions of the legend; in Auden's version he does little else. In the words of the ballad narrator who bridges the scene changes, Bunyan's physical size is impressive—"But let me tell you in advance, / His dreams were of greater significance." He is a dream who transmits his dreams to the collective unconscious that dreamed him into existence, and his dreams are so vast and archetypal that when he tells one of them to his men, "Young boys grew up and needed a shave, / Old men got worried they'd be late for the grave." Babe, the gigantic blue ox who is Bunyan's traditional familiar, appears at the moment Bunyan wakes from a dream of becoming the greatest logger ever. ("I conceive of her quite arbitrarily, as a symbol of his anima," Auden wrote when the opera was first performed in 1941.)

In these early stages of the work all dreams are benevolent and constructive. The archetypal dream needs the practical help of the waking world to achieve its ends, so Paul Bunyan summons the strong, unintelligent Hel Helson to be his foreman and the aimless, learned Johnny Inkslinger to be his bookkeeper, but they do not understand his purposes or why they can find their own purposes only through dreams. The night still knew better than the day.

Then, in December 1939, after Auden had written half the libretto and had gone to the cinema in Yorkville, everything changed. The daemon no longer knew where it was going, or why. "The Unconscious," Auden wrote in "Jacob and the Angel," "is blind; it knows it wants something, but cannot tell what it is until the right something is put into its hands." Auden had earlier typed a scene in which Bunyan brings on a quartet of failures (" 'Gold in the North,' came the blizzard to say") to warn the lumberjacks of the rigors of their civilizing task: "Here are some who will testify to the strength of her [earth's] reluctance." Now he revised the scene to make the quartet a nightmare of foreboding, and revised the first words of the introductory line to read: "Now as you fall asleep let a dream testify . . ." He added another episode in which the camp experiences a dream of the kind he had described in "Jacob and the Angel" as one of those secretions that "issue only at night or in popular entertainment as dreams, the mechanical properties of which betray their all too private origin." This dream took the form of a musical number for a chorus of figures called Lame Shadows and Animas.* These are the dream personae projected by the isolated self onto the photographic images of film stars and models. Meanwhile the real film stars and models sing that they are bored by the whole impersonal charade, in which they are reduced to "perfect nullities . . . / The heroes of the multitude / Their dreams of female pulchritude."

    In the second half of the libretto Auden dramatized the hopeful resolution he had sketched in "Jacob and the Angel," where "that wrestling bout of which the sex act and the mystical union are the typical symbols" brings about the daemon's transformation into an angel. Helson, tempted by four cronies, fights Bunyan for control of the lumber camp, while Bunyan's daughter, Tiny, and the camp cook, Slim (a Prolific who follows the way of love), sing a duet of satisfied longing, oblivious to the

---

* The Lame Shadow was Auden's name for the ideal figure that the wounded ego seeks in the world of the Alter Ego. He seems to have learned the name from his early psychological mentor John Layard, who had apparently adapted it from Jung; Jung's printed works use "shadow" in the same general sense but do not qualify it as "lame." The imaginary ideal is a shadow because its existence is merely an emanation from ourselves, a figure who is everything we are not, one whose powers compensate for our weakness. But the shadow is lame because it has no strength of its own and exists only through our weakness. In the "Epithalamion" Auden wrote in September 1939 he used "lame" in this same sense: "Shame at our shortcomings makes / Lame magicians of us all." Around the same time, in the letter in which he told Layard he had found love, he wrote: "My dear old Lame Shadow puts its arms round my neck and says 'Thank you. You *have* been an old Bore, you know, but let's forget about that. Now I can fly back to Heaven where I belong. So long. Remember me to John Layard. I always liked that man' " (British Library).

wrestling bout offstage that signifies their love's inherent darkness. The symbolism clanks discordantly when Bunyan wins the struggle with Helson, not because he is immeasurably bigger, but because, as the chorus keeps insisting, "Paul has the brains." Helson, enlightened through defeat, recognizes that he and Bunyan need each other, while Tiny and Slim also sing of their own mutual need. In the final scene, the human characters prepare to leave for sophisticated urban roles awaiting them elsewhere: Helson to direct public works in Washington, Inkslinger (like Isherwood) to be a movie consultant in Hollywood, the lovers Slim and Tiny to manage a hotel in Manhattan.

The American frontier has been closed, and Bunyan must go elsewhere. Distant forests and deserts call to him to give them a purpose, and "I must hasten in reply / To that low instinctive cry / There to make a way again / For the conscious lives of men." In America the machine has now imposed a new pattern on the old instinctive life: "Gone the natural disciplines / And the life of choice begins." As "Jacob and the Angel" had predicted, the night brings forth the day, the unconscious It fashions the conscious forebrain, which it cannot command or guide. Bunyan warns his friends: "you / Have the harder task to do / As at freedom's puzzled feet / Yawn the gulfs of self-defeat."

Yet for all his talk of departure, Bunyan never makes his exit. As in "Spain," at a similar moment of crisis, the daemon of determined necessity speaks an effusive farewell, then quietly neglects to leave. In "Spain" the instinctive force named "the life" told its human listeners, who begged it to command them, "I am not the Mover, / Not today, not to you," for "the life" has abdicated its powers in favor of conscious human choice. Paul Bunyan abdicates in the same terms: "America is what we choose to make it." But as "the life" persisted through the natural, unconscious, instinctive metaphors that in "Spain" described the acts of the volunteers in the Spanish Civil War, so the night world in *Paul Bunyan* will persist in the day world of the American future. In the closing lines Inkslinger demands, for the first time, "Paul, who are you?" and Bunyan replies:

> Where the night becomes the day
> Where the dream becomes the Fact
> I am the Eternal Guest
> I am Way
> I am Act.

The transformed daemon remains forever, calling itself the Way, and speaking the language of angels. Like "Spain," this closing scene is grand, memorable, and false. Auden knew—and the shouts in the Yorkville cinema had reminded him—that the instinctive id neither fades away nor sets things right.

Paul Bunyan suffered from many inadequacies that combined to sink it when it was finally launched in a student production at Columbia University in May 1941. (A professional production tentatively planned for early 1940 fell through.) Auden's characters were American in the same way that the characters in *The Mikado* are Japanese, and American critics who were not bored were offended. Auden had given his lumberjacks the diction of English public school boys, and between the resonant moments of Bunyan's dreams the libretto offered little more than the frictionless romance of Tiny and Slim and stale jokes about bad cooking in the lumber camp (i.e., school). After the first production Auden revised the text to make it a political parable, in which Helson's cronies use Communist slogans to justify their lust for power, but he made no attempt to resolve the contradictions of the final scene. The libretto remained unpublished until Britten revived it after Auden's death. *Paul Bunyan* was Auden's last effort to follow the determined forces of history and the daemon to a utopian future that would never arrive.

At the same time, Auden was aware that Christopher Isherwood had found a different answer to the shouts in the cinema. Having settled in Hollywood, Isherwood had met the swami who had founded the Vedanta Society of Southern California and who was now instructing him (and Aldous Huxley and other British Californians) in techniques of withdrawal from the world and its passions. Auden had visited Isherwood in August just after this instruction had begun and tried to find ways he could act in sympathy with him. In the autumn he planned to take up yoga and, as he told Mrs. Dodds, was "doing a preparatory course of physical exercises"—"*most* painful, but illuminating"—with a physical therapist, Tania Kurella Stern. (She and her husband, James Stern, had become Auden's closest friends in New York.) He quickly dropped this idea, but worked to find ways to translate Isherwood's new beliefs into familiar Western terms.

In December he began to write intermittently about sainthood, which he imagined as a vocation consciously chosen by those who did not have enough talent to become artists. An artist, he wrote in a prose note, is "one whose desire for ethical perfection is *exactly* balanced by his cow-

ardice, his fear of what the attempt to achieve perfection will involve."
That balance could fail in two ways: "Were his talent a fraction greater,
he would certainly become a madman or a crook; were it a fraction less,
he would probably be compelled to attempt to become a saint." In the
same note he wrote: "Definition of a saint: One to whom ethics have
almost become aesthetics." Two weeks after going to the Yorkville cinema he wrote a startlingly unflattering letter to Harold Albaum (who also
called himself Harold Norse), a young man embittered by multiple failures, among them the failure of his sexual relationship with Chester Kallman before Auden arrived on the scene—although he remained on
friendly terms with Kallman and was on awkward but cordial terms with
Auden, who sent him money when a pickup stole his funds. Auden now
suggested to Albaum—absurdly enough—that failure had destined him
for sainthood:

> I have sometimes wondered if you are not, maybe, being shaped by life for the
> most arduous of all callings, that every hole but one is not being stopped up,
> that every possibility but one is not being eliminated by the certainty of failure,
> in order to force you on to the one destiny which you can accept or refuse, but
> cannot change, i.e. to be a saint, one of those rare beings whom, when they
> die, the people who knew them remember not for any particular act, but for
> their existence, beings whose presence was enough to make others convinced
> that human life has not been an entirely vain experiment.

(This tone, as Auden seems to have guessed from his knowledge of Albaum, succeeded in breaking the ice between them. Their relations became far more cordial and Auden hired Albaum to type his next book.)

Auden found it easier to recommend sainthood *faute de mieux* than
to imagine what a saint might actually be like. In "The Icon and the
Portrait," published early in January 1940, he used an assignment to
review two cartoon books, one by James Thurber, the other by William
Steig, as an excuse for a brief essay about the modern conflict between
two kinds of visual representation, "iconography and portraiture, the
symbolic and the unique, the God and the mortal." Until the middle of
the sixteenth century, he wrote, the two kinds "coexisted in a fruitful
tension and equilibrium." Realistic portraits functioned as icons when
they occurred "in religious pictures," and the significant landscapes in
the background were signs of a secure relation between man and the rest
of nature. Then came an age of portraiture, followed more recently by a
revival of iconography in children's art, imitations of primitive sculpture,
and the work of Disney and Thurber. "Yet a synthesis of icon and por-

trait is still far off. The former remains non-representational, the latter accidental"—either abstract anonymous figures (like Paul Bunyan) or individual ones with no meaning beyond themselves (like Inkslinger and the lumberjacks). "Logos and Eros," he concluded, applying these terms as shorthand for the two kinds of representation, "have yet to be reconciled in a new Agape."

This way of writing about conflict and reconciliation was very different from metaphors of daemonic wrestling bouts. Auden's allusions to the faceless daemon turned perfunctory and finally ceased early in 1940. In a review of Carl Sandburg's life of Lincoln, he wrote that geniuses "are conscious of how little depends on their free will and how much they are vehicles for powers they can never fully understand but to which they can listen"; and in "New Year Letter," in a passage of empty affirmations, "the powers / That we create with are not ours." The daemon made a last sardonic bow under its own name in another passage in "New Year Letter," where "Our evil *Daimon*" is personified in Hitler.

The daemon had not been transformed into an angel, but Auden now used the word "angel" where he had once spoken of the daemon or the gift. In a book review in July 1940, he addressed an author who had sided with the Nazis: "Consider who you were: endowed by your angel with great gifts of imagination and expression." This new angel quickly settled into a poetic synonym for good luck. The hero of a sonnet in the sequence "The Quest," written in the summer of 1940, eludes deadly peril because "The angel of a broken leg had taught him / The right precautions to avoid a fall." Auden provided a gloss in a review a few months later:

> Psychotherapy will not get much further until it recognizes that the true significance of a neurosis is teleological, that the so-called traumatic experience is not an accident, but the opportunity for which the child has been patiently waiting—had it not occurred, it would have found another, equally trivial—in order to find a necessity and direction for its existence, in order that its life may become a serious matter. Of course it would be better if it could do without it, but unconsciously it knows that it is not, by itself, strong enough to learn to stand alone: a neurosis is a guardian angel; to become ill is to take vows.

Auden wrote "New Year Letter" partly to understand, partly to induce the transformation of his beliefs. He began the poem early in January

1940, finished drafting its seventeen hundred lines in March, and revised it until late in April. The poem describes itself as written during the hours from late New Year's Eve to the dawn of New Year's Day, and the early drafts make explicit that the impulse to write it was the familiar New Year's resolve toward reform and self-knowledge. "For I relapse into my crimes, / Time and again have slubbered through / With slip and slapdash what I do, / Adopted what I would disown, / The preacher's loose immodest tone." The New Year "occasion," he wrote in the drafts, must "lead me to / Ask who I am and what I do." He added elsewhere in the drafts:

> And once again this New Year's Eve
> I have a purpose to achieve,
> To use a language as one way
> To re-investigate today[,]
> Find what I think by seeing what I say.*

When "New Year Letter" appeared in book form in 1941, in *The Double Man* (the British edition was titled *New Year Letter*), Randall Jarrell began his review: "In 1931 Pope's ghost said to me, 'Ten years from now the leading young poet of the time will publish, in *The Atlantic Monthly*, a didactic epistle of about nine hundred tetrameter couplets.' I answered absently 'You are a fool'; and who on this earth would have thought him anything else?" Critics have followed Jarrell's lead in treating Auden's poem as too neoclassical and abstract for its own good—"within certain limits, a great success," Jarrell called it—and few readers have been attracted to it by the standard capsule summary, in which the poem's three parts are mechanically linked to the aesthetic, ethical, and religious stages in Kierkegaard, who was nothing more than a name to Auden when he wrote most of it.

What Jarrell and everyone else failed to notice about "New Year Letter" was the way in which the conservative order of its syntax and metre struggled to restrain the anarchic whirlwind of its ideas. Rhymed octosyllabic couplets give it the air of a patterned, rational argument, but this

---

* The last line paraphrases a remark attributed by E. M. Forster to an old lady: "How can I tell what I think till I see what I say?" (*Aspects of the Novel*, Chapter 5). The line has ten syllables, while the earlier lines have eight, because in draft the poem followed the seventeenth- and eighteenth-century convention of adding a foot to the third line of a rhymed triplet in a poem mostly written in rhymed couplets. In the published text only the final line of the poem has an extra foot, although many triplets occur earlier.

eighteenth-century manner (emphasized by proper names printed in small capitals in the American edition, in italics in the British) masks a restless idiosyncratic exploration of vast historical changes and uncertainties. Phrases from a half-dozen languages, and quotations from Plato, Augustine, Wagner, Eliot, and dozens of others, fall neatly into metrical step at Auden's command, but the poem cannot contain his thought or allusions, so still more quotations, together with verses and aphorisms by Auden himself, spill over into eighty-five pages of "Notes," where they are mixed more variously than anything in *The Waste Land* or *The Dunciad Variorum.*

Auden addressed his verse letter to his friend Elizabeth Mayer, a German refugee with literary and artistic interests who was living on Long Island with her psychiatrist husband. She was twenty-four years older than Auden; when they first met in September 1939 (Britten and Peter Pears, whom she had met earlier, were living in her cottage on the grounds of a psychiatric hospital) Auden instantly adopted her as an ideal surrogate for his mother. She balanced convention and disorder in a life that was simultaneously grand and rebellious. Her father had been chaplain to a grand duke, but she had outraged her family by marrying a Jew; her four children bore her husband's name, but one had been fathered by someone else. Her taste for geniuses was the quality least appreciated by her children, some of whom still lived at home as young adults and were obliged to vacate a room for Britten and Pears. She treated Auden as a favored son during his weekend visits, although he, seeing the effect on the children, befriended them and went out of his way to help them through rough patches in their personal and family lives. During the year after Auden met her, his erotic vision of Kallman was absent from his poetry, perhaps because he felt sufficiently secure in it to ignore it, while the image of Elizabeth Mayer—an icon more than a portrait—glowed through the visionary lines about her in his poem.

"New Year Letter" is Auden's *Faust*. The doomed Gretchen of Goethe's *Faust, Part I* has no counterpart in Auden's poem, but Elizabeth Mayer takes the place of the transfigured Gretchen of *Faust, Part II.* Like its model, the poem begins by renouncing old formulae, then ranges eclectically through distant epochs and conflicting ideas, searching, not for a place of rest, but for a labor that will issue in eternal and unending progress. The poem relies on a tempter named Mephistopheles to provide political delusions and ethical errors for us to use as "half-truths we can synthesize." Like *Faust* descending to *die Mütter*, Auden looks

"Down to . . . / The Terrible, the Merciful, the Mothers."* Faust's
wager binds him to yield his soul to Mephistopheles the first time he
says to the passing moment, "Linger awhile, thou art so fair"—that is,
when he first wants to *retain* a moment of happiness. Auden understands
happiness and vision as transient glimpses of a "perfect Being" that
"must be lost to be regained"—must be lost because, "if he stop an
instant there, / The sky grows crimson with a curse . . . / For he has
sprung the trap of Hell."

Near the end of Goethe's drama the aged Faust hopes to build a city
whose citizens, surrounded by natural perils, must daily regain their life
and freedom; when and if he could see such a city, Faust says, he could
ask the passing moment to linger—because, paradoxically, the moment
would be an eternal process, not a pause for stability and rest. Auden,
near the end of his poem, hopes to learn "To what conditions we must
bow / In building the Just City now," and knows that the act of building
must go on forever, because no human act can "bring the far horizon
near," and "any skyline we attain" in our endless journey "Reveals a
higher ridge again." Because Faust wanted to build a city of unceasing effort, Auden prays near the end of the poem to be instructed "in the civil
art / Of making from the muddled heart / A desert and a city where / The
thoughts that have to linger there / May find locality and peace." The
reading eye expects to see "A garden and a city," but the poem prays instead for the desert that will every day demand to be rewatered.

Like Faust's spirit ascending through the skies in his final scene, Auden
in his final lines hopes to rise toward a vision he can never grasp. In the
last lines of *Faust*, "*Das Ewig-Weibliche / Zieht uns hinan*"—the eternal
feminine leads us onward—embodied in the summoning person of the
risen Gretchen. In the last lines of "New Year Letter," Auden too is led
onward as he prays to Elizabeth Mayer, "May the truth / That no one
marries† lead my youth / Where you already are." In her "learned peace-

---

* The metrics of this line have confused more than one critic; one who noticed that it has
eleven syllables pounced on it as a stray pentameter intruding on a poem written entirely (until
its final line) in tetrameter. When scanned in isolation, the line is a trimeter (two second paeons
and an amphibrach), but the metrical expectations created by the surrounding lines cause a
reader to perceive it as a tetrameter by imagining four stresses in the line rather than the actual
three.

† A number of critics misread this phrase as meaning "the truthful statement that asserts that
no one marries"—an absurd contradiction of plain fact. The context makes clear that the phrase
means that you cannot marry the truth. In the same way, earlier in the poem, the *lex abscondita*
"evades / The vigilantes in the glades," and when one vigilante claims to have caught her, the
rest find him "With just a torn blouse in his hands."

fulness," she, like the penitent heavenly Gretchen, spreads "A warmth throughout the universe." Many years later Auden was asked by a friend what he saw in Elizabeth Mayer, who was snobbishly unpleasant to those outside her favored circle. He hesitated, then answered: "*Das Ewig-Weibliche*."

"New Year Letter" is sinuous, various, and far more elusive than its formal style suggests. When Auden had finished more than half of it, he wrote to Elizabeth Mayer, "Your poem creeps along but versified metaphysical argument is very difficult." He compounded the difficulty by trying to resist a temptation that had ruined two poems of metaphysical argument he had written earlier: the temptation to follow an accurate diagnosis with a reckless prescription for a cure. In 1932 he had abandoned an untitled alliterative poem in cantos, based loosely on Langland and Dante, at the point where its structural logic required him to compose a third canto portraying the Communist paradise to follow the capitalist hell and revolutionary purgatory of the first two. In 1938 he had completed a verse commentary to his sonnet sequence "In Time of War" with a prayer in which "the voice of Man" asks the forces of the will to build "a human justice," the work of "the just." Like the just who exchange their messages in "September 1, 1939," these unportrayable figures of political fantasy were called into being by the rhetoric of poetic endings, and by 1940 Auden was no longer willing to entrust them with the future. In "New Year Letter," therefore, he vacillated repeatedly between an analysis of the past and the urgent question of what to do in the present, but stopped short of answering his question. The prayer that concludes the poem asks nothing of the just, or of any other plural class; it does not even try to imagine that the just exist. Instead, it asks an unnamed divine power to "convict our pride of its offense / In all things, even penitence"—because penitence brings the temptation to count ourselves among the just. The poem's deliberate uneasiness and uncertainty arise from Auden's simultaneous refusal to offer a plan of action and his concern that he has put himself in the same position as Mephistopheles, who knows "he's lost if someone ask him / To come the hell in off the links / And say exactly what he thinks." As he wrote in a note to the poem: "The Devil, indeed, is the father of Poetry, for poetry might be defined as the clear expression of mixed feelings. The poetic mood is never indicative."

The poem's Faustian attention to its author's mixed feelings created structural problems that could not be entirely resolved by its use of a deliberately unresolvable dialectic. Ten years later Auden wrote about the "defects" of Goethe's *Faust*, but also about those of his own poem, when he said they were "not, of course, due to any lack of dramatic talent in Goethe but to the nature of the Faust myth itself, for the story of Faust is precisely the story of a man who refuses to be anyone and only wishes to become someone else. Once he has summoned Mephisto, the manifestation of possibility without actuality, there is nothing left for Faust to represent but the passive consciousness of possibilities." *Faust*, he continued, "is full of great poetry and wise sayings but it is not dramatically exciting." This explains why the three longer works Auden wrote after the first-person meditations of "New Year Letter" were all verse dramas about conflicts among persons who are emphatically themselves and never think of being someone else.

"New Year Letter," like *Faust*, is an epic, but less a national epic than a modern epic of the international and psychological kind introduced by *Faust* and Wordsworth's *The Prelude*. Without making public statements about it, Auden wrote the poem that Ezra Pound, after much self-advertisement, had failed to write in *The Cantos*. The epic, whether classic or modern, distinguishes itself from other modes of literature by calling into question the whole social order in which it is written. The novel and drama (except when they explicitly adopt an epic manner) regard the social order as a given, even when, as in Dickens or Balzac, they focus on its faults and contradictions. The epic incorporates social orders other than the poet's—both worse and better ones—and portrays the transformation of an old social order into a new one. Troy, the peaceful city of marriages and temples, must fall to the bachelor warrior camps of the besieging Greeks. Odysseus on his voyage home encounters societies with radically different conceptions of the relationship between host and guest, the relation that in the *Odyssey* defines a society's character. In worthy societies, like those of Eumaeus, Telemachus, Penelope, and the Phaeaceans, the host feeds the guest; in the unworthy societies of the Cyclops and the Lestrygonians, the host eats the guest. "New Year Letter" looks back to the emergence of the modern era in the Renaissance, when medieval "unity had come to grief / Upon professional belief," and "Another unity was made / By equal amateurs in trade." But the "Empiric Economic Man," even at the height of his success, has never fully dominated. "*Blake* shouted insults, *Rousseau* wept, / . . . / While *Baudelaire* went mad protesting / That progress is not interesting."

Today, though "the World ignored them," their "grapevine rumor" has come true: one era has again been transformed into another. The economic and scientific foundations of the past four centuries have been broken; the classical physics that assumed the separation of observer and observed, like the classical economics of profit and loss, has proved more tangled than Newton or the countinghouse thought. The manipulated objects of Renaissance science and psychology have avenged themselves, for the "guess" of outsiders like Blake and Baudelaire has proved true:

> It is the Mover that is moved.
> Whichever way we turn, we see
> Man captured by his liberty,
> The measurable taking charge
> Of him who measures . . .
>   old men in love
> With prices they can never get,
> Homes blackmailed by a radio set.

This entrapping crisis proves that "the special tasks begun / By the Renaissance have been done." Now we must begin to build another era. Indolence, not ignorance, is the only barrier that stands in our way:

> Three quarters of these people know
> Instinctively what ought to be
> The nature of society
> And how they'd live there if they could.
> If it were easy to be good,
> And cheap, and plain as evil how,
> We all would be its members now.

But the Just City will never be cheap or easy, and the poem's hopes for justice are repeatedly interrupted by its distrust of utopian shortcuts —a distrust so intense that it erupts even in the poem's final line, at the climax of an apotheosis of Elizabeth Mayer:

> And love illuminates again
> The city and the lion's den,
> The world's great rage, the travels of young men.

That closing line, by adding a single letter, takes Shelley's utopian vision in *Hellas* of "The world's great age" and transforms it into something more sadly plausible as the international background of Auden's journeys far from home.

Like *Faust* after its prologue in heaven, "New Year Letter" starts on the small stage of a writer's study and the streets outside, then moves to the large stages of history, evolution, and eternity. The citizens who walk about on Easter in the early pages of *Faust* reappear as New Year's Eve crowds who walk "In loose formations of good cheer." Faust first appears in his study, laboring over the relation of word and deed; Auden in his first hundred lines labors over the relation of art and life. On the day the war began, he recalls, he and Elizabeth Mayer played duets in her cottage. The keyboard music of Buxtehude (then an esoteric taste, and a sign of her learned sensibility) made

> Our minds a *civitas* of sound,
> Where nothing but assent was found,
> For art had set in order sense
> And feeling and intelligence,
> And from its ideal order grew
> Our local understanding too.

When Auden wrote "New Year Letter"—all but the last few hundred lines of it—he still attributed to both the conscious and unconscious wills an impulse toward order and a drive toward that wrestling bout that transforms daemon into angel:

> To set in order—that's the task
> Both Eros and Apollo ask;
> For Art and Life agree in this
> That each intends a synthesis.

Where the clever hopes of the 1930s were wrong, he thought, was in their belief that a synthesis could be willed—"For will but wills its opposite" as thesis gives rise to antithesis. Art's wish to imitate life produces not an imitation but an "abstract model of events" that, like all abstract models, cannot guide anyone who is trying to build a real future.

> Art in intention is mimesis
> But, realized, the resemblance ceases;
> Art is not life and cannot be
> A midwife to society
> For art is a *fait accompli*.
> What they should do, or how or when
> Life-order comes to living men
> It cannot say, for it presents
> Already lived experience

> Through a convention that creates
> Autonomous completed states.

Even if art cannot prescribe the future, artists, at least in the early stages of "New Year Letter," are still the most adept diagnosticians of the present: "Great Masters who have shown mankind / An order it has yet to find," masters who "challenge, warn and witness." The poem praises the same heaven of the great that had been praised in Auden's "Epithalamion" a few months before. Although Auden imagines himself, like everyone else whom "The greatest of vocations chose," stammering and hanging his head as he appears before a tribunal of greater poets (led, in his case, by Dante, Blake, and the ambiguously accusing example of Rimbaud, who gave up poetry for action), he finds courage to rise before them in the first place because he is gifted with sufficient skill to investigate the present through language. He claimed that gift in a passage that he discarded from the drafts, perhaps because its self-deprecating playfulness was too clearly a mask for a self-important boast:

> So though not painstaking like *French*
> Who with a railway-guide unties
> The watertightest alibis,
> Though I shall never, I confess
> Have *Peter*'s fabulous success
> With women, sonnets, cars and waiters
> Nor *Priestley*'s skill with apparatus
> Nor feel the brilliant flash that sears
> *Poirot*'s cerebral hemispheres
> Nor know as much about Chinese
> As *Vance* or Information Please
> I too shall try to [*illegible*] with what
> Small technical resource I've got
> Use poetry to reconstruct,
> Question, intuit, and deduct.*

Only after presenting the detective's résumé does the poem turn to the matter that needs investigating: "The situation of our time / Surrounds us like a baffling crime." The more we examine the evidence, the

---

* The superior detectives are Freeman Wills Crofts's Inspector French, Dorothy Sayers's Lord Peter Wimsey, John Rhode's Dr. Lancelot Priestley, Agatha Christie's Hercule Poirot, S. S. Van Dine's Philo Vance, and the panel of experts on the American radio program *Information Please*. Auden later analyzed his addiction to detective stories; see p. 256.

more we recognize that "the guilt is everywhere," that "all are suspects," that in the larger world as in our local parish, "Vast spiritual disorders lie." Even the best among us (in a generalized autobiographical confession) "feel / Their politics perhaps unreal / And all they have believed untrue." The images of the past decade are inescapable: "The Asiatic cry of pain, / The shots of executing Spain, / . . . / The Jew wrecked in the German cell, / Flat Poland frozen into hell, / The silent dumps of unemployed." Remembering this, all, even the best, are tempted by apocalyptic dreams of vengeance "In which the persecutors scream / As on the evil Aryan lives / Descends the night of the long knives." The just exchange mixed messages.

The first part of the poem ends with a double statement about the powers of the investigating poet: "No words men write can stop the war" or relieve "its immeasurable grief"; yet when "heart and intelligence" reach an impasse in their inner debate, "the good offices of verse" may bring about an accord. If art cannot recommend action, it can at least promote an atmosphere in which heart and mind can choose their acts harmoniously. The rest of the poem confounds this pious hope.

When "New Year Letter" turns from investigation to action, in its second part, it brings in a figure who looks and acts like an obstacle but also serves the deeper purpose of impelling us to overcome him. This is Mephistopheles, the poem's name for every temptation and constraint that works together with ourselves "to / Prevent the actions we could do." Mephistopheles' arrival opens a convoluted argument that the poem sustains almost to the end. Reduced to summarizing prose (as Auden himself did more than once in the notes that accompany the published poem), the argument runs like this. Human wishes are divided and contradictory. Each partial wish seeks to deny or prevent the satisfaction of all other wishes. The Devil is a convenient name for the cause and agent of this inner division but, as the poet tells Mephistopheles, only a name: "You have no positive existence, / Are only a recurrent state / Of fear and faithlessness and hate, / That takes on from becoming me / A legal personality." "Do you know what the Devil looks like," Auden asked a Sunday-school class in 1942, and answered, "The Devil looks like me."

By dividing the human will against itself, the Devil is the instrument of his own defeat:

> For as the great schismatic who
> First split creation into two
> He did what it could never do,

> Inspired it with the wish to be
> Diversity in unity.

Mephistopheles does more than simply inspire a wish for unity: he personifies a universal impulse to move toward it. Auden never says so explicitly, but the Devil is his name for the dialectic, a name that so thoroughly disguises this impersonal involuntary force that the poem's underlying determinism is rendered almost invisible. "Who, though, is the Prince of Lies / If not the Spirit-that-denies," the poem asks, giving Mephistopheles the name that Goethe gave him. The spirit that denies is the dialectical impulse toward a thesis-denying antithesis. "Poor cheated *Mephistopheles*" tells himself he chooses freely, but the poem taunts him with the truth: "the Determined uses you, / Creation's errand-boy creator." The Devil's involuntary errand is to bring us to salvation whether or not we want it.

> For how could we get on without you
> Who give the *savoir-faire* to doubt you
> And keep you in your proper place,
> Which is, to push us into grace?

Auden wrote a few months later: "Faust is saved because he is never content, he is never content because Mephistopheles will never let him rest: the devil is the cause of losing his own wager." Faust is never content because he is in the grip of the dialectic.

The Devil's greatest skill—indeed his only one—is his ability to convince us temporarily that a part is really a whole, that by satisfying one of our conflicting wishes we are satisfying all of them, that, for example, a poet who satisfies his wish to serve the revolution will also thereby satisfy his wish to write better poems. All our sophisticated efforts to find a false wholeness, whether through politics, philosophy, psychology, or art, merely give the Devil new ways of tempting us into division. His rapid shifts, as he counters each of Auden's intellectual defenses against him, are traced in one of the poem's most compressed passages. Auden (calling himself "we") first tries to elude division by renouncing the limited perspective of the individual mind: like everyone else in the twentieth century, he is too shrewd to suppose "our *idées fixes* to be / True of a fixed Reality," or to suppose he has direct access to any reality. We have no need for such access, he tells the Devil; we can admit the likelihood that "we love, not friends or wives, / But certain patterns in our lives, / Effects that take the cause's name." Yet, he continues confidently, we are too clever to be disturbed by this, because we know love occurs in the realm of experience, not certainty, that we need not find rational proofs of perceived phenomena. "If in this letter that I send / I write 'Elizabeth's my friend,' / I cannot but express my faith / That I is Not-Elizabeth." This kind of argument from phenomena was, Auden hoped, ingenious enough to counter nihilistic despair, and it builds on the same logic he had used in "In Memory of Ernst Toller": "existence is believing / We know for whom we mourn and who is grieving."

The Devil flatteringly agrees with every up-to-date word of it. "I see it now," he says. "The intellect / That parts the Cause from the Effect / And thinks in term of Space and Time / Commits a legalistic crime, / For such an unreal severance / Must falsify experience." This is exactly the antidualistic point that the poet was so proud to make a moment ago. The Devil follows up by urging us to reject intellect and its inherent dualism, and in its place, "Recover what appreciates, / The deep un-snobbish instinct which / Alone can make relation rich." And so he leads us into blood-consciousness, a dualism that favors flesh over mind, and thence into all other refusals of intellect, all other abdications to the moral philosophy of a Hitler.

The Devil's method is to get us to confuse successive half-truths with the truth. This confusion he finds both philosophically and politically convenient.

> The False Association is
> A favorite strategy of his:
> Induce men to associate
> Truth with a lie, then demonstrate
> The lie and they will, in truth's name,
> Treat babe and bath-water the same.

Throughout the centuries he has taught his victims to associate their wish for justice with their expectation of revolutionary change, and to lose faith in justice when they lose hope for change. The early Christians, when apocalypse failed to arrive as expected, abandoned "their early agape" for the comforts of "a late lunch with Constantine." Words-worth, having waited for the "Parousia of liberty" after the fall of the Bastille, "ended as the Devil knew / An earnest Englishman would do, / Left by Napoleon in the lurch, / Supporting the Established Church."

Those who believed the Russian Revolution would begin a new era of millennial justice now faced the same disillusioning temptation.

The aftermath of the 1917 revolution prompts the poem's most carefully nuanced ethical argument. Auden honors Marx as one of the "Great sedentary Caesars," the intellectual conquerors "Who brought an epoch to a close." An earlier conqueror was Galileo, who put an end to the "slaveowners' mechanics," their belief that nature operated differently on the great and the small; another was Newton, who "drew up a Roman code of Force" that replaced eccentric local ideas of physical law with universal law; a third was Darwin, who "brought / Man's pride to heel at last and showed / His kinship with the worm and toad," shattering the fantasy of ordained human dominion over nature. Like them, Marx demolished vast intellectual errors used by the unjust to justify themselves:

> As he explored the muttering tomb
> Of a museum reading room,
> The Dagon* of the General Will
> Fell in convulsions and lay still;
> The tempting Contract of the rich,
> Revealed as an abnormal witch,
> Fled with a shriek, for as he spoke
> The justifying magic broke.

Marx transformed his angers into triumph:

> The father-shadow that he hated
> Weighed like an Alp; his love, frustrated,
> Negated as it was negated,†
> Burst out in boils; his animus
> Outlawed him from himself; but thus,
> And only thus, perhaps, could he
> Have come to his discovery.

Marx's despairing hatred was the opposite of that "heroic charity" that might stimulate a voyage of intellectual discovery, but it served equally well:

---

* The god of the Philistines.
† In *Capital* Marx called the Communist revolution "the negation of the negation"—the negation of capitalism, which was itself a negation of feudalism.

> Heroic charity is rare;
> Without it, what except despair
> Can shape the hero who will dare
> The desperate catabasis
> Into the snarl of the abyss
> That always lies just underneath
> Our jolly picnic on the heath
> Of the agreeable, where we bask,
> Agreed on what we will not ask,
> Bland, sunny, and adjusted by
> The light of the accepted lie?

However heroic and enlightening was Marx's sense of the present and past, the poem has no illusions about his sense of the future. "We hoped; we waited for the day / The State would wither clean away, / Expecting the Millennium / That theory promised us would come. / It didn't." Great theories of economics, science, and history are no better guides to action than great works of art. The future refuses to be built on Marx's anger and despair. In arguing this point, Auden combines two kinds of metaphors, some from the unarguable observations of cell biology, others from the tendentious teleologies of creative evolution. The energies of the great theories (here called "Logos") are described as acting like cosmic rays that cause mutations in chromosomes, but these sterile mutations are rejected by the cellular apparatus of the centrosome, which sorts the genetic material transmitted to the next generation. "The rays of Logos take effect, / But not as theory would expect, / For, sterile and diseased by doubt, / The dwarf mutations are thrown out / From Eros' weaving centrosome." Logos and Eros remain unreconciled, and Eros, builder of cities, alone decides what and how to build.

While Marx's hatred rendered his sense of the future sterile and false, the moral force of his historical vision remains fruitful and true. "Loosed from its shroud of temper, his / Determinism comes to this: / None shall receive unless they give; / All must cooperate to live." Near the end of the poem, in its culminating vision of democracy, Auden translates into English Marx's most resonant formula about ability and need: "all have needs to satisfy / And each a power to supply."* Marx's failure as

---

* This is lifted almost directly from the translation of Marx's slogan that Auden had used as the final line of the published text of *The Dog Beneath the Skin* in 1935: "To each his need. From each his power." (The standard translation reads: "From each according to his ability, to each according to his need.")

a prophet does not discredit his exposure of tyranny or his revelation of the prerequisites for justice. Thanks to the sobering inadvertent lessons of Mephistopheles, we can learn the conditions we must accept in "building the Just City." And the dialectic will assure that it gets built in the end, even if Marx was wrong to imagine that a political party could draw the plans for it.

At this point, the Devil, using his favorite debating tactic of false association, rushes in to convince us that the Moscow trials and Stalin's massacres in Spain discredit the idea of the Just City itself. Knowing that we have woken from our intoxicating night of revolutionary hope "With swimming heads and hands that shake / And stomachs that keep nothing down,"

> He calls at breakfast in the role
> Of blunt but sympathetic soul:
> "Well, how's our Socialist this morning?
> I could say 'Let this be a warning,'
> But no, why should I? Students must
> Sow their wild oats at times or bust.
> Such things have happened in the lives
> Of all the best Conservatives.
> I'll fix you something for your liver."
> And thus he sells us down the river.
> Repenting of our last infraction
> We seek atonement in reaction.

And our attempts to find salvation in politics end in the same damnation we accepted when we tried to find it in philosophy.

Yet at the end of the second part, the poem transforms the Devil's temptation into a gift. It was he, we remember, who first tempted us in one direction, then in the opposite direction, and "He cannot always fool us thrice." "Time and memory are still / Limiting factors on his will." We can use his temptations as dialectical half-truths awaiting not only their antitheses but the creative synthesis that follows:

> So, hidden in his hocus-pocus,
> There lies the gift of double focus,
> That magic lamp which looks so dull
> And utterly impractical
> Yet, if Aladdin use it right,
> Can be a sesame to light.

The gift of double focus was more than a dialectical ability to see both sides of a question. Auden wrote in his review of Sandburg's Lincoln, "The one infallible symptom of greatness is the capacity for double focus." Those who lack it are "half-men and half-women, the little either-or people," the same population that in "New Year Letter" are called "The either-ors, the mongrel halves / Who find truth in a mirror."

The poem leaves them behind at the end of the second part, along with their patron the Devil, and in the third part introduces a way of thinking different from theirs. History had thus far in the poem been a realm where knowledge was altered (by Galileo, Newton, Darwin, Marx), but ethical action repeated itself (as in the recurring disillusionments after the French and Russian revolutions). This perennially dialectic history, in which one error merely breeds another, now drops away to be replaced by a realm of free action in an eternally changing condition to which the poem gives two names: Purgatory, a name Auden had not used before, and the simpler word "time."

The structure of Auden's sense of time was the same as it was in the mid-1930s, when he wrote of human uncertainty and anxiety framed between the perfection of the animals. "They are our past and our future: the poles between which our desire unceasingly is discharged," he wrote in 1936, using the metaphor of an electric circuit. But the ethical burden of that structure had now changed. In 1940, one pole is the heaven of perfect freedom, which we glimpse in moments of visionary happiness; the other is the hell of unfreedom, which we enter and become when we deny all possibility of change. The purgatorial realm of time is where we work to undo our incompleteness and error, an effort in which we are encouraged by our glimpses of heaven and warned by our descents into hell.

The brief experience of heaven, the momentary return to a lost Eden, "happens every day / To someone." Access to it is not restricted to the aesthetically initiated or to the ignorantly instinctive, as it is in Yeats, Eliot, and Pound. Such an experience happened to Auden a week before the nominal date of "New Year Letter," at a Christmas dinner with Elizabeth Mayer, and he describes it in the same vocabulary of unanticipated grace that he had used to describe his 1933 vision of the feast of Agape. "I felt the unexpected power / That drove our ragged egos in / From the dead-ends of greed and sin / To sit down at the wedding feast." But vision is inseparable from temptation. To ask it to linger a while is an act that denies the reality of time and springs the trap of hell. Like heaven, hell is a realm outside time, but unlike heaven it is built on a denial of time: it is "the being of the lie / That we become if we deny / The laws of consciousness and claim / Becoming and Being are the same / . . . / Its fire the pain to which we go / If we refuse to suffer."

Auden's prose note to these lines imagines that the gates of hell are always wide open; the lost stay in hell only because they refuse to admit that another life is possible. "They know that they are free to leave and know why they do not. This knowledge is the flame of hell." (Auden later observed that if there are any souls in hell, "it is not because they have been sent there, but because Hell is where they insist upon being.") In the Eden of momentary vision "grow the tree / And fruit of human destiny, / And man must eat it and depart / At once with gay and grateful heart." The fruit of that tree grants the knowledge of time, which brings about both banishment from the Garden and a promise of forgiveness and return, because return is possible only in the realm of error and reconciliation that is time itself: "In Time we sin. / But Time is sin and can forgive." Another note glosses these lines:

> Forgiveness of sin does not mean that the effect of an act is annulled, but that we are shown what that effect is. This knowledge, that we have been punished but not judged, removes our burden of guilt, for guilt is, in part, ignorance of the exact effect of our act upon others and, in part, a dread that upon ourselves it has had no effect at all, that we are so unimportant as to be beneath the notice of Divine Justice, that, as we have not been punished, we must do what God never does, judge the past.

An almost identical passage had appeared in *The Prolific and the Devourer* but without the final phrases about God and our guilty attempt to judge the past. After expressing his need for forgiveness in poems and prose for almost ten years, Auden had now given a name to the ultimate source of forgiveness.

"New Year Letter" admits, as the either-or ideologues cannot, that we are "a trifle / Relieved to wake," after a brief glimpse of heaven, on the damp earth of purgatorial time:

> It's been our residence since birth,
> Its inconveniences are known,
> And we have made its flaws our own.
> Is it not here that we belong,
> Where everyone is doing wrong . . . ?

Here we can at least believe that our future errors can help undo our past ones:

> O once again let us set out,
> Our faith well balanced by our doubt,
> Admitting every step we make
> Will certainly be a mistake,
> But still believing we can climb
> A little higher every time.

This exhortation gives courage while saying nothing about specific actions. But at the time Auden wrote it, around February or March 1940, he was confronting demands from within and without that he return to wartime Britain—still in the nervous quiet period of the "phony war," but under increasing threat. Anthony Powell had printed in *The New Statesman* a four-line squib against Auden and Isherwood for leaving England; they had been told by English friends that similar attacks were circulating privately. Auden had earlier resolved to return only if he were needed for military service, and he now expressed this position in an exchange of letters with E. R. Dodds. One of his letters took the form of a catechism on personal and national loyalties. He asked himself, "Do you care what happens to England?" and replied:

> Qua England, not in the least. To me England is bits of the country like the Pennine Moors and my English friends. If they were all safely out of the country, I should feel about the English as I feel about the Spanish or the Chinese or the Germans. It matters what happens to them as it matters to all members of the human race, but my concern is as a fellow human being not as a fellow countryman.

In his drafts for "New Year Letter" he made the same point, but with an emphatic one-sidedness that hinted at inner doubt. At one point he wrote: "The country I must not betray / Is not Great Britain"—and then broke off. In a passage that survived in the published text, he asked himself which among the competing calls to conscience he must obey, which among many challenges is "the *athlon* I must not refuse." His reply, in the drafts, was detailed and insistent about the nationalist calls that he must *not* accept:

Louder than all the others roar
The governments that run the war,
Camorras claiming each to be
The *patrios* of civility
For which no man will question why
It's sweet and decorous to die.
I hear them; no, it is not they
Whom all but traitors will obey.
"England," "La France, "Das Reich," their words
Are like the names of extinct birds
Or peasant-women's quaint old charms
For bringing lovers to their arms,
Which would be only pretty save
That they bring thousands to their grave.

In the published text this was reduced to a couplet: "Whatever wickedness we do / Need not be, orators, for you." But the question of which call to obey remained urgent. "The flares of desperation rise / From signallers who justly plead / Their cause is piteous indeed"—quite different flares from the messages of the just in "September 1, 1939." For the moment, Auden had no answer beyond a withdrawal into private loyalties and an unfocused wish to find larger ones: "We can at least serve other ends, / Can love the *polis* of our friends / And pray that loyalty may come / To serve mankind's *imperium*." This was an empty prayer to serve an abstraction that has never asked anything in return. Auden's next line asks, with apt puzzlement, "But where to serve and when and how?"

Unlike Auden's propagandistic poems, "New Year Letter" continually defers the question of what to do next. Hitler has a ready answer suitable to collective action: the "metaphysics of the Crowd," the imperative of mass resentment. Yet Auden's rejection of the nationalist answer is not absolute: "maps and languages and names / Have meaning and their proper claims." The answer sought by the poem is local and individual, but not walled in by privacy, not closed off from the proper claims of named places on a map. A plausible individual decision can be made only by accepting and embracing the shared impersonal conditions of nature, culture, and language in which individual choices are made. For Auden, in exile from his English origins, England still provides the metaphors through which he judges and understands alternatives. "England to me is my own tongue, / And what I did when I was young." Its local errors and disasters are the means by which he recognizes error and disaster elsewhere:

> Thus squalid beery *Burton* stands
> For shoddy thinking of all brands;
> The wreck of *Rhondda* for the mess
> We make when for a short success
> We split our symmetry apart,
> Deny the Reason or the Heart,
> *Ye Oldë Tudor Tea-Shoppe* for
> The folly of dogmatic law.

These newsworthy or familiar places are the signs of past failure. The closer the poem approaches the deferred question of success, the more deeply it explores the private landscape of Auden's childhood memory. His symbol of "the human creature we / Must nurse to sense and dignity" is "an English area," "a locality I love, / Those limestone moors that stretch from *Brough* / To *Hexham* and the *Roman Wall*." He returns there in memory in order to find the hidden springs of his future choices. The exploration begins in the primal realm of myth, in a geological and moral pun that imagines Auden's childhood explorations as sited below the cliffs where "Man faulted into consciousness." It proceeds to the mining country where Auden first recognized his individuality, to the same fields of abandoned machines that had prophesied his vision of Eros. He remembers the place now for its gift of isolation:

> In *Rookhope* I was first aware
> Of Self and Not-Self, Death and Dread:
> Adits* were entrances which led
> Down to the Outlawed, to the Others,
> The Terrible, the Merciful, the Mothers;
> Alone in the hot day I knelt
> Upon the edge of shafts and felt
> The deep *Urmutterfurcht* that drives
> Us into knowledge all our lives,
> The far interior of our fate
> To civilize and to create,
> *Das Weibliche* that bids us come
> To find what we're escaping from.
> There I dropped pebbles, listened, heard

---

* An adit is the horizontal opening of a mine.

The reservoir of darkness stirred:
"O deine Mutter kehrt dir nicht
Wieder. Du selbst bin ich, dein' Pflicht
Und Liebe. Brach sie nun mein Bild."*
And I was conscious of my guilt.

Disquietingly, this event remembered from an English childhood is interpreted in the German language that Auden learned ten years after it occurred, and that he now shared with Elizabeth Mayer and their wartime enemies. *Das Weibliche* (the feminine) and the Mothers are from *Faust*; *Urmutterfurcht* (primal maternal fear) and the voice of darkness are from *Siegfried*. The voice that speaks from the well to urge the young poet toward adulthood—*deine Mutter kehrt dir nicht / Wieder*—speaks in the language the young man learned in order to break away from her into psychological and sexual autonomy.

His English past established the conditions under which he must act, but the bond between himself and his past "is not an Ought" that can tell him which act to choose, "Only a given mode of thought, / Whence my imperatives were taught." In the present moment, when "we are conscripts to our age / Simply by being born," we are left to our own decisions, left with the question "how / To be the patriots of the Now?" Instead of answering this question, the poem once again makes a dialectical turn: away from the present's confrontation with the future and toward the past's evolution into the present through the rise and fall of Empiric Economic Man. Only after this final swerve does it confront the question of our present responsibility—the New Year question with which it opened thirteen hundred lines before.

Here the dialectic of the earlier lines reaches a closing but inconclusive synthesis. First the poet refuses the temptation to evade responsibility by blaming the public realm alone—the excuse that society made me do it. "The politicians we condemn / Are nothing but our L.C.M."—the lowest common mean or denominator of the sum of our individual selves. "Upon each English conscience lie / Two decades of hypocrisy, / And not a German can be proud / Of what his apathy allowed." Every society

---

* The German lines are loosely adapted from speeches in Wagner's *Siegfried*. The first two sentences may be translated roughly: "Your mother no longer cares for you: I am yourself, your duty and love"; Auden invented and added *Pflicht und Liebe* (duty and love). The third sentence is a subordinate clause that means, in its original context, "though it has shattered my image." Auden perhaps thought his sentence meant either "My image now is shattered" or "Now shatter my image."

is the product of private actions: "Even true lovers on some bed / The
graceful god has visited" know that their own failure to achieve "True
reverence contributes much / Towards the soldier's violent touch."

In the intellectual history of the public realm, "The flood of tyranny
and force / Arises at a double source": Plato's lie of intellect that gives
the elect the right to rule, and Rousseau's lie of the flesh that makes us
seek unity in irrational instinct. But when we look up from the map of
political history, we find that the waters that flow from this double source
are, ultimately, "scattered from one common cloud," the solitary ego
that claims "the right to lead alone / An attic life all on her own."* In
its radical solitude, the ego can find no reason to choose, no reason to
"will / This more than that," and because it refuses to live in and for
others, it is seized by panic when it asks "who would care / If she were
dead or gone elsewhere." In its panic, the ego can see no alternative but
its own dissolution: "She worships in obscene delight / The Not, the
Never, and the Night, / The formless Mass without a Me, / the Midnight Women and the Sea"—everything that symbolically dissolves the
unique person whom the ego had tried to become, seeking no goal other
than its own uniqueness.

If the ego could put aside its egoism, it would discover its freedom to
do something other than destroy itself. In 1940, that freedom is most
evident in America, "This raw untidy continent / Where the Commuter
can't forget / The Pioneer." Here, as at the end of *Paul Bunyan*, the
machine has destroyed the false necessities of class, party, neighborhood,
and nation from which we once tried to "learn our good." It has "publicized among the crowd / The secret that was always true / But known
once only to the few, / Compelling all to the admission, / Aloneness is
man's real condition." In that aloneness, choice is inescapable, and communities can form only by voluntary association. "New Year Letter"
endorses the Marxist analysis of Fascism as a throwback to a collectivism
no longer possible in the machine age. But it rejects the promise of a
different collective future fashioned by a vanguard party of philosopher-
kings; the knowledge that the vanguard party claimed as its special privilege is now everyone's knowledge.

The first part of the poem claimed for the artist the special vision that
was denied to the politician; the third part of the poem renounces the

---

* The ego takes the feminine pronoun because Auden has begun to adopt the Latinate grammar
of theology. The ego corresponds to the grammatically feminine soul, or *anima*, in contrast to
the grammatically masculine spirit, or *spiritus*.

claim in lines that Auden could not have imagined writing a few weeks
earlier. Even the artist's privileged access to nuance and myth now belongs equally to factory workers, commuters, scientists, and industrialists:

> In labs the puzzled *Kafkas* meet
> The inexplicable defeat . . .
> All the operatives know
> Their factory is the *champ-clos*
> And drawing-room of *Henry James*
> Where the *débat* decides the claims
> Of liberty and justice; where,
> Like any Jamesian character,
> They learn to draw the careful line,
> Develop, understand, refine.

In these lines, Henry James, the American who in Auden's version of
literary history first portrayed a world in which all acts that matter are
invisible inward ones, begins to rise to the heroic stature he maintained
in Auden's thought for the next half decade.

Immediately after this passage, the poem makes another dialectical
turn—this time to the realm of brutal fact. No matter how many millions
of Kafkas and Jameses "know / Instinctively what ought to be / The
nature of society," the New Year's Eve of hopeful resolutions ends in a
morning no different from the day before. As the poem's night journey
ends, "Day breaks upon the world we know / Of war and wastefulness
and woe." As for the New Year, it "brings an earth afraid, / Democracy
a ready-made / And noisy tradesman's slogan." The artists—who fifteen
hundred lines earlier had been chosen by the greatest of vocations—
debase their calling in obscene surrender: "Culture on all fours to greet
/ A butch and criminal *élite*." Dawn brings no enlightenment. All hope
of renewal dissipates into the repetitive dreariness of the familiar: "the
heart, / As *Zola* said, must always start / The day by swallowing its toad
/ Of failure and disgust." And where we once imagined ourselves in a
dialectic ascent, now "we seem altogether / Lost as our theories, like
the weather, / Veer round completely every day." This seems an accurate
statement of Auden's condition a few weeks before, but it makes clear
that the dialectic is still at its constructive work. Our theories veer round
"completely," not randomly, but toward their antitheses. And when Auden wrote these lines of alienation and despair, he did so in full knowledge that the lowest point of a visionary journey is also the turning point.

CHAPTER FIVE

It Without Image

Inevitably, "New Year Letter" ended in prayer—all of Auden's plays and long poems since the end of 1936 had ended in prayer—but until he had almost finished the poem he had no idea of what or whom his prayer would address. The prayers he placed at the end of the "Last Will and Testament" that he wrote with Louis MacNeice for *Letters from Iceland*, at the end of *On the Frontier*, and at the end of the "Commentary" to "In Time of War" were all addressed to no one in particular. They asked for forgiveness without knowing who might provide it. Now, while he was drafting the last few hundred lines of "New Year Letter," he found a dozen names for the recipient of the prayer he wrote to end the poem. But one prayer was not enough. A few weeks after writing it, he appended a second prayer to a recipient very different from the first.

Eighty lines from the end of "New Year Letter," at the point where hope fails and theory founders, the poem names a free act that, unlike all the acts described earlier, does not induce an antithesis that destroys it:

> true democracy begins
> With free confession of our sins.
> In this alone are all the same,
> All are so weak that none dare claim
> "I have the right to govern," or

"Behold in me the Moral Law,"
And all real unity commences
In consciousness of differences.

But in these lines "true democracy" and "real unity" are built more by adjectives than by acts, and this whole concluding passage retains something of "the preacher's loose dishonest tone" that Auden had renounced at the start of the poem. When, in the next few lines, we are taught to build the Just City by discarding the abstract utopian icon for the individual democratic portrait, the portrait lacks all particularizing features:

We need to love all since we are
Each a unique particular
That is no giant, god, or dwarf,
But one odd human isomorph;
We can love each because we know
All, all of us, that this is so.

As Auden wrote in "Jacob and the Angel," the strength we use in building the Just City issues from instinctive Eros: we "can live because we're lived, the powers / That we create with are not ours." But instead of insisting that we could find a purpose for our powers only by wrestling with them, he now imagined for the first time a divinity worth praying to for guidance.

He invokes that divinity under multiple names. "O Unicorn among the cedars, / To whom no magic charm can lead us" is the first of a long series of invocations, followed by: "O Dove of science and of light," "O Ichthus," "O sudden Wind," "O Voice," "O Clock and Keeper of the years, / O Source of equity and rest." All these titles are appropriate because the divinity addressed can accurately be called, as it is in the next few lines, "It without image," the one being that cannot be represented by something because it is the pattern of everything that it is not: "paradigm / Of matter, motion, number, time," even of the despair, lust, and pride that deny it, "The grinning gap of Hell, the hill / Of Venus and the stairs of Will."

As in more orthodox prayer, petition follows invocation: "Disturb our negligence," "Convict our pride," "Instruct us," "Send strength sufficient for our day, / And point our knowledge on its way, / O *da quod*

jubes, Domine." This last petition—Give what you command, Lord—
invokes a hierarchical title, not a name. At this point, Auden's fair-copy
manuscript of "New Year Letter" comes to an end, after more than thirty
lines addressed to a deity with every quality except a face.

The dense rush of names and thoughts in this closing passage derives
mostly from a single book, *The Descent of the Dove: A History of the Holy
Spirit in the Church,* by Charles Williams, a writer of poems, plays, novels,
and literary and historical studies on theological themes. Auden had met
him in 1937 when Williams, who worked at the Oxford University Press,
agreed to publish Auden's *Oxford Book of Light Verse.* Auden read Williams's book in February 1940, shortly after it appeared, and was emotionally and intellectually overwhelmed by it. Williams interpreted all the
great changes in Western history as the Spirit's intervention to correct
destructive imbalances. He did not call this process dialectic, yet the
structure of his thought was dialectic throughout. Auden, like everyone
educated in the school of Marx, had for years seen the dialectic at work
in history, and had just written hundreds of lines about it in "New Year
Letter." Now he found in Williams's book a new understanding of its
meaning and goal.

Writing of the collapse in the early Renaissance of the Church's efforts
to induce conversion through obedience, Williams wrote: "Christianity
had betrayed itself again, as, since St. Peter, it was always doing. There
was to be, as there always had been, a sharp and violent recall. It was
not for nothing that Messias had uttered one of his most appalling and
ambiguous sayings, 'Behold, I am with you always.' " The dialectic between self-betrayal and recall was already so important to "New Year
Letter" that Auden almost immediately (certainly by the middle of
March) chose a phrase from Williams for the title of the book that would
include the poem: *The Double Man.* Williams, who seems to have forgotten his source, quoted "a certain brother": "It is right for a man to
take up the burden for them who are near him . . . to put his own soul
in the place of that of his neighbor, and to become, if it were possible,
a double man." But Auden used the word "double" in a different sense,
which he found elsewhere in *The Descent of the Dove,* in a passage that
quoted Montaigne's "De la Gloire": "We are, I know not how, double
in ourselves, so that what we believe we disbelieve, and cannot rid ourselves of what we condemn." This sentence became the epigraph to *The
Double Man.*

Many years later, Auden, without naming Williams, recalled the effect
of their first meeting:

In a publisher's office, I met an Anglican layman, and for the first time in my life felt myself in the presence of personal sanctity. I had met many good people before who made me feel ashamed of my own shortcomings, but in the presence of this man—we never discussed anything but literary business—I did not feel ashamed. I felt transformed into a person who was incapable of doing or thinking anything base or unloving. (I later discovered that he had a similar effect on many other people.)

This, he wrote, occurred shortly after he found himself unexpectedly disturbed at finding the churches closed in socialist Spain, and although the meeting left no obvious traces in his work at the time, it perhaps helped lead him six months later to his speculation that "the two worlds" could be brought together only by "the exercise of what Christians call Charity."

Yet Auden apparently knew nothing of Williams's religious thought until he read *The Descent of the Dove*. In March 1940 Williams wrote his wife that he "had an extraordinarily moving note from W. H. Auden in America," that "he just wanted to tell me how moved he was by the Dove (and he no Christian)." Meanwhile, in "New Year Letter," Auden started quoting phrases from the book about a hundred lines from the end, just before the poem reaches its most hopeless moment. (A few words taken from Williams that occur earlier in the text were probably inserted at a late stage of composition.) Williams wrote: "In the Crucifixion of Messias necessity and freedom had mutually crucified each other, and both . . . had risen again. Freedom existed then because it must; necessity because it could." Auden saw in his vision of the Just City "a more conscionable dust / Where freedom dwells because it must, / Necessity because it can." Auden's formulaic-sounding phrase, "true democracy begins / In free confession of our sins," echoed Williams's closing meditation on the humility that Christians must achieve in relations among their churches and with those outside them: a 1920 conference of Anglican bishops, Williams wrote, "was remarkable for one thing at least: for the first time a 'great and sacred synod' . . . admitted its own spiritual guilt. 'It has seemed good,' they said . . . 'that we should confess that we have sinned.' " In the poem's first concluding prayer Williams was the source of Auden's quotations and paraphrases from Origen ("*Quando non fuerit, non est*": there is not when He was not), Dionysius the Areopagite ("It without image"), and, in the last line of the manuscript version, Augustine ("*O da quod jubes*").

About the being whom Dionysius the Areopagite and Auden called "It," Williams wrote: "this is not the kind of being to whom man can

pray."* Belatedly acknowledging this, Auden added a second prayer after
he had finished his handwritten text, this one addressed to the recipient
of his letter, the dialectical antithesis of an impersonal It:

> Dear friend Elizabeth, dear friend
> These days have brought me, may the end
> I bring to the grave's dead-line be
> More worthy of your sympathy
> Than the beginning . . .

Auden hoped to receive instruction and strength from the divinity he
had prayed to earlier. But it was Elizabeth Mayer to whom he looked
for forgiveness:

> We fall down in the dance, we make
> The old ridiculous mistake,
> But always there are such as you
> Forgiving, helping what we do.

This second prayer responds to an aspect of Williams that Auden had
at first ignored. Williams's Christianity was romantic and erotic, intensely
focused on "the figure of Beatrice" (the title of one of his later books),
who, he said, exemplified the doctrine that "without the body the soul
cannot be consummated in God." Elizabeth Mayer is both Gretchen
and Beatrice, a slightly blurry archetypal figure who casts on the lives
around her "a calm *solificatio*"—a word borrowed by Jung from medieval alchemy for his *Integration of the Personality*, where it means an
illumination of the unconscious by the anima.

The final sentence of the prayer, and of the published text of the poem,
begins: "O every day in peace and labor / Our life and death are with
our neighbor"—which adapts Williams's quotation from Athanasius,
"Your life and death are with your neighbor." But Auden wrote this
communal sentiment without quite believing it, and the line is haunted
by sixteen hundred earlier lines in the same poem that argued vividly that
"Aloneness is man's real condition, / That each must travel forth alone
/ In search of the Essential Stone." Like all visionary epics, "New Year
Letter" returns in the end to the waking world of alienation and disunity,
the world from which Dante, writing the final line of the *Paradiso*, saw

* In "Diaspora," written around the same time, the deity is "the Unconfined" and "It."

the sun and the other stars. But after a journey to another world, a new light seems to shine on this one: "Love illuminates again / The city and the lion's den." During the summer of 1940, when Auden compiled his notes to the poem, he wrote, as a note to the couplet "Where Freedom dwells because it must, / Necessity because it can," this brief acknowledgment: "For this quotation, and for the source of many ideas in the poem, v. *The Descent of the Dove* by Charles Williams." The ideas had been in the poem before Auden found them in Williams, but they looked different in the light that Williams reflected on them.

═══════

Before Auden finished "New Year Letter," with its antiquated couplets and civilized mode of argument, he began work on its antithesis, an up-to-the-minute example of the new genre of the radio play, a dramatic monologue that expressed all the reaction and hatred that the autobiographical monologue of "New Year Letter" tried to escape. A few months earlier, he and a producer at CBS had discussed the possibility of his writing a play for an experimental radio series called the Columbia Workshop. Auden now dusted off a brief cabaret sketch, "Alfred," written in 1936, and expanded it into a half-hour one-character play, a compressed saga of resentment and violence, which he entitled "The Psychological Reactions of the Woman who Killed the Goose that Laid the Golden Egg." CBS renamed it "The Dark Valley," a phrase short enough to fit into newspaper radio listings. No one had attempted a thirty-minute radio monologue before this, and the risks of monotony were great; Jean Cocteau, in his one-character play *La voix humaine*, had the advantage of onstage action with which to ward off boredom. As in "Alfred," the speaker of "The Dark Valley" is an old woman who, as a stage direction in "Alfred" specifies, "has something about her that reminds us of certain prominent European figures." Her monologue does not entirely reassure the goose whom she prepares to slaughter in the final moments.

Whereas "New Year Letter" used eighteenth-century verse to create an air of polite order, "The Dark Valley" intermittently adopts the alliterative *Beowulf* metre that Auden had used early in his career to evoke a world pervaded by violence; the metrical passages were drafted in verse although set out as prose in the finished text. Like "New Year Letter," the play looks back to betrayed heroes: the old woman remembers her miner father, dead in a drunken accident or, as she imagines, murdered

by the mine owners who envied his powers. "New Year Letter" spoke
of the industrial horror of boys trained in factories to nurse helpless
machines and girls married off to typewriters; the old woman savors the
irony that, in return for having received the modern gift of freedom, "all
we have to do . . . is address envelopes or take dictation or pull levers."
The prayers at the end of "New Year Letter" have their ironic counterpart in the old woman's explanation to the goose that "the All-Father is
proud of his pretty world, and takes her on his knees, Nana, as I take
you now, and strokes her back . . . and she looks into his eyes and is
ever so happy . . . though she wonders a little why his loving hands are
gripping so tightly that she gasps for air."

"The Dark Valley" gets a sentence or two in most books about Auden,
but he knew it deserved better. When Monroe K. Spears, in a book
published in 1963, praised it in perceptive detail, Auden told him: "I'm
delighted that you should say a good word for 'The Dark Valley,' a piece
which is virtually unknown and for which I cherish a secret affection."
He cherished a similar affection for everything in his imaginative work
that darkly challenged the sunnier public affirmations in his prose. In-
terpolated in the play are two of his most disturbing poems, "Eyes look
into the well" and "Lady, weeping at the crossroads," quiet-sounding
lyrics that drastically violate the expectations raised by their genres. When
he asked Britten to write music for them, he specified that it must be
"of folk-song character," and "beautiful," and must "gain sinister effect
from being sung by an old old woman with a cracked voice."

With the lucid abstract calm of a contemplative lyric, "Eyes look into
the well" presents a world of brutality and disaster:

> Under the midnight stone
> Love was buried by thieves;
> The robbed heart begs for a bone,
> The damned rustle like leaves.
>
> Face down in the flooded brook
> With nothing more to say,
> Lies One the soldiers took
> And spoiled and threw away.

And "Lady, weeping at the crossroads" begins as a conventional quest
lyric: the lady is urged onward to heroic tests she must endure before
she can "meet her love / In the twilight with his greyhounds, / And
the hawk on his glove." Her tests are the traditional timeless journeys

to the end of the world, the bottom of the sea, and the perilous castle. But the end of the quest is discordantly unlike anything feared or desired by chivalric heroes:

> Cross the silent empty ballroom,
> Doubt and danger past;
> Blow the cobwebs from the mirror,
> See yourself at last.
>
> Put your hand behind the wainscot,
> You have done your part;
> Find the penknife there and plunge it
> Into your false heart.

Auden went out of his way to cast a skeptical shadow over his own liberating self-discoveries at the end of "New Year Letter."

Søren Kierkegaard was the subject of only four pages in *The Descent of the Dove*, but for Auden they offered the first plausible answer to the questions he had begun to ask himself in the Yorkville cinema. How could Nazism have arisen in one of the great centers of European education and culture? Kierkegaard, Williams said, understood the modern era "as an effort to be without 'the unconditional,'" and Williams quoted him on the inevitable consequences. (The passage he chose is from *The Point of View*, an English translation of which Williams had recently shepherded through the Oxford University Press.)

> Let the race, let each individual, make the experiment of doing without the unconditional—it is a whirlpool and remains such. In the meanwhile, for a longer or shorter period, it may seem otherwise, it may seem like stability and security. But at bottom, it is and remains a whirlpool . . . To live in the unconditional, inhaling only the unconditional, is impossible to man; he perishes, like the fish forced to live in the air. But on the other hand, without relating himself to the unconditional, man cannot, in the deepest sense, be said to "live."*

---

* A few weeks after reading this, Auden wrote "The Maze," a poem that dramatized the condition of humanity lost without the absolute. "Anthropos apteros"—wingless man—finally realizes he is lost in the maze. Solutions offered by metaphysics, theology, sense data, mathematics, history, aesthetics, introversion, and the philosophically fashionable Positivist Logic leave him exactly where he began. So anthropos apteros, in his perplexity, "Looked up and wished he were the bird / To whom such doubts must seem absurd" (revised in *Collected Poems*, p. 303).

Auden later phrased one of his questions to himself: "If, as I am convinced, the Nazis are wrong and we are right, what is it that validates
our values and invalidates theirs?" Kierkegaard's unconditional was not
the answer, because in relation to the divine absolute, nothing human
can be valid, Nazi or anti-Nazi. As Williams quoted Kierkegaard: "Before
God man is always in the wrong."* Yet the idea of the unconditional
made it possible to distinguish between two radically different degrees
of error. The Nazis, who settled the question by equating might and
right—who justified killing by their power to kill—were absolutely in
the wrong because they did not believe themselves to be wrong. Those
who knew they could never be right—the Christian heirs of skeptical
Socrates—were at least potentially right about that. As Auden now wrote
in "New Year Letter": "True democracy begins / In free confession of
our sins," even if its achievement is impossibly distant.

Kierkegaard's existential Christianity offered two strengths that psychoanalysis and politics could not: it perceived its relation to an absolute
value; and it understood that it could never claim to know or embody
that value. Freud allowed the psychoanalyst and Marx the Communist
to claim special knowledge and authority, one through privileged access
to a determining private past, the other through privileged access to a
determined public future. But Auden in his skepticism distrusted all such
claims as the masks of an egoistic wish to dominate and control. He
began reading anthropology, he said later, partly in order to confirm his
sense of the provincial narrowness of all universal claims to authority.
Both Freud and Marx had appealed to his sense of justice because they
brought to light his own hidden motives and private errors while exposing those of others, yet both had also helped him justify his "preacher's
loose immodest tone." In Kierkegaard Auden found an absolute refusal
of evolutionary or relative ideas that made it possible to flatter oneself
with a sense of leading others into the light, an absolute refusal of a
fantasy of superiority to other people's struggles that encouraged the
temptation to pacifism. Kierkegaard, Auden told a friend later, "knocked
the conceit out of me." Auden scarcely needed Kierkegaard's absolute
to know that Hitler was in the wrong, but because it obliged him to
acknowledge that he too was in the wrong, he could believe its implicit

* In fact, this paraphrases a sentence in Kierkegaard's *Journals*, another book shepherded
through the press by Williams: "Before God, I am always in the wrong" (p. 114). The thought
is ancient: "There is none righteous, no, not one" (Romans 3:10) recollects "there is none that
doeth good, no, not one" (Psalm 14:3).

judgment against Hitler more thoroughly than he could believe judgments that gave secret consolations to vanity.

In *The Prolific and the Devourer* Auden had emphasized that over the course of time "the lives of individuals become more and more unique"; and for a year he had been arguing that the machine age had at last revealed to everyone the solitude in which individual choices must be made. But Kierkegaard had seen this a century earlier: his was an "age of disintegration," he wrote, when everyone had become an isolated individual, and, as in the fortunate fall, it was therefore possible to undo that isolation. "The individual can signify the unique and it can signify every one." Vulgar misreadings of Marx and Freud interpreted humanity in terms of collective or involuntary or archetypal categories, but Kierkegaard had shown that all such attempts were anachronistic and futile. He had put into aphoristic prose everything that the disintegrated culture of America made plain but left unspoken.

When Auden reviewed a translation of *Either/Or* in 1944, he wrote that the existential quality of Kierkegaard's philosophy was something he shared with "what is most valuable in Marx and Freud":

> In contrast to those philosophers who begin by considering the *objects* of human knowledge, [*viz.*] essences and relations, the existential philosopher begins with man's immediate experience as a *subject*, i.e. a being in *need*, an *interested* being whose existence is at stake . . . There is . . . no timeless disinterested I who stands outside my finite temporal self and serenely knows what there is to know; cognition is always a specific historical act accompanied by hope and fear. To realize this is not . . . to abandon as hopeless the search for common sharable truth and surrender to a subjective relativism: on the contrary, it is precisely in the interest of such a common truth, that it is necessary for the individual to begin by learning to be objective about his subjectivity, . . . to become conscious every time he asks calmly of an object or event, "What are you?" of his urgent, simultaneous aside, "Be this. Don't be that."

Kierkegaard, unlike Freud and Marx, insisted that each subjectivity must make its own choice. He offered no message or prescription for others to follow; he had no taint of the Devourer:

> What he would teach is an approach to oneself, not a conclusion, a style of questioning to apply to all one's experience, including the experience of reading him. The fatal follies of Marxists and Freudians should forewarn us from becoming Kierkegaardians, even if we will not listen to his own repeated warning, which Freud and Marx conspicuously fail to give, that he is a genius, not an apostle.

A subjective faith in the absolute seemed inseparable from a belief that everyone was inadequate before an unconditional standard. Unlike all the apostleships that Auden had hoped to make himself trust in, this faith required no belief that history can be driven by unseen providential forces, compelled no allegiance to corruptible institutions, promised its followers no earthly rewards, and demanded no credence in mythic entities like the proletariat or the super-ego.

In the spring of 1940 Stephen Spender wrote Auden a letter (now lost) in which he evidently guessed at Auden's belief in a "center" that gave meaning to everything else. Auden replied:

> What you say about "center" is probably true. I believe it to be there but am very shy about revealing [that I believe] it, partly because the nearest I can get now to expressing it directly is Kierkegaard's statement, *"Before God we are always in the wrong,"* and carelessly made such a remark appears misleading and defeatist.

Much of the indirection and elusiveness in Auden's poetry in the next few months was the product of this shyness. Having once adopted the preacher's immodesty in order to champion his own self-deceptions, he was now reluctant to claim to speak in the name of a truth that no one could speak for, a "truth that no one marries."

Auden began reading Kierkegaard as soon as he read about him in *The Descent of the Dove*. Probably early in March 1940 he told E. R. Dodds, "Am reading Kierkegaard's Journal at the moment which is fascinating." The first trace of the *Journals* in his work appears in a line in "New Year Letter" about Baudelaire's sense of himself as the grand pariah who by dying atones for the bourgeois "*Verbürgerlichung* of / All joy and suffering and love." This echoes Alexander Dru's phrase in the introduction to the *Journals* about "the Verbürgerlichung of Protestantism." Auden's adaptation occurs a few lines after a couplet derived from Williams: "Ironic Kierkegaard stared long / And muttered 'All are in the wrong.' "

In the *Journals* Auden found passages like this one:

> The fundamental error of modern times (which runs into logic, mathematics, dogmatics, and the whole of modern life) lies in the fact that the yawning abyss of quality in the difference between God and man has been removed. The result in dogmatic theology . . . is a mockery of God such as was unknown in paganism . . . and in ethics an impertinent indifference, or better still the complete absence of ethics.

A stumbling block for Auden's political beliefs in the 1930s had been the "absence of ethics"—a preference for expedience over truth—in the political parties he had hoped to believe in. A year after the collapse of his partisan hopes he found Kierkegaard writing in this strain: "After the individual has given up every effort to find himself outside himself in existence, in relation to his surroundings, and when after that shipwreck he turns towards the highest things, the absolute, coming after such emptiness, not only bursts upon him in all its fullness but also in the responsibility which he feels he has."

Auden's sudden recognition of the absolute put an end to the joking egotistic tone he had toyed with in early drafts of "New Year Letter." Around the time he started the poem, he had also written, in "The Icon and the Portrait," "We shall never earn the right to lift our heads till we have learned to hang them," and in another review a few days later he concluded, "Among the qualities required to create or to appreciate art of any style or age, the most necessary of all is an unlimited capacity for reverence and repentance." One way he acted on this conclusion was by sacrificing the coherence of "New Year Letter" in order to suppress its fascination with himself. He dropped the lines in which he played detective, cut most of the details of his meetings with Elizabeth Mayer, and removed every passage that claimed for any artist the power to bridge the gulf between art and life. In the final version, he emphasized his own susceptibility to intellectual temptation and error, and removed most of the passages that accused others of temptations and errors of their own. He crossed out wide swatches of the poem until it approached the spare, intense, unyielding style that he was to use for most of his work in the next two years. Now the existential drama of absolute choices occurred in a human world with no comfort and no guidance, in a universe that accepted neither compromise nor half measures. Even the lethal old woman in "The Dark Valley" understands the absolute, although she can only imagine it as destructive: as she prepares to kill the goose, she paraphrases Kierkegaard's contemptuous dismissal of the modern kind of minister for whom (in her words) "God is a mathematician and much like a man, and understands perfectly and expects little."

Kierkegaard wrote in his *Journals*:

Man has a natural dread of walking in the dark—what wonder then that he naturally has a dread of the absolute, of having to do with the absolute, of which it is true that no night and "no deepest gloom is half so dark" as this gloom and this night, where all relative ends (the common milestones and signposts), where all relative considerations (the lanterns which are normally a help to us), where even the tenderest feelings of devotion—are quenched . . . for otherwise it is not unconditionally the absolute.

In March or April 1940, when Auden wrote the verse "Prologue" to *The Double Man* (the poem that begins "O season of repetition and return"), he used Kierkegaard's metaphors for an inescapable state of darkness and dread. Not even war, "That last attempt to eliminate the strange" by uniting us in a terror of something we know, can "stop us taking our walks alone / Scared by the unknown unconditional dark." The poem closes the divisions of the double man in the only way Auden could now imagine: through an indivisible recognition of the absolute. He had written in *The Prolific and the Devourer*—and repeated in the notes to "New Year Letter"—that we have not one self but a number of contradictory selves, that we generally act in the false interests of one of these selves against the interest of the others. But in "O season of repetition and return," all those selves reunite in their common distance from the unconditional. Although they dream that they are scattered,

> Our bones cannot help reassembling themselves
> Into the philosophic city where dwells
>   The knowledge they cannot get out of
>   And neither a Spring nor a war can ever
>
> So condition his ears as to keep the song
> That is not a sorrow from the Double Man.

"The song that is not a sorrow" is the answer to the stark realization about the world that Auden had written into a sestina seven years earlier: "It is the sorrow." Now our distance from that song and our ability to hear it represent the sum of our sorrows and our hope of release: "O what weeps is the love that hears, an / Accident occurring in his substance."

In these closing lines, Kierkegaard's faith in the darkness of the absolute begins to brighten into the vision of Dante. In *La vita nuova* Dante used a scholastic vocabulary to affirm that love was not a substance, not a being in itself, but "an accident in a substance," meaning a property not essential to the substance it occupies. In the theology of Auden's poem, love is a gift from the absolute, given so that the absolute may be heard. What weeps is the love that hears the absolute, the same love that wept in the last days of August 1939.

===

Kierkegaard remained as a great warning and accusing presence in Auden's work for years, but after the first flush of shame, Auden was willing to listen also to voices that forgave as much as they accused. In the early summer of 1940 he worked on "The Quest." This was the most successful of the gnomic poems he wrote during his first years in America, and the first in which he imagined a garden where one might stay longer than an instant. The quest is typically the subject of heroic epic and romance; Auden rendered it in the miniature form of a sonnet sequence. The poetic form used generally to evoke private dramas of love and longing was Auden's proper form for "The Quest" because in industrial modernity the hero's solitary journey is everyone's private journey. As Auden had written in "New Year Letter": "Each salesman now is the polite / Adventurer, the landless knight / *Gawaine-Quixote*, and his goal / The *Frauendienst* of his weak soul"—the chivalric service imposed on him by that inner lady, his anima.

The twenty sonnets make up a narrative not of a specific quest but of an archetypal one. Each temptation that occurs along the way, each reward or failure that might end the quest, is portrayed as if experienced by a different individual (a "he" who sometimes succeeds, sometimes fails) or by a group (a "they" who always fail).

Auden wrote "The Quest" partly on the model of his 1938 sonnet sequence "In Time of War," partly as a corrective to it. The earlier sequence was largely composed in terms of generalities and collectives; the simple pronoun "he" represented a psychological or political type that persisted across centuries. But in "The Quest" each "he" is an individual example of a type (identified in the sonnet titles as "The Traveller," "The Hero," "The Average," "The Lucky," and others), a unique person who faces an existential choice. Auden was also making a pointed contrast with Eliot's version of the grail quest in *The Waste Land*. Both poets portrayed the quest as a series of incidents without a single unifying hero, but where Eliot treated the episodes in terms of impersonal myth and ritual, of emotional states misunderstood by those who experienced them, Auden treated them as a set of parables about consciousness and decision.

The parables in "The Quest" are compressed variations on themes expounded at length by Kierkegaard. "The Presumptuous," for example, depicts the failed questers who "set forth alone / On what for them was not compulsory." Or, as Kierkegaard wrote in a passage quoted in the notes to "New Year Letter": "A man cannot in reason embark upon 'the voluntary' . . . unless he has an *immediate* certainty that it is required of him *in particular*. From the point of view of the universal require-ments, 'the voluntary' is in fact presumption; and consequently one must have immediate certainty that the particular is required of one in order to be able to risk embarking upon it." "The Hero" portrays the counter-example, the successful quester who, in the eyes of those who never risked their lives as he did, "looks too like a grocer for respect." Kier-kegaard wrote in the same way of the Knight of Faith: if you met him on the street, "you would think he was a shopkeeper," because his hero-ism has nothing to do with *virtù*. The one visibly unique quality of Auden's hero is "his delight in details and routine," his capacity for absorption.*

Auden relied on Kierkegaard when he listened to the stern voice of the absolute, but the conclusion of "The Quest" required other, more celebratory voices. The sequence recognizes with mystical awe those who aid the hero—figures whom Kierkegaard, in his existential solitude, never noticed—and sees, as Kierkegaard did not, the coherence in the created world that makes it possible for the quest to succeed. In "The Waters," the penultimate sonnet and a masterpiece of philosophical dramatization, the waters are the world of perception and experience. Poets and wits, fishing "like unsuccessful anglers," fail to catch the truths for which they hunger because they bait their hooks with the wrong questions, and "at nightfall tell the angler's lie." Elsewhere, "the saintly and the insincere" are equally tempest-tossed on "rafts of frail assump-tion," while "Both sufferer and suffering" are inundated by waves of "enraged phenomena" in vast confusion. The closing lines of the sonnet are a riddle:

---

* Auden wrote a few years later that one of Byron's apparently unlikely characteristics was his "very 'un-Byronic' obsession with a clock routine": Byron's hours were bohemian but his regulation of them "was bourgeois, as, indeed, is essential to any writer who hopes to leave a substantial body of work." The artist and the hero had something in common after all, but only if the hero were understood to be a grocerlike Knight of Faith, not the Sherlock Holmes or Hercule Poirot of the drafts of "New Year Letter" (*The New Yorker*, 26 April 1958).

> The waters long to hear our question put
> Which would release their longed-for answer, but.

The puzzling final syllable (an echo of the inconclusive "but—" that cuts off Humpty Dumpty's song in *Through the Looking-Glass*) stops the poem before an answer can be spoken. Yet the unyielding and turbulent waters would be life-giving and clear if we, like any quest hero, could bring ourselves to yield to them instead of fighting or fishing them.

Everything is transformed in the setting of the final sonnet, "The Garden." Secret guilt becomes shared enjoyment as "children play at seven earnest sins." When one lover accepts another's erotic consent, "flesh forgives division." Unthinking nature enjoys temporary freedom from the human will, as dogs, unleashed by their masters, "believe their tall conditions dead." Souls burdened by hopelessness are blessed with triumph: "round some old maid's desolation / Roses have flung their glory like a cloak." And those burdened by success are blessed by a sense of shame that gives them a focus outside themselves to attend to:

> The gaunt and great, the famed for conversation,
> Blushed in the stare of evening as they spoke,
> And felt their center of volition shifted

—as, for Augustine (Charles Williams wrote), "the universe . . . had shifted in a garden."

By the summer of 1940 Auden had begun to render Kierkegaard's sense of absolute unworthiness in a new tone of exaltation. In July he wrote a "Song for St. Cecilia's Day" as a gift to Benjamin Britten, who had been born on the saint's day of the patroness of music. The title was the same as Dryden's 1687 ode in praise of music's power to harmonize the spheres and compel human emotion—Auden was again claiming, as he did with *Paul Bunyan*, that he and Britten were heirs to Dryden and Purcell—but in place of Dryden's playful baroque formality, Auden wrote in calm triumphant wonder, treating music as an invisible image of the absolute, with power to heal and transform. In Dryden's ode, as in his "Alexander's Feast," also written for Cecilia's day, music is the greatest of manipulators. In Auden's ode, music grants the truth-telling courage needed for forgiveness: "O weep, child, weep, O weep away the stain, / Lost innocence who wished your lover dead, / Weep for the lives your wishes never led."

In draft versions of the poem, Auden began by overturning the theory of art he had expounded in "New Year Letter." Art was still innocent and autonomous but no longer disinterested, and Auden now imagined it as begotten, not made. Cecilia, music's embodiment, is the "dear daughter of our double misery / Whole innocence begotten by our crime." In other abandoned lines (in the manner of the bombastic free-verse oratory that had disfigured his 1930s plays), Cecilia's beauty is "a witness" to the Kierkegaardian "reality of the Required," but she offers nurture, not rebuke: "For what the heart-beat of a mother promises her unborn child, your rhythm shall repeat; that the otherness of the universe is not against us."

The published text discards all this, and opens with a buoyant chorus that, while recounting Cecilia's invention of the organ, attributes to her many of the powers of Christ: power to command the luxurious gods of paganism ("Blonde Aphrodite rose up excited, / Moved to delight by the melody"); power to make the temporal world sacred ("the angels dancing / Came out of their trance into time again"); power even over hell ("around the wicked in Hell's abysses / The huge flame flickered and eased their pain"). Six months after he had tried to imagine sainthood for Harold Albaum, Auden found it easier to imagine it for the mythical figure of Cecilia.

In the middle section, Cecilia, speaking for music itself, sings gnomic quatrains that Auden made metrically strange by rhyming the penultimate syllable of the third line with the final syllable of the fourth: There is no one "Whom I belong to / Whom I could wrong." She sings from a world beyond time—"I cannot grow . . . I cannot err"—but ends with an appeal that bridges the gulf between her world and ours: "I shall never be / Different. Love me." Music does not change, but, in the concluding choral section, it gives, to those who hear it, the courage to change themselves:

> O law drummed out by hearts against the still
> Long winter of our intellectual will.
> *That what has been may never be again* . . .
>
> O trumpets that unguarded children blow
> About the fortress of their inner foe.
> *O wear your tribulation like a rose.*

Dryden's ode imagined trumpets heralding the end of time. Auden's ode imagines them as heralds of forgiveness.

During the same summer months of 1940 when Auden wrote poems celebrating the visionary glories of music and the quest (the final image in both the Cecilia ode and "The Quest" is a rose), his prose adopted an urgent tone of moral and political exhortation. Kierkegaard had given him courage to write about politics again after a year of introspection. In a review published in July he made a point of refusing the twentieth-century prejudice that dismissed the moral realm as trivial or empty because its logic was unprovable:

> One of the most disquieting intellectual developments of the last fifty years has been the exaltation of Causal Necessity and the denial of Logical and Moral Necessity. The discovery that the *intensity* with which men have believed in ideas and values has often been due, not as they imagined to their logic, but to their cultural or economic environment, instead of teaching them greater logical caution and moral vigilance, has led many people, and not only professed fascists either, to deny the possibility of making any judgment except one of practical expediency.

The war had now taken a sudden turn for the worse. On 10 May the "phony war" ended when Hitler's armies invaded the Low Countries; two days later they crossed into northern France. Churchill, in his first speech as prime minister, on 13 May, called for victory at all costs. But in early June all British forces in Europe were being evacuated from Dunkirk in a massive effort that was celebrated as if it had been a victory. By 14 June, the Germans had marched into Paris.

Auden had found in Rilke and Kierkegaard what he now called "the strength to resist the treacherous temptations that approach us disguised as righteous duties," but he was sharply conscious that the argument skirted the edge of complacency, that in wartime as in all other times, resistance to temptation was not enough. Shortly after the German invasion of France, Auden (who was now thirty-three) made contact with the British embassy in Washington to report that he was "willing to do anything when and if the Government ask me," only to be told that "only technically qualified people are wanted back" (a policy that stayed in effect for the remainder of the war). His offer was never publicized, and during the summer sneering comments in the British press about his and Isherwood's safe haven in the United States became frequent and virulent. "Letters from home," he told James Stern, "are beginning to take a sharper note about my absence." On 13 June a question was asked in Parliament whether Auden and Isherwood would be summoned back for military service and deprived of their British nationality if they failed to register as conscientious objectors; the minor parliamentary dogsbody who replied to this question thought it was about the tennis star H. W. Austin, and the matter went nowhere. Writing to his brother John a few days after the exchange in Parliament, Auden dismissed it with slightly clenched teeth as "some minor personal unpleasantness." He added that he did not see how he would serve the war effort by "writing in a cottage waiting for the parachutists."

The friendly challenges he received from E. R. Dodds earlier in the year had troubled him enough to prompt elaborate replies in his drafts of "New Year Letter," but he seems almost to have been reassured by the attacks in Parliament and the press, which seemed motivated more by anger at his politics, sexuality, and success than by any serious thought about civil obligation. He never bothered to defend himself in public or private, and in July he wrote an olympian attack on a writer who, he believed, had yielded to the dangerous temptations to serve an official cause. After the Nazis conquered Norway in battles against Norwegian and British forces in the spring, Knut Hamsun, the popular Norwegian novelist who had won the Nobel Prize in 1920, had written articles welcoming the German conquerors and the Norwegian puppet administration headed by Vidkun Quisling. Auden's "Open Letter to Knut Hamsun," published in the magazine *Common Sense*, speculated on Hamsun's motives: "No doubt the inducements were many; the human ambition to transcend the limits of a special field and become an all-round success, a lust for prophetic fame, an, in itself laudable, impatience with social evils that baffle even the experts." Auden did not hesitate to identify himself at the end of his letter as a British subject, "one who belongs to that nation of gamblers and coachmen [this was Hamsun's phrase] who came to the aid of your country, but thanks to you and a few of your misguided associates, too late to save it."

When Auden had written to Spender in May that he was shy about revealing his Kierkegaardian belief because the best statement he could make might sound misleading or defeatist, he had in mind public circumstances and obligations that Kierkegaard had not foreseen. Kierkegaard emphasized the urgency of the individual's relation to the absolute; he had less to say about the individual's relation to the community or the state. Auden hesitated to speak about the absolute until he could imagine ways in which societies as well as persons could find their relations to it. This seemed an insoluble problem in a century when every formula for describing the absolute was tainted by the prejudices and limits of the "cultural or economic environment," and in a season when hourly news bulletins reported a further triumph of moral relativism and aggressive power.

"His guardian-angel / has always told him / What and Whom to read next," Auden wrote in a late autobiographical poem. In this moment of intellectual uncertainty, his guardian angel seems to have arranged for the publication of the book he needed. *An Essay on Metaphysics*, by the philosopher and historian R. G. Collingwood, had appeared in Britain in March and reached the United States about a month later. Auden had read Collingwood's history of Roman Britain when working on his radio play *Hadrian's Wall* in 1937, and Collingwood had interpreted *The Ascent of F6* with unique penetration in *The Principles of Art* in 1938. Now, in his new book, Collingwood argued that metaphysics was not the study of the absolute itself, as philosophy assumed it to be, but the study of "absolute presuppositions," the unverifiable (but not always unexamined) assumptions about the universe that in every society underlie the sum of available knowledge. "All events have causes," for example, is an absolute presupposition, once taken for granted in all natural sciences and now taken for granted only in medicine and a few others. Metaphysics, for Collingwood, is a means of historical understanding, not the science of timeless truth. Its aims are to discover the absolute presuppositions of earlier cultures and our own, and to understand the processes through which these presuppositions change over time.

Auden had been writing for some months about "orthodoxy," which he had defined as the "interdependent whole" formed by human knowledge at any one time; in a review titled "Heretics"—about Rimbaud and D. H. Lawrence—he had described heresies as "eccentric deviations" from this orthodox whole. In his review of Sandburg's life of Lincoln, he had argued that although absolutes are "heretical"—incomplete distortions of a complete truth—"one can only act in a given circumstance by assuming one." Now Collingwood gave him the intellectual catalyst he needed to make sense of the relation of orthodoxy, heresies, absolutes, and the possibilities of justice. Or so he thought.

Collingwood addressed his argument beyond the circle of academic philosophers to everyone beleaguered by the current crisis. Modern European civilization, he wrote, frowned on metaphysics and denied even the existence of absolute presuppositions, but if the "neurosis" of this denial should succeed, then science and civilization would inevitably die. He did not need to add that they had already been murdered in the countries where strength had taken the place of truth. Auden immediately adopted Collingwood's terms as his own—sometimes giving them his own meanings—and adopted Collingwood's historical analysis, which identified Christian orthodoxy with the presuppositions that first enabled modern science. But he also began an inner debate over Collingwood's argument that the same orthodoxy remained the unacknowledged basis of modern science and must remain the basis of knowledge and justice in the future. "The basic weakness of the democracies," Auden told Spender in May, "is the failure to realize that if you give up Catholicism—and I think we must—one has to discover one's base again and that is a very long and exhausting job." The policymakers of the democracies were typified, he said, by the "lazy protestant living off the fat of his Catholic past and imagining that metaphysics and mysticism are unnecessary—the virtues will be kept alive by good form." They are baffled "that a rather nice man like Goering can behave in such an extraordinary way," and even more baffled when trying to think of an answer to him.

The greatest moral urgency, Auden now said at every opportunity, was the need to find a metaphysical absolute. On 17 June he made this the sole subject of a commencement address he delivered at Smith College in Massachusetts. It was the day France capitulated to Germany, when "the war is in the dreadful background of the thoughts of us all, and it is difficult indeed to think of anything except the agony and death going on a few thousand miles to the east and west of this hall." When those whom we love are in terrible danger, he said, "the overwhelming desire to do something this minute to stop it makes it hard to sit still and think. Nevertheless that is our particular duty at this hour," a duty to "try to understand what has come upon us and why."

Auden then addressed the Smith graduates in terms probably never heard at an American college commencement before or since. The present conflict, "in which we are all willy-nilly engaged," was one between the temptation to take refuge in closed societies copied from the past and the obligation to build open societies, which are the inevitable fruit of "social evolution." (The distinction between "closed" societies and the "open" ones favored by evolution had been made by Henri Bergson in *The Two Sources of Morality and Religion* in 1932; Auden was still invoking Bergsonian inevitability in his prose, though he had temporarily abandoned it in his verse.) "The failure of the human race to behave in the way that an open society demands, if it is to function properly, has led an increasing number of people to the conclusion that an open society is impossible and therefore that the only escape from economic and spiritual disaster is to return as quickly as possible to a closed type of society." Yet an open society was now indeed possible, because the technical means existed to overcome the inequalities of hunger and disease, and any failure to create it would be a "metaphysical failure." We lazily "go on applying habits of mind which were more or less adequate to the relatively closed society of the eighteenth century to an open society that demands completely new ones." An open society

> is a protestant society in the sense that it believes that logical necessity can be recognized by everybody and that, in consequence, the truth is best arrived at by free controversy. But it will recognize that no thinking or voluntary behavior is possible without making some absolute presuppositions, or acts of faith. The intellectual will regard it as his social responsibility to state what these presuppositions are, and to revise or restate them should fresh knowledge render them no longer absolute in their old form.

These alterable presuppositions sound much like the "divine laws" in *The Prolific and the Devourer*, with the difference that we make our presuppositions for ourselves.

Auden spoke at bewildering length, apologizing halfway through for being "very long-winded and pedantic," about the relation of presuppositions to society. Civilization itself came into being when "in the mythology of a nation, behind the plural figures of the gods who can appear to men and have affairs with their wives, there emerged the singular horizon of Fate against which even the gods play their parts—of the One, the Unknowable, the Unconditional." The discovery of that horizon must continually be renewed: a society comes to grief "when its members are confronted by problems for which their technique or their metaphysics, or both, are inadequate." Today's crisis is not "due to the appearance of some unusually wicked men"; it came about because the absolute is denied "unconsciously by most of us":

> We are rightly shocked when we hear the fellow countrymen of Goethe and Dante and Cervantes make remarks like . . . "Death to intelligence!" But we do not realize that when we say, "I can't be expected to behave well. I had an unhappy childhood," or "I can't be expected to work hard. I come from an

oppressed class (or a decaying class)"; when we that are writers think that only emotive expressions matter and that grammar hinders our originality and self-expression; whenever we treat personal relations as a kind of sleepwalker's journey from one bed to the next, we are every whit [as much] the enemies of democracy as those who speak of German science or Fascist justice.

This merely told the Smith graduates to follow absolute presuppositions in their private lives. Anyone who followed the intricacies of Auden's four-thousand-word speech would have heard a dozen variations on the statement that society as a whole needed absolute presuppositions, but not a word—beyond a vague gesture toward "free controversy"—about how it might get them.

Collingwood had an answer to this problem: the great Church councils fifteen hundred years ago had already found the presuppositions that we need. Local and temporary modifications had occurred, Collingwood wrote, "against a background that has remained unchanged: the constellation of absolute presuppositions originally sketched by Aristotle, and described more accurately, seven or eight centuries later, by the Patristic writers under the name of the 'Catholic Faith.' " These had been consciously chosen and explicitly stated as presuppositions: the Church Fathers made statements of what they believed, not statements that purported to describe ultimate reality. Auden embraced (and never abandoned) the idea that the absolute could be talked about only in statements that implicitly began with *credo*—I believe—but it was less easy for him to imagine how societies today could devise presuppositions that, like those formulated in the Nicene Creed, began with the first-person-plural form *credimus*.

He worried over the question for six more months in his essays, lectures, and reviews. When he next spoke before a lecture audience, at Columbia University in September 1940, he glided over the difference between the fifth and twentieth centuries. Classical civilization, he said, had never found presuppositions to replace its lost faith in the plural gods. But the Christian Church, through a conscious metaphysical decision to reject "as heresies both Arianism and Manichaeism"—each of which denied a relation between God and the physical world—"was able to relate the universal and the particular, the spiritual and the material, and made the technical advance of civilization possible." Modern science, similarly, based itself on the presupposition that there is a world of nature to be studied, when it "might well have wasted its time trying to prove that nature existed." This was a slippery argument. Auden neglected to mention that the Church had chosen its presuppositions in councils with supreme doctrinal authority, while science had made no such organized choice, and, unlike the Church, had never succeeded in relating its presuppositions to moral imperatives.* At the end of his lecture, he acknowledged the problem he had glided over earlier. "Some new form of catholic belief," he said, was "highly recommended by many" as a way out of our dilemma, but any attempt to achieve it would produce only "crude slogans imposed by ruthless force."

While Auden was arguing from the lectern for public absolutes, he had few illusions that he was accomplishing anything. "And write I do," he told E. R. Dodds in July, "hoping it is not only a deceptive form of idleness." Less idly, he worked with the organization that found American homes for British children sent abroad to escape the war, and told his mother to use the money in his English bank account for war relief. Meanwhile, his poetry, instead of echoing the call for absolutes he was making in his prose, offered only a skeptical comment from offstage. Probably late in the summer that began with his lecture at Smith and ended with his lecture at Columbia, he wrote "The Council," a parable for the times based on the sixteenth-century Council of Trent. In its task of formulating absolute presuppositions, the council succeeded brilliantly:

> For weeks their spiritual and temporal lordships met
> To reconcile eternity with time and set
> The earth of marriage on a sure foundation . . .
> The formulae essential to salvation
> Were found for ever, and the true relation
> Of Agape to Eros finally defined.

But it failed to make them stick:

* Collingwood, whom Auden was adapting in this argument, wrote as if the modern counterpart of a Church council were the senior common room of an Oxford college. The central chapters of his book systematically demolish the philosophical heresy of logical positivism (its radically empirical worldview excluded absolutes) and its heresiarch, A. J. Ayer. Auden joined the debate in his poem "The Maze," where "Positivist Logic," instead of seeking a way out, is content to say, "In theory there is no solution." But when the poem was in galley proof (as one of the notes to "New Year Letter" in *The Double Man*), Auden realized he was no longer interested in fighting Collingwood's battle, and replaced "Positivist Logic" with "certain educators."

As they dispersed, four heralds galloped up with news:
"The tribes are moving on the Western Marches.
Out East a virgin has conceived a son again.
The Southern harbors are infested with the Jews.
The Northern provinces are much deluded
By one who claims there are not seven stars, but ten."

Who wrote upon the council-chamber arches
That sad exasperated cry of tired old men:
—*Postremum Sanctus Spiritus effudit?*

The last line is adapted from an inscription at Trent quoted by Charles
Williams in *The Descent of the Dove*: "Here the Holy Spirit [spoke] for
the last time."

In his prose Auden wrote in an ever more convoluted style about the
need to find an absolute. In his poems he hoped to be found by one.
"Oh what sign can we make to be found?" he asked in the "Epilogue"
to *The Double Man*, the poem he later retitled "The Dark Years." The
Horatian stanzas of this orotund poem are heavy with adjectives, but
enlivened by enough joking and extravagance to avoid high seriousness.
In his speeches Auden asked his listeners to turn from the immediate
horror of the war to consider metaphysical questions. In this poem, written in October 1940, when German bombs were falling over England,
"this year the towns of our childhood / Are changing complexions along
with the woods," and the local and metaphysical disasters are inseparable.
"The waste is a suburb of prophets," all offering warnings and answers,
"but few have seen Jesus and so many / Judas the abyss." (The first of
these names had appeared often in Auden's prose but never before in his
poems.) Every route to the comforts that once soothed the "inflamed
ego" now leads to a crisis of belief, "that labyrinth where either / We
are found or lose ourselves for ever."

The "Epilogue" ends in prayer, the first of Auden's verse prayers in
which he imagined who or what might find him. Death, in the closing
stanzas, "is probable," but the personal speech that informs all poetry
and prayer must not be silenced: "Let the lips do formal contrition /
For whatever is going to happen." Borrowing the sacramental language
of T. S. Eliot in "Burnt Norton," the poem proceeds to hope that
"Time remembered [may] bear witness to time required." Then, using
a vocabulary in which every word is taken from the first chapter of the
Gospel According to John, the final stanza offers a prayer that

the shabby structure of indolent flesh
Give a resonant echo of the Word which was
From the beginning, and the shining
Light be comprehended by the darkness.

In September 1939 Auden had tried to imagine ironic points of light flashing out human messages into the surrounding dark. A year later, the shining light was as eternal and universal as the Word, and the uncomprehending darkness was the human will.

CHAPTER SIX

Imaginary Saints

In October 1940, as he was making his last revisions to *The Double Man*, Auden "began going, in a tentative and experimental way, to church." These were the words he used to describe the event many years later; at the time, there was little that was tentative or experimental about the display of theology and dogma in his poems. "I started going to church again," he told a student later, "just about October," after a period of nine or ten months when he worked on *The Double Man* and "was beginning to think seriously about such things" as churchgoing "without committing myself." At the beginning of October he had begun sharing a house in Brooklyn Heights with his brother-in-law Golo Mann, Benjamin Britten, Peter Pears, and George Davis (who as fiction editor at *Harper's Bazaar* paid Auden high fees for poems and essays); Chester Kallman remained in Manhattan with his father. "On Sundays," Golo Mann wrote later, Auden "began to disappear for a couple of hours and returned with a look of happiness on his face. After a few weeks he confided in me the object of these mysterious excursions: the Episcopalian Church."

His return at thirty-three to the Anglican Communion he had abandoned at sixteen put into practice the "adequate and conscious metaphysics" he had been recommending to artists and others in his prose. On Sundays he participated in the form of worship that was the nearest equivalent in the United States to the Anglo-Catholicism he had learned from his parents, but he found the doctrines and terms of his belief in a radical form of Protestantism that he learned from Paul Tillich and other, mostly German, theologians in their forties and fifties whose work had become widely known in Britain and America. Their theology began, as Kierkegaard's did, by making a clear separation between divine judgment and human inadequacy. But unlike Kierkegaard, who said nothing about social questions, they found in the meaning of the Gospels an absolute command to serve divine justice by working toward an inevitably flawed and incomplete justice on earth. They denounced the nineteenth-century liberal religion of their teachers' generation, and of many Protestant churches in their own era, for disguising injustice behind its sentimental glorification of humanity and for ignoring its own promises of reform; Communist writers, followed by Auden, had made the same objections to liberal politics. Tillich, like his friend Reinhold Niebuhr, who had brought him to New York in 1933, had worked actively with labor and socialist groups, and had woven Marxist thought into his theology. In the disputatious world of radical Protestantism, Tillich and Niebuhr maintained a running argument against the tendency to otherworldliness in the work of the best-known and most extreme figure in the movement, Karl Barth.

Auden had been peripherally aware of radical Protestant theology since around 1933, the year when an English translation was published of Barth's 1919 commentary on Paul's Epistle to the Romans. (Some of Barth's lesser works and a few specialist books about him had appeared in English earlier.) In 1934, in a footnote about "intellectual *avant-garde*" movements that seek a dictatorship by the unconscious, Auden briefly described surrealism and D. H. Lawrence, and added: "As a specifically religious movement, there has been that of Barth in Germany, with its insistence on Grace." In Britain and the United States in the early years of the century, Auden wrote later, "Protestant theology (and, perhaps, Catholic too) was at a low ebb; Kierkegaard had not been rediscovered and Karl Barth had not been translated." Then Barth's appearance in English was quickly followed by a wave of Kierkegaard translations until, by the early 1940s, the theologians who claimed Kierkegaard as their ancestor had become, to a remarkable degree, intellectually fashionable in a culture that was generally skeptical about the whole field. More significantly, because Tillich and Niebuhr were public figures (Niebuhr later appeared on the cover of *Time*), radical Protestantism established itself even outside theological circles as a focus of intellectual resistance to Nazism. In the same essay in which Auden recalled the enlightening effect of Kierkegaard and Barth, he pointed to the different effect of a rival theology: he attributed the anti-Semitism of the English Catholic writers G. K. Chesterton and Hilaire Belloc partly to "the pernicious influence, both upon their generation and upon the succeeding generation of Eliot and Pound, exerted by the *Action Fran-çaise* Movement"—a Catholic nationalist movement founded in 1898, which the Vatican, after giving it implicit support, had belatedly condemned only in 1926.

Auden returned to Christian belief in 1940, after thinking for three years about doing so, when he began to see it as a religious doctrine in which the limits of human justice could not be excused by citing the infinitude of divine justice. Literary history tends to assume that Eliot's otherworldly Anglicanism of the still point and the rose garden was the norm among twentieth-century writers who considered themselves Christians. But Auden's sense of Christianity's ethical and political meanings was insistently different from Eliot's, although both worshiped in the same church and recited the same creed.*

Before Auden delivered *The Double Man* to his literary agent in October 1940, he made a few last-minute changes. He appended Paul Tillich's *The Interpretation of History* to the list of "Modern Sources" and inserted an extract from Tillich's book, which he quoted without comment. "The fundamental Protestant attitude," it said in part, "is to stand in nature, taking upon oneself the inevitable reality; not to flee from it, either into the world of ideal forms or into the related world of supernature, but to make decisions in concrete reality."

Auden found in Tillich a dialectical religious understanding that he

---

* Auden treated Eliot with reverential gratitude for his support and friendship, but went out of his way to dispute Eliot's religious ethics and politics. In 1934 Eliot sent Auden a copy of *After Strange Gods*, the book in which Eliot wrote of "the society that we desire" that its "population should be homogeneous," and that "more important is unity of religious background; and reasons of race and religion combine to make any large number of free-thinking Jews undesirable." Auden said in his thank-you letter: "Some of the general remarks, if you will forgive my saying so, rather shocked me, because if they are put into practice, and it seems quite likely [they will be], would produce a world in which neither I nor you I think would like to live." In 1954, reviewing Eliot's *Complete Poems and Plays*, Auden objected to an "occasional discordant snobbish note" in the religious allegory of Eliot's later plays, adding politely that he believed "this is not a matter of sensibility but of technique." With equal politeness he demolished what he saw as Eliot's perversion of Christianity's sense of an inner calling: "I am absolutely certain that Mr. Eliot did not intend us to think [in *The Family Reunion*] that Harry is called and not John because John is stupid, or that [in *The Cocktail Party*] Celia is called but not Lavinia because she is of a higher social class, but that is exactly what the comedy convention he is using is bound to suggest" (*The Griffin*, March 1953).

could reconcile with his own earlier understanding of history and psychology. In place of the either-ors, the mongrel halves—on one hand, followers of Barth who renounced all hope of earthly justice because they believed the Kingdom of God to be "purely transcendent," and, on the other hand, believers in an earthly utopianism that "must end with a metaphysical disappointment"—Tillich saw an unchanging infinite God who made changing, finite demands on humanity. He described the relation between God and humanity in much the same way that Auden in *The Prolific and the Devourer* had described the divine laws that change over the course of history. "The struggle for a new social order," Tillich wrote,

> cannot lead to a fulfillment such as is meant by the Kingdom of God, but . . . at a special time special tasks are demanded, and one aspect of the Kingdom of God appears as a demand and expectation. The Kingdom of God will always remain as transcendent; but it appears as a judgement to a given form of society and as a norm to a coming one. Thus, the decision for Socialism during a definite period may be the decision for the Kingdom of God, even though the Socialist ideal remains infinitely distant from the Kingdom of God.

Through all his later religious changes Auden retained this sense of Christianity's integration with social justice. When Peter F. Drucker's *The Future of Industrial Man* appeared in 1942, with its vision of the workplace as a community with personal dignity and status for every worker, Auden urged it on friends as an example of Christian thought applied to the practicalities of management. In 1950, the editors of *Partisan Review*, in their introduction to a symposium on "Religion and the Intellectuals," posed the question whether the renewed interest in religion might not be due "to a renunciation of hopes for any fundamental social improvement." Auden had no patience with the ignorant prejudice implied by the question. "The abandonment of hope for a general social improvement which the editors suggest as a possible cause for a religious revival will lead a man not to Christianity but to one of those religions which hold that time is an illusion or an endless cycle." Other beliefs, he added, claimed the name of Christianity but were as distorting and incomplete as, in earlier centuries, gnosticism or docetism had been: "the typical 'modern' heresy is . . . a Barthian exaggeration of God's transcendence which all too easily becomes an excuse for complacency about one's own sins and about the misfortunes of others."

Marx and Kierkegaard had been Tillich's ethically transforming teachers (as they had been Auden's), and from them he learned to expect no relief from the disorienting turbulence of modern thought. "I owe to Marx," Tillich wrote, "the insight into the ideological character, not only of idealism, but of all systems of thought, religious as well as profane, which as the servants of power hinder, even though unconsciously, the more righteous form of social reality." And he saw Kierkegaard as "the first to break through the closed system of the idealistic philosophy of essence" from Plato to Hegel. From both Marx and Kierkegaard, for Tillich as for Auden, "a new conception of truth arises: truth is bound to the situation of the knower, to the individual situation in Kierkegaard and to the social situation in Marx." The only authentic relation between the divine and the human was private and subjective; atheism would be right, Tillich said, "in the face of an *objectively* existing God."

"I find T[illich] very exciting," Auden told a friend a few months later, and in a letter to a student, around the same time, he emphasized his German intellectual influences, notably Georg Groddeck, Wolfgang Köhler, "and more recently theologians like Paul Tillich." The theology he learned from Tillich did not recommend a comforting return to the religion of his childhood. Christians of every faith, Tillich wrote, must obey God's command to Abraham to go out from his country "into a land that I shall show thee." The home they leave behind them, he added, may be "home in the sense of soil and national community"; or "ruling powers, social and political tendencies," which must be resisted in thought and action; or "one's habitual way of believing and thinking." Auden later made a point of quoting Lichtenberg's aphorism: "There is a great difference between *still* believing something and believing it *again*." As he returned to the forms of faith he had learned on his native English soil, he adopted a theology that Tillich had defined in these terms:

> The substance of my religion is and remains Lutheran. It embodies the consciousness of the "corruption" of existence, the repudiation of every social Utopia, including the metaphysics of progress, the knowledge of the irrational demonic character of life, and appreciation of the mystical elements of religion, and a repudiation of Puritan legality in individual and social life.

The "irrational demonic" was the subject of a long chapter in *The Interpretation of History*, in which Auden found his own unformulated belief that, in Tillich's words, "the demonic is the perversion of the creative."

———

Auden's religion in 1940 made strong ethical and intellectual demands, but for all his insistence on subjective faith—"an internal necessity consciously decided," as he called it in a lecture on criticism in November —it was not quite a personal religion, and was more an alternative to his personal demons than a means of confronting them. Immediately after he began going to church, he again began writing love poetry, ending a year of poetic silence about his relations with Kallman. But these new poems took the form of abstract theological meditations on love, treating the relation between two human lovers in the terms in which Kierkegaard treated the relation between the individual and the absolute; and when they addressed the beloved, they tended to preach.

"In Sickness and in Health" is a large-scale rhymed essay on the theology of marriage (a subject much debated by theologians in response to late-nineteenth-century social upheavals), a study in the metaphysics of belief written in a "metaphysical" style blatantly imitating Donne. The poem opens in a bewildering synaesthesia: "Dear, all benevolence of fingering lips / That does not ask forgiveness is a noise / At drunken feasts where Sorrow strips / To serve some glittering generalities." (Briefly: love speech that does not confess the speaker's guilt is sentimental gush.) It ends in an updated version of Donne's "The Litanie," a poem Auden was urging on friends at the time. Auden's first seven stanzas are an anatomy of the temptations that threaten marriage; the last seven are a prayer for the salvation of marriage, addressed to a deity identified as "Love," "Essence of creation," "Fate," and *"Felix Osculum."* After reading Tillich on the relation between demand and expectation, Auden was no longer shy about quoting Kierkegaard's "Before God we are always in the wrong." The central stanza of the poem* finds in the personal and erotic realm the same demand and expectation made by the Kingdom of God in the social and political one:

> Beloved, we are always in the wrong,
> Handling so clumsily our stupid lives,

———

* The symmetry breaks down in a later version, which omits a stanza that ends by asking the beloved to pray that love may use its power to "lay your solitude beside my own."

Suffering too little or too long,
Too careful even in our selfless loves:
The decorative manias we obey
Die in grimaces round us every day,
Yet through their tohu-bohu comes a voice
Which utters an absurd command—Rejoice.

The last couplet is an elaborate triple allusion that states Auden's new loyalties by explicating the Bible, paraphrasing Kierkegaard, and contradicting Yeats. The command to rejoice is the same creative imperative that brings light to the tohu-bohu ("without form and void") in Genesis 1:2. It is an absurd command because Abraham, as Kierkegaard described him, "believed by virtue of the absurd"; and, as Auden writes later in the poem, "All chance, all love, all logic, you and I, / Exist by grace of the Absurd." But the voice that issues it is emphatically not the same oracular voice of which Yeats had written in "The Gyres" that it is indifferent to nightmare and blood because "all it knows is that one word 'Rejoice.' "

Celibate Kierkegaard presides over the central stanzas of this marriage poem, but he shares the other stanzas with notably uncelibate figures from the world of myth. The seducer Don Juan, who denies the unchanging reality of spirit as he pursues a different body every night, and the mutually idealizing Tristan and Isolde, "the great friends" who deny the reality of flesh by endlessly postponing sexual satisfaction,* personify the temptations faced in the first part of the poem. Auden had found this pairing of mirror opposites in Denis de Rougemont's paeans to Christian marriage and denunciations of romantic love in *Love in the Western World*, which had appeared in English a few months earlier. (In Britain its title was *Passion and Society*.) The closing litany offers a dialectical prayer to be tempted precisely in the ways that doom Don Juan, Tristan, and Isolde, but that strengthen the marriages of unmythical human beings. In a metaphysical conceit, "this round O of faithfulness we swear" is a wedding ring, and the poem prays that through the enlivening dangers of temptation the ring "May never wither to an empty nought" in mere habitual affection, "Nor petrify into a square" in pious parodies of virtue.

---

* Tristan and Isolde are "great friends," not "great lovers," because, for Auden, they typify the romantic fantasy of spiritual friendship (typically between two members of the same sex); this is not a disguised or sublimated homosexual desire but an attempt to evade bodily sexuality in favor of something imagined to be higher and purer.

As a portrait of a marriage, the poem has many faults. It displays the domineering quality of Spenser's "Epithalamion," one of the few earlier instances of a marriage song sung by the bridegroom; and its language has what Donne called "my words' masculine persuasive force." Auden, after taking the title "In Sickness and in Health" from the Anglican marriage service, imposes Christian imperatives on the skeptical Jewish Kallman: "Rejoice, dear love, in Love's peremptory word"; "beloved, pray / That Love, to Whom necessity is play, / Do what we must yet cannot do alone." The poem was so unspecific and impersonal that Auden was willing to comply when one of his friends, reading it three years after it was written, insisted that he dedicate it to her and her husband.* But as a metaphysical poem—an ingenious, scholastic, passionate ratiocination on the meaning of marriage, a witty and artificial meditation on the moral and erotic complexities of a relation of equals—it is an almost unique example in its century of a memorable poem about marriage that is not about a marriage's failure. It convinces us despite its delusions, because it admits that we are tempted by them and makes no claim that they can be resisted without help.

"In Sickness and in Health" makes the large affirmations that Auden often put into his long discursive poems. His shorter lyrics tended to be more elusive or more doubtful. A dry villanelle written in October 1940, "Time will say nothing but I told you so," follows Auden's epithalamion in its passage from sorrow to rejoicing, but in a language of mystery rather than wit. In the first few stanzas, Time, which "only knows the price we have to pay," repeats its gloating I-told-you-so whenever we weep or stumble. Love poems often promise a faithful future; this poem would make that promise if it could: "There are no fortunes to be told, although, / Because I love you more than I can say, / If I could tell you I would let you know." Time offers no meaning, but meaning must exist nonetheless: "The winds must come from somewhere when they blow, / There must be reasons why the leaves decay; / Time will say nothing but I told you so." And the two final stanzas, in the least "masculine persuasive" language possible, imagine a peaceable kingdom that may astonish even Time:

---

* All published texts of the poem are dedicated to this couple, Maurice and Gwen Mandelbaum, from whom he rented a room from 1943 to 1945, during his second and third years of teaching at Swarthmore College. Maurice Mandelbaum said later that his wife apparently hoped that the dedication would magically help ward off the impending failure of their marriage.

Perhaps the roses really want to grow,
The vision seriously intends to stay;
If I could tell you I would let you know.

Suppose the lions all get up and go,
And all the brooks and soldiers run away;*
Will Time say nothing but I told you so?
If I could tell you I would let you know.

Auden perfected his gnomic style when writing this poem. Each statement, taken by itself, is lucid and colloquial, but each is connected to
the next more by implication than by any clear emotional or intellectual
logic. He used this style during the next few months to write some darker
lyrics that responded with awe to a divine absolute while demanding with
increasing urgency that Kallman do the same.

When Auden praised endangering temptation in "In Sickness and in
Health" he may have been making a virtue of necessity. Kallman's eyes
and hands still roved as they had done when he and Auden took their
honeymoon journey. Auden seems not to have been conscious of Kallman's casual infidelities, but he apparently understood more than he admitted to himself. "The sense of danger must not disappear" is the
opening line of a brief dry lyric in quatrains that he wrote in December
1940. It purports to be a meditation on the leap of faith required by
personal love; but this leap is as terrifying and lonely as the Kierkegaardian leap into faith in the Unconditional. The poem's disturbing strangeness arises from its double vision of the leap: it does not merely accept
the condition in which Kierkegaard imagined the Christian believer,
"constantly out upon the deep and with seventy thousand fathoms of
water under him," but repeatedly imposes it on the beloved. In the
opening stanza, "The way is certainly both short and steep, / However
gradual it looks from here; / Look if you like, but you will have to leap."
Auden had closed "In Sickness and in Health" by praying paradoxically

---

* In Auden's poems in 1939 and 1940, brooks are strikingly and invariably associated with
disaster and death. "The brooks were frozen" in his elegy for Yeats; the murdered in "Eyes
look into the well" lay "Face down in the flooded brook" (in Auden's poems, killing is always
an *effacement*); and in this villanelle "brooks and soldiers" make a lethal pairing. Perhaps the
point is that any conventionally gentle site in nature is just as lethal as any other place; sylvan
nature has no moral value. As Auden put it in his sonnets from China in 1938, "The mountains
cannot judge us when we lie" (*The English Auden*, p. 257).

"hold us to the voluntary way"; now he seemed ready to hold Kallman
to it.

> A solitude ten thousand fathoms deep
> Sustains the bed on which we lie, my dear:
> Although I love you, you shall have to leap;
> Our dream of safety has to disappear.

But of the two of them, only Auden had such a dream, and knew he
must lose it.

═══════

Auden's prose gave few signs of a new religious commitment during the
first months after he began going to church. He repeated his arguments
for a conscious choice of absolutes, with slight but significant changes in
his standard phrasings. In a lecture on criticism in November 1940 he
spoke of the critic's need to admit "original sin" in order to avoid delusions of infallibility, and concluded that "every act of critical judgement, like every other act in life, like life itself, rests on a decision, a
wager which is irrevocable and in a sense absurd." His studiedly casual
use of the phrase "original sin" marked a watershed in his prose. It
repudiated all the essays in which he had experimented with doctrines
inherited from the Enlightenment and romanticism that held that people
suffer mostly because of their environment and can be improved by successive generations of schooling. It affirmed instead a doctrine that he
had expressed in his poetry from the start, which held that human beings
suffer because in every generation they have an equal predisposition to
act against themselves and (what is the same thing) against everything
else. He had said as much in "Our Hunting Fathers" in 1934, where the
processes of evolution lead to a human "love *by nature* suited to / The
intricate ways of guilt," but until now he had been unwilling to give this
doctrine a name.

Yet he remained unwilling to give a personal name to the absolute,
and as he tried to describe a basis for values that was more secure than
liberalism, his prose became ever more polysyllabic and opaque. In October the literary editor of *The Nation* invited him to write an essay on
the problems of the writer. Auden agreed; then, in November, he turned
in "A Note on Order"—a throwaway title that gives no hint of the

essay's almost impenetrable density. Disentangled from its abstractions, this was another statement that a just society needs absolute presuppositions but also needs to understand that they are never final and can be found only through democratic debate. "In a civilized society, that is, one in which a common faith is combined with a skepticism about its finality . . . orthodoxy can only be secured by a cooperation of which free controversy is an essential part." His language was more religious than it had been when he addressed the Smith graduates six months earlier, but the argument was the same, and remained no less a utopian fantasy than the Marxist delusions it was meant to correct.

Auden again built his argument on a foundation given by Collingwood, but he seems to have sensed that the structure was dangerously shaky. He now propped it up with new arguments that he took from Alfred North Whitehead's *Process and Reality* (1929), a philosophical account of (among many other metaphysical and scientific matters) a society's need for an order that is inevitably mutable and imperfect. Whitehead's vocabulary—with such negatives as "triviality" and "vagueness" and such positives as "actuality" and "order"—saturated Auden's work for the next few months, and never entirely disappeared from it.

Whitehead, more subtly and convincingly than Collingwood, found a common language for social order and personal order. He emphasized that both are inherently dynamic and that the same principles apply to each; in arguing this, he called attention to the intellectual trap in which one kind of order is treated as the subordinate or image of the other, as in the myth of the "body politic," where society has a single ruler because the body has one. Whitehead's double focus, and the explicit theological basis of his thought, gave Auden hope that he could at last integrate private and public matters in ways that he had not been able to learn from Marx or Freud. But his argument in "A Note on Order," with its numbered propositions and proliferating qualifications ("every orthodoxy, in fact, is, in an absolute sense, heretical"), rose to a level of abstraction and imprecision in which the psychological and political dilemmas that had first prompted it seemed to disappear. Generalizing about a Christian doctrine it refused to identify, the essay collapsed into empty exhortations that few readers were likely to understand and none likely to follow.

His first clear statement of his new beliefs, outside his circle of intimates, was in a letter to T. S. Eliot on 17 December 1940. He enclosed a list of errata for "New Year Letter"—Eliot was his editor at Faber & Faber—and reported, at the end of his cover-letter courtesies, "I think

a lot about you and whether you are safe, the more so because, thanks
to Charles Williams and Kierkegaard, I have come to pretty much the
same position as yourself, which I was brought up in anyway. (Please
don't tell anyone about this.)" He added that he "must stop and review
Niebuhr's *Christianity and Power Politics*. It's all right but a little glib
like an army chaplain."

In telling his secret to Eliot he made his first step toward telling it to
everyone else, and took the next step in his review. Reinhold Niebuhr,
it began, "has long been one of the most gifted writers on the relation
of Protestant Christianity to politics"; his new book was "lucid, just and,
I believe, theologically unexceptionable, and yet it leaves me a little uneasy." With the aggressive certainty of a new convert, Auden complained
that the book lacked "the sense, as Kierkegaard puts it, of always being
out alone over seventy thousand fathoms." Auden endorsed Niebuhr's
attack on the pacifist movement as a bogus religion; pacifism, Auden
paraphrased, "blasphemes by denying original sin and pretending that
perfection can be acquired in a progressive school." The paraphrase was
accurate, although its terms were taken from Auden's private argument
with his own earlier writings on politics and education.

But despite Niebuhr's accurate strictures, Auden continued, a genuine
and saintly pacifism might really exist:

> The danger of being a professional exposer of the bogus is that, encountering
> it so often, one may come in time to cease to believe the reality it counterfeits.
>   One has an uneasy suspicion that, were Dr. Niebuhr to meet the genuine,
> he might be as embarrassed as an eighteenth-century bishop or an army chap-
> lain. The question is: Does he believe the contemplative life is the highest
> and most exhausting of vocations, that the church is saved by the saints, or
> doesn't he?

Niebuhr, as Auden learned when he met him soon afterward, believed
nothing of the kind, and tended to think of personal sanctity as all but
impossible for anyone conscious of the moral complexity of the self and
the world. Auden shared Niebuhr's view, although he worked hard not
to. Starting with this review, the contemplative saints briefly but disastrously took over much of his work, and they ruined every poem they
touched. Because he insisted on bringing in the saints, Auden's first public statements about Christianity in verse and prose showed the same
kinds of confusion and improbability that marked his first statements
about Communism in the 1930s—and that marked his lines about the

just in "September 1, 1939." The world will be saved, he now tried to argue, not by the revolutionaries or the just, but by the saints, while the rest of us look on.

Each time he rushed into a fantasy of unnamed and unnameable heroes, he had no one to blame afterward but himself, but in each case he was trying to serve someone else—a beleaguered proletariat or a despairing citizenry, or his one friend who had become a committed pacifist and was trying to live the contemplative life. Christopher Isherwood had realized he was a pacifist while he and Auden crossed the Atlantic to New York in 1939, and he had been drawn to Vedanta partly by its withdrawal from the realm of passion and anger. He intended to declare himself a conscientious objector if he were drafted, and moved in and out of various retreats and monasteries until the end of the war. In November 1940, a few weeks before Auden wrote his review, Isherwood had been formally initiated into Vedanta as his guru's disciple.

Before the European war began, Auden seems to have half convinced himself that "my position forbids me to be a combatant in any war"; he wrote this in a quasi-dramatic dialogue on politics in *The Prolific and the Devourer* in which the pacifist speaker expresses views that are partly Isherwood's. Even then he rejected as mere luxury any simple refusal to bear arms: "To think that it is enough to refuse to be a soldier and that one can behave as one chooses as a private citizen, is to be quite willing to cause a war but only unwilling to suffer the consequences." Now, in 1940, Auden became convinced in every detail by Niebuhr's attack on pacifism, which confirmed what he already believed, and had begun to admit to himself that he regarded Isherwood's religion as a moral and intellectual nullity of the kind he later called "Southern Californian." But he loved Isherwood enough as a friend to defend his pacifism in the pugnacious style of someone defending a loved one who is in the wrong.

Auden tried to have it both ways. He declared his own religion in terms that glorified the contemplative saints, while making clear that pacifism would be a selfish delusion for everyone else, including himself. In a symposium in the monthly magazine *Decision*, edited by Klaus Mann, another of his brothers-in-law, Auden dismissed his own earlier conviction that the most helpful course for a writer is to sit still and pray. "As far as writers are concerned, their problem is not *What should I do as a writer?*—the answer to that is the same under all circumstances, *Write as well and truthfully as you can*—but only, *Have I any other capacities, e.g., physical strength, which are of direct military value and which I ought therefore to offer to the state?*" In a letter to Stephen Spender in March 1941 he asked rhetorically: "What has to be done to defend Civilization?" His answer, "in order of immediate importance," was un-hesitatingly militant: "(1) to kill Germans and destroy German property; (2) to prevent as many English lives and as much English property from being killed and destroyed; (3) to create things from houses to poems that are worth preserving; (4) to educate people to understand what civilization really means and involves." He went out of his way to defend Isherwood's position, but in terms that did not quite endorse it:

> What he is trying to do must seem meaningless unless one believes, and I do, firstly that there is such a vocation as the mystical contemplative life, and sec-ondly that of all vocations it is the highest, highest because the most difficult, exhausting and dangerous . . . I know that I am not fit for such a vocation; Christopher feels that he is called . . . I think his friends should have enough faith in him to trust his judgment for himself.

When he wrote to Isherwood he was more skeptical. "If you are *certain* you are called, then you must of course obey, but you *must* be certain, otherwise it is just presumption." He added that he himself "must fight if asked to," and said he believed "America should enter the war." To the extent that he supported Isherwood's choice he refuted himself with his own public-platform smarminess: "As you know, I re-gard the contemplative life as the highest and most difficult of vocations, and therefore the one to which very few people are called—fewer even than are called to be creative artists, among whom, rightly or wrongly, I believe my place to be: for the other I am not good enough."

The saints appear, sometimes lightly disguised, in a series of three long poems that Auden worked on from December 1940 through the follow-ing spring, "Christmas 1940," "At the Grave of Henry James," and "Kairos and Logos." While his briefer lyrics retained their clarity and focus, these three extended sermons in verse opened out into grandiose historical vistas. Auden was drawing from the murkiest chapters of *The Interpretation of History*, in which Tillich abandoned the issue of social justice for theological paradoxes about the ultimate identity of the eternal and the daemonic, of freedom and fate. Tillich's prophetic and dialectical invocations of "fate" gave Auden an excuse to cling to the idea of his-torical determinism after trying to renounce it. (An unpublished poem, "We get the Dialectic fairly well," which he sketched while working on the other three, is explicit: "Nothing is unconditional but fate. / To grumble at it is a waste of time, / To fight it, the unpardonable crime.")

He later abandoned part or all of these poems after publishing them, discarding more lines of verse from his religious poems than he did from his political ones.

"Christmas 1940," the first and least salvageable of the three, purports to be a dialogue between two voices—a long speech in the middle is framed within quotation marks—but they say exactly the same thing. The voices echo Whitehead's sober vocabulary of "structure," "extension," and "occasion," but their magniloquent eight-line stanzas (the same form used for "In Sickness and in Health") expound Tillich's prophecies of fate. The first voice begins by portraying a present time of vagueness and collapse. Then the improbably learned voice of "some deeper instinct" cries out a summary of geological and evolutionary history in which the gradual emergence of consciousness finally led to "the Great Exchange" between Word and Flesh at the moment of the Incarnation; "now to maturity must crawl that child" who is ourselves, in order to learn the "self-annulment" of the contemplatives and bring about the apocalyptic end of time.* The first voice returns, explaining that in the breakdown of external order, "this modern Void where only Love has weight," nothing in the world of matter can block "our reasonable and lively motions" toward the end chosen for us by the Spirit. (Auden had used this pattern before—of a present moment of crisis framed by a predestined past and future—in "Spain.") The closing lines are a labored metaphysical attempt to reconcile faith and works through paradoxes comprehensible only to readers who can spot arcane allusions to Kierkegaard.

In 1932, while thinking in a tentative, experimental way about Communism, Auden had written a hectoring poem, "Comrades, who when the sirens roar," in the style he imagined a Communist might use. In "Christmas 1940," he wrote in the style he imagined might be used by a Christian. With its two voices of instinct and reason endorsing each other's optimism, the poem wishes away the recalcitrance and evil that Auden hoped to understand by returning to Christian belief. Worse, through a theological sleight-of-hand, he defined evil out of existence. In the long poems he wrote around this time, evil was not the product of willed choices but merely the less culpable product of passive consent. "In Sickness and in Health" has lines about "the dream" that makes

* As if to highlight his own long-windedness, Auden alludes to the vivid solidity of Shakespeare's Sonnet 60: "Nativity, once in the main of light / Crawls to maturity."

the "human matter" of our bodies ill "Not by our choice but our consent." "Christmas 1940" twice repeats the point: negation, says the voice
of instinct, is mere emptiness, without form or feature, and its "lust to
power is impotent" unless the actual world "consent"; and the other
voice echoes, "We may, as always, by our own consent, / Be cast away."

When Auden tried to describe the contemplative life in even minimal
detail, the best he could do was portray an aesthetic withdrawal from the
world. Early in 1941 he wrote an ode to the patron saint of writers, as a
few months earlier he had written an ode to Cecilia, patroness of music;
but because no patron of writers was commemorated in the calendar, he
beatified Henry James, and claimed him as his patron in a dismayingly
loquacious poem, "At the Grave of Henry James." The poem ends with
an appeal for a saint's intercession: "Master of nuance and scruple, /
Pray for me and for all writers living or dead." James could safely be
called upon to pray when he was dead, however seldom he had prayed
in life.

James, as he is addressed in this poem, is a patron and protector whose
powers are the fruits of his purity:

> O with what innocence your hand submitted
> To those formal rules that help a child to play
>   While your heart, fastidious as
> A delicate nun, remained true to the rare *noblesse*
> Of your lucid gift.

(Auden first showed a Jamesian weakness for French nouns in "Christmas 1940," in which the world no longer has "a *faiblesse* . . . for the
dull / To swim in.") James gives strength to resist the vagueness Alfred
North Whitehead warned against—"Yours be the disciplinary image that
holds / Me back from agreeable wrong / And the clutch of eddying
muddle"—and inspires the order Whitehead required: "Suggest: so may
I segregate my disorder / Into districts of prospective value."

But the elegy tends to portray James in the same way Yeats, in his
most fancifully aristocratic moments, portrayed himself. When Auden
applied his ideas about sainthood to an artist like James, he revived his
fantasies about the unique greatness of the artist's vocation—only a year
after Kierkegaard had silenced them. Having argued that the machine
had revealed the unique subjectivity of every individual, Auden now
erupted with a Yeatsian denunciation of the "resentful muttering mass,"

> Whose ruminant hatred of all which cannot
> Be simplified or stolen is still at large;
>   No death can assuage its lust
> To vilify the landscape of Distinction and see
> The heart of the Personal brought to a systolic standstill,
>   The Tall to diminished dust.

In the presence of Charles Williams in 1937 Auden had "felt transformed into a person who was incapable of doing or thinking anything base or unloving." In the presence of James's tombstone in 1941, forgetting Williams, he dramatized himself as "Despising Now yet afraid of Hereafter." And he attributed to James the tone that Yeats adopted when writing about Coole Park:

> What but the honour of a great house, what but its
> Cradles and tombs may persuade the bravado of
>   The bachelor mind to doubt
> The dishonest path.

The real James cared more for honor than for love, but he cared nothing for the honor of a house. Auden's lines about the great house used the Yeatsian technique of assertion-by-rhetorical-question, and he quickly repented them; between sending the poem to an American magazine and to a British one he replaced "What but . . . what but" with "Perhaps . . . perhaps." He dropped the whole stanza (and three others) when he revised the poem for book publication in 1944. When he revised it again in 1965 he cut fourteen more stanzas, reducing it to half its original length. But all his cuts and second thoughts could not salvage a poem that had been overburdened from the start by its heavy sinuous phrasings that imitated James's complexity but not his wit. Twenty years after writing it, Auden quoted two lines from the poem, "Lightly, lightly, then, may I dance / Over the frontier of the Obvious," as an example of ridiculous poetic badness, and asked: "How *could* I, a martyr to corns, have written it?"*

Writing to Spender at about the same time, Auden described himself

---

* The answer is that he found the idea in Kierkegaard's description in *Fear and Trembling* of the knight of the infinite resignation, who is one step away from becoming a knight of faith: "The most difficult feat which a dancer can attempt is said to be to leap up and take a definite attitude, so that at no particular moment does he appear to be trying to take up this position . . . Perhaps there are no dancers who can perform this feat—but the knight performs it" (translated by Robert Payne, 1939, p. 52).

("in Jung's terminology") as "a Thinking-Intuitive type," who "accordingly . . . can only develop along the abstract systematic formalist line (like Henry James and Valéry)." This line was the most obvious means of escape from his old political entanglements, but Auden was perhaps less convinced than he claimed to be that it was the only escape. His poetic prayer to James for artistic purity has the characteristic windiness of his attempts to write what he could not make himself believe. It repeatedly asks James for private salvation—"O dwell ironic at my living centre"; "Then remember me that I may remember"—but it seems to have been written largely in the service of Isherwood's withdrawal and at least two other causes that were not Auden's own. The poem takes sides in the public critical battle then being fought in, among other places, the pages of *Partisan Review* (where the poem first appeared in the United States) to canonize American literature as a precursor of English and European modernism. This battle was led by Auden's acquaintance F. O. Matthiessen, a Harvard professor who had published a laudatory book about T. S. Eliot and was now finishing his *American Renaissance* (1941), a book that defined an American tradition like the metaphysical tradition defined in English literature by Eliot. But Auden had long since turned away from the lonely idealizing modernism of Eliot's generation, and only his friendship for Eliot and his liking for Matthiessen led him to promote it now.

The poem seems also to have been written as a private offering to Mina Curtiss, the sister of Auden's friend Lincoln Kirstein; she made a cult of the higher aestheticism, and Auden had made a point of praising her grand and "beautiful house" in a thank-you letter. Auden's perennial doubts about the higher aestheticism were confirmed during a visit he and Kallman made to her a few months later, when she referred to Kallman as "just a Brooklyn kike." (She too was a Jew.) At the time this occurred, Auden's relations with Kallman were obviously strained, but Auden decided, as he told her, that although he was still fond of her (and "if one likes a person, one takes them as they are") his loyalty to Kallman made it impossible for him to continue to see her.

Once again, after writing a long poem overstuffed with empty affirmations, Auden deflated them in a laconic, dark lyric. It opened by dismissing the hierarchical pretensions of the poem to James: "Jumbled in the common box / Of their dark stupidity, / Orchid, swan, and Caesar lie." Time had laid its honors at poets' feet in Auden's elegy for Yeats. Now it made no exceptions: "Time that tires of everyone / Has corroded all the locks, / Thrown away the key for fun." Artistic purity is unthink-

able ("a jackass language shocks / Poets who can only pun"); so is
religious vision ("Prophets . . . in days gone by / Made a profit on each
cry"). The poem is burdened with guilt and dread, but carries them with
an air of quick ironic comedy more memorable than high seriousness.
Auden's poem to James ended in an elevated vocabulary of prayer; this
lyric ends with the words of a children's tongue-twister:

> Once too often you and I
> Did what we should not have done;
> Round the rampant rugged rocks
> Rude and ragged rascals run.

Around the same time, in January 1941, Auden also wrote the first of
his love poems to Kallman in which he used a vocabulary of departure.
"Atlantis" is one of his strangest works, part love poem, part Kierkegaardian preaching, part playful reinterpretation of myth. Its complex
short-lined stanzas, resembling those of his two essays on man,
"Wrapped in a yielding air" and "Underneath the leaves of life," offer
a series of warnings to a quester "set on the idea / Of getting to Atlantis." Auden wrote the poem after reading C. P. Cavafy's "Ithaca" in
a French translation by Marguerite Yourcenar, whom he had come to
know in New York; he translated into English two of her other render-
ings of Cavafy's Greek and had them published in *Decision* in February.
He had first read Cavafy in translation ten years before, and admired and
imitated Cavafy's unemphatic personal tone of amused seriousness, his
erotic verse that, as Auden wrote later, "neither bowdlerizes nor glam-
orizes nor giggles," his sense of "the comic possibilities created by the
indirect relation of poets to the world" when the world refuses to cooperate with the poet's vision of it, and his sense that poets are "citizens
of a small republic in which one is judged by one's peers and the standard
of judgment is strict."

In "Atlantis" Auden copied the shape and tone of "Ithaca," but instead of making the unattainable goal of the poem the secular Ithaca of
Cavafy's poem or the *civitas dei* invoked in his own more grandiose
works in this period, he named Atlantis as the place of "salvation." He
said nothing in the poem about Atlantis itself, only about the places that
distract from it or counterfeit it, all of which must be embraced if the
real Atlantis is ever to be found. The poem offers no theological doctrine,

only a double sense that Atlantis is a shining place, and that, in this poem at least, its shining is perceptible only as a "poetic vision."*

The poem is written in the second person, with six stanzas of detailed instructions guiding the quester past all likely obstacles. "Stagger onward rejoicing," and if, in the end, you can only see Atlantis but not reach it, "Give thanks and lie down in peace, / Having seen your salvation." Then, in the final stanza, using the same technique of a delayed declaration of intimacy that Auden had used in "Law Like Love," the poem reveals itself as a love poem, addressed to "my dear" in one line, "dear" in another.† But it is a love poem that sends away the beloved in a tone of sadness and hope, not quite in the way that "Lay your sleeping head, my love" sent away an earlier beloved. In "Atlantis," the beloved, who this time is fully awake, is told: "All the little household gods / Have started crying, but say / Good-bye now, and put to sea. / Farewell, my dear, farewell." The earlier poem ended by invoking "every human love" to watch over the beloved; the new one invokes divine love in the person of "the Ancient of Days"—a figure from the Book of Daniel and the common title of an engraving by Blake that Auden had been given by an admirer—"Lifting up, dear, upon you / The light of his countenance."‡ The private occasion of this loving farewell was Kallman's decision to spend a year at the University of Michigan; Auden told Isherwood that Kallman, who had just turned twenty, would "be there by himself, as he has never been away from home or me . . . Being a real Victorian wife, I don't relish the prospect of being parted at all." The beloved in the poem sets sail while the poet remains on shore with the sad knowledge that the place of vision can be found only by those who travel alone.

In the dry Dantesque triplets of the poem he wrote next, Auden admitted for the first time the degree to which the beloved of his dreaming vision differed from the one he saw when awake. This was not a moralizing distinction between wish and reality: the beloved he dreamed

---

* Auden, who was reading German romantic writers around this time, may have had in mind E.T.A. Hoffmann's *Der goldene Topf*, which ends with the hero transported magically to Atlantis, where he lives a "life in poetry."

† "My dear" was commonly used among English upper-middle-class male friends, without sexual connotations, until around the middle of the century, but "dear" was used among sexual or family intimates. Auden reduced both terms in a 1957 revision to "dear friend" and "friend."

‡ Among the poem's faint disturbing notes is that the Ancient of Days in Blake's engraving does nothing of the kind: he looks down on the void and measures it.

about was distorted by his wish, but the beloved he perceived in daylight
was equally distorted by the reflecting lens of his conscious will:

> Each lover has some theory of his own
> About the difference between the ache
> Of being with his love, and being alone.
>
> Why what, when dreaming, is dear flesh and bone
> That really stirs the senses, when awake,
> Appears a simulacrum of his own.

Different perceptions of one's beloved are the products of different presuppositions. At one extreme, "Narcissus disbelieves in the unknown"
and cannot find union because "he assumes he is alone." At another
extreme, "The child, the waterfall, the fire, the stone, / Are always up
to mischief," interfering unlovingly with everything else because they
"take / The universe for granted as their own." Lovers, unlike these
solipsists and pantheists, know there is such a thing as another person,
yet "every lover has a wish to make / Some kind of otherness his own."
After asking why this is so, the poem closes with a quiet guess at a
theological explanation: "Perhaps, in fact, we never are alone." The unspoken idea is that the "light of his countenance" makes visible the other
person whom we cannot see by ourselves. But when Auden later gave
titles to this poem he chose doubting ones: "Are You There?" and then
"Alone."

   Not content with a compact and complete lyric on this theme, Auden
restated it in the imposing form of a quadruple sestina in "Kairos and
Logos." The outer two stanzas are booming, idealizing, and mostly
empty, yet the inner two are magnificent, heartbreaking, and profound.
Auden dropped the whole poem in the 1960s but, near the end of his
life, became reconciled with its rough strengths and decided to restore
it. The title, and the theme of the outer two sestinas, derives from the
"Kairos and Logos" section of Tillich's *The Interpretation of History*,
where the biblical "concept of Kairos, the fulfillment of time," is interpreted in terms of the special tasks demanded by the Logos, the Kingdom
of God, at a specific historical time. The inner sestinas portray two ways
those tasks are evaded, in each case by choosing one of the loveless
extremes Auden had evoked in "Alone." These sestinas describe the ethi-

cal temptations faced by two different artists, with no Henry James to intercede for them.

The opening sestina presents, in abstract technical language, a potted theological history of the West. The birth of Christ is "the condescension of eternal order" that occurred when "predestined love / Fell like a daring meteor into time." In Lutheranism, "condescension" is the term for God's free act of Incarnation, but in this poem the event is neither personal nor free. The sestina's history assigns a central role to the contemplative saints, who appear as abruptly and improbably as revolutionaries and "the just" did in Auden's earlier poems: "The fair, the faithful and the uncondemned / Broke out spontaneously all over time," inducing the order Whitehead called for, "Setting against the random facts of death / A ground and possibility of order."

The second sestina seems almost to have been written by a different poet. With a fairy tale's haunting lucidity and effortless economy, it tells the story of a young girl whose dream suddenly seems real, who convinces herself that her dream is the world. "There stood the unicorn declaring—'Child.' " This illusory address darkly parodies George Herbert's poem "The Collar," where a divine voice uses the same word of comfort. The childish imagination that "took the earth for granted as her garden" (as the child in "Alone" took the universe for granted as its own) finds itself defenseless when it grows up enough to learn that the world no longer cooperates, when "the day came the children of the garden / Ceased to regard or treat her as a child"—and she turns "Frightened and cruel like a guilty child."

The third sestina is a modern short story, told with knowing and laconic dryness, about an adult temptation that mirrors the child's temptation. A twentieth-century intelligence, having lost faith in the power of words to indicate reality ("One notices, if one will trust one's eyes, / The shadow cast by language upon truth"), imagines itself in a world of mere objects whose only order is the arbitrary one imposed by the observer. "The bright and brutal surfaces of things / Awaited the decision of his eyes." At the inevitable ironic conclusion, this poet of objective imagination is left only with his chosen exile, having lost even the passive earth he hoped to rule by imaginative fiat: "instead of earth / His fatherless creation; instead of truth / The luckiest convention of his eyes." This was the first of several portraits in Auden's work of an imaginary poet (in later poems explicitly modeled on Wallace Stevens) who is a late-romantic heir to Mallarmé: the type of an artist for whom the ethical vocabulary of personal and social relations has no meaning, whose narcissistic task is to discover the patterns created by his own mind, and whose fantasy leaves him (as it later left many twentieth-century philosophers of language) with no hope of escape from his self-condemned loneliness. "Narcissus disbelieves in the unknown."

The final sestina of "Kairos and Logos" moves, far less convincingly, from abandonment to salvation. The "broken ladders of our lives" point nowhere; the mythic "nymphs and oracles have fled away"; but the cold and absence they leave behind is the same "blessing of reproach" that Auden had found in the abandoned machinery of Rookhope. The poem ends with a less confident version of the optimistic closing of "Christmas 1940" that Auden had written a few weeks before. "The flora of our lives could guide occasions"—Whitehead's vocabulary again—"Without confusion on their frisking way / Through all the silences and all the spaces." "Frisking" has the same unintended absurdity as the dancing in "At the Grave of Henry James," but the sestina is partly rescued by the hesitant "could." Auden was no longer sure enough of the future to say of it that it *will*.

═══

Auden's prose lost its turgidity and evasions once he made his Christianity explicit. He quickly dropped the saints from his reviews and essays (while continuing to invoke them in his poems), dropped his demands for unidentifiable absolutes, and dropped his vague appeals for public debate and private goodness.* His next review—the first he wrote in 1941—was an essay on Kafka that also served as a summary statement of his new beliefs. This was the review in which he wrote that "the Jews have for a long time been placed in the position in which we are now all to be, of having no home," and that "a neurosis is a guardian angel." In the same review, almost in passing, he renounced the self-interested, self-driven frame of mind in which he had begun "New Year Letter" a year earlier. Faust, he wrote, is faithful to the motto "To thyself be true," regards his own arbitrary personality as the necessity he must follow, and succeeds because (like the children in "Alone" and "Kairos and Logos") he has "the primitive animal faith of the child, and does not ask where he is going, but enjoys the ride." Faust was the "Renaissance Man" who,

---

* He wrote in 1955 about the "personal sanctity" of Charles Williams (see p. 125), but the idea of sainthood had by that time lost its earlier associations.

in trying to reconcile his relation with himself and his relation to others, is tempted "to return to the aesthetic pantheism of the fairy story." (In other words, the "unicorn among the cedars" to whom Auden prayed at the end of "New Year Letter" was the same one who reappeared in the child's deceiving dream in "Kairos and Logos.") Faust flattered himself that he was exceptional; but in his faithfulness to himself he is "the type of the unreflective common man (if such a person exists any more)." Kakfa's "K., the Modern Man," recognizes the arbitrariness of the universe around him; he has become reflective, conscious of himself as isolated, therefore exceptional; but his predicament is everyone's because "industrial civilization makes *everyone* an exceptional reflective K."

In a universe where everything appears arbitrary, where there is no orthodoxy to cling to, the danger for K., Auden continued, is the danger of losing his faith. Auden did not need to mention that this was a faith that had nothing to do with sainthood, and he ended with a sentence from *The Castle* that speaks "in a voice which is equally Jewish and Christian: 'There are many places of refuge, but only one place of salvation; yet the possibilities of salvation are as many as all the places of refuge.' "

Auden was finding his mature prose voice—lucid, conversational, and unaggressively confident in its opinions. He relaxed enough to review Gertrude Stein's *Ida* in an affectionate parody of Stein's voice ("That is what Ida is. I like Ida."), and he ceased to veer off into extremes of banal grandiosity and embarrassing intimacy. He wrote lectures, essays, and reviews, he said later, "because I needed the money." But, he added, he hoped "some love went into their writing," and he almost always found a way to write about issues that mattered to him. The task of reviewing a biography of Shaw, for example, he claimed was "a pleasant excuse for writing an essay on *Christianity × Bergsonism* = ?" He began treating prose as a professional craft, filling notebooks and five-by-eight-inch cards with extracts and references for possible use when he needed them. (Unlike his essays, he said, "all the poems I have written were written for love; naturally, when I have written one, I try to market it, but the prospect of a market played no role in its writing." This conceals that he had also treated poetry almost from the start as a journeyman craft, and throughout his career filled hundreds of notebook pages with metrical diagrams and long lists of words and phrases. He eventually deployed only a tiny fraction of these reserves.)

His prose now took as its subject the rights of the personal realm against the demands of plural, corporate, and deterministic ones. In a review on nineteenth-century theories of universal history, he wrote that the success of Marxism and of Social Darwinism "is unpleasant evidence of what happens when the Absolute is dismissed with a damn and the problem of human 'anxiety' ignored. It returns not in its proper theological shape, but exactly where it has no business to be, in epistemology, moralism, and aestheticism." The real business of the Absolute is to provide a basis for personal belief: " 'Trust in God and take short views,' said Sydney Smith.* The possibility of the second half of his sentence depends upon the first."

He made the same point in a political context when he opened a review of Ortega y Gasset's pluralist theorizing in *Towards a Philosophy of History*: "A real society can only be composed of persons. A person is an individual who knows his place, i.e., who understands the nature of his relations to God and his fellow creatures, for it is by these relations that his individuality is defined." (The phrase "knows his place" is used with a careful sense of its shock value for politically pious readers.) And, in a long review of *Love in the Western World*, he took up the same themes in the erotic realm: "In the last few chapters of his book Mr. de Rougemont states the Christian doctrine of marriage, which will seem absurdly straitlaced to the hedonist and shockingly coarse to the romantic. But perhaps the unpleasant consequences of romantic love and romantic politics are making thoughtful people more willing to reconsider it than they were while a bourgeois convention [of marriage], which professed to be Christian but was nothing of the kind, was still à la mode."

Auden's prose responded to Whitehead's themes of order and vagueness in terms more pointed and polemical than the abstract ruminations in his poems. In a brief essay on James Joyce (who died in January 1941), in which he took care to distinguish "one's admiration for Joyce as a human being" from "one's taste for Joyce's work," Auden devoted much of his attention to the substitutes for Christian beliefs that artists had tried to find since the late nineteenth century:

> Either, abandoning the belief in Original Sin, they became liberal optimists who foresaw the Good Life becoming easy for all, apostles of a great march toward the dawn *all together*; or abandoning the belief in Free Will, they returned

---

* Here and in his poem "Under Which Lyre," Auden slightly misremembers a phrase in a letter from this eighteenth-century clergyman and wit to his sister-in-law Lady Holland.

to the pagan view of the Good Life being only possible to *some*, the intellectual, the proletariat, the aryan; or, abandoning the belief in Grace, they became romantic pessimistic determinists who regarded the Good Life as being impossible to all, and declared that we were lying in the swamp of the Accidental *all together*.

The great protagonist of the first view, he continued, was Walt Whitman; of the second, Richard Wagner "and perhaps D. H. Lawrence"; of the third, Proust and Joyce. Joyce's shock value is political not aesthetic, revealing "to each of us those layers of his soul which are susceptible to the ambiguous and hypnotic Hitlerian cry." But, Auden continued, "one's taste for Joyce's work . . . will depend, therefore, on whether or not one accepts the flux as the Thing-in-Itself. If one does, then Joyce must seem the supreme master; but if, like myself, one does not, then, apart from the haunting beauty of accidental phrases with an accidental dream-like appeal, he ceases to interest as soon as he ceases to shock." (Later, when Auden read through all of *Finnegans Wake*, he found it interesting enough to dispute and imitate in *The Age of Anxiety*, and joked that it had immortalized him by a footnote that used his name: "bolt the thor. Auden.")

Auden's challenge over the saints had given no offense to the austerely Protestant Reinhold Niebuhr, and shortly afterward Auden accepted an invitation from Niebuhr's wife, Ursula, an English-born Anglican theologian. This began a lifelong friendship with the Niebuhrs, who introduced him to most of his other friends in theological circles. Niebuhr published Auden's "Atlantis" in the quarterly he edited, *Christianity and Society*, and commissioned a review of *The Double Man* that took the poem's theology seriously enough to question it in detail. During the next few years, most of Auden's political and ethical positions were indistinguishable from Niebuhr's; many sentences in the reviews each wrote for *The Nation* might be mistaken as the work of the other. Both interpreted Nazism as simultaneously unique to Hitler and potential in everyone; in Niebuhr's words (echoed repeatedly by Auden), "Hitler is of course a brother to all of us, in so far as his movement explicitly avows certain evils which are implicit in the life of every nation. Yet it is not unfair to regard him as, in a special sense, the evil fruit of the German romantic movement. The greatness of that movement is not refuted by the fact that Nazism is really its fruit; but neither can the relation of the fruit to the tree be denied." Both argued publicly against the anti-Semitism of most American churches; both warned that Allied propaganda that demonized all Germans had the effect of encouraging political attitudes akin to those of the Nazis themselves.

In May 1941 Auden reviewed in *The New Republic* the first volume of Niebuhr's theological *summa*, *The Nature and Destiny of Man*, in a tone of admiring gravity, calling it "the most lucid and balanced statement of Orthodox Protestantism that we are likely to see for a long time." Around the same time, in response to a note from Ursula Niebuhr asking what she should say to others about his theology, he identified his position as, "I think, the same as your husband's, i.e. Augustinian not Thomist," that is, concerned as Augustine and most Protestant theology is with the personal experience of sin and grace, rather than concerned as Thomas Aquinas and most Catholic theology is with systematic philosophical understanding. He "would allow a little more place, perhaps, for the via negativa," he added, in a mild parenthetical defense of contemplatives. His liturgical practice, in contrast with the Protestantism of his theology, was "Anglo-Catholic, though not *too* spikey, I hope." ("Spikey" is Anglican slang meaning excessively Catholic, ritualistic, "high.") As to forms of church organization, he continued, "I don't know what to think. I'm inclined to agree with de Rougemont [now a friend] that it will be back to Catacombs for all of us. As organizations, none of the churches look too hot, do they?"

Auden had found his way to a Christian frame of mind that was generous and sane, but he formulated it in terms more theoretical than personal, and seemed dissatisfied with his attempts to translate it into poetry. For three or four months after March 1941 he apparently wrote no poems at all. He was distracted in April and May by the long-delayed production of *Paul Bunyan*—for which he now added a brief speech for Bunyan that describes the night as the time of dream when "the saint must descend into Hell; that his order may be tested by its disorder"—but did not return to his lyric verse afterward. His most ambitious poems in the earlier months of 1941 had expressed a guiltless religiosity in which evil was never chosen and for which the most suitable images were plaster saints and a faceless absolute. He later characterized this episode of his life and work in a single word: "frivolity."

CHAPTER SEVEN

The Absconded Vision

A tlantis, after appearing in a poetic vision, sank beneath the sea. In July 1941 Kallman ended his sexual relations with Auden, said he could no longer endure the constraints Auden placed on him, and announced that he had already been unfaithful.

Auden had accepted the risks of time and change and the uncertainties of Kallman's roving eyes. Having thought of their relation as a marriage, he believed that challenges and dangers served to protect it, as they protected other marriages, from rigidity and inertia. But he had never imagined this kind of abrupt ending; he felt it as the destruction not only of his private happiness but of a morally coherent world. He regarded his relation with Kallman as a sacrament, in the way that marriage is regarded in Christian doctrine: as a visible confirmation in one's private life of an invisible universal order. His first response was the only physically violent act of his life, an act that was less than murder but something more than an unexpressed intention to murder.

Kallman, as he later told a friend, fell asleep after confronting Auden with his infidelity and his decision to separate, and half-woke to feel Auden's hands on his neck. He pushed them aside and went back to sleep. In his Christmas letter to Kallman written later in a heightened, quasi-liturgical poetic prose, Auden remembered: "On account of you, I have been, in intention, and almost in act, a murderer." He inserted the phrase "and almost in act" above the line as an emphasizing afterthought. For a few days after that first night his fury persisted in histrionic though less violent form. Eventually he came to interpret the episode as the discovery, not the loss, of a morally coherent world. He could no longer imagine that the impulse to murder was felt only by other people—by devouring politicians or jeering crowds. Fifteen years later, in his autobiographical essay about his return to Anglicanism, he identified this episode as the concluding stage. After describing his experiences in Spain, his first meeting with Charles Williams, his first readings in Kierkegaard, and his "tentative and experimental" churchgoing, he ended with this laconic sentence: "And then, providentially—for the occupational disease of poets is frivolity—I was forced to know in person what it is like to feel oneself the prey of demonic powers, in both the Greek and the Christian sense, stripped of self-control and self-respect, behaving like a ham actor in a Strindberg play."

At the time, he managed to distance himself from "The Crisis" (as he called it in the chronology of poems about "l'affaire C" that he later prepared for a friend) long enough to write a poem about it, although in other poems during the next few years, he rebuked himself for his own act of withdrawal into aesthetic detachment. The song "Though determined nature can," with its tight fabric of metre and rhyme, only hints at the agonies it subsumes into a formal order. It deliberately treats the special incidents of Auden's private suffering in generalized terms that might apply to anyone; but by withholding every hint of its occasion, by excluding specific dramatic incidents, it fails to justify its generalizations, as his earlier love poems had justified theirs.

The poem's central argument is that everything desirable, including truth, has its cost; more, that *only* that which is desirable has a cost. Because we have a language that can point toward a truth outside itself, we must also endure the ambiguities, falsehoods, and doubts that language brings with it. "All truth, only truth / Carries the ambiguous lies / Of the Accuser." A vision of love cannot escape the fears that shadow it, and we cannot know "how / Evil miracles are done / Through the medium of a kiss." All the signs that lovers make to each other "Summon to their meetings One / Whose name is Legion," and the crisis we endure today is the fulfillment of all we did before. The poem prays to the beloved—and to no one else—for the power to resist the evil that love itself called into being, the unspecified evil of a single night:

> We, my darling, for our sins
> Suffer in each other's woe,
> Read in injured eyes and hands
> How we broke divine commands

And served the Devil.
Who is passionate enough
When the punishment begins?
O my love, O my love,
In the night of fire and snow,
Save me from evil.

"Poor cheated *Mephistopheles*," as Auden called him in "New Year Letter," had returned in triumph.

Auden's wish for stability and faithfulness, not any recent action by Kallman, was the immediate cause of the Crisis. Despite all contrary indications, Auden had retained his faith in Kallman's essential loyalty; although he and Kallman had seen each other almost daily for more than two years, they had lived separately, and Auden knew little of the life Kallman led when they were apart. And he had no desire to satisfy the masochistic sexual tastes that Kallman indulged clandestinely with casual pickups. Auden could not overcome a doubleness in his feelings about Kallman: he imagined their relation as a lasting marriage of equals, yet, as he admitted to a friend, he simultaneously thought of Kallman as a "boy" with whom his relation was by definition transient. Kallman, aware of these double feelings, took revenge by inducing jealousy, although, until now, he had kept his revenge within tactful limits.

The infidelity that led to the Crisis had begun and ended some months earlier. In late 1940 an upper-middle-class English sailor, Jack Barker, had called on Auden with a letter of introduction, probably from Stephen Spender, with whom Barker had had an affair in 1939. Auden enjoyed Barker's company and invited him to stay at the house in Brooklyn Heights while his ship was in New York Harbor. Kallman and Barker fell into an affair with each other; Kallman concealed it from Auden and, until shortly before Barker left New York in January 1941, concealed from Barker that he and Auden had a relation of their own that Auden regarded as a marriage. Barker later said (perhaps truthfully) that although he sensed that Auden and Kallman were in a relation of some kind, he had not guessed its significance, and he did not learn until some time afterward the consequence of Kallman's revelation about their affair.

When the Crisis occurred, Auden regarded Barker as its innocent cause (he revised his opinion some years later, after observing Barker's relations with others) and blamed himself more than he blamed Kallman. The poems he wrote at the time speak of impending danger, treating it confidently, like "Atlantis," or theatrically, like the nightmare nursery rhyme

"Jumbled in the common box." (Auden listed both these poems in his chronological record of "l'affaire C.") After the confrontations in July, he spent a desolate ten days at the end of the month at a writers' conference he had agreed to attend at Olivet College, in a small town in Michigan. The tension continued into August, when he returned to New York, and then spent a month together with Kallman in Jamestown, Rhode Island, as guests of Caroline Newton, a literary patroness who collected geniuses and seems to have been in love with Auden but who, unlike Elizabeth Mayer, expressed her love in money, not warmth. Auden had sold her some of his manuscripts and kept up a didactic correspondence with her about psychoanalysis.* He and Kallman now stayed with her in her summer home; Isherwood joined them briefly in an attempt to mediate; Kallman told him he would never resume sexual relations with Auden.

On 21 August, when Auden, Kallman, and Caroline Newton were preparing to go to dinner with an admiral, Kallman, gently dividing the news into separate phases, told Auden they would not be going out, and that a telegram had arrived reporting the death of Auden's mother. He had not seen her since leaving England almost three years before. After a long pause he said, "How like her that her last act on earth should be to get me out of a social engagement I didn't want," and burst into tears. Later he told Spender, "It was a much greater shock to me than I expected."

Auden already knew that his earlier rebellions were more deeply entangled with his mother than he had presented them in *Paid on Both Sides* and *The Ascent of F*6, plays in which a mother wields the stifling power of a dead past. He wrote James Stern in 1942: "It's a pity we can't swap childhoods for a week; you would be surprised how unpleasant too much parental love and interest can be, and what a torture of guilt it makes breaking away." Now, in 1941, in the course of a few weeks, he was severed first from erotic love, then from maternal love. He believed his loss of the first resulted from his egoistic betrayal of the obligations of love; his loss of the second seemed to confirm his sense of guilt. He had lost first his future, then his past.

---

* The relation ended after a dispute in 1944, when she declined to pay Tania Stern for physical-training sessions on the ground that a friend should not be expected to pay another friend; she asked Auden not to take sides, but he insisted that she apologize and broke with her when she refused. (Tania Stern and James Stern were scraping along on income from her classes and his journalism.) Auden portrayed Caroline Newton, not entirely unsympathetically, as "The huge sad lady" in his poem "The Duet" in 1947; see page 264.

Partly through guilt, partly because of his sacramental sense of marriage, Auden still thought himself bound by his vows despite Kallman's defection. Two years earlier, he had written in a review that civilized society was based on the principle that "a treaty, a contract, an agreement must be kept, not because it is rational or just—it is rarely either—but simply because one's word has been given." Now he committed his deepest emotional loyalties to Kallman—whose intelligence and wit never stopped giving pleasure—even while he began seeking sexual friendships elsewhere. Kallman accepted these terms without protest.

In September 1941, after Auden and Kallman returned to New York, Kallman left for California "to find his own life," as Auden put it in a letter to Harold Albaum.* Kallman had dropped his plans to go to Ann Arbor to study at the University of Michigan, although it is unclear whether he did this before or after Auden (apparently during his visit to Olivet College in July) had arranged to spend the next academic year in Ann Arbor as a visiting lecturer in English. In the soap-opera tone Auden adopted when writing to Albaum, he said: "I feel as if I were scattered into little pieces. And if the Devil were to offer him back to me, on condition that I never wrote another line, I should unhesitatingly accept." With the Devil's offer not forthcoming, and with no prospect that he could now sacrifice the vocation of poetry for the vocation of marriage, he set to work on "For the Time Being," a long dramatic poem in which he interpreted his double loss as the end of a sacramental vision.

———

Auden chose to write a dramatic poem because he began to consider his relationship with Kallman as the dramatic performance of a marriage rather than a real one. He had been the author and director of the play, and had performed it for an audience that consisted mostly of himself. It would have been nothing worse than frivolous self-dramatization had it not required a second actor obliged to remain cast forever in a role he did not want to play.

"A Christmas Oratorio," later the poem's subtitle, was its working title while Auden was composing it and for a year thereafter. He wrote it with the idea that Britten would set it to music for chamber or radio

* According to one report (an unpublished interview with John Grierson, formerly the head of the film unit for which Auden wrote "Night Mail"), Auden was sustained during a period of intense mental anguish—probably at this time—by long private talks with Reinhold Niebuhr.

performances. It is divided into nine episodes from the Christmas story, each comprising one or more choruses, narrations, dialogues, songs, chorales, recitatives, meditations, and proclamations, most in regular verse forms, some in prose. The characters include—in addition to Joseph, Mary, Wise Men, and Shepherds—a narrator who speaks in relaxed fourteen-syllable lines, and a chorus that variously takes the part of the general populace, unborn children, Roman soldiers, tempting desert voices, and exultant angels. A song for Rachel, mourning the innocents, expands on the verse in Matthew that describes the massacre as the fulfillment of the prophecy in Jeremiah of Rachel weeping for her children. The Star of the Nativity, the angel Gabriel, and the four Jungian faculties of Intuition, Feeling, Sensation, and Thought also speak in verse. Extended prose meditations are spoken by Herod and by Simeon, the devout old man in Luke who takes the infant Jesus in his arms and exclaims to God that he has seen salvation. Auden's typescripts specify Joseph as a bass, Mary as a soprano, the Star of the Nativity as a contralto, and so forth, but the fifteen hundred lines of the completed text were far too vast and literary to be sung. When he prepared it for publication, Auden dropped all indications that he had ever intended it for music.

The Christmas story, for all its richness of incident, could hardly be made to include the details of Auden's recent history. He treated the story as a parable of the advent and departure of a vision, and his juxtaposition of the secret private meaning of the poem and its religious public meaning was simultaneously audacious and devotional. He placed his own story in the poem for the same reason that a donor of a religious painting typically had himself portrayed kneeling to the manger or the cross, slightly behind the saints: he, like the donor, was as implicated in the sacred events as the central characters were. "For the Time Being" is a rare twentieth-century instance of the tradition in which the erotic and religious elements of a work of art cast light on each other—the sacred story is retold in the familiar vocabulary of the flesh, and the flesh is understood as an image of the sacred—but works of this kind were frequent in earlier centuries, especially in the European baroque. Bernini's portrayal of Teresa's ecstasies, and Bach's cantata "*Wachet auf!*" in which Christ the bridegroom sings duets of longing and satisfaction with his bride, the soul, are the most familiar examples. In each case, the erotic relation is dignified enough to serve as a symbol of the relation of the soul to God; and the two relations are joined by the Christian understanding of matrimony as a sacrament, not merely a symbol of grace but a means of grace. Traces of this convention survived into *Jane Eyre* (where adultery is rebuked and marriage rewarded by a maternal lunar goddess and by patriarchal religion) before it was supplanted in the late nineteenth century by the avant-garde convention that deploys the erotic elements in a work of art for the purpose of unmasking the religious ones.

"For the Time Being" takes for granted the argument Auden set forth explicitly twenty years later in his essay on mysticism, where he analyzed Dante's vision of Eros and his own. The erotic element of the vision prefigures a "final vision" in which "Eros is transfigured but not annihilated." Christian orthodoxy, unlike Platonic idealism, he wrote, affirms that love "involves the whole of our being," including the body, and "whatever else is asserted by the doctrine of the resurrection of the body, it asserts the sacred importance of the body." In Auden's oratorio, that sacred importance is asserted by the doctrine and event of the Incarnation; and the birth of the Christ Child reveals, among many other things, that idealism is thin-lipped and ultimately trivial. God feels no shame or diminution in occupying a body that is no less susceptible to suffering and death than the bodies occupied by everyone who experiences erotic love. Because of the Incarnation, the body is honored by orthodoxy in a phrase in the Anglican marriage ceremony spoken by the husband and wife to each other, a phrase Auden echoed in his Christmas letter to Kallman: "With my body I thee worship."

"For the Time Being" also takes for granted that its private meanings are as appropriate to prayer as its public ones. It accepts, perhaps more fully than any other work of modern writing, the Christian belief that while worship is a public ritual act, every person participating in it has a unique voice with unique overtones, and these private voices, no matter how eccentric or unconventional, are equally valuable. The poem does not suggest that the poet's love is more guilty or shameful than anyone else's; Joseph is made to suffer for the sexual conceit of all males, no matter whom they desire; and, when a chorus of soldiers demonstrate their expertise in homosexual slang before going off to massacre the innocents,* the poem rebukes a special kind of indifference, not a special kind of love. (A more explicit statement of the value of any praise and prayer, no matter whose, occurred in Auden's commissioned poem "The Ballad of Barnaby," written decades later, in 1968, for a performance

---

* The homosexual sense of the slang is unmistakable, but the words themselves—debutante, numero, flybynight, Emperor, matador—had not been used in real homosexual slang: Auden created an ingeniously unsettling effect by inventing a slang based on common themes in the slang in actual use. A knowing reader easily recognizes the secret meanings, but the unknowing reader can find no clues in a slang dictionary. The poem identifies its reader as much as its author.

at a girls' school. Barnaby—based on the unnamed tumbler in the thirteenth-century *Tombeur de Notre-Dame*—prays to a statue of the Virgin in the only way he knows, by tumbling, and when he falls faint, she steps down and wipes his brow. Later the Abbot, observing from the shadows after being summoned by a worried monk, recognizes Barnaby's unconventional prayers as "holy and humble.")

When "For the Time Being" was published in 1944—in a book with the same title that also included his next long poem, "The Sea and the Mirror"—the only direct suggestion of personal meaning was the dedication of the oratorio to the memory of Auden's pious mother. But this dedication concealed more than it revealed, because the oratorio's erotic allegory was invisible to everyone except Auden and Kallman. In case Kallman should miss the point, Auden made it clear in the letter he wrote to him on Christmas Day, 1941, when the oratorio was half-finished—a year after the impersonal bombast of "Christmas 1940." "Dearest Chester," the letter began:

> Because it is in you, a Jew, that I, a Gentile, inheriting an O-so-genteel anti-semitism, have found my happiness:
> As this morning I think of Bethlehem, I think of you.
>
> Because it is you, from Brooklyn, who have taught me, from Oxford, how the most liberal young man can assume that his money and his education ought to be able to buy love;
> As this morning, I think of the inn stable, I think of you.
>
> Because, suffering on your account the torments of sexual jealousy, I have had a glimpse of the infinite vileness of masculine conceit;
> As this morning, I think of Joseph, I think of you.
>
> Because mothers have much to do with your queerness and mine, because we have both lost ours, and because Mary is a camp name;
> As this morning I think of Mary, I think of you.
>
> Because the necessarily serious relation of a child to its parents is the symbol, pattern, and warning of any serious love that may later depend upon its choice, because you are to me, emotionally a mother, physically a father, and intellectually a son;
> As this morning I think of the Holy Family, I think of you.
>
> Because, on account of you, I have been, in intention, and almost in act, a murderer;
> As this morning I think of Herod, I think of you.

Because even les matelots et les morceaux de commerce instinctively
pay you hommage;
> As this morning I think of the shepherds, I think of you.

Because I believe in your creative gift, and because I rely absolutely
upon your critical judgement,
> As this morning I think of the Magi, I think of you.

Because you alone know the full extent of my human weakness, and
because I think I know yours; because of my resentment against being
small and your resentment against having a spinal curvature, and because with my body I worship yours;
> As this morning I think of the Manhood, I think of you.

Because it is through you that God has chosen to show me my
beatitude,
> As this morning I think of the Godhead, I think of you.

Because in the eyes of our bohemian friends our relationship is absurd;
> As this morning I think of the Paradox of the Incarnation, I
> think of you.

Because, although our love, beginning Hans Andersen, became
Grimm, and there are probably even grimmer tests to come, nevertheless I believe that if only we have faith in God and in each other,
we shall be permitted to realize all that love is intended to be;
> As this morning I think of the Good Friday and the Easter Sun-
> day already implicit in Christmas Day, I think of you.

None of this is visible in the oratorio itself, which makes a great point
of retelling the Christmas story in the language and setting of a contemporary public world known to everyone. The Shepherds push levers and
wear ready-made clothes; the Wise Men are followers of Bacon, Bergson,
and Bentham who now hope to find a better wisdom. In Caesar's empire,
credit replaces barter and synthetic chemicals conquer disease and de-
pression.* Joseph worries in a well-lit bar. The purpose is not to make
the story of the Incarnation palatably up-to-date but to make the reli-

---

* The fugal chorus in praise of technological and propagandistic Caesar—"When he says, This
is good, this is loved; / When he says, That is bad, that is hated"—updates the young man's
praise of the king in I Esdras 4: "If he command to smite, they smite; if he command to make
desolate, they make desolate."

gious point that the story is always contemporary, and that contemporary events are most fully understood in its terms.

"For the Time Being" is a mixed success, with long-winded and dutiful-sounding passages scattered among memorably vivid ones. The poem's most profound and witty moments are those in which events from the Christmas story, the contemporary public world, and Auden's private erotic history precisely coincide. Auden's version of the story of Joseph consists of Joseph's lonely meditation in a bar followed by a chorus that rebukes him for his masculine conceit and for all clubroom anger against women, all forms of "insistence on a nurse, / All service, breast, and lap." A special personal meaning is hidden in Joseph's despairing plea for "one / Important and elegant proof / That what my Love had done / Was really at your will / And that your will is love." And the chorus's feminist lecture to Joseph is also Auden's rebuke to his own exploded claims to erotic and emotional privileges justified by his superior age and class. (The section of the oratorio devoted to Joseph was another of the poems Auden listed as part of the record of "l'affaire C.")

In retelling the Christmas story in contemporary terms, Auden adopted the content, vocabulary, and rhetorical technique of a historical study published in 1940, *Christianity and Classical Culture*, by Charles Norris Cochrane. This book is a massive elaboration on an argument that had briefly been sketched by Cochrane's teacher Collingwood in *An Essay on Metaphysics*, to the effect that the early patristic writers had solved the metaphysical problems that had baffled classical philosophy, and that the world was converted to Christianity because Christian thought was more coherent and accurate than the clutter of half-believed ideas that pagan thinkers themselves scarcely bothered to defend. Auden told Spender that Cochrane's was "one of the most exciting books I have ever read," and in 1944 he persuaded *The New Republic* to let him review the corrected second printing: "I have read this book many times, and my conviction of its importance to the understanding not only of the epoch with which it is concerned, but also of our own, has increased with each rereading."

Cochrane's book is a notable example of historical double focus. Without mentioning any event later than the fifth century, Cochrane uses a dense vocabulary of contemporary allusion to make clear that he is writing about the present as much as the past. An obvious example is his reference to the "new deal (*nova concordia*)" of the Augustan era, but most of the book is subtler. Cochrane lets his readers infer his Christian perspective, but he is no apologist for the Church, and as Auden emphasized in his review, he makes no suggestion that political crises can be solved by organized religion. Cochrane portrays Constantine's official endorsement of Christianity as a catastrophic disaster. "Our period," Auden wrote in his review,

> is not so unlike the age of Augustine: the planned society, caesarism of thugs and bureaucracies, paideia, scientia, religious persecution, all are with us. Nor is there even lacking the possibility of a new Constantinism; letters have already begun to appear in the press, recommending religious instruction in schools as a cure for juvenile delinquency; Mr. Cochrane's terrifying description of the "Christian" empire under Theodosius should discourage such hopes of using Christianity as a spiritual benzedrine for the earthly city.*

Cochrane spoke directly and accusingly against beliefs that Auden had once prized more than any others. In a passage about the "intermediate beings" that Plato and others postulated between the ideal and the real, he denounced "the most vicious of heresies, the heresy of two worlds, the discontinuity of which paganism seeks with this feeble expedient to bridge." Of demons, he wrote: "Thus, though in fact delusion, they are terribly and disastrously real to those who believe in them."

Other phrases from Cochrane's book appear more or less whole in Auden's poem. The narrator's phrase "fiscal grief" appears in Cochrane's account of the depreciation of currency in third-century Rome.† The warning to Joseph, "There is one World of Nature and one Life," adapts Cochrane's report that for Christianity "there was but one world of experience and that common to all human beings on precisely the same terms." "Powers and Times are not gods but mortal gifts from God" adapts Cochrane's quotation from Ambrose, "Victory is not a power but a gift," and his paraphrase of Augustine, "Time is not a *principium*." Auden's Baconian Wise Man, who disciplines his intelligence with an "Ascesis of the senses," echoes Cochrane's account of Plotinus's "rigorous programme of *ascesis*, variously described as a progressive 'evacuation' by the soul of all elements of complexity, i.e. of sense-perception and positive knowledge." The same Wise Man, who put nature to the question and found that "Her answers were disjointed," is no less alienated from her than his predecessors were when, "to the assiduous ques-

---

* This last metaphor is perhaps an oblique reproach to Auden's use of benzedrine as a stimulus for his writing since 1939. He was still using it as late as 1967, but apparently heeded his doctor's warnings and gave it up shortly afterward.

† Auden referred to this subject again in 1966 in his review of E. R. Dodds's *Pagan and Christian in an Age of Anxiety*, reprinted in *Forewords and Afterwords*.

tions with which the Hellenic intellect plied her, nature had returned but ambiguous answers." Some of the parallels in the poem between the Christian story, Cochrane's narrative, and Auden's experiences are so elaborate and strained that the verse collapses under its own weight and dozens of lines of chorus or narration sit inert on the page.

Auden justified the poem's double focus in a letter to his father, who had found it puzzling:

> Perhaps you were expecting a purely historical account as one might give of the battle of Waterloo, whereas I was trying to treat it as a religious event which eternally recurs every time it is accepted. Thus the historical fact that the shepherds were *shepherds* is religiously accidental—the religious fact is that they were the poor and humble of this world for whom at this moment the historical expression is the city-proletariat, and so on with all the other figures. What we know of Herod, for instance, is that he was a Hellenised-Jew and a political ruler. Accordingly, I have made him express the intellectual's eternal objection to Christianity—that it replaces objectivity with subjectivity—and the politician's eternal objection that it regards the state as having only a negative role. (See Marcus Aurelius.) . . .
>
> I am not the first to treat the Christian data in this way; until the 18th Cent. it was always done, in the Mystery Plays for instance or any Italian paintings. It is only in the last two centuries that religion has been "humanized," and therefore treated historically as something that happened a long time ago; hence the nursery picture of Jesus in a nightgown and a Parsifal beard.
>
> If a return to the older method now seems more startling it is partly because of the acceleration in the rate of historical change due to industrialization— there is a far greater difference between the accidents of life in 1600 AD and in 1942 than between those of 30 AD and 1600.

The unspoken point of Auden's distaste for the "humanized" religion of the past two centuries is that it was also, paradoxically, an impersonal religion, in which all the important events occurred a long time ago to somebody else, and the believer was untroubled by the unique personal demands of guilt and action. Its proponents, in fact, boasted of its impersonality as an advance over the naïveté of earlier forms of Christian belief. In 1841, for example, Ludwig Feuerbach wrote that "active love is and must of course always be particular and limited . . . yet it is in its nature universal, since it loves man for man's sake, in the name of the race. Christian love, on the contrary, is in its nature exclusive" and therefore to be transcended, for Christ was the primitive "substitute for the consciousness of the species." In the opening sentences of his "Theses on Feuerbach," Marx had famously responded that reality was conceived "even by Feuerbach" as an object, as something to be contemplated, not in terms of practice, "not subjectively"—a phrase that could have been written by Kierkegaard.

In the vision of the Incarnation in "For the Time Being," as in Auden's vision of Eros, divinity manifests itself in the body of a unique person. When Auden began the poem, in October 1941, he had not rid himself of the abstract impersonal theology he had expounded for the past year. The least convincing parts of the work occur in its first half, where almost every dramatic voice—except Joseph's—is collective or angelic or otherwise inhuman. As he continued to work on the poem in early 1942, unique subjective voices increasingly broke through its longueurs, and by the end it had survived its lapses. Its traditional gestures of faith seem perfunctory, but even these are rescued by the ironic tone of disenchantment that surrounds them. Literary versions of the Christmas story almost invariably treat it as a narrative of irreversible transformation: the miser learns how to keep Christmas, once and for all, but Auden points insistently to the loneliness after the feast. When Joseph is beset by doubts, the chorus tells him that his unhappiness reveals only his faithless errors, not some bleaker reality in the world outside: "Sin fractures the Vision, not the Fact." A sentence in a 1934 essay about the social visions of Christianity and Communism proved true in Auden's own person eight years later: "A truth is not tested until, oppressed and illegal, it still shows irresistible signs of growth."

———

The action of "For the Time Being" is a passage from despair to exultation and then to the ordinary condition of anxiety and doubt. "Advent," the baffling and murky opening section, seems to be about a kind of despair that never actually occurred, for the narrator insists that it is an "outrageous novelty" unprecedented in personal or historical time. He finds it hard to say what it is:

> I mean
> That the world of space where events re-occur is still there
> Only now it's no longer real . . .
> I mean that although there's a person we know all about
> Still bearing our name and loving himself as before,
> That person has become a fiction; . . .
> That is why we despair . . .

Writing this around October or November 1941, and still working on it in early December, when the Japanese bombing of Pearl Harbor brought the United States into the war, Auden went out of his way to deny in the poem an equation between wartime dread and the dread that precedes the Incarnation. "If, on account of the political situation, / There are quite a number of homes without roofs, and men / Lying about in the countryside neither drunk nor asleep," the narrator begins, "That is not at all unusual for this time of year." War is one of "our familiar tribulations," not this new horror but something we manage to use as a futile defense against it, "Like a juke box tune that we dare not stop."* He was so intent on treating the Incarnation as an event that can be experienced at any time that he made no connection between it and the specific events of the present or any plausible reader of the poem.

The sudden novel experience of "this Void" is based on the familiar, and not at all sudden, experience of modern disjunction and dislocation, but the narrator calls it "the Abomination" and "the wrath of God." This alludes to the despair Auden had experienced before he met Kallman—*de profundus exclamavi*, as he told his brother—but he kept all trace of his personal experience out of this opening section. The narrator and chorus borrow images of dread from Cochrane's account of a "crisis of despair," but Cochrane was writing about pagan Rome three centuries after the Incarnation, not the first century before it. In a later essay on Kierkegaard, Auden wrote—as if to justify the narrator's vocabulary—"The wrath of God is not a description of God in a certain state of feeling, but of the way in which I experience God if I distort or deny my relation to him." This has little to do with the tone of abrupt melodramatic horror in the poem; the narrator's speech is theatrical in the way in which Auden was now regarding his relation with Kallman as theatrical. A few months after behaving "like a ham actor in a Strindberg play," he found himself writing like one.

In his review of Niebuhr's *The Nature and Destiny of Man*, Auden had described in more plausible terms the mood that preceded the birth of Christ. Adapting an argument he found in Cochrane, he wrote that the Incarnation "occurred precisely at that moment in history when an impasse seemed to have been reached." Imperial Rome had united the world politically, but social division seemed permanent and intractable. "Philosophical dualism divided both society and the individual person-

---

* He had made the same point in the "Prologue" to *The Double Man*; see p. 134.

ality horizontally, the wise from the ignorant, the Logos from the Flesh; the only people who did not do this were the Jews, but they divided society vertically, themselves from the rest of the world."

The most exultant passages in "For the Time Being" celebrate the Incarnation as the means by which this impasse was dissolved, just as Auden's visionary love lyrics in 1939 celebrated his vision of Eros for breaking the impasse between the two worlds. In the Gospels the aged Simeon's few words of praise make explicit the universality of Christian revelation. Jesus, he says, is "a light to lighten the Gentiles and the glory of thy people Israel." In the oratorio Simeon speaks in resplendent, copious paragraphs about the universal meaning of the Incarnation to flesh and mind, and to all of philosophy, science, and art. It could not have occurred, Simeon says, until all varieties of emotion and experience had been explored, until the high roads of classical philosophy had issued in dead ends and forking paths, until there was nothing left to learn but an inescapable awareness of isolation and guilt. Now that it has occurred, a personal relation has become possible between oneself and God, "and that which hitherto we could passively fear as the incomprehensible I AM, henceforth we may actively love with comprehension as THOU ART."*

Now, he continues, our relation to the rest of the universe is revealed as a civil one. The Incarnation assures the flowering of the subject matter of art—something that did in fact occur in the wake of Christianity. No longer was the exceptional hero the only figure worthy of awe and the low-born clown the only butt of comedy, "for since of themselves all men are without merit, all are ironically assisted to their comic bewilderment by the Grace of God."† Imagination, he adds, "is redeemed

---

* The personal address of this last phrase, perhaps suggested by Martin Buber's Kierkegaardian meditations in *I and Thou* (English translation, 1937), was introduced when Auden reprinted the oratorio in his 1945 *Collected Poetry*. In its first publication in 1944, Simeon's sentence ended "HE IS."

† In his essay on James Joyce, Auden wrote that the Christian, unlike the pagan, believed "the Good Life was pretty difficult for all, but impossible to none. The effect of this on the subject matter of art was enormous . . . what mattered was the intensity of effort with relation to the capacity of a given character to make it: Christianity introduced the tea-table into literature." The last phrase alludes to the novelistic technique of E. M. Forster as it was praised by Isherwood's literary mentor Edward Upward. Forster's technique, Upward said, was "based on the tea-table: instead of trying to screw all his scenes up to the highest possible pitch, he tones them down until they sound like mothers'-meeting gossip" (Isherwood, *Lions and Shadows*, 1938). Upward, now a staunch Communist (who had infuriated Auden by upbraiding Isherwood for turning to religion), would have been surprised to learn he had made a theological point.

from promiscuous fornication with her own images"—the "*fantastica fornicatio*, the prostitution of mind to its own fancies" that Augustine (quoted by Cochrane) wrote about, and that Auden saw in the Mallarmésque self-infatuated turn of late-romantic writing. As in art, so in science, the future of which is assured by the revelation that the infinite can be perceived through its manifestation in the finite, so that experimentation with local objects can reveal universal law. The Incarnation frees science from the barbarian error that denies unity, "asserting there are as many gods as there are creatures"; from the Platonist error that denies multiplicity; and from the error of Judaism, which limits "the co-inherence of the One and the Many to a special case." (Co-inherence is a doctrinal name both for the three-in-one quality of the Trinity and for the mutual presence in Christ of the human in the divine and the divine in the human; Auden found the word in Charles Williams, who made it the central theme of his theology, and also in Cochrane.) Simeon accepts Collingwood's argument in *An Essay on Metaphysics* that the "guardianship of the European 'scientific frame of mind' is vested in the religious institutions of European civilization." And his meditation on art and science expands on a phrase of Whitehead that Auden quoted earlier, when the chorus prays to learn to put its trust in God and be persuaded by the brutal facts of the created world "to / Adventure, Art, and Peace." These are three of the five qualities that Whitehead described in *Adventures of Ideas* (1933) as essential to civilization. (The other two were Beauty and Truth, which Auden presumably omitted because another poet had got to them first.)

Auden gave Simeon's prose meditation the same shape he had given "Spain." Each opens with an inclusive panorama of the entire period up to the present: "Yesterday all the past," as "Spain" calls it. Each then turns to the present, in "Spain" "Today the struggle," in Simeon's meditation the "here and now" of the Incarnation. But the two works look forward to different futures—"Spain" to the abrupt collective polity of "the sudden forest of hands" and the impersonal triumphs of History; Simeon to "the perpetual recurrence of Art," "the continuous development of Science," and a morally comprehensible history unlike anything in Auden's abandoned fantasies about fate and determinism, "for the course of History is predictable in the degree to which all men love themselves, and spontaneous in the degree to which each man loves God and through Him his neighbor." "Spain" ends in an empty universe where the stars are dead and the animals will not look and we are left alone with our day; Simeon ends his meditation in a world where "we may no longer desire God as if he were lacking," for he "is always and everywhere present." History in "Spain" cannot help or pardon; the chorus that gives a brief response to each section of Simeon's speech ends in a prayer for precisely that good which History had refused to grant: "Its errors forgiven, may our Vision come home."

Auden deliberately offended liberal rationality when he had Simeon name Christian revelation as the guardian of secular science. But Stalin's endorsement of the politically driven theories of Lysenko and Hitler's rejection of any intellectual work done by a Jew were, Auden believed, the inevitable effects of the forcible removal of that guardianship. He understood that the Enlightenment was not, as its heirs imagined, a rejection of Christianity so much as a flowering of its Protestant strain, a fulfillment of Simeon's prophecy that the One could now be sought in the study of the Many. The rebuke to Enlightenment rationality in "For the Time Being" is even more pointed elsewhere in the poem: Simeon's exalted *nunc dimittis* is followed immediately by a second prose speech, in which Herod states the plausible argument that rationality makes against revelation, and ends by wringing his hands over the necessary murder as he calls in the army to defend civilized values.

Writing in 1942, Auden had an abundance of plausible models—mostly German—to choose from when he portrayed Herod. Any of them would have flattered his readers' sense of their own contrasting moral superiority. Instead, he made Herod a well-meaning liberal reformer, dedicated to the task of bringing light to barbarian darkness. Herod foresees the consequences of the Incarnation in the same way that any well-meaning rationalist perceives an eruption of absurd irrationality. He cannot imagine it as a manifestation of a universal absolute, only as an apotheosis of individual uniqueness. "Reason will be replaced by Revelation," he warns, and subjective feeling will take the place of knowledge. "Idealism will be replaced by Materialism," and every private fetish will take the place of civic virtue. "Justice will be replaced by Pity," and "all fear of retribution vanish." His conclusion that civilization must be saved even if this means sending in the army is the logical consequence of his argument, and the self-pity of his final lines—"How dare He allow me to decide? I've tried to be good. I haven't had sex for a month. I object. I'm a liberal"—is the inevitable effect of his confrontation with an absolute that he cannot understand but that his own idealism makes it impossible for him to ignore.*

Herod's speech restates in dramatized form Auden's argument that liberalism, which exposed the workings of power behind moral systems, had left itself without an answer to Hitler, who went a giant step further by dropping all pretense of morality and acknowledging power as his sole means and motive. At around the same time, Auden wrote an essay on poetry and war for *The Chicago Sun*, a new daily paper notable at the time for its intellectual prose and liberal politics. His argument was an implicit answer to the "where are the war poets" questions being asked in England and elsewhere, often with direct reference to Auden himself:

> It is always silly to generalize, but I think it not unlikely that the aspect of this war which will be most reflected in the poetry of the next few years is the danger that, in order to win it, the democracies will construct an anti-fascist political religion, and so, by becoming like their enemies, lose the peace.
>
> If the poet, qua poet, has any other social function than to give pleasure, it is, in the words of the greatest poet produced by the last war, "to warn,"† so that, in one sense, the serious poetry of any given moment is always at odds with the conscious ideas of the majority.
>
> The louder the voices grow that demand strong beliefs, universal values, and nothing more, the more necessary it becomes to warn, "It is not enough that a belief be strong—it must also be true. It is not enough that a value should be universal—it must also really be unconditional."

To be at odds with the conscious ideas of the majority meant bringing to light uncomfortable truths about the majority and oneself. This was a matter different from Auden's endorsement in 1939 of Rilke's withdrawal; the poet's task was now more public. Later in the war, in November 1944, Auden praised a new edition of Grimms' fairy tales for, among other things, its potential to overcome "our poverty of symbols," a poverty that was largely responsible, he thought, for "half our troubles,

---

* Auden's Herod combines liberalism with classical stoicism, another philosophical position that made no room for the unconditional. Herod's opening catalogue of those who helped him become himself spoofs the catalogue in Marcus Aurelius' first book of *Meditations*. Herod thanks, among others, "the stranger on the boat to Sicily—for recommending to me Brown on Resolution," as Marcus thanks Rusticus for a copy of Epictetus. But "Brown on Resolution" is not a treatise by a Mr. Brown on the virtues of resolution: it is the title of a middlebrow adventure novel by C. S. Forester.

† Wilfred Owen wrote in an introduction to his poems in 1918: "All a poet can do today is warn. That is why true Poets must be truthful."

both individual neuroses and collective manias like nationalism." If everyone learned these stories and told them to their children, with embellishments, "then, in a few years, the Society for the Scientific Diet, the Association of Positivist Parents, the League for the Promotion of Worthwhile Leisure, the Cooperative Camp of Prudent Progressives and all other bores and scoundrels can go jump in the lake." Randall Jarrell furiously missed the point when he complained that "these prudent, progressive, scientific, cooperative 'bores and scoundrels' were the enemies with whom Auden found it necessary to struggle. Were *these* your enemies, reader? They were not mine." But no one needed to be warned against enemies who loudly threatened to kill or enslave. The enemies Auden warned against were the voices that threatened to lose the peace by establishing a political religion—as in the anti-Communist inquisition of the 1950s—and the voices that sought to reassure Auden and his readers by telling them their enemies were so clearly evil that they themselves could comfortably congratulate themselves on being good.

Auden's letter to Kallman on Christmas Day, 1941, closes by looking toward an Easter season of crucifixion and resurrection. "For the time Being" closes with neither dread nor hope, looking instead toward the ordinary world from which vision and intensity have been withdrawn. The Christmas feast has left us with little but leftovers ("Not that we have much appetite, having drunk such a lot"), a sense of having failed to love all our relatives, and a mild distaste for gloomy self-denial as "the mind begins to be vaguely aware / Of an unpleasant whiff of apprehension at the thought / Of Lent and Good Friday which cannot, after all, now / Be very far off." This least theatrical of the narrator's speeches is also the most moving and successful speech in the poem. The comedy of the narrator's disillusionment shades imperceptibly into a profound evocation of the ordinary difficulty of faith in a world where the Christmas decorations have been put back in their boxes ("some have got broken") and not even the slightest afterglow improves daily existence. The kitchen table "seems to have shrunk during the holidays. The streets / Are much narrower than we remembered." Faith was easy when it was rewarded by happiness. Now

the Spirit must practice his scales of rejoicing
Without even a hostile audience, and the Soul endure
A silence that is neither for nor against her faith
That God's Will will be done, that, in spite of her prayers,
God will cheat no one, not even the world of its triumph.

After this, the oratorio concludes with a chorus of nine lines that is less a reaffirmation of faith than an unassertive reminder of what it might be like:

> He is the Life.
> Love Him in the World of the Flesh;
> And at your marriage all its occasions shall dance for joy.

Auden told his friend Theodore Spencer, a poet and English professor at Harvard, five years older than Auden, who from the early 1940s until his death in 1949 acted as Auden's private critic and censor: "I tried to introduce the sweeter note in the last section, i.e. if the light is to be seen again, it is by going forward (to the Passion perhaps) and not by nostalgic reminiscence. One cannot *be* a little child; one has to *become like* one, and to do that one has to leave home, to lose even what now seems most good." In the first glow of his vision of Eros in 1939 Auden had written that now he had the answer from the face "that never will go back into a book," that he and his beloved "the life-day long shall part no more." But the meaning and purpose of his vision revealed itself only after it irrevocably withdrew.

═══

"For the Time Being" is more plausible at the end than at the beginning because, while writing it, Auden was working to discard the props, masks, and poses that had once sustained him. In the spring of 1942, when he had finished about half the oratorio, he wrote a long accusatory autobiography that he disguised as an appreciative review of a new book of poems by his friend Louise Bogan. As poetry reviewer for *The New Yorker* she had championed Auden's work, and her technically adept, ironically lyrical verse was sufficiently like his for him to write a credible account of her poetic development that applied equally well to his own.

The ostensible theme of his review was the relation between a poet's life and a poet's work—one of the themes of the adult education course he had taught in his first year in New York—and Bogan's success in understanding what that relation must be. In past centuries, he began, a poet's "self-development" arose at least in part from his life as an assenting or dissenting member of a community; now, in an age when there is no community, "only a public," the poet gets no help from outside. If he refuses, rightly, to please an anonymous crowd, he is tempted instead to write about "The Interesting, which in practice means his childhood and his sex-life, so that he escapes being a journalist who fawns on the public only to become a journalist who fawns on his own ego." Good poetry, like Bogan's, "represents today therefore a double victory, over the Collective Self and the Private Self."

At this point the review turns to autobiographical specifics, although the generalizing tone continues. "Wherever there is a gift, of whatever kind, there is also a guilty secret, a thorn in the flesh, and the first successful poems of young poets are usually a catharsis of resentment." The identity of the secret thorn is not named (as Paul did not name the "thorn in the flesh" that he was given "lest I should be exalted above measure," in II Corinthians 12:7), but Auden's more attentive readers could guess it was some variety of sexual and intellectual loneliness. "Poems at this stage are usually short," he continued, evidently remembering his early verse, "made up of magical lyrical phrases which seem to rise involuntarily to the consciousness, and their composition is attended by great excitement." Poets like A. E. Housman and Emily Dickinson, excellent as they are, "never get beyond this stage, because the more successful the catharsis, the more dread there must be of any change in either one's life or one's art." The failure of his own attempts at catharsis is implied in the next stage of his account by the persistence of the thorn:

> The poet who escapes from the error of believing that the relation of his life to his work is a direct one, that the second is the mirror image of the first, now falls into the error of denying that there need be any relation at all, into believing that poetry can develop autonomously, provided that the poet can find [for] it a convenient Myth. For the myth is a set of values and ideas which are impersonal and so break the one-one relationship of poetry to experience by providing other standards of importance than the personally interesting, while at the same time it is not a religion, that is to say, it does not have to be believed in real life, with all the effort and suffering which that implies.

Any reader who had followed Auden's career would recognize in this a rejection of his political poems. He underlined it by listing, among the myths favored by modern poets, Yeats's lunar cycles and the deifications, by "Yeats's younger and less-talented colleagues," of "the Id or Miss History." (The camp name signals his lack of awe before the stern un-

pardoning power he had honored in "Spain.") But, he continues autobiographically, "the escape from the Self without the surrender of the
Self is, of course, an illusion, for it is the Self that still chooses the particular avenue of escape." The personal note in the poetry remains, "only
now in the form of its denial, in a certain phoney dramatization, a 'camp'
of impersonality. Further, the adoption of a belief which one does not
really hold as a means of integrating experience poetically, while it may
produce fine poems, limits their meaning to their immediate context; it
creates Occasional poems lacking any resonance beyond their frame."*
To confront and resist the temptation of impersonality "is to realize that
the relation of Life to Work is dialectical, a change in the one presupposes
and demands a change in the other, and that belief and behavior have a
similar relation, that is to say, that beliefs are religious or nothing."

Up to this point, the review sounds like the argument Auden made
for religious absolutes around the time he began going to church, but
the next few words make clear that he now included among his mythical
and camp-impersonal poems the ones he wrote in the afterglow of his
vision of Eros and his first readings in Kierkegaard: "A religion cannot
be got out of books or by a sudden vision, but can only be realized by
living it." This realization is both the theme and the method of "For
the Time Being": the theme of the lonely difficulty of belief after the
vision fades, and the method, however imperfectly achieved, in which
events in the poet's private life and events of public history cast light on
each other.

During the previous few years Auden had interpreted more than one
event in his life as a decisive break with the past—his departure from
England, his commitment to Kallman, his return to the Church—but in
each case he had been able to dramatize himself in the act of making a
triumphant, voluntary change. Now, in the undramatic aftermath of an
unlooked-for crisis, he had found the total change that he had earlier
only imagined. In January 1942 he wrote to his publisher, Bennett Cerf
at Random House, proposing "a *Collected Poems* which would include
the lyrics from the Iceland and China books, lyrics from the plays, some

---

* This was precisely the objection he raised against Yeats in a review of a biography a few
months later: "Magnificent as is their diction, I cannot but feel that his poems lack a certain
inner resonance. Each exists solidly enough in its frame of reference, but rarely transcends it"
(*Chicago Sun Book Week*, 7 February 1943). After 1939 he sensed that Yeats's work was the
product less of a large mysterious gift than of a narrow deliberate will, and was less willing to
endorse the argument he had written for the defense in "The Public v. the Late Mr. W. B.
Yeats."

alterations and omissions, and a few new poems."* He wanted to gather all his past work in a single book, because he expected all his future work to be different. In April he told Stephen Spender in a letter:

> The next step for us, as poets, lies in opposite directions. You have to get over your camp of pity and accept your strength, I over my camp of tough aggressiveness, and accept my weakness. I.e., your poetry has to lose its whiff of the yearning school-girl, and mine its whiff of the hearty scoutmaster. Technically this probably means that I should deprive myself of the support of strict conventional forms, while you should impose them on yourself, in other words, we should both attempt the *difficult* (for us each).

A year earlier he had remarked to Spender that because of his personality type, "I can only develop along the abstract systematic formalist line." He had now abandoned this fantasy of inherent destiny, renounced his Yeatsian and pious masks, repudiated his familiar lyric technique, and was prepared, as he told Theodore Spencer, "to leave home, to lose even what now seems most good."

The final episode from the Christmas story represented in "For the Time Being" is the Flight into Egypt. Mary and Joseph return to the place of Israel's enslavement in order that they may "hide from our pride / In our humiliation," that "our future may be freed from our past," that they may "fly from our death with our new life" in the person of a child. By the time Auden finished the oratorio, in July 1942, he still considered himself bound to Kallman by vows, but he was beginning to think of the emotional link between them less as a marriage than as a relation of parent and child. He was substituting one kind of theatrical performance for another, rather than renouncing theatrical relations altogether, but at least he had stopped demanding that Kallman play a role inconsistent with his personality.

In February 1942 Kallman had followed Auden to Ann Arbor after all, where they shared a house but not a bed during Auden's second semester at the University of Michigan, and he became a student in the same department where Auden was teaching. Two months later, Auden told

* His publisher's initial reluctance, then his own commitments, kept him from putting the book together until the summer of 1944. It was further delayed by wartime paper shortages until 1945, when it appeared (with twenty-five new poems written after 1940) under the title *The Collected Poetry of W. H. Auden*. This was almost exactly the title he had originally proposed, but he now objected to it: "As to the title, I want *Poems 1928–1945*. The word Collected suggests finality which I *hope*, anyway, is incorrect" (Letter to Saxe Commins, his editor at Random House, 20 January 1945, Columbia University Library).

Spender that in his relation with Kallman, "my mistake was demanding that he should be my Mother-Father, and one has no right to ask that of another, least of all someone fourteen years younger." During the next few years Kallman accepted Auden's treatment of him as a child even while rebelling against it. He let Auden pay his school bills during his year at Michigan (he stayed one more semester to finish his M.A. after Auden left), and after losing miscellaneous jobs in New York during the next few years (at one point he worked for the U.S. Army censoring soldiers' letters home), he lived mostly on Auden's income for the rest of his life. But he also subjected Auden to individuating tantrums and blatant inducements to jealousy. Auden tried, sometimes successfully, to endure these episodes with parental patience, even to the point of asking Tania Stern to find out from Jack Barker "whether his feelings for Chester are what Chester thinks they are." Eventually he made the camp element in this role-playing explicit by referring to himself among friends as "your mother." And he seems to have tried, perhaps consciously, to deflect his sexual desire for Kallman by opposing it with the taboo against incest.*

Virtually everything Auden wrote during this time paid homage to a child. "For the Time Being" was addressed, in the words of the three Wise Men, to the "Child, at whose birth we would do obsequy"; two of the three shorter poems he wrote while working on the oratorio, "Many Happy Returns" and "Mundus et Infans," were about children. (The third, "In War Time," was a commission from Caroline Newton for a poem to be read aloud at a gathering at her summer home in 1942; this halfhearted exercise was the last poem Auden wrote that he discarded after including it in one of his books.)

"Many Happy Returns" is ostensibly a set of birthday maxims addressed in February 1942 to the seven-year-old son of a couple who befriended Auden in Ann Arbor. But it was also addressed privately to Kallman a few weeks after his twenty-first birthday, and to Auden himself as a rebuke to his own parental ambitions. The seven-year-old will soon realize we are all like actors, so the poem warns him that "Deliberate interference / With others for their own good / Is not allowed the author / Of the play within The Play." The self-knowledge that comes with growth "Tempts man into envy." Therefore, may you, the

---

* "The triple situation," he wrote to his friend Rhoda Jaffe in 1947, "of being sexually jealous like a wife, anxious like a mamma, and competitive like a brother is not easy for my kind of temperament. Still, it is my bed and I must lie in it" (14 July 1947; Berg Collection).

poem hopes, "Love without desiring / All that you are not." Auden included this poem also in his list of the published record of "l'affaire C."

Shortly before he wrote the poem, Auden had been rebuked by another of the objects of his "Deliberate interference / With others for their own good." At the end of January he had sent Benjamin Britten some newly written sections of "For the Time Being" with a cover letter prompted by Britten's decision to return to England. "I have been thinking a great deal about you and your work during the past year," he wrote. "As you know I think you the white hope of music; for this very reason I am more critical of you than of anybody else, and I think I know something about the dangers that beset you as a man and as an artist because they are my own." He then sketched a theory of art that reads like a meditation on the form and content of "New Year Letter." "Goodness and Beauty," he began, "are the results of a perfect balance between Order and Chaos, Bohemianism and Bourgeois Convention." Bohemianism alone produces "a mad jumble of beautiful scraps." Bourgeois convention was the source of an artist's technical skill, but by itself "ends in large unfeeling corpses." For middle-class Englishmen like Britten and himself, "the danger is of course the second." Britten denied and evaded the demands of disorder, Auden said, through his attraction to "the sexless and innocent," through his psychosomatic attacks of ill health, through his habit of surrounding himself with adoring nurses and acolytes, and through his temptation to build "a warm nest of love." Britten must abandon all this, Auden warned, if he hoped to develop to his full stature. Britten, not unreasonably, took offense, and Auden rushed to explain in his next letter that he "didn't mean to suggest that your relationship with Peter [Pears] was on the small-boy level." Cordial relations were temporarily restored, and Britten set Auden's "Song for St. Cecilia's Day" to music later that year as planned. But he never set anything else Auden wrote, beyond two brief fragments of "For the Time Being," and repeatedly snubbed Auden's later attempts to resume their friendship.

A newborn child transforms the social order of its family and realigns old patterns of power and obligation. "Mundus et Infans," written in August 1942, proclaims the birth of a child in stanzas that imitate Pindar's praises of triumphant athletes in a vocabulary germane to modern dictators. Auden dedicated the poem to another couple in Ann Arbor. Albert Stevens was an English professor; Angelyn Stevens, when Auden met her, was suffering from allergies that, she thought, were preventing her from conceiving another child. Auden believed he charismatically cured her by talking with her about her allergies; she became pregnant soon afterward. Auden wrote his poem when he heard the news—Wystan Auden Stevens, as his parents named him, was born six months later— but the family politics of the poem referred both to the Stevens family and to the less traditional family of Auden and Kallman.

In "Mundus et Infans," the child's mother's "role / In the New Order must be / To supply and deliver his raw materials free." The baby himself is "Resolved, cost what it may, to seize supreme power and / Sworn to resist tyranny to the death with all / Forces at his command."* Among the morals the poem draws from infancy is what it means to become like a little child. The baby's "loud iniquity is still what only the / Greatest of saints become—someone who does not lie." (Following Niebuhr, Auden now associated sainthood with unknowing innocence.) We love the baby, he continues, "because his judgements are so / Frankly subjective that his abuse carries no / Personal sting." After listing a dozen ways in which the child differs from the adult, the poem closes with one that carried a distinct personal sting for Auden himself: the adult, having lost childhood unity, is the one who has "learned to distinguish between / Hunger and love." This line records the end of the epoch in Auden's work in which he wrote about "the drives of love and hunger," as he called them in "Letter to Lord Byron." For the next twenty years Auden's implicit excuse for Kallman's actions was that Kallman had not yet learned to distinguish between hunger and love. But Auden lived with the adult knowledge that his own love would not be satisfied, and in "The More Loving One," written in 1957, he preferred it that way: "If equal affection cannot be, / Let the more loving one be me."

As Auden tried to transform his relation with Kallman into a parental one, he reaffirmed his sense of the solemnity and importance of the marital relation he no longer imagined he could have. A year after the Crisis, Auden wrote to James Stern: "You can't imagine what a source of strength your marriage has been to me during the past year, a bright little light in a naughty world of greedy romantics and castrated pussycats." Two years later, he told Stern: "I've long cherished a secret wish to collaborate with you on a play about marriage, the *only* subject." (He

---

* In 1931 Auden had written another Pindaric ode to a newborn dictator, the ode in *The Orators*, "Roar, Gloucestershire, do yourself proud." But the infant tyrant in that poem was imagined as marching on London and transforming England, and the parents did not appear at all.

used almost the same phrase in a letter to Isherwood.) And, much later, he famously observed that, "like everything which is not the involuntary result of fleeting emotion but the creation of time and will, any marriage, happy or unhappy, is infinitely more interesting and significant than any romance, however passionate." He had no fantasy that even the happiest marriage was a condition from which the furies had been banished, and he dismissed the opposite fantasy, exemplified in D. H. Lawrence, that through marriage the instinctive flesh can redeem the corrupt mind:

> By always presenting the "white" spiritual love and the love of the "Dark" God as irreconcilable enemies, Lawrence has encouraged people in fact—though not of course in intention—to divide their lives between "white" relations and "dark." This is to deny the possibility of a happy marriage, for, however difficult to achieve, marriage is by definition a reconciliation between the two.

Auden now began to insist that because marriage was a form of vocation, anyone who had first been called to the vocation of writing was forbidden to attempt a second vocation in marriage. He told a lecture audience in 1943: "To acknowledge vocation is, like marriage, to take a vow, to live henceforth by grace of the Absurd, to love for better or worse, for richer or poorer, in sickness and in health, until death do us part." Late in 1944, in a review of Henry James's stories about writers and artists, he wrote:

> There are many callings, but whichever one chooses you, to that you must be faithful, "for better, for worse, for richer, for poorer, in sickness and in health, till death do you part," for only those who are so dedicated have a real history; only they have the art which makes out of a tangled mass of mere moments the figured carpet of a significant life.

Repudiating his earlier beliefs that (as he had told his father in 1939) to be a writer was "the most difficult and honorable occupation a human being can have," or that (as he had told Spender in 1941) the "mystical contemplative life" was the highest vocation "because the most difficult, exhausting and dangerous," he now wrote that it is "my belief that the vocation to which the majority of mankind is called is also the highest and hardest, and that to be a good husband and father is a larger achievement than becoming the greatest artist or scientist on earth." And he endorsed a commandment that he claimed to find implicit in James's example: "If you *are* called to the intellectual life, then you had better remain single and, if possible, celibate." Give an artist a family "and in

many cases he will soon be faced with the choice between being unfaithful to the demands of his work and unfaithful to his responsibilities for
those he has promised to love, and will only too often end up by being
faithful to neither."

A few years later he dropped the metaphor of vocation and wrote
about the poet's relation to language simply and directly as the poet's
true marriage. Before a poet finds his own style, he wrote, "the poet is,
as it were, engaged to language and, like any young man who is courting,
it is right and proper that he should play the chivalrous servant . . . and
defer to his beloved's slightest whims, but once he has proved his love
and been accepted, then it is another matter. Once he is married, he
must be master in his own house and be responsible for their relationship." As the husband of his language, "the poet is the father who begets
the poem which the language bears." The marriage of poet and language
was no more inherently ideal than natural marriage: "Poets, like hus-
bands, are good, bad and indifferent . . . For all of them, there are periods
of tension, brawls, sulky silences, and, for many, divorce after a few passionate years."

"True Love enjoys / twenty-twenty vision, / but talks like a myopic,"
Auden wrote many years later. In his prose and discursive verse, whenever
he portrayed moral weakness and self-centeredness, he was portraying
Kallman as he knew him to be; in his lyrics, he continued to infuse
Kallman's image with a myopic glow. And Kallman was also the model
for a curious recurring motif in which Auden paraphrased an aphorism
by Marx: "The only antidote to mental suffering is physical pain." Auden
first made this point in the narrator's final speech in "For the Time
Being." The feeling that remains after the exaltation of Christmas is guilt
over its loss; craving the remembered sensation of a visionary escape from
the self, but forgetting that the escape was a gift of vision, "We look
round for something, no matter what, to inhibit / Our self-reflection,
and the obvious thing for that purpose / Would be some great suffering." Auden readily blamed himself for real and imagined misdeeds, but
he neither feared nor wanted physical punishment for them. Kallman,
who felt histrionic shame but apparently little conscious guilt, sought
and enjoyed physical punishment, and Auden interpreted this wish to
suffer as a refusal of self-reflection, a perversion of the wish to find meaning. Near the end of Caliban's speech in "The Sea and the Mirror," the
"important persons at the top of the ladder" turn to Ariel, the spirit of
art, for release from the disorder of life, but end in a fate more appro-

priate to Kallman's prospects: "a rising of the subjective and subjunctive to ever steeper, stormier heights," at last seeking relief at "the Black Stone on which the bones are cracked, for only there in its cry of agony can your existence find at last an unequivocal meaning and your refusal to be yourself become a serious despair, the love nothing, the fear all."

Kallman's stormy and theatrical egoism was, in Auden's eyes, the outer sign of the inner disorder he described in a 1947 essay, "West's Disease." The heroes of Nathanael West's novels cannot make their wishes issue in desires, and therefore live in a state of "wishful self-despair." The sufferer from West's Disease, Auden wrote, is not selfish—because wishes refer to nothing real. The sufferer has no designs on other persons or things—but is "absolutely self-centered."* The disease in its final stages "reduces itself to a craving for violent physical pain—this craving, unfortunately, can be projected onto others—for only violent pain can put an end to wishing *for* something and produce the real wish of necessity, the cry 'Stop!' " Kallman's preference for rough trade was less a sensual desire than a wish for self-affirming sensation.

While Auden was writing these calm diagnostic accounts of Kallman's psyche, he addressed him in lyrics that combined gratitude and resignation. The last of the poems listed in 1947 as the published record of "l'affaire C" was "Few and Simple," a brief lyric from 1944 that affirmed the persistence of his love. The dialogues of lover and beloved having ended, this poem records a dialogue among three aspects of the poet himself: the perceiving mind, the impulsive flesh, and the "I" incompletely ruling over them. (In "On the Circuit," twenty years later, these were the three who shared "our snug / Apartment in New York.") The mind, in the opening stanza, "Amazes me with all the kind / Old such-and-such it says about you, / As if I were the one you / Attach unique importance to, / Not one who would but didn't get you." Both I and the mind are in turn startled by the flesh (which "mind insists is ours, / Though I, for one, by now know better") when, in its erectile moods, it "Gets ready for no-matter-what / As if it had forgotten that / What happens is another matter." In the final stanza "the most ingenious

* In a notebook (now in the Berg Collection) he wrote in the late 1940s: "Freedom of wish is infinite, though not really freedom. To wish = to wish that what is, should not be. Which is impossible. To will is to choose a possible future based on the existing present." Wishing, not willing, is the condition he asked the moon to prevent in his 1953 lyric "Make this night loveable": "Shine lest tonight any, / In the dark suddenly, / Wake alone in a bed / To hear his own fury / Wishing his love were dead" (*Collected Poems*, p. 577).

love"—subtly ingenious in its search for satisfactions it cannot have—knows enough to "think twice of trying to escape" these few and simple facts of unceasing liking and desire.

   That love was ingenious enough to find new expressions, although more successfully in Auden's poems than in his daily life. In *The Age of Anxiety*, around 1945, Auden's representative, Malin, has subdued his sexual desires into a "hunger for a live / Person to father." When the young man Emble bicycles off with someone else, Malin says, "In youth I would have cared, / But not now," expressing an indifference Auden had not quite convinced himself to feel. In the 1950s, when a friend told him about two Austrian boys in their early teens who could not afford to stay in school, Auden, who had not met them, paid their fees; afterward, he paid for the university educations of two war-orphaned young men chosen for him by a social agency; he continued to do this, with different beneficiaries from different countries, until the end of his life. Ten years after his crisis with Kallman, in "Their Lonely Betters," Auden contrasted the animals and birds with their human betters who live in historical time and are therefore conscious of loss—"Who count some days and long for certain letters." The love of those who count days until a loved one returns and who long for letters from the departed one is not the love of one spouse for another, or the love of one partner for another in a relation of equals. It is the love a parent feels for a child who has grown old enough to stay long months away from home.

CHAPTER EIGHT

The Murderous Birth

"The Sea and the Mirror," to all appearances, is a poem about poetry. Its subtitle describes it as "A Commentary on Shakespeare's *The Tempest*," as if it were a work of literary criticism. In form it is a long quasi-dramatic work in verse and prose in which the characters of Shakespeare's play comment on their experiences and most of them have strong opinions about the relation between art and life. Prospero and Caliban, who are given the longest speeches, talk about little else. Auden confirmed this interpretation in letters to friends. He told Ursula Niebuhr that "The Sea and the Mirror" was "really about the Christian conception of art," and to Theodore Spencer he wrote that it was "my Ars Poetica, in the same way I believe *The Tempest* to be Shakespeare's, i.e., I am attempting, which in a way is absurd, to show, in a work of art, the limitations of art."

His explanations are accurate but incomplete. He described the theme, as he generally did with poems that probed deeply into himself, in terms that make it sound theoretical and dry, yet the poem itself is a turmoil of moral and emotional intensities. Each of the characters, despite their elaborate variety of style and theme, illuminates a different aspect of one central figure: an artist whose work exploits the suffering of others, a dramatist who manages his characters for his own ends, a poet whose skill in shaping language tempts him to give shape to the lives of those around him. And concealed within the apparently plotless series of disconnected monologues is a single narrative about an inner journey back to the mystery of birth and a doubtful act of murder.

The action of *The Tempest* takes place at sea and on Prospero's island. The action of "The Sea and the Mirror" takes place in a theater after a performance of *The Tempest*. The poem's "Preface," spoken by "the Stage Manager to the Critics" (as specified in a stage direction beneath its title), is an ironic lyric about performance and reality. The "Postscript," spoken by Ariel to Caliban, is a metaphysical lyric on the inextricability of art and life. Between these brief lyrics are three large "chapters."* In the first, "Prospero to Ariel," Prospero speaks in regular syllabic lines (the form Auden henceforth preferred for his more meditative poetry) interspersed with compressed accentual lyrics. In the second, "The Supporting Cast, *Sotto Voce*," the other human characters in *The Tempest* think to themselves, each in a different stanza form. Prospero and the supporting cast are more or less the same characters as they are in Shakespeare's play, and unaware of their status as dramatic fictions. But in the third chapter, "Caliban to the Audience," written in an extravagantly artificial prose style, Caliban knows himself to be a dramatic fiction, and his themes concern the fictions that the real audience, actors, and dramatist choose as the shapes and textures of their lives.

In "For the Time Being," Auden had reimagined his relation to Kallman as a stylized drama that rescued and idealized the wreckage of the relation itself; the narrator's closing speech acknowledged that the drama had ended, but everything else in "For the Time Being" had performed it. At the start of "The Sea and the Mirror," the curtain has fallen and the revels are ended. In his relation with Kallman, Auden had been playwright, director, producer, manager, and actor all at once, and now that the theater had closed, the one role remaining was that of reviewer. He performed that role in the voice of Caliban:

> Now it is over. No, we have not dreamt it. Here we really stand, down stage with red faces and no applause; no effect, however simple, no piece of business, however unimportant, came off; there was not a single aspect of our whole production, not even the huge stuffed bird of happiness, for which a kind word could, however patronizingly, be said.

And at "this very moment," Caliban continues, we "at last see ourselves as we are."

This bleak moment of self-knowledge was now explicitly at the center

---

* The word "chapter" appeared in the headings of the first published text, in 1944, but disappeared in later versions, apparently at the fiat of a book designer. Auden referred to the parts as "chapters" in his letters to friends.

of Auden's religious beliefs. Four years earlier, in *The Prolific and the Devourer*, he had identified Jesus as the greatest of historians: "Neither the heathen philosophers, nor Buddha, nor Confucius, nor Mohammed showed his historical insight." As recently as "For the Time Being" he had written (in the voice of Simeon) about Jesus as the intellectual patron of the arts and sciences. Now, in an essay, he proposed two statements that might plausibly be made by a Christian about his belief that Jesus is the Christ: "I believe because He fulfills none of my dreams, because He is in every respect the opposite of what He would be if I could have made Him in my own image," and, if asked why Jesus and not Socrates or Buddha or Confucius or Mohammed, because "None of the others arouse *all* sides of my being to cry 'Crucify Him.' "

On 1 September 1942, after settling his affairs, Auden reported to be drafted into the U.S. Army; the deferral he had received while teaching at Michigan had expired. An examining psychologist recognized his homosexuality and assigned him the 4F classification that excluded him from service on medical grounds. (He had told Tania Stern that he would not try to escape the draft by announcing his homosexuality but would not conceal it if questioned.)

Shortly after he was turned down by the Army, he accepted a teaching job at Swarthmore College, near Philadelphia, where he remained for the next three academic years. He enjoyed the friendships he made there—especially with Wolfgang Köhler, whose work on Gestalt psychology he had incorporated in *The Orators* ten years before—but never felt at home. "Small towns, my dear, are HELL," is the camp judgment made by Adrian and Francisco in an abandoned draft of "The Sea and the Mirror." Among Auden's duties during his second and third years at Swarthmore were classes for Chinese naval officers, war work that scarcely appeased his guilt over his safety. "Could you find out for me the details of where and how to get into the Merchant Marine," he asked James Stern in November 1942, a few weeks after he started teaching. "The more I think about the future and how they are going to take the adolescent and the married, the more uncomfortable I feel sitting on my 4F bottom." Nothing came of this, but Auden's request was consistent with the interest in risky war service he had expressed earlier, when he told the student newspaper at the University of Michigan that if he were drafted he wanted to volunteer for submarine duty. (This was not a simple matter of heroics. As he had written in "Letter to Lord Byron" about his childhood love for abandoned mines: "Today I like a weight upon my bed; / I always travel by the Underground.")

Auden's wartime guilt and sense of obligation were the latest variation on a theme that had manifested itself from the time he began writing poems. He had always insisted that his good fortune and the good fortune of those like him could not be divided from the suffering of others left outside. Someone's success invariably required someone else's failure. In the 1930s he saw his good fortune as the bourgeois privilege he enjoyed at the expense of the unemployed. In "A Summer Night," written during the economic distress of 1933, he and his schoolmaster friends did not stop to "ask what doubtful act allows / Our freedom in this English house, / Our picnics in the sun," while the "gathering multitudes outside" stayed hungry. When the Spanish Civil War began in 1936, success and failure became matters of life and death. Success required "the conscious acceptance of guilt in the necessary murder" that occurred in every armed battle, while failure would receive from history neither help nor pardon. Those who were defeated were generally plural in number: an overthrown social class, a conquered army. But by 1938, after Auden had written his meditative sonnet sequence on the war in China, "In Time of War," and had begun to ask himself questions that called for religious answers, he understood success and failure in very different terms. Defeat and suffering no longer seemed to occur in the grand decisive struggles of "Spain," but happened almost without being noticed, while someone else was eating or opening a window or just walking dully along. The expensive delicate ship in "Musée des Beaux Arts" had *somewhere to get to*—as history did in "Spain"—but the defeated victim it left behind, a boy falling out of the sky, was a unique and vulnerable person, neither a class nor an army.

Soon Auden was applying this general pattern of purposive departure and abandoned victim to the events of his own life. An early sign appears in his letters to Harold Albaum. In 1939, he had accepted the justice of Albaum's resentments:

To you, perhaps, I seem a representative of that Other World of success who has taken Chester away from you, one who has been lucky and suffered little, born into a home where I was loved, given the best education that money could buy, acquainted with the Right People, and living at exactly the right time for my work to receive notice as the new poetic model, one in fact for whom everything possible has been done to make his life easy. And yes, you are right. Everything has been done.

In 1941, after Kallman had left Auden as he had earlier left Albaum, Auden answered a letter from Albaum with a long meditation on the temptations of unhappiness, and offered advice that he could not have written, he said, had Kallman not gone away. Yet even now he made no pretense to share the griefs of Albaum's self-pity: "The terrible thing about success, even in the very modest degree to which I know it, is the way it cuts one off from those who have not known it, i.e., the vast majority of mankind. Worldly success is like sex, an experience which you can only share with those who have known it."

"The Sea and the Mirror" repeatedly makes the same distinction between the prosperous and the wretched. Caliban speaks for the audience:

We should not be sitting here now, washed, warm, well-fed, in seats we have paid for, unless there were others who are not here; our liveliness and good-humor, such as they are, are those of survivors, conscious that there are others who have not been so fortunate, others who did not succeed in navigating the narrow passage or to whom the natives were not friendly, others whose streets were chosen for the explosion or through whose country the famine turned aside from ours to go . . .

The catalogue of failure extends to those who are alive but wrecked by their own psyches, those "who lost their suit against their parents or were ruined by wishes they could not adjust or murdered by resentments they could not control"—but even these were, in the insistent metaphor of Caliban's prose, "murdered," and the crucial distinction made by the poem is that between those who are alive and those whose death made possible the guilty prosperity of the living.

"The Sea and the Mirror" began to take shape during Auden's first weeks at Swarthmore, when he sensed that some poems he had already written might be part of something larger. (*Paid on Both Sides* had taken shape in the same way in 1928.) In August 1942 he had written a lyric, "The Aged catch their breath," which ended in a cluster of allusions to Shakespeare, who knew that in contrast with the noisy world of fact, "All the rest is silence / . . . / And the silence ripeness, / And the ripeness all." Auden seems to have begun writing about Shakespeare partly so that he could talk about him with Theodore Spencer, who was a professional Shakespearean. In 1946–47, two years after writing "The Sea and the Mirror," Auden gave a yearlong series of lectures on Shakespeare at the New School in New York but, after Spencer's death in 1949, wrote almost nothing about Shakespeare for eight years. "The Aged catch their breath" is a poem about the gap between audience and stage actor and, by explicit analogy, between the contemplation of action and the act itself—the same issue that had engaged Auden when he added the words "and almost in act" to his statement that he had been in intention a murderer. The work of art makes us "wet with sympathy,"

> but how
> Shall we satisfy when we meet,
> Between Shall-I and I-Will,
> The lion's mouth whose hunger
> No metaphors can fill?

These lines darkly imply the guilt of all action. The choice to do something cannot be fulfilled by a metaphor, only by an act. The "lion's mouth" that demands acts, not words, was the name of the repository set up by the Republic of Venice to receive secret accusations of criminal acts.

While he was writing "The Sea and the Mirror" Auden's prose continued, as in previous years, to adjudicate between two ideas of the artist, the autonomous romantic hero and the responsible moral educator. Introducing his selection from the poems of Tennyson, published in 1944, he contrasted Baudelaire, who since the mid-1930s had been the representative of the first category whom Auden most admired, and Tennyson, whom Auden had begun praising, to the annoyance of modern-minded friends, during the same period. Tennyson, he now wrote, was "undoubtedly the stupidest" English poet (although he had "the finest ear, perhaps"); Baudelaire made himself greater than Tennyson by developing "a first-rate critical intelligence." Yet there are other standards of merit:

> Baudelaire was right in seeing that art is beyond good and evil, and Tennyson was a fool to try to write a poetry which would teach the Ideal; but Tennyson was right in seeing that an art which is beyond good and evil is a game of secondary importance, and Baudelaire was the victim of his own pride in persuading himself that a mere game was

le meilleur témoignage
Que nous puissons donner de notre dignité.

As intended, this infuriated partisans of both sides of the question, but the argument was a diversionary tactic, one of many that Auden employed in his prose while in his verse he was conducting an unnoticed but far more outrageous and extreme critique of his own poetry and of artists in general.

A few months earlier, Auden had tried to draft a long blank-verse speech for Simeon in "For the Time Being." In the final, published version of the oratorio, he cast Simeon as a theologian who speaks in visionary prose. In the abortive draft Simeon is an aged, subdued poet whose themes are his relation to his gift and his discovery, through the Incarnation, of the limits of his gift. His speech is an imaginary self-portrait of Auden as an old man, forty-five years older than he was when he wrote it. "I have been certain of something twice in my life," Simeon remembers. His first certainty was his discovery of his vocation as a poet. Auden's own awakening as a poet occurred in a field among the salt marshes near Gresham's School in Norfolk when he was fifteen.* Simeon's discovery occurs in the same way:

> Once when I was fifteen years old, and I walked
> At three o'clock on a Sunday afternoon
> On a narrow causeway in the middle of a saltmarsh
> When I suddenly knew what I was going to be.
> I was surprised because poetry
> Was nothing I had thought about, but not in the least
> Excited or alarmed. I simply felt
> I had been given the task which I was able to do.

* Auden described the event in "Letter to Lord Byron," and Robert Medley, the school friend who had awakened Auden's sense of vocation by asking if he had ever written poetry, recalled it in his memoir *Drawn from the Life* (1983):

> I embarked on an attack on the Church . . . Expecting a sympathetic response to my ardently expressed, logical but unoriginal views, I was taken aback to discover Wystan flushed, frowning and offended. Wystan, I thus discovered, was devout . . . To break the tension . . . I found myself offering to share an intimate secret. Confessing that I wrote poetry I asked if he wrote himself and was oddly surprised to find that he had never tried. I suggested that he might and that started things off.

Simeon's new certainty of the Incarnation has nothing to do with poetry. "I am glad," he says, that "it was not my gift," to which until now he has dedicated all his life, "But my weakness that was able to see this child." This paraphrases the letter Auden wrote to Spender around the same time, in which he said he must "accept my weakness." In another draft passage, Simeon is "glad that for the first time in my life, I have seen / Something I could not imagine for myself." His gift and its strength have been supplanted by a new demand and a new expectation:

> And now today, I walked home with a similar certainty
> That the task is no longer required, and I can die.
> I have not done it well. I wish I could accuse
> Myself of presumption, a mistaken belief in my gift;
> That would be a kind of excuse. That would be better
> Than knowing I had largely wasted what I had.
> For the gift was not really mine,
> But the sixty years of impatience and idleness were.

Today Simeon "can believe I can really die." With his knowledge of mortality comes an understanding that without guilt there would have been no gift, and that without the gift he could not have understood his guilt:

> Now that our partnership is about to be dissolved
> I am beginning to understand
> Why wherever there is a gift there is a guilty secret
> A thorn in the flesh, that our gift
> Is the strength by which our weakness knows of its guilt,
> Its intuition of a lost perfection that is ever present.

But the poet-Simeon recognizes his humility as a subterfuge of pride. He is concerned more with his gift and its interesting limits than with the vision the biblical Simeon was unselfconsciously grateful to receive. The poet-Simeon knows this, but is too enraptured by his gift to be able to change:

> What we never realize until too late
> Is that there is no escape from temptation
> For the will with which we scourge ourselves is itself corrupt.
> The lust restrained becomes the pride of resistance

The repentant tears and the vow to reform
Tricks for avoiding the present. All I know
About the Evil One is that whenever I cannot see him
He is staring me right in the face as my unawareness,
And whenever I think I see him, he is really behind my back
As the challenge to battle what he makes me see.

The echoes of Eliot's *Four Quartets* in these lines seem to be Auden's disguised means of praising himself for joining Eliot in Christian belief.

When he replaced Simeon-as-poet with Simeon-as-theologian, Auden did not abandon Simeon's poem, but reused much of it to make an acid rebuke to his own vanity in posing as Simeon in the first place. The poet-Simeon's draft describes "one of those winter days, cold, brilliant, utterly still / When the bark of a shepherd's dog carries for miles, / The great wild mountains come up quite close to the house / And the mind feels intensely awake." After making a few trivial changes, Auden found these phrases perfectly suited the thoughts of the figure in the Christmas story who least resembled Simeon, and inserted them into the prose speech for Herod.

Auden tried to take seriously his renunciation of the poet-Simeon's vanity. When he published a set of theological pensées titled "Lecture Notes" in five issues of the Roman Catholic weekly *The Commonweal* in November and December 1942, he signed them with the pseudonym "Didymus," the Greek name of Doubting Thomas, and never took public credit for them, although they included some of his most profound aphoristic prose.

In the earliest draft of "For the Time Being," the abandoned speech of the poet-Simeon is followed by another abandoned poem, a lyric in which the poet's gift speaks in the first person. The gift addresses its song to the imperfect artist whose thorn in the flesh first called the gift into being. Now, in "The Sea and the Mirror," Auden found a place for this lyric as the "Postscript" spoken by Ariel to Caliban: "Weep no more but pity me, / Fleet persistent shadow cast / By your lameness." He also found a place for "The Aged catch their breath," the Shakespearean lyric he had written in August, by making it the "Preface" spoken by the Stage Manager to the Critics. Having given a few of the poet-Simeon's lines to Herod in "For the Time Being," he gave many of the rest to the lonely, self-isolating Prospero, who readily admits he has much in common with Herod.

The poet-Simeon knew that the living made use of the dead, but he understood this as a pandemic fault of the conscious mind, not as the unique fault of the artist:

> Consciousness, they say, cannot conceive of its negation, death.
> A bird's still carcass agitates the eye
> With novel images, a stranger's sudden end
> Is the beginning of much lively speculation.
> At eighty bereavement has become a familiar experience
> But every time some dear flesh disappears
> What is real is the arriving grief.

(This is a variation on a sentence Auden quoted frequently from Augustine's *Confessions*: "I would rather have been deprived of my friend than of my grief.")

When these lines reappeared as Prospero's address to Ariel in "The Sea and the Mirror," they became a specific accusation against the artistic imagination. Prospero is glad to have freed Ariel, glad to have renounced his art,

> So at last I can really believe I shall die.
> For under your influence death is inconceivable:
>   On walks through winter woods, a bird's dry carcass
> Agitates the retina with novel images,
>   A stranger's quiet collapse in a noisy street
> Is the beginning of much lively speculation,
>   And every time some dear flesh disappears
> What is real is the arriving grief.

The poet for whom a stranger's collapse gives rise to lively speculation is the same poet who can "make a vineyard of the curse" in Auden's elegy for Yeats, but he has abandoned his Yeatsian pretensions.

Someone always gains from the death of an innocent in Auden's poems, and Auden insisted on his guilty complicity. The death he wrote about was literally and legally murder only in dramatically charged circumstances like Herod's. Generally murder in his poems is invisible, a matter of intention that never erupts into action, or a projected image of his own survival and success. The audience in "The Sea and the Mirror"—in the speech made on its behalf by Caliban—takes the trouble to remind Shakespeare that he, like the successful hero in Auden's "The Quest," had stepped across a predecessor's skull.

And shouldn't you too, dear master, reflect—forgive us for mentioning it—
that we might very well not have been attending a production of yours this
evening, had not some other maybe—who can tell?—brighter talent married a
barmaid or turned religious and shy or gone down in a liner with all his manuscripts, the loss recorded only in the corner of some country newspaper below
A Poultry Lover's Jottings?

The thorn in the flesh that drives all these reminders of the artist's
survival is Auden's accusation against his own treatment of Kallman in
their first years together, when (as he now saw it) he tried to reshape an
autonomous person into the Galatea-spouse required by his wish for
marriage. He told his audience at a lecture about Shakespeare's sonnets
in 1946: "Art may spill over from creating a world of language into the
dangerous task—the dangerous and forbidden task—of trying to create
a human being." His impulse to murder had revealed the meaning of
his impulse to be married: an effort to shape the life of another person
seemed innocent enough as long as the other went through the motions
of cooperating, but it was no less an effacement of the other's reality
than the murderous wish that burst forth when the cooperation stopped.

═══

Auden's theme when he began "The Sea and the Mirror" was the isolating disaster of success. While planning this longer poem he wrote a
group of notably obscure shorter ones whose subject was, in the overheated words of one of them, "The hot rampageous horses of my will."
"Canzone," the least readable of these, has the cramped knotted style
Auden favored when writing in the first person about emotional agonies
he did not want to identify. Far from renouncing strict conventional
forms, as Auden told Spender he now must do, he made a grand show
of technical bravura by adopting the stanza form of Dante's *canzone* from
La vita nuova (still the model and rebuke for Auden's new life), in which
the same five end-words are used repeatedly through five twelve-line
stanzas and a five-line *envoi*. The poem is the most blatant instance of a
kind of verse Auden attempted during moods of existential intensity,
when he seemed deliberately to banish intellectual wit and verbal pleasure, as if a reader's mere enjoyment were incompatible with the perception of truth. Yet the technical challenge of working in a form like the
canzone was always deeply pleasurable for him, and the poem luxuriates
in its air of self-reproach. Written in the first person, it bristles with

accusations against its author, and fails partly because it never says what
he is accused of. "The Sea and the Mirror," in contrast, says nothing
about its author, but makes its accusations overwhelmingly clear.

"Canzone" presents itself as a cry of gratitude for the defeat of its
author's will. The poet's love was an instrument of that will, but "Love
/ Gives no excuse for evil done for love." The will wants the security of
possession and control: "What we love / Ourselves for is the power not
to love." (Or, as Auden wrote some years later, Narcissus finds self-
delight less in his own image than in "the satisfaction of not desiring the
nymphs.") The defeat of the will confirms a world of justice and love:

> If in this dark I less often know
> That spiral staircase where the haunted will
> Hunts for its stolen luggage, who should know
> Better than you, beloved, how I know
> What gives security to any world
> Or in whose mirror I begin to know
> The chaos of the heart as merchants know
> Their coins and cities, genius its own day?

Yet the similes in the last lines reveal that the poet's will has triumphed
in the act of proclaiming defeat. His knowledge of the chaos of his heart
is to him what coins and cities are to merchants, the medium and market
of his special wealth. The whole poem protests that artists gain no profit
from suffering, but Auden had been making poetry out of his suffering
from the moment he experienced it. He said so, elliptically but unmistakably, in the first of his pseudonymous "Lecture Notes," a few weeks
after writing "Canzone":

> Every child, as he wakes into life, finds a mirror underneath his pillow. Look
> in it he will and must, else he cannot know who he is, a creature fallen from
> grace, and this knowledge is a necessary preliminary to salvation. Yet at the
> moment that he looks into his mirror, he falls into mortal danger, tempted by
> guilt into a despair which tells him that his isolation and abandonment is irrev-
> ocable. It is impossible to face such abandonment and live, but as long as he
> gazes into the mirror he need not face it; he has at least his image as an illusory
> companion.

Auden seldom left his self-deceptions unanswered for long. In three
memorable and mysterious sonnets that he gathered under the title "The
Lesson," three dreams teach the poet to be grateful for defeat, but unlike

the histrionic "Canzone," these dreams are gentle, elusive, and deflating. At the end, in a seven-line demi-sonnet, the poet understands that all three dreams intend "one rebuke":

> For had not each
> In its own way tried to teach
> My will to love you that it cannot be,
> As I think, of such consequence to want
> What everyone is given, if they want?

The will to love brings none of the heated existential crises imagined in "Canzone"; it is what everyone is given if they want to love—which is not the same as wanting to be loved by someone else.

The three sonnets in "The Lesson" are studies in the egoism of romantic love. They are inverted sonnets, with the sestet preceding instead of following the octave, and the inversion is a sign that they turn back to the lover instead of outward to the beloved. In the dream in the first sonnet, "we were in flight" from civil war, but when we sought shelter in a "tall house,"* a clerk refused to admit us: our fantasy that romantic love can escape the chaos of the outer world was rebuked. In the second dream, after a kiss, "sudden flame and wind / Fetched you away" and left a silent empty plain where

> On a high chair alone
> I sat, a little master, asking why
> The cold and solid object in my hands
> Should be a human hand, one of your hands.

The pride of the poet's love is rebuked for making the loved one into an object, nothing more than a hand that can be held. And the third dream imagines the poet and his beloved at a "Victory Ball / After some tournament or dangerous test." The two lovers must have been the victors: "though there were crowns for all, / Ours were of gold, of paper all the rest." Then their triumph reveals its isolating punishment: "A sea of paper crowns rose up to dance; / Ours were too heavy; we did not dance."

What these poems do not say—although "The Sea and the Mirror" repeatedly does—is that success isolates because, in requiring another

---

* As in the dogs' "tall conditions" in "The Quest," "tall" is a relative term, here signifying the tall state of adulthood seen from the vantage point of a child.

person's failure, it is *criminal*. A single step divides the sense that one is alive because someone else is dead from the sense that one has success- fully willed someone else's death through the simple act of living. This was a matter too deep and dangerous for direct speech: Auden wrote about it at this time only in the analogical world of dramatic poetry, not in the expressive world of his first-person lyrics. A chorus in "For the Time Being" had taken an extreme view of the sinfulness even of the fertilized zygote's division into the undifferentiated cells of an embryo: "in / The germ-cell's primary division / Innocence is lost and sin, / Already given as a fact, / Once more issues as an act." In "The Sea and the Mirror" the speech that identifies this originating act as murder is the most morally and emotionally concentrated moment in the poem, the sestina spoken by Sebastian in which he identifies his wish to murder his brother, Alonso, as the same wish that willed him into his own life:

> To think his death I thought myself alive
> And stalked infected through the blooming day.

The only hint in *The Tempest* that Sebastian learns anything at all is his exclamation "A most high miracle!" when Ferdinand is seen alive and playing chess with Miranda. In "The Sea and the Mirror" Sebastian has been in intention, and almost in act, a murderer, and is now grateful that his own defeat has confirmed the reality of justice. For both Sebas- tian and his twentieth-century author, justice is the sign of mercy:

> Nothing has happened; we are all alive:
> I am Sebastian, wicked still, my proof
> Of mercy that I wake without a crown.

The judgment on Sebastian is also a gift of security and peace that lib- erates him from the anxiety of a world that had seemed disordered, un- predictable, and unjust:

> O blessed be bleak exposure on whose sword,
> Caught unawares, we prick ourselves alive!
> Shake Failure's bruising fist! Who else would crown
> Abominable error with a proof?
> I smile because I tremble, glad today
> To be ashamed, not anxious, not a dream.

The reality of defeat frees him from his fantasy of murderous success: "In dream all sins are easy, but by day / It is defeat gives proof we are alive." Or, as Caliban says near the end of the poem, only after all of life's various routes end in empty failure can we recognize their single alternative in a "Wholly Other Life," and see in its negative image of judgment the positive visage of mercy.

By writing "The Sea and the Mirror" as a series of monologues for fictional characters borrowed from Shakespeare, Auden could write autobiographically in a deeper and more comprehensive way than in his first-person lyrics. He expressed a different aspect of himself in each character, without masking that aspect behind a self-consciously public face. Sebastian's sestina, written in Auden's most stark and unornamented style, would, if paraphrased as a prose statement, seem almost identical to Auden's first-person "Canzone," but it achieves all the grandeur and intensity that "Canzone" heatedly fails to approach.

The sestina form is based, like the form of "Canzone," on a recurring pattern of end-words instead of rhymes. The cycle of end-words is as fixed and inescapable as judgment; and the Sebastian who accepts judgment is the one figure in the poem who made the choice to enter the formless amoral freedom of dream while knowing, unlike the unrepentant Antonio, that the waking world of judgment and mercy really exists.*

To think his death I thought myself alive. The murder that never quite occurs in "The Sea and the Mirror" was a murder that repeatedly did not quite occur in the thirty-five years of Auden's life. In 1944, a few months after he finished the poem, he wrote a letter to a friend, Beata Wachstein, one of Elizabeth Mayer's two daughters, commiserating on her miscarriage in a blithe tone that concealed the private depths of his theme: "Just a note to say how sorry I am about your misfortune, and to wish you better luck next time. My mother had a miscarriage before me, for which I cannot be sorry, because, if she hadn't, perhaps I shouldn't exist." Or, as he has Caliban say: "We should not be sitting here now, washed, warm, well-fed . . . unless there were others who are

---

* Because Auden altered the sequence of stanzas while revising his early drafts, the sestina slightly violates the traditional formula that governs the shifting position of end-words from one stanza to the next. The lucky effect of the change was to create a form that imitates Sebastian's moral status: "wicked still," as he says, but close enough to the moral order to know he stands outside it.

not here . . . others who have not been so fortunate, others who did not succeed in navigating the narrow passage."

Children make guilty equations. "The Sea and the Mirror" expiates the guilt of a child who believes his existence depends on the absence of another child, and who, somewhere outside the realm of conscious thought, suspects that, in defiance of the adult logic of space and time, he murdered the absent child in order to achieve his own birth afterward. When the adult Auden imagined the service he could perform in wartime, when he might be required to yield his life to protect others, he thought of enclosed places where he would be surrounded by water: the submarine service, the merchant marine. Looking at a Breughel in a museum a few years earlier, he had thought about a splash, a forsaken cry, and an expensive delicate ship that must have seen something amazing—a boy falling out of the sky—but had somewhere to get to and sailed calmly on. Auden wrote to Beata Wachstein some weeks after her miscarriage, almost certainly many days after he heard about it. His letter is dated 6 June, the day on which he and everyone else in America woke to the news of the invasion of Normandy, where thousands would die while he continued to live.

The obscure unarticulated struggle between Auden and himself in "The Sea and the Mirror," in which he simultaneously accused and vindicated himself, produced emotional splendors with few parallels in modern literature. The finished poem has the triumphant quality he wrote about in "Song for St. Cecilia's Day" when he praised the "trumpet that unguarded children blow / About the fortress of their inner foe." In his darkest imaginings about himself, he connected his illusory sense of guilt about his own birth with his inescapable sense of guilt about his homosexuality, his sense of it as criminal and isolating. The crime that was his sexuality was itself a punishment for an earlier crime. The obscure offense against childbirth that he had committed by being born was now punished, through a Dantesque *contrappasso* of the original act, by another obscure offense against childbirth. "About / blended flesh, those midnight colloquia of Derbies and Joans, / I know nothing," he wrote in "The Cave of Nakedness" in 1963, "about certain occult / antipathies perhaps too much." The occult antipathies of homosexuality were the punishment for a murderous crime; during the war years, his homosexuality, by keeping him out of combat, was his means of repeating the original crime as he preserved his life while others died.

Even the deepest motives change over time, and the deepest illusions can be broken. Auden's political and social sense of guilt in the 1930s (and again in works like "Horae Canonicae" in the 1950s) was not simply a disguised version of the personal guilt he felt during the war. The mind has no ultimate center of meaning to which all other meanings refer or from which they are derived: Auden's exemption from the draft and his revulsion against his efforts to reshape Kallman's personality combined to give a recurring pattern of thought and feeling a private erotic tinge that it had not had earlier and that, for many reasons, it would not have again. It is at least possible, however remotely, that his mother's miscarriage never occurred, that Auden's belief in it was projected back from his guilt over a murderous impulse. (His older brother John had never heard that his mother had miscarried until he was told much later about the letter to Beata Wachstein. Yet if the miscarriage in fact occurred, the child who preceded it might have had less motive to remember it than the child who came later.) A person who feels guilty for an imaginary crime simultaneously accepts guilt and revolts against it. In "A Summer Night," Auden wrote that his own comfort in an English house was allowed by a "doubtful act." The act may have been doubtful in two senses of the word: on one hand, it was doubtful and faithless in moral terms; on the other hand, it may never have happened at all.*

In the early 1940s Auden adopted the multiple voices of "For the Time Being" and "The Sea and the Mirror" partly in order to answer his false accusations against himself. The lonely, solitary voice of his lyric poems and "New Year Letter" was not so double as he claimed when he gave one of his books the title *The Double Man*. That single voice made accusations and found no answer. But the voices in Auden's dramatic poems include some who have much to feel guilty about—Herod, Sebastian, Prospero—and others who suffer no burden of shame or guilt—Mary, Ferdinand, Miranda. Sebastian says of his brother, "To think his death I thought myself alive," because he cannot imagine both their lives in the same world. But he is part of an implicit dialogue in which Miranda speaks of a lover who brought her to life without dimin-

---

* Auden's guilt about a miscarriage before he was born may help make sense of the baffling dream sequence at the end of *The Ascent of F6*, written in 1936. The climber Michael Ransom dreams he is playing chess with his rival brother when the brother suddenly dies; Ransom shouts that he didn't do it, that the Demon (revealed later in the scene as the brothers' mother) "gave the sign"; he then rushes to protect the Demon while the other dream figures proclaim the Demon's guilt. Auden and Isherwood dedicated the play to Auden's brother John, an expert mountaineer.

ishing or harming anyone else: "He kissed me awake, and no one was sorry."*

Outside his poems, Auden's moral vocabulary in the early 1940s—as it did throughout his life—attended to civil and political matters, always with a special focus on those who were unjustly excluded from the safe enclosing city. His letters to E. R. Dodds during the war regularly included brief reports on domestic American issues. In February 1944, while working on Caliban's speech, he told Dodds:

> The political outlook for postwar America is not too good. The race feeling (Negro in the South, Japanese and Mexican in the West, and Jewish in the East) is very bad indeed—incidentally, I hear Anti-Semitism is growing in England. Is this true?—and the Labor situation extremely dangerous. One of the troubles is that men go into Union organizing as a business and not from conviction—half of them could just as well be corporation lawyers . . . Anyway, there is a real danger, I think, of an anti-labor war-veteran movement after the war.

And six months later, in August 1944:

> My odds at present [on the November election] are 6–5 on Roosevelt. We are in, anyway, for a strong swing to the right, though, fortunately, the Southern Bourbons and the Northern Tycoons can never quite get together . . . I don't know if the British Press reported the Philadelphia Transit Worker strike which was a bad business. The strike [by white workers] was against the upgrading of Negro workers, and though their union leaders opposed the strike, it seems pretty clear that the majority of the rank and file approved.

When Auden began working on "The Sea and the Mirror," he recognized that Shakespeare was the writer who best understood the moral and aesthetic issues he was now trying to shape into a poem. Each of Shakespeare's comedies ends with one character pointedly excluded from the resolving dance. The triumph of a restored society, the education of a just ruler, the mutual recognition of chastened lovers—all these occur after someone else has been laughed offstage. Shakespeare's comedies nurture the darkness of tragedy, just as the solitary agonies of his tragedies end in a shared, renewing dawn. Mocked, discontented Malvolio sees himself as eloquent misunderstood Hamlet. No society achieves the coherence of the dance without convincing itself that the excluded de-

---

* "*Er küsst dich wach*": Siegfried, speaking of himself in the third person, sings this to Brünn-hilde in *Götterdämmerung*, Act 3. And everyone was sorry.

serve their exclusion, that nothing tragic has occurred, that the arbitrary line dividing insiders from outsiders is a natural border that must always be defended. Prospero, in *The Tempest*, forgives the faults of his brother, Antonio, in the same breath in which he refuses him brotherhood: "you, most wicked sir, whom to call brother / Would even infect my mouth." Caliban, speaking on behalf of the audience in "The Sea and the Mirror," knows that "without these prohibitive frontiers" between Us and Them, "we should never know who we were or what we wanted." Auden's private myth about a murder committed before he was born is transformed by the end of the poem into a public truth about real and continuing injustice.

In the last act of *The Tempest*, Prospero resolves to bury his staff and drown his books. In "The Sea and the Mirror," Auden, speaking through Prospero, Gonzalo, Trinculo, and Caliban, repeatedly resolves to renounce the powers of his art. But each time, he also says what he has Prospero say to Ariel after claiming to have set him free: "Stay with me, Ariel, while I pack." This was the same plea Auden had made to another departing figure two years earlier. Each time he renounced poetry he was turning away from one kind of poetry so that he could learn to write another. Prospero asks Ariel to sing

> To man, meaning me,
> As now, meaning always
> In love or out,
> Whatever that mean,
> Trembling he takes
> The silent passage
> Into discomfort.

In these lines Auden is also asking to be sustained by art while he begins to "attempt the *difficult*," as he called in it his letter to Spender. In the same letter he had suggested that his own "weakness" could help him: he was not (as he said Spender was) "jealous of someone else writing a good poem because it seems a rival strength," but felt instead that "every good poem . . . is a strength, which is put at my disposal." In the 1940s Auden, like Shakespeare before him, learned to write his best work—and was most himself—in voices he learned from others.

Both Auden's Prospero and Auden himself knew that art can be truthful in ways an artist cannot. In "New Year Letter" poets produce from
their "soiled, shabby, egotistic lives" masterworks that remain "large,
magnificent, and calm." In Prospero's speech in "The Sea and the Mirror" art is again a unique source of clarity, order, and truth, but is simultaneously available for corrupt misuse. Prospero has begun to learn
"the difference between moonshine and daylight," between the magical
enchantment that claims the status of art and art itself. In private life this
was the difference between the love that interferes with another person
for the other's good and the love that desires another's self-fulfillment.
Prospero renounces his power over others because he "knows now what
magic is:—the power to enchant / That comes from disillusion." Enchantment imposes one will upon another, but art imposes nothing on
anyone, and "makes nothing happen." As Prospero says to Ariel,

> we have only to learn to sit still and give no orders,
> To make you offer us your echo and your mirror;
> We have only to believe you, then you dare not lie;
> To ask for nothing, and at once from your calm eyes,
> With their lucid proof of apprehension and disorder,
> All we are not stares back at what we are.

The authentic work of art, because it has no designs on its reader, no
wish to seduce anyone into collusion or flatter anyone into action, can
see behind the masks of a reader's fear:

> For all things,
> In your company, can be themselves: historic deeds
> Drop their hauteur and speak of shabby childhoods
> When all they longed for was to join in the gang of doubts
> Who so tormented them.

A few months later, Auden restated this as the opening of a review of
T. S. Eliot's selection of Kipling's verse but added a further point:

Art, as the late Professor R. G. Collingwood pointed out, is not Magic, i.e., a
means by which the artist communicates or arouses his feelings in others, but
a mirror in which they may become conscious of what their own feelings really
are: its proper effect, in fact, is disenchanting.
    By significant details it shows us that our present state is neither as virtuous
nor as secure as we thought, and by the lucid pattern into which it unifies these
details, its assertion that order is *possible*, it faces us with the command to make
it *actual*. In so far as he is an artist, no one, not even Kipling, is intentionally

a magician. On the other hand, no artist, not even Eliot, can prevent his work from being used as magic, for that is what all of us, highbrow and lowbrow alike, secretly want Art to be.

In "The Sea and the Mirror" Prospero understands only half of this. Speech, as he perceives it, is either indicative or subjunctive, not imperative, not the voice of an absolute demand or expectation. The only truth he can imagine is the truth of silence. It does not occur to him that others, like Alonso and Gonzalo, can hear an unconditional command and a promise of peace in the sounds he understands only as the sweet and dangerous songs of Ariel.

But until these other voices are heard later in the poem, everything Prospero says seems plausible. His disenchanted understanding of the artist's cold manipulation of his material is eloquent and truthful, and corresponds exactly to Auden's publicly stated views on art. Yet "The Sea and the Mirror" repeatedly invites its reader to assent to one character's plausible argument, then brings in another character who explodes it. The poem is designed to educate and disenchant through a progressive sequence of disillusionments. Art, Auden wrote in his review, is not a means by which an artist induces his own feelings in others, yet the disillusionment and disenchantment induced by "The Sea and the Mirror" duplicate Auden's disenchantment with his own manipulative powers. Like Prospero, he retained his powers in the act of renouncing them.

Prospero's judgments on the other characters in the play are among the most cunning instances of Auden's disenchanting technique. Prospero knows so much about his own limits—"Can I learn to suffer / Without saying something ironic or funny / On suffering?"—that we inevitably assume he also knows about everyone else's. His quick, lucid portraits of the other characters are convincing to anyone who has met them in *The Tempest*:

> weak Sebastian will be patient
> In future with his slothful conscience—after all, it pays;
>   Stephano is contracted to his belly, a minor
> But a prosperous kingdom; stale Trinculo receives,
>   Gratis, a whole fresh repertoire of stories and
> Our younger generation its independent joy . . .
>   Will Ferdinand be as fond of a Miranda
> Familiar as a stocking? Will a Miranda who is
>   No longer a silly lovesick little goose,

When Ferdinand and his brave world are her profession,
Go into raptures over existing at all?

The only trouble with these portraits is that they are wrong. The characters of "The Sea and the Mirror" are not quite those of *The Tempest*, and their inner voices reveal greater depths than Auden's Prospero imagines. Some years later, in liner notes for a recording of *Cavalleria Rusticana* and *I Pagliacci*, Auden wrote: "We can never be certain that we know what is going on in the hearts of others, though we usually overestimate our knowledge—both the shock of discovering an infidelity and the tortures of jealousy are due to this." This names the source of Prospero's errors and identifies the suffering that Prospero was able to avoid because Ariel, unlike Kallman, was not a figure of flesh and blood.

Auden's Sebastian, far from accepting virtue because it pays, as Prospero thinks he does, combines a religious dread of absolute judgment with religious gratitude for absolute mercy. The taut metaphysical paradox of his closing line—"The sword we suffer is the guarded crown"—states that the sword of judgment is inseparable from the crown of glory, but not as he imagined when he hoped to usurp a crown by wielding a sword. The judgment against him manifests a mercy that guards itself against him, while it crowns "abominable error with a proof"; and the guarded crown is, as Auden wrote of the will to love in "The Lesson," "what anyone is given, if they want." Stephano, too, in his address to his belly, demonstrates a less sophisticated but more profound understanding of the body-mind dualism than anything in Prospero's aesthetics: "When mind meets matter, both should woo . . . / The will of one by being two / At every moment is denied": through the marriage of body and mind, the isolating will of each is defeated, to the benefit of both.

Ferdinand's love for Miranda is sustained by his religious sense that his erotic love depends on "another tenderness," which he hears "Pleading with ours for us"—a divine love that lovingly desires fulfillment for its human counterpart. For Auden's Christian Ferdinand, the mutual relation of human and divine love means that neither of these two tendernesses "without either could or would possess" the object of its love. Miranda will indeed become as familiar to Ferdinand as a stocking, but the divinity whom Ferdinand identifies (in phrases that he evidently found in the tales of Henry James) as "The Right Required Time, the Real Right Place, O Light," retains forever its love-sustaining awe.

Miranda herself, closing the middle chapter of "The Sea and the Mirror" with a villanelle that is the most subtle and delicate of all Auden's lyrics, defends her love against precisely the suffocating ordinariness that Prospero casually assumes must leave her defenseless. Miranda knows better. Two lines in her final stanza—

> So to remember our changing garden, we
> Are linked as children in a circle dancing

—quietly acknowledge a power stronger than change. Their linked dance is the type and prophecy of remembrance and commitment, and its strength is the same strength inherent in the circle Miranda will soon wear on her left hand, the strength of remembrance that, because it is prepared for change, will not alter when it alteration finds.*

Her lines generously locate in that dancing circle all the voices of the central chapter of the poem, voices that alternate between the courtly elevation of Ferdinand, Gonzalo, Alonso, and Sebastian, and the plebeian bluntness of Stephano, Trinculo, and the Master and Boatswain, and even the camp triviality of Adrian and Francisco.† With her nursery-rhyme language, she alone understands the link between love and polity: "My Dear One is mine as mirrors are lonely, / As the poor and sad are real to the good king." Her stanzas close with one of two recurring lines: "My dear one is mine as mirrors are lonely" (early drafts have "true" instead of "mine"), alternating with "And the high green hill sits always by the sea." The second affirms as a physical fact the marriage of the two sexes; the first points to a troublingly ambiguous mystery of love that in "The Sea and the Mirror" (and here) can be explained only near the end.

Just as Prospero underestimates the moral depth of the other characters, he fails to notice that he is not the only artist in the cast. Gonzalo

---

* At around the time Auden was writing Miranda's poem he wrote the most agonized of his surviving statements about his sexuality. He told Elizabeth Mayer on 20 February 1943: "Being 'anders wie die Andern' [*Anders als die Andern*, "Different from Others," was the first sympathetic film treatment of homosexuality, made in 1919] has its troubles. There are days when the knowledge that there will never be a place which I can call home, that there will never be a person with whom I shall be one flesh, seems more than I can bear, and if it wasn't for you, and a few—how few—like you, I don't think I could." This last phrase identifies the private meaning of his lines to her in "New Year Letter": "Always there are such as you / Forgiving, helping what we do."
† Adrian and Francisco's line "It's madly ungay when the goldfish die" alludes to an anecdote told among Auden's English friends about a young man who was heard to remark at a lunch party during the Spanish Civil War that it was "madly ungay in Spain this summer."

repents his "booming eloquence," in which "Honesty became untrue," just as Auden repented his public voice, and he also regrets his "interference" that "by speculation froze / Vision into an idea, / Irony into a joke," leaving him "convicted of / Doubt and insufficient love." (This booming eloquence is the same interference with others for their own good that Auden warned himself against in "Many Happy Returns.") Gonzalo has been restored by crisis: "a storm's decision gave / His subjective passion back / To a meditative man." Like Auden isolated by his art, Trinculo, "the cold clown / Whose head is in the clouds," knows that the emotion provoking his art differs from the emotion his art provokes:

> A terror shakes my tree,
> A flock of words fly out,
> Whereat a laughter shakes
> The busy and devout.

As Auden's Prospero renounces art so that "at last I can really believe I shall die," Trinculo hopes to return to the realm of the living and dying:

> Wild images, come down
> Out of your freezing sky,
> That I, like shorter men,
> May get my joke and die.

The unrepentant villain Antonio, refusing in Dantesque triplets to join in the harmonies made by Prospero's art, knows more about the motives and powers of art than Prospero can guess. Prospero imagines that reconciliation can be achieved by knowledge alone, and has never heard of mutual forgiveness: "Both of us know," Prospero says of himself and Antonio, "That both were in the wrong and neither need be sorry." Every word of this is wrong. Prospero does not understand that Antonio in his enmity insists on staying outside the artist's tidy circle, and that this eternal refusal forces the artist to persist in a futile attempt to make his artistic harmonies permanent and complete. "Break your wand in half, / The fragments will join; burn your books or lose / Them in the sea, they will soon reappear, / Not even damaged."

Theologically and psychologically shrewd as he is, Antonio is unconvincing as the speaker of a monologue, because he embodies the motiveless malignity that, after it is revealed, withdraws into total silence.

Like Iago, who says he "never will speak word," Antonio says of himself, "One tongue is silent . . . / My language is my own." In his final lines, Antonio gloats over the peace he refuses his brother, Prospero, who therefore will

> Never have time to curl up at the center
> Time turns on when completely reconciled,
> Never become and therefore never enter
> The green occluded pasture as a child.

But the interweaving of child and pasture—a metaphor borrowed from Tillich's account in *The Interpretation of History* of Christ as the center of time—is something the Antonio of the rest of the speech is too malignant to imagine.* Antonio becomes convincing only by ceasing to be Antonio. Near the end of "The Sea and the Mirror" Caliban acknowledges the paradox Auden confronted in writing a harmonious poem for the discordant Antonio—the same paradox faced by any writer who understands that "the brighter his revelation of the truth in its order, its justice, its joy, the fainter shows his picture of your actual condition in all its drabness and sham." Like all great poems, "The Sea and the Mirror" provides the means of understanding its own flaws.

Antonio has chosen to stand outside, and from there he interjects after every speech by the other members of the cast a mocking refrain that begins with "One," ends with "alone," and asserts variously that "My will is all my own," "My person is my own," that his nature, language, audience, empire, compass, conscience, humor, and magic are all "my own." "One link is missing," he says after Miranda speaks of children linked in a circle dancing. But Antonio is another poor cheated Mephistopheles who brings about exactly what he thinks he is preventing, for it is his recurring refrain that links the speeches of all the others and draws the circle that Miranda delights in. Antonio is right in whispering to Prospero: "while I stand outside / Your circle, the will to charm is

---

* To Isherwood, Auden described "Iago-Antonio" as "the man made demonic by art and failure because he cannot forgive forgiveness," in contrast to Sebastian, who is "the man redeemed by art and failure." Other summary portraits in the same March 1944 letter included Adrian and Francisco, who represent the "flight from anxiety into chic," the Master and Boatswain as the "flight from anxiety into passivity and circumstance," Stephano as the "flight from anxiety into unconsciousness (body)," and Trinculo as the "flight from anxiety into wit (mind)." But Auden's explanations have an after-the-fact air, and his terminology refers less to "The Sea and the Mirror" than to the poem he began a few months later, *The Age of Anxiety*.

still there." But neither the gloating, persistent Antonio nor the weary, cynical Prospero knows what Ferdinand and Miranda know, which is that in a universe of forgiveness, an imperfect, incomplete circle is enough.

═══

After the characters demonstrate how wrong Prospero is about all of them, Caliban strips the masks from their faces. The delicate emotion and fairy-tale language of Miranda's villanelle is followed immediately by Caliban's disenchanting reminder of the artifice that made her: "If now, having dismissed your hired impersonators with verdicts ranging from the laudatory orchid to the disgusted and disgusting egg . . ." This disjunctive moment continues to bother Auden's readers, but as he told Theodore Spencer, "Your irritation at the disunity is, justifiably or not, the effect I intend." Shakespeare's Caliban, he continued,

> does disturb me profoundly because he doesn't fit in; it is exactly as if one of the audience had walked onto the stage and insisted on taking part in the action. I've tried to work for this effect in a non-theatrical medium, by allowing the reader for the first two chapters not to think of the theatre (by inversion, therefore, to be witnessing a performance) and then suddenly wake him up in one (again by inversion, introducing "real life" into the imagined).

The astonishing variety of style and metre in the earlier chapters served to demonstrate that formal verse can express any experience and sympathize with any personality. Caliban's flexible, inclusive prose demonstrates by contrast the narrow limits of verse. And his lush, logical demolition of everyone's hopeful pretenses—Auden's included—exposes the comfortable self-deception of an audience that sympathizes with fictional characters and forgets about real ones.

Caliban speaks in a hypertrophied version of the late style of Henry James, a style that in Auden's hands accommodates sentences three pages long, shifts effortlessly between Latinate elevation and rude slang, and, while echoing James's moral seriousness, also imitates (as Auden's poem about James three years earlier did not) his lethal wit. Despite the artifice of Caliban's voice, he embodies everything that is not artifice. The id is one name for him; he identifies himself at one point as Eros, son of Venus; and Auden identified him to Spencer as the allegorical figure of "the Prick."* The id has no language, and at first Auden was "completely stuck" (as he told both Spencer and Isherwood) when trying to find one for him in May 1943. In July he told Elizabeth Mayer that he had "struck oil on the third part of the Tempest stuff after fruitless prospecting of 3 months." He spoke too soon. He had begun and abandoned verse speeches variously addressed to Caliban and about him, and now drafted a speech for Caliban himself that began with a reminder of the existential darkness beyond the well-lit stage:

> Ladies and gentlemen, please keep your seats,
> An unidentified plane is reported
> Approaching the city. Probably only a false alarm
> But naturally, we cannot afford
> To take any chances.

But this led nowhere, and as he told Spencer, he needed another three months before he "suddenly got the James idea; it seemed blindingly 'right,' and bar[ring] outside distractions the writing went without a hitch."

What was blindingly right to him was his realization that (as he explained later) "since Caliban is inarticulate, he has to borrow, from Ariel, the most artificial style possible, i.e. that of Henry James." Because this style need not express Caliban's personality—the id has none—it is free to express and include everything that comes to hand. Twenty years after Auden wrote this, academic literary theorists began to argue that all literary language must be understood as written, not spoken, that it issues from no human voice. In his lonely months of prospecting in 1943, Auden arrived at the same theory and devised a practice for it, but he also understood that a writer's choice of one kind of artifice rather than another is an expression of personal depths. In a lost letter to Auden, Spencer seems to have recognized this. "I'm extremely pleased and surprised," Auden replied, "to find that at least one reader feels that the section written in a pastiche of James is more me than the sections written in my own style, because it is the paradox I was trying for, and am afraid that hardly anyone will get."

Auden admired James's style for the same reason he admired James's

---

* "It's OK to say that Ariel is Chester," Auden told Isherwood in a letter in 1944, "but Chester is also Caliban . . . Ariel is Caliban seen in the mirror."

content. He told a lecture audience in 1946: "Without exception, so far as I know, the characters in Henry James are concerned with moral choices; they may choose evil, but we are left in no doubt about the importance of choosing it." The "exquisite formal beauty" of James's style is the product as well as the vehicle of choices, Auden thought; it exists solely for the sake of fiction and serves no practical purpose. In 1943, when Auden was working to give up his "camp of tough aggressiveness," James's style, because its artifice was so emphatic, was paradoxically the least "camp" style he could imagine: it was *all* pose, therefore no one's real posture, and could never be taken as a dramatic impersonation—or so he believed until James's notebooks appeared in print in 1947. Auden, like most other readers, realized then for the first time that James's style was not so much an artifice devised for the sake of fiction as it was his native mode of thought. Auden told a friend: "The notebooks show he was writing like that all the time. And I find that a very suspect attitude for an artist." And he remarked a few years later, in a praising review of Keats's letters: "Reading Rilke's letters or the Journal of Henry James . . . there are times when their tone of hushed reverence before the artistic mystery becomes insufferable and one would like to give them both a good shaking."

Caliban's eight thousand words are continuously surprising and exhilarating when read sentence by sentence, but only intermittently convincing in the dialectical argument that shapes the whole. They are organized as an elaborate series of monologues and dialogues in which Caliban impersonates all the voices. He speaks first (he explains) as the audience's echo; he interrupts himself to adopt the voice of Shakespeare, no less; then, among further interruptions in his own voice, he speaks for the two classes into which audiences are traditionally divided, crude sensation-seekers in the pit and elite intellectuals in the gallery; and he ends on behalf of Ariel and himself.

The audience, in the first section, pleads with Shakespeare to answer their baffled questions about *The Tempest*. They are dismayed to find Caliban, the embodiment of anarchic physical disorder, let loose in the decorous world of art, which they had always imagined as an aristocratic realm of fantasy that gave them pleasure precisely because it was so different from reality. If the world of art should suddenly be afflicted by the same anxieties and uncertainties that afflict their own, it would no longer offer them a pleasurable myth of escape. Even more dismaying is their fear that when Ariel, the principle of abstract aesthetic order, was set free at the end of *The Tempest*, he may have been let loose into the world of life, "breaking down our picket fences in the name of fraternity, seducing our wives in the name of romance, and robbing us of our sacred pecuniary deposits in the name of justice."* The playgoers happily applaud anyone who serves fraternity, romance, and justice in art, so long as no one requires them to serve the same ends in life.

As he begins the second part of his speech, Caliban asks the audience's patience while he delivers "a special message" from Shakespeare to any young writer (Auden's earlier self, for example) who came to this performance of *The Tempest* in the hope of learning "more clearly just how the artistic contraption works." The lesson is not about impersonal craftsmanship, however, but about the personal significance to the writer of Prospero's relations with Ariel and Caliban. Shakespeare's message takes the form of a summary life story of a dramatist or other writer of fictional plots; it is told in the second person because it is the typical story of any writer, including the young writer to whom it is addressed. The story opens (Shakespeare says) on the day when, "in the middle of a salt marsh or at the bottom of a kitchen garden or on the top of a bus," Ariel called you to your artistic vocation. Since then, with Ariel's faithful aid, you have won ever greater victories over problems of form and content, and the collaboration between "magician and familiar" has grown deeper and more intimate. Then, one day, the relation turns faintly sour. Ariel's persistence in "standing around, waiting for orders," seems oppressive, because (Shakespeare unmistakably implies) you now want ordinary human embraces instead of the Midas touch that transforms everyone into material for your art. "You finally manage to stammer or shout 'You are free. Good-bye,' but to your dismay He whose obedience through all the enchanted years has never been less than perfect, now refuses to budge." After nurturing your artistic imagination for a lifetime, you cannot wish it away, and are appalled to discover that its shaping aesthetic power is, and has always been, an elegant camouflage for the resentful fury of the id:

> Striding up to Him in fury, you glare into His unblinking eyes and stop dead, transfixed with horror at seeing reflected there, not what you had always expected to see, a conqueror smiling at a conqueror, both promising mountains and marvels, but a gibbering fist-clenched creature with whom you are all too

* The picket fence, like many other details in the speech, signals Auden's growing wish to write in American. A few pages later, as he told Theodore Spencer, he took the "sugarloaf sea" (having huge pyramidal waves) from *The American Thesaurus of Slang*, by Lester V. Berrey and Melvin Van den Bark, published in 1942.

unfamiliar, for this is the first time indeed that you have met the only subject
that you have, who is not a dream amenable to magic but the all too solid flesh
you must acknowledge as your own; at last you are come face to face with me
[Caliban], and are appalled to learn how far I am from being, in any sense,
your dish.

That gibbering creature sounds remarkably like Auden as he later described himself: "forced to know in person what it is like to feel oneself
in the prey of demonic powers . . . stripped of self-control and self-
respect." Caliban ends by telling the young writer that in the punishing
loneliness after their crisis, "we shall have, as we both know only too
well, no company but each other's."

These opening sections of Caliban's speech are organized as an antithesis of audience and artist, but Auden's subtle and luxurious style makes
the parallels between them almost imperceptible. In the sections that
follow—the final third of the speech—the dialectical machinery clanks
loudly into view as Caliban addresses the two classes in the audience:
"assorted, consorted specimens of the general popular type" and "important persons at the top of the ladder." In making this distinction,
Auden seems to have forgotten his own lesson that modern industrial
civilization makes everyone an exceptional reflective K., and the latter
parts of the speech seem shaped more by arbitrary oppositions than by
knowledge or experience.

The specimens of the general popular type are still dismayed (as they
were before Caliban interrupted himself to address the young artist) by
the obligations imposed on them by abstract order. Caliban cannot help
them, he says, because their dismay shows that they know they have
entered adulthood, and must therefore now confront the accusing difference between what they are and what they should be. They are still
in an undifferentiated "Grandly Average Place," something like a railway
terminus, but the choice they are obliged to make will transport them
"far outside this land of habit" to one of the many "despotic certainties
of failure or success."

When they arrive there, Caliban tells them, they will almost inevitably
beg to be taken back on his fleshly shoulders. Their wish takes the form
of nostalgia for a childhood of sensual satisfaction that never was, and
which they can only imagine as the absence of adult constraint. As in a
fairy tale, their wish is granted, but what they get is not what they need.
Instead of arriving at the "specific Eden which your memory necessarily
but falsely conceives of as the ultimately liberal condition," they find

themselves in a barren isolating landscape of random geysirs and extinct volcanoes, where "your existence is indeed free at last to choose its own meaning." Having refused the possibility of any meaning or obligation outside themselves, they can choose only to "plunge headlong into despair and fall through silence fathomless and dry."

Meanwhile, the successful few in the audience—executives, scholars, professionals, heirs to great fortunes—have chosen an alternative route toward a different kind of release. Too sophisticated to look back to a fetishistic Eden, too sated to imagine they can find satisfaction in sensual particulars, they long for the unchanging realm of abstract order, the "Heaven of the Really General Case," where everything can be clarified into one overarching idea. Ariel, Caliban tells them, must instantly grant their wish to be taken there, because they break their relation to the world in the act of wishing to transcend it. Yet, he continues, because they cannot rise above the world of matter, they remain among the particularities of their lives, but now so alienated from them that everything seems meaningless. They can go anywhere they want, but "any sense of direction . . . is completely absent." (Auden presciently described this elsewhere as the idol of the present age: "a belief, approaching superstition, in the presentational immediacy . . . of a fact, and a doubt, approaching denial, of its having any further meaning or value." This is what made the typical contemporary literary production "the diary, the true confession, the autobiographical novel" forms "as 'factual' and without pattern as a telephone directory.")

Caliban's wholesale accusations of failure do not exempt the poet who wrote them, and his relentless logic leads to the paradox that a work of art fails to the degree that it succeeds. The goal of art, Caliban says, is "to make you unforgettably conscious of the ungarnished offended gap between what you so questionably are and what you are commanded without any question to become." (Caliban omits pleasure from his theory of art because, being inhuman, he does not know what it is.) The more convincingly an artist portrays an imaginary realm of order and coherence, the more he distracts attention from the aimless disorder of the real world. Conversely, "the more truthfully he paints the condition, the less clearly can he indicate the truth from which it is estranged." An artist who understands this paradox knows he can be rescued from it only by a power outside himself. Renouncing magic, he must hope that "some unforeseen mishap," like an absurd misprint, will "ruin his effect, without, however, obliterating . . . the expectation aroused by him that there was an effect to ruin." (This is Auden's moral justification for the low puns and comic asides in his most serious poems.)

Auden still imagined he was tracing a via negativa in which a sense of total estrangement leads to a saving leap of faith. When Caliban ends, everyone has been forced to admit failure—even Ariel and Caliban himself, who are, the latter says, "just as deeply involved as any of you." This is "when we do at last see ourselves as we are . . . swaying out on the ultimate wind-whipped cornice that overhangs the unabiding void— we have never stood anywhere else." With no place to turn, we finally acknowledge "that Wholly Other life"—the *ganz andere*, as Rudolf Otto named the holy, in a phrase echoed throughout the theology of Barth, Niebuhr, and Tillich. The "contrived fissures of mirror and proscenium arch"—the self-regarding theatrical performances that have been our whole lives until now—can be understood not as mere falsehoods but as "feebly figurative signs" of a truth beyond signs and figuration, the "essential emphatic gulf" between ourselves and the Wholly Other.

In the realm of the Wholly Other, Caliban continues, "all our meanings are reversed and it is precisely in its negative image of Judgment that we can positively envisage Mercy." This restates Sebastian's theme that mercy is implicit in judgment, but in a vocabulary that is generalized, impersonal, and plural: no individual person experiences judgment in the flesh; no personal god uses words to promise mercy. In our total failure, we may "rejoice in the perfected Work which is not ours," yet that work has no name. It can be described only by abstract adjectives: the Unconditional, the Unconfined, the Absolute. When Caliban tries to describe it, he turns uncharacteristically vague.

> Its great coherences stand out through our secular blur in all their overwhelmingly righteous obligation; its voice speaks through our muffling banks of artificial flowers and unflinchingly delivers its authentic molar* pardon; its spaces greet us with all their grand old prospect of wonder and width; the working charm is the full bloom of the unbothered state; the sounded note is the restored relation.

Near the beginning of "The Sea and the Mirror," Prospero said he had never suspected until he freed Ariel that "the way of truth / Was a way

---

* Auden found this word in a book by Wolfgang Köhler, *The Place of Value in a World of Fact* (1938), which he had cited in the notes to "New Year Letter." Köhler refers to "the 'macroscopic' or 'molar' aspect of the physical world" (p. 169).

of silence." This is the poem's explanation for loquacious Caliban's inability to be convincing when he turns to matters of ultimate truth. But the hollow grandeur of Caliban's climactic lines is perhaps an early sign that Auden was not so convinced as he thought by the theology of an inexpressible Absolute.

Because Caliban is a voice without a face, he assumes that an abstract theological system is more illuminating and true than concrete personal experiences. Yet throughout his final paragraph are reminders that Auden had already found a more humane and less objective language of judgment and mercy, and had used it in the same poem when writing speeches for mere human voices. Caliban completes the partial thoughts of the other characters by explaining what they had left unsaid, although he cannot experience what he explains. The mystery of Miranda's formula—"My dear one is mine as mirrors are lonely"—explains itself at last when Caliban refers to "our contrived fissures of mirror and proscenium arch" as signs of the gulf that divides us from the Wholly Other. For Caliban the theologian, that dangerous gulf is bridged, as soon as we perceive it, by the antithetical relation of judgment and mercy. For Miranda, it is bridged by love: my dear one can be mine because in my lonely act of looking in a mirror—a truthful, not a flattering, one—I recognize my need for him. The gulf Miranda crosses when she acknowledges her loneliness is the same gulf bridged by Ferdinand in his sonnet when he hears "pleading with ours for us, another tenderness."

Caliban's map of the "alternative routes" by which human fear seeks release through either Ariel or Caliban is a redrawing in theological terms of the political and poetic map Alonso draws in the long letter he writes to Ferdinand halfway through the middle chapter, at the poem's structural center. Caliban's unyielding vision is appropriate to an impersonal principle, but Alonso's more humane vision is the work of a chastened father and king who loves his son the prince. The dialectical structure of abstraction and instinct that seems chilly and arbitrary when expounded by Caliban is plausible and moving when Alonso uses it to understand his own suffering.

As an expert reader of Alfred North Whitehead, Alonso knows civilization to be a precarious balance of trivial order and barbaric vagueness. On Ferdinand's coronation day, the young king may wish to forget the wastes beyond his borders, but he will be threatened nonetheless by "the waters where fish / See sceptres descending with no wish / To touch them," and "the sands where a crown / Has the status of a broken-down / Sofa or mutilated statue." Alonso can imagine, as Caliban cannot, a civilized middle way "Between the watery vagueness and / The triviality of the sand," because Alonso has experienced time and change, not instantaneous antitheses. He sees the way of adult voluntary life as a passage through time "From loose craving to sharp aversion, / Aimless jelly to paralyzed bone," between the extremes of vagueness at birth and triviality at death.

"Tao is a tightrope," Auden had warned the seven-year-old boy he had addressed in "Many Happy Returns" a year earlier.* Now Alonso warns Ferdinand: "The Way of Justice is a tightrope / Where no prince is safe for one instant / Unless he trust his embarrassment." Ferdinand's "embarrassment" is that half of himself that he most dreads and by which he is most tempted. Alonso does not pretend to know whether Ferdinand will try to repress his lusts by fleeing into abstract thought or try to forget the loneliness of thought by fleeing into sensuality. Both temptations are delusory: "the fire and the ice / Are never more than one step away / From the temperate city." Both lead to private and public grief: "Many young princes soon disappear / To join all the unjust kings."

Alonso, having survived the tempest, knows that Ferdinand too, by choosing one or the other temptation, may come to a crisis "Where thought accuses and feeling mocks." At the climax of his letter, he draws the lesson that Auden learned from his own crisis:

> Believe your pain: praise the scorching rocks
> For their desiccation of your lust,
> Thank the bitter treatment of the tide
> For its dissolution of your pride.

Your suffering, Alonso continues, can transform itself into a gift of freedom from the disappointments of power and lust. Accept it,

> That the whirlwind may arrange your will
> And the deluge release it to find
> The spring in the desert, the fruitful

---

* "By the by," Auden asked Ursula Niebuhr on 19 December 1941, "have you ever read Arthur Waley's *The Way and Its Power*, a translation of the Quietist Tao Tê Ching? It has some wonderful stuff in it" (Library of Congress).

Island in the sea, where flesh and mind
Are delivered from mistrust.*

In Alonso's experience of the restored relation, each of the two partial realms of flesh and mind is rescued and redeemed not by an Absolute, immeasurably distant from both, but each by the other. As Miranda knows, the high green hill sits always by the sea.

In a closing stanza suffused with pardon and miracles, Alonso recalls his release from crisis as a vision of resurrection. He can now face death without fear, "rejoicing in a new love, / A new peace, having heard the solemn / Music strike and seen the statue move / To forgive our illusion." The statue is that of Hermione in *The Winter's Tale,* which, at the words "Music, awake her; strike!" steps down from its pedestal as a living woman, restoring a wife to her husband and a mother to her child. Caliban's theology saw no reconciliation of art and truth, but Alonso can give thanks for his vision in the same lines in which he admits to being a fictional character in a book of plays.

———

While Auden was writing Alonso's letter, in the spring of 1943, he was teaching a seminar at Swarthmore on "Romanticism from Rousseau to Hitler" (the printed catalogue more tactfully called it "Romanticism"), in which he handed out to his students manuscript pages of quotations and pensées (including some that later appeared in his pseudonymous "Lecture Notes"). One day, without comment, he put on the seminar table a diagram of the two alternative routes described in Caliban's speech and in Alonso's letter, and the middle route between them. The chart, reproduced here, is perhaps the most provocative and intelligent page of notes about a poem ever given to a college class by an instructor.

---

* For Stephano, Alonso, and Caliban, the mutual mistrust of flesh and mind leads to crisis. But the same mistrust had briefly dissolved, without benefit of crisis, in "The Model," a shorter poem Auden wrote in the autumn of 1942, when he was beginning work on "The Sea and the Mirror." The solution he imagined in the poem was not one available to Auden himself, because "The Model" describes an eighty-year-old woman, sitting for a portrait, whose "body . . . exactly indicates her mind." At eighty "Even a teeny-weeny bit of greed" (the phrasing dates from the other end of her life) "Makes one very ill indeed / And a touch of despair is instantaneously fatal." Time forgives her, not because she worshiped language, but because "she forgave; she became." Being coherent in herself, she can make the world cohere around her. The painter can please himself by putting any objects he likes into the background: "She will compose them all / Centring the eye on their essential human element" (*Collected Poems,* p. 329).

PARADISE
(Eden)
Essential Being

The Fall

	HELL of the Pure Deed — Power without Purpose	← Search for Salvation by finding refuge in Nature — THIS WORLD Dualism of Experience, Knowledge of Good and Evil, Existential Being — Search for Salvation by finding release from Nature →			HELL of the Pure Word — Knowledge without Power
Primary Symbol	Sea — Common Night	Forest	City	Mountain	Private Light — Desert
Secondary Symbols	Blood — Tears — Serpents	Wild Beasts	Domestic Pets	Birds	Machines — Insects — Abstract shapes
Myth Symbols	Dragons — Sirens — Hidden Treasure	Dwarves, Giants	The Hero, The Ring	Witches	Ghosts — The Magician's Castle
Metaphysical Condition	Pure Aesthetic Immediacy / Pure Ethical Potentiality	Art	Actualization of the Possible / Growth / Soul=Spirit	Science	Aesthetic Nonentity / Pure Ethical Actuality
Order	Monist Unity (water) / Barbaric Vagueness	Rivers / Country	Differentiated Unity / Civilization	Roads / Town	Dissociated Multiplicity / Decadent Triviality
Time	Natural Cyclical Reversible Everlasting — Circle change (○)	Historical	Irreversible Process Change — Spiral	Static	Eternal Unchanging — Turbine (◎)
Relation between Selves	Mutual Irresponsibility Encroachment	The Vow	Conscious relations Neighborliness	The Contract	Mutual Aversion Desertion
Relation to Self	Self-sufficiency	Low brow Masses	Self-Realization	High brow Rulers	Self-negation
Mental Life	Stream of Sensations	Sensation / Memory / Intuition	Generalized patterns of feeling / Important facts	Thinking / Logic / Feeling	Empty Abstractions
Requiredness	Objective Instinctive Determined	Venere Vulgare / Blind Eros	Subjective Grace / Agape	Venere Celeste / Seeing Anteros	Conscious lack of requiredness / The void of Indecision or Self-Reflection
Sin	Sensuality	{ Criminals / Bohemians	Anxiety	Police / Bourgeois Pharisees }	Pride
Sex	Incest (The Walsung)	Romantic Adultery (Tristan)	Marriage	Sophisticated Adultery (Figaro)	Promiscuity (Don Giovanni)
Physical Diseases	Cancer	Digestive-Venereal		Sensory-Respiratory	Paralysis
Mental Diseases	Idiocy	Epileptics Manic-Depressives		Paranoiacs Schizophrenics	Dementia Praecox
Religion	Blind Superstition (Animism)	Pantheism	(Cath.) Faith (Prot.)	Deism	Lucid Cynicism (Logical Positivism)
Theories		Irrational Emotionalism		Rational Legalism	
Art	Dada Art	Surrealism		Cubism	State Art
Politics	Tyranny (Fascism)	Feudal Aristocracy		Laissez Faire Democracy	Anarchy (Economic Collapse Class War)
Political Slogans	Fraternity		Justice		Liberty
Hero	The Tragic Hero-Outlaw with S[ex] A[ppeal] / Flying Dutchman / Vamp	Marx Bros.	The Comic or Ironic Hero / Don Quixote / The Beggar / The Idiot (Dost.) / The Child (Alice)	Byron's Don Juan / Detectives (Holmes)	The Demonic Villain without natural S[ex] A[ppeal] / Iago / Stavrogin / The Grand Inquisitor / Depraved or Cissy Master-Crooks
The Quest	The Voluntary Journey of the corrupt mind through the Sea. Purgation of pride by Dissolution	Fertilizing the Wasteland / The Island	PURGATORY / Forgiveness	Draining the Swamp / The Oasis	The Voluntary Journey of the corrupt body through the Desert. Purgation of Lust by Dessication

PARADISE
(The City of God)

It combines a commentary on Alonso's letter and a structural literary analysis of the Quest, with its heroes, temptations, and transforming ordeals. Out of Eden, the adventurer enters either the hell of pure deed that is the realm of Caliban, or the hell of pure word that is the realm of Ariel—or, between them, This World. But the middle way is a tightrope, and only those who accept their inevitable fall can find the island or oasis waiting to rescue them.

In the postscript to "The Sea and the Mirror"—the same lyric that Auden had first composed for the voice of Simeon's gift in "For the Time Being"—Ariel sings to Caliban, "Helplessly in love with you, / Elegance, art, fascination, / Fascinated by / Drab mortality." Like the theories, politics, and styles in Auden's diagram, art exists only where the two ways balance imperfectly. There can be no art where no drab mortality exists to be transfigured by it. Attempts to make Ariel meet Caliban's needs—as Auden once tried to make art serve political ends—are temptations that, if accepted, would corrupt Ariel's vision of the truth he cannot be. "Tempt not your sworn comrade," Ariel sings. "Only / As I am can I / Love you as you are." The differences between them will dissolve only at the end of time. Caliban can never hope to say farewell to Ariel, for the one event that can divide "our falsehoods" is the apocalypse that ends flesh and art, matter and spirit, in "One evaporating sigh."

At the end of each stanza is a Brechtian "echo by the Prompter," as a subtitle describes it. This echo is the single syllable *I*, spoken by an ordinary unimpressive human voice. This was a voice Auden could hardly have imagined in the 1930s, when he reiterated in verse and prose that existence was divided between the two worlds of mind and flesh, and that the love of one for the other was as hopeless as the love of Ariel for Caliban. Now, in his diagram, he identified marriage as the love that joined the two worlds, and navigated a middle way between the romantic adultery of the flesh and the sophisticated adultery of the spirit. When he referred in letters to his first years with Kallman he now used the word "relationship" rather than "marriage," and when he wrote about marriage he made a point of using phrases like "husband and father." He thought of himself as irrevocably excluded from the sacrament of which his Anglican prayer book said: "First, it was ordained for the procreation of children." Yet this bleak and lonely belief gave rise to a greater and more profoundly affirmative poem than anything he had written before.

CHAPTER NINE

Asking for Neighborhood

When Auden began *The Age of Anxiety* in July 1944, he had in mind the same themes of theatricality and murder that had pervaded "The Sea and the Mirror," but his new long poem seemed to have ideas of its own. By the time he finished it early in 1947, it had proved to be less about isolating guilt than about an almost instinctive wish for a shared community we can imagine but never achieve. During these three years Auden's poems and essays tried to find the unifying grail given many names in "The Sea and the Mirror"—Caliban's "restored relation," Alonso's spring or island where body and mind are "delivered from mistrust"—but the reconciling words remained elusive.

More than at any other time, the events in Auden's life that he recognized as significant and transforming were not "immediately incorporated, however obscurely, in a poem," as he put it later to James Stern. His most harrowing experience in these years was a three-month government mission undertaken in the summer of 1945 to the devastation that had once been Germany; almost no trace of this appears in the poems he wrote at the time, although it flooded into his work in 1949 and after. And his most gratifying experience in the same period, the one that most altered his sense of himself, was a yearlong sexual relation with a woman, the only one of its kind in his life. It too scarcely touched the surface of the poems he wrote while it occurred, although it suffused the new tone and content of the poems he wrote afterward. He was still justifying in his poetry the lonely existential faith that had sustained him in a time of personal and political crisis but that seemed partial and distorting in a time of relative calm. He wrote some memorable poems in these years, and collaborated with Kallman on an opera libretto that even without music is a satisfying work of art. But he was troubled by a new sense of detachment and division, not unlike the one he had experienced in the late 1930s, when he wrote poems that justified political answers because he knew of no better ones.

The Age of Anxiety, the longest of his poems, takes the form of a dialogue among four characters, three men and one woman, who meet by chance in a New York bar in wartime. The poem has nothing specific to say about anxiety—that fear of an undefined nothingness that Kierkegaard anatomized in *The Concept of Dread*, first published in English in 1944—but its four characters endure in different ways the immediate anxieties of war and the deeper anxiety of alienation from themselves. Unlike the vividly differentiated characters in "For the Time Being" and "The Sea and the Mirror," who have already chosen who they are and speak in distinctive metres and forms, the characters in *The Age of Anxiety* all exhibit the same indecisiveness, and speak at first in the same verse form, a four-stress alliterative line adapted from *Beowulf*. Through the anachronistic strangeness of its metre, *The Age of Anxiety* calls attention to its artifice and self-consciousness as thoroughly as Caliban's speech does with its pastiche of Henry James. For the later sections of the poem (and for brief lyrics scattered throughout), Auden reshaped this four-stress metre into fifty stanzaic forms, some borrowed from medieval Wales, some invented for the occasion; he subtitled the poem "A Baroque Eclogue," and he dedicated it to the most famous exponent of Victorian ornament and extravagance, John Betjeman, who had been a friend since their Oxford days. The whole poem is simultaneously justified and haunted by a dictum Auden found in Kierkegaard's journals: "It is characteristic of the present time always to be conscious of the medium. It is almost bound to end in madness, like a man who whenever he looked at the sun and the stars was conscious of the world going round."

When Theodore Spencer read the typescript he commented on the "made-up" quality of some of the verse. Auden replied that he had set out precisely "to devise a rhetoric which would reveal the great vice of our age which is that we are all not only 'actors' but know that we are

(reduplicated Hamlets)* and that it is only at moments, in spite of ourselves, and when we least expect it, that our real feelings break through."
In the lyric "Few and Simple," a few months earlier, Auden had written
of the kind of "startling" moment that "amazes" him with his own real
feelings, but those moments seemed rare. Auden reported in a letter
to Isherwood that a friend who had visited England shortly before the
Allied victory had confirmed "by first-hand observation what I suspected
from occasionally reading *Horizon, New Writing, New Statesman*, etc.,
that our English friends have learned nothing from the war"—nothing,
that is, about the horrors committed on both sides when local interests
and private angers are disguised as real ethical imperatives. In "The Sea
and the Mirror," tempestuous suffering destroys theatrical artifice and
prompts a transforming moment of self-recognition. But, as Auden told
Isherwood, nothing of the kind seemed to have happened in England:
"It is terrifying to realize that even great and real suffering can be turned
into a theatre and so be no help." The rhetoric Auden devised for *The
Age of Anxiety* gave voice to the ingenuity with which feelings are turned
into theater, rather than the surprising moments when they reveal themselves. It was the one long poem of Auden's later years that offered no
consoling image of enduring love.

The Age of Anxiety is theatrical in tone but almost entirely without
drama in its action. The four solitaries who meet in the opening pages
spend the night talking, first in a bar, then in a taxi, then in the woman's
apartment, finally separating and forgetting each other before dawn. But
for two of the four—the woman and one of the older men—the stakes
of these minor inconclusive actions are infinitely high. At the end, in
verse that far surpasses in energy and excitement everything that comes
before, they separately confront the relation of their anxious selves to an
unconditional God. For the older man, the unconditional is the Christian
one, the crucified redeemer; for the woman it is the God of Moses.

The dramatic point of making the four speak in effectively the same
voice—at times in unison—is that, until two of them differentiate themselves at the end, they separately experience the same estrangement. In
wartime, as the first of the poem's discursive prose stage directions explains, "everybody is reduced to the anxious status of a shady character
or a displaced person." And so business thrives in bars like the one where

* Hamlet, that is, unlike the histrionic stage players, can bring himself to neither passion nor
action, and his inability is redoubled in those who think of themselves (as he did not) as stage
players.

the poem opens, "an unprejudiced space in which nothing particular ever happens," where patrons find "a choice of physiological aids to the imagination whereby each may appropriate it for his or her private world of repentant felicitous forms." The poem is an urban eclogue, but the shared formal diction of the four speakers has a motive different from that of the learned shepherds in traditional eclogues, where rustic pastoral themes disguise sophisticated urban sensibilities. In *The Age of Anxiety* the dense vocabulary of detail and concrete extravagance of metaphor are not a disguise but a representation: they indicate the irony and clutter of everyone's modern sensibility. The archaic metre suggests the common archetypal depths beneath the individualizing surface of the urban psyche. Interruptions by a radio announcer offer music

> By brutal bands from bestial tribes,
> The Quaraquorums and the Quaromanlics,
> The Arsocids and the Alonites,
> The Ghuzz, the Guptas, the gloomy Krimchaks,
> The Timurids and Torguts,

whose names (lifted from Arnold Toynbee's *A Study of History*) bring into the present the futile violence of an unimaginably distant past. (In August 1944, a few weeks after he started work on the poem, Auden told Isherwood he was "making my way through six volumes" of Toynbee.) The same radio voice also reads news bulletins from the most modern of wars.

When Auden began planning the poem, he apparently intended to bring its archaic violence closer to home. His first sketches, near the end of a notebook used mostly for drafting "The Sea and the Mirror," include a list of four *dramatis personae*: Civilian, Doctor, Girl, Merchant Seaman. In some sketches he added a disembodied voice identified as Radio. All five appear in the final version, where the Civilian is Quant, an aging widower who drudges as a shipping clerk while his imagination feeds on fragments of ancient myth; the Doctor is Malin, a middle-aged medical intelligence officer in the Canadian air force; the Girl is Rosetta, a buyer for a department store, nostalgic for a dream-image of her English childhood; and the Merchant Seaman is Emble, a young naval recruit "fully conscious of the attraction of his uniform to both sexes." The early sketches also included a plot outline that Auden discarded when he began writing the poem itself:

The murder
The stories of the suspects
The exposure of their lies (contradictions and fresh evidence)
The discovery of the murderer.

He did not lose interest in this murder plot—he wrote an essay on detective stories, "The Guilty Vicarage," around January 1946, when he had finished most of the poem—and traces of it persist into the finished poem in scattered phrases like Malin's "A crime has occurred, accusing all"; Rosetta's "Question his crimes till his clues confess"; and the prose narrator's description of Rosetta's daydream landscape as one "familiar to all readers of English detective stories," a place inhabited by charming eccentrics "to whom, until the sudden intrusion of a horrid corpse onto the tennis court or into the greenhouse, work and law and guilt are just literary words." But Auden was not yet ready to write the long poem he wanted to write explicitly about murder, perhaps because he thought he had not yet found a proper language for it. His imagination remained caught in an opposition of irreconcilable extremes: the solitary inner drama of existential choice, and the impersonal archetypal generality of the human species; but a murder involves two persons who are simultaneously unique in themselves and alike in their common humanity.

The characters in "For the Time Being" and "The Sea and the Mirror" live in the focused, uncluttered realm of sacred and literary texts. Almost all of them have already been transformed by revelation or crisis. In *The Age of Anxiety*, Auden made a conscious effort to give artistic clarity and moral intensity to characters who were too modern, secular, and anxious to experience anything of the kind. He told Spencer:

The Elizabethans and even the Victorians could be rhetorical without realizing it. We have lost that naiveté, at the same time we have to go on being rhetorical, so that for us sincerity is almost a matter of luck.

I find Yeats' poetry boring and faux because he claims to be naive and isn't. On the other hand the attempt of a poet like Laura Riding to dispense with *all* rhetoric and be absolutely honest, seems to me a false over-simplification in the other direction.

What I'm after in my non-lyrical work is to find a valid way of presenting the modern consciousness, which not only embraces other times and spaces but reflects itself in itself. No doubt I haven't found it, and perhaps the problem is insoluble but at any rate it's fun trying.

Even the lyrics sung by the characters (or chosen by them from a jukebox in the bar) fit closely into what Auden called his "non-lyrical work." They are mannerist variants on popular, traditional, and ancient forms, intricate and oddly airless songs that seem designed to imitate but not achieve the condition of being moving: "Deep in my dark the dream shines / Yes, of you, you dear always; / My cause to cry, cold but my / Story still, still my music."

Without hope of revelation or crisis, the characters in *The Age of Anxiety* escape self-consciousness by joining in a partly illusory, partly authentic shared vision of unconscious unity. As he worked on the poem, Auden was repeatedly on the point of finding a quality that human beings all have in common and that he could use to signify the authentic element of this vision. Meanwhile, he tried to make do with an inadequate substitute, Jung's system of four archetypal faculties, Intuition, Thought, Feeling, and Sensation. He had alluded to this system in the mid-1930s (the four climbers in Ransom's party in *The Ascent of F6* seem to be modeled on it), and when he found it again in Jung's *The Integration of the Personality*, published in 1939, he adopted it as the most detailed and reliable map of the human psyche. But the verse in which he expressed this idea was unconvincing or worse. In "For the Time Being," the speeches of the Four Faculties sound tediously irrelevant to everything else in the poem. In *The Age of Anxiety*, they are represented by the four characters, but the allegory quickly turns repetitive and mechanical. Quant is Intuition (which makes quantum leaps and perceives the *quantum* or whole of things); Malin, Thought (*malin* is French for "shrewd"); Rosetta, Feeling (the rose of love and the mysterious congruence of languages on the Rosetta Stone); Emble, Sensation (aware of the visible, emblematic aspect of things). As in *The Orators*, where, as Auden said later, he let certain of his tendencies run riot in fantasy in order to exorcise them, he gave the Four Faculties in *The Age of Anxiety* the freedom to talk at such length that he finally lost interest in them. (In 1963, as he was looking through a copy of "For the Time Being," he wrote in the margin of the speeches of the Four Faculties: "Bosh, straight from Jung.") The conscious side of the double man, driven by unique choices, is not integrated in the poem with the instinctive side, driven by archetypal powers. Kierkegaard and Jung stare incomprehendingly across the divide.

Like "For the Time Being" and "The Sea and the Mirror," *The Age of Anxiety* perceives its characters simultaneously at widely different points in time. In the two earlier poems, events that occur in the distant past are portrayed in contemporary terms, because the meaning of the Christmas story reoccurs whenever it is experienced, and the dilemmas of *The Tempest* reoccur in every experience of a work of art. But *The Age of Anxiety* reverses the equation: instead of universally known historical figures demonstrating their modern significance, the poem is about anonymous contemporary figures whom no one would notice outside the poem, but who demonstrate a significance transcending time's limits. It translates into art the Christian aesthetics expounded by Simeon, in which "every tea-table is a battlefield littered with old catastrophes."

The whole poem revisits, somewhat skeptically, the sense of visionary unity Auden had described in "A Summer Night." The four friends who in 1933 sat "Equal with colleagues in a ring" reappear as the four strangers who meet by chance in a Third Avenue bar. In his prose account of the 1933 vision Auden emphasized that no one had been drinking, but in *The Age of Anxiety* the four characters enter "a state of semi-intoxication" before they glimpse "that rare community which is otherwise only attained in states of extreme wakefulness," "a rapport in which communication of thoughts and feelings is so accurate and instantaneous, that they appear to function as a single organism."

———

"We who are four were / Once but one," the Faculties say in "For the Time Being," adding that they alone can still look into paradise and tell mankind what happens there. The four characters in *The Age of Anxiety* arrive at their vision as they shed their uniqueness. They begin as isolated exponents of their faculties, conscious of themselves before they become aware of each other. In the "Prologue" Quant speaks first and, in a later section, "is the first to see anything," because, as Jung wrote in *Psychological Types*, intuition "follows directly from the given circumstances."* Malin, the representative of thought, thinks first in the disconnected propositions that, in Jung, characterize passive thinking ("No chimpanzee / Thinks it thinks. Things are divisible. / Creatures are not") and

---

* Quant intuits that the world in the barroom mirror is different from his own in ways that cannot be known through reason or sense data. "What flavor," he asks his image, "has / That liquor you lift with your left hand?" Auden was evidently aware that because the flavor of liquor is determined by asymmetrical molecules, mirror-liquor presumably tastes different from its real counterpart. In the opening chapter of *Through the Looking-Glass*, Alice makes a similar but less scientific guess: "Perhaps Looking-glass milk isn't good to drink."

then comes to what Jung called "a recognition of their directedness," when his propositions coalesce into one realization: "singular then / Is the human way." It is Malin who will lead the other three in the second section of the poem, "The Seven Ages," where they explore the experience of human time. Rosetta, driven by feeling, begins by glorifying nostalgically the English landscape of her childhood. Emble, the voice of the differentiating faculty of sensation, is the only one who looks at his surroundings, but he does so in order to isolate himself; in his youthful self-conscious nervousness, he disdains the "malcontented" patrons of the bar, forgetting he is one of them.

Then an "official doctored message" of radio news breaks in, "compelling them to pay attention to a common world of great slaughter and much sorrow." The four strangers now become aware of each other, through the common focus of an impersonal, anonymous, inauthentic announcement from which every trace of the first-person singular has been banished: "Now the news. Night raids on / Five cities. Fires started. / Pressure applied by pincer movements." (Auden told friends he detested wartime radio.)

In this and many other passages, *The Age of Anxiety* acknowledges the force of every modern skepticism about individual freedom and autonomy: the affirmations at the end of the poem would be trivially easy if it did not. Indeed, the poem makes a point of insisting that individuals are in part artifacts—created by involuntary forces of language and culture, shaped by unseen social and symbolic systems, and subject to the radio announcer's impersonal voice. Malin, in his opening speech, knows the volitional *I* is produced through relations with others, knows it is not the sign of some imaginary essential self: "for the ego is a dream / Till a neighbor's need by name create it." The prose narrator explains that speech cannot be a direct personal statement, because "Human beings are, necessarily, actors who cannot become something before they have first pretended to be it; and they can be divided, not into the hypocritical and the sincere, but into the sane who know they are acting and the mad who do not." Even one's own body is not directly accessible because it can be perceived only after it has been translated into a symbolic landscape (represented in the poem by the dream-place visited in the third section, "The Seven Stages"). The erotic ritual of the fifth section, "The Masque," ascribes Rosetta's and Emble's sexual choices to the impersonal instinctive powers of Venus; experience of the world is perceived through the distorting, reflexive, and paradoxical lenses of language: "for all gestures of time / And all species of space respond in our own /

Contradictory dialect, the double talk / Of ambiguous bodies." Our bodies retain, in their ordinary everyday existence, all the doubleness and ambiguity of mind and matter, wave and particle, finitude and connectedness.

In its concluding affirmations, the poem recognizes all these dilemmas as the condition of personality, not its refutation. The individual person—despite all his paradoxes and limits—is finally the only possible counterweight to the vast brutal engines and official doctored message of the faceless state. As in "The Sea and the Mirror," this final realization follows a long series of failures: of ambition and nostalgia in the second and third parts; of authority and Eros in the fourth and fifth.

In "The Seven Ages," the second part, Malin describes the ambitious man's advance from clumsy youth to triumphant age when "Recognition surrounds his days," and then to his decline into death when he "joins the majority . . . and is modest at last." But this futile progress instructs only Malin: the three others, after serving as an echoing chorus to his reports on childhood and youth, lose the thread and start arguing among themselves when he reaches his midlife success. Malin, ignoring their digression, goes on to the age when his subject "pines for some / Nameless Eden where he never was," but the others, having forgotten their historic quest, turn their thoughts to the journey to Eden, a quest in the opposite direction from Malin's world of thought. Quant has the intuition to ask Rosetta, the voice of feeling, to lead it.

The shape of "The Seven Ages" is clear enough, but the shape of the Edenic quest in "The Seven Stages" has baffled even Auden's most sympathetic readers. Rosetta leads a quest not through historical time but through a dream landscape, where the four seek "that state of prehistoric happiness which, by human beings, can only be imagined in terms of a landscape bearing a symbolic resemblance to the human body." (This prose description was added to the typescript almost at the last minute—"to make it easier," Auden told his student and secretary, Alan Ansen.) For this part of the poem, Auden invented a narrative sequence that alludes in no way to traditional fictions of a journey or quest; the four travel across the outer surfaces of the human body, places that (except in erotic contexts) are almost never thought of as stages along a way, although since the time of Jonah the body's *inner* passages have served as suitable routes for a quest. He made his task harder by avoiding any sense that the journey has a goal, and by giving the landscape a symbolic rather than an allegorical relation to the body, so that the features in the dream do not much resemble the bodily features that suggested them. For example, while walking across the "sad plain" that symbolizes the belly, Rosetta sees a "tacit tarn" that perhaps recalls the navel, but the water inside it and the "beehive mounds" nearby are obscuring embellishments of dream.

The physiology of "The Seven Stages" was "really quite straightforward," as Auden told Ansen in 1947:

> It begins in the belly, the center of the body, goes on to the general region around the heart, then to the hands (symmetrically, [the four characters] two by two), then to the nose and throat (the capital), then north to the eyes where Rosetta goes in and the others describe it from outside, then to the forehead complex (the museum), the ears (gardens) through which one receives spiritual direction, the hair (woods), and finally they look down the back, the desert—there's nothing farther.

"It's all done in the Zohar," he explained, referring to the greatest of Jewish cabalistic books, but the journey in the poem plays extravagantly on the Zohar's use of anthropomorphic symbolism to describe the anatomy of the divine, instead of imitating any journey in the Zohar itself. Auden's explanation omitted some of the few obvious details, like the smooth-surfaced "twin confederate" mountains "Where the great go to forget themselves." The symbolic body that the four travelers visit is an imaginary Eden remembered from infancy: it has breasts but no sex. The details Auden described explain the structure and wit of "The Seven Stages," but knowing them does not help make it memorable or convincing. Auden's efforts to write a poetry of the body were frustrated by his insistence on writing about symbols of the body instead of the body itself.

As the travelers cross the desert on the last of the seven stages, "this waste / Which is really empty" proves the failure of their search for Eden. "The world from which their journey has been one long flight rises up before them . . . in all the majesty of its perpetual fury." Their first two quests have led nowhere. In the next two sections of the poem they will mourn another failure and be tempted by an illusory success. "The Dirge," spoken by the four in unison as they ride in a taxi to Rosetta's apartment, laments the death of "some semi-divine stranger with superhuman powers, some Gilgamesh or Napoleon, some Solon or Sherlock Holmes," that mythical hero who, everyone is convinced, must once have rescued nature and humanity from their inadequacies and who, "long or lately, has always died or disappeared."

When Auden published this section separately under the title "Lament for a Lawgiver," it sounded like an ironic echo of the public mourning for Franklin Roosevelt, but its Pindaric catalogue of the mythical achievements of "Our lost dad, / Our colossal father," makes a precise psychological point: the dead hero who "harrowed hell, / Healed the abyss / Of torpid instinct and trifling flux" is a Jungian imago who encompasses all the imaginable feats of a lost hero, and who exists solely as a projection of the failures and dissatisfactions of those who mourn him. Auden's lament is a parody and refutation of Jungian mythographies of the kind popularized by Joseph Campbell—first in the opening pages of Campbell and Henry Morton Robinson's *A Skeleton Key to Finnegans Wake* (which Auden read when it was published in 1944), where Joyce's H. C. Earwicker is the "great progenitor" who manifests himself as Woden, Thor, St. Patrick, and Cromwell; later in Campbell's *The Hero with a Thousand Faces* (1949).* At the end of *The Age of Anxiety* Rosetta and Malin rediscover their relations with a god who is a historical person, not a recurring myth, but before they can remember their obligations to their personal god, they must endure the disappointments of their nostalgia for this projected collective archetype.

After "The Dirge" looks back to a lost fatherhood, "The Masque" looks forward to a "millennial Earthly Paradise." In Rosetta's apartment, prompted by "alcohol, lust, fatigue, and the longing to be good," the four find themselves in that "euphoric state in which it seemed as if it were only some trifling and easily rectifiable error" that prevents Paradise from being built on earth. In their private erotic way they are as convinced of inevitable progress as they had been convinced of inevitable loss in "The Dirge." Malin invokes "Heavenly Venus" while Rosetta and Emble dance together, and encourages them to dissolve their personalities into myths: "Be to him always," he tells Rosetta, "The mother-moment which makes him dream / He is lord of time." But the two lovers' wish to translate themselves into archetypes, abetted by the two older men, ignores the awkward fact that they remain persons. When Malin and Quant make a tactful departure, Rosetta returns from the door to find that Emble "had gone into her bedroom and passed out."

---

* Probably in 1953, Auden attended a public lecture at which Campbell said that Christ and Buddha were the same because spears had been used against both, although the ones used against Buddha had been transformed into flowers. Auden, as his friend Wendell Stacy Johnson recalled, "exclaimed quite loudly that on Good Friday the spears were real ones."

At the end of the poem Rosetta and Malin overcome their anxiety—Rosetta in her monologue at the close of "The Masque," Malin in his solitary meditations in the "Epilogue." During the past few years, Auden's prose had studied the condition from which they are released, that of the "anxious subject," but except in a phrase or two in "The Sea and the Mirror" he had not confronted it in his poems. In 1943, shortly after he stopped writing his pseudonymous "Lecture Notes," he wrote his long philosophical and religious essay, "Purely Subjective," in which

> I wake into my existence to find myself and the world that is not myself already there, and simultaneously feel responsible for my discovery. I can and must ask: "Who am I? Do I want to be? Who do I want and who ought I to become?" I am, in fact, an anxious subject. That is my religious problem. I experience subjective requiredness,* i.e. a requiredness the source of which I cannot identify with anything I can call an object, and which concerns the meaning and value of my existence to myself. That is my immediate religious experience which allows me no rest until I believe that I have understood it.

As in *The Age of Anxiety*, most of the essay explores a series of attempts to evade this problem, to escape subjective anxiety by denying subjectivity itself.

One common denial is the immersion of oneself in a *public*. Auden portrayed this variety of escape in "A Healthy Spot," a brief unpleasant poem written in 1944 about his Swarthmore colleagues; a typescript version is entitled "Swarthmore." "They're nice," it begins. They have all the civic virtues. Yet "One is constantly struck by the number of / Happy marriages and unhappy people." Their corporate selves are contented enough; their personal selves are not. In their subdued unhappiness they ignore "by tacit consent our hunger / For eternal life"—the same hunger that Malin names when he describes human beings as "Temporals pleading for eternal life with / The infinite impetus of anxious spirits." This hunger, in "A Healthy Spot," is the "caged rebuked question" occasionally released in the saturnalia of clambakes and college reunions, "and which the smoking-room story / Alone, ironically enough, stands up for," through its tribute to uncontrollable Eros.

* The phrase is from Wolfgang Köhler, who used it in a much weaker sense in *The Place of Value in a World of Facts*. Köhler wrote that among his favorite colors is a very dark green, and that he cannot explain its strong attraction for him: "This, I suppose, is an example of 'subjective' requiredness" (p. 353).

The effort to escape anxiety by denying subjectivity inevitably fails; in *The Age of Anxiety*, as in virtually the whole Protestant tradition, the only possible way to escape is to embrace subjectivity in all its loneliness and risk. Auden wrote in 1946, in his introduction to Henry James's *The American Scene*, that the one way to attain the Good Place is to "desire it with sufficient desperation to stand a chance of arriving." Embracing the subjective does not make one self-centered, but allows for a relation with another subject—most of all, Auden believed, with the God who is a person, not a myth, abstraction, or power. Malin, in his final speech, calls this God "the whole subject / Of our not-knowing." Quant is too immersed in ancient myth to worry about his subjectivity, and disappears cheerfully from the poem singing an impromptu ballad about impersonal movements of civilizations (a fantasia on themes by Toynbee) and cycles of nature. Emble is so fearful he can do nothing but pass out. The poem reserves the subjective for Rosetta, who finds it in her Judaism, and for Malin, who finds it in his Christianity.

Auden had described himself in his essay on Hardy as a "thinking-intuitive" type, as opposed to those like his father who came from "that other world of feeling and sensation." But in *The Age of Anxiety* he divided his self-portrait between thinking (Malin) and feeling (Rosetta). The Jungian mechanism that connects them is the relation between the masculine persona and its complementary inner opposite, the feminine anima. "Where the persona is intellectual," Jung wrote in *Psychological Types*, "the soul is quite certainly sentimental." In his inner life, Malin, like Auden, endures sexual loneliness and the isolation of success. In his job as a medical intelligence officer and his interests in scientific and moral psychology, he was modeled on a British psychoanalyst named John Thompson, whom Auden apparently met at Swarthmore and who became a close friend. Thompson had converted to Catholicism at about the same time that Auden returned to Anglicanism. In July 1943 Auden wrote Elizabeth Mayer about a visit from Thompson,

who is now a British liaison officer for medical air-research and keeps flying between England, Canada, USA and Russia, and in his spare-time defends psychiatric offenders [i.e., homosexuals] at court-martials (with great success).

He had so much to say; some depressing, e.g. anti-semitism is growing in England by leaps and bounds; some cheering, e.g. many German prisoners (Infantry not Luftwaffe) are asking to become Canadian citizens; and some heart-breaking, e.g. Thompson was nursing a mortally-wounded gunner in one of the raids over Cologne, who just kept asking over and over again, "Why have They killed me?" (What psychological insight Edward Lear had.)*

In the person of Malin, Auden remembered the gunner's question: " 'Why have They killed me?' wondered our Bert, our / Greenhouse gunner, forgot our answer, / Then was not with us."

Malin's speech at the end of *The Age of Anxiety* was Auden's last statement of his theology of the Wholly Other and his first attempt to find a less distant divinity. As at the end of Caliban's speech, God is acknowledged only when all else fails, in what Malin calls "the flash / Of negative knowledge" that occurs when all other knowledge proves fruitless. Caught in our anxiety, we are "unwilling to say Yes / To the Self-So which is the same at all times, / That Always-Opposite." But this God is not purely Other. He is also a person whose acts are voluntary, who "from no necessity / Condescended† to exist and to suffer death / And, scorned on a scaffold, ensconced in His life / The human household." Or, as Auden had written in his "Lecture Notes" in 1942: "Faith for Christianity means the power to endure the paradox that Jesus, the individual historical man, was and is, as He claimed, Christ, the only begotten Son of the Father." Malin can endure this paradox because he recognizes the voice of forgiveness and atonement sounding through his own experience of pain and abandonment: "It is where we are wounded that is when He speaks / Our creaturely cry." Malin's line sounds a new note in Auden's poetry. In "For the Time Being" Auden knew all about the Incarnation, and in "The Sea and the Mirror" he knew all about the Wholly Other. *The Age of Anxiety* was the first poem in which he expressed religious dread before the cross. This was far from the last stage of his religious feelings—in later works he imagined both a deeper guilt and a broader community than he did in *The Age of Anxiety*—but it pointed, somewhat overemphatically, in the new direction his poems were now ready to take.

Compared with Auden's straightforward self-portrait in Malin, his more complex identification with Rosetta is a profound act of imaginative

---

* Many of Lear's limericks referred to "They," who denounced or misunderstood all particularity or eccentricity. "There was an Old Man of Whitehaven, / Who danced a quadrille with a raven; / But they said 'It's absurd / To encourage that bird!' / So they smashed that Old Man of Whitehaven." In his sonnet on Lear, Auden called them "The legions of cruel inquisitive They."

† For the theological meaning of "condescension," see p. 169.

sympathy, and for her final monologue he wrote some of his greatest verse. (Around this time, he spoke to friends admiringly about the psychology of Robert Browning's monologues.) Superficially Rosetta is everything Auden was not: a Jewish woman with enough sense of fashion to work as a buyer for a department store. But the poem gives her a lower-middle-class childhood in the same Birmingham where Auden had his upper-middle-class one,* and gives her the same fantasy as his of an innocent landscape in the Yorkshire vales. Her self-deceptions dissolve when she at last remembers her inescapable obligation to her Judaism. The poem does not mention Rosetta's faith until she names it in her final speech, just as Malin says nothing about his Christianity until he returns to the solitude and silence that prompt his credo. The moral point of not identifying her earlier as a Jew is that the poem does not categorize her by ethnicity or race: her Judaism is a creed, and the poem takes no interest in it until she does.

Rosetta—evidently helped by psychoanalysis—understands that her fantasy world is a daydream through which she tries to deny the reality of her past and her exclusion from the world of the gentiles:

> Should I hide away
> My secret sins in consulting rooms,
> My fears are before Him: He'll find all,
> Ignore nothing. He'll never let me
> Conceal from Him the semi-detached
> Brick villa in Laburnum Crescent . . .
>   for He won't pretend to
> Forget how I began, nor grant belief
> In the mythical scenes I make up
> Of a home like theirs, the Innocent Place where
> His Law can't look, the leaves are so thick.

The deeper source of her daydream is the same one that Auden, in his essay on murder mysteries, "The Guilty Vicarage," identified as the cause of his own. "The fantasy . . . which the detective story addict indulges is the fantasy of being restored to the Garden of Eden, to a state of innocence, where we know love as love and not as the law." (The detective, that is, routs the criminal from the vicarage garden, and the

---

* The "semi-detached / Brick villa in Laburnum Crescent" is not literally in Birmingham, which has no Laburnum Crescent, but is laced with far more streets named Laburnum (Laburnum Avenue, Close, Drive, Road, Street, Villas, etc.) than any other English city.

forbidden fruit is magically restored to the tree.) Rosetta's daydream takes her from the realm of Old Testament Law to that of New Testament Love, but she wakes from her dream into the exile of Israel. As Auden wrote in "The Guilty Vicarage," "The fantasy of escape is the same, whether one explains the guilt in Christian, Freudian, or any other terms"—that is, in terms of original sin or sexual guilt. "One's way of trying to face the reality, on the other hand, will, of course, depend very much on one's creed."

Auden went out of his way to understand Rosetta's creed on its own terms. He devoted the last of his five sets of "Lecture Notes" in 1942 to Judaism and anti-Semitism:

> The difference between a genuine Judaism and a genuine Christianity is like the difference between a young girl who has been promised a husband in a dream and a married woman who believes that she loves and is loved. The young girl knows that the decisively important thing has not yet happened to her, that her present life is therefore a period of anticipation, important not in itself but in its relation to the future . . . To the married woman, on the other hand, the decisively important thing has already happened, and because of this everything in the present is significant . . . Faith for Judaism is the power to endure the suffering of waiting.

Rosetta's power is strong enough to maintain her faith despite sufferings far more brutal than those of waiting. "We'll point for Him," even if He chooses to do nothing "to defend us now / When bruised or broiled our bodies are chucked / Like cracked crocks onto kitchen middens / In the time He takes. We'll trust. He'll slay / If His Wisdom will."* When she finds Emble asleep on her bed, she understands the difference between the security he will wake to and the anticipation she must endure. "You'll build here," she thinks as she looks at him, "be / Satisfied soon, while I sit waiting / On my light luggage to leave if called / For some new exile." She recognizes in Emble the same failure of Christian faith that Auden described in his "Lecture Notes" as the characteristic failure of a cradle-Christian who has no personal relation to his nominal God, refuses the paradox of Jesus as both historical man and son of God, and lets the Gospels and church affirm his faith for him; "What

---

* Although the action of the poem occurs during the war, when the mass murders in Nazi concentration camps were only partly known, Auden wrote these lines—perhaps the first references to the event in English and American poetry—when the war was over and the full truth about the camps was known to all.

it all means," he says, "I can safely leave to the theologians." For Emble, Rosetta observes, "Niceness is all and / The rest bores. I'm too rude a question." Emble can find the rest boring because smug secular culture calls itself Christianity, and his "Christian luck" lets him "joke now, / Be spick and span, spell out the bumptious / Morals on monuments."

When Auden began *The Age of Anxiety* he read through two great visions of cyclical history, one by a historian, the other by an artist. In the same letter in which he told Isherwood he was reading Toynbee, he also reported reading *Finnegans Wake* "with the help of the just pub-lished guide" by Campbell and Robinson. For the lines of daughterly nostalgia in Rosetta's final speech, he purloined rhythms and motifs from Anna Livia's concluding monologue. (Anna Livia: "It's sad and wear I go back to you, my cold father, my cold mad father." Rosetta: "I shan't be at peace / Till I really take your restless hands, / My poor fat fa-ther.")* But he followed his usual practice of contradicting in the act of borrowing. At the end of *Finnegans Wake* Anna Livia Plurabelle flows into the sea so that the river can repeat the circular passage it began at the start of the book. At the end of *The Age of Anxiety*, as in all of Auden's longer works, the poem returns to the world of chosen events and linear history "where time is real and in which, therefore, poetry can take no interest." Rosetta's time, unlike Anna Livia's, moves from a past of exile through a present day of destruction and slaughter toward a promised messianic ending. She cannot receive the future, cannot find shelter, until she takes the hands of the past; conciliation with the past is the only psychological means of moving forward. "Moses will scold if / We're not all there for the next meeting / At some brackish well or broken arch, / Tired as we are. We must try to get on." The promised future will arrive, not through the turning of historical cycles, but after a cataclysmic change still unimaginably remote: "I'll be dumb before / The barracks burn and boisterous Pharaoh / Grow ashamed and shy." And this last half-line continues alliteratively with the Jewish credo, "Sh'ma Yisrael, / Adonai elohenu, adonai echod" ("Hear O Israel, the Lord our God, the Lord is one")—a startling and convincing link be-

---

* Auden had looked at Joyce's final pages earlier, apparently in the 1935 pamphlet edition of *Anna Livia Plurabelle.* Caliban's impersonation of the common herd in "The Sea and the Mirror" includes the cry: "Carry me back, Master, to the cathedral town where the canons run through the water meadows." Anna Livia cries to her father: "Carry me along, taddy, like you done at the toy fair!"

tween Old English metre and ancient Hebrew, in a line that looks to the end in the language of the beginning.

The two endings of *The Age of Anxiety*, one Jewish, one Christian, point to the depth and complexity of Auden's religious interests at the time. In the first years of the war, he had sought an answer to Hitler in the absolutes of Kierkegaard and Tillich, and continued in the next few years to read widely in the Protestant tradition. But during the later years of the war and immediately afterward, when Hitler's genocidal rage against the Jews emerged as one of the central facts of the age, Auden began reading more widely in Judaism and its many varieties of mysticism and law. In the autumn of 1945, after three years at Swarthmore and three months in Germany, he found an apartment in New York, resumed his freelance life of reviewing and lecturing, and immersed himself in the intense, argumentative intellectual life of Jewish exiles. "I've been increasingly interested in the Jews," he told Alan Ansen; "I wonder what would happen if I converted to Judaism."* The only people he could talk to in America, he added, were Jews. He was tentatively finding his way from a private, existential religion to a communal one. The integrated vision of justice he had hoped to find in radical Protestantism seemed ever more distant, and he began wondering if it might be sought elsewhere. Jewish Rosetta thinks about Pharaoh and the death camps. Protestant Malin is too preoccupied with anxiety and faith to notice them.

Auden discovered a central theme of *The Age of Anxiety* only after writing almost all of it. In mid-1946, when he had been working on the poem for almost two years, he came across a far more sympathetic and resonant means of writing about the shared condition of humanity than the Jungian archetypes he had used until then. He wrote his discovery into the prose narratives and the title-page epigraph of the poem, but he had not yet found a way to fit it into the verse. Most critics who write about *The Age of Anxiety* mention the last line of the opening prose narration, "It was the night of All Souls," and some observe that the epigraph is from the *Dies Irae* sung in the Mass for All Souls: "*Lacrimosa dies illa / Qua resurget ex favilla / Iudicandus homo reus*" (Tearful will be that day when guilty man rises again from ashes to be judged). But the relation of these details to the rest of the poem makes sense only in terms of the little-known book in which Auden found them.

---

* Around the same time, he made a practice of retelling jokes in Yiddish, in an accent that usually rendered them incomprehensible.

The book was Eugen Rosenstock-Huessy's *Out of Revolution* (1938), an eccentric, panoramic study of history of a kind Auden always found stimulating and sympathetic. He first encountered it, he wrote later, when a friend (probably Reinhold Niebuhr) gave it to him around 1940, and "ever since I have read everything by him that I could lay my hands on." It was a book of that rare kind that "gives me the impression of having been written especially for me."* But at first only a few traces of it appeared in his prose and verse. Then, around April 1946, he apparently read another book by Rosenstock-Huessy, *The Christian Future*, soon after it was published, and was stimulated to reread *Out of Revolution*. Much as Auden admired Toynbee, after reading six volumes of recurring tragic histories, he was transfixed by Rosenstock-Huessy's teleological linear vision of a series of unique events culminating in the Second Coming. The final phrase in verse in *The Age of Anxiety*, "His World to come," was suggested by passages in *The Christian Future* stating that "to be a Christian is to think primarily in the language of time rather than of space, as shown by the favorite biblical phrase, 'the world to come.' "†

Out of Revolution identifies All Souls as one of the great transforming moments in European history. It was established in 998 as the feast in which the Church celebrates the faithful departed. Traditional accounts of it focus on the prayers offered by the living to assist the multitude of the dead on their way through Purgatory. During the Reformation it was abolished in most Protestant churches, but it was later restored in the Anglo-Catholic liturgy as a celebration of the whole mystical body of Christ. For Rosenstock-Huessy, the novelty of All Souls was its general intercession on behalf of all dead souls instead of a few specific ones:

> All Souls established the solidarity of all souls from the beginning of the world to the end of time . . . The first universal democracy in the world was a democracy of sinners, united by their common confession of sins in expectation of the Last Judgment . . . Europe started with a new experience when All Souls

---

* Another such book, he said, was Hannah Arendt's *The Human Condition* (1958), which he evidently valued less because it gave him new ideas than because it systematically expounded his existing ideas about vocation and alienation, the private and public worlds, and the relation between speech and responsibility.

† Cochrane made the same point on the last page of *Christianity and Classical Culture*, where he wrote that, to the Christian, "history is prophecy; i.e. its true significance lies not in the past, nor in the present, but in the future, the life of 'the world to come.' "

was added to All Saints. For it gave comfort to innumerable people in the loneliness of their hearts to celebrate the truth that death was universal and that all men would be rallied at the Last Judgment.

Auden echoed this interpretation repeatedly, for example in a lecture in 1956, when he told his audience that the essays of W. P. Ker aroused in him a "vision of a kind of literary All Souls Night in which the dead, the living and the unborn writers of every age and in every tongue were seen as engaged upon a common, noble and civilizing task."

For a few years after 1946 Rosenstock-Huessy had the same significance in Auden's thought that Gerald Heard had had in the early 1930s. Both were polymath generalizers who rushed breathlessly across vast tracts of history, tracing patterns unimagined by others and finding decisive changes in events that were slighted by more-plodding historians. Their authority in Auden's eyes depended on a special combination of qualities: on one hand, their overwhelming range of useful information; on the other, their wildly implausible claim to unique insight. (Rosenstock-Huessy, Auden wrote later, at times "seems to claim to be the *only* man who has ever seen the light about History and Language.") Their prophetic manner made both Heard and Rosenstock-Huessy faintly and unintentionally comic, so that Auden found it possible to accept the authority of their ideas, in a subjunctive and experimental way, without being tempted to hero-worship the authority they claimed for themselves. Both were parodic variations on Auden's father, who had the same catholic variety of learning but none of their intellectual extravagance or pride.

Auden hinted at the changes in his theology when he sent to Ursula Niebuhr in August 1946 one of the lyrics from "The Seven Stages" section of *The Age of Anxiety* and, alluding to its lush accumulation of sensual images of "sweet-smelling borders," "random rose-walks," and "wanton groves," entitled it "Baroque" and described it as "a counter-Reformationary number" for possible publication in Niebuhr's magazine *Christianity and Crisis*. (Niebuhr turned it down.) He probably chose "A Baroque Eclogue" as the subtitle for *The Age of Anxiety* at around the same time. The notes Auden gave his Swarthmore seminar in romanticism a few years earlier had defined the baroque as "the counter-reformation's theatrical use of *matter* against the abstract and *earnest* thinking of the Reformers." The lyric points in the direction Auden took in his life and work two years after he wrote it: "How tempting," it begins, "to trespass in these Italian gardens."

While Auden was working on *The Age of Anxiety* he wrote only one other poem, on commission from Harvard University, where he was invited to deliver the Phi Beta Kappa poem at the 1946 graduation ceremony. "Under Which Lyre: A Reactionary Tract for the Times," like *The Age of Anxiety*, is a defense of subjectivity. The rival musical instruments of its title are the lyre of subjective, illegal, prolific Hermes and the lyre of objective, official, devouring Apollo. As Auden saw it, the war between these two gods, after a pause when they had allied themselves against a common enemy from 1939 through 1945, had now resumed in all its comic fury.* The followers of "precocious Hermes"—Auden among them—have no wish to win; they only want to be left alone with their subjective passions. It is "pompous Apollo" who wants dominion.

> If he would leave the self alone,
> Apollo's welcome to the throne,
>   Fasces and falcons;
> He loves to rule, has always done it;
> The earth would soon, did Hermes run it,
>   Be like the Balkans.

Apollo's success, in 1946, is almost complete, because his forces have learned to camouflage themselves as Hermes' forces. The then-fashionable intellectual imitators of French existentialism, having nothing

---

* Sometimes not so comic. Early in 1946 Auden's American publisher, Bennett Cerf at Random House, announced he was excluding Ezra Pound's poems from an anthology of American poetry because Pound was a traitor. Auden wrote Cerf on 29 January that whatever the merits of Pound's poems ("I do not care for them myself particularly") Cerf's actions were intolerable:

Begin by banning his poems not because you object to them but because you object to him, and you will end, as the Nazis did, by slaughtering his wife and children.

As you say, the war is not over. This incident is only one sign—there are other and far graver ones—that there was more truth than one would like to believe in Huey Long's cynical observation that if fascism came to the United States it would be called Anti-fascism. Needless to say, I am not suggesting that you desire any such thing—but I think your very natural abhorrence of Pound's conduct has led you to take the first step which, if not protested now, will be followed by others which would horrify you.

He added that he saw "no alternative for me but to sever my connection with your firm" and, despite repeated pleas from Cerf, held to his position until Cerf abandoned his.

in common with the affirming existentialism of Kierkegaard, serve only the pomposity of Apollo:

> In fake Hermetic uniforms
> Behind our battle-lines, in swarms
>   That keep alighting,
> His existentialists declare
> That they are in complete despair,
>   Yet go on writing.

The poem swears defiance, confident that the prolific impulse embodied in "white Aphrodite is on our side." Aphrodite makes common cause with the Hermetics, but not for the trivial reason that the sexuality she embodies can erupt into anarchic disorder; a Dionysiac orgy is as faceless, impersonal, and objective as an Apollonian committee. Aphrodite is "on our side" because, like everything else on the Hermetic side, sexuality is most fulfilled and fulfilling when it is *personal*.

To assure the morale of his allies, Auden closes the poem by reciting the Hermetic Decalogue. Among its commandments are: Thou shalt not do as the dean pleases nor sit with statisticians; instead thou shalt "Read *The New Yorker* [then in its most irreverent era], trust in God; / And take short views." Auden read the poem aloud in a ceremony organized by Apollonians: he was followed by Harvard's University Orator, recently returned from his wartime post as director of censorship. Earlier in the day, when he met Harvard's president, James Bryant Conant, he thought, as he later told Alan Ansen, "This is the real enemy." He suspected Conant (a member of the Interim Committee of advisers to President Truman in the last months of the war) of having made the final decision to use the atomic bomb against Japan. But the war in which Auden took Hermes' side was also a war within himself. Remembering Prospero's chilly management of those around him, Auden told Ansen he had "a bit of Apollo" in himself.

In 1947, after he finished *The Age of Anxiety*, he wrote a group of shorter poems in which the subjective could be heard, if at all, only as a still small voice. The first of these was a miniature, elusive vision of pandemic disaster, "Nursery Rhyme," about a daydreamed past, when "Their learned kings sat down to chat with frogs," that has yielded to an actual present where "The blinded bears have rooted up the stoves." The technical complexity of its form—a cycle of interlocking triplets, not unlike those of a villanelle, based on a medieval Portuguese lyric sent to

Auden by Theodore Spencer—is more striking than anything in it, and like much of his work in 1947, its worst fault is its triviality.

He managed to avoid triviality a few months later when he returned to the theme of "Nursery Rhyme" in "The Fall of Rome." In this poem the subjective speaks only in a realm where officialdom can contain and ignore it, where "an unimportant clerk / Writes I DO NOT LIKE MY WORK / On a pink official form."* In both fifth-century and twentieth-century empires, rule and rebellion are impersonal and collective: "Cere-brotonic Cato may / Extol the Ancient Disciplines / While the muscle-bound Marines / Mutiny for food and pay." The doom of empire—one impersonal dominion falling to another equally impersonal one—is prefigured in the reindeer that "altogether elsewhere" are displaced by unnamed hordes of warriors approaching from the steppes.

In other poems he wrote in 1947, Auden praised the small, unimpressive particulars of the subjective world, but he did so in language that was too precious and unfocused to be convincing. He was trying to find a way to celebrate everything human that was neither grand nor successful nor ascetic nor extreme nor decisive nor compelling—everything that was part of the common humanity united in the feast of All Souls; but the examples he chose had the effect of making readers merely feel distant from them—probably because he felt the same way. "Music Is International," written on one week's notice as the Phi Beta Kappa poem for Columbia University's graduation ceremony, is more wordy than memorable. "In Schrafft's" fails to glorify the visionary moment it tries to praise, the moment when a middle-aged woman's smile in a New York coffee shop (one of a popular chain) "attested / That, whomever it was, a god / Worth kneeling-to for a while / Had tabernacled and rested." And in "The Duet" the rich and aesthetic "huge sad lady" pities herself in overripe diction while "a scrunty beggar," tipsy and out of tune, "Cried Nonsense to her large repining"; the beggar's praises are no more convincing than the lady's complaints. Auden's insistence that the beggar's "scrannel music-making" was the true voice of praise was his means of renouncing the Miltonic claims he had made in his elegy for Yeats: "scrannel" was the dismissive adjective in "Lycidas" for songs that were lean, flashy, grating, and false. He was renouncing old errors without finding plausible truths to put in their place. In July 1947, while writing these po-

---

* The rhyme *clerk/work* serves as an elliptical announcement of Auden's American citizenship, which he had received in 1946. He told Alan Ansen that he wanted the language of *The Age of Anxiety* to be thoroughly American; when Ansen made a typed copy to give to the publisher, the only Britishism that slipped past him was the spelling "Quiz Programme."

ems, he told Elizabeth Mayer, "Work sticks a bit as I am in one of those necessary but unpleasant periods when one is full of ideas but is looking for the right focus for them and the right form of expression." He was finding his way to new complexities through these simple parables of the incursion of collective and official life on the personal realm.*

Before he could find the "right focus" and "form of expression" he was looking for, Auden felt he needed to change his deepest relations with himself. During the mid-1940s, at around the same time he was considering a conversion to Judaism, he also called into question his attitudes toward his sexuality and the guilt that seemed inseparable from it. In the past he had occasionally gone to bed with one or another of his women friends when it was clear she would be disappointed by a refusal (talking with him about homosexuality, Kallman exulted in the camp taunt, "At least *I'm* pure"), but late in 1945 he seems to have made a deliberate decision to have a heterosexual affair. His first steps were tentative, extending no further than inviting for the evening a woman friend who failed to show up. Then, early in 1946, while still working on *The Age of Anxiety*, he began an affair with a friend who was doing some work for him as a secretary and who had been the model for all the features of Rosetta he had not found in himself. Rhoda Jaffe was Jewish, like Rosetta, and like Rosetta she had a mother who had died young and a father who had failed financially and was emotionally opaque; he had managed an orphanage and she had imagined herself as one of the orphans. In 1946 she was planning to change her job from employment director at a restaurant chain to department-store buyer, the job that in the poem Rosetta does well. She had been friendly with Kallman at Brooklyn College and had known Auden since his first months in New York. In 1944,

---

* His introduction to a Modern Library selection of fairy tales by Grimm and Andersen, written in 1947 but not published until 1952, warned against the dangerous tendency to shift children's education from parents to schools. "If people are sincere when they say that the great contemporary menace in every country is the encroachment of the power of the State over the individual citizen, they must not invite it to mold the thinking of their children in their most impressionable years by refusing to help with their education themselves." The tales of Grimm and Andersen are ideal examples of "the personally told tale which permits of interruptions and repeats," and their publication in an inexpensive volume, he hoped, "will be a step in the campaign to restore to parents the right and the duty to educate their children, which, partly through their own fault, and partly through extraneous circumstances, they are in danger of losing for good."

at her wedding to another of Kallman's college friends, Milton Klonsky, Auden was one of the four men who held the ceremonial canopy, the *huppah*. She was strikingly attractive and, although she insisted on talking at length about her psychoanalysis ("Should I hide away / My secret sins in consulting rooms"), her character had, at the time, a generous warmth that was otherwise rare in the sharp-tongued literary circle she moved in. Her marriage had disintegrated, within a year or two, into a series of trial separations, and she tried to argue Auden into bed by asking if he intended to go through life without heterosexual experience. In the spring of 1946 Auden was teaching for one semester at Bennington College in Vermont, occasionally returning to New York for the weekend. Their affair apparently began during one such weekend. After a later visit he wrote to her: "The weather is lovely here but the bed is lonely and I wish you were in it. Aren't men BEASTS. No finer feelings."

"I have pencilled on envelopes / Lists of my loves," Emble confesses in a guilty moment in *The Age of Anxiety*. His lines conceal Auden's self-rebuke for writing similar lists in moods of retrospective analysis. Around May 1947, he listed in a notebook the great emotional milestones of his life. He framed each name with the calendar year and his age at the time:

1922	Robert	15
1926	Christopher	19
1932	[The subject of "Lay your sleeping head"]	25
1939	Chester	32
1946	Rh[oda]	39

These names commemorate the sexual loves that had had the greatest effect on his work and life; infatuations and mere sexual friendships are omitted. Robert Medley had first given him the idea that he might write poetry when they walked together across a salt marsh near their school. Christopher Isherwood had been, at first, an object of sexual passion and literary discipleship. The young man named next to the date 1932 had inspired Auden's series of love poems from 1933 to 1937.*

---

* Auden deleted two names while writing the list: "Mr. Newman," the school chaplain with whom he seems to have had his first sexual experience at thirteen, during the episode he later called his "period of ecclesiastical *Schwärmerei*" (*Forewords and Afterwords*, p. 517), and "Bill C.," the heterosexual painter William Coldstream, with whom he worked at the General Post Office Film Unit in 1935 and with whom he devised his materialist aesthetic in the mid-1930s. He told a friend he "had a pash" for Coldstream but never consummated it.

When Auden began seeing Rhoda Jaffe, he was creating in Rosetta the first female character in his work who was neither demonized (like the mothers in *Paid on Both Sides* and *The Ascent of F6*) nor idealized (like Mary and Miranda). And he made amends for these earlier portraits by writing "The Mythical Sex," a casual-seeming prose piece he wrote for *Harper's Bazaar* about the impersonal myths of Infernal Venus and Celestial Venus, which mask the personal reality of beautiful women. These myths arose, he said, from the assumption that romantic love is the most interesting thing in the world, which "may or may not be true . . . but most of us, even if we are a little ashamed of doing so, believe it, and in consequence beautiful women become more 'fictionalized,' less like their living originals, than any other kind of human being."

His affair with Rhoda Jaffe did not alter the fact of his homosexuality—he casually refers to himself as "a queer" in a letter to her—but it transformed his interpretation of it. Having once defined his sexual inclination as both a crime and a curse, he could now think of it as a voluntary choice. If even for a brief interval he could choose an alternative, then it was not a curse after all. The clearest note that sounds through his letters to Jaffe is one of grateful admiration: "Lots and lots of love, darling. You are *so* good, and I'm a neurotic middle-aged butterball."

After about a year and a half, sometime in late 1947 or early 1948, she apparently brought the affair to an amicable end. In April 1948 he wrote to her: "I can't tell you, my dear, how I feel about all your goodness to me during the past winter—I don't deserve it and I never shall."*

Once in 1938, when Isherwood was raging against religion, Auden had told him: "Careful, careful, my dear—if you keep going on like that, you'll have *such* a conversion, one of these days." (Isherwood converted to Vedanta a few months later.) Auden had briefly been a "homosexual chauvinist," as Edmund Wilson described him in 1945, and "homosexual to an almost fanatical degree," as Wilson noted again early in 1946, but

* A renewed sense of unworthiness led him many years later to regret having encouraged another person to offer sexual love that he could not fully return. "I tried to have an affair with a woman, but it was a great mistake. It was a sin," he told Margaret Gardiner (*A Scatter of Memories*, 1988). And he insisted to friends that it was morally contemptible for a homosexual man to marry a heterosexual woman, because of the inevitable inequality in their love. But he had gone to bed at least once more with an insistent woman friend who had followed him to Italy from New York. And in 1952, in the afterglow of a dinner party but with entirely serious intent, he proposed marriage to Thekla Clark, a friend on Ischia who, as friends who knew both women observed, somewhat resembled Jaffe.

after his affair with Jaffe was over, he found militant homosexuality harder to maintain. "I've come to the conclusion that it's wrong to be queer," he told Ansen in October 1947: "all homosexual acts are acts of envy."* When the Kinsey Report, *Sexual Behavior in the Human Male*, appeared in January 1948, he first considered writing an anonymous article attacking the book, he told Ansen, from "the standpoint of a representative of the Homintern."† But he never wrote the article, and in 1954, after the first of the British parliamentary debates on homosexuality, he told James Stern: "I tried writing an anonymous essay in the summer for *Encounter* but it turned out so *anti* homintern that I tore it up." In 1950, he headed his review of a new biography of Oscar Wilde with the barbed title, "A Playboy of the Western World: St. Oscar the Homintern Martyr."

The one love poem Auden wrote during his months with Rhoda Jaffe renounced much of the rhetorical reticence of *The Age of Anxiety*. The "Serenade" that begins "On and on and on" claims first that all things, "with or without a mind," from waterfalls to diplomats, have an ax to grind and rights to declare. "Not one is man enough / To be, simply, publicly, there." But that same self-assertiveness is the means by which "my embodied love"—despite its rhetorical excess, despite being "like most feeling . . . Half humbug and half true"—"Asks neighborhood of you." Theatricality and rhetoric have become a medium of love, not a falsifying obstruction. And the adjective in the phrase "my embodied love" is an early sign of an integrated sense of self unlike anything in his work before.

Auden now felt a new sense of release from the isolating superiority of rhetoric and the isolating inferiority of guilt. This was a frame of mind

---

* That is, all such acts are based on the envy of a partner's greater strength, whether physical, intellectual, or social—as in Auden's theory in the late 1930s of the unhappy love that one world feels for another. Heterosexual partners, in Auden's implicit contrast, each have strengths that the other does not have at all, and that each can therefore give the other. Auden wrote to Spender in April 1942: "What *I* envy are strengths which by their nature I cannot make use of as support, e.g. your prick."

† The Homintern was the name, modeled on the Comintern, devised in Auden's circle for the informal network of homosexual chauvinists and propagandists that included many of Auden's acquaintances. Credit for originating the term was much disputed. Auden's dislike of the Kinsey Report arose partly from its distortions—"too many male whores," he told Ansen—but mostly from its pseudo-scientific statistical approach to personal intimacy, its treatment of its objects of study as numbers not faces. He wrote to T. S. Eliot that the book was "the most extreme example of pseudo-science I have ever seen. Men have 'outlets,' one of which is called 'Petting to climax.' Do the ladies have 'intakes' or what?" (19 February 1948).

in which, he thought, he could at last achieve a relation of equals with Kallman. Matters between them had become increasingly bitter since the time Auden moved back to New York in the autumn of 1945, after three years of almost continuous separation, and during the winter of 1945–46 Kallman had aired his contradictory feelings in the columns he wrote as opera reviewer for *The Commonweal*—a job he almost certainly got on Auden's recommendation. Writing about Wagner's *Die Meistersinger*, Kallman described Hans Sachs as a tired old man, "bitter about his age, disappointed in love, unsatisfied with his art . . . a recluse trying to be one of the boys." But writing about Donizetti's *Don Pasquale* a few weeks later, he rejected the "exuberant cruelty" of its "assumption that old men who want love are naturally comic." Both comments were accurate hits at Auden's newly parental manner, yet Auden was not yet thirty-nine.

Then, in September 1947, Igor Stravinsky invited Auden to write an opera libretto for him, to be based on Hogarth's series of engravings *The Rake's Progress*. He seized on Stravinsky's invitation as the opportunity to write a drama different in every way from the unemphatic inwardness of *The Age of Anxiety*. Instead of dramatizing the great rhetorical vice of the age—our self-conscious acting that allows feelings to break through only "at moments, in spite of ourselves, and when we least expect it"— he began to plan a work in which acting and feeling would be the same. Opera, as he later wrote in essays and reviews, "is an imitation of human wilfulness: it is rooted in the fact that we not only have feelings but insist upon having them at whatever cost to ourselves." While visiting Stravinsky in Los Angeles in November 1947 he devised a scenario that combined Stravinsky's musical ideas with his own aesthetic and moral ones, and during the next few weeks he talked excitedly with friends about the complex challenge of collaborating with someone so grand, so Russian, so Orthodox, so entirely unlike himself. Without troubling to consult Stravinsky, he invited Kallman to collaborate on the libretto. Though they could never become one flesh, no impediment barred them from the relation between collaborators that Auden later referred to as a marriage of true minds. The same theatricality that he believed had wrecked their relationship earlier could now be redeemed by restoring it to the proscenium arch and bright lights where it belonged.

In *The Rake's Progress*, as in all their later collaborations, Kallman had an equal—sometimes more than equal—share in the "composite personality" of joint authorship. When an early critical essay about *The Rake* failed to mention Kallman, Auden dictated most of a reply that appeared over Alan Ansen's name. "Though the scheme of the work was largely

Mr. Auden's," the letter acknowledged, "its execution was in equal measure his responsibility and that of Mr. Kallman."

Auden had given *The Age of Anxiety* a mood of repressed inwardness. Working with Kallman, he gave *The Rake's Progress* a mood of feelings so intense and public that they erupt into song—although opera directors took almost half a century before they learned not to treat the work as a frigid neoclassical pastiche. In a theory of opera that Auden set out in print at the time of the premiere in 1951, he argued that a libretto can be concerned only with simple feelings, not with the complexity and multiformity of real persons:

> Opera . . . cannot present character in the novelist's sense of the word, namely, people who are potentially good *and* bad, active *and* passive, for music is immediate actuality and neither potentiality nor passivity can live in its presence . . .
>
> The quality common to all the great operatic roles . . . is that each of them is a passionate and wilful state of being. In real life they would all be bores, even Don Giovanni.

But the libretto Auden and Kallman presented to Stravinsky only pretends to have little room for psychological depth. Like many works by great writers that seem to have the schematic form and conventional tone of fairy tales, it is subtle and profound in its thought and witty and gorgeous in its language. It comprises a double allegory, one public, one private. In the public allegory, which is the plot accessible to the audience, Tom Rakewell, too restless and ambitious to be content with the absolute devotion of Anne Trulove, is tempted by the Devil in the person of his servant Nick Shadow. Shadow offers Rakewell a series of pleasures, all of them tempting in their promise of freedom, all of them empty in their impersonality. When Rakewell wishes for money, Shadow appears with news of an inheritance that lets him purchase the tedium of impersonal sex and impersonal sensation, while, under Shadow's tutelage, he childishly parrots romantic theories in praise of pagan cyclical nature. When Rakewell wishes for happiness, Shadow offers him the disinterested *acte gratuit* that had come into philosophical vogue when André Gide recommended it as the key to freedom from passion and obligation— although its real attraction is its release of the temper-tantrum impulse to have one's own way at all costs. Shadow uses the idea of the *acte gratuit* to persuade Rakewell to marry the bearded lady Baba the Turk precisely because he neither desires her nor is obliged to her—so in choosing her he is perfectly free and therefore happy. (In his 1951 essay on opera, Auden wrote that we have "learned that we are less free than nineteenth-century humanism imagined, but also have become less certain that freedom is an unequivocal blessing, that the free are necessarily the good.") When, more to give satisfaction to himself than to help anyone else, Rakewell wishes to benefit humanity, Shadow ruins him in a swindle that promises to end poverty and want—and therefore, Rakewell believes, to restore humanity to Paradise—by making and selling a machine that transforms stones into bread. This something-for-nothing fantasy casts a sardonic glance at the political programs Auden had brought himself to endorse in the 1930s. (And Rakewell's cheerful justification for laziness—"Have not grave doctors assured us that good works are of no avail for Heaven predestines all?"—alludes to theories more recent than Calvinism.)

Through all this, Anne Trulove remains constant, and although she cannot rescue Rakewell from madness and death, she can save him from dying in guilty torment and despair. But all her attempts to save him are futile until he reaches a moment of absolute hopelessness, when he makes a leap of faith and believes in the impossible. In the last act, Shadow offers to play a game of cards with Rakewell, with Rakewell's soul as the stake. In each round of the game, Rakewell must guess a card. In the first round, he remembers Anne and guesses—correctly—the Queen of Hearts, which Shadow then throws aside. In the second round, Shadow again throws aside a card after Rakewell guesses it correctly. Then, in the third and last round, when Rakewell hears Anne's voice singing offstage, although he knows that Shadow has discarded the Queen of Hearts and cannot possibly be holding it, he names it again—and wins back his soul, because Shadow had snatched up the card while Rakewell was looking away. (The Devil cannot resist cheating, and loses because he does.) Shadow had observed earlier that Rakewell was childishly and easily bored, that "repetition palls him." But when Rakewell, by naming the same card twice, accepts repetition, it proves to be, as it is in Kierkegaard, the image of eternity in the world of time.

As Shadow descends into hell he curses Rakewell into madness, but Shadow wields "power to pain" only because Rakewell himself chose the mad belief that his wishes could come true. In the final scene in Bedlam, where Rakewell believes he is Adonis, Anne sings a lullaby over him, and he dies in a return to infancy. Anne's name literally means *grace*—it derives from the Hebrew name Hannah—and in the final scene she is grace's embodiment. Her song is a lullaby, because in relation to grace, everyone has the status of a child who receives unconditional, unearned love. In the opera's closing moments the characters sing moralizing limericks to the audience, reminding them that the Devil finds work for idle hands, "A work, dear Sir, fair Madam, / For you and you." Ever since the premiere, reviewers—evidently disconcerted by an opera that offers neither a romantic male villain nor a triumphant male hero—have complained that Tom Rakewell is a cipher. But he was deliberately written as a mirror of everyone's temptation to evade adulthood. *De te fabula*: the story is about you.

Concealed within this public allegory was a private allegory about Kallman's relations with Auden, for the Rake's self-destructive choices correspond to Kallman's erotic ones. Tom Rakewell, Auden wrote, "is a manic-depressive, elated by the prospect of the future and then disgusted by the remembrance of the recent past"; Auden had written helplessly about Kallman's manic-depressive cycles in letters to Rhoda Jaffe shortly before. Anne Trulove's constancy, and her insistence that "It is I who was unworthy," represent in abstract style Auden's self-denying decision to continue supporting Kallman in financial and other ways after the end of their sexual relations.

The allegory was rendered more complex by the division of labor in the writing. Auden wrote most of Rakewell's faithless lines while Kallman wrote most of Anne's faithful ones. Auden as lover appears in the libretto as Anne Trulove, but Auden as artist appears as Baba the Turk. Her beard is her gift, and she recognizes it as her vocation—a glory, not a curse. The beard, Auden said in a broadcast, "represents her genius, something which makes her what she is and at the same time cuts her off from other people." In accepting Rakewell's proposal, her mistake "is that she tries to fit into an ordinary family life, to be an ordinary person, and of course the whole thing breaks down." Her triumphant exit—when she returns to dominate the stage after her "self-indulgent intermezzo" with Rakewell—crushes into cowed subservience the auctioneer who had tried to reduce her unique exotic treasures (each one given by an admirer whom she names) to the anonymous numbered lots of a sale. Before she leaves she restores Anne to hope and encourages her search for the ruined, absconded rake.

Like any artist in Auden's meditations on art in the 1940s, Baba is too wounded and exceptional for marriage. (Although Auden never spelled out the resemblance, she is clearly an imaginary portrait of Henry James.) But when she accepts celibacy, she makes herself the defender and patroness of those who love. She is the only character who recognizes

Shadow for what he is, and her judgment of the relative guilt of Rakewell and Shadow is the same judgment Auden now made on the impulsively self-revealing Kallman and the smoothly plausible Jack Barker: "I can tell who in that pair / Is poisoned victim and who snake." The willful exuberance of the libretto, its insistence on expressing a personal history of crisis and abandonment in a language of joy, was the outer sign of an inner reconciliation. In 1949, a year after the libretto was finished, when Auden was sharing a house with Kallman after they had lived apart since 1942, he wrote to Rhoda Jaffe from Ischia that he found himself, to his "great delight," "completely untroubled by sex," that "Chester, too, is quite changed," and that the relation between them was, "for the first time, a really happy one."

═══

Auden's affair with Rhoda Jaffe, with its "embodied love," suggested to him the answer to a poetic and religious problem that had troubled him for years. He had tried repeatedly, and without success, to find poetic images for the state of reconciliation and fulfillment that Christianity promises under such names as the Kingdom of Heaven and the peace of God which passeth all understanding. In his drafts for *The Age of Anxiety* he had devised an image even less convincing than the grandiose formal garden described by Caliban at the end of "The Sea and the Mirror." In the typescript, the poem ended with fifteen lines of verse (following Malin's phrase "His World to come") in which Malin describes that ultimate moment "When the whole creation shall give out another sweetness, / Nicer in our nostrils, a novel fragrance / From cleansed occasions in accord together / As one feeling fabric, all flushed and intact." In the work of a poet who had recently (in the Hermetic Decalogue in "Under Which Lyre") warned against making love to "those / Who wash too much," this imagery seemed less than authentic. At the last minute, and at Kallman's urging, Auden dropped these fifteen lines and replaced them with a deliberately anticlimactic prose paragraph in which the narrator reports that Malin has returned to duty, "reclaimed by the actual world," whose apocalyptic self-destruction was, "as usual, postponed."*

---

* He adapted the original verse ending for use as an anthem he had been commissioned to write for the dedication of an English church in 1946. He did not include the anthem in any of his books until 1972, when, with the addition of an opening line from Caedmon's Hymn, he printed it in *Epistle to a Godson* under the title "Anthem."

Like Caliban's description of "the unbothered state," Malin's abandoned lines define that state by its novelty, difference, and otherness. But
after the recent changes in his sense of himself, Auden realized that
everything he had hoped to find in the realm of the Wholly Other was
waiting for him closer to home—in the same way he had realized in 1939
that he had been wrong to look for love in the world of the Alter Ego.
He already knew where to look. A signpost could be found in Malin's
meditative verses (metrically imitated from Bach's passion chorales, as a
sign of the Protestant faith they express) that precede his final speech in
The Age of Anxiety:

> For the new locus is never
> Hidden inside the old one
> Where Reason could rout it out,
> Nor guarded by dragons in distant
> Mountains where Imagination
> Could explore it: the place of birth
> Is too obvious and near to notice,
> Some dull dogpatch a stone's throw
> Outside the walls, reserved
> For the eyes of faith to find.

The place of birth—no longer a place of murder—was now a place
where the two halves of the divided self might find their relation. In
Auden's poems after 1947, the vocabulary of division that had governed
his work since 1939 suddenly altered, and the incoherent structure in
which he had yoked Kierkegaardian choice to Jungian archetype disappeared. As Auden imagined Herman Melville saying, in a poem of 1939,
"All that was intricate and false." The world and the self were still divided
against themselves, but the metaphors for their division were no longer
the metaphors of a wholly other life, or an impossible heaven, or a walled
archetypal garden. The other part of the self and its means of access to
the world were to be found in a local and specific landscape, one that
Auden, like everyone else, had occupied from the moment he was born,
a place that until now had been too obvious and near to notice, a changing landscape, with a surface fragrance of time and, beneath, a secret
system of caves and conduits.

PART TWO

The Flesh We Are

1948–1957

CHAPTER TEN

The Murmurs of the Body

In 1948, the year Auden first summered in Italy, he began to write poems about the inarticulate human body. His work had an exhilarated air of discovery, as if he had found what he called "the missing entry in Don Giovanni's list": the body that never asks to be regimented or idealized, feels no abstract hatred or intellectual envy, believes no theories, and is moved by impulses that, fortunately for us, are not exactly the same as our own. He dedicated to the body some of his most profound poems, works whose depth and breadth have been underestimated because their treatment of their subject matter was novel and unexpected in an age whose writers hesitated to see the body as "simply, publicly, there." And because he learned to value the body as sacred in itself, Auden learned to believe in it as the means and promise of salvation. For his most sustained poetic meditation on the body, "Memorial for the City," he chose a visionary epigraph by the fourteenth-century anchoress Julian of Norwich, who wrote: "In the self-same point that our soul is made sensual, in the self-same point is the City of God ordained to him from without beginning."

Auden said later about the existentialist philosophy he had admired in Kierkegaard that it had "done all it can, and is now a danger"; he was perhaps speaking about the danger to himself as much as to the intellectual climate. "I think it's a form of gnosticism. It doesn't pay proper attention to the body." In place of the weightless archetypes and faculties that he had admired in Jung, in place of the daemon and the mysterious forces, he now wrote about an ordinary human shape. Caliban in "The

Sea and the Mirror" had not been body but flesh: a personification of impulse and id, not something that could be wounded or embraced.

Auden's reconciliation with the body as a poetic subject reflected a conciliation he had made with his own body. Neither party to this marriage of equals could hope to dominate or reform the other, and each must learn to live with the other's annoying habits. After 1947, when Auden found himself tempted to commit "the sin of the high-minded, sublimation," he remembered the corns with which he had long been afflicted, and wrote about them, sometimes explicitly, sometimes not. "A martyr to corns," he regarded his martyrdom as fortunate. In the most solemn of all his poems, "Nones," during the appalled silence after the Crucifixion, the crowd that shouted for the event experiences its effect in their own bodies: "We are left alone with our *feat*." And in "Under Sirius," the promised world to come is one in which the body regains its pedal graces and "the reborn *featly* dance." The last time Auden's body had been present in his serious poems in this way was in "A Summer Night," after his vision of Agape in 1933, when he wrote of his sleeping posture: "my feet / Point to the rising moon."

This sense of a restored relation with the flesh led him to other integrations. He found in the Communion service the action and symbol of membership in the human community. In the ritual act through which the communicant receives wine and bread as the body and blood of Christ, he understood a means of participation in the "Body of Christ" that was the living church. In Auden's earlier Kierkegaardian prayers, the absolute had seemed impossibly distant, but now (as in the phrase reported in the Gospel of Matthew), "where two or three are gathered together in my name, there am I in the midst of them." By 1947 Auden had read, and began recommending to friends, *The Shape of the Liturgy*, by Dom Gregory Dix, a tendentious but revelatory history of Christian worship, first published in 1945. At the center of Dix's book is an argument that modern individualist prayer both impoverishes and falsifies the corporate prayer of the Church. Through increasingly private ideas of prayer introduced in the later Middle Ages, Dix argued, the laity had lost "the notion of the priestly prayer of the whole church, as the prayer of Christ the world's Mediator through His Body." This loss was inadvertently worsened when the laity's instinct that they had "a more effective part to play in intercession than listening to someone else praying" was stifled; this drove them "to *substitute* private and solitary intercession for the prayer of the church as the really effective way of prayer, instead of regarding their private prayer as deriving its effectiveness from their membership of the church. So their hold on the corporate life is weakened and their own prayers are deprived of that inspiration and guidance which come from participating in really devout corporate prayer."*

One of the first poems Auden wrote in 1948 was "The Love Feast," a meditation on the Communion service lightly disguised as a sardonic survey of a late-night drunken party in which all "worship" is private: "Jack likes Jill who worships George / Who has the hots for Jack." The title of the poem is a common translation of the Greek word *agape*, and the party takes place, like the Last Supper, in "an upper room." "Catechumens make their entrance," but we are "gathered on behalf / Of love according to the gospel / Of the radio-phonograph." A stanza in the original text reads: "Who is Jenny lying to / By long-distance telephone? / The Love that made her out of nothing / Tells me to go home." When Auden revised the poem he changed the first two lines to: "Who is Jenny lying to / In her call, Collect, to Rome?" Besides correcting a false rhyme, this sharpens the poem's point about the absence of inspiration and guidance that might be gained through a petitionary prayer (a Collect) in a church service.

Dix's argument in *The Shape of the Liturgy* integrated liturgy, theology, and justice. "A 'high' doctrine of the sacrament," he wrote, a doctrine in which the body of Christ is believed to be really present in the bread and wine and really present in the body of the Church, "has always been accompanied by an aroused conscience as to the condition of Christ's poor." As in his conversion to radical Protestantism in 1940, Auden's new beliefs about sacrament and liturgy included the imperatives of social justice. During the next few years he wrote his great sequence "Horae Canonicae," which focuses its attention on the murdered victim excluded from the prosperous city.

At the same time, his statements of Protestant faith and dismissals of Catholic doctrine began to disappear from his prose. In September 1947, replying to a student's question about his religious beliefs, he proposed a new formulation:

I am a member of the Episcopal Communion, i.e. Anglican. I myself do not take the differences between the Churches who basically share the same doctrines (i.e., who recite the Nicene and Athanasian Creeds and believe in the

* Auden's remarks to Alan Ansen in March 1947 paraphrase a recurring theme in Dix: "When you go to Mass, it makes absolutely no difference whether you're emotionally excited or not. Religious emotion, like any other kind of emotion, is irrelevant to religious duty" (Ansen, *The Table Talk of W. H. Auden*, 1990, p. 34).

sacraments) very seriously. If I had been, say, a Frenchman, I would obviously have returned to Roman Catholicism. As I was born in Englishman, I returned to a church whose split with Rome is largely an historical accident. Thus, since in the creed I say, *I believe in the Holy Catholic Church*, I suppose I call myself a Catholic.

And in the early 1950s, as he wrote increasingly about the world of nature, his poems began sketching a theology of the Madonna, although with an allusiveness and tact that spared his Protestant friends from feeling scandalized.

Around 1947 Auden began to take on shared and corporate responsibilities, some of them tedious, all of them in service to causes with no political ambition. He became active in a small theological discussion group called The Third Hour, which met mostly in living rooms,* and in the larger Guild of Episcopal Scholars, which met every year at the General Theological Seminary in New York. He enjoyed serving on a criminal grand jury in New York and did his best to frustrate the over-eager district attorney who sought indictments from it. When the Readers' Subscription book club was founded in 1951 as a selective alternative to mass-market operations like the Book-of-the-Month Club, Auden was brought into the editorial board with the first two members, Jacques Barzun and Lionel Trilling, and shared the work of choosing monthly selections and writing reviews for the club's monthly bulletin, *The Griffin*. (The young man who organized the club had been Barzun and Trilling's student at Columbia.) Auden took enough pleasure in the work to produce some of his best critical prose, and was friendly with his fellow editors without always sharing their academic tastes; Trilling, he complained privately, did not really like literature. Auden was the only board member who understood the club's finances well enough to warn of problems that forced a reorganization, and the board's departure, in 1959. Soon afterward, with different managers, the three editors founded the Mid-Century Book Society and its bulletin, *The Mid-Century*; this lasted only three years before sinking under financial losses that Auden had again gloomily predicted to his sanguine colleagues.

---

* "And it was the third hour, and they crucified him" (Mark 15:25). The group was organized mostly by the Russian Orthodox writers Nicholas Berdyaev, Helene Iswolsky, Vassily Yanovsky, and others, but its highly ecumenical membership included at various times Father Martin D'Arcy (the Oxford theologian who had befriended Auden when he was an undergraduate), Dorothy Day, Denis de Rougemont, Jacques Maritain, and other Roman Catholics, and the very Protestant Marianne Moore.

Auden made himself available throughout this period as a judge for literary prizes and fellowships, especially ones that favored younger writers and translators. From 1947 through 1959 he was the editor of the Yale Series of Younger Poets, the best-known series of its kind, for which he chose a first book of poems by a different poet each year, and wrote encouraging letters to many of those he turned down. He took time to settle into his editorship. The first volume that appeared during his tenure was a posthumous book by Joan Murray, who had studied with him when he first taught in New York and had died at twenty-five; Auden brought the book to the Yale University Press when he found nothing worth printing among the manuscripts submitted directly by their authors. In 1948 he again passed over the submitted manuscripts and chose a book by Robert Horan, a poet and writer on dance whom he had met through Lincoln Kirstein. Horan was loosely associated with a small group of poets in California who called themselves Activists—a label that had nothing to do with politics and everything to do with the intensity of their style. After this, Auden chose from submitted manuscripts, and in 1949 selected one by Rosalie Moore, who was even closer to the Activists and perhaps had been encouraged by Horan to send in her poems. Although Auden acknowledged in his foreword that there were "dangers in the Activist approach, as in any approach," he found it useful illustrative propaganda for his anti-utopian aesthetics. The Activists' conception of poetry, he wrote, "is a reaction—and a healthy one—against the conception of poetry as the defender of humanist values of intelligence and order against irrationalism, such as has been put forward by that very fine poet Dr. Yvor Winters, and the conception of poetry as an instrument for arousing proper public emotions about political and social issues, such as was common during the 'thirties.'" But he recognized that the Activists tended toward rhapsodic nonsense in the manner of Hart Crane, and although he visited the group during a lecture tour a few years later, he never mentioned them again.*

He found none of the 1950 submissions to the Yale series worth printing, although he told the leader of the Activists, Lawrence Hart, that a submission from another member of the group was the best of the lot. Then, in 1951, he began selecting manuscripts marked by the formal fluency, emotional subtlety, and intellectual clarity that, largely under his own influence, was becoming characteristic of much American poetry.

---

* Horan was the only member of the group represented in Auden's selection for *The Faber Book of Modern American Verse*, published a few years later.

The eight poets he chose from 1951 through 1959 (he found nothing he liked in 1955) were Adrienne Rich, W. S. Merwin, Edgar Bogardus, Daniel Hoffman, John Ashbery,* James Wright, John Hollander, and William Dickey. Seven of them (Bogardus died young) vindicated Auden's choice by going on to establish prolific and widely honored careers, but Auden had doubts about the poetic style that took his own as its model and had now become the quasi-official voice of American verse. The best poetry in America, he wrote in 1954, was composed not in an official voice or in any other conventional voice but in each poet's own: "The first thing that strikes a reader about the best American poets is how utterly unlike they are . . . The danger for the American poet is not of writing like everyone else but of crankiness and a parody of his own manner." He appended his warning doubts in a footnote: "The undeniable appearance in the States during the past fifteen years or so"—the period that happened to begin when he arrived in 1939—"of a certain literary conformity, of a proper and authorized way to write poetry is a new and disquieting symptom, which I cannot pretend to be able to explain fully." An official style helped further Apollo's will to regimentation even when the style itself originated in the service of Hermes.

In the 1930s Auden had been mostly exasperated by his work with the Group Theatre in London, which had been cobbled together—organized is too strong a word—by the dancer Rupert Doone and Auden's school friend Robert Medley; and he felt frivolously subversive when he worked for six months in the General Post Office's serious-minded documentary film unit. But in the 1950s he was exhilarated by his collaboration with a pioneering early-music group, the New York Pro Musica, efficiently organized and imaginatively led by a young labor activist named Noah Greenberg until Greenberg's death in 1966. Auden read the verse in the group's concerts—and a recording—of Elizabethan verse and music in 1954 and 1955. He and Kallman collaborated with Greenberg on *An Elizabethan Song Book*, published in 1955. He wrote the verse narration for the Pro Musica's production of the hitherto-unknown medieval music-drama *The Play of Daniel*, and in 1958 joined in the preparations for its first performance in the churchlike setting of the Cloisters in New

---

* In 1956 the manuscripts submitted by Ashbery and Frank O'Hara were among those weeded out by the Yale University Press before sending the rest to Auden, who, then, for the second year in a row, found nothing worth choosing. When he later heard from Kallman that Ashbery and O'Hara had submitted work he had not seen, he sent word to them asking for copies and chose Ashbery's.

York. Audiences were startled to encounter a sacred medieval work with the musical variety and emotional intensity of grand opera, and the production became an international success. It was typically performed in churches, with the narrator, costumed as a monk, reading from the pulpit; Auden delighted in playing the narrator in a series of performances at an Oxford church in 1960. The rewards of shared effort that he had imagined he could find by submerging himself in political work in the 1930s finally came to him in the 1950s through musical and theological work.

Through his new interest in the liturgical aspects of his religion he found in collective worship a source of forgiveness that he had never found in private individual faith. In 1947 he manifested the seriousness of his interest in the Church Visible by making an elaborately frivolous joke about it. In Cherry Grove, a largely homosexual summer colony on Fire Island, near New York, a Carnival was celebrated every August; costumes were obligatory, and almost all the costumes were drag. Auden, after some days of thought, dressed himself up (he told Ursula Niebuhr) "as a Bishop, mitre, cape and all"; Kallman accompanied him as a "very rococo guardian angel." As in all of Auden's theological camp, the joke simultaneously affirmed the absolute seriousness of the subject and the limited, artificial, therefore ultimately frivolous approach to it, which was, he thought, the most that any individual could achieve.

Theologically more to the point, he told other friends that he had dressed for the Carnival as Ronald Firbank's lascivious Cardinal Pirelli. Firbank's butterfly-like novels, with their elliptical comic plots, suggestively witty dialogue, and brief concluding glimpses of real suffering, had developed a sophisticated cult following when they appeared between 1915 and his death in 1926. A few titles had been reprinted in the United States, but were now mostly unavailable. In 1947 Auden lobbied American publishers to reprint them, and after he finally persuaded New Directions to issue a one-volume edition of five Firbank novels in 1949, he arranged to review it in *The New York Times Book Review*. "Firbank's extraordinary achievement," he wrote, "was to draw a picture, the finest, I believe, ever drawn by anyone, of the Earthly Paradise, not, of course, as it really is, but as, in our fallen state, we imagine it to be, as the place, that is, where, without having to change our desires and behavior in any way, we suffer neither frustration nor guilt." Firbank's recognition—as Auden generously imagined it—that the Earthly Paradise appears in unique ways to every unique person inspired Auden's descriptions of his own private Eden ("Public Statues: Confined to famous defunct chefs") during the next few years. The point of the comedy was the same point Auden attributed to Firbank: "The fact that Firbank's novels are so funny is proof that he never lets us forget the contradiction between life as it is and life as we should like it to be, for it is the impossibility of that contradiction which makes us laugh."

A prior contradiction, between the absolute and the human, makes no one laugh, but it is the cause of the comic contradiction between life as it is and life as we should like it to be. Auden's theology now recognized that for real human beings frivolity was a sign and symbol of seriousness. He chose a line from Firbank as the epigraph to *The Age of Anxiety*: " 'Oh, Heaven help me,' she prayed, 'to be decorative and to do right.' " He then accepted Theodore Spencer's suggestion that he drop it: "*I* think it very serious but no one else will unless I write an essay to explain why." But finally he restored it as the epigraph to "The Masque" instead of to the whole poem, and wrote his explanatory essay a few years later (without mentioning Firbank) under the title "Notes on the Comic," the last section of which is headed "The comic presentation of the state of Grace." Where the seriousness of Auden's religion of imaginary saints in 1941 had been a mask for a frivolous self-dramatizing fiction, now Firbank's frivolity was a mask for a seriousness of purpose too thorough to make claims for itself. By choosing Firbank for a brief term as his literary master Auden permanently banished his earlier master, Rilke, who (he wrote later) had tempted him into "making some of my poems too *schöngeistig*, too much Poetry with a capital P."*

===

Auden was finding other integrations between poetry and experience, and now he belatedly recorded in his published work the suffering and despair he had witnessed on his mission to postwar Germany in 1945. He had acknowledged it privately, from the start, as one of the most wrenching experiences of his life. "I keep wishing you were with us to help," he had told Elizabeth Mayer soon after he arrived, "and then I think perhaps not, for as I write this sentence I find myself crying."

---

* Rilke, like Blake and Yeats, was a writer whom Auden used as an example when he needed him and then lost interest in him. Referring to Rilke's bodiless visionary ecstasies, Auden called him (in conversation among friends in 1964) "the greatest lesbian poet since Sappho" (Robert Craft, *Stravinsky: Chronicle of a Friendship*, 1972, p. 258). In the more public setting of an interview he called him one of the "Promethean madmen" among modern writers (interview with Philip Hodson, *The Isis*, 8 November 1967).

He had gone to Germany as a uniformed civilian attached to the United States Strategic Bombing Survey, established at the end of 1944 by the Secretary of War to gauge the military, economic, and psychological effects of Allied bombing in Germany and Japan; it was directed by about a dozen management and financial experts (among them, George Ball and Paul Nitze), economists (John Kenneth Galbraith), sociologists (Rensis Likert), and corporate executives (Henry Alexander). Auden had been recruited for the large staff of German-speaking interviewers by one of his Swarthmore colleagues, the social psychologist Richard S. Crutchfield, and was given the "equivalent" rank of major by virtue of his academic salary and status. At Auden's suggestion, James Stern also joined up, and until the end of July they worked together in the Morale Division, with Auden as Research Chief for one of the teams, interviewing a random sample of the population in six cities in and near Bavaria. Auden said later that "we asked them if they minded being bombed." But he also recalled that the survey's final report, *The Effects of Strategic Bombing on Civilian Morale*, indicated that the policy of massive bombing had done less to hasten victory than its proponents claimed. As he told Elizabeth Mayer: "Washington is going, I know, to say that the people we've interviewed have pulled the wool over our eyes, but it is not so."

While in Germany he compiled reports on his team's findings and, as he implied in brief letters to friends, made unspecified bureaucratic maneuvers to engineer assignments for himself to write a report on the 20 July 1944 plot to kill Hitler and "a *very* high-brow" report on Christianity and Nazism.* Yet the verse he wrote in 1945 after his return to New York gave no hint that he had ever left home. Before they left, he and Stern had contracted with a publisher to collaborate on a book about their experiences, but he showed no interest in working on it when they got back, and Stern eventually wrote it alone. (*The Hidden Damage* was published in 1947; Auden makes brief appearances as an Englishman named Mervyn.) He waited four years before he first evoked the demolished cities, the barbed wire, the captives led away, and the crow on

---

* Auden apparently did not write a report on juvenile delinquency during the war that he is sometimes reported to have written, but he did liberate such a report from a cache of Gestapo documents. Later in his mission he told Kallman he was going to see an Old Etonian for information on juvenile delinquency and underground movements in Munich, and perhaps he appended this information to the German report. None of Auden's reports has been identified, despite extensive research by Jacek Niecko in the National Archives.

the crematorium chimney—all of which appear in the opening lines of
"Memorial for the City."

Auden was able to write about these matters in this poem because he
had learned to write about the body. The flesh that belongs to everyone
in the same way became a means of understanding the corporate society
everyone belongs to in common. And because the body is an attribute
of each individual person, Auden interpreted the city as a set of persons
in relation to each other, not as a statistical average or a sociological
generalization. The uprooted isolates of *The Age of Anxiety* are interesting as persons only to the degree that they make or avoid existential
choices; the poem has only a cursory interest in the civil space where
each person has a role, profession, economic status, and a unique and
shifting balance of the securities and uncertainties of citizenship. But
now, in Auden's poems after 1948, these attributes are essential aspects
of personality, not arbitrary accidents (like Rosetta's or Quant's job,
which could have been any job).

Auden had portrayed in his earlier poems the fact of civil guilt—over
the unjust exclusion of an outsider or over the injustice of society at
large—but he had never quite succeeded in portraying the excluded victim as anything more than a hypothetical or metaphoric projection of
the guilt itself, a figure unknown and unknowable, often a literary image
(like the victim of sexual murder—"the body half undressed / We all
had reason to detest"—who represented "The situation of our time" in
"New Year Letter"). When he wrote "The Guilty Vicarage," his essay
on detective stories, in 1946, he had begun to recognize this as a moral
evasion. The "magical satisfaction" that a reader—someone "like myself,
a person who suffers from a sense of sin"—seeks in these stories is "the
illusion of being dissociated from the murderer." But this satisfaction is
merely magical, and the stories are "escape literature, not works of art."
The private purpose of Auden's essay was to remind its author that the
works of art he wanted to write, but did not yet know how to write,
should provide no magical illusion of dissociation. By May 1948, Auden's
birthday poem for T. S. Eliot referred to "the bloody corpse"—still a
literary image, but for the first time stained with real blood; two years
later, he was alluding explicitly to "this mutilated flesh, our victim." The
ancient imagery of the Communion service had become urgent and
contemporary.

Auden saw that the "magic formula" of the detective story ends with
a "real innocence from which the guilty other has been expelled, a cure
effected, not by me or my neighbors, but the miraculous intervention of

a genius from outside"—Sherlock Holmes, Inspector French, Father Brown, or any of the heroes whose loss is mourned in "The Dirge" in *The Age of Anxiety*. But in the real world, he knew, restored innocence is a magical illusion. In "A Walk After Dark," written in August 1948, the victims, those whom the present has "wronged," "whimper and are ignored." The poem ends with the poet, looking outward from self to society, "Asking what judgement waits / My person, all my friends, / And these United States."

These essays and poems explicitly deny that sexuality and the body are necessarily implicated in Auden's own sense of guilt, or in anyone else's. The sin and guilt explored in his later work were shared by all people, and could be forgiven *because* of shared bodily realities, not, as in Manichaean fantasies of sinful flesh, in spite of them. "Without me," the body says in "Memorial for the City," "Adam would have fallen irrevocably with Lucifer; he would never have been able to cry *O felix culpa*."

This new theme in Auden's work coincided with new ways of thinking about history. He was returning to the idea of revolutionary change he had adopted in his English years, but he hoped to find truer versions of it than those he had rejected earlier. In his early twenties, he had written about an impending revolution which he described partly in Marxist terms as the overthrow of a class, partly in visionary terms as a restoration of the first-century community of agape. Now he wrote about a series of past revolutions, each successively revealing different aspects of the relation of individual persons to the full community of man and God.

In both instances, he adapted his revolutionary vision from the religious theories of an extravagant polymath—Gerald Heard in the 1930s, Eugen Rosenstock-Huessy in the 1940s. The Agape, as Heard had described it in *Social Substance of Religion* (1931), ignited a psychic revolution:

> The small group of about a dozen . . . formed an inward-looking group—perhaps a ring. There was a great cry of Sursum Corda . . . It was the outbreak of exultation as the worshipers realized they were in the formed psychic field . . . What has been described [here] is the minimum manifestation of the force which suddenly precipitated somewhere in the Levant and spread along the veins of the tired Empire like a new wine.

This was the basis of the revolution of love that Auden half seriously had hoped could be achieved by what he called in 1931 "the smaller group, the right field of force." In Heard's version of liturgical history, the bureaucratic Church replaced the ecstatic Agape with the ritualistic Mass, and Auden did not try to convince himself for long that the loving group would survive as a social unit under the rule of a bureaucratic party.

In 1946 he found a different revolutionary vision in Rosenstock-Huessy's account of All Souls in *Out of Revolution*.* In *The Age of Anxiety* Auden borrowed the idea of All Souls as a recurring ritual of universal communion, but Rosenstock-Huessy also interpreted All Souls as a unique historical event in the same way that Heard interpreted the Agape: as a sudden revolutionary impulse in the midst of a tired empire. Rosenstock-Huessy saw All Souls, with its implications of inclusive democracy, as an instrument and symbol of a papal revolution in the tenth and eleventh centuries, when Pope Gregory VII established the primacy of pope over emperor. No other historian had described these events as a revolution, but Rosenstock-Huessy saw it as the first in the linked series of Europe's great revolutions, and by early 1948 Auden had rewritten this idea for his own purposes.† It emerged fully formed in February in a lecture, "Poetry and Freedom," and recurred in much of his published prose over the next two years.

In "Poetry and Freedom" he surveyed four revolutions and the characteristic heroes of each. The first three were the papal revolution, the Reformation, and the French Revolution, all described in terms taken from Rosenstock-Huessy. But his account of the twentieth-century revolution turned away from Rosenstock-Huessy's focus on the Russian Revolution; Auden named a broader revolution with a different significance:

> We are now, as we are all painfully aware, in the middle of a fourth revolution, which is concerned, I think—and this passes beyond any particular political view which we may have—with the right of every physical body, natural body, to health and leisure, which shall give the individual to whom that body belongs the best chance to form the best kind of community and the more [i.e., most] efficient kind of society. We, too, have our symbolic figure. It is not [as it was in earlier revolutions] the knight or the warrior; it is not the professional man; it is not the man of genius; it is the naked, anonymous, numbered figure.

* He seems also to have found a new significance for the small group. In 1951 he told a lecture audience that modern poets no longer address a whole class or community, and (as a student newspaper somewhat obscurely paraphrased him) "the largest group successfully used is limited to twelve" (*Mount Holyoke News*, 19 January 1951). The idea disappeared from published versions of this lecture.

† Rosenstock-Huessy's idea of a papal revolution was taken up in the 1960s by Norman Cantor and other historians, but it was entirely unorthodox at the time.

Now one of the things that makes our revolution particularly acute is that as bodies we are all members of a crowd, for bodies in themselves can make no choices. Individual differences are irrelevant. Hence you can see in this revolution why there is emphasis on uniformity . . . this is true in every country, right or left.

Nonetheless, he continued, "if this revolution is to succeed, the successes, the conquests of the previous three revolutions have to be defended," and the individualizing impulse of earlier revolutions must be maintained. The present challenge was to recognize the universality of the vulnerable, enumerable body while retaining the freedom from totalizing authority that had been won in the past. Totalizing authority in the twentieth century claimed to speak for the anonymous body—then broke or enslaved it.

===

"Italian sunshine, Italian flesh" prompted Auden to write his poetry of the body, but he had been preparing himself to write it for many months before he arrived in Italy, at the age of forty-one, in May 1948. A century and a half earlier Goethe had achieved sexual awakening on a visit to Italy, and Auden's visit had a comparable effect, though a more subtle and interior one. When Auden translated Goethe's *Italienische Reise* with Elizabeth Mayer in 1961, he introduced it with an essay that treated Goethe's experience in terms he had learned from his own. Goethe's book was "a psychological document of the first importance dealing with a life crisis which, in various degrees of intensity, we all experience somewhere between the ages of thirty-five and forty-five." Goethe had made his European reputation by writing *The Sorrows of Young Werther* (as Auden had made his reputation with his early political verse), and although "he had come to Weimar to get away from *Werther*, it was as its author that Weimar had welcomed and still regarded him" (as Auden was welcomed in America for the political poems he had written in England). "The stability which Weimar had given him was threatening to become a prison. Though it had enabled him to put *Werther* behind him, it had failed to give him any hints as to what kind of thing he should be writing instead." Both went to Italy to learn what they had been unable to learn in their secure and honored positions in the places they had chosen as home.

Auden's journey to the warm south renewed his relations with the cold north of his childhood. Seen in the afterglow of his relationship with Rhoda Jaffe, Italy seemed to bring to an end the long isolation of his poetry from the maternal flesh he remembered from his infancy. Auden and Kallman sailed from New York on 7 April 1948, on a voyage Auden had begun planning a year earlier, around the time he turned forty. During two weeks in England they visited Auden's father in the Lake District; by 8 May they had arrived in Florence. Auden wrote to Elizabeth Mayer: "I hadn't realized till I came how like Italy is to my 'Mutterland,' the Pennines. Am in fact starting on a poem, 'In Praise of Limestone,' the theme of which is that that rock creates the only human landscape." The poems he wrote in his first summers in Italy—he returned every year until 1958 to the village of Forio, on the island of Ischia in the Bay of Naples—repeatedly overlay the local image of Ischia with the remembered image of an English motherland. He told a lecture audience in 1950 that his lines in "Prime" about "The flat roofs of the fishing village / Still asleep in its bunny" referred to both countries:

> It is true that the particular Italian village is a fishing village and it has flat roofs. It is not however situated in a bunny—which is a little ravine between sand hills and cliffs; that image actually comes from memories of fishing villages in the south of England. But for the particular picture I wanted to build up it seemed right.

In 1947 he thought about writing a guidebook to England in collaboration with John Betjeman, whose topographic poetry Auden admired and whose verse he introduced to American audiences the same year by editing a selection titled (at Betjeman's suggestion) *Slick But Not Streamlined*. Auden also considered writing a book called *Underground Life*, about the mines he had visited as a child. Instead, he blended English and Italian landscapes. The site of the abandoned lead mines in "Not in Baedeker" cannot be found in any guidebook because it is compounded of elements from the south and the north: from Italy, a bus driver who greases his hair and dreams of America, and an annual festival of St. Cobalt, patron of mines; from England, a shot tower in Alston, Cumberland, a paraphrase of a descriptive passage in *An Account of the Mining Districts of Alston Moor* (1833), by Thomas Sopwith, and a memory of "two English cyclists" who visited the shot tower on a September day. The older of the two is probably Auden's school friend Robert Medley; in August 1923, they visited ancient lead mines in Yorkshire,

                          where the younger
         (Whose promise one might have guessed even then
         Would come to nothing), using a rotten
         Rickety gallery for a lectern,
         To amuse his friend gave an imitation
         Of a clergyman with a cleft palate.

Auden's parenthetical dismissal of his earlier self in these lines amounts
to a renunciation of his earlier ways of writing about the English landscape. The lead-mine country is no longer the setting for archaic imaginary feuds or the place that silently prophesies a future love. What it loses
in dramatic effect it gains in its integration into a real history of real
persons. It now "can strike / Most if not all of the historical notes /
Even (what place can not?) the accidental," a quiet personal note that
sounds more truthfully than the grand mythical chords he heard there
in the past. His "first image of Italy," he wrote in 1952, "is associated
with an aunt whose devotion to the country led her into building her
dream Italian house in one of the wettest parts of England. It was dread-
fully damp and draughty and the veranda shut out the sun; even so, I
thought it beautiful." This was not quite his *Mutterland*, but it was the
house of the aunt closest to his mother, who had spent a few weeks
recuperating there shortly before her death.

     The landscape Auden first wrote about in Italy was human in a double
sense: it was the landscape of the human body itself and the landscape
in which human beings belonged. The United States, he thought, vital
as it was as a place of existential freedom, offered few human landscapes
in the second of these senses, and he had complained about the lack.
"Nature never intended human beings to live here," he wrote in 1946
in his introduction to Henry James's *The American Scene*. This was the
same year when he wrote in *The Age of Anxiety*, "How tempting to
trespass in these Italian gardens." The poems he wrote in Italy were the
first that noticed the daily ordinariness of a place where he actually lived.
In his verse letter to Richard Crossman written in 1936 for *Letters from
Iceland*, he had hoped to be able to see in Iceland's local details "the
growth, the wonder, / Not symbols of an end, not cold extremities /
Of a tradition sick at heart"—the symbols he had seen in England when
he chose to wear red-tinted glasses. But it was only now that he lived up
to this hope. In Italy he began to recognize ordinary life as an adequate
sign of the absolute—an idea suggested to him by Kierkegaard's Knight

of Faith, who looks like a shopkeeper—rather than as its enemy. In place of the glaciers and crossroads that fill the maps of his early poems, his Italian townscapes had real barbers and buses in them; instead of symbolic winds in allegorical deserts, a real sirocco and long dog days; instead of titanic struggles in mythical arenas, a tangible landscape you could settle into.

"In Praise of Limestone," the first of these poems suggested by Italy, overwhelmingly justifies Auden's decision to abandon his camp of tough aggressiveness. This extraordinarily beautiful and unemphatic poem, with its long syllabic lines and meditative essayistic manner that gradually turns urgent, sounds like nothing he had written before. He devised a style for it that accommodates the largest questions of universal meaning while speaking in the conversational voice that is the twentieth century's closest possible approach to an authentic personal tone. Even the oratorical imperatives in the opening lines sound more leisurely than commanding:

> If it form the one landscape that we, the inconstant ones,
>   Are consistently homesick for, this is chiefly
> Because it dissolves in water. Mark these rounded slopes
>   With their surface fragrance of thyme and, beneath,
> A secret system of caves and conduits; hear the springs
>   That spurt out everywhere with a chuckle,
> Each filling a private pool for its fish and carving
>   Its own little ravine whose cliffs entertain
> The butterfly and the lizard; examine this region
>   Of short distances and definite places . . .

Readers found the poem memorable; anthologists reprinted it; but even the critics who praised it did not pretend to understand it. Those who, without quite knowing why, felt grateful to it were perhaps responding to its secret, unexplicit defense of a part of themselves that almost everything else written in their century was teaching them to discredit or deny.

Ostensibly, the poem praises an agreeable and unimportant landscape, a place whose voluble Italian villagers have never faced natural disasters or moral crises. They are "unable / To conceive a god whose temper-tantrums are moral / And not to be pacified by a clever line / Or a good lay." They have "never had to veil their faces in awe / Of a crater whose blazing fury could not be fixed" as one fixes a parking ticket or

a local election. Their "eyes have never looked into infinite space /
Through the lattice-work of a nomad's comb." And the limestone landscape is truly human because, as Auden put it in a letter to Elizabeth
Mayer, it is the one in which "politics, art, etc., are on a modest un-
grandiose scale. What awful things have been suggested to man by huge
plains and deltas."

Much more is at stake here than the affirmation of a human scale
against postwar bureaucracy and imperial conflicts. The poem treats the
limestone landscape as an allegory of the body and of the body's relation
to ultimate questions. "What could be more like Mother," it asks of this
place of rounded slopes and, beneath them, caves and conduits.* It is a
region not of great public works but of minor local modifications "from
weathered outcrop / To hill-top temple, from appearing waters to /
Conspicuous fountains, from a wild to a formal vineyard." (It is also the
fittest background for "the nude young male who lounges / Against a
rock displaying his dildo"—called that, instead of the name of its real
counterpart, because in this poem the body is inherently feminine and
the dildo is an object of artifice and display, like the hilltop temple and
conspicuous fountain.) It has "a surface fragrance of thyme" because it
is in the hands of time: it dissolves in water and is therefore the one
landscape the inconstant ones are consistently homesick for. Those who
are not inconstant, whose hearts have one purpose alone, feel no sympathy with their own changing bodies; the "best and worst," the two
varieties of the constant ones, "never stayed here long but sought /
Immoderate soils" where they could escape the humanizing world of the
ordinary. Saints-to-be left for the sterner imperatives of granite wastes,
whose rocky voices cry: "how accidental / Your kindest kiss, how permanent is death." (The "accidental" is one of the notes struck by the
limestone landscape of "Not in Baedeker.") Intendant Caesars left for
the passive plasticity of clays and gravels that purr: "soft as earth is mankind and both / Need to be altered." And the "really reckless" follow
the "oceanic whisper" of "the solitude that asks and promises nothing."

Auden found his vocabulary of nomads, clays, and gravels—all that

---

* This derives from Anthony Collett's *The Changing Face of England,* which Auden had plundered in 1935 for the choruses of *The Dog Beneath the Skin.* He told Alan Ansen in April 1947
he was looking for a copy of the book; evidently he found it by 1948, when he adapted Collett's
sentence "The chalk is not riddled, like the grey limestone, with a network of caves and conduits" (p. 138).

limestone is not—in Toynbee's *A Study of History.** He was still excited by the scope and ambition of Toynbee's vast unfolding work, but felt the same ambivalence about Toynbee's claims to have tamed history into a system that he felt about Rosenstock-Huessy's claims. ("It is a major work I think," he wrote of the *Study* to Elizabeth Mayer; the slight hesitation at the end of the sentence is expressive.) Large-scale visions of historical cycles had come into intellectual fashion with Spengler's *The Decline of the West* in the 1920s and offered a pessimistic counterpoint to visions of evolutionary progress that thrived around the same time; Auden had absorbed Spengler's sense of the West in its final decay in his early poems and made it the background of his historical summaries in "Spain" and "In Time of War." But he also knew that an intellectual climate propitious to theories of macrocosmic change made it all too easy to justify great destroyers like Hitler or Stalin and that any cyclical theory was a counsel of despair. In a letter to a friend in 1962, Auden, in his only recorded comment on Spengler, called *The Decline of the West* "an evil book." Toynbee's vision seemed more learned and plausible than Spengler's, for it combined an authoritative sense of geopolitical change with almost lyrical passages of praise for humane, domestically scaled societies where one could feel at home. In the symbolic topography of "In Praise of Limestone" Auden adopted Toynbee's double focus on large and small scales, and echoed Toynbee's refusal to be over-awed by the larger while admitting its power to crush the smaller. Within a few years, Auden no longer gave credence to grand patterns in real history, but he continued to find pleasure in them when they occurred in fiction. The same double focus he had tentatively admired in Toynbee he praised wholeheartedly in J.R.R. Tolkien's *The Lord of the Rings*.

The voices that summon the best and worst to ocean, granite, clays, and gravels "were right / And still are," for the indisputable reason that, as Auden wrote in "Under Which Lyre," without Apollonian authority the earth would be a fratricidal nightmare "like the Balkans." Is the limestone landscape, the poem asks, therefore nothing more than "A backward / And dilapidated province, connected / To the big busy world by a tunnel"—is it, in other words, a womb one can never return

---

* The mysterious "nomad's comb" that no one in a limestone landscape ever looked through perhaps comes from Toynbee, but I have not been able to find it; it may be a recollection of Toynbee's description in his third volume of the nomads' long, straight, wiry hair. Two tribes whose names Auden gave to dance bands in *The Age of Anxiety* are mentioned in Toynbee's "annex" on nomadism in the same volume.

to, a place with only a "*seedy* appeal"? Not quite, is the poem's answer:

> It has a wordly duty which in spite of itself
> It does not neglect, but calls into question
> All the Great Powers assume; it disturbs our rights.

It reminds us, when we indulge in Platonist fantasies of transcendence or Baconian fantasies of detachment, that our inescapable home is our own flesh. The poet who elevates his mind over the glories of the created world, who is

> Admired for his earnest habit of calling
> The sun the sun, his mind Puzzle, is made uneasy
> By these marble statues which so obviously doubt
> His antimythological myth.*

Similarly the scientist, looking too far out as the poet looks too far in, is pursued by local gamins with "lively offers" of sexual pleasure—offers that "rebuke his concern for Nature's / Remotest aspects." (This was the same concern Auden identified in "Spain" as "the inhuman provinces" visible only to the microscope or the telescope, "the virile bacillus / Or enormous Jupiter finished.")

After these errors comes a third. "I, too, am reproached for what / And how much you know." The *I* of "In Praise of Limestone" can be reproached by *you* because the poem has turned into a love poem, and has done so at the precise moment that it acknowledges the claims of the inhuman landscapes which have no love: "They were right, my dear, all those voices were right / And still are." When the poem admits the rights of inhuman abstraction, it dialectically affirms physical human love.

---

* The poet who calls the sun the sun (and not, say, Phoebus) is a portrait of Wallace Stevens —Stevens himself, not the generic version portrayed in "Kairos and Logos." The first section of "Notes toward a Supreme Fiction," from Stevens's *Transport to Summer* (1947), dismisses mythical names—"Phoebus was / A name for something that never could be named"—and proposes a different "project for the sun. The sun / Must bear no name . . . but be / In the difficulty of what it is to be." In "Someone Puts a Pineapple Together," published in *Partisan Review* in 1947, Stevens in effect identifies his mind as creating "the sum of its complications"—something that could appropriately be named as the mythical beast Puzzle. Stevens perhaps noticed Auden's allusions to him: in a letter in 1953 he described "The Comedian as the Letter C" as "what may be called an anti-mythological poem" (*Letters of Wallace Stevens*, 1977, p. 778).

Poet, scientist, and "I" are reproached for refusing to look directly at a real person, for wishing to escape the solid reality of the flesh. Everyone makes this refusal, everyone yields to this wish:

> not, please! to resemble
> The beasts who repeat themselves, or a thing like water
>   Or stone whose conduct can be predicted, these
> Are our Common Prayer, whose greatest comfort is music
>   Which can be made anywhere, is invisible,
> And does not smell.

Music, that is, is everything the body is not. And "in so far as we have to look forward / To death as a fact, no doubt we are right"—right to wish for transcendence out of the realm of that which merely dies and decays. The muted sadness that gives the poem a flavor unlike anything else in English verse derives from the elegy for the changing body that the poem intertwines among its meditations on landscape.

But death may be more than a mere fact; it may have other meanings visible only to the eye of faith. Near the end, the poem turns away from the fact of death in the way that elegies turn toward the promise of immortality. The closing passage names the double promise of Christianity—forgiveness and resurrection—as the reason to be grateful to the flesh, and represents that flesh as a garden built with Italian limestone on a human scale:

> if
> Sins can be forgiven, if bodies rise from the dead,
>   These modifications of matter into
> Innocent athletes and gesticulating fountains,
>   Made solely for pleasure, make a further point:
> The blessed will not care what angle they are regarded from,
>   Having nothing to hide.

Having nothing to hide is an entirely different state from the Sunday-best pomposity Auden had imagined in his two earlier attempts to describe blessedness—at the end of Caliban's address to the audience, and in the lines he dropped from Malin's concluding speech. It is the same state he was to write of in "Compline," six years later, when he prayed that on the Last Day "we too may come to the picnic / With nothing to hide." The body without shame is the condition of blessedness and forgiveness; more, it is the likeness of a divine and universal order, the true image of eternity:

> Dear, I know nothing of
> Either, but when I try to imagine a faultless love
> Or the life to come, what I hear is the murmur
> Of underground streams,* what I see is a limestone landscape.

In a world where forgiveness is imaginable, language bears less of a burden than it does in a world where it alone is the conduit for relations among the isolated, for in that harsher world, love cannot survive the inadequacies of language. In 1937, in "As I Walked Out One Evening," Auden had seen nothing but futility and failure in a lover's inflated declaration that he would love forever, until China and Africa meet. By 1953, in "The Willow-Wren and the Stare," love potentially surpassed all errors of vocabulary and intention. When the lover in this poem addresses his beloved in overwrought diction, the listening willow-wren asks skeptically, What does he want? "Much too much," replies the starling, making a judgment on language that only wordless nature can make. When the lover hopes that the "brats of greed and fear" who dwell within him may still be a sign "for all they fall so short of," the willow-wren asks, Does he mean what he says? "Some of it," says the stare, who knows that *some* may be enough. When the lover briefly suspends his verbal acts to engage in the sexual one, the willow-wren asks, Is it only that? "It's that as well," says the stare, who knows that desire is only one of the inescapable elements of love, that the lover's extravagant praises are among its other elements. Finally, waking contented in his beloved's arms, the lover celebrates the sexual act in the broken metre of an only partly misplaced prayer:

> "I have heard the high good noises
>   Promoted for an instant,
> Stood on the shining outskirts
>   Of that Joy I thank
> For you, my dog, and every goody."

---

* Those underground streams had a further religious resonance. Late in life, when reviewing a hymn book, Auden introduced "a digression." Because he knows no Hebrew, he said, he does not notice when Coverdale mistranslates the English Psalter. In Psalm 42, for example, "I understand that the phrase, 'because of the noise in the water-pipes' really means the noise, presumably faint, made by underground streams in a limestone country" ("Praiseworthy," *The New Statesman*, 29 June 1973).

Ferdinand, in "The Sea and the Mirror," had said the same thing in more dignified style when he thanked "another tenderness." But the level of style no longer signifies the authenticity of a prayer, and this lover's authenticity, like everyone else's, cannot be measured by human standards of decorum:

> *Did he know what he meant?* said the willow-wren—
> *God only knows*, said the stare.

Auden declined to use a decorous or idealizing language for the flesh, because he hoped to honor it for what it is. As he argued a few years later, the bird-catcher Papageno in *The Magic Flute* refuses to endure the trials welcomed by Prince Tamino in his quest to free Pamina, but is nonetheless rewarded with marriage and children because he has "the heroic humility to acknowledge that he lacks" the heroic passion that transcends bodily pain.

In December 1948, a few months after he had celebrated the maternal aspects of the flesh in "In Praise of Limestone," Auden celebrated the male flesh in a less sacramental style. "Deciding that there ought to be one in the Auden corpus"—his choice of the noun is deliberate—"I am writing a purely pornographic poem, *The Platonic Blow*," he told Kallman. He borrowed the nameless syncopated metre ("It was a Spring day, a day for a lay, when the air / Smelled like a locker-room") invented by Charles Williams for the poems in his highly sacramental *Taliessin through Logres*, but the word "Platonic" in Auden's title was an ironic spoof. The sexual act described by the poem in microscopic physiological detail is "Platonic" only in the popular sense that it is perfect of its kind—Auden asked friends to contribute their relevant ideas of perfection—and not in the sense that the bodies that perform the act are in any way transcended. "In Praise of Limestone" had combined in the same way the artifice of display and the actuality of flesh in "the nude young male who lounges / Against a rock displaying his dildo." Nine years later Auden applied a fig leaf when he revised this to read "the flirtatious male who lounges / Against a rock in the sunlight." The original text had been rendered superfluous by the longer, but at the time unpublishable, poem on the subject he had now concealed.*

---

* Around 1965 one of Auden's friends lent a copy of the typescript of "The Platonic Blow" to someone who transcribed it and gave copies to others. Printed editions began circulating in New York and London, and an erotic magazine published the poem; Auden sent back its check and publicly refused to acknowledge the poem—although he did so freely to friends and once, inconsistently enough, to a newspaper interviewer.

"Since / Nothing is free, whatever you charge shall be paid," Auden wrote, addressing the patron saint of Ischia in the poem he wrote about the island when he arrived there in May 1948. (He and Kallman stayed in a *pensione* for ten weeks, then rented a house together the following summer and all their remaining summers in Italy.) And, in the first poem he had written on his European holiday, the birthday tribute to T. S. Eliot, he identified the present as the time when we wait "for the Law to take its course / (And which of us shall escape whipping?)." The Italian summer in which Auden looked forward to the day when sins are forgiven and bodies rise from the dead was also the summer when the doom of judgment darkened his brightest poems. This doom was tangible, as the *Dies Irae* theme tacked onto *The Age of Anxiety* was not.

The price that must be paid was a theme in other poems composed that summer. In the song "Deftly, Admiral," written in June, two lovers embrace on a bridge between the "properties" of an aged admiral and an aged ambassador, who have seen their public triumphs overrun or decayed. "In its glory, in its power," this hour belongs to the young lovers. The shock of the poem's final lines is all the greater because the fate of the old men has already made clear the doom of power and glory. "Nothing your strength, your skill, could do," the poem tells the two old men,

> Can alter their embrace
> Or dispersuade the Furies who
> At the appointed place
> With claw and dreadful brow
> Wait for them now.

"A Walk After Dark," written in August 1948, asks "what judgment waits / My person, all my friends, / And these United States," and wonders whether indeed judgment has already begun.

> Occurring this very night
> By no established rule,
> Some event may already have hurled
> Its first little No at the right
> Of the laws we accept to school
> Our post-diluvian world.

This world feels safe in the covenant that followed the Flood, and in the physical laws that claim to account for past and future. But "Pleasure Island," begun in Ischia and finished on Fire Island (where Auden and James and Tania Stern shared a summer cottage they had bought together in 1945), proposes that this "Lenient amusing shore . . . is in / Fact our place, namely this / Place of a skull where the rose of / Self-punishment will grow." Fire Island is a Golgotha because the predawn sufferings of loneliness that occur there are chosen freely by the sufferers, thanks to an unconstraining grace.

Auden gave thanks in the opening lines of "Ischia" for the island's human scale, its variety and mildness, its restorative powers—and at the end acknowledged that nothing is free. The patroness of the island is named, suitably, Santa Restituta, and her "annual patronage, they say, is bought with blood. / That, blessed and formidable / Lady, we hope is not true." What the poem hopes is not true is different from the truth that the poet knows. "Without a cement of blood," Auden wrote a few years later in "Vespers," another poem with an Ischian setting, "no secular wall can safely stand." But Santa Restituta filled another, more generous, role. "The nature which Americans . . . had every reason to fear could not possibly be imagined as a mother," Auden wrote after seven summers on Ischia. In contrast, he thought, the nature known to Europeans "is humanized, mythologized, usually friendly," and he had returned to it on an Italian island protected by a saint who was both maternal and, in ways his familiar English motherland could not be, indifferent.

The judgment Auden awaited for himself, his friends, and these United States was a judgment on inner tyrannies as well as outer ones. After he returned to New York in September 1948, he devised an allegorical psychology entirely unlike his earlier Jungian ones. In place of Jung's fourfold personality, Auden now imagined a trinitarian self, and he mapped the individual psyche not as a set of balances and imbalances between binary opposites but as a set of relations among three persons. As he told a lecture audience some years later:

> It has been my experience that often the most important matters are most aptly explained in comic terms. A number of years ago I invented a parlor-game called Trinities. Each player had to take someone either known to them personally or, in the case of a writer, through their work, and describe them in terms of a household of three persons, who can be of any age and of either sex.

These household trinities were on a homely and domestic scale, like his vision of the world to come in "In Praise of Limestone." He twice used this parlor game as a method of interpretation in his writings: first in a poem, "A Household," which portrayed the grim household of his inner self; then, a few months later, in the spring of 1949, in a review, "Port and Nuts with the Eliots," in which he described the comic disordered household embodied in the author of *Notes toward the Definition of Culture*.

Auden found the idea of the household in Cochrane's *Christianity and Classical Culture*; the trinitarian analysis of it was his own invention. Augustine, as Cochrane reported, wrote that the secular order, the *pax terrena*,

> manifests itself in at least three phases. The first is that of the *pax domestica*, the order which determines life in the household. This order depends ultimately upon the union of male and female . . . But this union, as the source of offspring "according to the flesh," may at the same time be regarded as the seedbed of the city . . . Accordingly, the order of the household gives rise to a second and more comprehensive order, the *pax civica*. A third phase of human association emerges as household and city expand on a world-wide scale . . . to blossom forth as the imperial state. Differing as they do both in constitution and objectives, these three forms of secular society have this much at least in common, that their existence depends upon will. The will in question, however, is not that of an "oversoul," nor may it be described as "general" except in so far as it marks "a composition or fitting together of individual human wills with respect to such objects as pertain to mortal life." This being so, such order as is evolved within secular society can hardly be more than imperfect.

The inner household of the psyche was Auden's modern counterpart of Augustine's household. Auden's poem and review on the household were the first in a series of increasingly ambitious works in which he explored the relations of all three orders of society—domestic, civil, and imperial.

His poem about himself and his review about Eliot each portray a household distorted by inner tyranny. The household in the poem is destroyed by the breadwinner to assure his success. The household in the review suffers milder, more amusing forms of the same kind of imperfect order. The review is a playful act of lèse-majesté that treats its organizing metaphor as an illuminating joke, while the poem is an unsmiling work of self-analysis that conceals that it is an extended psychological metaphor and not an account of three separate human beings. "Like most important writers," the review begins,

> Mr. T. S. Eliot is not a single figure but a household. The household has, I think, at least three permanent residents. First, there is the archdeacon, who believes in and practices order, discipline and good manners, social and intellectual, with a thoroughly Anglican distaste for evangelical excess . . . And no wonder, for the poor gentleman is condemned to be domiciled with a figure of a very different stamp, a violent and passionate old peasant grandmother, who has witnessed murder, rape, pogroms, famine, flood, fire, everything; who has looked into the abyss and, unless restrained, would scream the house down . . . Last, as if this state of affairs were not difficult enough, there is a young boy who likes to play slightly malicious practical jokes. The too earnest guest, who has come to interview the Reverend, is startled and bewildered by finding an apple-pie bed or being handed an explosive cigar.*

The review is largely a polite argument against Eliot's view of history (Eliot was wrong, Auden said, to associate the transmission of culture with specific social classes, because, until the eighteenth century, culture in Europe had in fact been transmitted by the Church) and a gentle reminder of the blinkered nostalgia of Eliot's perspective. "The value of Mr. Eliot's book is not the conclusions he reaches, most of which are debatable, but the questions he raises." The review returns only intermittently to its household metaphor to point out passages in Eliot's book where the boy or the grandmother seems to interrupt the archdeacon's monologue. But Auden's poem does not stray from its household theme or present itself as anything other than a portrayal of family unhappiness, perhaps drawn from the life. By the time it appeared in print, in *Nones* in 1951, readers had had two years to forget the review, although anyone who placed the poem next to the review would have guessed its secret at once. Auden seems to have waited more than ten years before he told anyone (other than Kallman, from whom he apparently kept no secrets) that the poem was a self-portrait.

---

* Auden modified this trinity when he lectured on Eliot to an English-speaking audience in Vienna, probably in September 1968, three years after Eliot's death. Eliot, he said, "consisted, firstly, of the American pre-Jackson aristocrat of a kind which died out in 1829 . . . Then there was the little boy aged 12, adoring practical jokes such as cushions which fart when you sit on them." Finally, he added, in an indecorous challenge to the prejudices he encountered in both Eliot and Austria, "there was the Yiddish momma who wrote the poems" (reported in Stella Musulin, "Auden in Kirchstetten," *Auden Studies* 3, 1995). In Auden's draft, in a notebook in the Berg Collection, this third person is further characterized as "a wildly emotional and melancholic Yiddish Momma who cries Oi Weh!"

The analyses in both poem and essay draw on the theology of the Trinity in order to show what is wrong with the psychological trinities they portray. In both the Christian Trinity and Auden's households, three persons occur in a single substance. The substance of the poet, whether Eliot or Auden, comprises a father and a son and a third person who is the father's mother. Her role bears some relation to Augustine's account in *De Trinitate* of the Spirit as the product of the mutual love of the father and son, but the relation is one more of parody than of analogy. The psychomachia of the poem is Auden's adult rethinking of a comic parable about himself that he wrote in 1933, when he was twenty-six, but never published. This earlier poem, which begins "The month was April," describes the good ship *Wystan Auden Esquire* as captained by a woman who displays the domineering anger of Auden's mother. In "A Household," which Auden wrote at forty-one, the head of the household is the poet's masculine ego, and the mother's angers are reduced to the mad ravings of "a slatternly hag," who "spits / And shouts obscenities from the landing." A cabin boy was one of the crew in the earlier poem; in the later one he reappears as "a miserable runt / Who wets his bed . . . / A tell-tale, a crybaby, a failure."

The visitor to the Eliot household in Auden's review is unsettled by the presence of the screaming grandmother and mischievous boy. But no visitor sees the inside of the Auden household. The ego conceals it from the world by holding up for public view a picture of a household that never existed. The adult ego of the poem is a successful corporate executive (an anonymous friend, probably Spender, remarked of Auden: "He sees himself as a giant private firm, Auden, Auden, Auden & Co.") who knows which secrets not to give away. At business meetings he speaks proudly of his spirited son and saintly mother, while stoically keeping silent ("A reticence for which they all admire him") about his dead and worshiped bride. "Whom, though, has he ever invited for the weekend? / Out to his country mansion in the evening, / Another merger signed, he drives alone."

Auden received the Pulitzer Prize for *The Age of Anxiety* in May 1948 (it was the first of his books published since he took American citizenship and became eligible for the prize), a few months before he told the world under his breath, in "A Household," just whom they had honored. The elegant mansion—closed to a public that repeatedly renewed its contract to supply praise and fame at bargain prices—concealed an emotional shambles. The adult ego who defeats all rivals in the outer world returns home to find the other two persons in his trinity "in an unholy alliance,

/ Youth stealing [for] Age the liquor-cupboard key, / Age teaching Youth to lie with a straight face." Rivals outside, "envying his energy and his brains / And with rattling skeletons of their own," would, if they could look within, conclude that the successful ego was "the villain of this household, / Whose bull-voice scared a sensitive young child, / Whose coldness drove a doting parent mad." Their judgment is the same as Auden's own judgment on his camp of tough aggressiveness: in the furthest reaches of the poem's allegory, it was this toughness that turned Kallman's affection into resentful fecklessness and refused to nurture the gentler voices of Auden's native gift. But, more subtly, the poem also rebukes Auden's sense that the disordered hatreds of his inner household are the conditions that allow it to exist at all, the conditions that make possible his public success. Without the thorn in the flesh, the ego of this poem believes, there would be no success and no self, and like the aging initiate in *The Orators* who wrote a letter to his wound, the ego is half in love with it:

> He half believes, call it a superstition,
>
> It is for his sake that they hate and fear him:
> Should they unmask and show themselves worth loving,
> Loving and sane and manly, he would die.

The repetition of *loving* is a sign of gratified wonder. If *they* are worth loving, then he too would prove loving and sane and manly, but these swelling affirmations that begin the final line of the poem yield quickly to the reminder, in the final word, of the price he still believes must be paid. Were he to recognize the maternal and instinctive parts of himself as worthy of love, he would destroy the whole structure of himself that he had built upon the failures of his love.

There is a deeper point, which the ego of this poem does not recognize, although the poet does: if he allowed the structure of himself to be overthrown, he would achieve the self-love that is not pride but the self-recognition and self-forgiveness without which no love of others is possible. Augustine, writing on the Trinity, described the generation of the Son as analogous to human self-knowledge and the generation of the Spirit as analogous to human self-love. For the executive in the trinity of "The Household" to achieve self-knowledge and self-love—neither was possible without the other—he would need to renounce his public and private falsehoods, would need to stop thinking in the terms that

Malin parodied in *The Age of Anxiety* as "Miserable wicked me, / How interesting I am." The poem recognizes Auden's continuing belief— "call it a superstition"—that he, like Yeats, had been hurt into poetry, as his present anxiety had hurt him into writing this poem. He had shrugged off the denunciations in the British press and Parliament that followed his departure for America in 1939, but he could not so easily shrug off the inner wound inflicted by public honor in 1948.

The two inner victims in "A Household," the old woman and the young boy, in earlier poems had also been imaginary victims of Auden's will. In the obscure crime hidden behind the metaphors of "The Sea and the Mirror" they were the mother and the unborn child who suffered in order that the living child might be born. Now they were the victims not of a private sexual crime but of public acts of Apollonian power. A few months before Auden wrote "A Household," he portrayed the same victims in the early drafts of "A Walk After Dark":

> Our present, meanwhile, is about
> Our business here and abroad:
> A boy is whipped in a cell,
> An old woman is bustled out
> Of the house she loved so well;
> Both whimper and are ignored.

The tormentor in "A Household" is a successful businessman. In the drafts of "A Walk After Dark" it is our present time that is successfully performing "Our business" by tormenting others. Auden judged the cruelties and ambitions of his age in the same terms in which he understood the divisions of his own psyche. This was a moral achievement he had last attained in the sonnets of "In Time of War" in 1938, a few weeks before he turned most of his poetic attention away from the public and political realm. Now, as he learned to attend to the cruelties he inflicted on the persons within himself, he was preparing to write about the more lethal cruelties that, for his benefit and the benefit of his fellow citizens, were committed by his city against persons outside.

CHAPTER ELEVEN

Waiting for a City

In the verse and prose Auden wrote in 1949, history made its own choices and pursued its own goals. Earlier in his career, he had repeatedly imagined a teleological purpose in history, and had then abandoned this as a fantasy that evaded personal responsibility and furthered partisan injustice. Now he tried to recover it in the service of the apolitical human body. Among the strongest impulses of his imagination was an urge to find parallels and connections between events that occur on a local, human scale and events that occur on the vastly larger scale of history, evolution, and cosmology. Having set out to write about the involuntary flesh common to us all, he also sought a theory and vocabulary for writing about the shared involuntary forces that shape the larger world around it.

In the mid-1930s Auden had debated with himself the truth and justice of the Marxist prophecy of revolution, alternately accepting and disputing it in poems written within weeks of each other. A few months after arriving in New York, he had briefly tried to revive a more generous prophecy based on his reading of the Gospels; then he halfheartedly sketched a sacred, providential theory of history in "Christmas 1940" and "Kairos and Logos." But the brutal evidence of war could no longer be wished away, and until 1947, both conventional and purposive history all but disappeared from his published work. "In the war years a poet had to be other-worldly. At any rate, I did," he said to a friend in 1948. His long dramatic poems focused on the present moment in its relation to eternity; they looked back at the historical past in order to demonstrate that the past was simultaneous with the present in relation to the absolute, that Simeon and Prospero were contemporaries of Rosetta and Malin. The large historical changes Auden had delineated in "Letter to Lord Byron," "Spain," "In Time of War," and "New Year Letter" disappeared from his long poems, and chronological history was supplanted by analogical history. But his long explanatory letters to his father and Theodore Spencer about these poems were filled with sober historical speculations on the causes and effects of modernity. But when chronological history abruptly returned to his poems and essays, his speculations had a different tone.

In the autumn of 1947 Auden compiled an anthology of Greek literature, *The Portable Greek Reader*, for the Viking Portable Library,* and wrote a long introduction for it at the end of the year. The introduction emphasizes the strangeness of the classical Greeks from the perspective of the twentieth century, but it makes most of its points through analogies that collapse centuries of change. He appended to it a "Chronological Outline of Classical Greek Civilization," laid out in two columns, one with dates of births and deaths, the other with dates of "events." The standard format of the Viking Portable series did not call for anything like this table, but Auden commissioned Alan Ansen, who was polymathically learned, to compile it (and a longer table for the five-volume Viking *Poets of the English Language*, which he edited two years later). He told Ansen which categories to include and was pleased to add some of the more obscure dates himself. This was a clear renunciation of the nonhistorical alphabetical arrangement he had used for two earlier collections, the school anthology *The Poet's Tongue* in 1935 and his own *Collected Poetry* in 1945.

Traces of an outline of history that is both chronological and teleological appear in Auden's notebooks in the same year, 1947, though an explicitly teleological history did not emerge in his printed work until 1949. His theories of art and civilization translated fluently into "The Sea and the Mirror," just as his theories of the body translated into "In Praise of Limestone," but his moral intelligence resisted this revived teleology, as it had resisted the Jungian archetypes he favored earlier. During these years, his initial impulse to write about history—to analyze the order of the city and the empire as he had analyzed the smaller order of "A Household"—flowered from tentative outlines and sketches into

---

* This book evolved out of an abandoned plan, which Auden had worked on in 1945–46, for an anthology of poetry in translation from various languages.

the sequence "Horae Canonicae," arguably his greatest work and certainly the one that occupied his attention longer than any other. Yet by
the time he wrote the first of its seven poems, in August 1949, he was
already jettisoning the historical theories that had shaped his plans for
the sequence when he first conceived it.

As in earlier years, Auden had tried to resolve intellectual and moral
problems by immersing himself in theories of necessity when the solution
he needed was more difficult and less systematic. Troubled in his own
person by the conflicting goals of voluntary mind and involuntary body,
he set out to understand them through the more general relation of the
historical and natural worlds. "In the summer of 1947," he told a lecture
audience in 1950,

> I had the idea of writing a series of poems corresponding to the church offices
> . . . Why I was interested in this was that the [prayers in the] offices celebrate
> historical events, particularly events of the passion of Christ, and these are re-
> peated daily. So what I had in mind was that it might be possible to write a
> series of poems which were to be, in some sense of the word—I don't know
> how—about the relation of history and nature.

This relation was "a problem which has fascinated me for at least ten
years," but he apparently had been unable to write about it earlier. He
added that in the three years since first thinking of the sequence, he had
written only one of the poems planned for it, "Prime."

He had chosen to treat the relation of historical and natural events in
Christian terms: Christianity associates unique divine actions like the Incarnation or Crucifixion with recurring natural events like birth or death,
and in the relation between prophetic types and fulfillments it sees both
recurrence and uniqueness. But he did not treat this relation in "Horae
Canonicae" in quite the way he suggested in his lecture. The seven poems in the sequence are arranged in a pattern that echoes the pattern of
events on Good Friday, but the content of the poems is concerned less
with Christ's passion—his suffering and death—than with the narrower
subject of his judicial murder: the authorities who permit and decree it,
the craftsmen who make the instruments for it, the crowds who shout
for it, and the detached citizen who tries to imagine he had nothing to
do with it. Auden understated this theme in a similar way in a lecture in
1949 in which he contrasted the characteristic hero of the romantic era
with that of the ironic present, who is "the less exciting figure of the
builder, who renews the ruined walls of the city." This consoling sen-

tence hides an unpalatable truth about the builder's materials, a truth Auden insisted on exposing in the final line of the last poem he wrote for "Horae Canonicae," where the mortar needed to build or renew any secular wall is a "cement of blood."

The canonical hours, as Auden interpreted them, gave a universal framework to ordinary daily life. They introduced into Western society a measure of time that applies to the whole world, unlike measures that apply differently to separate localities. They had the same universalizing effect on the routine experience of time that All Souls (as Rosenstock-Huessy described it) had had on the apocalyptic expectation of judgment. Citizens in a Greek city could agree to gather for a public ritual at dawn or at noon, but no one who lived outside its walls was obligated or even affected by their choice. The hours of the Church offices (which Rosenstock-Huessy, incidentally, did not mention) were constructed on the novel assumption that it was a matter of sacred importance to perform certain acts at the same moment everywhere. "I have heard it suggested," Auden wrote in 1954, "that the first punctual people in history were the monks—at their Office hours. It is certain at least that the first serious analysis of the human experience of time was undertaken by St. Augustine, and that the notion of punctuality, of action at an exact moment, depends on drawing a distinction between natural and historical time which Christianity encouraged if it did not invent."* He added that no classical author had described "The Punctual Man (the type to which I personally belong)" and that the classical world thought of time objectively as the realm of fate, or chance, "a factor in our lives for which we are not responsible, and about which we can feel nothing." It is only when we begin to think about time subjectively that "we feel responsible for *our* time, and the notion of punctuality arises." (He had long since quietly abandoned his attempts to follow Tillich in imagining a Christian version of fate.)

Prince Hal taunts Falstaff, "What a devil hast thou to do with the time of day?" Auden moralized on this line: "Not to know the time of day is to be governed, like animals and children, by the immediate mood of

---

* With a glance back at his poem "Kairos and Logos," Auden appended a footnote: "The Greek notion of *kairos*, the propitious moment for doing something, contained the seed of the notion of punctuality, but the seed did not flower."

the self. To know the time of day, to structure the passage of time, is to submit the self to the ego which takes purposive decision with a view to attaining some future good; it signifies that a person is conscious of a vocation, of the kind of person he intends to become." Auden in his later years made a theatrical display of punctuality, to the great annoyance of his friends, but it had originated in deliberate humility. To be punctual is to affirm responsibility to an order larger and greater than oneself, an order that requires an exacting homage from those whose isolating acts violate it.

Auden's commissioned essays and reviews were always more comforting than his poetry (his rare uncommissioned prose works, like "Purely Subjective," which no one offered to pay for, tended to be deeply disquieting), but their calm surfaces and didactic clarity were achieved only after bitter debates that he conducted in verse. In three long theoretical essays published in the Roman Catholic quarterly *Thought* in 1950, 1952, and 1954, he wrote in aphoristic and philosophical style about issues he was struggling to untangle in his seven years' labor on "Horae Canonicae." He wrote the essays at the request of the editor of *Thought*, William F. Lynch, S.J., another of his theologian friends in New York and a fellow member of the Third Hour discussion group. All three essays—"Nature, History and Poetry," "Notes on the Comic," and "Balaam and the Ass: The Master-Servant Relationship in Literature"— were theological meditations, but in a tone different from those he wrote in the early 1940s. They had little to say about his earlier Protestant themes of existential faith and much to say about the more Catholic themes of hierarchy and the body.

The first essay opens with an absolute distinction on which the argument of all three essays depends:

Temporal events may be divided into two classes: natural events and historical events.

A natural event (a) is recurrent, i.e., a member of a class of similar events; (b) occurs necessarily according to law.

An historical event (a) is once only, i.e., the unique member of a class of one; (b) occurs not necessarily according to law but voluntarily according to provocation; (c) is a cause of subsequent historical events by providing them with a motive for occurring.

This distinction seems straightforward enough, but its hidden polemical purpose was to counter Auden's recent temptation to believe that historical events can occur by necessity, that history has a predestined goal that it is determined to achieve. When he had first thought about the Church Offices, in 1947, he was willing to treat his temptation as at least a poetic possibility, for he was still inclined to organize his poems according to cyclical and archetypal patterns, was still breathing the Joycean atmosphere that stayed with him after he plundered *Finnegans Wake* for Rosetta's final speech in *The Age of Anxiety*. His early outlines for "Horae Canonicae" resemble the table of correspondences in *Ulysses* that Joyce directed Stuart Gilbert to include in *James Joyce's "Ulysses"* in 1930.

Auden's outlines took the form of two charts sketched in a notebook around May 1947.* The first of these was a table of revolutionary events in secular history, in reverse chronological order, followed by a table of the events of Good Friday and a mostly illegible table of typological events including "The prophecy" and "The proclamation." Two pages later, this chart flowered into another, more elaborate one, which reproduced most of the first and added the names of the canonical hours:

One household	Matins	Arrested	Creation of Matter	1917	The naked body
	Prime	Mocked	Fall of Man	1789	The individual genius
	Tierce	Condemned	Noah's Covenant	1776	The law-abiding
One world	Sext	Nailed	Old Testament	1649	The Elect god-fearing
	Nones	Pierced	New Testament	1517	The faithful professional
One God	Vespers	Descent	Church	1075	The [?believers]
	Compline	Burial	Last Judgement	998	The saved

Auden found his historical details in Rosenstock-Huessy's *Out of Revolution*. The two right-hand columns (which roughly match the history of revolutions in Auden's lecture "Poetry and Freedom" a few months later) are lifted almost whole from a chart listing the Orders of the Sacraments of Divinity as described by Hugo de St. Victor—a twelfth-century writer who appealed to Rosenstock-Huessy by building his theology on the Bible's historical meanings. Rosenstock-Huessy printed Hugo's list of sacraments side by side with a column of dates in reverse chronological order, representing each of the great revolutions in his historical schema: for each sacrament, a matching revolution. But at the

---

* They seem to have been preceded by a simpler chart, sketched on the endpapers of another notebook, now in the British Library, which lists eight canonical hours (including Lauds in addition to Matins), each associated with events from Good Friday and miscellaneous events and prayers. Auden presumably settled on a sequence of seven poems, each associated with a historical event, shortly after sketching this earlier outline.

top of Hugo's list was the culminating sacrament, the Sacrament of the Creator, which Rosenstock-Huessy associated only with a blank space, making clear that the coming revolution (the as yet unimagined one that will follow the revolution of 1917) would correspond to Hugo's ultimate sacrament and, in effect, bring history to completion. Like most apocalyptic thinkers, Rosenstock-Huessy could not resist the flattering belief that he had the good fortune to live in the last and most interesting phase of history. And he borrowed Hugo's claim for the list of sacraments: "This is the whole Divinity, this is the whole spiritual building." Auden's chart shares the apocalyptic expectations implicit in Rosenstock-Huessy's, but as in his "Poetry and Freedom" lecture, he substitutes "the naked body" for Rosenstock-Huessy's "everybody" as the symbol of the revolutionary period that began in 1917. This was already a significant turn away from the apocalyptic generalities of his source and toward the local specificity of the body.

In July 1947 Auden asked Ursula Niebuhr, "Where can I get texts of the Offices (Lauds, Prime, etc.)? Also their historical origins." In another letter he explained he had "a possible scheme in mind for a series of secular poems based on the Offices"; the word "secular" was evidently a warning not to expect anything liturgical or devotional, although Auden's schemata, from the beginning, emphasized the liturgical and theological dimensions of the work.

He produced an even more elaborate version of his chart probably a year later, in 1948, by which time he had come to associate it with even vaster reaches of time; the new chart shared a notebook page with a table of geological eras (among them the Pre-Cambrian one named in "A Walk After Dark" in the summer of 1948). The twelve columns of the new chart incorporate the earlier version, but extend its range of reference to broad questions of social order and narrow details of the body and its organs. (In the transcript shown here, the leftmost column of the chart is repeated for the sake of clarity on all three staves.)

Lauds	Creation		Arrested		3.00 a.m.	10
Prime	Fall	one household	Denied		6.00	20
Terce	Noah's Covenant		Sentenced		9.00	30
Sext	Abraham Covenant	one world	Crucified	nailed	Noon	40
Nones	Christ N.T.		Died	pierced	3.00 p.m.	50
Vespers	Church	one god	Brought off cross		6.00	60
Compline	Last Judgement		Buried		9.00	70

Lauds	1917	Russian Rev	Matter. Nature	Head
Prime	1789	Romanticism / French Rev	Will. Consciousness	Lungs

Terce	1776	Industrial	Reason	Hands
Sext	1649	English Rev	Law	Ears
Nones	1517	Luther Rev	Secular Works	Eyes
Vespers	1075	Papal Rev	Local and universal space	Tongue
Compline	998	[*blank*]	Time. History	Prick

Lauds	Time is [the] real good and to [be] redeemed	The saved
Prime	Society is real good	The believing
Terce	Work is real good	The [?hard]-working
Sext	The state is real good	The [?responsible] citizen
Nones	The Individual reason " " "	The neighbor
Vespers	The Individual will " " "	The individual genius
Compline	The body " " "	The naked body

In "Horae Canonicae," when Auden finished it six years later, only a fraction of this program remained. The events of Good Friday and the hours of the day survived intact, although with some events half-concealed. In "Terce," for example, the sentencing of Christ is sketched lightly by the presence of a judge and hangman who do not yet know what sentence they will pronounce or execute. The burial is shifted from "Compline" to a phrase in "Vespers" about a hill called "Adam's Grave." Many details disappeared because, between preparing the chart in 1948 and starting the poems in 1949, Auden changed his central historical idea. The chart portrays a linear sequence of events from Lauds to Compline, Creation to Apocalypse, dawn to dusk. But a strictly linear time ignores the repetitive physiology of the body. The finished sequence, with Lauds at the close, integrates linear history with cyclical nature: Lauds heralds the natural recurrence of the next day's dawn—a moment when, through both recurrence and forgiveness, the solitary human figure, roused from bed by his own inner will in "Prime," is now, on the following day, awakened in "Lauds" by the song of birds, "*In solitude, for company.*" The Roman Catholic Church at that time celebrated the first Easter Mass on the morning of Holy Saturday, and thus in "Lauds" "Already the mass-bell goes dong-ding" in a first celebration of resurrection and renewal. Furthermore, the column of separate body *parts*—suggested by a similar column in Stuart Gilbert's chart for *Ulysses*—was replaced in the finished poem by an evocation of the body as a whole. The kind of schema devised by Joyce had little relation to the historical world of persons. The professors, as Joyce hoped, are kept busy for centuries; readers who confuse literature with puzzles enjoy the satisfaction of finding hidden patterns; but no one is any wiser after sorting out the details.

Auden needed a change of air before the poems of "Horae Canonicae" could get written. He had first planned the sequence in 1947, at around the same time he planned his trip to Europe, but he did not begin writing the poems until his first full summer in Ischia in 1949. His two years of preparation were spent unlearning mistaken presuppositions, experimenting unsuccessfully with new ones, and cleaning others off his workbench, not because they were wrong, but because they had outlasted their usefulness. During this time he also established the seasonal schedule he followed for the rest of his life, with rural summers in Europe, where he wrote most of his poems, and urban winters in New York, where he wrote most of his prose. During the winter of 1948–49 he worked on a series of lectures to be delivered at the University of Virginia in March (these were published as *The Enchafèd Flood*); in them he set out in systematic prose the issues he had been exploring for the past seven years in symbolic poetry and other issues he had left hovering around the edges of his poems.

The first lecture, "The Sea and the Desert," spelled out the opposition between barbaric vagueness and trivial order that gave shape to Alonso's letter to Ferdinand in "The Sea and the Mirror." The second, "The Stone and the Shell," presented itself as a study of the contrast between Euclidean transcendental truth and symbolic prophetic vision; Auden's symbols for these were the stone and shell carried by the Arab of the Desert in the fifth book of Wordsworth's *The Prelude*. Yet except in the opening and closing paragraphs, this lecture concerned itself with another subject entirely: the ship as a metaphor of society, a metaphor he described as suitable to a closed imaginary society, of the kind he described in "The Guilty Vicarage" and dramatized in the four-person society of *The Age of Anxiety*—not the open extended one, far more difficult to represent, that became the subject of "Memorial for the City" and "Horae Canonicae." The third lecture, "Ishmael—Don Quixote," examined the varieties of the romantic artist-hero, and at the end closed the door on him as a subject for poetry:

We live in a new age in which the artist neither can have such a unique heroic importance nor believes in the Art-God enough to desire it, an age, for instance, when the necessity of dogma is once more recognized, not as the contradiction of reason and feeling but as their ground and foundation, in which the heroic image is not the nomad wanderer through the desert or over the ocean, but the less exciting figure of the builder, who renews the ruined walls of the city. Our temptations are not theirs. We are less likely to be tempted by solitude into Promethean pride; we are far more likely to become cowards in the face of the tyrant who would compel us to live in the service of the False City. It is not madness we need to flee but prostitution.

In April 1949, after delivering his lectures, he again sailed for Italy and continued to work toward his sequence on the hours by writing a short poem about the problems he needed to solve before he could turn to the longer ones. The riddling poem "One Circumlocution" confronts the central difficulty of a secular poem on sacred themes: How can a verbal fiction express an ineffable truth? He had worried over this problem ever since his return to Christian belief, but he had been dissatisfied with all his attempts to solve it until he found the answer where he least expected it—in the apparent byway of his reconciliation with his body and the novelty of feeling (as he told Rhoda Jaffe that summer) "untroubled by sex."

God the Creator cannot be portrayed without using an image, and when Auden wrote "For the Time Being," "The Sea and the Mirror," and *The Age of Anxiety*, he felt obliged to be an image-breaker in the final lines of each. Then, in "In Praise of Limestone," having arrived at a recognition that his own creatureliness could be forgiven, he recognized the creature as the image of the Creator: "Imago Dei who forgot his station," as he wrote in 1953. In the same way, the falsehoods of language could now be forgiven by the truths they indicate, as Auden implied in "The Willow-Wren and the Stare," and poetic fictions no longer needed an apology—or at least seemed not to need one. The fictions Caliban derides as "indescribably inexcusably awful" are the same ones Auden justified a few years later in a poem titled with a line taken from Shakespeare's Touchstone: "The truest poetry is the most feigning." Where Caliban sees the human condition as "drabness and sham," estranged from the absolute, the poems Auden now wrote, especially "One Circumlocution," accept the drabness and sham and rename them *ordinariness* and *play*, states not of estrangement but of inadequacy and need, and open to forgiveness.

Auden placed "One Circumlocution" immediately before "Horae Canonicae" when he arranged his *Collected Shorter Poems 1927–1957*. It earns its position as gatekeeper through its extraordinary richness of theme and allusion. Yet the sheer difficulty of the poem has always confounded readers, and even when its riddles are solved, it remains more ingenious than moving. It is one of those poems, like "In Schrafft's" and "The Duet," that Auden seems to have written in order to learn how to write better ones.

The subject of "One Circumlocution" is the way in which every work of art is a riddle—the solution of which can be named only outside art, or perhaps not named at all. Auden derived the poem's cryptic, riddling wit from William Empson, whose *Collected Poems* had appeared in the United States a few weeks earlier, and some of its style and matter from the philosophical abstractions of Heidegger. As he put it in an article for *Mademoiselle*, in which he described the change in the typical young, female reader of the magazine over the past fifteen years, "At her parties existentialism has replaced Marxism as a controversial topic; her notions of what Kierkegaard, Heidegger, Sartre, et cetera, actually wrote are probably vague but she knows it has something to do with anxiety, guilt and making choices."

> Sometimes we see astonishingly clearly
> The out-there-now we are already in;
> Now that is not what we are here-for really.
>
> All its to-do is bound to re-occur,
> Is nothing therefore that we need to say;
> How then to make its compromise refer
>
> To what could not be otherwise instead
> And has its being as its own to be,
> The once-for-all that is not seen or said?

Auden had mentioned Heidegger in a review as early as 1942; in *The Age of Anxiety* the phrase "the Nothing who nothings" is an echo of *"das Nichts nichtet"* in Heidegger's 1929 essay "Was ist Metaphysik?" and "thrown into being" translates a central idea in *Sein und Zeit*, a book Auden seems to have looked at in the mid-1940s and absorbed more thoroughly in late 1948 or early 1949. Auden's phrase about the "being-there-ness of a fact," in a 1945 foreword, echoes the common English version of Heidegger's *dasein*, a word borrowed from Hegel. (Heidegger's work had been widely discussed in English, but no translations appeared until the selection *Existence and Being* was published late in 1949.) Auden told Alan Ansen that he had tried to make his *Enchafèd Flood* lectures as difficult as Heidegger—apparently to dazzle anyone in his professorial audience who might be skeptical about a poet's intellectual authority.

With Heidegger, as with other philosophers and poets, Auden responded to an ideological enemy by appropriating and subverting him. Through the use of compound simple nouns as terms for universally common feelings and purposes, he took over Heidegger's technical vocabulary in order to refute Heidegger's secular existentialism. He invented Heideggerian compounds like "here-for," and made the informal word "to-do," meaning business or fuss, sound like something found in philosophy. The opening stanzas—the hyphenated vocabulary disappears in the later stanzas, as if its refutation had been accomplished—assert that the problem of finding an authentic external world, an out-there-now, is not the massive problem philosophy sometimes takes it to be. In fact, as the first lines observe, sometimes we see that world "astonishingly clearly," but our seeing it "is not what we are really after."* All the to-do of the natural world has no choice except to reoccur in empty repetition, a "compromise" in which natural events can exist but must renounce all claims to uniqueness. Heidegger had repeatedly pronounced that the earth was the foundation of morals.† But Auden refuses the romantic fantasy that nature can take the place of the divine being-in-itself (Tillich's phrase), which manifests itself in the once-for-all of historical time. "Once for all" is the standard translation of Heidegger's *einmalig,* but for Heidegger the once-for-all is revealed by repetition, while for Auden the phrase has an entirely different sense, derived from Rosenstock-Huessy. (He and Heidegger had both adapted it from Hegel.) Rosenstock-Huessy used the phrase in a passage in *The Christian Future* that Auden effectively paraphrased in these first three stanzas of his poem: "In the cyclic, pagan view of History, there is nothing new under the sun; everything we do has happened before, will happen again; nothing of any permanent value is achieved; there is only change, without beginning or end. Christianity, on the contrary, has shown how man can be eternal in the moment, how he can act *once for all."* (The limestone landscape, like the recurring landscape of the body, occupies a different world of time. "In Praise of Limestone" acknowledges that the peace of

---

* This is the phrasing of Auden's early pencil draft, now in the Berg Collection, replaced in the published text by "not what we are here-for really."

† Auden explicitly refused this same romantic temptation in a sonnet in his sequence "In Time of War," written in 1938, that alludes to the same lines by Hölderlin that Heidegger cited when he accepted the temptation. See *Early Auden,* p. 354.

the poem's landscape is *not* "the historical calm of a site / Where something was settled once and for all.")

The next two stanzas of "One Circumlocution" explore the ways art has usually tried to invoke infinitude. Images of potent miracles—"to thunderclaps / The graves flew open"—fail because they are so clearly imaginary: "such staged importance is at most perhaps." The once-for-all that matters is an invisible act of choice, not a visible act provoked by it in the out-there-now. Awed visions of beauty—"moonlight on a spiral stair . . . light-boned children under great green oaks"—acknowledge the excellence of the created world, but they omit change, that vector toward an end which is present in all choice. In mere aesthetic visions there is "wonder, yes, but death should not be there," or the whole aesthetic effect is lost.

The only remaining method of referring to the infinite, or absolute, relies neither on miracle nor on beauty, but on "one circumlocution as used as any"—a riddling phrase that unfolds to reveal the basic aesthetic theory of much of Auden's later work. At its heart is his persistent sense that judgment proves mercy: our local failure is the sign that confirms universal success:

> One circumlocution as used as any
> Depends, it seems, on the joke of rhyme
> For the pure joy; else why should so many
>
> Poems which make us cry direct us to
> Ourselves at our least apt, least kind, least true,
> Where a blank I loves blankly a blank You?

The solution to this riddle appears at the end of the essay Auden drafted a few months later, "Nature, History and Poetry." The verbal order of a poem, he wrote there, "is an attempt to present an analogy to that paradisal state in which Freedom and Law, System and Order are united in harmony . . . An analogy, not an imitation; the harmony is possible and verbal only." A poem refers to the absolutes of Paradise not by naming or imitating them but by talking around them, by using a kind of speech in which the formal order, not the content, is the analogy to the divine order. It depends "on the joke of rhyme / For the pure joy." Rhyme is a joke because it is both comic, bringing things together (tragedy tears them apart), and fictional (not a direct image of the real).

The *content* of the poem, on the other hand, must remind us that in our fallen world and mortal time, our lies do not and cannot imitate the order of rhyme or of paradise:

> The effect of beauty . . . is good to the degree that, through its analogies, the goodness of created existence, the historical fall into unfreedom and disorder, and the possibility of regaining Paradise through repentance and forgiveness are recognized. Its effect is evil to the degree that beauty is taken, not as analogous to, but as identical with goodness, so that the artist regards himself or is regarded by others as God, the pleasure of beauty taken for the joy of Paradise, and the conclusion drawn that, since all is well in the work of art, all is well in history. But all is not well there.

Or, as Auden wrote at the end of a lecture on *Don Quixote*: "Analogy is not identity. Art is not enough."

The blank I who loves blankly a blank You (the Empsonian phrasing adopts the convention of saying "blank" to indicate a missing letter in a crossword puzzle: blank, I, blank, U) reminds us that, in the real history of private life as of public life, "all is not well." Yet we weep for joy because the beauty of the verbal structure, combined with the sadness of the content, makes up the one circumlocution that points toward the same universal order that Auden called in "Compline" "some hilarity beyond / All liking and happening."

This antiromantic sense of ordinary life as the image of Paradise gave a special edge to the lyrics Auden wrote during the next few years when he rested between larger projects. "Music Ho!" (the original title of a 1948 poem that begins "The Emperor's favorite concubine") is a brief comic essay on the Incarnation: at the close of a tedious stage performance at the Emperor's court, a transformation scene is brought off by a "rather scruffy-looking god" who misplaces his rustic rhymes. And in "Cattivo Tempo," written in 1949, the minor devils of "ga-ga and bê-tise," of gossip and spite, cannot be defeated by an existential act of choice and will, because that merely plays into their domineering over-dramatic hands.* "The proper riposte is to bore them" with chat about the weather or dull correspondence, "Outwitting hell / With human obviousness." The obvious, the ordinary, the scruffy-looking god in the

---

* The poem names these devils Tubervillus and Nibbar, which were Auden's mistranscriptions of similar names listed in Maximillian Rudwin's *The Devil in Legend and Literature* (1931). He also miscopied from this book the first of the two devils named in the title of his later poem "Merax & Mullin."

yawn-inducing play—all prove themselves closer to the truth than severe Caliban ever guessed.

In June 1949 Auden disassembled the elaborate structure he had devised for his sequence on the hours and at the same time wrote explicitly about historical destiny. He began by detaching Rosenstock-Huessy's thousand-year scheme of revolutionary history from his plans for "Horae Canonicae" and writing it into a separate poem, "Memorial for the City," a four-part work in verse and poetic prose that approached in ambition and scale the not-yet-written sequence originally designed to include much of its material. It contains some of his most eloquent writing about the body and the city, and some of his least convincing writing about history. While he was working on it, he incorporated the same scheme of revolutionary history into his introductions to the five volumes of the Viking Portable *Poets of the English Language*.* In the first he wrote: "Christendom was not a unity which grew out of the preceding unity of the Roman Empire, but a new structure created by the Papal Revolution of 1000–1200 . . . The Papal Revolution established once and for all that a man may have two loyalties, a local loyalty to the region where he is born, lives, and dies, and a universal loyalty to the truth which is the same for all." The vocabulary and interpretation are taken directly from *Out of Revolution*, as, to a lesser extent, is Auden's denigration of the idea of a European renaissance in favor of "the real revolutionary events, namely, the publication of Luther's ninety-nine Theses in 1517, of Machiavelli's *Prince* in 1513, and of Descartes's *Discours de la Methode* in 1637." Though not all the history derives from Rosenstock-Huessy—Auden mentions "the Cathar Movement with its doctrine that matter was incapable of salvation" which he learned about in Denis de Rougemont's *Love in the Western World*—the idea of history as a series of revolutions, each with its characteristic hero, was Rosenstock-Huessy's, just as the idea of the small group that Auden wrote about in the early 1930s had been Gerald Heard's.

In the introduction to the fifth volume of the Viking anthology, Auden treated the highly charged subject of the twentieth-century revolution

* He selected the contents of the anthology in collaboration with Norman Holmes Pearson, an American professor of English literature at Yale whom he had met in the early 1940s through Elizabeth Mayer, but he wrote the introductions alone. Pearson had earlier edited an anthology of American literature, the field in which Auden was least confident of his expertise, and the publisher wanted an academically respectable co-editor to help assure sales to university classes.

and its future outcome. "In 1914 a revolution was set in motion which has involved the whole world and is still going on." In this revolution it is the exceptional man, the man who works alone, "the man whom the French Revolution liberated and admired, who has become the object of the greatest suspicion." In place of this solitary romantic hero, the new revolutionary symbol is "the naked anonymous baby," and "It is for the baby's right to health, not for the freedom of any person or class to act or think—for a baby is not yet a person and cannot act or think—that the revolution is being fought everywhere in one way or another." Because the values of the new revolution "are really derived from medicine, from a concept of health, it is hostile to any nonconformity—any deviation from the norm."

This was a more sophisticated—but, Auden soon recognized, equally specious—version of his prewar sense that he was on the wrong side in a just revolutionary struggle. In "A Summer Night" his metaphor for the new revolutionary order had been "a child's rash happy cries." Now he imagined himself the nonconformist enemy of a revolution fought once again for a baby's rash happiness. The symbol of revolution in his lecture "Poetry and Freedom" in 1948 was the "naked, anonymous, numbered *figure*." By changing that phrase to the "naked anonymous baby" he identified the revolutionary cause with the imaginary victim in the background of "The Sea and the Mirror," the anonymous baby who dies so that the poet may be born—exactly as Auden had identified an earlier revolution with the wretched multitudes excluded by the walls of his class and comfort.

In less ambitious essays and reviews, Auden was describing the condition of the modern artist in terms of the artist's voluntary opposition to a society whose goals he was nonetheless sane enough to recognize as just. But in the grand historical sweep of his introduction to *Poets of the English Language*, he described this opposition not as voluntary but as the product of a teleological necessity that culminated in love:

> Perhaps history is forcing the intellectual, whether scientist or artist, into a new conception of himself as neither the respectable bard nor the anarchic aesthete, but as a member of the loyal opposition, defending, not for his own sake only but for all, the inalienable rights of the individual person against encroachment by an overzealous government, with which, nevertheless, even though the latter deny it, he has a bond, their common love for the Just City.

Governments and individuals, Apollonians and Hermetics, were moving toward a goal that both desired, and impersonal history was *forcing* them there.

"Memorial for the City" also looked toward a vision of the Just City of the future, but it devoted most of its attention to the unjust cities of the present and past. The poem as a whole seems so craggy and various that readers and critics have largely ignored it, but its experimental ambitions make it one of Auden's richest and most memorable works. It is another instance of "the fair notion fatally injured," in the phrase he used to describe an earlier miscellaneous work, *The Orators*.

Each of the poem's four parts adopts a different style and treats events on a different scale. Where "Horae Canonicae" integrates its scales—from the local to the apocalyptic—in the course of each poem, "Memorial for the City" segregates them. The meaningless destruction of war occupies the first part; a thousand-year revolutionary period the second; the third portrays the divisions of the world and the self; and the fourth is spoken by the body in language it might use if it were autonomous, able to observe mind and spirit from outside.

The problem the poem poses is the central one preoccupying Auden at the time: the relation of nature and history. The poem treats the body as the victim who is sacrificed repeatedly to historical hatreds, yet history is also the field in which the body, after long eras of suffering, must ultimately triumph. The poem identifies the anonymous body with the incarnate Christ: the epigraph from Julian of Norwich* identifies the moment when the soul takes on a body as the moment when Paradise is promised and therefore regained. And by writing the poem Auden confronted, for the first time in his work, the devastation he had seen in Germany four years earlier.

"To Augustine," Cochrane wrote in *Christianity and Classical Culture*, "body is neither absolute reality nor absolute appearance; it is the organ by which mankind establishes contact with the objective world." "Memorial for the City" traces four ways of perceiving the objective world, and of valuing or debasing it, and four corresponding historical epochs. The first part describes wartime destruction and injustice as seen through "the eyes of the crow and the eye of the camera"; it is a world

---

* Auden identifies her as Juliana of Norwich to make clear to readers unfamiliar with her that she was a woman; he found the epigraph (from Chapter 55 of her *Sixteen Revelations of Divine Love*) in *The Descent of the Dove*, where Charles Williams, following the title of a 1924 book about her by R. H. Thouless, referred to her with an invented honorific, "the Lady Julian."

without meaning and therefore without hope. The irregular, unrhymed verse of most of this section imitates the disconnectedness of pre-Christian or non-Christian worldviews, which is also the camera's view —and Heidegger's:

> The eyes of the crow and the eye of the camera open
> Onto Homer's world, not ours. First and last
> They magnify earth, the abiding
> Mother of gods and men; if they notice either
> It is only in passing: gods behave, men die,
> Both feel in their own small way, but She
> Does nothing and does not care,
> She alone is seriously there.

The plural gods merely *behave* in the behaviorist sense; they make no choices. Men merely die. The perspectives of "The crow on the crematorium chimney / And the camera roving the battle" are those that make possible the crematorium in the death camp. They record a world where personal history does not exist, "a space where time has no place":

> On the right a village is burning, in a market-town to the left
> The soldiers fire, the mayor bursts into tears,
> The captives are led away, while far in the distance
> A tanker sinks into a dedolent sea.
> That is the way things happen . . .
> One enjoys glory, one endures shame;
> He may; she must. There is no one to blame.

(Sexual power relations in this world without value are stark and simple: he *may* enjoy glory; she *must* endure shame.) The whole passage quietly rebukes the "I am a camera" mood of Isherwood's early fiction and the equally indifferent timelessness of Isherwood's more recent belief in Vedanta.

To the camera's modern eye and the crow's impersonal one—as dedolent (ungrieving, insensible, callous) as the sea—there is no one to blame. But the moral argument of Auden's whole career, and the explicit argument of the later sections of this poem, is that *someone* is to blame. The suffering the camera records as inevitable might have been otherwise, had someone chosen otherwise. As Auden wrote in "A Walk After Dark," "Somebody chose their pain, / What needn't have happened did." And the first part of "Memorial for the City" ends by affirming that the camera always lies:

> The steady eyes of the crow and the camera's candid eye
> See as honestly as they know how, but they lie . . .
>   Even now, in this night
> Among the ruins of the Post-Virgilian City
> Where our past is a chaos of graves and the barbed-wire stretches ahead
> Into our future till it is lost to sight,
> Our grief is not Greek . . .

The Post-Virgilian City (which can no longer enjoy the *Aeneid*'s fantasy of unending Roman triumph) has learned once and for all a Christian sense of linear, historical time, which it can refuse or deny but never forget. The experience of Christian time teaches that even these disasters have meaning because someone *chose* them, that they are human acts subject to judgment, that our pain is felt as punishment, not abandonment. (As Auden noted in his contribution to a *Partisan Review* symposium on "Religion and the Intellectuals" in 1950, Christianity found ingenious ways to ignore its own lesson. With a glance at Karl Barth, he wrote of a "too easy acceptance of the Doctrine of Original Sin" in modern religion, a conviction of absolute human helplessness which "is, of course, not Christianity at all, but simply another variant of the pessimism we find in Homer.")

The poem proceeds, speaking of those who are no longer simply *the* dead as in earlier lines, but *our* dead:

> As we bury our dead
> We know without knowing there is reason for what we bear,
> That our hurt is not a desertion, that we are to pity
> Neither ourselves nor our city;
> Whoever the searchlights catch, whatever the loudspeakers blare,
> We are not to despair.

This says: I am not a camera. And: do *not* consider this and in our time as the hawk sees it or the helmeted airman.* In a broadcast talk on Graham Greene's *The Ministry of Fear* in January 1949, Auden wrote about "the vice of pity, that corrupt parody of love and compassion,"

---

* When Auden wrote a poem titled "I Am Not a Camera" around 1969, he took its epigraph from Rosenstock-Huessy: "Photographable life is always either trivial or already sterilized" (*Collected Poems*, p. 840).

and traced its connections to the genocidal crimes that he described a few months later in his poem: "Behind pity for another lies self-pity, and behind self-pity lies cruelty. To feel compassion for another is to make oneself their equal; to pity them is to regard oneself as their superior and from that eminence the step to the torture chamber and the corrective labor camp is shorter than one thinks." As he had written in "The Prophets" about the mine country he loved in childhood, "There was no pity in the adit's face."

The second section of "Memorial for the City" records the city's history from the papal revolution to the late romantic revolution, and does so in the syncopated metre and internal rhymes Auden learned from Charles Williams and trained himself to write in "The Platonic Blow." Many of the details are virtuoso improvisations on Rosenstock-Huessy's themes. In the first line, for example, "Pope Gregory whispers his name" has behind it Rosenstock-Huessy's notion that Gregory VII "combined two purposes in the choice of his name. One was a protest against the imperial action which had forced Gregory VI out of office in 1046 . . . Then, Gregory I . . . was the pope who more than any other was quoted and appealed to by his great revolutionary successor." Auden makes Gregory's first act as pope—a verbal act—the first act in the poem's historical drama. The opening stanza records the rise of "the New City" upon the opposition of rival allegiances to emperor and pope. Each of the following stanzas records the revolutionary rise of a later city: the Sane City of the Renaissance,* the Sinful City condemned by Luther, the Rational City of the eighteenth century, the Glittering City of the nineteenth, and the Conscious City for which the lonely heroes of romanticism died, after making known "the forbidden, / The hidden, the wild outside."

The Conscious City proved neither just nor happy. The third section of the poem, which Auden thought well enough of to include in his 1957 selected edition under the title "Barbed Wire," opens with an image of an abolished city, the city Auden found in postwar Germany. Civil and religious institutions have been destroyed, but the ignorant camera is given a hotel's comforts and privileges:

---

* "Framed in her windows, orchards, ports, / Wild beasts, deep rivers and dry rocks / Lay nursed on the smile of a merciful Madonna." Or, in Rosenstock-Huessy's words: "The Madonna, the fixed visual center of the divine service in the church, is framed by the political vision of the new city-state: the Landscape . . . The Mother Church, and the citizen protected by her, were felt to be the center from which light shone into the darkness of the world. A landscape is the country viewed from within the city" (*Out of Revolution*, p. 583).

> Across the square,
> Between the burnt-out Law Courts and Police Headquarters,
> Past the Cathedral far too damaged to repair,
> Around the Grand Hotel patched up to hold reporters,
>   Near huts of some Emergency Committee,
>   The barbed wire runs through the abolished city.

The barbed wire that divided postwar Vienna and Berlin into occupation zones enforced a principle of arbitrary exclusion and sundered what human voice and choice once brought together.

Four years after the war, Auden's war poetry retains all the commitment to self-rebuke that so annoyed his critics during the war itself. The wire that runs across the city also runs "Across our sleep," where it is the sign of our divisions against ourselves:

>   It trips us so we fall
> And white ships sail without us though the others weep,
>   It makes our sorry fig-leaf at the Sneerers' Ball,
>   It ties the smiler to the double bed,
>   It keeps on growing from the witch's head.

It ties the smiler to the double bed: the division of the self from the body does not manifest itself simply as an isolating shame that makes us put on a sorry fig leaf, but also takes the form of a sexual complacency that treats the sexual relation as adequate to itself, and imagines that because all is well in the double bed, all is therefore well in the world outside. Auden's understanding of sexuality now included a double recognition: of the body's ability to restore division, and of its inability to do so without help from something beyond itself.

The last two stanzas look across the barbed wire to the body, named by the poem "our Image," the part of us that is visible. This is a rare instance in which Auden followed the tempting example of Heidegger by using a common word in a distinct and idiosyncratic sense that calls attention to the strangeness and difficulty of his argument. (His use of "our Double" to refer to the body in "Horae Canonicae," a year later, is another.) The language lacked a word that exactly described the quality of the body he wanted to evoke, so for better or worse he chose a deliberately eccentric sense of an existing word. This impersonal image, unaffected by consciousness, is the body as it exists prior to will and choice, prior even to the distinguishing qualities of sex or age:

> Behind the wire
> Which is behind the mirror, our Image is the same
> Awake or dreaming. It has no image to admire,
> No age, no sex, no memory, no creed, no name,
> It can be counted, multiplied, employed
> In any place, at any time destroyed.

The same naked, numbered anonymity that makes it the proper symbol of a revolution based on a concept of health makes it equally subject to mass destruction in the name of that revolution.

Throughout the 1930s Auden had insisted that the instinctive force of Eros had abdicated its authority when it took on human form. He now understood the body in a different and—for a brief period—quasi-mystical way. It has an agenda of its own, and its autonomy guarantees nothing less than our salvation. "Is It our friend?" is the question that begins the last stanza of this section of the poem, and the answers are unsettling. Against a reader's expectation, the first answer is "No"; and another surprise follows: "that is our hope." Only the body's refusal of our goals gives us any hope of being rescued from those goals. Our hope is that "we weep and It does not grieve" because it knows that for it, "the wire and ruins are not the end." The body can triumph over our doubts about it: it is "the flesh we are but never would believe, / The flesh we die but it is death to pity; / This is Adam waiting for His City."

The flesh waits because it knows it can neither choose nor provoke the end. In the final section of the poem, the flesh itself at last speaks its prophesies. Like Caliban, it speaks in an artificial voice, for it has no voice of its own; its voice, unlike Caliban's, is straightforward and unironic; it remembers no historical events, because in this poem (although not in later ones) it experiences them as undifferentiated moments of pain. It remembers instead the events of myth, Scripture, and fiction.* The poetic form it uses is the variable line divided into two phrases, derived from the Hebrew Bible, a line Auden had used in print in the disembodied moralizing choruses of *The Dog Beneath the Skin* and *The Ascent of F6* in the 1930s, and had not attempted since his abandoned drafts of "Song for St. Cecilia's Day" in 1940.

The body begins by defining its difference from spirit—its need for

---

* The one historical event it remembers is the reference Christ makes to his body in the biblical accounts of the Crucifixion: "To me the Saviour permitted His Fifth Word from the cross; to be a stumbling-block to the stoics." (The fifth of Christ's seven words—i.e., sentences—from the cross was "I thirst.")

warmth, its susceptibility to injury and death, and its indifference to art:

> Without me Adam would have fallen irrevocably with Lucifer; he would
>   never have been able to cry O Felix Culpa.
> It was I who suggested his theft to Prometheus; my frailty cost Adonis
>   his life.
> I heard Orpheus sing; I was not quite as moved as they say.

The body ignores oracles ("Had he listened to me Oedipus would never have left Corinth"); has no interest in legal disputes (like the trial of Orestes); falls asleep when Diotima talks of an ascent from physical beauty to the idea of beauty; is baffled by the spirit's decision to remain chaste, although it, not the spirit, must live with the choice ("I rode with Galahad on his Quest for the San Graal; without understanding I kept his vow"). The body has no use for soliloquy and indecision ("With Hamlet I had no patience"), and "forgave Don Quixote all for his admission in the cart" (when he said he had soiled himself: acknowledging for the first time the reality of his flesh). The body has no wish to murder and prefers comfort to revenge ("I was innocent of the sin of the Ancient Mariner; time after time I warned Captain Ahab to accept happiness"). Above all, as it says in the final lines, it refuses to accept the bodiless generalizing sociology and politics of the modern city:

> As for Metropolis, that too-great-city; her delusions are not mine.
> Her speeches impress me little, her statistics less . . .
> At the place of my passion her photographers are gathered together;
>   but I shall rise again to hear her judged.

The camera's eye, which finds no meaning in life or death, treats the insult to the flesh as a spectacle. But the flesh knows it will rise again on the last day to hear this judgment pronounced on its tormentors: as in "A Walk After Dark," somebody chose its pain and "What needn't have happened did."

———

Magnificent as this is, Auden knew all too well that prophetic expectations were not enough. The body need not act or choose, but the mind must. The solution he proposed for the problem of nature and history was incomplete—and he told himself so in the poem he wrote next.

"Under Sirius" seems pleasant but pointless when read in isolation from the poems written just before and after it, but it has a sharp and stinging point when read as the rebuke Auden hurled against his own errors.

The poem takes the form of an address to the sixth-century poet Venantius Fortunatus, whom Auden had read about in two books by F.J.E. Raby that he plundered throughout his career: *A History of Christian Latin Poetry from the Beginnings to the Close of the Middle Ages* (1927) and *A History of Secular Latin Poetry in the Middle Ages* (1934). The Fortunatus of Auden's poem lies in bed till noon, his "much advertised / Epic not yet begun," in the same way that Auden had not yet begun the sequence on the canonical hours that he had discussed at length with Ursula Niebuhr. The historical Fortunatus, who died a bishop, wrote Easter hymns in demotic metres (English versions were in the Anglican hymnal from which Auden sang on Sundays) as well as panegyrics to pleasure in a learned epicurean style. The much-advertised unwritten epic seems to be Auden's invention, as is Fortunatus's luxurious willingness to let the future take care of salvation for him. Auden portrays him drowsing in dog-day passivity, waiting for the world to alter itself. "All day, you tell us, you wish / Some earthquake would astonish, / Or the wind of the Comforter's wing / Unlock the prisons."

But while "it is natural to hope and pious, of course, to believe / That all in the end shall be well," Fortunatus would be wise to remember that "first of all . . . / The rotten fruit shall be shaken":

> Would your hope make sense
> If today were that moment of silence,
> Before it break and drown,
> When the insurrected eagre hangs
> Over the sleeping town?

(An eagre is a tidal wave in the Humber or Severn River, unknown to Fortunatus.) What will you answer if you hear, breaking from the heavens, the riddle "Who are you and why?"

Fortunatus's passivity before a wished-for predestined end ensures his exclusion from a real, fortunate one:

> For when in a carol under the apple-trees
> The reborn featly dance,
> There will also, Fortunatus,
> Be those who refused their chance.

The jaunty syncopation of "Under Sirius" suggests that Auden sensed, in writing it, that he had escaped the fate it threatened.

In the spring of 1950, about six months after he absorbed this warning to himself, Auden went out of his way to praise Tocqueville in a review as "one of the noblest examples of an attitude which may be called the Counter-Revolution":

> This must not be confused with Reaction, which refuses to recognize the just element in the Revolution and wishes to regard it as a simple rebellion. The Counter-Revolutionary has no wish to return to the condition which preceded the outbreak of revolution; he wishes rather to save the revolution from failure through the inevitable over-emphasis and over-simplification of the revolutionary party.

As in his introductions to *Poets of the English Language*, he named the central issue in the world revolution of today as the right of "every human body to the food, light, housing, medical attention, and so forth necessary to health," and identified its central symbols as the "naked anonymous baby and the tomb of the Unknown Soldier."

> The body knows nothing of freedom, only of necessities, and these are the same for all bodies. Hence the tendency of the revolutionary party in concentrating on this one goal to deny all liberty and all minority rights. In so far as we are bodies, we are or ought to be revolutionaries; in so far, however, as we are also souls and minds, we are or ought to be counter-revolutionaries.

This was no longer, as it had seemed to him a year earlier, a position that history had forced him into, nor did he now imagine that history had pushed intellectuals to one side of the argument while everyone else was on the other. His argument was built on a subtle, liberating dialectic of necessity and freedom, body and spirit, a dialectic that he believed every soul and mind participated in, not only the souls and minds of those who praised themselves for having a distinguished character and then pitied themselves because it was also their isolating fate.

A few years later, in 1954, Auden asked in a review why Albert Camus, who took seriously the antithesis of nature and history and believed passionately in the reality and value of personal freedom, should

> defeat himself by accepting the Hegelian-Marxian use of the word History which robs it of all meaning, since for them all historical events are natural events? To believe in freedom and the reality of the person means to believe in

an order of unique (though analogous) events which occur, neither necessarily nor arbitrarily, but voluntarily, according to motive and provocation and for which, therefore, the actor is responsible (since history is something man *makes*, it is meaningless to talk of *obeying* it).

By escaping precisely that tempting meaninglessness, by freeing himself from the unwilled necessities of history—necessities that no one but he had forced him to accept—Auden freed himself to write the richest and deepest of his poems about the fatal irreversible acts of the human will.

CHAPTER TWELVE

The Great Quell

The subject of "Horae Canonicae" is murder and its aftermath. The murder is the Crucifixion, but the sequence Auden wrote about it remained the "series of secular poems based on the Offices" that he had originally planned. The event at their center is the specific historical act that was performed in first-century Jerusalem and, simultaneously, any apparently trivial act you may do that harms another person when you did not consciously intend to do harm. The sequence's emotional and moral force can be felt by a reader who has no interest in religion but who remembers having said hurtful words and then, with a sudden painful knowledge of the irreversibility of historical time, wished them unsaid.

"Horae Canonicae" is the most ambitious and successful of Auden's encyclopedic poems, works in which he tried to integrate patterns of world history and local personal detail. He had repeatedly tried to write poems of this kind, first in 1932, when he began and abandoned his long poem in cantos on the model of Dante and Langland; then in 1937 and in 1938, when he was able to finish the miniature historical epic "Spain" and the longer verse commentary to "In Time of War" only by leaving himself out of both. "New Year Letter" in 1940 was far more successful, but when he looked back on it later, he found it emotionally and intellectually diffuse—partly because he now wanted to write something different. In a letter to E. R. Dodds in 1945 he said of "New Year Letter": "My only defense is that I wanted to write one discursive bookish essay and it doesn't pretend to be anything more than that" (although of course it did). What all these poems lacked was a sense of continuity between, on one hand, the macrocosmic scales of geological aeons and historical centuries and, on the other, the microcosmic scales of human life and daily experience.

"Horae Canonicae," more intellectually systematic and emotionally intense than these earlier poems, found that continuity in the body. The seven prayer services that give the sequence its large structure punctuate the events of twenty-four hours from dawn to dusk, then the new dawn that follows; this structure also encompasses the decades of a human life from birth to death, the history of a city from its founding to its dissolution, and all time from the creation of the world to the Last Judgment. The opening word of the opening poem—"Simultaneously"—sets the tone for the rest. The sequence begins with the risks and hopes of a new day, a new birth, and a new creation, and closes with the promise of a wholly other kind of beginning. The day in which the events occur is Good Friday, and also any day; and the place where they occur is Jerusalem with its law court and temple, and also the Italian fishing village where the poems were written, or anywhere. In the hours after the Crucifixion an empty blue bus in an empty pink square fills up and departs.

At the center of the sequence, giving coherence to the whole, is the unique historical event of Jesus' crucifixion: an act of murder which, as Auden wrote in his essay on detective stories, is the only act that, once it has been committed against a unique person, can never be performed a second time. "Crane and pickaxe wait to be used again / But how can we repeat this?" Among the themes of the poem are the real virtues and comforts of urban civilization—without it "how squalid existence would be, / tethered for life to some hut village"—and the exclusion, injustice, and violence, the "cement of blood," which every civilization denies or misrepresents but which sustains them all, even the least unjust. The sequence deliberately invites the objection that no one is wounded by the act of writing a poem, and it answers that even the quiet room in which that act occurs has that same cement in its walls.

The canonical hours were instituted in monasteries as occasions for prayer specified by rule (canon). "Seven times a day do I praise thee," sang the author of Psalm 119, whose example was followed by the early Church until an eighth canonical hour became standard around the sixth century. The eight were Matins, Lauds, Prime, Terce, Sext, Nones, Vespers, and Compline. Auden dropped Matins (typically sung in the middle of the night) almost from the start of his plans for the sequence, perhaps because Matins was usually combined with Lauds, perhaps because seven is a symbolically richer number than eight. Lauds, sung at sunrise, uses the text of a group of psalms in which the word *laudate* (praise ye) is prominent. Prime, at six A.M., was originally sung in the monastery's dormitory, followed in the choir by Terce at nine, Sext at noon, Nones at three, and Vespers at sunset; each of these consists of a hymn, prayers, and passages from the psalms. Compline (*completorium*) completes the sequence at nine P.M. by adding a confession to the hymn, prayers, and psalms. By shifting Lauds to the end of his sequence Auden gave his poem two beginnings: Prime represents, among many other beginnings, the Fall of Man; Lauds represents a new beginning of forgiveness and praise.

Auden began the sequence with "Prime" in August 1949, a few weeks after reminding Fortunatus that his much-advertised epic was not yet begun. He then deferred writing the poems that he planned as the second and third, and in 1950 wrote the fourth, "Nones." By writing it, he also finished a book of poems he entitled *Nones*; it resumed the quinquennial sequence of thin volumes of verse that had been interrupted by his *Collected Poetry* in 1945. He gave no hint in *Nones* that "Prime" and the title poem were part of something longer. In the next two years he wrote no other poems for the sequence,* although he later went back to the one-act libretto "Delia," which he and Kallman wrote in 1952, and rewrote its final chorus as "Lauds." ("Delia" was a sixteenth-century pastiche with a plot borrowed from *The Magic Flute*; Auden and Kallman hoped Stravinsky might want a second libretto that combined ancient and modern sensibilities in the manner of *The Rake's Progress*, but Stravinsky had turned to serialism and declined to set it.)

Auden resumed "Horae Canonicae" late in the summer of 1953, after writing "Bucolics," a companion sequence of seven poems, far more relaxed in tone and content, three of which were written in 1952, the rest in 1953. His mood had now changed from the one in which he wrote the first two poems, and "Terce," using a far less clotted and intense

---

* In 1951 Auden wrote only two poems; this was fewer than in any other year since he began his career. He was distracted first by the scandal that broke in June when the Soviet spies Guy Burgess and Donald Maclean fled from London to Moscow. Just before their flight, Burgess, who knew Auden slightly, had tried unsuccessfully to reach Auden by phone at Stephen Spender's house in London. He made no further attempt to reach him, but after Spender told the story to the press, Auden, by then in Ischia, was shadowed for weeks by reporters and police. Later in the summer he and Kallman worked on preparations for the premiere of *The Rake's Progress* in Venice, where, among other distractions, he struggled to coach the Italian chorus in English pronunciation.

style, expresses a less personal and more universal sense of guilt. He finished in 1954 with "Compline," "Sext," and "Vespers," poems that are conscious of guilt and blood but are ready to accept forgiveness in ways the earlier poems were not. Each is metrically less formal than the preceding one: "Prime," "Nones," "Terce," and "Compline" use increasingly relaxed variants of the syllabic metre Auden favored for meditations on history and nature; "Sext" is in free verse; "Vespers" in cadenced prose.

"Nones"—set at the hour named in the Bible as the moment of Jesus' death—is the poem's turning point. The event is acknowledged here as the murder that it is, and our body begins its work of "restoring / The order we try to destroy, the rhythm / We spoil out of spite." In "In Praise of Limestone" the body (not mine or yours but a generalized one) was the image of perfect love and the life to come; similarly, in "Memorial for the City" the body was innocent of crimes of the will and knew it would rise again to hear those crimes judged. But in "Nones," the body is "our own wronged flesh," not the quasi-allegorical body these earlier poems treated as something not quite ours.* The first three poems in "Horae Canonicae" are written under the shadow of judgment, the same judgment for which Fortunatus in "Under Sirius" is unprepared but which for the poet of "Nones" will arrive "Sooner than we would choose." Having named in this poem the wound that damaged both his victim and himself, he would turn in the later poems to the calmer landscape of forgiveness, where he remained, despite some unnerving dislocations, for the rest of his career.

When Auden published the sequence as a whole in 1955 he gave it an epigraph: *"Immolatus vicerit"*—"the sacrificed one triumphs." The phrase is from the passion hymn "Pange lingua," by Venantius Fortunatus, who had apparently roused himself from his dog-day languors. In Auden's later editions of his poems, he consistently placed "Horae Canonicae" in a position that emphasized its importance: in a volume of selected poems published by Penguin Books in 1958 and the Modern Library in 1959, he violated an otherwise generally chronological arrangement by putting it at the end, and in his 1966 *Collected Shorter Poems 1927–1957*, he again ignored chronology and put it at the end, followed

---

* When Auden first published "Memorial for the City" in 1949, the speech of the body was headed *"Let his weakness speak"*—i.e., the weakness of Adam waiting for his city. When he revised the poem for *Nones* in 1950, around the same time he wrote the poem "Nones," he changed the heading to read *"Let our weakness speak."*

only by the valedictory coda to his Italian years, "Good-bye to the Mezzogiorno." The arrangement seems designed to make clear that he had
gone to Italy in order to write the kind of poems that made up the
sequence, and when he finished them he was ready to move on.

═══

Unlike Auden's earlier long poems, with their bravura displays of polyglot information, the sequences he wrote in the fifteen years from 1948
to 1963—"Horae Canonicae," "Bucolics," and "Thanksgiving for a
Habitat"—are informed by the kind of knowledge that, because it so
successfully integrates personal and universal themes, deserves to be
called wisdom. These fifteen years were conducive to wisdom because,
except for one distorting episode halfway through, they were a time of
the most sustained equilibrium, stability, and calm in all of Auden's life
and work, when his private life was happy enough to let him write without the burdens of obsession, and his public fame gave him confidence
in a large appreciative audience. The poems he wrote in these years
achieved a level of ambition in design and assurance in execution that
suggests his secure knowledge of their greatness, even when conventional
opinion ranked them lower than the work of elder statesmen like Eliot
or Yeats.

Auden first wrote explicitly about wisdom in 1948, when, in a review,
he praised the philosopher Paul Weiss for having the "moral courage"
to claim that "philosophy is what the layman thinks it is, not a highly
specialized technical investigation of highly specialized problems, but a
search for wisdom, an attempt to answer such questions as What can I
know? What ought I to do? which also presupposes that such questions
are real and can have real answers." It was appropriate, he added, that
Weiss's book should be reviewed by "as complete a layman as this reviewer, since it is to laymen, I believe, that his words are addressed."

Without abandoning his sense of a clerical literary vocation, Auden
increasingly addressed his poems after 1948 to what might be called a
literary laity.* "Horae Canonicae" offers its wisdom with an ironic tone

---

* He expressed his earlier, quite different opinion on the subject in 1947: "The ideal audience
the poet imagines consists of the beautiful who go to bed with him, the powerful who invite
him to dinner and tell him secrets of state, and his fellow-poets. The actual audience he gets
consists of myopic schoolteachers, pimply young men who eat in cafeterias, and his fellow-
poets. This means that, in fact, he writes for his fellow-poets" ("Squares and Oblongs," *Poets
at Work*, introduced by Charles D. Abbott, 1948, p. 176).

that works against any implicit claim that poetry enjoys privileged access to truth. The last poems written for the sequence, "Terce," "Compline," and "Vespers," explicitly acknowledge the aestheticizing perspective favored by all artists, including Auden, but these poems lack the private accusations against himself that he had ventriloquized in Prospero's speech ten years earlier. Prospero understood art and was wrong about everything else; the artist in "Horae Canonicae" no longer wields Prospero's wand and no longer suffers from Prospero's delusions. These poems, like the "Bucolics," recognize the poet as no more and no less guilty than the judge and hangman empowered by the state—and no more and no less innocent than the lovers in "Hunting Season," another poem written around this time, whose hidden angers erupt through the calm surfaces of their affection. Can poets be saved? Auden asked in "Compline," as he had implicitly asked in the earlier poems he had written for Prospero and the poet-Simeon in his drafts of "For the Time Being." But now he phrased the question with a deflating parenthesis: "Can poets (can men in television) / Be saved?"

As the sequence developed, its subject expanded to include the guilt shared by everyone who enjoyed the secure comforts of the United States and Western Europe. "Horae Canonicae" is a Cold War poem, haunted by secular and religious apocalypse, conscious that the victories of the last war gave no protection against the horrors of the next, insistent that neither side could claim a monopoly on virtue. Like Beckett's *Endgame,* written a few years later, "Horae Canonicae" imagines the apocalypse in terms different from those in which it had been imagined before the era of atomic weapons. Yeats recognized the dismal horror of civil war but treated ultimate apocalyptic change as an aesthetically thrilling renewal, as a rough beast's cyclical rebirth; Eliot imagined a concluding whimper; Frost either fire or ice. Auden, after 1945, imagined it in terms that combined theology and recent history: "the end, for me as for cities, / Is total absence," because "sooner than we would choose / Bread will melt, water will burn, / And the great quell begin"; and he saw these events occurring not through inevitable forces but as the result of deliberate human choice. Auden chose his metaphoric name for the Day of Judgment with precise literary tact: "The great quell" predicted in "Nones" is a quotation from the lines in which Lady Macbeth, plotting Duncan's murder, plans to let Duncan's drunken officers "bear the guilt / Of our great quell." As in every *contrappasso,* the crime is its own punishment, and judgment repeats the murder that provoked it.

"Simultaneously, as soundlessly, / Spontaneously, suddenly," the gates
of dream close, and the "kind / Gates of the body fly open to its world
beyond." These opening lines of "Prime" record the transition from
sleep to waking, from the "rebellious fronde" of dreams to the understanding that Auden identified in "Spain" as "the conscious acceptance
of guilt in the necessary murder." Auden had already recoiled from the
idea that inevitable revolution was the motive power of history, so the
rebellion he chose to name was the unsuccessful one of seventeenth-
century France, the Fronde—mentioned only in passing by Rosenstock-
Huessy and absent from Auden's early plans—instead of the successful
Revolution of 1789, one of Rosenstock-Huessy's predestined stages in
the prophetic structure of divinity, and the revolution associated with
"Prime" in Auden's seven-part diagrams.

"Prime" records the transition from the chaos that precedes creation,
then to an Edenic unity, then to the Fall and its division between spirit
and flesh, a mutual betrayal by partners in crime: "this ready flesh" is
"my accomplice now, / My assassin to be." The opening stanza is a rush
of beginnings, taut with the internal rhymes which in Auden, as in Gerard
Manley Hopkins and Charles Williams, indicate dense moral connectedness. The eyes and ears and other sense organs that fly open are the
kind gates of the body in that they are its *natural* gates; this was Auden's
first use of "kind" in its archaic sense (it recurs in his allusion to "Dame
Kind" in "Sext" and in his later poem titled "Dame Kind"). As they
open, the Homeric and Virgilian gates of true and false dreams, "The
horn gate and the ivory gate," close on the disorder and falsehood (as
the conscious world wants to imagine it) of all dreams. Ten years earlier,
those dreams had occupied the archetypal world of the daemon. Now,
to the ego that suppresses them in the act of waking, they seem mere
tohu-bohu, the "nocturnal rummage" that must be shut away before
the historical world of daylight can be attained. The fronde of dreams
are "ill-favored, ill-natured, second-rate"; without rights as citizens of
the psyche ("disenfranchised"); disconnected from past and future
("widowed and orphaned"); and condemned to this state by "an historical mistake," the Fall that initiated history itself. But the act of waking
quells these dreams—"The horn gate and the ivory gate / Swing to,
swing shut, instantaneously / Quell the nocturnal rummage / Of its
[the body's] rebellious fronde." The uncivilized outcasts so tidily dis-

posed of at dawn will not be so easily forgotten later in the day, when the victim of a different quell is neither an archetype nor a dream.

Auden almost never wrote or lectured about his own work, but he found the genesis of this poem illuminating enough to lecture about it on college campuses early in 1950. He illustrated his lecture by handing out a transcript of his working drafts for the poem; this was fifteen years before a well-organized market for modern literary manuscripts emerged and Auden voiced disapproval of their publication and display. "In regard to this poem," he said,

> the experience of waking up is something that has always interested me: the problem of returning to consciousness and the return of memory and identity, the whole relation of [knowing] ego and [known] self* . . . Then there's a general theological problem which interests me and has for some time—to what extent we have any kind of recollection, or imagination, or intuition of what life was like before the Fall. Now since the Fall is a condition of human history . . . it seems to me we cannot imagine an unfallen action, but only the state preceding action—and action, of course, includes not only the physical action, but the actual intention of the will. And that, you see, began to link up with the business of waking up.

The second stanza of "Prime" pauses over a prelapsarian moment of waking when the "I" of the poem is "here, not alone, / But with a world," because "the will has still to claim / This adjacent arm as my own, / The memory to name me." The intact world has not separated into nameable objects; the light's outcry is wordless; the body is no more or less present than is the natural landscape of which it is still a part; and

---

* The distinction between ego and self has exasperated virtually every reader of Auden's prose because he seems to have treated it almost as self-explanatory. In a response to a letter from Clement Greenberg on 16 December 1944, he wrote of "our lack of a vocabulary to distinguish clearly and invariably between the I (Ego. Logos. ♂) and the Me (Self. World. ♀)" (Archives of American Art). In the aphorisms he collected under the title "Hic et Ille" (in *The Dyer's Hand*) he wrote in more detail:

> Every autobiography is concerned with two characters, a Don Quixote, the Ego, and a Sancho Panza, the Self . . . If the same person were to write his autobiography twice, first in one mode and then in the other, the two accounts would be so different that it would be hard to believe that they referred to the same person. In one he would appear as an obsessed creature, a passionate Knight forever serenading Faith or Beauty, humorless and over-life-size: in the other as coolly detached, full of humor and self-mockery, lacking in a capacity for affection, easily bored and smaller than life-size. As Don Quixote seen by Sancho Panza, he never prays; as Sancho Panza seen by Don Quixote, he never giggles.

the "I" of the poem is "Adam sinless in our beginning, / Adam still previous to any act."

Then everything divides. The final stanza opens with the first act of will, a conscious drawing of breath that deliberately claims life, and in doing so claims its separation from other life:

> I draw breath; that is of course to wish
>   No matter what, to be wise,
> To be different, to die and the cost,
>   No matter how, is Paradise
> Lost of course and myself owing a death.

The pattern of internal rhymes tells a fatal story. As Auden explained to his lecture audience in 1950, the irregularly placed internal rhymes were designed to set up a counterpoint with the stops at the ends of lines; this counterpoint was impossible in standard rhymed verse, where rhymes and line ends coincide. Lines 2–5 exploit this technique to splendid effect by creating the expectation of an *abab* rhyme scheme through the end-words, "wise," "cost," and "Paradise," and then fulfilling that expectation prematurely in the opening word of the next line, "Lost." The rhyme occurs—as Auden wrote in "Nones" about the apocalypse— "sooner than we would choose," yet because it is part of the phrase "Paradise Lost," it occurs exactly when it should. The stanza is dense with literary history: the fifth line begins with an allusion to Milton, then explains the allusion by echoing Shakespeare in the punning (and pro-verbial) phrase "we owe god a death/debt" which occurs in both parts of *Henry IV*.

The action of the will changes the landscape for the worse. The mountain, sea, and village,

> Though as fresh and sunny still are not friends
>   But things to hand, this ready flesh
> No honest equal, but my accomplice now,
>   My assassin to be, and my name
> Stands for my historical share of care
>   For a lying self-made city,
> Afraid of our living task, the dying
>   Which the coming day will ask.

The condition of physical objects as "things to hand" is an echo and critique of Heidegger's *Sein und Zeit*, where things *zur Hand* are the equipment of the world that indicates our separation from Being.* But Auden gives this idea a moral dimension by understanding these things as the tools of the criminal conspiracy of self and body. His "care" for a city fearful of its murderous task also derives from Heidegger, but it has a greater moral significance than anything Heidegger imagined. In *Sein und Zeit* care is "Being-toward-death," an awareness of one's own death; in "Horae Canonicae" the word is redefined to include our will to bring about someone else's death.

Auden arrived at this sense of "care" by transforming "Prime" from the love poem it was in its early drafts into a poem that offered no consolation to loneliness. In the transcript he gave his lecture audiences in 1950, the poem ended, in its first version:

> No honest companion but my accomplice
>> For now, my assassin to be:
> Once more I claim in my name, and yours
>> Stands, my beloved, for that care
> Which can neither pretend to be love
>> Nor stop me wishing it were.

Here "care" is the private self-awareness that perceives others as instruments, not as selves—another name for the pity Auden wrote about earlier the same year. But after writing this draft, as Auden told his lecture audience, he showed it "to someone" (Kallman had now taken over Theodore Spencer's role as private literary advisor) who said, "You kept most of the poem dealing with the general problem; now to make it a unique and personal problem is all wrong." Auden then wrote a new ending, which integrated the poem into the sequence of Good Friday meditations, and (as he could not say in his lecture because he had not yet written the other poems) left all trace of love poetry deferred until the sixth poem in the sequence, "Compline."

———

"A great psychological division," Auden told his lecture audience, separates "those of us who feel depressed when we wake up and feel better at night" from those, including himself, "who feel better in the morn-

———

* In his lecture Auden said that a poem—any poem—"cannot be properly said to exist except when it is being read or remembered. At all other times it is only, as Heidegger would say, 'on hand.' "

ing . . . The bad period for me is the afternoon, between two and four, and one day I have to write a poem about that too." He told friends that his low ebb at three in the afternoon was a remembrance of the Crucifixion. "Nones," the second poem written for "Horae Canonicae," a few months after his lecture in 1950 (but fourth in the published text), is set at the moment when "it is barely three, / Mid-afternoon, yet the blood / Of our sacrifice is already / Dry on the grass."

The foreshortened drama of recognition and discovery in "Nones" corresponds exactly to the theory of drama expounded by Aristotle in the *Poetics*: in Auden's poem as in Aristotle's generalization, action, not character, is the essential element of a dramatic plot. The drama of "Nones" is made up of separate miniature dramas; one of these imitates a complete action but has no characters at all. In this action, now that the murder has occurred, our understanding of our acts has changed irreversibly; from now on we shall,

<blockquote>
under
The mock chase and mock capture,
The racing and tussling and splashing,
The panting and the laughter,
Be listening for the cry and stillness
To follow after.
</blockquote>

In the midst of a game as innocent as tag, the sudden accident occurs which reveals the violent intent masked and sublimated by our playfulness. Our intent is now visible everywhere, even in the act of writing this poem—"wherever / The sun shines, brooks run, books are written, / There will also be this death"—and the characterless drama in which it is manifested indicates that the poem is about everyone's individual acts, not the deeds of a named character who might be misidentified as someone other than oneself, someone conveniently available to take the blame.

"Nones" opens with a dense network of internal rhymes and an explanation of what those rhymes mean:

<blockquote>
What we know to be not possible,
Though time after time foretold
By wild hermits, by shaman and sybil
Gibbering in their trances,
Or revealed to a child in some chance rhyme
</blockquote>

Like *will* and *kill,* comes to pass
Before we realize it.

The chance rhyme reveals a truth that would be true even if there were no rhyme to express it. But one feature of an arbitrary system of linguistic signs is its power to bring to consciousness through chance relations of sound—the "joke of rhyme" in "One Circumlocution"—knowledge that might otherwise escape notice. The chance rhyme of *will* and *kill* reveals to a child a more universal truth about evil than the simpler proverbial wisdom Auden had cited in "September 1, 1939," where "all schoolchildren learn" that killing is a response to an outside stimulus, not an act inherent in the will, that it is those *to whom evil is done* who do evil in return. The chance rhyme in "Nones" completes the thought Auden began in "Musée des Beaux Arts," about the expensive delicate ship sailing away from drowned Icarus because it had somewhere to get to, sailing away on "urgent voluntary errands," as an earlier poem, "Look, stranger, on this island now," had put it. These were errands of *volonté,* of will, not curiosity or love, and in "Horae Canonicae" the goal that all willful acts are sailing away to is murder.

That is why, in the fourth stanza of "Nones," all human thought and action—"The spell of the asparagus garden, / The aim of our chalk-pit game; stamps, / Birds' eggs"—is now shaded by "This mutilated flesh, our victim." The garden in which we regiment nature, the game for which we establish legal rules, the stamps or birds' eggs we encase in our collections—these are signs of a will to direct, to possess, and to control. Likewise our erotic and religious feelings:

behind the wonder
Of tow-paths and sunken lanes,
Behind the rapture on the spiral stair,
We shall always now be aware
Of the deed into which they lead.

The sunken lanes and the towpaths at the edge of the canals in Oxford and Birmingham were charged with Auden's memories of adolescent sexual excitements, which, the poem implies, arose from a will to possess, a *care* that could not pretend it was love. The rapture on the spiral stair—a glancing allusion to the bodiless solitude of Eliot's religion in *Ash-Wednesday* and after—has the guilt of any experience that excludes not only other persons but the whole created world.

After the Crucifixion at noon and the death at three, after the world returns to its surface normality—"The shops will re-open at four"—everything looks the same yet feels different. We can deny the historical uniqueness of this murder. We can pretend it was not final but merely one phase in a recurring cycle. "We have time / To misrepresent, excuse, deny, / Mythify, use this event." Yet the fact that we experience a linear historical time in which to make these denials is enough to refute them. To live in historical time is to be banished from Eden: "It would be best to go home, *if we have a home*, / In any case good to rest." The home that "Prime" took for granted (and is still taken for granted in the second poem in the finished sequence, "Terce") is suddenly in question. Through the act whose meaning we deny, we have the status of displaced persons: "Under a hotel bed, in prison, / Down wrong turnings, its meaning / Waits for our lives." It waits everywhere except in our abolished home.

The meaning that waits is nothing less than apocalypse, now understood in terms that combine erotic degradation and nuclear catastrophe:

> Sooner than we would choose,
> Bread will melt, water will burn,
> And the great quell begin, Abaddon
> Set up his triple gallows
> At our seven gates, fat Belial make
> Our wives waltz naked.

Meanwhile, at this moment, it is "good to rest" in order that two things may happen. "Our dreaming wills," in the sixth stanza, may "seem to escape / This dead calm," and "our own wronged flesh," in the seventh stanza, "May work undisturbed, restoring / The order we try to destroy." The dreaming will can witness, in an incomplete and distorted way, the work of restorative labor that its accomplice, the body, does when, in the passivity of sleep, the will stops directing it. The will's dream is a nightmare of anxiety and crime. It wanders on knife edges, "in mazes / Of string and penitent cones,"* then "Through gates that will not relatch / And doors marked private, pursued by Moors / And watched by latent robbers, / To hostile villages at the heads of fjords." But its dream ends in an image that is more uncanny than threatening:

---

* The literal meaning of "penitent cones" derives from geography: they are spikes of ice found in the Andes and Antarctica.

in "a room / Lit by one weak bulb, where our Double sits / Writing and does not look up."

The dream cannot say that the Double is the body, because the will has no way of knowing the meaning of dreams (a point made explicitly in "Compline"). But in the same way that "our Image" in "Memorial for the City" is the body that does not cooperate with the will (is not "our friend"), so the Double quietly ignores us. The body has its own work to attend to, and in the poetic world made up of words, the body does not look up from its work of making because, in dreams, the will cannot summon the body to act on the will's behalf.

Auden took the image of the impassive writing "double" from Henry James's story "The Private Life," where the narrator, after leaving the great writer Clare Vawdrey at dinner downstairs, goes up to Vawdrey's room to find Vawdrey's double sitting in the dark, writing, and not responding to the narrator's greetings. In "Nones" this becomes an image of the flesh at its serious work, a work more serious than anything Auden claimed for any artist in the years when he paid homage to James. In James's story the double is someone else's double; in Auden's poem it is our own.

It is good to rest and dream, the poem continues, so that "our own wronged flesh / May work undisturbed, restoring / The order we try to destroy, the rhythm / We spoil out of spite." The body's work is described in lines with no poetic metaphors, only a simple vocabulary of reportage: "valves close / And open exactly, glands secrete, / Vessels contract and expand."* The body, as the body itself had said in "Memorial for the City," was not much moved by Orpheus's song.

The healing work of sleep is a respite not merely from the anxieties of the will but also from the taut condition of existential choice in which, without the relief of sleep, choice finally becomes impossible. "One of the most horrible, yet most important discoveries of our age," Auden wrote, "has been that, if you really wish to destroy a person and turn him into an automaton, the surest method is not physical torture, in the strict sense, but simply to keep him awake, i.e. in an existential relation to life without intermission."

---

* These lines pay homage to two quite different authors whom Auden admired. Wolfgang Köhler wrote in *The Place of Value in a World of Facts*: "Muscles contract, action potentials travel along nerve paths, glands secrete" (p. 64). And Paul Valéry, whose published notebooks, Auden told his lecture audience in 1950, had helped suggest the subject of "Prime," wrote: "Every heart beat, every secretion, every night's sleep blindly resumes the task of remaking the body" ("Suite," published in *Tel Quel I* [1941]) and elsewhere).

As the will only half understands the hidden work of the body, so the body does not understand the work of the will. It does its sleeping work "Not knowing quite what has happened, but awed / By death like all the creatures now watching this spot." The poem ends by drawing back from the human, civil village to the animal kingdom around it, a world the poem observes in a cinematic montage. The body responds to death

> like the hawk looking down
> Without blinking, the smug hens,
> Passing close by in their pecking order,
> The bug whose view is balked by grass,
> Or the deer who shyly from afar
> Peer through chinks in the forest.

The animals display the traits that, when combined with the uniquely human personal will, made the Crucifixion possible: cold cruelty, hierarchical authority, exclusion, and mere distance and detachment.

Auden deployed all his resources of verbal and structural virtuosity when he wrote "Nones," and some of his most impressive feats were the least obvious. The poem incorporates in its seven stanzas a microcosm of the full sequence of seven poems. The first stanza, with its child and wild hermits, and its question "What shall we do till nightfall?" summarizes the dream outsiders, the chorus of beginnings, and the anxious fears of "Prime." The second stanza, in which the angry crowd that gathered for the Crucifixion melts away into harmless individuals, mirrors "Terce," where each person is in transition between a private self and a public role. The third stanza, in which "the Madonna of the green woodpecker, / The Madonna of the fig-tree, / The Madonna beside the yellow dam" turn their faces away from us to look on the completed act of murder,* is echoed in "Sext" by the crowd that "sees only one thing," only the manifestation of force in the act of judicial murder. The fourth stanza, in which the victimized flesh makes clear the intentions of the will, is both formally and emotionally at the exact center of the sequence, a miniature version of "Nones" itself. The fifth stanza, in which we misrepresent and use the event, is echoed in the systematic denial of guilt detailed in "Vespers." The dream in the sixth stanza is echoed in "Compline" by a return to sleep, when "A stride from now will take me into

---

* "It is permissible, and even right, to endow Nature with a real face, e.g., the face of the Madonna, for by so doing we make Nature remind us of our duty towards her" (*The Dyer's Hand*, pp. 62–63).

dream," and that second dream, like the one in "Nones," simultaneously reveals and conceals a guilty act: "youths in an oak-wood / Insulting a white deer." And the seventh stanza, with its restoring body and its animals and plants, anticipates "Lauds," where "Among the leaves the small birds sing; / The crow of the cock commands awaking." Five of the seven poems in the sequence had not been written when Auden composed this miniature version of the whole.

Auden waited three years before he began to fill in the remaining outlines of "Horae Canonicae." "Terce," in 1953, relaxed the mood and tempo of "Prime" and "Nones" by adopting longer syllabic lines (eight and eleven syllables instead of seven and nine) and by omitting the internal rhymes that had tightened the fabric of the earlier poems. This relaxation of tone serves a dramatic effect: the turbulence of creation is past; the turbulence of destruction has not yet occurred. The moment of "Terce" is the calm interval of transition between private familial relations and public official ones. The hangman, after kindly shaking paws with his dog, sets off briskly over the heath; the judge, henpecked at home, descends his marble stair on his way to the court of justice;

> And the poet, taking a breather
> Round his garden before starting his eclogue
> Does not know whose Truth he will tell.

A public role, even the artist's role that Auden had guarded so jealously a few years before, is inevitably performed on behalf of someone else: state, patron, audience. At this moment, therefore, each prays to be free from both public and private roles, simply to be left alone. And the prayer of each is addressed, therefore, to a private protective god, to "his image of his image of himself." "Let me get through this coming day / Without a dressing down from a superior, / Being worsted in a repartee." Insofar as this is our wish, "we all might be anyone," because we want to live in a world without consequences, a world without any moral requirements imposed on our private selves. We wish, therefore, for a world with no dimension beyond the aesthetic: "Let something exciting happen" and "Let me hear a new funny story." We enjoy, therefore, the fantasy of living in an amoral world of magic: "Let me find a lucky coin on a sidewalk." These are wishes in the sense that Auden used the word in "West's Disease": absolutely self-centered fantasies of a world in which reality has been suspended in one's own favor. In the moral climate of "Horae Canonicae" the wishes in "Terce" cannot be innocent. You can move through the world untouched only if others stay out of your way. Because they never do, you must, in order to have your wish, move them out of your way. On this day, our wish will "for once" be granted completely, and the one person who most unforgivably and offensively stands in our way—"None of the others arouse *all* sides of my being to cry 'Crucify Him,' " as Auden wrote in "Purely Subjective" in 1943—is "our victim who is without a wish," who knows that "by sundown / We shall have had a good Friday."

By noon, in "Sext," we have long since adopted our public roles. Some citizens have vocations; some have authority; some can do no more than join the crowd. Those with vocations—the Prolific—perform them without will or animus. The eyes of "a cook mixing a sauce, a surgeon / making a primary incision, a clerk completing a bill of lading, / wear the same rapt expression, / forgetting themselves in a function." Vocation, as always in Auden, is the most innocent form of love, a voluntary loss of self in an object, a renunciation of appetite that does not offer the compensating flattery that one has renounced something worth having. "There should be monuments, there should be odes . . . / to the first flaker of flints / who forgot his dinner, / the first collector of sea-shells / to remain celibate." Civilization began in their prodigious impulse to "ignore the appetitive goddesses" such as Aphrodite or Demeter, to devote their lives to something other than instinctive hungers, "to pray instead to St. Phocas, / St. Barbara, San Saturnino," or whichever little-known saint is patron of their particular guild. Saturnino intervenes for fishermen in Auden's Ischian village. Phocas is patron of sailors, an innocent enough vocation in peacetime. But Barbara is patroness of artillery makers, and without the dedicated eye-on-the-object work of those summoned by a vocation, "at this noon, for this death, / there would be no agents."*

The hydrogen bomb gave a new shading to this theme in 1954, when Auden wrote "Sext," but he had written on the same theme in the 1930s:

---

* Auden named Barbara again in the poem he wrote about the saints in 1966, "Insignificant Elephants," where her domain, now explicitly identified ("a *Barbara* to bless the artillery"), deliberately shadows the poem's general mood of praise. The nameless saints Auden imagined in 1941 abandoned their pacifism when they gained their names.

in the ballad "James Honeyman" a chemist and his wife and child are killed by the poison gas the chemist had invented. Auden returned to the theme in 1951 in the gently elliptical lyric "Fleet Visit." Sailors on shore leave in an Italian port are severed from role or vocation: "They neither make nor sell— / No wonder they get drunk." Their inhuman ships, in contrast, "actually gain / From having nothing to do." The chance rhyme revealed to a child in "Nones" occurs again in "Fleet Visit," but makes its point by indirection: the poem says of the warships that "Without a human will / To tell them whom to kill / Their structures are humane." With guns and engines at rest, they "Look as if they were meant / To be pure abstract design / By some master of pattern and line"—nonrepresentational works of art of the kind snatched up by modern museums and traded on the art market at impressive prices, "Certainly worth every cent / Of the millions they must have cost." Or so they seem in their "Terce"-like days of inaction. The poem's multiple ironies make clear that the will is only provisionally absent. And "Sext" records the moment when it issues its command.

The first section of "Sext" points to the guilt of the Prolific; the second section points to the merits of the Devourer. Those in authority are "for the most part . . . very great scoundrels," whose greatest satisfaction is in "being right, an incarnation / of *Fortitudo, Justicia, Nous.*" But we owe them "basilicas, divas, / dictionaries, pastoral verse, / the courtesies of the city," with its order and safety. Now, without their judicial power, "there would be no authority / to command this death." The Devourer, with all his pride, is merely an accomplice of the will.

The poem shifts its perspective in its third section to the undifferentiated crowd with neither vocation nor authority. Auden had for years embraced Kierkegaard's argument in *The Point of View*: "The crowd is untruth." Now, in a desolate revision, he saw the crowd, although still the antithesis of personality, as the embodiment of a truth made manifest in those who shouted for the Crucifixion:

> but the crowd rejects no one, joining the crowd
> is the only thing all men can do.
>
> Only because of that can we say
> all men are our brothers,
>
> superior, because of that,
> to the social exoskeletons

—that is, superior to ants and bees. In "Nature, History and Poetry" Auden wrote that pluralities divide into three classes: crowds, societies, and communities. A community is a group of persons united by the love of something like music that is other than themselves. A society consists of a number of members who join in "a whole with a characteristic mode of behavior which is different from the behavior of its several members in isolation (e.g. a molecule of water or a string quartet)"; it is "a system that loves itself" and maintains its existence for its own sake. A crowd "loves neither itself nor anything other than itself." The sole characteristic of a crowd is the "togetherness" of its members.*

As always, this prose exercise in classification was more explicit but less revealing than the poem corresponding to it. The essay says nothing about the acts of the crowd—although Kierkegaard in *The Point of View* had defined the crowd by naming its acts of violence: "Not one single soldier . . . dared lay hands upon Caius Marius . . . But given merely three or four women with the consciousness or the impression that they were a crowd, and with hope of a sort in the possibility that no one could say definitely who was doing it or who began it—then they had courage for it."† "Sext" takes up Kierkegaard's statement that the " 'crowd' is an abstraction and has no hands; but each individual has ordinarily two hands." The crowd in the poem is not the aggregate of every *one* member of it. It "does not see what everyone sees"—a boxing match, a train wreck. It does not "wonder what everyone wonders," is "never distracted / (as everyone is always distracted)" by a dog or a smell or a mosquito. Only the crowd sees, as no one person can see, force and power in its pure elemental form, "an epiphany of that / which does whatever is done."

---

* Many readers have noted the resemblance of these lines to the opening sections of Elias Canetti's *Crowds and Power* and assumed that Auden borrowed from Canetti, although *Masse und Macht* (1960) was published six years after Auden wrote his essay. When the English translation of Canetti's book appeared in 1962, Auden evidently saw in it more of a celebration than a condemnation of power and wrote to his friend Geoffrey Gorer that, "apart from its errors, I thought it an evil book, like *The Decline of the West*" (17 September 1962, Sussex University Library). See also p. 294.

† The crowd is not quite the public, which Auden had named in "Nones": after the crowd that witnessed and demanded the Crucifixion dissolves, "we have lost our public." In his prose Auden quoted Kierkegaard: "Made of such individuals at the moments when they are nothing, a public is a kind of gigantic something, an abstract and deserted voice which is everything and nothing" (*The Dyer's Hand*, p. 82). Auden added: "A man has a distinctive personal scent . . . A crowd has a generalized stink. The public is odorless."

"Sext" is one of the few poems in English that try to understand power in its willed yet impersonal essence, as neither the manifestation of someone's personal wickedness or the instrument of unwilled historical forces. What it attempts is more difficult because less visible than the recognition that "Somebody chose their pain" which Auden wrote about in "A Walk After Dark": it acknowledges the social and bureaucratic powers that Kierkegaard dismissed as lethal untruths. The poem never names power directly—to name it is to give it a local habitation—but refers to it in the vocabulary of Christian myth. When, the poem asks about the social insects,

> have they ever ignored their queens,
> for one second stopped work
>
> on their provincial cities, to worship
> The Prince of this world, like us,
>
> at this noon, on this hill,
> in the occasion of this dying?

The Prince of this world is one of the names of the Devil, but his worship is not mere devil-worship. "The crowd collects to watch the wrecking-gang demolish the old mansion," Auden wrote around this time, "fascinated by yet another proof that physical force is the Prince of this world against whom no love of the heart shall prevail." Later he wrote: "When the New Testament speaks of 'The Prince of this world,' it certainly does not mean the Prince of the Cosmos nor assert that, so long as they are on earth, human souls have no option but to obey the orders of the Devil. By *this world* is meant, I should guess, Leviathan, the Social Beast." The same impersonal Roman force that had performed the Crucifixion remained on its throne, more powerful than ever. Auden wrote in 1952:

> To all of us, I believe, in the middle of the twentieth century, the Roman Empire is like a mirror in which we see reflected the brutal, vulgar, powerful yet despairing image of our technological civilization, an imperium which now covers the entire globe, for all nations, capitalist, socialist and communist, are united in their worship of mass, technique and temporal power. What fascinates and terrifies us about the Roman Empire is not that it finally went smash but that . . . it managed to last for four centuries without creativity, warmth or hope.

"Sext" leads to "Nones," and "Nones" is followed by "Vespers," which Auden wrote a few weeks after "Sext." "Vespers," the evening counterpart of "Terce," records the moment of transition back to the private realm that was left behind nine hours before, an unstable revelatory moment when the "conforming masks" of the public day and private night worlds are put aside, and "all must wear their own faces." "Terce" faces the coming day anxiously, but "Vespers" permits itself the relieved comedy of a safe return to the comforts of night.

The incident that provokes the poem is the casual encounter of two antitypes, an arcadian and a utopian, an encounter in which the old oppositions of Prolific and Devourer, Hermes and Apollo, are tentatively and momentarily resolved. The arcadian poet, who wants to be left alone to daydream about an aesthetic Eden, meets his utopian counterpart, who dreams of organizing everyone into the permanent ethical order of some future New Jerusalem. The comic literary conceit of their mirror-opposition leads gradually into a darker exploration of private guilt. Both figures seem harmless enough in their wish to deny the reality of the present, until their meeting reminds them of the mechanisms of injustice and murder which their evasions serve.

The poem begins with an image of their two opposing daydreams of time, both dreams embodied in the single figure of Adam, whose fall into time and death first divided the two dreams:

If the hill overlooking our city has always been known as Adam's Grave, only at dusk can you see the recumbent giant, his head turned to the west, his right arm resting for ever on Eve's haunch.*

* Auden converted to theological purposes a painting by Pavel Tchelitchew, *Fata Morgana*, in which a mountain has the shape of two sleeping giants, the man looking away from the woman but with his hand in her lap. (Auden had met Tchelitchew through Lincoln Kirstein.) Auden was generally not much interested in the visual arts, but during his Italian years he forced himself to think about the visible world in ways he had not done since the 1930s. In 1952 he spent much time photographing friends on Ischia with an expensive camera, and two of his three allusions in his later poems to specific paintings (the third was his 1954 allusion to Tchelitchew) occurred the same year: "Woods" opens by describing paintings by Piero di Cosimo (perceived mostly through an essay by Erwin Panofsky) and "Mountains" begins, "I know a retired dentist [Chester Kallman's semiretired father] who only paints mountains." The pageant of Time in "Delia," also in 1952, may have been suggested by Vasari's description of the *Car of Death* made by Piero di Cosimo for a Florentine pageant.

Adam's head looks toward evening and the future and the course of empire, but his hand rests on the backward-looking comforts of Eve's flesh. Only at dusk can you see their shapes, and only now, when all wear their own faces, "can you learn, from the way he looks up at the scandalous pair, what a citizen really thinks of his citizenship," what one's private relation to the city really is. Two examples of citizenship follow, each looking confusedly in two directions at once: the drunk, with his "rebel sorrows crying for a parental discipline," looks backward in time to find a stern utopian law, while the nostalgic solitary, whose "lustful eyes" desperately scan "all passing limbs for some vestige of her faceless angel who in that long ago when wishing was a help mounted her once and vanished," seeks her future in an illusory Eden. Both are too self-absorbed to recognize their double vision, so the poem turns to the pure arcadian and utopian types who meet and instantly recognize their opposites. "It is now that our two paths cross," and "both, simultaneously, recognize his Anti-type," each with his own vision of justice and peace: "He would like to see me cleaning latrines: I would like to see him removed to some other planet."

The next paragraphs catalogue the details of their opposing daydreams, with the wishes of the first-person narrator almost identical to those Auden listed when he described his own imaginary Eden in various essays in the 1950s. The Eden imagined by the first-person Arcadian in "Vespers" is a place where "a person who dislikes Bellini has the good manners not to get born," and "our only source of political news is gossip." In the Utopian's New Jerusalem, "a person who dislikes work will be very sorry he was born," and "there will be a special daily in simplified spelling for non-verbal types." Merely by imagining Eden, the Arcadian transports himself to that Firbankian Paradise: "I have only to close my eyes, cross the iron footbridge to the tow-path" (the same route remembered in "Nones"), "and there I stand in Eden again, welcomed back by the krum-horns, doppions, sordumes of jolly miners."* When the Utopian closes his eyes, "he arrives, not in New Jerusalem, but on some August day of outrage," the day of political upheaval when the obstacles to utopia will be swept away, "when the unrepentant thieves (including me) are sequestered and those he hates shall hate themselves instead." (An earlier unrepentant thief was Barabbas, who was set free when Jesus was

---

* The sounds of these obsolete musical instruments were among the pleasures Auden enjoyed when he began appearing in concert with the New York Pro Musica a few months earlier in 1954.

crucified.) In a lecture on literary Edens a few years later, Auden, without mentioning "Vespers," offered a detailed gloss on these lines:

> The psychological difference between the Arcadian dreamer and the Utopian dreamer is that the backward-looking Arcadian knows that his expulsion from Eden is an irrevocable fact and that his dream, therefore, is a wish-dream which cannot become real . . . The forward-looking Utopian, on the other hand, necessarily believes that his New Jerusalem is a dream which ought to be realized so that the actions by which it could be realized are a necessary element in his dream; it must include images, that is to say, not only of New Jerusalem itself but also of the Day of Judgement.
>
> Consequently, while neither Eden nor New Jerusalem are places where aggression can exist, the Utopian dream permits indulgence in aggressive fantasies in a way that the Arcadian dream does not. Even Hitler, I imagine, would have defined his New Jerusalem as a world where there are no Jews, not as a world where they are being gassed by the million day after day in ovens, but he was a Utopian, so the ovens had to come in.

In "Vespers" *I* interprets the world aesthetically; *he,* the Utopian, interprets it politically. "Glancing at a lampshade in a store window, I observe it is too hideous for anyone in their senses to buy: He observes that it is too expensive for a peasant to buy." Each knows exactly which kind of knowledge he prefers not to have. "Passing a slum child with rickets, I look the other way; he looks the other way if he passes a chubby one." In one of Auden's many ethical uses of *litotes,* the poem points to the diseased child while confessing the temptation of all art to aestheticize or to look away, but it refuses to hold up the child as a justification for one unjust utopia rather than another.

So, after the two antitypes meet and recede, "heading, incorrigible each, towards his kind of meal and evening," the poem considers two interpretations of their meeting. To "any god of cross-roads"—any of those pagan gods or spirits of myth who, as Auden wrote, "do not have real faces but rather masks, for a real face expresses a responsibility for itself, and the pagan gods are, by definition, irresponsible"—the meeting seems "simply a fortuitous intersection of life-paths, loyal to different fibs." (The juxtaposed latinate and nursery vocabulary signifies that evasion can be attempted in many ways, some straightforward, some polysyllabic.) Or, the poem asks, was it

> also a rendezvous between two accomplices who, in spite of
> themselves, cannot resist meeting

to remind the other (do both, at bottom, desire truth?) of that
half of their secret which he would most like to forget,
    forcing us both, for a fraction of a second, to remember our
victim (but for him I could forget the blood, but for me he could
forget the innocence),
    on whose immolation (call him Abel, Remus, whom you will, it is
one Sin Offering) arcadias, utopias, our dear old bag of a democracy
are alike founded:
    For without a cement of blood (it must be human, it must be
innocent) no secular wall will safely stand.

"At bottom" is a comic reminder of the body, in the same literary register as "our feat" in "Nones." With that saving remembrance of our
common flesh, the poem recollects two aspects of "our victim": the
blood, which in wishing to aestheticize the event *I* would forget; and
the innocence, which the Utopian *he* would forget in his legalistic fantasy
that anyone excluded from the city deserves his fate. There has never
been a society sufficiently just to exclude no one; in "Sext" "only the
crowd excludes no one," yet the crowd always finds its victim. Arcadia
and utopia require their cement of blood; so does our dear old bag of a
democracy. Auden made a similar personification in a broadcast a year
later: "Nobody would call Miss Democracy anything but a plain girl, but
when one compares her with the hags to whom millions are expected to
pay court, she seems a very Helen." His prose, with its distancing tone
of camp, once again omitted the crime and the blood that his poem
insisted on naming. The murders named in the closing lines of "Vespers"
initiated biblical and imperial history, and perhaps have a private significance suggested by Sebastian's sestina in "The Sea and the Mirror": in
each case, one brother is murdered by another.

At the end of the day, sleep returns in "Compline," the poem which
presents the evening counterpart to the waking hour of "Prime." The
stanza form of both poems is the same, but in "Compline" the rhythms
are slower, the diction more relaxed, and the internal rhymes less frequent and agitated. As the body joins "Plants in their chaster peace,
which is more / To its real taste," as the day ends, an instant of recollection can be expected "When the whole thing makes sense." That
moment comes, "but all / I recall are doors banging, / Two housewives
scolding . . . / Actions, words that could fit any tale, / And I fail to see

either plot or meaning." "Nones" insists that words, actions, tales all point toward the same meaning and the same plot, but now that meaning is indefinitely deferred. The restorative work begun in "Nones" has brought about its comforting results. Until now the sequence was engrossed in the moral connectedness of a plot—in plot itself, plot as an allegory of the moral connectedness that links one human event to another. Now the poem no longer recalls what its own story is about. "I cannot remember / A thing between noon and three."

With the return of sleep, the one language available is the language of the body. This is a language of numbers, not words, "a language of motion / I can measure but not read." The speculations that follow this statement concern the meanings of this wordless language, meanings that link the natural world to the human realm of judgment and mercy. The rhythms of the body perhaps admit the body's complicity in today's dying—"maybe / My heart is confessing her part / In what happened from noon till three"—while the rhythms of the constellations perhaps affirm "some hilarity beyond / All liking and happening." But no one can presume to know any of this. So, "scorning / All vain fornications of fancy,"* which might affirm as ascertainable truth what I want to believe the natural world is telling me, I can "accept our separations" from that world, and thank both heart and stars "for the sweetness of their cassations" while asking them for nothing more.

With the end of the day, the poem moves toward a vision of an ultimate ending, but in terms more hopeful than the grotesque image of judgment in "Nones." Dreams reveal nothing. Their symbolic censorship is a "magic cult to propitiate / What happens from noon till three." And, from the untruths of dream, there remains only

> one step to nothing,
> For the end, for me as for cities,
> Is total absence: what comes to be
> Must go back into non-being
> For the sake of the equity, the rhythm
> Past measure or comprehending.

In the final stanza of "Compline" the sequence completes its passage through the day and becomes the love poem Auden had first planned to make it when he drafted "Prime."

---

* These are the same *fantastica fornicatio* named by Augustine and translated by Auden's Simeon as the imagination's "promiscuous fornication with her own images."

It is not easy
To believe in unknowable justice
Or pray in the name of a love
Whose name one's forgotten: *libera*
Me, libera C (dear C)
And all poor s-o-b's who never
Do anything properly . . .

Those poor s-o-b's were last seen in "Sext," where "Few people accept
each other, and most / Will never do anything properly," although all
can join the crowd. Now, for the first time, Auden's poetry can pray for
All Souls as it simultaneously prays for someone named by the initial C.
As in the final lines of Dante's *Paradiso*, a vision of the universe coalesces
into a human face.

In its closing prayer to be spared "in the youngest day"—the last day,
identified by a riddling phrase that transforms its judgment into youthful
promise—"Compline" knows that the Crucifixion, like all murders, cannot be forgotten or denied. On the day "when all are / Shaken awake,
facts are facts, / (And I shall know exactly what happened / Today
between noon and three)," the new awakening will also be a transfiguration. Spare us, the prayer concludes,

That we, too, may come to the picnic
With nothing to hide, join the dance
As it moves in perichoresis,
Turns about the abiding tree.

The life to come is imagined not quite as it was in "In Praise of Limestone," as a human body, certainly not as it was in "The Sea and the
Mirror," as a formal garden, but as the shared mild communion of a
picnic. The resolving dance moves in "perichoresis": a reader can puzzle
out the word easily enough as a Greek borrowing that means "dancing
around," but it is also the name for the theological doctrine (referred to
by Simeon in "For the Time Being" under its English name) of the
mutual "co-inherence" of the human and divine in Christ. At the center
of both dance and doctrine, the cross abides in the living tree.

——

"Lauds," the coda to the sequence, welcomes the new day in ancient
verse. The poem's singsong rhythms, coarse-grained rhymes (*sing/*

awaking), and repetitive circular form (all but two lines occur twice, and those two are symmetrically balanced) derive from a thirteenth-century Galician *cossante* Auden found in Gerald Brenan's *The Literature of the Spanish People* when it was published in 1951. In Brenan's translation the refrain that follows each couplet reads, "Gladly I go my way." In the first version of "Lauds" (the final chorus for the libretto "Delia") Auden wrote the refrain as "*Day breaks for joy and sorrow*"; he rewrote it here as "*In solitude, for company.*" "Lauds" can move from the solitude of sleep to the company of waking because it records no acts of possessive will, only acts of grateful attention:

> Bright shines the sun on creatures mortal;
> Men of their neighbors become sensible:
> *In solitude, for company* . . .
>
> Already the mass-bell goes dong-ding;
> The dripping mill-wheel is again turning:
> *In solitude, for company.*
>
> God bless the Realm, God bless the People;
> God bless this green world temporal:
> *In solitude, for company.*

This naïve-sounding prayer for blessing, made possible by a free admission of guilt, is phrased with Auden's subtlest skill. It asks benediction neither on an impersonal crowd nor on impersonal authority, but on a Realm—a *royaume*—ruled by a person, and on a People, a plurality made up of persons, not an abstract impersonal public. It also asks, in a single phrase, benediction on two kinds of time, the cyclical time of the green world and the historical time of the temporal world. The final lines praise repetition and renewal in both worlds, the constructed economic world and the begotten natural one:

> The dripping mill-wheel is again turning;
> Among the leaves the small birds sing:
> *In solitude, for company.*

Men become *sensible* of their neighbors in this poem by putting to use the five senses that Auden celebrated in 1950 in an exuberant song of praise, "Precious Five," which took the form of invocations to each sense organ: to the tongue, that it praise the Earthly Muse of appetite (partly in honor of its "twin, your brother, / Unlettered, savage, dumb, / Down there below the waist"); to the hands, that they become "true hands" by making and giving; to the eyes, that they learn to love by believing that "There is a world to see," a belief that "sight can never prove" (this is what Auden earlier called the absolute presupposition of science); to the ears, that they drudge at the work of acceptance until all sounds "seem natural" and are signs of a pervading grace, "the luck you cannot place"; and to the nose, that its odd appearance "may provoke / To a mind-saving joke / A mind that would it were / An apathetic sphere" of Platonic autonomy and perfection. The verse paragraph addressed to the nose also asks that it point upward, as a guide on the purgatorial ascent which, when Auden wrote "New Year Letter," had seemed achievable by spirit alone, but for which the body now provides a comic signpost.

The presupposition that the senses take on faith is the same one that Auden described in "Nature, History and Poetry" as necessary to a poet: the procreative presupposition that the existence of the historical world "is a good, and every addition to the number of events, persons and relations is an additional good." The historical world is a fallen world— "though it is good that it exists, the way in which it exists is evil, being full of unfreedom and disorder"—but redeemable. So, when at the end of the "Precious Five" Auden writes that he, but not his senses, can "Find reasons fast enough / To face the sky and roar / In anger and despair / At what is going on, / Demanding that it name / Whoever is to blame," the sky will state the same truth in the imperative mood that the senses know in the indicative:

> That singular command
> I do not understand,
> *Bless what there is for being.*

In "Horae Canonicae" Auden answers that command by climbing the storm-beaten slope from fatal memory to unconditional hope. This is no transcendent escape from the physical world but an undignified, saving scramble back into it. In imagining it, he found himself at home not only in both his work and his body—their reconciliation is one of the private achievements of the poem—but also in the double world of nature and history, neither an imaginary past nor a visionary future, but the place he lived now.

CHAPTER THIRTEEN

Number or Face

"The problem of every man and writer," Auden wrote late in 1949, "is at all times essentially the same, namely first to learn to be himself and then to learn to be not himself." It is difficult for anyone to unlearn the tics and automatic responses through which a personality hardens into a parody of a person, a mere set of habits, and especially difficult for a writer with an established career. After years of analyzing and rebuking the egoism in his idea of love, he now quietly began working to change it. He confronted the problem by trying to find new ways of writing in the first person, by appearing in his poems less as the dramatic character of "the poet" and more as himself. Writing as *I* meant taking responsibility for language, and keeping its promises not only to oneself and to a religious absolute but also to an equally personal and vulnerable *You*. The personal *I* of Auden's poems of the 1950s was no less an artifact of language than the more self-dramatizing *I* of his earlier work, but it used its artifice more to be intimate than astonishing. It was an *I* who tried to escape the limits of the solitary self not by pretending to *be* something different but by learning to *become* something different.

The first person of Auden's poems after 1950 is more self-consciously idiosyncratic than the existential *I* of his shorter lyrics in the 1940s. For all their insistence on the unique relation of the individual to the absolute, these earlier poems, even when splendid and memorable, are deliberately impersonal on the page. They use either the spare metaphysical abstractions of "Time will say nothing but I told you so," or the ornate dramatic masks of "The Sea and the Mirror."* It was not quite true that (as Auden later wrote of Kierkegaard) "a planetary visitor might read through . . . his voluminous works without discovering that human beings are not ghosts but have bodies of flesh and blood," yet the person who speaks in these 1940s poems lives in a world almost entirely without weight and form. Auden's poems in the 1950s, however, speak from a body that suffers ordinary ailments and enjoys ordinary pleasures. Auden adopted for his poems' personal voice a grown-up version of the self-mocking voice he had used when most disaffected with his public role in the mid-1930s, the voice that caused others to say, in "Letter to Lord Byron," "It's such a pity Wystan never grows up." As he did then, he now wrote in a comic first person for an urgent political reason: to keep the first person out of the solemn, regimenting hands of politicians.

The intellectual and emotional temptations to abdicate one's personal voice tended to take different forms over the course of the twentieth century. When myths of inexorable historical destiny were discredited by the acts of their loudest exponents, Hitler and Stalin, they were gradually replaced in intellectual fashion by myths that required no belief in individual leaders. Historical theories of collective *mentalités,* cultural theories that attributed absolute power to impersonal forces of subjugation and restraint, literary theories that dissolved the idea of the author into patterns of language that did his writing for him, structural theories of universal patterns that governed apparently voluntary acts—all these myths were more sophisticated than earlier notions about the inevitable withering away of the state, and more difficult to dislodge. In the postwar world, a frame of mind in which one believed one's personal identity to be the product of unalterable genetic or subconscious processes, or to be the intersection of undefeatable social and historical forces, seemed sadly consistent with daily reality. The impersonal myths favored in the first half of the century had all too obviously served the ends of dictators, but the myths favored in the second half, although far more subtle, were equally conducive to passivity, equally useful to those who justified personal and political cruelty. In his own work and thought, Auden had

* Auden used the existential *I* when devising new titles in 1944 for the previously untitled lyrics he reprinted in his *Collected Poetry* (1945): "I Shall Be Enchanted," "Nobody Understands Me," "Which Side Am I Supposed to Be On?" and "Let History Be My Judge." The *you* or implied *you* in other titles in the book is equally abstract: "Make Up Your Mind," "Are You There?," "Please Make Yourself at Home," "Shut Your Eyes and Open Your Mouth," "What Do *You* Think?" and "Do Be Careful." He dropped almost all these titles when he compiled his next collected edition in 1965.

long since discarded his private myth about poet-heroes as a comic variation on public myths about supreme leaders. He now wanted to repu-
diate his lingering subtler myths while arguing against their public
counterparts.*

As Auden had foreseen in his essays during the war, the Western democracies were indeed adopting their own forms of collective persuasion
after defeating regimenting totalitarianism in 1945. The new international
mood of the 1950s exhibited none of the mass ecstasy of Nazi rallies or
the mass anger of Communist marches; the collective impulse was now
expressed in dispassionate conformity, mass communications, and statistical answers to ethical questions:

> Out of the air a voice without a face
> Proved by statistics that some cause was just
> In tones as dry and level as the place:
> No one was cheered and nothing was discussed;
> Column by column in a cloud of dust
> They marched away enduring a belief
> Whose logic brought them, somewhere else, to grief.

Thus "The Shield of Achilles" in 1952. Auden looked back in 1953 to the
war years in his brief "Epitaph for the Unknown Soldier"—the figure
he had earlier identified, together with the naked anonymous baby, as
the symbol of the contemporary revolution. The poem reminds the living
you—each individual citizen of the postwar world—of the personal
uniqueness that was once *this* soldier:

> To save your world, you asked this man to die:
> Would this man, could he see you now, ask why?†

Most of the poems Auden wrote in the early 1950s, whatever their
manifest subject matter, concealed arguments about personal and im-

---

* For example, Auden was no longer so confident as he had been in the 1930s about the moral
benefits of anthropology, a field of study that effectively dislodged local presuppositions but,
he now thought, left deeper prejudices unchanged. He told a lecture audience in 1947: "Anthropology is not a [good] beginning for eradicating race prejudice: one must arouse a passion
for treating one's neighbor as oneself" (transcript by Alan Ansen, Berg Collection).

† This is a more personal restatement of the words Auden used in 1941 in a review of a book
by Harold Laski: "Unless it is realized that the true necessity . . . is internal and absolute, then,
when Hitler is defeated and the external compulsion of war removed, the dead . . . will once
again be betrayed by the surviving" (*Decision*, January 1941, p. 52).

personal speech and hoped to refute the voice without a face. Speech, as Auden understood it, was the ground and instrument of personality, the means by which a face became itself and then voluntarily became not itself. This was the first of his central ethical beliefs that he did not spell out immediately in reviews and essays; he served it best by exemplifying it in his first-person poems instead of generalizing about it in his prose.

He made his most explicit statement on the subject many years later, in 1966, in a lecture, "Words and the Word," published in *Secondary Worlds*, where he contrasted first-person speech, the words of persons who speak in their own name, with third-person speech, the words of an anonymous he-or-she who takes no responsibility for words or acts.

> Whenever we use the pronouns *You* and *I*, not as mere convention, but meaning what we say, uttering them is accompanied by a characteristic feeling-tone.
>
> The You-feeling is a feeling of attributing-responsibility-to. If a boy says to a girl, "You are beautiful," and means what he says, he is asserting that she is, in part at least, responsible for her physical appearance: it is not merely the result of a lucky combination of genes . . .
>
> Similarly, the I-feeling is one of accepting-responsibility-for. To say "*I* love you" is to say that, whatever the causes or the origin of what I feel, I take upon myself the responsibility for them; I am not the passive and helpless victim of passion. Common to both the I- and the You-feeling is the feeling of being in the middle of a story with a personal past to remember and a personal future to make.

Third-person language has nothing to do with responsibility. "Can you tell me the way to the station?" uses first- and second-person pronouns only by convention; neither the question nor any plausible answer has anything to do with the persons in the dialogue. In some languages, as Auden observed, the question is typically phrased in the third person: Can the gentleman tell his humble servant the way to the station? The words are code, not speech, and the answer to the question can typically be stated in numbers: three streets east; five minutes away. This is the human counterpart of the language in "Compline" of the body and stars that "I can measure but not read."

These issues first became explicit in his poems in 1950. In "Their Lonely Betters" he returned to the contrast he had drawn in the 1930s between the natural world without choice and the voluntary human world, but restated it in terms of speech. The natural world, because it lacks a personal voice, takes no responsibility for past or future:

As I listened from a beach-chair in the shade
To all the noises that my garden made,
It seemed to me only proper that words
Should be withheld from vegetables and birds.

A robin with no Christian name ran through
The Robin-Anthem which was all it knew,
And rustling flowers for some third party waited
To say which pairs, if any, should get mated.

No one of them was capable of lying,
There was not one which knew that it was dying
Or could have with a rhythm or a rhyme
Assumed responsibility for time.

Let them leave language to their lonely betters
Who count some days and long for certain letters;
We, too, make noises when we laugh or weep,
Words are for those with promises to keep.

The immediate responses, laughter and weeping, need no language; the Robin-Anthem is as impersonal as a national anthem; the flowers make no personal choice when mating. The poem's echo of Robert Frost's "Stopping by Woods on a Snowy Evening" in the final line is simultaneously a tribute to another poet's verbal mastery and a claim to moral understanding deeper than his. Auden's subject is not his having promises to keep but the means through which he makes his promises, and who he is when he makes them. And the connection between first-person speech and the "Christian name" (lacked by the robin in the poem) is as important to poetry as it is to promises: in his 1956 lecture "Making, Knowing and Judging," Auden imagined himself judging literary critics by the answer they would give if asked if they liked—"and by like I mean really like, not approve of on principle"—long lists of proper names like Old Testament genealogies or the catalogue of ships in the *Iliad*. Your taste for the idiosyncrasies of personal names is perhaps a measure of your taste for the idiosyncrasies of persons.

Some years later, in 1963, when Auden wrote lyrics for the musical play *Man of La Mancha* (the playwright rejected them as insufficiently romantic and hired another lyricist instead), one was a "Song of the Devil," written for a Devil who fully understands the difference between code and speech. The Devil catalogues each illusion he offers his victims, but ends with a true statement of his feelings about them: "Believe while you can that I'm proud of you, / Enjoy your dream, / I'm so bored with the whole fucking crowd of you, I could scream." Audiences at some of Auden's public readings in the late 1960s were justifiably uncertain how to take this final line—because it was the last line of the last poem he recited, they found themselves clapping for it as he left the podium—but every word makes a serious point about personal and impersonal language. To be *bored* is to take no interest in particulars; the *whole fucking crowd* is the boundless undifferentiated group that performs mere sexual behavior instead of acts of love; to *scream* is to "make noises" instead of speaking words. The Devil does not intend to keep his promises.

Impersonal language issues from anyone who is a he or a she, not an I or a thou.* "Hunting Season," in 1951, illustrates the third-person relations of hunter and hunted that lie hidden beneath the more benign relations of first and second persons. A rifle shot opens the poem: "Some feathered he-or-she / Is now a lifeless bundle," to be brought proudly to a kitchen by an anonymous "example of our tribe." At the same moment, "Down in the startled valley / Two lovers break apart." The startled valley is an anatomical as well as a geographical place, and the two lovers suddenly sense the impersonal sexual hungers that drive their personal love:

> He hears the roaring oven
> Of a witch's heart;
> Behind his murmurs of her name
> She sees a hunter taking aim.

The third stanza records the response of the poet—that indifferent aesthete, not to be trusted as a moral authority, whom Auden, like a Renaissance painter, portrayed in the background of many of his canvases in the 1950s. The sound of the rifle shot reminds "One interrupted bard" only "of the hour / And that his chair is hard." He then heedlessly "Postpones his dying with a dish / Of several suffocated fish": an act in which his own life is preserved by multiple deaths. When he starts to eat, he leaves a "deathless verse half done"—a reminder that persons, whether first, second, or third, are not at all deathless.

Auden took over these ideas partly from Rosenstock-Huessy, partly

* Auden took this detail, and many others, from the opening sentences of Martin Buber's *I and Thou*: "the combination *I-It*; wherein . . . one of the words *He* and *She* can replace *It*."

from Rosenstock-Huessy's successor in his pantheon of encyclopedic thinkers, the German critic and philosopher Rudolf Kassner. Kassner, then living in Switzerland, had written many volumes of unclassifiable essays and stories in a rapid, allusive, difficult prose that traversed ancient philosophy and modern fashion in the space of a few sentences. His work combined existentialism and Christianity (he wrote a book about Kierkegaard in 1927), and was marked by bracing aphoristic contempt for the romantic and modern worldviews typified by Rousseau and Nietzsche, for all attempts to build ethics on blood and soil, for all varieties of collective and utopian thought. His central theme was "physiognomy," a word he used in the title of a half-dozen books; he defined it as "the doctrine that everything is expression and alteration and that there are no masks. It teaches, therefore, that we are not marionettes whose movements are controlled by an invisible hand." In the way other writers attempted an anatomy or genealogy of their subject matter, Kassner subtitled one of his books "An Attempt at a Physiognomy of Ideas." Auden wrote late in life that "half of what I now know about the difference between Personal Speech, based upon Proper Names, and Second and First Person Personal Pronouns, words of command and obedience, summons and response, and the impersonal 'objective' use of words as a communications code between individuals, I owe to Rosenstock-Huessy."* Much of the other half he owed to Kassner's 1919 study of "universal physiognomy," *Zahl und Gesicht.*

Kassner was (and remains) almost unknown in English except as a slightly condescending friend of Rilke; one of the few English translations of his essays appeared in *The Criterion* in 1930, where Auden (whose *Paid on Both Sides* had been printed in the same magazine a few months earlier) almost certainly read it and forgot it. He first read about *Zahl und Gesicht* in the translator's notes to Rilke's *Duino Elegies* in the edition he reviewed in 1939, and apparently read it in the mid-1940s, when he lifted a phrase from the beginning of the section "Das Gesicht" for Malin's opening meditation in *The Age of Anxiety*: "The faceless machine / Lacks a surround." Much of the rest of Malin's first speech is loosely adapted from the same passage. (The book had perhaps been given to him by Denis de Rougemont, who recalled feeling the "shock" of Kassner's "*authority*" when he read a French translation published in 1931.) Auden seems to have reread the book in 1950 and found that it illuminated exactly the problems of personality and impersonality that he had

---

* Rosenstock-Huessy's essays on language were collected in *Speech and Reality* (1970).

been facing in his poems. In a *Festschrift* published for Kassner's eightieth birthday in 1953 Auden wrote a brief note of thanks under the title *"Zahl und Gesicht"*: "Among all the books which a writer reads over the years, the number which have so essentially conditioned his vision of life that he cannot imagine who he was before he read them is, naturally, very small. But every now and then, perhaps by pure accident, he picks up a volume, opens it at random, and is immediately overwhelmed by the feeling that this voice is addressed to him personally, so much so that he is jealous lest it should speak to others."

In the course of a few weeks in the summer of 1950 Auden translated much of the vocabulary and argument of *Zahl und Gesicht* into English verse. His poem "The Chimeras," about persons who have been swallowed up into the anonymous public, is a gloss on the book's pages on chimeras.* When someone is possessed by the chimerical public, "of him, poor foolish fellow, / Not a scrap is left, not even his name"—which is to say, he loses his name and everything his name stands for. "Numbers and Faces," his second poem on this theme, translates the title of Kassner's book (the German phrase means roughly *quantity and quality,* but the two separate words mean *number* and *face*) and, in a comic fantasia on Kassner's themes, lists the ways in which those who live by number get everything wrong:

> Lovers of small numbers go benignly potty,
> Believe all tales are thirteen chapters long,
> Have animal doubles, carry pentagrams,
> Are Millerites, Baconians, Flat-Earth men.
>
> Lovers of big numbers go horribly mad,
> Would have the Swiss abolished, all of us
> Well purged, somatotyped,† baptised, taught baseball:
> They empty bars, spoil parties, run for Congress.

---

* Kassner's essay "Die Chimäre" equates chimeras with the unclean spirits who possess the demoniac in Mark 5:2–13, and whose "name is Legion: for we are many." The idea that membership in any collective group is a form of demonic possession recurs throughout Auden's later work.

† W. H. Sheldon's system of somatotyping persons as ectomorphs, mesomorphs, and endomorphs, employed most recently in his *Varieties of Delinquent Youths* (1949), was appealing enough as a wild generalization for Auden to use it in his brief two-part poem "Footnotes to Dr. Sheldon" ("Behold the manly mesomorph" and "Give me a doctor, partridge-plump") written during the same summer of 1950 when he wrote "Numbers and Faces" (*Collected Poems,* p. 570).

As in Kassner's book, there is one exception to the rule that numbers are impersonal: "One is always real." But among all numbers, "which could any face call good"? A possible answer—the infinity of the absolute—is dismissed in the final lines, and the personal face of the godhead reaffirmed, "for calling / Infinity a number does not make it one."

Faces are attributes of bodies. Kassner wrote about the physicality of Christ in *Zahl und Gesicht* and devoted other books and essays to the subject, notably *Die Gottmensch* (1938) and *Die Geburt Christi* (1951). When Auden prepared a selection from Kierkegaard, probably in 1951, he quoted *Zahl und Gesicht* in an epigraph: "About Christ it is significant, not that he sees, hears, and tastes, but that he is made flesh." This is unlike Zeus, who (Kassner continued), has identity, and sees, hears, and tastes, but has no individuality because he has no flesh; "When Identity reigns, there is still the Teacher," still an impersonal order of the universe that can be taught and learned like a skill. In contrast, "Christ sets up over against the teacher, the Witness, the Example, just as he replaces Identity by the Individual and Fate by the Sacrifice."

In *The Dyer's Hand*, a decade later, Auden quoted a related passage from Kassner's *Die Geburt Christi* on the opposition of Christianity and poetry. When, according to Christian theology, the Word was made flesh, it had no need for the shaping artifice of poetic metre because its incarnate form was complete in itself: as Kassner put it, "The God-man did not write down his words himself or show the slightest concern that they should be written down in letters . . . Over against the metrical structures of the poets stand the Gospel parables in prose, over against magic, a freedom which finds its limits within itself, is itself limit." Auden added: "I hope there is an answer to this objection [to poetry], but I don't know what it is." This response may sound like a polite formula, but Auden was struggling to answer Kassner's objection to poetry in most of the poems he wrote in the 1950s. He had in mind not only Kassner's objection but a larger biblical objection to aesthetics, typified by this passage in the Book of Amos: "Take thou away from me the noise of thy songs; for I will not hear the melody of thy viols. But let judgment run down as waters, and righteousness as a mighty stream."

Auden's implicit argument in these poems is a claim that their artificiality is a sign of the difference between themselves and a truth that can never be expressed in verse; he made the argument explicit in one poem, " 'The Truest Poetry Is the Most Feigning,' " a poem that proves to be even more feigning than it acknowledges. It advises a poet to feel no compunction over resexing a love poem to his mistress into a panegyric for a generalissimo whose tanks have suddenly taken over: "True hearts, clear heads will hear the note of glory / And put inverted commas round the story." But the final lines suggest that a further set of inverted commas should be placed around the whole of Auden's poem. Man's nature is feigning; what but tall tales, the poem asks, "Can trick his lying nature into saying, / That love, or truth in any serious sense, / Like orthodoxy, is a reticence?" The love of "your Beatrice"—both the love and the person had been praised a few lines earlier—is a reticent tall-tale version of a faith that needs neither metre nor rhyme.*

In the many versions of Auden's defense of poetry through a defense of feigning, he sometimes seems to have pretended to be more single-minded than he was. As war began in Korea and the great powers were threatening mutual atomic destruction, his poems somewhat over-assertively distinguished between the loud utopian aggressors who destroy civilization and the quiet arcadian defenders who preserve it—as if he had forgotten what he had written in "The Sea and the Mirror" about Prospero's illusory pride and culpable indifference. Mild unimposing aesthetes transform themselves into heroes in these poems. "Footnotes to Dr. Sheldon" first dismisses the manly mesomorph as an Achilles in the barroom but a coward who retreats "in the ditch of hopeless odds," then idealizes the ectomorph, "pink-and-white, / Fastidious, almost girl-ish," who covers his retreat and dies at his gun. In the baroque fantasies of "Ode to Gaea," in 1954, these aesthetes are civilization's last defense against the terrors of Achilles' many shields:

> Perhaps a last stand in the passes will be made
> By those whose Valhalla would be hearing verse by Praed
>   Or arias by Rossini
> Between two entrées by Carême.

* "Orthodoxy is reticence" is a phrase Auden attributed variously to an unnamed Anglican bishop (in *Forewords and Afterwords*, p. 71) and to "Anonymous" (in *The Viking Book of Aphorisms*). He may have heard the phrase in August 1953 at a seminar in Alpbach that he attended with the dedicatee of the poem, the Renaissance scholar Edgar Wind, on the subject "Was ist der Mensch?" Representatives of various religious organizations attended, but it may have been Wind who quoted the phrase from a bishop he had met elsewhere. When Auden sent the poem to Wind, he described it as "the result of our discussions." (Auden and Wind had become friends at Smith College earlier that year.)

Praed, not Hölderlin; Rossini, not Wagner: this is a pleasurable, idiosyncratic aesthetic that goes with a taste for Firbank. But Auden, who preferred meat and potatoes to the sculpted confections baked by
Talleyrand's chef, was exaggerating his aestheticism in a futile effort to
annoy the serious-minded. (In the same way, he liked to tell American
visitors to Ischia that he spent his time reading Firbank, when in fact he
was reading Rudolf Kassner "with a dictionary at my elbow.")

His statements of this theme became progressively less self-dramatizing. In "The Epigoni," in 1955, he wrote about the lesser poets of the
declining Roman Empire who wrote ever more intricate and pointless
elaborations of metre and rhetoric while foreseeing their "probable ending / As dog-food, or landless, submerged, a slave." They did nothing
for which later dark ages (including our own) could memorialize them,
yet an individual reader may honor their refusal to bewail their doom:

> To their credit, a reader will only perceive
> That the language they loved was coming to grief,
> Expiring in preposterous mechanical tricks,
> Epanaleptics, rhopalics, anacyclic acrostics:
> To their lasting honor, the stuff they wrote
> Can safely be spanked in a scholar's foot-note,*
> Called shallow by a mechanized generation to whom
> Haphazard oracular grunts are profound wisdom.

(For Auden as for others, Rome offered an infinitely adaptable model
for contemporary history, because one could find an image of the present
day in the Republic, the early Empire, the Pax Romana, or Rome's decline and fall. Auden tended to choose the decline for his model, as he
did in "Secondary Epic" in 1959, a poem that obliquely questions what
later writers called the "Pax Americana" by commenting on the failure
of Virgil's prophecy of the Roman future, a prophecy that missed the
irony of the name of the defeated last emperor, Romulus Augustulus.)

For each of his books of verse Auden wrote a dedicatory poem that
defends the kind of poetry in the book while purporting to characterize it as minor. The one he wrote for *Nones* in 1950 (later collected as

---

* The scholar was F.J.E. Raby, whose *History of Secular Latin Poetry in the Middle Ages* (the
source of Auden's "Under Sirius") dismisses these poets in a chapter on the "Rhetorical Tradition" of the fourth and fifth centuries. The footnote was the one in which Raby asks of some
lines by Dracontius: "What is all this but the rhetorical frivolity of the school-exercise?"
(I. 106).

"We Too Had Known Golden Hours") justifies an undramatic personal manner—"the wry, the sotto-voce / Ironic and monochrome"—as the only style of personal speech that had survived the disastrous triumph of falsehood and noise. He would prefer to have "sung from a resonant heart" in "the old grand manner," but grand, resonant speech had been degraded by the "promiscuous crowd" and by editors who use words like peace and love as "spells to befuddle the crowd."* Public impersonal speech is a leveling, destructive "pandaemonium"—a late work of the daemon. In its aftermath,

> where should we find shelter
> For joy or mere content
> When little was left standing
> But the suburb of dissent?

This was a fantasy of innocence, not unlike Auden's fantasy of the just exchanging their messages in "September 1, 1939." He had taken the image of "ironic points of light" from E. M. Forster's essay "What I Believe," in which the "unquenchable lights of my aristocracy" reassure each other in the darkness. Now he took the "suburb of dissent" from Forster's essay "T. S. Eliot," in which Eliot's tone of protest was "the more congenial for being feeble": "For what, in that world of gigantic horror, was tolerable except the slighter gestures of dissent?" When Auden made his most ambitious claims for the virtue of art—claims he renounced soon afterward—he put on Forster's mild, unassuming mask.

═══

Faces and names can take responsibility; numbers and crowds cannot. When Auden wrote that it was proper to give nature a real face in order to remind us that we have a duty to her, he added, using Kassner's vocabulary, that "we may only do this after we have removed the pagan mask from her, seen her as a world of masses and realized that she is not responsible for us." His poem "Nocturne" (he used the title for more than one poem; this one begins "Appearing unannounced, the moon") removes that mask and endows the moon with a face like a person's. Yet in writing the poem in 1951, Auden could not convince himself that it

---

* The dedicatory poem to *On This Island* in 1936 withdrew in the same way from a disordered public world: "Since the external disorder and extravagant lies, / The baroque frontiers, the surrealist police; / What can truth treasure, or heart bless, / But a narrow strictness?"

mattered exactly which face he chose: an early title for the poem was the algebraic formula "The Moon Like X."

The poem begins with the sudden apparition of the moon and the differing responses of "my heart" and "my mind." The heart says: "Adore Her, Mother, Virgin, Muse, / A face worth watching Who can make / Or break you as Her fancy choose." The mind answers, "You will not tell me, I presume, / That bunch of barren craters care / Who sleeps with or who tortures whom." (*That bunch care*: to the mind, the faceless moon is plural, not singular.) The mind's "baser frankness" wins, because only the mind has the honesty to admit that both it and the heart are "worshippers of force." The heart in this poem worships myths, not persons. As Auden wrote in an essay on themes taken from Henry Adams, "The Virgin & The Dynamo,"* when we worship natural forces which "we imagine to be responsible for our lives," we deny our own responsibility. The mind genuflects before the simple force of indifferent nature where no one is responsible for anything. And if both heart and mind worship force, then

> neither of my natures can
> Complain if I should be reduced
> To a small functionary whose dreams
> Are vast, unscrupulous, confused.

If I accept myself as a mere cog in an irresponsible social machine, I let my mental states serve as mere cogs in my incoherent inner machinery.

But the poem refuses to end without a counterhypothesis. "Supposing, though, my face is real / And not a myth or a machine." If I can accept the reality of my own face, then the image I project on the moon will be neither Venus nor dynamo, but the real face of some other real person: "The moon should look like *x* and wear / Features I've actually seen." The moon's disk is a neutral sign, but if its dark and light patches remind me of anything at all, let it be a responsible first person, not a third-person category, "Neither a status nor a sex." And as long as it looks like a face, it hardly matters which unheroic imperfect face it seems to resemble, "That gushing lady, possibly," or "That hang-dog who

---

* The essay observes that Adams "thought that Venus and Virgin of Chartres were the same persons. Actually, Venus is the Dynamo in disguise, a symbol for an impersonal natural force, and Adams's nostalgic preference for Chartres to Chicago was nothing but aestheticism; he thought the disguise was prettier than the reality, but it was the Dynamo he worshipped, not the Virgin." Hence the sentimentality of *Mont St. Michel and Chartres*.

keeps coming back / For just a temporary loan." What matters is that I
refuse to worship the faceless force which Auden called, in "The Shield
of Achilles," the "mass and majesty of this world" which "always weighs
the same," and that I find

> A counter-image, anyway,
> To balance with its *lack of weight*
> My world, the private motor-car*
> And all the engines of the State.

At around the same time he wrote this poem, Auden ended a book
review about manic-depression with a final renunciation of impersonal
necessity, proclaiming his loyalty to a unique named person about whom
he had not written before in prose but for whom he had written songs
of maternal love and awe in his Christmas Oratorio:

> The Christian conception of a unique revelation in history is as incompatible
> with Jung as it is with Marx, with cyclical theories of time as with doctrines of
> the Wave of the Future . . . One cannot, for instance, identify the cult of the
> Earth Mother with the cult of the Madonna; the former is a dynamo in disguise,
> the falsely personal image of the impersonal forces of nature; the latter, through
> her actual personal historical existence on earth, has become the type and pledge
> of the redemption of the natural order.

In the figure of the Madonna, he implied, history and nature, Logos and
Eros, are reconciled. He said as much in "Woods" in 1952, using a phrase
less conventional and casual than it sounds: "A well-kempt forest begs
Our Lady's grace." Our Lady, Mary, was both mother and virgin, but
she was not a myth or a muse.

A few years before Auden first read Kassner, he had independently
adopted some of Kassner's vocabulary when writing about sex without
love. As early as "The Sea and the Mirror," when he knew that his sexual
satisfactions must remain separate from his personal love for Kallman, he
used the word "number" in a slang sense that was also its precise moral
sense: in Ariel's world of imagination "every gorgeous number / May
be laid by anyone." In "The Love Feast," in 1948, after identifying all
the other guests at the party by first name, the poet postpones his exit

---

* The private motorcar encloses each person's solitary world in a faceless dynamo of random
irresponsible motion. Late in life, in 1972, he wrote a personal address to the faceless automobile
in the brief poem "A Curse."

to attend to "that Miss Number in the corner, / Playing hard to get."*
In "Numbers and Faces" he acknowledged that in intervals of sexual
hunger between loves for named persons, an effectively anonymous partner would perhaps be better than nothing: "True, between faces almost
any number / Might come in handy." The tone of these lines, with their
suggestive use of "handy," is the same rueful throwaway tone in which
Auden, in letters and conversations, accepted his celibacy during much
of this period. And the easy juxtaposition of theological meditation
and sexual slang in "Numbers and Faces" and other poems composed
around this time suggests his new understanding of the body's place in
a moral universe. Anonymous erotic numbers disappeared from his work
thereafter.

Auden commemorated their disappearance by writing, during the
course of the same summer of 1950, a set of obscene limericks that converted an often smirking and anonymous genre into something gentle
and particularizing:

> There was a young poet whose sex
> Was aroused by aesthetic effects;
>   Marvell's *The Garden*
>   Gave him a hard-on
> And he came during *Oedipus Rex.*

Dr. Kinsey had no statistics on this variety of sexual behavior in the
human male.

Auden's " 'posthumous' poems"—poems unpublishable in his lifetime which he sent to his friends in the 1960s as oblique reports on his
accomodations with Eros—emphasized the names even of those who
exchanged sex for money. In "Minnelied," a 1967 poem addressed to
Kallman, he made the point he had made earlier in "Numbers and Faces"
about the handiness of almost any number. But a *Minnelied* is a poem
that chivalrically idealizes the beloved, and the number now had a
name:

> When one is lonely (and You,
> My Dearest, know why,
> as I know why it must be),

* The poem perhaps echoes Kassner. The conventional phrase in the last stanza "The Love
that made her [Miss Number] out of nothing" is used emphatically in *Zahl und Gesicht*: *"Das
'Wort' hat die Welt aus dem Nichts geshaffen"* ("System und Ordnung," §20).

steps can be taken, even
a call-boy can help.

Tonight, for instance, now that
Bert has been here, I
listen to the piercing screams
of palliardizing cats
without self-pity.

Another of these "posthumous" poems, "Glad," written in 1965, was a
second-person address to "Hugerl, for a decade now, / My bed-visitor, /
An unexpected blessing." His relation with Hugerl* had been transformed from that of *"Strich und Freier"*—whore and john—after Hugerl
was arrested for stealing and "Both learned a lesson." Auden's lesson
presumably had something to do with an insight he had had thirty years
earlier, when he wrote about "theft, that attempt to recover the lost or
stolen treasure, love." But his idealizing or animalistic moods of the
1930s, when he addressed his beloved impersonally as "my dove, my
coney" or as "you, my swan," were gone, and not regretted.

———

From the moment it appeared in print in 1952 "The Shield of Achilles"
was welcome in anthologies for its sturdy unobjectionable sentiments
against violence and war. Yet the moral and technical intelligence of
Auden's poem rests in its deeper inexplicit argument about the relation
of language and act, and it is a greater and more disturbing work than
even its admirers suggest. Auden could not have written it without having read Kassner, but when he wrote it he no longer echoed Kassner's
vocabulary of numbers and faces, for he had absorbed Kassner's meanings
and made them his own.

   In Auden's poem, as in book 18 of the *Iliad,* the shield that Hephaistos
forges at Thetis's request for her son Achilles is a work of art within
another work of art. The scenes portrayed on the shield in both the
ancient and modern poems are vivid and plausible enough to make a
reader forget that they are works of art whose contents have been chosen
by an artist who might have portrayed something different at the whim
of his mood or patron. When Auden read the poem in public he ex-

---

* A diminutive of the name of Hugo K., a young Viennese auto mechanic. Auden remained
friendly with him (and with his wife) after their sexual relations ended.

plained that in Homer the shield portrays only beautiful scenes (a slight exaggeration: one of Homer's scenes is a besieged city); in his own poem Hephaistos forges "Quite another scene."

The two different stanza forms in "The Shield of Achilles" represent two different ways of using language that turn out to have more in common than they seem. The stanzas written in short lines describe a world of mythic grandeur in which Hephaistos forges the shield as Thetis watches; the stanzas in longer lines describe, entirely without mythic resonance, the modern scenes portrayed on the ancient shield:

> She looked over his shoulder
>   For vines and olive trees,
> Marble well-governed cities
>   And ships upon untamed seas,
> But there on the shining metal
>   His hands had put instead
> An artificial wilderness
>   And a sky like lead.

> A plain without a feature, bare and brown,
>   No blade of grass, no sign of neighborhood,
> Nothing to eat and nowhere to sit down,
>   Yet, congregated on its blankness, stood
>   An unintelligible multitude,
> A million eyes, a million boots in line,
> Without expression, waiting for a sign.

Thetis and Hephaistos have as yet no names—they are *she* and *he*— which means they are incapable of first-person responsibility. *She* neither acts nor speaks but only looks over *his* shoulder. The syntax of the poem makes *his* acts the impersonal work of his hands, not of himself. Because his work is impersonal, faces, names, and speech cannot exist in the world he creates on the shield. All is unintelligible, chimerical, expressionless: numbers like a million that are beyond the human ability to count; fragments and fetishes of persons—eyes and boots—instead of persons themselves. Precisely because the eyes and feet are expressionless, they are willing to obey the faceless voice that uses statistics to prove its own justice.

In the next short-lined stanza, Hephaistos and his hands do not act at all, and Thetis, again looking over his shoulder for ritual pieties, sees instead the parody Crucifixion described in the next two long-lined stanzas. The place is an "arbitrary spot" bounded by barbed wire. Three pale figures, with no visible signs of personality, watched by a silent "crowd of ordinary decent folk" too passive to shout for the death of one or the release of another, are destroyed first as individual persons, then as anonymous bodies: "they lost their pride / And died as men before their bodies died." In the third short-lined stanza Thetis looks over Hephaistos' shoulder for athletes and dancers—for aesthetic distinction, even if moral distinction is unimaginable on the shield—and finds that "his hands had set" a field choked with weeds. Loitering there is the ragged urchin for whom it is axiomatic that girls are raped, that two boys knife a third. The urchin's world lacks the first person, so he has "never heard / Of any world where promises are kept, / Or one could weep because another wept."

So, when Thetis and Hephaistos are at last identified by name in the final stanza, their names occur too late to be responsible for anything. "The thin-lipped armourer, / Hephaistos, hobbled away," leaving behind a work he made neither for himself nor for his vocation nor for love but only "to please her son." "Thetis of the shining breasts / Cried out in dismay": she makes noises when she weeps. But in earlier stanzas she had failed to speak, and her silence had accepted without protest the whole fated world of myth in which she, Hephaistos, and her son exist. Her world was no less impersonal than its modern counterpart on the shield. Both are places ruled by fate because choice has abdicated into silence. Both are the proper settings for doomed embodiments of power, "the strong / Iron-hearted man-slaying Achilles / Who would not live long." Both are settings where cruelty is divorced from conscience, because, as Auden wrote in "The Virgin & The Dynamo," "we tend to deprive of their faces any person whom we believe to be at the mercy of our will."

When Auden gathered his recent poems for the quinquennial volume he assembled for publication in 1955, he entitled the book *The Shield of Achilles*. The title implied that all the poems in the book, not just the title poem, portray a world shaped by the hands of Hephaistos.

———

The seven poems of "Horae Canonicae" expand on the chance rhyme *will* and *kill*. The seven poems of "Bucolics," written in 1952 and 1953 in an interval from his work on "Horae Canonicae," expand on *face* and *place*. The poems of the first sequence are set in village and city, the poems of the second in the countryside beyond. "Horae Canonicae" follows time's arrow in a single urban place where something was settled once and for all. "Bucolics," after the introductory poem "Winds," wanders without a plot from place to place: woods, mountains, lakes, islands, plains, and streams. Most of "Horae Canonicae" is written in Auden's grave syllabics; much of "Bucolics" is in playful iambics and acrobatically complex stanzas. It signals another aspect of Auden's escape from the narrow existential crises of his work in the 1940s: instead of recording decisions and consequences, it observes predilections and moods. It is a triumph of gentle, memorable comedy, and one of the rare proofs in modern verse of the profundity of laughter. Like all rural eclogues from the *Bucolica* of Theocritus, Bion, and Virgil to the lyrics of Hardy and Frost, Auden's sequence is the work of an urban sensibility that regrets its exclusion from the country while knowing its regret is an evasive fantasy.* After listing all the kinds of lakes that he might live near if he chose—"Moraine, pot, oxbow, glint, sink, crater, piedmont, dimple"— Auden concludes, in the tone of voice exactly suitable to this kind of evasion, "Just reeling off their names is ever so comfy." The whole sequence observes with an ironic eye the mood of domestic coziness Auden was experiencing, for the first time, all year round. He and Kallman had been sharing a summer house in Ischia since 1949, but until now they had wintered in separate New York apartments. In 1952 they moved in together, first in a loft on Seventh Avenue, then in an apartment on St. Marks Place which both of them treated as a more or less permanent home.

The rhyme *face* and *place* occurs in a poem about the condition of having neither. When Auden compiled his *Collected Shorter Poems 1927–1957* in 1965, he began the last section, dated 1947–1957, with the poem "In Transit" (which he had titled "Air Port" when he wrote it in 1950).† The opening stanza takes place in an airport itself, an arbitrary spot "selected / Jointly by general staffs and engineers." This anonymous place

---

* Auden evidently reread the Greek bucolic poets late in 1947 while preparing *The Portable Greek Reader*. In his scenario for *The Rake's Progress* the opening scene is described as "Pastoral comme Theocritus." The choral lament he wrote a few months later for the dying rake is an abridged translation of Bion's "Lament for Adonis."

† He flew from New York to Italy in 1950 after having sailed both ways in 1948 and 1949. He seems to have flown first in 1930, when apparently he was on the staff of a summer camp for schoolboys, and, after a few further flights in Europe during the 1930s, flew in 1945 from America to Europe and back with the Strategic Bombing Survey. He enjoyed claiming the historical status of being the first poet to fly the Atlantic.

is suffused by "new fresh air that smells / So strongly of soil and grass, of toil and gender." This is the impersonal world of he-or-she, not the world of the first or second person. We are treated here with "that fond peremptory tone reserved for those / Nervously sick and children one cannot trust." The impersonality of this non-place is a reminder that other places have personalities—not quite personalities of their own, but ones projected on them by our private memories of the personal acts we performed there:

> Somewhere are places where we have really been, dear spaces
> Of our deeds and faces, scenes we remember
> As unchanging because there we changed . . .
>
> Somewhere, too, unique for each, his frontier dividing
> Past from future, reached and crossed without warning.

In this airport, however, "we are nowhere, unrelated to day or to Mother / Earth in love or hate." We are unrelated to day because, by suspending our acts and choices, we have taken ourselves outside historical time: "our occupation / Leaves no trace on this place or each other." In lines that read like a first sketch for a crucial moment in "The Shield of Achilles," we do not act as individuals but are "controlled by a voice that from time to time calls / Some class of souls to foregather at the gate." When the plane takes off, we look down at a world where nature and choice both leave traces: "Motives and natural processes are stirred by spring" and "an ancient / Feud re-opens with the debacle of a river." "Debacle," used in its original sense of the breaking up of river ice, is a harsher echo of the floods that loosened frozen impulse in Auden's fantasies of revolution in the 1930s.

"In Transit" has the quietly unsettling tone of the poems in which Auden tried to reimagine a world of faces while admitting the strength of everything that wipes away individual features. This was a task too difficult to solve in verse, as he knew, and in his prose he wrote explicitly about the intransigence of the problem. His introductions to the Yale Series of Younger Poets surreptitiously reported on the latest round of his·private poetic agon while offering graceful praise to the poets he selected.

For Daniel Hoffman's poems in 1951, he wrote about the difficulty of writing nature poetry in the machine age. One of the main functions of poetry has always been "the preservation and renewal of natural piety toward every kind of created excellence, toward the great creatures like the sun, moon and earth on which our lives depend, toward the brave warrior, the wise man, the beautiful woman." A visible creature worthy to be celebrated by a poem must possess power—it must be "a real subject, a cause, not an effect"—but poetry cannot praise pure force. "The Earth Mother may be mysterious at times and cruel in her dealings with men, but unless there were a pattern discernable in her ways, she could only be hated and defied."

Ten years before, Auden had seen the machine as a liberator: it ended parochial loyalties and revealed to everyone the secret once known only to the few, that "Aloneness is man's real condition." Now he was more interested in the machine as a maker of nonpersons, like the modern rulers portrayed in his 1948 poem "The Managers," "working too hard in rooms that are too big," with "Heavy gait and careworn / Look":

> Technology, by transferring power from nature to the social collectivity, has deprived power of a face and left all personal excellence without visible power. Even when the collectivity is beneficent, showering on us some unequivocal blessing like the refrigerator, poetry cannot thank it as it can a king who made wine flow in the streets; and when it does harm it cannot be attacked, for it is faceless and makes no conscious-choice: in antiquity a tyrant could be satirized for his vices, but a modern dictator cannot really be praised or blamed, because he is an official or a medium rather than a person.

"The Managers" have been reduced to functionaries of their weapons, so detached from personality that they will not experience the consequence of their acts. In an age when their political guesses "can prove so fatally wrong," they alone will find "places on the last / Plane out of disaster."*

Technology alienates everyone from nature by replacing its rhythmic recurrences with "mathematically identical 'soulless' repetitions"; these induce a horror of recurrence and an obsession with novelty which, Auden argued, was an idolatry "more destructive than any traditional idolatry and harder to cure. Tristan may be led to see that there is something excessive about his love for Isolde by being reminded that she will die; Don Giovanni cannot be cured in this way, because you cannot tell him that the supply of ladies will run out."

Because of us each is a bodily person, our relation with nature persists,

---

* This had already occurred in 1945, when Gauleiters in Breslau and East Prussia took the last planes out as the Red Army approached, leaving ordinary Germans to suffer the disaster.

even if in forms different from those known in the past. "The ever growing popularity of hunting, fishing, and mountain climbing are evidence
of this," but because "they make the relation to Nature one of contest,
the goal of which is human victory, and limit contacts with her to those
of the greatest dramatic intensity, they may exacerbate rather than cure
that unnatural craving for excess and novel thrills which is the characteristic urban disease." With this sentence, Auden offhandedly but unequivocally repudiated the various quests in much of modern writing that
struggled for dominance over nature, the feminine, and the earth. In
another passage, he repudiated the distaste for nature and sexuality that
he also thought characteristic of the age. Politely blaming technology for
the inability of writers such as T. S. Eliot and Graham Greene to embody
in their work a central belief of the Christianity they professed—the belief
that the natural and temporal world is an analogue of the eternal one—
he wrote that they could not "portray, for instance, a temporal relationship like marriage as anything but sordid and corrupting." Instead of
domination or repulsion, he continued, "what is really needed is a much
more modest, passive, and reverent kind of approach."

Auden then interrupts himself. "At this point I hear the Accuser adopt
his 'honest Iago' voice: 'This is sentimental rubbish.' " He had heard
the same voice when his "baser frankness" derided his worship of the
moon in "Nocturne." The Accuser now makes the same argument in
greater detail:

> "You don't feel that Nature is holy and as a modern man you never can. Gen-
> uine art is the mirror of genuine feelings, and the only real feelings you have
> are of self-pity at your alienation. So be frank, be modern. Express your pity
> for yourself in the rhythmless language really used by metropolitan man."

The only way to counter this lie, Auden continues, "is to realize its half-
truth." It is too late to respond to nature in a prescientific or Wordsworthian mode, yet intimacy with nature, even in "our urban culture,"
is still possible, "a prize slowly and patiently to be won: we all start as
outsiders."

═════

The seven "Bucolics" are the products of an outsider's deliberately half-
successful attempts to regain intimacy with nature. Only six of them are
about places; after writing them, and finishing the sequence as he had

originally planned it, Auden added "Winds" as the opening poem. Winds are weightless and anonymous, but air—the breath of God, "His holy insufflation"—gave life to individual, tangible bodies. Now the human inheritors of that wind choose either solitude or company by responding variously to the wind's effects. "Winds make weather; weather / Is what nasty people are / Nasty about and the nice / Show a common joy in observing." The Accuser, reading this, prepares to dismiss it as sentimental rubbish, but the closing stanza may make him hesitate. There, the Madonna-faced "Goddess of winds and wisdom" is asked to fetch "Arthur O'Bower" (a nursery-rhyme name for wind) to clear the air when "your poet with bodily tics, / Scratching, tapping his teeth, / Tugging the lobe of an ear, / Unconsciously evokes You." The Accuser may be quicker than more naïve readers to notice that in these lines Auden wrote the only serious modern English verse about farting.*

The poem ends by praying that the poet may sense the goddess's presence, "That every verbal rite / May be fittingly done, / And done in anamnesis / Of what is excellent / Yet a visible creature, / Earth, Sky, a few dear names." This is one of Auden's indirect and incomplete answers to Kassner's objection to poetry as a realm of magical unfreedom and constraining rhythm that stands accused by the prose freedom of the Gospel. Poetry's verbal rites require the wind of breath; Auden wrote elsewhere that poetry is "essentially a spoken, not a written word." And when verbal rites are done in *anamnesis*—recollection—of something excellent yet visible, poetry is an analogue of the Eucharistic rite, which was initiated, in Christ's words (as rendered by Dom Gregory Dix in *The Shape of the Liturgy*), "for the *anamnesis* of Me." Later, at the end of "Plains," Auden acknowledges that although he "can't pretend / To think these flats poetic," they can at least remind him that "nothing is lovely, / Not even in poetry, which is not the case." That is, nothing is lovely which is not a visible creature in the world. The world, as Wittgenstein put it, "is everything that is the case."

The six poems that follow "Winds" are written by an urban visitor to countrysides that are very much "the case."

"Woods"—now that they are tamer than "those primal woods / Piero di Cosimo so loved to draw"—seem peaceful enough to encourage daydreams of "sylvan nature." But the innocent wood is a place where

---

* A year earlier, Auden told friends "that Edith Sitwell broke wind while she was recording *Façade* and did not notice it during playbacks though everyone else heard it distinctly" (Robert Craft, *Stravinsky: Chronicle of a Friendship*, revised edition, 1994, p. 83).

"Guilty intention still looks for a hotel / That wants no detail and sur-
renders none." The sexual semi-innocent, undone among woodland
charm, blames the nightingales whose song celebrated the happiness of
desire. To this fantasy of irresponsibility the next stanza answers: "Those
birds, of course, did nothing of the sort." The final stanza, with a "small
oak massacred to the last ash," returns to the murders of Piero di Cosimo's woods in the opening lines, "Where nudes, bears, lions, sows with
women's heads / Mounted and murdered and ate each other raw." The
wood is never distant from the city. "The trees encountered on a country
stroll / Reveal a lot about that country's soul." What they reveal about
ours is that "This great society is going smash." (The phrase echoes
Rosenstock-Huessy in *The Christian Future* on "the Great Society, this
speechless giant.")

"Mountains" can be a home only for those of whom it can be said
that "they have the balance, nerve, / And habit of the Spiritual, but
what God / Does their Order serve?"* Auden's attraction to high places
is a cultural artifact, first fashioned by the worship of wild nature that
arose in response to late-eighteenth-century urbanization. "Am I / To
see in the Lake District, then, / Another bourgeois invention like the
piano," he asks himself. His answer, "Well, I won't," is an annoyed
attempt to deny that this is exactly what he saw there in the act of asking
the question. Yet he still wins his argument with himself, because despite
everything he knows about the cultural prehistory of his emotions, he
still feels them: "I wish I stood now on a platform at Penrith, / Zurich,
or any junction at which you leave the express / For a local that swerves
off soon into a cutting." Human beings are born actors; their emotions
are constructed from materials already shaped by historical, social, economic, and linguistic powers larger than themselves. This does not make
their emotions any less real; a bourgeois invention like the piano is no
less authentic than a reed pipe.

"Lakes" offer human scale, privacy, delight, but the fantasy of benign
nature they encourage requires brutal means to keep at bay all that is
not benign. The dedication of "Lakes" to the Oxford philosopher Isaiah
Berlin, with whom Auden was friendly but not intimate, has a hidden
edge. Berlin's liberal ideals, eloquently asserted against the angry ex-

---

* This paraphrases Auden's remarks on Captain Ahab in *The Enchafèd Flood*: "We watch him
enact every ritual of the dedicated Don Quixote life of the Religious Hero, only for negative
reasons . . . His whole life, in fact, is one of taking up defiantly a cross he is not required to
take up."

tremes of left and right, coincided almost exactly with Auden's, but—
the poem gently suggests—Berlin's approach to them was ultimately
comfy. Against the violent totalitarian abysses, Berlin affirmed the superiority of moderation and reason, while Auden was impelled to refuse
large public abysses because he understood all too well the secret abyss
in himself. Berlin, that is, flattered his like-minded readers by ignoring
the uncomfortable truth the poem insists upon: "Liking one's Nature,
as lake-lovers do, benign / Goes with a wish for savage dogs and man-
traps."*

Among the many who seek refuge on "Islands" are old saints looking
for a solitude where "no female pelvis can / Threaten their agape." But
no island in Auden's poetry is ever a refuge. The place of escape dutifully
reproduces the inequities one goes there to escape from. The master-
slave relation remains when the conventional signs of it are left behind:
"In democratic nudity / Their sexes lie; except / By age or weight you
could not tell / The keeping from the kept." Islands appeal to innocent-
sounding egoism—"How fascinating is that class / Whose only member
is Me!"—but the poem's examples are not quite so innocent as they
sound. "Sappho, Tiberius, and I / Hold forth beside the sea": a poet
on Lesbos, another on Ischia (both attracted to their own sex), and a
tyrant on Capri enjoying the violent debaucheries described in leering
detail by Suetonius.

The thought of "Plains" prompts Auden to six horrified stanzas on
the emptiness of those unpoetic flats, which so appall him that he knows
them "Only as a landscape common to two nightmares," one of pursuing spiders, the other of "an abominable desolation" like that of "Tar-
quin ravished by his post-coital sadness." The allusion to the rapist's
penitence in Shakespeare's *Lucrece* suggests that Auden's nightmare is
the product of his own disordered loves. "If I were a plainsman I should
hate us all"—and this potential for lonely envy, like his two nightmares,

---

* When Auden reviewed Berlin's *The Hedgehog and the Fox* in 1954 he politely but pointedly
added a second distinction, borrowed from Lewis Carroll, to the "entertaining and illuminating" one that Berlin borrowed from Archilochus. "If all men may be divided into hedgehogs
and foxes"—those who relate everything to one central vision and those who pursue many
contradictory and unrelated ends—"they may also be divided into Alices and Mabels." This
distinction is concerned less with two styles of organizing intellect than with two kinds of moral
temptation. Alices "have strong nerves," but tend to convince themselves they are the Queen
of Heaven. Mabels are "a type that is becoming, unfortunately, commoner—the intellectual
with weak nerves and a timid heart, who is so appalled at discovering that life is not sweetly
and softly pretty that he takes a grotesquely tough, grotesquely 'realist' attitude" ("Holding
the Mirror Up to History," *The New Yorker*, 25 September 1954).

"goes to show I've reason to be frightened / Not of plains, of course, but of me." Yet he refuses self-pity, knowing his evil is not his own special daemon but the same as everyone's: "I should like / —Who wouldn't?—to shoot beautifully and be obeyed."

"Streams" occupies the kind of landscape that is least like plains, and least like all the other landscapes in the sequence, the only one without violence, the only one offering an unbroken fantasy of Eden. The closing stanzas of "Streams," and of the entire sequence of "Bucolics," are set in "that dale of all Yorkshire's the loveliest"—Swaledale, which Auden visited a few weeks before writing the poem, and which he described to his brother in a letter as "one of my holy places," honored in the poem with a name and creaturely character as the spot "where Kisdon Beck / Jumps into Swale with a boyish shouting." There, the poem recalls, when "I dozed for a second," a vision appeared. "The god of mortal doting," Eros himself, "promised X and Y a passion undying." In this vision, Auden's equation of the wedding ring and the circle of dancers, last heard in Miranda's villanelle, is heard again, as "round in a ring we flew, my dear on my right."* After he wakes, he remembers the day as "fortunate . . . and enlightened," when water's voice seemed to be "wishing, I thought, the least of men their / Figures of splendor, their holy places." These were the same "places we have really been" that he remembered in "In Transit." In the historical world of "Horae Canonicae," anonymous nature is awed by individual death; in the erotic and generative world of "Bucolics," it wishes happiness to all "dear names." At the end of the sequence, the prize of a recovered intimacy with nature has been won, but the poem is realistic enough to envision it only in the admitted artifice of a rococo dream.

In "Streams," Auden hears water speaking in the inarticulate "vocables" of its "innocent . . . outcry," but the poem itself speaks in the most elaborate verse form he devised, and almost the only one he took the trouble to explain in print. In liner notes to a recording published in 1954, he wrote:

> In each quatrain, lines 1 and 2 have twelve syllables each and masculine endings, line 3 has nine syllables and a feminine ending. A syllable within line 1 rhymes with a syllable within line 3, the final syllable of line 2 rhymes with the penul-

---

* "My dear" seems to be an amalgam of Kallman and the dedicatee of "Plains," Wendell Stacy Johnson, a young instructor at Smith College with whom Auden had had an affair earlier in the year and to whom he wrote at length about the "Bucolics."

timate syllable of line 4, and the penultimate syllable of line 3 rhymes with a
syllable within line 4.

(He neglected to add that line 4 has ten syllables and a feminine ending.)
Through this kind of blatant artificiality, the poem leaves no doubt that
it is feigning when it gives water credit for the same kind of sympathy
with lovers that the semi-innocents attribute to the nightingale in
"Woods." Yet the wishes of water, imaginary though they are, are the
poem's analogy for a real personal love that sees splendor in the names
and places where lovelessness sees only numbers and masses.* The comforts of water in the "Bucolics" are specifically maternal ones. In
"Lakes," everyone was "The genius of some amniotic mere" before being born. And in "Woods" that unfallen Paradise in the womb is remembered whenever

> late man, listening through his latter grief,
> Hears, close or far, the oldest of his joys,
> Exactly as it was, the water noise.

The fatal waters of "The Sea and the Mirror" had turned placid and
forgiving.

———

By 1954, a year after he finished the "Bucolics," Auden was less willing
to warm his hands over fictional analogies. In the spring, a few months
after returning to his dream Eden in "Streams," he remembered its
mood well enough to write a practical guide for travelers: an article for
the American edition of *Vogue* in which he described a six-day tour to
the Lake District, for him the "Innocent Place where no contradiction
has yet arisen between the demands of Pleasure and the demands of
Duty." But, later in the year, after he had written "Vespers" and acknowledged that his vision of the Innocent Place was his means of denying the urban sacrifice, the tone of "Streams" seemed less justifiable
than before. Immediately after finishing "Vespers" he wrote "Ode to

---

* Water weeps over a named beloved cat in the quatrain epitaph, "In Memoriam L.K.A.,"
written in October 1953. "At peace under this mandarin, sleep, Lucina," the poem begins; the
mandarin seems to be the mandarin blue of the waters off Ischia where Auden and Kallman
buried their cats at sea. "For you the Ischian wave shall weep / When we who now miss you
are American dust" (*Collected Poems*, p. 570).

Gaea," in which he recognized a far more indifferent earth than that depicted in the "Bucolics."

The opening lines of "Ode to Gaea" signify that something has gone wrong with the poet's relation to nature. The title promises an ode *to* the earth goddess, but the poem speaks of her as someone whom it would be pointless to address at all. Seen from "this new culture of the air" (as in "In Transit" four years earlier), the earth is still "far-shining in excellence," still "our Mother, the / Nicest daughter of Chaos." Now "she seems more mysterious" than she did in the long era of superstition and myth and "less approachable." Auden had ended "In Transit" by looking down on a world renewed by spring, the same renewing spring that also reopens an ancient feud. "Ode to Gaea" sees a world that nature neither helps nor hinders. "Earth, till the end, will be herself." The dreamer of "Streams" had seen a vision of Eros commanding a dance, but the waking poet of "Ode to Gaea" knows he lives "on this eve of whispers and tapped telephones / Before the Ninth Catastrophe," and answers his own dream of Eros with quick skepticism. ("Who on Cupid's Coming would care to bet?") The Lake Country, or any place imagined by someone as a private Eden, cannot impress the Earth itself. "What, / To her, the real one, can our good landscapes be but lies, / Those woods where tigers chum with deer." Like the three Madonnas in "Nones" who turned "their kind faces from us," Gaea, "the real one," takes no interest in the fictions of Auden's poems.

Any future worth living in will not be made by the grace of indifferent nature, and Auden knew he would not be happy if his Arcadian fantasies came true, however dire the prospects of civilization seemed. In "Bucolics," his most sensual fantasy of living in the mountains—"near enough, a real darling / Is cooking a delicious lunch"—would in reality "keep me happy for / What? Five minutes?" And in "A Permanent Way," written right after "Ode to Gaea," he is grateful to the railway for letting him imagine "some steep romantic spot" while keeping him from being disappointed by a real wilderness with no chance of cashing "at least a ten-dollar cheque." The jog-trot rhythm of the poem combines with a disturbing undertone in which the poem welcomes a security granted by rigid constraints. "Forcibly held to my tracks, / I can safely relax and dream" of intriguing dales. "Self-drivers" trap themselves in traffic jams created by their freedom of movement (and "curse their luck" because they prefer to blame an involuntary fate) but the train is protected by "the dogma of its rails." The poem ends on a deceptively cheerful note:

> And what could be greater fun,
> Once one has chosen and paid,
> Than the inexpensive delight
> Of a choice one might have made?

The train offers an illusory freedom of wish after real freedom has been voluntarily renounced.

In the last poem he wrote in 1954, Auden restated in stronger terms the price that civilization "has chosen and paid":

> Guard, Civility, with guns
> Your modes and your declensions:
> Any lout can spear with ease
> Singular Archimedes.

The warning was timely. A few months later, his private world of singular faces came under sudden attack, first from within, then from without.

CHAPTER FOURTEEN

The Altering Storm

In the mid-1950s Auden set out to write poems in homage to Clio, "muse of the unique / Historical fact," and at the same time found himself the object of hatreds provoked by historical memories. In the end he won his way to reconciliation and success, but six months of anxiety and upheaval put an end to the comforts of his Italian decade and left him with memories of living under siege. The accusations against him were no different from those he had once dismissed without much strain, but they gained sudden unexpected force because he had recently begun to make similar accusations against himself.

After the holiday excursions of "Bucolics," the landscape of his poetry was again urban and anxious. Neither nature nor art offered much safety. In 1954 and 1955, he repeatedly challenged himself in his poems to justify poetry against the urgent demands of historical fact. Then, late in 1955, this inner theoretical challenge was echoed by an external political one when he was nominated for the post of Professor of Poetry at Oxford; the possibility that he might return to England after seventeen years gave rise to renewed attacks in British newspapers for his decision to move away in the first place. He had earlier begun to speak privately about his psychological terror of the English, but their criticisms seriously affected him only after he won the election for the professorship in February 1956. Beyond his usual inner recriminations over any public success, he suffered from a new sense that he had been judged and found wanting by external powers he scarcely understood. He had ignored similar charges in 1940 because they came from distant, mostly anonymous voices at a time when the war was a larger preoccupation for everyone and the accusations accompanied no unusual public reward. Now he had to deliver an inaugural lecture at a university where some of the older dons publicly gloated over the fact that they had awarded him only a third-class degree in 1928. After enjoying for almost fifty years the psychological luxuries of a spoiled youngest son, he experienced for the first time "fits of blind sweating panic during which a printed sentence makes no sense and I do not take in what people say."

————

From the start of his career Auden had alternated between large prophetic claims for the powers of poetry and modest statements of its indirect ability to teach or amuse. Now, while he tried to justify poetry itself, he was questioning his own work in an increasingly probing and persistent way. His recent fantasies of the aesthete as the last defender of civilization seemed culpably frivolous. He imagined instead a debate between two parts of himself, the poet and the historian, and while he saw no need to teach the historian the skills of the poet, he felt obliged to teach the poet how to value the historian's knowledge. The poet's work sounds splendid, but what does it serve? Its *logos* never quite responds to the *kairos*:

> From bad lands, where eggs are small and dear,
> Climbing to worse by a stonier
> Track, when all are spent, we hear it:—the right song
> For the wrong time of year.

Auden wrote this quatrain in the summer of 1954, around the time he devoted much of a review—nominally about Isaiah Berlin's *The Hedgehog and the Fox*—to a consideration of Tolstoy's efforts to integrate historical thought into literature. "I have never been able to agree with those literary critics who, following Turgenev, have deplored the historical disquisitions in *War and Peace* as inartistic irrelevancies; they have always seemed to me not only of great interest in themselves but also an essential element in the novel." Historical thought was an essential element in almost every poem Auden wrote in 1955—"Makers of History," "Bathtub Thoughts" (earlier titled "C. 500 A.D."), "Homage to Clio," "The Old Man's Road," "The Epigoni," "The History of Science"—and in almost all his prose. As in his elegy in 1939, he recruited Freud as a propagandist for his current views: Freud's "essential revolutionary discovery," he now wrote in a review of the second volume of Ernest Jones's biography, was that "the life of the mind cannot be studied by the quantitative methods suitable to the study of brain events, for it is a historical life which, since it contains both objective and subjective elements, is neither a strict science nor a pure art."

The voluntary history he had in mind was the opposite of purposive Hegelian-Marxist History with an upper-case *H*. "The Old Man's Road," a series of terse couplets about an ancient English pathway whose forgotten builders rustics call simply "the old man," is a sly hymn of praise for a road that was once an imperial imposition on the landscape, but has since become a route used only by those who choose it freely— in the moral sense, a Way. Today, forgotten by the authorities, invisible on maps, it ignores ideology and frontiers; those who love it "never ask what History is up to, / So cannot act as if they knew"; those who wander with it slip across guarded borders at the point where the searchlight never squints. The road disappears where others have built over it but re-emerges at a point where no one notices its hidden continuity. Official guardians of virtue and efficiency have no interest in it, because it is indifferent to their goals. The poem's elusive statement is the same as the explicit one Auden made a few years later about the opposition of officialdom and historical freedom: "Plato would probably disapprove of historical studies even more than he disapproved of poetry, for 'what really happened' is even more crowded with bad examples, with the triumph of injustice and unrighteousness, than the feigned history of the poets. But he would be wrong."

In the spring of 1955 Auden broadcast under the title "The Dyer's Hand" a series of three talks for the BBC that focused on the contrasting powers of poetry and history. In the millennia-old debate between poet and historian—"fictitious beings from whom every trait except the one they typify has been removed"—the poet, Auden proposed, being neither moralist nor theologian, takes an interest only in aesthetic heroes, those who, like natural forces, exercise arbitrary power and are really themselves. The historian, on the other hand,

has no interest in nature, only in human beings, and . . . he is interested in them precisely because he does not believe their lives are pre-ordained by fate but that, on the contrary, what their future is to be depends on the choices that they make, for which they are personally responsible. Thus, while the poet, when he meets someone, thinks only in terms of the present moment . . . the historian is interested in the present only as it relates the past to the future.

The poet in this debate holds views that Auden held about opera when he and Kallman wrote the libretto for *The Rake's Progress*, and when he claimed that the plot of an opera issues from strong irrational feelings; that all great operatic figures are passionate, willful states of being; and that the most fully realized operas are found in the nineteenth-century Italian repertory. The historian, however, holds the position Auden expressed about opera when he and Kallman wrote their libretto *Elegy for Young Lovers* for Hans Werner Henze in 1959: the plot, he claimed, connects a remembered, unalterable past and various possible futures; young lovers sing not about the way they feel now but about a future they cannot have; and the most fully realized operas are the Hofmannsthal-Strauss collaborations.

History, Auden wrote elsewhere, did not merely concern but *was* the subjective, psychological, and moral realm. "Life, as I experience it in my own person," he wrote, "is primarily a continuous succession of choices between alternatives, made for a short-term or long-term purpose; the actions I take . . . are less significant to me than the conflicts of motives, temptations, doubts in which they originate." His experience of time, he continued, "is not of a cyclical motion outside myself but of an irreversible history of unique moments which are made by my decisions."

This was the first-person experience that Auden wanted to write about in his poems. But although the poet seems highly subjective, as Auden imagined him in his debate with the historian, he knows almost nothing about his own subjectivity. "Life," Auden imagines the poet saying, "is fleeting and full of sorrow and no words can prevent the brave and the beautiful from dying or annihilate a grief.* What poetry can do is transform the real world into an imaginary one which is godlike in its per-

---

* This lament is the subject of a limerick Auden wrote in 1950 and published in *Homage to Clio* under the title "The Aesthetic Point of View" (*Collected Poems*, p. 572):

> As the poets have mournfully sung,
> Death takes the innocent young,
>   The rolling in money,
>   The screamingly funny,
> And those who are very well hung.

manence and beauty, providing a picture of life which is worthy of imitation as far as it is possible." Imitation, the poet admits, is not possible, but "without the attempt the real world would get even worse." The historian, rightly seeing in this a temptation to build a static utopia, responds that "art cannot teach or even portray examples worthy of imitation. It can only hold a mirror in which each person sees his face reflected . . . The way for each person is unique."

Auden had argued the historian's position since the 1930s, and had devoted much of "The Sea and the Mirror" to this metaphor of art as the mirror of the face. But he had not until now confronted a major difficulty: if poetry's ultimate subject is the choices made by its readers, then poetry is about something it can never portray. Faces and acts are visible; decisions are not.

That problem, Auden said, did not bother poets of the pre-Christian era who were interested more in myth than in history, awed more by power than by decision. In secular literature the first traces of the historical element began to appear in Roman literature around the time of Christ's birth. Aeneas "is not only a hero but has a mission as the founder of Roman civilization," and nearly all poems written since Virgil's time have been the product of a collaboration in "uneasy tension" between the poet and the historian: "Essentially poetry is an affirmation of being, and the main negative motive for writing it is a dread of non-being." Like Prospero, who makes art out of someone else's death, the poet transforms transience and absence into unchanging objects.

> His very medium, language, is ill-fitted to describe becoming. I can describe fairly accurately . . . inorganic objects like stones, which either are or are not . . . But when I come to describe even the non-human organic world which does not even have a real history but only a cycle of growth, I run into difficulties. I may possess names for certain stages, e.g. acorn, sapling, oak, but the exact point at which I abandon one term to use the next is arbitrary.

These lines contain a hint of Auden's later interest in Goethe's writings about the metamorphoses of plants and animals. But at the time, what mattered most to him in history was that which he could not describe because it was inaccessibly silent and unnameable. In 1955 he wrote "Homage to Clio," a poem in which he gave that silence a personal voice and a proper name.

The silence at the core of things was a noisily fashionable subject in the period bounded by Beckett's *En attendant Godot* (1952) and Jerzy Peter-kiewicz's *The Other Side of Silence* (1970). Auden chose a characteristically parallel but distinct course for his own exploration of the subject. He wrote about silence as he wrote about other existential matters, using the same vocabulary that everyone else used, but with a moral understanding that emphasized the existence of other persons as well as the existential ego, and a historical understanding that focused on the reality of change instead of projecting onto the past an image of the egoistic present. Late in 1954 he went out of his way to distinguish his approach from more news-worthy ones by writing an exasperated review of Camus's *The Rebel*, under the title "Fog in the Mediterranean" (possibly an editor's title, but more likely his own). Camus's intentions, Auden wrote, were generous, but when they were combined with his massive ignorance of history, the prod-uct was "this well-meaning but maddeningly woolly and verbose essay."*

"Homage to Clio" is a tribute offering to the "merciful silence" of historical choice, not an existential emptiness but the silent medium in which free acts are possible, neither interrupted nor restrained by words of command. Clio's silence requires nothing, but gives love and forgive-ness an open place in which to occur; this is a place that "No explosion can conquer but a lover's Yes / Has been known to fill."† Without the unique historical facts that Clio defends, human life would consist only of an instinctive struggle for survival, in which "Only the first step would

---

* Camus imagines, Auden wrote, that "history begins in 1789" and therefore fails to understand earlier contributions to human liberty, and writes about monarchy "as if Philip V had held the same view of his function as Louis XIV." In writing about Christianity, Camus adopts the views of its nineteenth-century opponents instead of performing the more useful task of identifying the heresies that afflict Christianity now (Auden had written earlier about the Barthian heresy of an absolutely distant god). Camus defeats his own love of freedom by accepting the Marxist view of historical necessity, an error that has occurred "all too often in revolutions," when revolutionary theoreticians "accepted without question the most pernicious premises of their enemies . . . It never occurred to Marx, for all his insight into the influence of thought and behavior on modes of production, to ask whether there might not be something hostile to life in the factory system as such, which no change from private to state ownership could cure, an oversight which was later to cost millions of peasants their lives."

† Rosenstock-Huessy made the same point about the historical significance of "a lover's Yes." "In every-day life the most similar event [to a nation finding its eternal role] was perhaps the act of the bride who passed from her parents' house into that of her suitor by the one word 'Yes.' . . . The bride's single word of reply has a power as divine as 'Let there be light' of the world's first day. Like the cry in an hour of revolution, her 'yes' carries a weight as heavy as the most heroic action" (*Out of Revolution*, p. 709).

count, and that / Would always be murder." The "unconstraining
voice" Auden had once attributed to poetry found its true expression in
Clio's unconstraining silence.

"Our hill has made its submission and the green / Swept on into the
north." The poem opens with a tribute to the inexorable springtime powers of nature. This is the poet's world, not the historian's. All around are
birds, insects, and other genera who live "by observations . . . / In space,
as unaware of silence / As Provocative Aphrodite or her twin, / Virago Artemis, the Tall Sisters / Whose subjects they are." In a world ruled by
these appetitive goddesses everything is instinctively itself, "nothing is too
big or too small or the wrong / Color," and even an earthquake cannot
disrupt as an act of will disrupts. (Not far away may be seen the *précieux* nature of Marvell's "Upon Appleton House," where grasshoppers are giants.)

But for we who are "brought face to face" with Clio's silence—her
world consisting of unique faces, not impersonal numbers—"nothing is
easy." Her silence stands between us and the bucolic dream of "phallic
pillar or navel-stone / With twelve nymphs twirling around it," or some
"magical centre / Where things are taken in hand." (There are twelve
nymphs because numbers have resonance in the impersonal world of
myth.) But, the poem asks, are we really as sorry about this as we pretend
to be? Artemis and Aphrodite are "Major Powers" in the same sense that
the United States and the Soviet Union were in 1955. No one looks to
them for change or forgiveness. Therefore,

> it is you, who never have spoken up,
> Madonna of silences, to whom we turn
>
> When we have lost control, your eyes, Clio, into which
>   We look for recognition after
> We have been found out.

Artemis and Aphrodite are instantly recognizable from "the perfect buttocks, / The flawless mouth too grand to have corners." But when we
look for the muse of history, we can find her only in unique personal
incarnations:

> I have seen
> Your photo, I think, in the papers, nursing
> A baby or mourning a corpse: each time

You had nothing to say and did not, one could see,
Observe where you were.

"What Icon / Have the arts for you," the poem asks, and gives the answer in verbs of action—nursing and mourning. These acts are prompted by the beginning or end of a unique life; each values another person and asks nothing in return. The poem—unlike "In Memory of Ernst Toller," fifteen years earlier—never questions whether Clio knows for whom she mourns and who is grieving. Her feminine acts of love counter murderous acts of will like those that dominated the masculine world of "Horae Canonicae," a world where historical events occur but no one is visibly present to mourn or forgive. The poem, like almost everything Auden wrote in the last twenty years of his life, has no use for the conventional equation of the feminine with nature in its determined, cyclical, involuntary aspects. It understands the feminine principle as one that values unique particulars, while its only image of masculinity is "A cock pronouncing himself himself / Though all his sons had been castrated and eaten." Auden told Tolkien that "Homage to Clio" "is really, as you will see, a hymn to Our Lady."* The plural Madonnas who turned their faces from us in "Nones" have come into focus as a singular Madonna who returns our gaze; she is transfigured from an icon of nature into the guardian of history. Newspaper photos of women nursing or mourning are contemporary images of nativity and *pietà*.

Unlike birds and insects, who live by observation, Clio cannot detach herself enough to observe anything at all. Instead, the poem imagines her "defending with silence / Some world of your *beholding*": the word recalls the active, transitive, responsible sense of "beholden" that is absent from detached observation. The world of power is the same as the world ruled by natural forces. The rulers, "The Short, The Bald, The Pious, The Stammerer" (designations of miscellaneous kings related to Charlemagne), come and go in their cycles, "round and round like the

---

* In the same letter he praised Tolkien for having solved in *The Lord of the Rings* the problem he had implicitly set for himself in writing this poem: "how to write a 'Christian' piece of literature without making it obvious or 'pi' [exaggeratedly pious]." He wrote to Ursula Niebuhr about the "Anglican problem" of composing a "hymn to B.V.M. . . . The Prots don't like Her and the Romans want bleeding hearts and sobbing tenors" (9 June 1955; Library of Congress).

Laxey Wheel."* These are the same impersonal rulers who in another poem written in 1955, "Makers of History," are melded into a collective myth, a "composite demi-god" made up from "mere commanders." The very different figures whom Clio loves are unique historical *makers*, those who "bred . . . better horses, / Found answers to their questions, made their things."

In "Homage to Clio," lives that obey the Muse of History do so freely: they "move like music, / Becoming now what they only can be once, / Making of silence decisive sound." (These lines restate Auden's Kierkegaardian, and willfully paradoxical, argument that music imitates history because "a succession of two musical notes is an act of choice: the first causes the second, not in the scientific sense of making it occur necessarily, but in the historical sense of provoking it, of providing it with a motive for occurring"; the rhythmic recurrence of Western music, with its time signatures and metronome beat, is explained, or explained away, as "a strictly natural or cyclical time," which serves as a "framework" for the "irreversible historicity of the notes.") Of such voluntary historical life, the poem continues, "It sounds easy," then adds, in a casual-sounding play on words, "but one must find the time." This laconic phrase, in context, makes a breathtakingly compressed and moving statement of the myriad challenges and regrets of private life.

The poem's closing invocation asks Clio to "forgive our noises"—the inarticulate sounds we share with the animals—and to "teach us our recollections." But the poem immediately revises this pious wish, because forgiveness requires an ability to forget, an ungrudging willingness "to throw away / The tiniest fault of someone we love." The feuding clans in *Paid on Both Sides* were taught to remember every ancient resentment, but Clio chooses what to remember and what to throw away.

Auden had concluded "Makers of History," probably written a few weeks before, by claiming that Clio loved "even those fulsome / Bards"

---

* This machinery was built for the lead mines on the Isle of Man; Auden saw it during a 1935 holiday visit, together with the family of the young man who was the subject of "Lay your sleeping head, my love." This allusion is the first of several to this early love in Auden's later poems. The pattern of events that resembles the Laxey Wheel is characterized by Charles Norris Cochrane in *Christianity and Classical Culture* as "a sense that the rhythm of human history depends on forces, which, whether friendly or hostile, are at any rate alien to mankind. In modern times these 'forces' have generally been regarded as 'progressive', although recent events have tended to shatter this naïve belief. Antiquity thought of them as, on the whole, circuitous; representing them accordingly either as an 'upward and downward path' or as a wheel" (p. 483).

among the *poētes* who serve "mere commanders." "Homage to Clio"
closes on a more self-doubting note:

> Approachable as you seem,
> I dare not ask you if you bless the poets,
> For you do not look as if you ever read them,
> Nor can I see a reason why you should.

This is an elliptical way of saying, as Auden repeatedly said after 1939,
that no work of art ever had any effect on history; that, as he replied to
praise for his political poems, "nothing I wrote prevented one Jew from
being gassed." ("The only person who really benefited from it was me,
because it gave me a certain literary reputation," he added.) Clio does
not merely ignore poetry, but refuses it her blessing. In the same way,
in "Ode to Gaea" a year earlier, nature—"our Mother . . . her, the real
one"—dismissed the poet's good landscapes as lies. Two maternal deities, intent on the real work of nursing and mourning, had judged the
solitary act of verbal *poēsis* and found it wanting.

Auden always felt free to expunge from his earlier poems any "wicked
doctrine" that later he judged himself to have used merely for rhetorical
effect. In the summer of 1955, he found an opportunity to expunge what
he judged to be a wicked doctrine from a work written two centuries
earlier. He and Kallman, working on a translation of *The Magic Flute*
commissioned for American television, threw out everything in the original libretto that celebrated the triumph of masculine reason over feminine passion. The eighteenth-century text, in Auden's view, was an
example of history written by the victors. As if to redress an old wrong,
Auden's Sarastro explains, in a newly written soliloquy, that he too must
die when the Queen of the Night is defeated.* At the final curtain,
Tamino and Pamina ascend together to the two thrones specified in
Auden's stage direction, and the long war of the sexes ends in a mutual
sympathy of equals. In a "Metalogue to *The Magic Flute*," which Auden
wrote to be printed between the first and second acts of the translation,
he mocked the silly vanities of, among other self-important aesthetes,

---

* In the one-act libretto "Delia," in 1952, he and Kallman had simply reversed the ending of
The Magic Flute by retelling its basic plot from the perspective of the Queen of the Night.
Delia, held captive by Sacrapant the Mage, is released to marry the knight Orlando when
Sacrapant is defeated by the Queen "of Night and Elfland" ("Whom some Diana, some Dame
Nature call"), who seems to be his mother.

Conductor *X*, that over-rated bore
Who alters tempi and who cuts the score,
Director *Y* who with ingenious wit
Places his wretched singers in the pit
While dancers mime their roles, *Z* the Designer
Who sets the whole thing on an ocean liner.

Yet *A* and *K*, not mentioned in the poem, had claimed an ethical justification for far more momentous changes.

———

The events of the months in Auden's life immediately after he wrote
"Homage to Clio" seem distinctly uncanny, as if, by privately considering a problem in the abstract, he caused it to emerge in public form.
He finished "Homage to Clio" in June 1955. Early in July he read a new
book by his friend Geoffrey Gorer, *Exploring English Character*, and
wrote Gorer an eight-page letter about it. He focused on the characteristically English fear of one's own aggressive impulses—the theme of his
review of the American edition of the book later in the year—and on his
own response to a kind of aggression he regarded as peculiarly English.
Under the heading "Shyness" he wrote:

> I wouldn't call myself particularly shy but I can feel terrified sometimes in En-
> glish and in no other company, and all foreigners I know say the same, that
> the English are socially formidable. I.e., I don't think that I just project onto
> them my own feelings of ill-will—I just feel I am being looked over and judged,
> not by individuals, but by the English as a people, and that they may be as
> right in their judgements as they obviously believe that they are.

He added in a postscript: "Apropos of aggression, here is a little poem,"
and he wrote out "Merax & Mullin," a poem in which the more obvious
of two devils prompts fearful souls to write savage satires, while the subtler one (whose victims deceive themselves by repressing impulses of hatred they find too fearful to acknowledge) "eggs on / Laodicean lovers
till they swear / Undying love."

Less than a month later, on 5 August 1955, Auden received a letter
from Enid Starkie, Reader in French at Somerville College, asking him
to become a candidate for Professor of Poetry, the only chair at Oxford
chosen by an election—in which everyone who held an M.A. degree was
eligible to vote. Although the duties were light—three lectures each year

plus an oration in Latin every second year to thank the benefactors of the university—the quinquennial election had become a widely publicized affair. Starkie had successfully managed Cecil Day-Lewis's election in 1951, and now she wanted to devote her energies to Auden. At first Auden refused, for two reasons:

I am an American citizen. Even if the statutes do not automatically exclude me, this would be a fatal handicap in any election.

The winter months are those in which I earn enough dollars to allow me to live here [Ischia] in the summer and devote myself to the unprofitable occupation of writing poetry. I do not see any way in which I could earn the equivalent if I had to reside in England during that period.

Starkie had no patience with this. Her second letter led Auden to reply that "the fit person for the Chair is Robert Graves"—whose two decades of public accusations that Auden was both incompetent and a plagiarist had caused no visible hard feelings—but, he said, "your continued interest on my behalf is weakening my reluctance." Oxford graduates with a bachelor's degree received their M.A. merely by applying for it, and Auden asked her the procedure for obtaining his M.A. in the United States. After a further assault from Starkie, he capitulated on 7 November 1955, and told her he was willing to stand.

His rivals for the chair were Sir Harold Nicolson (a diplomat and author of polite books on Tennyson, Byron, and Swinburne, whose chief qualifications were seniority and good temper) and the visionary Shakespearean scholar G. Wilson Knight (who was too much of an outsider to receive strong support). Much of the sentiment in favor of Nicolson derived from two facts: first, he was not Auden and, second, he had worked for the government during the war while Auden had gone to America. (He had been friendly with Auden before then, but in 1940 had published an attack on British intellectuals who withdrew to American ivory towers.) Nicolson's most prominent support came from the classicist Maurice Bowra, an old antagonist of Auden's friend E. R. Dodds, and from the essayist and editor John Sparrow, who had attacked Auden in print as early as 1934. Auden's supporters included his old tutor Nevill Coghill, the socially impeccable Lord David Cecil (who in 1935 had diplomatically saved *The Dog Beneath the Skin* from being banned from the stage by the Lord Chamberlain's Office), and most of Oxford's dons who taught classic and modern literature. He also enjoyed the vocal but nonvoting support of the undergraduates, who viewed the election as a symbolic battle, a generational struggle for the soul of the university between insular convention and cosmopolitan intelligence. As the campaign was in progress, Auden received another of his American honors, the National Book Award for Poetry for *The Shield of Achilles*. The award ceremony occurred two days before the Oxford election.

When the votes were counted on 9 February 1956, Auden received 216 to Nicolson's 192 and Wilson Knight's 91. Writing to Starkie about the outcome, he again alluded to his sense of unworthiness: "Entre nous, I'm surprised that the anti-Americans didn't have the political sense to put up a really distinguished academic scholar, for, if they had, I should immediately have withdrawn." Winning the election had called for no effort on his part; by a decorous tradition, candidates did nothing for themselves while their campaign was conducted by friends and supporters. But his inaugural lecture—scheduled for 11 June—was an ordeal he would now have to face alone. And he saw it as only the first of his ordeals. "Now the economic headaches start," he replied to a letter of congratulations from Spender. "How am I to live?"

Three weeks after the election, on the morning of 1 March, he read in *The New York Times* that the charitable shelter maintained by Dorothy Day's Catholic Worker organization, not far from his own apartment, had been fined $250 for failing to conform to city fire regulations and had been ordered to evict its sixty impoverished residents. Dorothy Day was a close friend of John Thompson, the model for Malin in *The Age of Anxiety*; Auden saw her occasionally in theological circles and had given a poem to the Catholic Worker's monthly paper two years before. As she left the shelter for the courthouse a few hours after the newspaper story appeared, Auden, who had been waiting outside, handed her a check for the full amount of the fine—for him a large sum, especially when he expected to spend his next five winters in England away from his American sources of income. Not expecting to see him, she mistook him for a Bowery bum, and when he said "Here's two-fifty," she thought he was giving her two dollars and fifty cents. She realized her mistake by the time she reached the courthouse, and told a waiting reporter that Auden had saved the day. The judge then commuted the fine, but Auden insisted that she keep the money to help pay for the necessary repairs. The story was spread across the front page of the next day's *New York Times* under the headline POET AND JUDGE ASSIST A SAMARITAN. Auden was given a few minutes of a television game program called *Strike It Rich* to appeal for funds for Dorothy Day, but the producer refused to let him say on the air that her great merit was charity to "the undeserving poor."

A few months later, Auden wrote in a review that the triumphant third son in folktale quests "is the one who stops to share his crust with the old beggar woman or free the trapped beast, thereby securing magical aid, when his proud and impatient rivals pass by and in consequence come to grief." (Auden was the third son in his family, and at forty-eight the youngest of the three candidates in the Oxford election.) But he also said to a friend about his television appearance—and about the published reports of his charity—that "theologically it was all wrong." The third son in the folktale performs his charity anonymously, not under spotlights.

As he drafted his lecture, after returning to Ischia in April, his shyness before the English intensified into dread. He told Spender: "I have been discovering surprising things about myself in relation to England and to Oxford in particular while working on my inaugural lecture." He hoped his panic would pass, he said, but, meanwhile, "Why are the English so terrifying?"

Auden concealed the answer to this question behind the urbane and modest tone of the lecture he delivered in the Sheldonian Theatre in June. Scattered among his audience were those he described later as "my enemies," but his lecture, indirectly but unmistakably, acknowledged that he was facing down internal enemies as well. He chose as his title a characteristic triad, "Making, Knowing and Judging," and emphasized the third.

His text was organized on the model of classical oratory, opening with a disingenuous statement of incapacity for the task at hand and ending with stirring universal affirmations. The explicit means he used to disarm his enemies were intelligence and wit, but he implicitly employed magic spells against them. Speaking apotropaically—a word he had used a few months earlier in "The Old Man's Road," referring to the magical technique of warding off future evil by pretending to suffer already—he began with his sense of inadequacy:

> Even the greatest of that long line of scholars and poets who have held this chair before me—when I recall the names of some, I am filled with fear and

trembling—must have asked themselves: "What *is* a Professor of Poetry? How can Poetry be *professed*?"

I can imagine one possible answer, though unfortunately it is not the right one. I should be feeling less uneasy at this moment than I do, if the duties of the Professor of Poetry were to produce, as occasion should demand, an epithalamium for the nuptials of a Reader in Romance Languages, an elegy on a deceased Canon of Christ Church, a May-day Masque for Somerville or an election ballad for his successor. I should at least be working in the medium to which I am accustomed . . .

If I am in any way to deserve your extraordinary choice for what one of the noblest and most learned of my predecessors so aptly called *The Siege Perilous*,* then I must find some topic about which I cannot help knowing something simply because I have written some poems.

And he continued to take every opportunity to refuse any claims to unique learning or vatic authority.

Another variety of self-judgment, in the figure of the poet's internal critic, that inner faculty with which he gauges the merits of his own work, "might be a possible topic," he suggested. "Anyone who writes poetry ought to have something to say about this critic who is only interested in one author, and only concerned with works that do not yet exist. To distinguish him from the critic who is concerned with the already existing work of others, let us call him the Censor." Presenting his audience with the poet's internal critic, he deprived external ones of much of their power. He then defanged, for the benefit of resentful listeners, his own undergraduate generation, with its fantasies of itself as revolutionary moderns. ("Really, how do the dons stand it, for I'm sure this scene repeats itself year after year.") The Censor helps a poet outgrow the excesses of his youthful manner; but the poet must not be immodest enough to confuse his changing tastes with dispassionate judgment: "I still think Rilke a great poet," he said tactfully, "though I cannot read him any more." He then repeated his formula from 1949: "Having spent twenty years learning to be himself, he finds that he must now start learning not to be himself."

After drawing these self-deprecatory lessons from his own career, he turned to the real subject of his lecture, the poetic imagination itself. The work of poetry, he said, is involuntary praise. It responds with a

* W. P. Ker, whose inaugural lecture in 1920 opened with sentences that had a special resonance for Auden: "I wish I could say how deeply I feel what I owe to the sanguine friends who have elected me to this most honorable Chair. It would be less difficult to find words for the danger of the task; this is the Siege Perilous" (*The Art of Poetry*, 1923).

passion of awe to encounters with sacred beings—those beings or events that to any individual imagination make an impression of "an over-whelming but undefinable importance." Sacred beings are of many kinds, and so is the awe that responds to them.

> This awe may vary greatly in intensity and range in tone from joyous wonder to panic dread. A sacred being may be attractive or repulsive—a swan or an octopus—beautiful or ugly—a toothless hag or a fair young child—good or evil—a Beatrice or a Belle Dame Sans Merci—historical fact or fiction—a person met on the road or an image encountered in a story or a dream—it may be noble or something unmentionable in a drawing room, it may be anything it likes on condition, but this condition is absolute, that it arouse awe.

He did not add what he had already said in a broadcast lecture a year before, that this kind of awe was an impersonal awe of power, which the poet is morally obliged to unlearn by attending to history. Nor did he tell his audience that they had made themselves into one of his sacred beings by inspiring exactly the "panic dread" that he named as one of the extremes of imaginative awe. The English were terrifying partly because, being one of them, he had imaginatively projected on them the daemonic powers he most dreaded in himself.

Auden's final note of praise encompassed not only sacred beings but everything:

> Whatever its actual content and overt interest, every poem is rooted in imaginative awe. Poetry can do a hundred and one things, delight, sadden, disturb, amuse, instruct—it may express every possible shade of emotion, and describe every conceivable kind of event, but there is only one thing that all poetry must do; it must praise all it can for being and for happening.

This was enough to put any lingering antagonism at an embarrassed loss for words, and concludes the text as Auden published it in *The Dyer's Hand*. When he spoke in the Sheldonian Theatre, however, he proceeded without a pause to read, "as an epilogue to this lecture," Thomas Hardy's "Afterwards," because, he said, it illustrated all his points and, "but for the man who wrote it, I should not now be here." (Hardy, as he had written in 1939, was his "poetical father" whom he now seldom read.) The poem describes the poet as someone moved by imaginative awe—"He was a man who used to notice such things"—but also served to ward off the anger of Auden's audience by portraying the poet as already dead. When Auden stopped speaking, anyone who refused to join in the loud applause found himself in the awkward position of insulting the memory of Thomas Hardy.

"Never in my life have I been so terrified," Auden wrote to Kallman afterward, "but thanks to Santa Restituta, I had a triumph and won over my enemies." The third son perhaps calculates slightly more than is reported in the folktales.

═══

After his lecture Auden settled into a routine that he followed for the next five years. Oxford permitted him to deliver his annual three lectures over a period of three weeks instead of across the full academic year, so he was able to go on earning his living in New York. (In the first year he had already sublet the apartment he and Kallman shared in New York, because he expected to be obliged to live in Oxford, so he spent a lonely winter in Ischia while Kallman lived mostly with friends in New York.) Yet despite spending far less time in Oxford than most of his predecessors, he was the first Professor of Poetry who felt obliged to do more for students than lecture at them. He visited the same coffee shop each afternoon, ready to make conversation with anyone who wanted to join him, and he gave shrewd advice to undergraduates who sought his help in problems of love and work.* He gave a refrigerator to Christ Church's senior common room with the excuse that it would allow him to drink properly chilled martinis, but his gift had a private, charitable motive: the wish to share what he had called in his preface to Daniel Hoffman's poems "some unequivocal blessing like the refrigerator." For his biennial Latin orations, he wrote playfully ornate English texts which a don translated for him, and was pleased to be the first occupant of his chair "ever to use Church Latin pronunciation"; this, he said, was "the only living Latin . . . and, besides, one can speak it much faster than the official Oxford dialect." He made it clear he was having the time of his life.

Auden's happiness was real, but not strong enough to topple the for-

---

* Dom Moraes, then an undergraduate poet, told Auden he was having trouble writing poems, and Auden suggested that he work on translations until the trouble passed. When Moraes reported that he was unable even to translate, Auden told him, "Perhaps you ought to be in love." Moraes replied that he already was. After a pause Auden said, with exact psychological acuity, "Then it's the wrong person" (Dom Moraes, *My Son's Father*, 1968, p. 192).

tress of his inner foe. "That winter," his friend Thekla Clark said of his lonely months in Ischia in 1956–57, "was the only time I heard him express any doubts about his work, not a single piece, but the whole thing." He had always been able to answer his inner accusers by writing poems that debated or accepted the justice of their charge, but his new experience of feeling threatened from outside left him shaken. He doubted everything he had ever done, while at the same time he thought himself falsely accused and justified in resisting.

He wrote no poems in the panicky months before his inaugural lecture, but when he returned to Ischia in June 1956, he wrote one addressed to himself, "There Will Be No Peace." This was one of the few in which he did not translate or universalize the experience that had prompted it into something accessible to a sympathetic reader, and was perhaps the least successful poem he had written in fifteen years. "I don't know why critics have disliked this poem so much. However, I can't be objective about it, since it is one of the most purely personal poems I have ever written," he remarked some years later. "It was an attempt to describe a very unpleasant dark-night-of-the-soul sort of experience which for several months in 1956 attacked me." *Attack* was the key word. When he read the poem in a BBC broadcast he prefaced it with a more general allusion to its "theme of paranoia."

When the poem begins, the attack has been repulsed, but its scars remain:

> Though mild clear weather
> Smile again on the shire of your esteem
> And its colors come back, the storm has changed you:
>   You will not forget, ever,
> The darkness blotting out hope, the gale
>   Prophesying your downfall.

The attackers are vague daemonic forces, far beyond questions of grammatical identity and debates about number and face: "Beings of unknown number and gender: / And they do not like you." When he asks himself what he did to his accusers, and answers "nothing," he knows he will come to believe, as he warns himself, "That you did, you did do something." But he refuses both accusation and defeat: "Fight back," he tells himself, "with such courage as you have / And every uncharitable dodge you know of," battling with a clear conscience because "Their cause, if they had one, is nothing to them now; / They hate for hate's sake."

"Reflections in a Forest," written in 1957, presents itself as a meditation on the reticent indirectness of human speech as contrasted with the blatant visual language of trees, but the closing stanzas insinuate a curiously phrased defense of unchivalrous human dodges:

> My chance of growing would be slim,
> Were I with wooden honesty
> To show my hand or heart to Him
> Who will, if I should lose, be Me.*

This stanza makes no sense if it refers to ordinary rivalries: if you defeat me, you do not *become* me. But it makes sense if it refers to the imaginary struggle implied in Auden's letter to Beata Wachstein of 6 June 1944, but unmentioned since, about the unborn child who preceded him, and who might have been Wystan Hugh Auden. Now what matters is the mere Darwinian struggle for survival: "Our race would not have gotten far, / Had we not learned to bluff it out."

—————

Auden knew that the uplifting sentiments of awe that he had described in his inaugural lecture were less easy to translate into poetry than he had implied. All poems, he told his Oxford audience, praise sacred objects. He said nothing about the difficulty of writing sacred praise in a secular century, yet he worried over the subject in virtually everything else he wrote during 1956. He tried to identify the kinds of praise that could still be spoken, and, to avoid slipping into sentimentality or gush, made the task as intellectually difficult for himself as possible. He readily accepted, as he always had, the idea that language was an autonomous system of arbitrary signs, but he complicated this skepticism (in ways that later theoreticians of language generally did not) by understanding that however artificial language may be, the pain or pleasure it can induce is real. In the poems he now wrote, he turned inward to find a way to

---

* "Wooden honesty" is the simple visible presence of the trees in the forest of the title. The capitalized "Him" has confused some readers into finding biblical meanings, but Auden was in the habit of capitalizing pronouns to point to their status as substitutes for names (as in the same stanza's capitalized "Me").

justify his defense against the inarticulate opposition he imagined staring at him from the darkness outside.

All these poems try to solve the double problem of finding subjects worth writing about and a language they deserve. Auden wrote a prose manifesto on this problem, in the form of his foreword to John Ashbery's book in the Yale Series of Younger Poets, *Some Trees*. In it he named the many difficulties a modern poet faces that he had studiously ignored in his Oxford lecture a few weeks earlier.

"A poet," he began, returning to the slightly disreputable figure described in his broadcast lectures in 1955, "is perhaps the only kind of person who can say, honestly and knowing what he means, that he would rather have been born in an earlier age than the present"—an age before the advent of Platonic philosophy and monotheistic religion, with their ethical imperatives that call his art into question. "Then, real meant sacred . . . Real events are sacred ritual actions, ritual marriages, sacrifices, and so on, by means of which a universe is sustained in being and repeatedly reborn: a rite is a public, not a private, act, not an act of personal choice but that which has to be done." In such a world, individual people and particular historical events, do not matter: "a man or woman is only real when he or she impersonates a god or goddess," and the whole moral question of voluntary choice and first-person language—the central subject of Auden's poetry—simply does not exist.

Today, when history and individuality cannot be evaded, we live in two separate worlds, external and internal, each with different ideas of reality. In the outer world, no object is more sacred and therefore more real than any other: "only concrete particulars seem real, and all concrete particulars seem equally real." Time is experienced not as a cycle of ritual moments in which "an event that does not re-occur is nothing," but "as a succession of unique moments, each of which is novel and will never recur." But in the inner world, "in childhood largely, in dreams and daydreams entirely, the imaginative life of the human individual stubbornly continues to live by the old magical notions. Its world is one of sacred images and ritual acts . . . a numinous landscape inhabited by demons and strange beasts." This world provides the mythical subject matter of many modern poets "from Rimbaud down to Mr. Ashbery." Unlike ancient myths, which explained recurrent events of nature that were visible to all, the myths of private psychic worlds refer to "the unique particulars of the individual's personal history."

Many successful modern poems (including, although he did not say so, some early ones by Auden) make use of these mythologies. "Every imagination has its holy places," and a reader, by "active re-creation," can often translate a poet's myth (of, for example, some unique remembered happiness in a foreign city) into a corresponding myth of his own. But while acknowledging Ashbery's preference for the subjective as one of the few plausible ones available to a modern artist, Auden tactfully dissociated himself from it. Because a poet in the school of Rimbaud, in order to be true to his experience, builds his poetry upon "strange juxtapositions of imagery, singular associations of ideas," he is inevitably "tempted to manufacture calculated oddities as if the subjectively sacred were necessarily and on all occasions odd. At the same time he cannot avoid the question of how to reconcile truth to nature with accuracy of communication, for the writing of poetry presupposes that communication is possible; no one would write if he were convinced of the contrary."

The introduction ends abruptly with this observation: "It is not surprising, then, that many modern poems, among them Mr. Ashbery's entertaining sestina 'The Painter,' are concerned with the nature of the creative process and with posing the question 'Is it now possible to write poetry?'" Auden's poems of the time answered this question while facing, as Ashbery's had not yet done, the great poetic subjects of love, history, and death.

Auden now composed one of his most unsettling poems in an attempt to confront these issues. It was pointedly not in the manner of Ashbery, but it experienced and criticized the same mental states and poetic patternings that Ashbery and many of his contemporaries took for granted. "First Things First" is an impressive example of Auden's ability simultaneously to conduct a complex argument about language and to write a love poem whose emotional subtleties make it different from any other. Like much of Auden's later work, it has been ignored by critics and anthologists, perhaps because its method and content have virtually no precedents through which they might easily be understood.

"First Things First" treats the problem of writing poetry in the era of subjective uniqueness as exactly parallel to the problem of writing a love poem to an irrevocably absent beloved. The poem assumes a world in which public myth is no longer available; therefore, in a chaos of concrete particulars, we attribute to them meanings that may or may not be their real ones. The poetic myths that now matter most are likely to be subjective ones in which unique proper names have special significance, and the imaginative life continues to live by the old magical notions:

> Woken, I lay in the arms of my own warmth and listened
> To a storm enjoying its storminess in the winter dark
> Till my ear, as it can when half-asleep or half-sober
> Set to work to unscramble that interjectory uproar,
> Construing its airy vowels and watery consonants
> Into a love-speech indicative of a Proper Name.
>
> Scarcely the tongue I should have chosen, yet, as well
> As harshness and clumsiness would allow, it spoke in your praise,
> Kenning you a god-child of the Moon and the West Wind
> With power to tame both real and imaginary monsters . . .

The poetry of the subjective mind communicates indirectly and by example. Auden wrote in his foreword that when he reads a poem by Ashbery about Mexico, "I who have never been to Mexico and have no wish to go there translate this into images of the happy life drawn from quite different cities." (The glint of cosmopolitan snobbery is a late trace of the *épatant* aestheticism he had espoused a few years earlier.) So, in "First Things First," the noisy storm, which has no sacred public associations, is translated by "active re-creation" into the memory of a sacred personal moment of silence in a quite different landscape. And it speaks, as a modern poem speaks, to a solitary listener:

> Loud though it was, alone though it certainly found me,
> It reconstructed a day of peculiar silence
> When a sneeze could be heard a mile off, and had me walking
> On a headland of lava beside you, the occasion as ageless
> As the stare of any rose, your presence exactly
> So once, so valuable, so here, so now.

But to reconstruct this moment is to indulge in a private myth, and all private myths are called into question by the official voice of modern rationality, which in the poem is the voice of the tempter:

> This, moreover, at an hour when only too often
> A smirking devil annoys me in beautiful English,
> Predicting a world where every sacred location

Is a sand-buried site all cultured Texans do,
Misinformed and thoroughly fleeced by their guides,
And gentle hearts are extinct like Hegelian Bishops.*

Auden had written in his foreword that "a modern poet who celebrates his inner mythological life cannot escape asking himself: 'Do I really believe in my mythology and, if I do, ought I to believe it?' " Ashbery had glanced at these questions, without answering them, in some of his poems. Auden closed his poem with a complex, elliptical answer. The world of concrete particulars finds nothing of interest in psychological myths—"Grateful, I slept till a morning that would not say / How much it believed of what I said the storm had said"—and points wordlessly to visible events. The morning light, that is,

  quietly drew my attention to what had been done
—So many metres the more in my cistern
  Against a leonine summer—, putting first things first:
  Thousands have lived without love, not one without water.

The final line, with its renunciation of "We must love one another or die," admits that poetry has no power over the brute public facts of life and death, while the poem as a whole affirms that poetry is a proper medium for speaking about voluntary private matters, such as the value of one person for another, that are neither concrete particulars nor egocentric myths. Auden's foreword had mentioned the zodiacal signs as an example of public mythography; the allusion to a sign of high summer in the word "leonine" points, with cunning ambiguity, to the irrepressible resurgence of myth in the midst of fact.

The absent beloved in this poem was not Chester Kallman but someone else, whose absence was far more complete and decisive. The private sacred moment on "a headland of lava beside you" had occurred in Iceland twenty years before, and the beloved was the same person Auden

* The Hegelian Bishops (evidently standing in for anyone in the clergy who tries to reconcile old faith with new philosophy) seem to have been suggested by Bishop Ernest William Barnes of Birmingham, the low-church priest who had been the *bête noire* of Auden's high-church mother. Barnes's book *Scientific Theory and Religion* tried to unify relativity and Christianity through a lightly disguised Hegelian dialectic. In 1970 Auden called him "the ineffable Bishop Barnes" (*Forewords and Afterwords*, p. 402).

addressed in his love poems of the mid-1930s* and to whom he later addressed further poems, notably "Since," which reconstructs another private sacred moment in a sacred place thirty years before the poem was begun in 1964. The ritual quality of these recollections, each occurring a round number of years after the event, marks them as elements in a private myth, the privacy of which is further circumscribed by the poems' evocation of a love for a young man who has long since grown to adulthood and marriage and the familiarity of long-term friendship, yet also (unlike Kallman, who had refused to be treated as a myth, not a person) remains an unchanging private image of sacred glory, an inaccessible godchild of the Moon and the West Wind.

═══════

As pendants to this imposingly great poem, Auden wrote three jewel-like sonnets, "Objects," "Words," and "The Song," in which he explored different aspects of its theme in a condensed, theoretical style. All three concern the limits of language in relation to concrete particulars, and the powers of language to sustain private myths. "Objects"—the title refers to everything impervious to words, all that "lies outside our sort of why"— seems to be about the comforting persistence of wordless matter, in contrast to the "mourning" and "grief" that afflict those who use language. But (like "Prospero to Ariel") it also seems to be about the hidden satisfaction felt in the midst of grief when someone else takes on the status of an object by dying: "somewhere, a soul / Light in her [the soul's] bestial substance, well aware, / Extols the silence of how soon a loss."†

"Words" meditates abstractly on the autonomy of language ("A sentence uttered makes a world appear"), with the proviso that because we are language-using creatures, the "verbal chance" of language in effect expresses "our fate," because we choose our fate by choosing our words. Language expresses our life by analogy, not identity (as "the joke of

* In a letter to Lincoln Kirstein, who was always grateful for gossip, Auden gave a different account: the poem "refers," he said, to a "new little heart flutter," a young musician in whom he had taken a protective interest (8 March 1957). This new brief interest perhaps prompted him to write the poem, but the subject of the poem itself is a deeper affection that had begun decades earlier.

† Auden had told Stephen Spender earlier that Spender's poems of mourning for the dead were masks over "a very strong, ruthless character . . . I suspect for instance that your *real* personal feelings about the deaths of others are: Goody. He's dead and I'm alive" (10–12 April 1942; Berg Collection).

rhyme" expresses pure joy in "One Circumlocution"): "fact [is] fiction for us at its best." But the gulf between words and facts notwithstanding, the analogy holds, "As rustics in a ring-dance pantomime / The Knight at some lone cross-roads of his quest." The crude marriage celebration is an adequate sign of the salvation sought by the knight on his solitary journey; and the juxtaposition of ring and cross—a bloodless, almost Yeatsian symbolism of the kind Auden avoided everywhere else—is appropriate to a self-consciously mythical poem of the kind Auden had acknowledged as especially difficult to write in a secular age.

"The Song," a bravura sonnet made up of two unpunctuated sentences, proclaims again that poetry can do nothing but praise, even if its initial impulse may be denunciation and complaint (an acknowledgment that Auden had omitted from his inaugural lecture). The song tries to rebel against "whiteness drabbed" and "glory said away," but it exists in a verbal world that "lacks all picture of reproach," because a work of art glorifies its subject through the glory of its artifice, and so "it ends / Denying what it started up to say."

These three poems insist on language's inherent contradictions, its autonomy, its denial of its own statements, its concern with that which is inherently absent from it. In these and other poems, Auden transformed Rudolf Kassner's religious vocabulary and large religious themes into secular meditations that anticipate by twenty years the themes of later philosophies of language. For Auden these issues had a personal, moral resonance which is absent from his successors, who tend to claim a moral high ground only after digging it out from under their feet. The relation of language to world in Auden's poems is not a permanent condition that can be defined in the timeless, unchanging terms of philosophy, but a historical one that alters as cultures alter and, within a culture, varies from one person to the next and, in each individual life, from one moment to another. These changing, contradictory personal relations of language and world are not proofs of fragmentation or incoherence, as they became for later writers, but of the inherently historical quality of personality, of the integration of personality with a language of responsibility that looks to both a past and a future.

The subtlety and intelligence of Auden's poems about poetry evidently restored much of his lost confidence. In 1957, a year after his Oxford lecture, he was no longer imagining vague daemonic accusers; they had been reduced to the equally vague, but now powerless, inhabitants of "Limbo Culture." This poem returns to the nightmare landscape of "There Will Be No Peace" (Auden placed the two poems next to each other in his books) and observes it through awakened, ironic eyes. The tribes of Limbo, as travelers report, "seem much like ourselves," with the one difference that their world consists of everything that is *almost* the case. "They keep their houses practically clean, / Their watches round about a standard time." Their language "Has many words far subtler than our own / To indicate how much, how little, something / Is pretty closely or not quite the case, / But none you could translate by *Yes* or *No*." The poem reports that none of the travelers to Limbo "says he saw a Limbo child."

In the language of Limbo, pronouns "do not distinguish between Persons," and without first-person speech, there are perforce no historical personal choices, no lover's Yes that could fill Clio's silence. Why, the poem asks at the end, does Limbo culture have such a "love for inexactness"?

> Could it be
> A Limbo tribesman only loves himself?*
> For that, we know, cannot be done exactly.

This poem, like much of Auden's work at the time, makes the claim that the precise language of poetry is allied by analogy with the loving Yes and defiant No, with all the dignity and freedom sustained by the First Person speaking to the Second; and, like its allies, it stands opposed to the inarticulate noise of power and force. But after his Oxford election and inaugural, Auden could no longer imagine for himself the honorable status of an outsider who slips easily under the searchlights of authority like travelers on the Old Man's Road. He had been the target of enmities he imagined as lethal, and resolved to be prepared for them in the future with active and, if need be, unchivalrous dodges—an entirely different way of proceeding from the one he imagined during the many years when he thought of the poet as an otherworldly counterpart of the chivalrous knight.

After ten years in Italy, in the civil Mediterranean sunlight where (as he wrote in "In Praise of Limestone") everyone knows everyone else "too well to think / There are any important secrets," he began for the first time to feel the need of a walled defensible fortress.

---

* Auden seems to have conflated the Limbo of the virtuous heathen with Dante's vestibule of the neutral, "who were for themselves" and chose neither salvation nor damnation (*Inferno* 3.39); the passive Fortunatus of "Under Sirius" risks joining them.

PART THREE

Territorial
1958–1973

CHAPTER FIFTEEN

Poet of the Encirclement

In June 1957, while he was giving his first series of lectures at Oxford, Auden won the Feltrinelli Prize for Literature and was suddenly richer by twenty million lire, or $33,000. This was more than enough to buy a comfortable house anywhere in rural Europe. He had already told friends that his Italian interlude could not and should not last, and now he acted quickly to end it. Arcadia, he had repeatedly warned himself, transforms itself into a prison when one tries to remain there. He chose to move north into German-speaking territory, but he narrowed his choice to regions where wine, not beer, was the preferred drink and an opera house was in easy distance. Three weeks after he won the prize, and a few days after he returned to Ischia, he wrote to an Austrian friend to ask her help in finding a house within forty kilometers of Vienna. The friend was Christa Esders; she was the daughter of Hedwig Petzold, whom Auden had stayed with (and had been willingly seduced by) during his first stay in Austria in 1926 and whom he had intermittently visited since. In September 1957 he went to Vienna for a few weeks, saw a newspaper advertisement for a farmhouse in Kirchstetten, a village forty kilometers west of the city, and bought the house on 28 September for one-third of his prize money. He stayed there for a month in the following summer, but returned to Ischia for a few weeks while a modern kitchen was installed for Kallman's expert but disorganized use. In September 1958 he left Ischia for the last time and traveled north to Kirchstetten; he was to stay there every summer for the rest of his life.* "What I dared not hope or fight for," he wrote in "Thanksgiving for a Habitat" in 1962, "is, in my fifties, mine, a toft-and-croft / where I needn't, ever, be at home *to* / those I am not at home *with*."

He underlined some of the meanings of his move from Mediterranean sunshine to the southern limits of the gothic north, and was silent about others. "Good-bye to the Mezzogiorno," one of the first poems he wrote after settling into Kirchstetten in 1958, contrasts an Italy of public space to a *Germania* of private time:

> between those who mean by life a
> *Bildungsroman* and those to whom living
> Means to-be-visible-now, there yawns a gulf
> Embraces cannot bridge.

In twenty-three flowing stanzas of syllabic verse (only the final stanza ends with a punctuation mark stronger than a comma), this unpretentiously profound poem interprets the relations of north and south, borrowing the sweeping geopolitical scale of Toynbee and the precise personal details Auden attributed to the Sicilian novelist Giovanni Verga, of whose books he wrote in a review: "Everything has been observed at first-hand with the loving attention one gives to a way of life which, whatever its sorrows and crimes, is worth living."† In the south, according to this poem, existential isolation and other "metaphysical threats" do not occur; one does not see even so benign an isolation as that of "an only child engrossed / In a game it has made up." Instead, "in streets packed solid / With human flesh," the northerner can be shocked into learning "That surfaces need not be superficial / Nor gestures vulgar," that the body has its own dignity and substance.

The south in this poem is the realm of space, the north the realm of time. Auden, as he describes himself, is one of those who journey south for a special kind of plunder: not for gold or Old Masters like "our fathers," or in a futile summertime quest for sex or health, but for "spiritual loot." By moving away from his English past, he could find a

---

* He almost became a homeowner in New York the following winter, when he expected to buy a four-story house in Long Island City, one subway stop away from Manhattan; but either he changed his mind or the sale fell through.

† Verga is one of the poem's "sacred meridian names, *Vico, Verga,* / *Pirandello, Bernini, Bellini*," a list that covers a range of styles and manners from Vico's grand historical patternings through the undemanding pleasures of the composer favored by the Arcadian in "Vespers."

possible future, like all who go to Italy "In middle-age hoping to twig from / What we are not what we might be next." The future is "a question / The South seems never to raise": no one is worried there by judgment, "yet (if I / Read their faces rightly after ten years) / They are without hope." Having come south to find one answer, Auden was now leaving to find another before the blessing became a curse: when northerners try to " 'go southern,' we spoil in no time, we grow / Flabby, dingily lecherous, and / Forget to pay bills." In "Serenade," written a year before he came to Italy, Auden had complained about everything that refused "to be, simply, publicly, there." Having been "there" for a decade, he knew it was time to be somewhere else.

In going north, Auden was interested more in the *Innigkeit* of the German tradition than in anything in recent German history. "Yes, it is a German Age," he had written to a friend in 1943, "and the chances are, I have a suspicion, that after the war it will continue to be. What other country in our century has produced anything comparable to the cumulative effect of—to name only a few—Rilke-Kafka-Berg-Strauss-Barlach-Klee-Husserl-Heidegger-Scheler-Barth-Groddeck-Koehler."

The German language had a deeper personal meaning to him, which Auden did not mention but that obscurely mattered when he was building a refuge against external enmity. German was for him the language of disapproval and judgment: in his later years, in conversation with bilingual and English-speaking friends, he often switched into German when he criticized others in ethical, not aesthetic, terms. "*Sie sind alle Verbrecher*" ("They are all criminals"), he said to Golo Mann about publishers in a conversation otherwise conducted in English. "*Christoph ist falsch*," he said to Spender about Isherwood. Of his other languages, he wrote in 1947 that "English may be the language of Heaven, but in the Earthly Paradise, I am quite sure, nothing but Italian will be spoken or sung."

The erotic principle to which the Mediterranean world—and Auden's poems until 1957—had given the imposing names of Aphrodite and Venus now took on Germanic northern names, Frau Minne and Dame Kind. Auden gave Dame Kind a poem of her own in 1959, a "slightly unpleasant" poem, as he called it. The "Coarse Old Party" it describes is very different from the blond Aphrodite who "rose up excited, / Moved to delight" by Cecilia's melodies in 1940, and different also from the white Aphrodite who was "on our side" in the war between Hermetics and Apollonians in 1946. "Dame Kind" opens with her appearance in crude stone prehistoric fertility images: "Steatopygous, sow-

dugged / and owl-headed." In that guise, she was the first deity prayed
to for rain, and the recipient of the first sacrificial murder, the one "To
Whom—Whom else?—the first innocent blood / was formerly shed."
(The story of Cain and Abel is ignored as a later patriarchal invention.)
Today, still, when we spot "Her Picked Winners," our response is an
envious "ONE BOMB WOULD BE ENOUGH." The poem matches its harsh
rhythms with an uncharacteristically ugly layout, where the short rhyming lines are exaggeratedly indented from the margin of the longer unrhymed ones. Because Dame Kind is who she is, the one without whom
we should not exist at all, the poem ends in thanks for all the sexual
unions that were required to bring us about, but its vision of the
sexual life is germane to a world where there will be no peace. It remarks, without a trace of idealizing, "How many hundreds / Of lawful,
unlawful, both equally / loveless beds, / Of lying endearments, crooked
questions, / crookeder answers,* / Of bawling matches, sarcastic silences, / megrims, tears, / How much half-witted horse-play and sheer /
bloody misrule" comprise the prehistory of even the most solemn acts
of love. In *Homage to Clio*, published in 1960, "Dame Kind" precedes,
and sets the tone for, the skeptical treatment of language and eros in
"First Things First."

—————

The refuge Auden had dared not hope or fight for had been on his mind
for five years. "Lakes" had imagined a possible landholding by denying
it was probable:

> It is unlikely I shall ever keep a swan
>   Or build a tower on any small tombolo
> But that's not going to stop me wondering what sort
>   Of lake I would decide on if I should.

In poems like "The Shield of Achilles," "Streams," and "Vespers," he
had wished for a secure aesthetic Eden while knowing himself to be in
a world of insecure violence. Now that he had his refuge, he denied
himself even a fantasy of Arcadia. As he had written earlier, a lake-lover's

---

* Auden had by now stopped using the word "crooked" in sexual contexts as a code word for
homosexuality.

preference for benign nature goes with a self-protective "wish for savage dogs and man-traps." Over the next few years Auden's poems evoked unsettling images of a violence that was everywhere in the modern world because it was everywhere in the human spirit. In "The Sabbath," written in 1959, humanity apparently destroys itself in war, leaving only "holes in the earth, / Beaches covered with tar, / Ruins and metallic rubbish in plenty." Yet when the wordless beasts try to resume the paradise that Man interrupted, "A rifle's ringing crack / Split their arcadia wide open, cut / Their sabbath nonsense short. / . . . That fellow was back, / More bloody-minded than they remembered, / More god-like than they thought." In 1964, observing the peaceable landscape of suburban Europe through the dry haiku of "Et in Arcadia Ego," he wrote:

> I might well think myself
> A humanist,
> Could I manage not to see
>
> How the autobahn
> Thwarts the landscape
> In godless Roman arrogance,
>
> The farmer's children
> Tiptoe past the shed
> Where the gelding knife is kept.

A wartime beheading by the Nazis is recorded in "Josef Weinheber" in 1965, but the evil embodied in the Nazis had not been defeated: "never as yet / has Earth been without / her bad patch, some unplace with / jobs for torturers."

"Walks," one of the first of Auden's Kirchstetten poems, professes to make a mild contrast between two kinds of path: the historical purposive time of the straight "road from here to there," which, even when he returns by the same road, "looks altogether new / Now that is done I meant to do"; and the determined repetitive time of a circular walk taken "for walking's sake." The final stanzas name a third path:

> The heart, afraid to leave her shell,
> Demands a hundred yards as well
> Between my personal abode
> And either sort of public road.

That additional distance adds the second stroke that makes the straight road a T and the circular one a Q, and it allows him "To call both walks entirely mine." A path that goes only to one's house gives an assurance of privacy: "a lane no traveller would use, / Where prints that do not fit my shoes / Have looked for me and, like enough, / Were made by someone whom I love." Like enough, but far from certain.

Auden had written in 1943 about Kipling as "the poet of the encirclement": "Poem after poem, under different symbolic disguises, presents the same situation of danger without, the anxiety of encirclement—by inanimate forces, the Picts beyond the Roman Wall." Kipling's "whole concern is to show that the moment of special emergency is everlasting." In such a view, there is no history, only nature, and if there is no history, then, Auden asked, "how can Nature and Man, the Jungle and the City, be opposed to each other, as Kipling is clearly certain that they are?" Kipling's answer is that civilization consists of "the People living under Law," but if one asks about the source and meaning of that law, "he refers one back to Nature, to the Darwinian law of the Jungle . . . or to the Newtonian law of the Machine." Kipling, Auden wrote, managed to "avoid the embarrassment of this paradox" by concentrating on the special emergency, for "it is precisely when civilization is in mortal danger that the immediate necessity to defend it has a right to override the question of just what it is we are defending." These remarks—in his review of T. S. Eliot's selection from Kipling's verse—were one of Auden's many warnings during the war about the worldview that could be expected from the victors. Yet Auden had chosen Kipling's poems to read aloud to surprised left-wing audiences in 1939, and in his elegy for Yeats he had named Kipling as a poet whom Time had already pardoned "for his views." Now, when he, too, felt "the anxiety of encirclement," he returned to Kipling's metaphors and chose to confront the question he believed Kipling had evaded.

In 1960, in a review of Kafka's *The Great Wall of China: Stories and Reflections,* Auden wrote: "To give some idea of what these later stories are like, I must content myself with describing one, *The Burrow.*" The story Auden chose is narrated by

some sort of badger-like animal, except that he is carnivorous. He lives by himself without a mate and never encounters any other member of his own species. He also lives in a perpetual state of fear lest he be pursued and attacked by other animals—"My enemies are countless," he says—but we never learn what they may be like and we never actually encounter one. His preoccupation is with the burrow which has been his life-work.

The story breaks off after the narrator-beast hears a faint whistling noise that he cannot identify.

> From now on, he is in the grip of a hysterical anxiety . . . Edwin Muir in his introduction suggests that the story would have ended with the appearance of the invisible enemy to whom the hero would succumb. I am doubtful about this. The whole point of the parable seems to be that the reader is never to know if the narrator's subjective fears have any objective justification.

Until now Auden had often written of the intimacies of the private world as a refuge from the hatreds of the public one, although he never pretended that privacy was enough. When someone woke "alone in a bed," he wrote in a lyric in 1953, there was every chance he might "hear his own fury / Wishing his love were dead." But the worst thing Auden had said of marriage in print or conversation was a remark he made among friends to the effect that marriage was the only quest in which the ordeal was also the reward. Now his vision of the private life took on the same dark shading as his vision of public life. He counted himself—he wrote in "Fairground" in 1966—one of those who "with their wander-years behind them" avoid the noise and the people of the fairground, one of those who prefer silent coigns where they "play chess or cribbage, / games that call for patience, foresight, manoeuvre, / like war, like marriage." Auden's vision had become more comfortless than it was even in the late 1930s, when his expectations of apocalypse were comforted by an artist's characteristic pleasure at the prospect of well-lit destruction. After 1956 the happiness celebrated and praised in his poems was always threatened by its opposite. Even the act of writing had the tone of a struggle against antagonistic outsiders:

> Each year brings new problems of Form and Content,
> new foes to tug with: at Twenty I tried to
> vex my elders, past Sixty it's the young whom
> I hope to bother.

Reviewers in these years complained that Auden had sunk into cozy optimism. Philip Larkin's review of *Homage to Clio* was titled "What's Become of Wystan?"—a play on Browning's "What's become of War-

ing," the first line of a poem about a sudden and mysterious disappearance.* But the tone the reviewers decried was part of an elaborate effort
at concealment. Auden had perfected a technique of writing about the
darkest possible subjects in a tone that deceived real or imaginary enemies
into thinking him too mild and avuncular to bother contending with.
He apparently learned his tactics from Robert Frost, whose combination
of folksy diction and bleak content was a cunning version of pastoral that
Auden greatly admired, and he had quickly set to work studying the
lessons of this master. The title and subject of his first Oxford lecture
after his inaugural—the first of the three he delivered in 1957—was
"Robert Frost."

In Kipling's world, Auden had written in his review, "The important
figure in society is, of course, the man on guard, and it is he who, in
one form or another, from the sentry on the Afghanistan frontier to the
gardener . . . is the Kipling hero. Unlike the epic hero, he is always on
the *defensive*." In Auden's work, poetry and the poet now became
guardians of personal truths they could not embody and the defenders
of a public language they did not speak. Like Kipling's guardians, they
have little sympathy with city dwellers safe inside the walls, but unlike
them, they defend a possible city that does not yet exist. When Auden
wrote "The Garrison," in 1969, he claimed guardian status, while also
making clear that he was defending not the empty power of a state but
the different strengths of the personal voice:

> Time crumbs all ramparts, brachypod Nemesis
> catches up sooner or later with hare-swift
> Achilles, but personal song and language
> somehow mizzle them.

"Mizzle," an obsolete dialect word Auden found in the *Oxford English
Dictionary*, means "to confuse, muddle . . . to give (one) wrong information." Personal song and language practice every unchivalrous dodge
they know of.

The guardians defend neither the "Present, / so self-righteous in its
assumptions and so / certain that none dare out-face it," nor the rulers,

---

* Auden claimed, perhaps not quite accurately, that he never read reviews of his work "unless
they happen to appear in papers or periodicals I happen to take" (letter to Monroe K. Spears,
14 June 1963; Berg Collection). A few months after Larkin's dismissive notice appeared in July
1960 in *The Spectator*, a paper Auden almost certainly took, Auden reviewed Larkin's first widely
published book, *The Less Deceived*, and praised it without reservation.

for "Whoever rules, our duty to the City / is loyal opposition." Their deepest loyalties are historical ones—to the past, which communicates with the present through personal song and language, "Thanks to which it's possible for the breathing / still to break bread with the dead"; and to the future that they themselves imperfectly image, serving "as a paradigm / now of what a plausible Future might be," even in a house shadowed by painful histories. The typical soldier-guardian in Kipling would be familiar with the mood but baffled by the thought. The magazine to which Auden gave the poem for publication was a theological one, the journal named for his discussion group, *The Third Hour.*

Auden's religious thought, which had always focused on the dialectic of human freedom and absolute commandment, now treated the absolute as more distant than ever and human freedom as more powerful to do harm. He had written of Kipling: "It is noteworthy that the *interested* spirits are all demonic; the Divine Law is aloof." Now he evoked a similar universe in "Friday's Child," a bleak, profound, strange, and haunting poem written in 1958 as a memorial to Dietrich Bonhoeffer, the pastor and theologian who had been active in the resistance against Hitler and was killed by the Nazis in 1945. The poem was partly a reminder to himself about the recent history of the part of the world he had moved to, partly a return to the Good Friday themes of "Horae Canonicae" in an even darker tone.

Bonhoeffer's posthumous *Letters and Papers from Prison*, first published in 1948, and one of the most radical and influential theological works of its time, expounded a "religionless" Christianity suitable to a humanity that had at last "come of age" by outgrowing the traditional structures of worship and reassuring images of a paternal God by which Christian belief had been sustained until now. The only plausible Christianity, Bonhoeffer wrote, would be a "worldly" one, built in ways as yet unknowable on a revelation of the incarnate and humiliated Christ, and on a sense of Christ's agony and powerlessness as the condition of humanity. "It is not some religious act which makes a Christian what he is, but participation in the suffering of God in the life of the world." In this attack upon "Christendom" Bonhoeffer built on a long Protestant tradition, but his writings had a special plausibility in an age that had seen the depth of Fascist evil. And, having left behind a refuge secured for him in the United States by Reinhold Niebuhr, to return to wartime Germany and work actively and dangerously for the resistance movement, he wrote with the authority of a martyr.

"Friday's Child" adopts the themes and moods of Bonhoeffer's letters

from prison. The poem's apparently simple manner manifests the incom-
mensurability of language and truth: it adopts the rhythms of the nursery
while confronting the total absence of any divine check or limit on human evil. "He told us we were free to choose," it begins, in a plain
statement of Christ's psychological teaching. But "children as we were,"
we convinced ourselves that we were free *only up to a point.* We thought
we were free to do *almost* anything, that we would be stopped before we went too far. "Paternal love will only use / Force in the last
resort / On those too bumptious to repent." In that happy conviction,
"It never crossed our minds He meant / Exactly what He said." But
because He did in fact mean we were free to perform any evil, without
limit, what sort of reverence should be paid "to a Divinity so odd / He
lets the Adam whom He made / Perform the Acts of God?"*

We have no direct access to this odd divinity, and therefore "All proofs
or disproofs that we tender / Of His existence are returned / Unopened
to the sender." The only access to Him the poem can imagine is through
dread:

> Now, did He really break the seal
> And rise again? We dare not say;
> But conscious unbelievers feel
>   Quite sure of Judgment Day.
>
> Meanwhile, a silence on the cross
> As dead as we shall ever be,
> Speaks of some total gain or loss . . .

For eighteen years Auden had written in his poems and prose about
the "total gain"—a shorthand phrase for the Christian themes of re-
demption and love offered to a sinful world. The only other time he had
paired it with the alternate possibility of total meaninglessness and loss
was a year earlier, when he made a rueful joke in "The More Loving
One" about his ability to aestheticize lovelessness: were all the stars to
disappear, "I should learn to look at an empty sky / And feel its total
dark sublime, / Though this might take me a little time."

The abstraction of its argument notwithstanding, "Friday's Child" expresses a more complex and emotional relation with a personal god than
anything he had written before; it tries to find an answer to the question,

---

* As Auden wrote in a haiku a few years later: "The God of Love / Will never withdraw our
right / To grief and infamy" (*Collected Poems*, p. 737).

asked insistently by Bonhoeffer, not *what* Christianity is to us but *who* Christ is to us, at a time when (in Bonhoeffer's phrase) we are all nihilists.

Around the time Auden wrote this poem, he seized on a passage in Charles Williams's posthumous collection of essays, *The Image of the City*, published in 1958.* The Crucifixion, Williams wrote, makes God "tolerable as well as credible. Our justice condemned the innocent, but the innocent it condemned was one who was fundamentally responsible for the existence of all injustice—its existence in the mere, but necessary sense of time, which His will created and prolonged." The injustice of the Crucifixion, he continued, makes sense only when understood as a response to "something terribly like injustice" committed by God in creating the world as it is. Auden quoted these sentences in his review of the book, with comments that unabashedly put his own ideas into Williams's mouth: "I think he would almost go so far to say that, but for the Crucifixion, it would be *morally* impossible for us to believe either in the Incarnation or in the Divine origin of the world." In "Friday's Child," God creates an Adam—humankind—who performs "Acts of God" (in the legal sense of destructive occurrences like fires or floods) that include the revenge murder of God himself. In the year he wrote the poem, Auden began saying to friends that the one Christian heresy he believed in was Patripassianism, the doctrine that God the Father suffered with the Son on the cross.

"You and I are free," he wrote in the final stanza of "Friday's Child,"

> To guess from the insulted face
> Just what Appearances He saves
> By suffering in a public place
> A death reserved for slaves.

"The insulted face"—the phrase combines the medical and social senses of "insult"—had become Auden's image of divinity; this was at the farthest possible distance from the sweet-smelling gardens of the Wholly Other Life at the end of Caliban's speech written fifteen years before.

---

* Auden may have had the passage in mind when he wrote the poem, or he may have encountered it shortly after. Williams's book appeared in November, and the exact date in 1958 when Auden wrote the poem is unknown. Auden almost certainly received a proof copy before it was published; he is named in the introduction, and his review of the book was published in January 1959 (by the American right-wing biweekly *National Review*, a magazine Auden had never seen until he received the issue with his review; he was annoyed with the editor for not having told him about the magazine's politics and never wrote for it again).

And to "save the appearances," in the traditional language of natural philosophy, means to find a hypothesis that accounts for events perceived by observation—as appearances of planetary motion in the night sky were "saved" by the hypotheses of Copernicus. For Auden, the appearances saved by the crucified Christ are the unjust acts of murder and degradation that every civilization inflicts on its victims; and the saving hypothesis is that the face of each of those victims is the image of God.

In May 1957, a year before Auden wrote this poem, a book had been published under the title *Saving the Appearances*, by the English writer Owen Barfield; it was widely noticed in theological circles and apparently ignored elsewhere. Auden had admired Barfield's earlier books on language, and later wrote a preface to a reprint of Barfield's *History in English Words*. Although he seems not to have mentioned *Saving the Appearances* in letters or essays, Auden used its vocabulary and thought in "Friday's Child" and many other poems in the next few years. Barfield gave Auden the intellectual means with which to unify a variety of theological and literary issues he had confronted earlier; and in Auden's imagination the morally inseparable acts of Creation and Crucifixion, and their shared implication in injustice, now corresponded to the mutual relation of the believer and the object of belief, the observer and the thing observed, the artistic maker and the thing made.

Barfield organized his book as a brief history of ancient and modern efforts to save the appearances of the physical world. The conventional understanding of observed events "as objects in their own right, existing independently of human consciousness" is, he wrote, an idolatry that was becoming ever more prevalent and extreme. Even the most advanced physicists quickly forget their knowledge of the inextricability of observer and observed, and treat subatomic particles in quantum theory as if they existed without observation. Barfield proposed instead a new (yet also ancient) understanding based on imaginative "participation" between observer and observed, a participation culminating in the "final participation" of full religious faith, when all the idols of detached observation are swept away.

This book was as timely for Auden as *Zahl und Gesicht* had been a few years earlier. He had focused increasingly on the arbitrariness and autonomy of perception and of any language built on perception—as in "First Things First," or in "Words," where a sentence uttered makes a world appear. At the same time he felt ever more certain that only a participatory, undetached, first-person language had the power to overcome the isolation of the ego, because objective, detached language only increases the isolation it is intended to break. This intersection of ideas developed new urgency through Auden's sense that his poetic language and vocation were besieged from outside by inarticulate hatred. It was morally imperative to avoid Kipling's error of defending a civilization without knowing what, if anything, made it worth defending.

Any defense of the poetic and personal realms must fail, Auden believed, if it adopts the methods of its adversaries. Most modern literature and thought had done precisely that: had insisted on plainspoken realism in art and on scientific detachment in ethics, or had withdrawn into opiate symbolism in art and existential drama in ethics. In "The History of Truth," another poem from 1958, Auden wrote of truth in the distant past having taken the participatory form that Barfield called original perception; "when being was believing," truth was not a scientific absolute but one among many ways of belief, "the most of many credibles." Today, in the era of technological power, "Truth is convertible to kilowatts," on one hand, while on the other hand the scientific universe has no relation at all to its appearances: "Some untruth anyone can give the lie to, / A nothing no one need believe is there."

The only way out of this dilemma is to acknowledge, together with modern science itself, the gap between perception and reality—and then to refuse to accept it as if it were itself reality. Auden paraphrased Barfield in "Friday's Child":

> Since the analogies are rot
> Our senses based belief upon,
> We have no means of learning what
> Is really going on.

Barfield had written that the gap could be closed by faith that appearance and meaning had been joined when the Word became incarnate—and by a faith that the relation between the two is real, even if it cannot be fully understood until the end of time. The meaning of the Word, Barfield argued, had been made potentially available at the moment of the Incarnation, a moment he named "the Event." As Auden wrote in an epigraph in *Homage to Clio*:

> Between those happenings that prefigure it
> And those that happen in its anamnesis
> Comes the Event, but that no human wit
> Can recognize till all happening ceases.

The language is that of Auden's earlier poems about shared liturgy—the Last Supper prefigures the Incarnation, the Communion service occurs in its anamnesis—but the full participatory meaning of these acts is now impossibly distant.

Shakespeare's comedies that adapted earlier stories in prose or verse always included, when it was absent in the original, a threat of death that shadows the festivities. Similarly, whenever Auden adapted a philosophical treatise into one of his poems, he always added the fact of murder. Barfield had noted that appearances, as perceived by the modern scientific worldview, had been transformed into idols—"They had no 'within.' " Auden saw an analogue of this idolatry in the moral detachment that made possible the prison camp where Bonhoeffer had been martyred. Barfield recalled the Baconian understanding of knowledge as *operative* knowledge, or power, and compared it to the way one can partially "know" an automobile by experimenting with its levers and dashboard; Auden added the truth that this partial knowledge can be murderous. The "observing Mind" in "Friday's Child" "cannot clearly understand / What It can clearly do," but it does not need to understand itself to use its power; it performs the Crucifixion with "instruments at Its command" that "Make wish and counterwish come true."

Auden insisted that if any religious meaning is possible, it must accommodate the violent degradation that, in the Christian story, divinity accepted for itself when an incarnate god was crucified by human powers—and the violent degradation that it permitted Auden's German-speaking neighbors to inflict on millions of innocent victims, Bonhoeffer among them. (Auden addressed his poem "Josef Weinheber" to the memory of a fellow poet, also by a remarkable coincidence a householder in Kirchstetten, who had collaborated with the German invaders and had killed himself at the end of the war.) As the Nazis' efficient machinery proved, inarticulate violence allied itself with the exact, autonomous vocabulary of science. Both were failures of participation. Inarticulate violence and the language of scientific and social power both revel in their detachment from their objects, and although separately and together they are doomed to destroy themselves, they are all too likely to leave behind the atomic desolation Auden pictured in "The Sabbath" as holes in the earth, beaches covered with tar.

The question that closes "Friday's Child"—"Just what Appearances He saves" by dying his humiliating death—cannot finally be answered, Auden believed, except by complete participation in its meaning, which is impossible in human time. The personal language of poetry can achieve only an incomplete participation, and its attempts can easily be deflected—either into sealed associative mazes (of the kind Auden saw in the poetic school of Rimbaud and Ashbery) or into "haphazard oracular grunts" (as he called them in "The Epigoni"). But in a brief epigraph a few years later, Auden restated his first-person commitment to a language greater than his own:

> A moon profaned by
> Sectarian din, death by
> Fervent implosion:—
> Possibles. But here and now
> Our oath to the living word.

Auden knew that in writing poems like this one, he faced the temptation of aesthetic pride, the fantasy that the writer is innocent because words draw no blood. In order to resist it, he reminded himself that even the most personal words can never be wholly innocent. The curse of Babel, the disintegration of shared speech into the mutually incomprehensible languages of division, may have been undone (as the Venerable Bede was the first to notice) by the miracle of Pentecost, when the apostles spoke in their own language and were heard in the languages of each person who listened; yet when Auden commemorated Pentecost in "Whitsunday in Kirchstetten," he did not let himself forget the antagonisms of the curse. "Since this morning," since Pentecost, even prayers are spoken "with a vocabulary / made wholesomely profane, open in lexicons / to our foes to translate."

Auden's double subject was now the defense of the word from its enemies and the word's incapacity to say what it wanted to say, two issues that he treated as inseparable. His morally intelligent distrust of his own motives drew from these two a third subject: the artist's temptation to pervert the word into an instrument of power disguised as a personal voice.

He had explored these themes in the prose and verse of *The Orators* in 1931, and he now returned to them with the same formal and verbal inventiveness he had used then, but with another half-lifetime of experience. He wrote two large-scale works in 1959, one in luminous aphoristic prose, "Dichtung und Wahrheit," published as an "Interlude" to the lyric poems in *Homage to Clio*, the other an opera libretto in collaboration with Kallman, *Elegy for Young Lovers*; the first of these explored the limits of the word, the second the ruthlessness of those who claim to defend it. Both were written in the aftermath of the most severe strain in his relations with Kallman since the crisis of 1941.

"Dichtung und Wahrheit"—the title duplicates that of Goethe's autobiography—is a meditation in fifty numbered sections, forty-nine of them expanding on the text of the first:

> Expecting your arrival tomorrow, I find myself thinking *I love You*: then comes the thought—*I should like to write a poem which would express exactly what I mean when I think those words.*

The sections that follow are elaborations on the emotional grammar set out in the essays on language Auden had been writing for several years: the differences between first-person speech and third-person code, the I-feeling and the You-feeling; the relation between the ego that knows and the self who is perceived; the linguistic impossibility of making "I love You" into a statement that is both true and *self-evidently* true; the ease of the promise "I will love You forever" and the difficulty of the promise "I will love You at 4:15 P.M. next Tuesday"; and the related difficulty of the promise to love a person, not a set of qualities (as in: "I will love You whatever happens, even though you put on twenty pounds or become afflicted with a moustache"). The last of the fifty sections closes with a transition to the poem that follows it immediately in *Homage to Clio*, the verse tribute to Dame Kind which Auden had written a few months earlier:

> This poem I wished to write was to have expressed exactly what I mean when I think the words *I love You*, but I cannot know exactly what I mean; it was to have been self-evidently true, but words cannot verify themselves. So this poem will remain unwritten. That doesn't matter. Tomorrow You will be arriving; if I were writing a novel in which both of us were characters, I know exactly how I should greet You at the station:—*adoration in the eye; on the tongue banter and bawdry.* But who knows exactly how I *shall* greet You? Dame Kind? Now, that's an idea. Couldn't one write a poem (slightly unpleasant, perhaps) about Her?

The impersonal realm of Dame Kind has none of the paradox and ambiguity of personal speech, and is, as Auden wrote in an essay, "fully and accurately described by the more brutal four-letter words."

The "You" who was arriving in Kirchstetten was not Kallman, who was already there, but Adrian Poole, later an academic sociologist, then a twenty-five-year-old student working toward an honors degree in jurisprudence at Oxford, where Auden had met him, and who visited Kirchstetten for about two weeks in September 1959. Poole enjoyed Auden's company but felt no sexual attraction to him; Auden, who sensed Poole's feelings, never made a closer approach, but enjoyed an exhilarating sexual attraction to the younger man without intruding on him by expressing it. In the eighteen years of Auden's sexless relations with Kallman, no one whom he had loved, with the sole exception of Rhoda Jaffe, had prompted him to write so rich a poetic tribute. Auden gave the subtitle "An Unwritten Poem" to "Dichtung und Wahrheit," but it is better described as the happiest of his love poems, the one least afflicted by the anger, transience, wreckage, and fear that in almost all his other poems are inseparable from love.

After Poole left Kirchstetten, Auden began work on "Dichtung und Wahrheit." Kallman, who had treated Poole's visit as a routine matter, now understood that Auden had rebelled against his emotional subservience to him and was writing for someone else a love poem which Kallman believed by rights should be his. For the first and only time in their relations, Kallman did what Auden had imagined himself doing many years before in "Dear, though the night is gone": he "felt / Unwanted and went out." In a postcard to Thekla Clark, Kallman reported, without explanation, that he was "running away from home." He then sent a telegram from Lisbon: FOR THE MOMENT TREACHERY IS PROSPERING, MUCH TO MY DISAPPOINTMENT. A few days later he settled into a house in the Algarve but in another postcard to Clark complained about local dullness, adding: "I may confuse the issue and go back to Austria." He did. The crisis passed, and Poole, who became a lifelong friend of both Auden and Kallman, did not know until long after Auden's death that it had even occurred. But the relations between Auden and Kallman had permanently changed. The same resistance that Auden had sworn to maintain against persecutors from outside in "There Will Be No Peace" he had carried out against someone he had begun to see as a persecutor within his walls.

———

After Kallman returned in late September 1959, he and Auden began work on a libretto they had offered to write for Hans Werner Henze, whom they had met in Ischia in 1953. Their relation with Henze was the opposite of their relation with Stravinsky: Auden was now the senior and more famous collaborator who initiated each new project and chose the subject. (After their experience with the financially rapacious Stravinsky, who arranged for his music publisher to retain the copyright on their words for *The Rake's Progress*, Auden and Kallman pointedly copyrighted their libretti for Henze in their own names.) Henze responded to Auden and Kallman's offer by asking for a libretto for a "chamber" opera for small orchestra and soloists but no chorus. Auden and Kallman made various false starts before they were able to devise a plot and characters. They found their efforts interesting enough to describe them in a prose epilogue to the printed libretto of *Elegy for Young Lovers*.

"Genesis of a Libretto," probably written by Auden although jointly signed by both librettists, refers directly to Auden's recent interests and indirectly to events in his career. He and Kallman first thought of a plot with "five or six persons, each of whom suffered from a different obsession so that, while all inhabiting a common world, each would interpret that world and the actions of the others in a completely different way." This extreme example of the privacy of perception was extreme only in degree, not in kind; it corresponded to the common linguistic idea, which Auden endorsed, that each person speaks a private idiolect, a personal linguistic system subtly different from the system of a shared language like English. They then "toyed with the idea of a ladies-maid masquerading as a great lady. The interest in this situation was to have come from showing that, though she was, socially speaking, an imposter, by nature, in her sensibility and instinctive behavior, she was really the great lady she was impersonating." This idea survived only into the essay, where it stands as one of Auden's allegories about poetic language that, although inescapably feigning and deceptive, can also be true to a reality it cannot directly express. Auden and Kallman's next wrong move was an attempt to make a great actor the "mature, worldly, and cynical rival" of an idealistic young man in a love triangle. Finally the plot fell into place when they set the scene in 1910 and made the older man a poet, an example of "the artist-genius of the nineteenth and twentieth century."

The poet, Gregor von Mittenhofer—the librettists wanted to name him Hinterhofer after their Austrian electrician, but Henze balked at the undignified sound of it—is a monster of egoism, "a cross between W. B. Yeats and Stefan George," and, as a compound portrait of them, "very libellous," Auden said in a letter to James Stern. (Auden later told Spen-

der that Yeats had become for him "a symbol of my own devil of unauth-
enticity, of everything which I must try to eliminate from my own poetry,
false emotions, inflated rhetoric, empty sonorities.") Compared to the
Prospero of "The Sea and the Mirror" he is a far more dangerous variety
of coldhearted artist. Prospero misunderstands the personalities of others
and uses their suffering as matter for his art. Mittenhofer, in order to
complete the poem he is writing, "(morally) murders two people and
breaks the spirit of a third." He does so without guilt, not simply because
he is monstrous, but because he accepts one of the central myths of his
age, the distinction between personal speech and artistic "production":

> Aesthetically speaking, the personal existence of the artist is accidental; the essen-
> tial thing is his production. The artist-genius, as the nineteenth century conceived
> him, made this aesthetic presupposition an ethical absolute, that is to say, he
> claimed to represent the highest, most authentic, mode of human existence.
>
> Accept this claim, and it follows that the artist-genius is morally bound as a
> sacred duty to exploit others whenever such exploitation will benefit his work
> and to sacrifice them whenever their existence is a hindrance to his production.

The distance is not great between the nineteenth-century artist-genius
who defends the primacy of his art against the philistine mass and the
twentieth-century poet-professor who defends the word against its
collective and official enemies. Like Ransom in *The Ascent of F6* twenty
years before, Mittenhofer is Auden's private warning to himself against
his own temptations, an illustration of what might have occurred if he
could have translated tempting wishes into completed acts. Mittenhofer's
relentless exploitation of his patroness, Carolina von Kirchstetten, parodies the relation that Auden first accepted, then found morally intolerable, between himself and Caroline Newton in 1939–44. The triangle that
links Mittenhofer and the young lovers echoes the triangle that linked
Auden, Kallman, and Jack Barker in 1941—but seen through the lens of
the events of September 1959. Auden's moment of rage against Kallman
in 1941 is judged mercilessly: Mittenhofer lies to the alpine guide who
asks him if he knows of anyone who might be trapped on the mountain
by an impending blizzard—after Mittenhofer had asked the lovers to go
there to find the mountain flower he uses as a stimulus to poetic vision.*

* Kallman insisted on edelweiss over Henze's objections that German-speaking audiences would
find this absurdly sentimental for a poet of Mittenhofer's sophistication. For the German text
Henze changed it to alvetern, a flower apparently unknown outside a few square miles of eastern
Switzerland.

The lovers' death in the blizzard repeats Ransom's death in the blizzard in *The Ascent of F6*, but where Ransom dies in service to his own ambition, the lovers die in service to the ambition of a poet who lives on after them, and whose work, without their death, would not exist. The obscure connection that Auden had made many years earlier between theater and murder he now made explicit on an opera stage: in the closing scene, at a celebration of his sixtieth birthday, Mittenhofer takes deep delight in public triumph as he reads his elegy to a theater audience in Vienna that includes the Emperor and the Minister of Culture—and the elegy is sung not by him but by the disembodied voices of those he murdered or destroyed in order to complete it. A few years later, Auden wrote that he found in "so much 'serious' poetry . . . an element of 'theatre,' of exaggerated gesture and fuss, of indifference to the naked truth, which, as I get older, increasingly revolts me." The uncharacteristically strong verb was a sign of his revulsion from something deeper than literary style. "Every writer," he told an interviewer (in German) around the same time, "is menaced by his own latent monstrosity."

"Genesis of a Libretto" ends by disclaiming any idea that Mittenhofer's acts are specifically Austrian. "As a matter of fact, the only things about him which were suggested to us by historical incidents were drawn from the life of a poet—no matter whom—who wrote in English." Mittenhofer's egoism came from Yeats, but the "historical incidents" came from Auden. In the libretto, Carolina's misreading of Mittenhofer's handwritten "port" as "poet" is a direct lift from Isherwood's misreading of that word in Auden's "Journey to Iceland." (Unlike the furious Mittenhofer, Auden found the misreading preferable to the original.) A scarf knitted endlessly by a woman for her absent husband was based on one knitted by Tania Stern for James Stern when he was away at a writers' conference. Mittenhofer could never have written "There Will Be No Peace"—although he rages at reviewers' insufficient praise—but he too uses unchivalrous dodges. When he reads his elegy in the theater, the poem is represented not by words but by instruments and wordless vocalizing (because, Auden explained, a great poem cannot be represented by the words of another poet, but its greatness can be suggested by music). Yet the idea of an unspoken poem is a variation of the unwritten poem which the medium of prose pointed to in "Dichtung und Wahrheit," and it serves as an extreme illustration of how every poem—as Auden wrote in "The Song"—cannot express "what it started up to say."

In the following year, 1960, Auden was occupied mostly with his public roles. He gave three lectures at Oxford in May and then two more in October to complete the fifteen required in his five-year term. During the election campaign for his successor, in February 1961, he wrote a newspaper article on his professorship, and although another article on the same page quoted the undergraduate magazine *Isis* in praise of his lectures—"by far the most entertaining and provoking" of any recently given in Oxford—Auden, with the same tact he had demonstrated in his inaugural, refused to take himself seriously. "Oxford," he said, "should feel very proud of herself for having anything so comically absurd as a Chair of Poetry." He imagined a Bardic College ("Who would pay for it? Who would staff it? What jobs would there be for its graduates?"), where a poetry professor could train apprentices instead of lecturing to future teachers of literature; the curriculum would include instruction in prosody, courses in geology, liturgics, and cooking, and "every student would be required to take personal charge of a domestic animal and a garden plot." Only after laughing himself out of his professorship did he take up the delicate question of who should be his successor. Someone whom Oxford audiences would not otherwise have a chance of hearing seemed preferable to someone already there; between a scholar and a poet, the scholar was the safer choice.

> Since, however, the chair is such an oddity, it would be cowardly not to take risks in filling it . . . If a scholar is to be chosen, why not elect a learned crank, a Baconian or a Rosicrucian? But why not a poet? He may mumble, but that can be rectified by a microphone.* He may talk nonsense, but it will probably be interesting nonsense. There is only one topic upon which no poet is ever worth listening to, his contemporaries; it is highly unlikely that he has read most of them.

This amounted to an implied endorsement of the candidacy of Robert Graves, who duly won the election, but Auden's closing sentence was an apotropaic attempt to ward off evil: Graves had delivered a notorious jeremiad against Auden and other contemporary poets in a lecture at

---

* Auden had complained about the acoustics in his lecture hall and had urged unsuccessfully that the authorities install a microphone.

Cambridge six years before, and whether or not Graves read Auden's article, he chose not to repeat himself at Oxford.

Auden wrote only one poem, "You," during all of 1960, although he and Kallman also translated Brecht's *Mahagonny* for a production that never took place. He had never written so little poetry for so long a period. "You," a poem addressed to his own body—in an ironic refusal of the You-feeling promised by the title—complains that although he was "born for / Sacred play" in his vocation of poetry, he is obliged to write lectures, essays, and translations to earn food and shelter, "Turn base mechanic / So that you may worship / Your secular bread, / With no thought / Of the value of time."

In "You," sexual urges no longer signify love—"you plague me / With tastes I was fool enough / Once to believe in"—and the senses leave the ego isolated by false appearances:

> I suspect strongly
> You hold some dogma
> Of positive truth,
> And feed me fictions:
> I shall never prove it.

Auden knows that evolutionary changes between two ice ages gave his body a "sinner's cranium," conscious of itself. "That explains nothing." When he asks "Who tinkered and why," to make evil exist, his question is shadowed by the thought of a god who, as Williams wrote, was fundamentally responsible for all injustice. But his answer finds an explanation in his own sense of guilt: "Why am I certain / Whatever your faults are, / The fault is mine . . . ?"

Like most of Auden's work at this time, the poem is a reminder of dissociation and separation. His body and his voice, which addresses his body in the second person, are estranged. Auden needed to live through a year of almost complete poetic silence before he could look back as he did the following year, and write:

> Corns, heartburn, sinus headaches, such minor ailments
> Tell of estrangement between your name and you,
> Advise a change of air . . .

He had already changed his air from England to the United States to Italy to Austria, but the change he now had in mind was a more subtle,

almost invisible one. "To go Elsewhere is to withdraw from movement, / A side step, a short one, will convey you thither." This was
exactly the opposite of the advice he had written about in "Reflections
in a Forest" in 1957, where he imagined the blatant language of trees
telling him to "Keep running if you want to reach / The point of knowing where you stand." The change of air he needed now was not something he could find by moving swiftly somewhere else. It was so near
that finding it was as simple as going home.

CHAPTER SIXTEEN

The Air Changes

After five years of concealment and reticence, Auden's poems now regained their brightest plumage. Released from the public terrors of his Oxford professorship, secure in his house in Kirchstetten, he wrote the twelve poems of "Thanksgiving for a Habitat," and after collecting these and other short poems in 1964 for publication in *About the House*, he described the book to friends as the happiest he had ever written and the least disguised. "For the first time I have felt old enough and sure enough of myself to speak in my own person." The few dark-toned poems in *About the House* were balanced with spirited crowd-pleasers like "On the Circuit." Auden's friends privately doubted his claims of happiness, but they may not have noticed that the poems in which he made those claims were written about someone they had never met—not the man they joked with over dinner, but the poet who worked alone in a study "more private than a bedroom even," behind a closed door that no one but he was allowed to open.

A house was the product of personal choices. But compared with the invisible inner acts of faith that Auden wrote about twenty years earlier, a house was more enduring, more tangible, more dependent upon the choices of other persons and the impersonal qualities of inanimate matter. Houses built by human beings were unlike anything in the world of nature: among insects and animals, he wrote in "The Birth of Architecture," were "masons and carpenters / who build the most exquisite shelters and safes, / but no architects, any more than there are heretics or bounders." The passage from "gallery-grave and the hunt of a wren-king / to Low Mass and trailer camp," although incomprehensibly vast, was consistently human. "To construct a second nature of tomb and temple, lives / must know the meaning of *If.*"

The first of the poems Auden later called his *Hausgedichte* was "On Installing an American Kitchen in Lower Austria,"* written in 1958, the year he moved in. It was a celebration of the conscious choices that had made the place his own. The kitchen, in the past "an abhorrent dungeon," was now "numinous"—the proper subject of poetry's sacred awe. It was the focus of a democratic household, where choice and action, not ancestry and title, determine one's status: "if I am / banned by a shrug it is my fault, / not Father's, as it is my taste whom / I put below the salt." The exuberantly complex stanzas commandeer the form in which Pindar praised victors in masculine tests of strength and apply it to the feminine nurture that welcomes everyone to the feast. (He had made similar ironic use of Pindaric stanzas in "Mundus et Infans" to praise a newborn infant in 1942.) The opening stanza explicitly rejects the Greek model of heroism as masculine, aggressive, and self-assertive, as Auden had implicitly rejected it in "Homage to Clio": should the shade of Plato visit us, we could tell him that poets now praise figures who never "bore arms or / made a public splash," and then, "we would point, for a dig at Athens, 'Here / is the place where we cook.' "

Auden at this time was self-consciously taking lessons from feminine nurture and the feminine imagination. In his introduction to Phyllis McGinley's collection of poems *Times Three*, written probably in late 1959 or early 1960, he speculated on two not quite parallel questions: "What does the poetry men write owe to the influence of women, whether as mothers, sisters, and wives, or as women authors whom they admire?" (he listed Jane Austen, Colette, Virginia Woolf, Laura Riding, and Marianne Moore), and "What can women who write learn from men and what should they beware of imitating in masculine literature?" He dismissed any idea that masculine and feminine imaginations were mutually exclusive—"the hundred-per-cent male and the hundred-per-cent female are equally insufferable"—but proceeded to describe the kind of poetry that each might write if it existed in isolation. The faults of the masculine imagination sound much like the ones he saw in his earlier life and work; the virtues of the feminine imagination sound much like the ones he was

---

* When he incorporated the poem into his sequence "Thanksgiving for a Habitat," he retitled it "Grub First, Then Ethics." This was his rendering of a famous line by Brecht, "*Erst kommt das Fressen, dann kommt die Morale,*" from *Mahagonny.*

now trying to achieve in his poems. "Left to itself the masculine imagination has very little appreciation for the here and now; it prefers to dwell on what is absent, on what has been or may be." It writes good love poems, because, like Auden's love poems in the 1930s, these are less about real persons than about generalizable qualities: men "are always aware that the girl they happen to be in love with might be someone else (and often one suspects that they are thinking of several girls at the same time.)"* Relations with real persons require a different way of seeing: "the feminine imagination accepts facts and is coolly realistic," which is why "women write better than men about marriage. When a husband does write about his wife, which is rare, he is apt to become weepy."

The masculine imagination, by itself, could not have found the way to the poetry of the ordinary body that Auden had learned to write: it "lives in a state of a perpetual revolt against the limitations of human life. In theological terms, one might say that all men, left to themselves, become gnostics." (The corresponding feminine error, which sometimes occurs in Auden's later theories about poetry, has a moral rather than a gnostic quality: "Left to itself, the feminine imagination would get so serious that it would look down on the arts as unworthy frivolities.") He identified three different ways of writing about children: fathers write about their children's futures; "bachelors" like Lewis Carroll, "with their masculine nostalgia for their own childhood, are better than women, perhaps, at understanding the fantasy life of children, but only a mother can convey a sense of their physical presence." (He perhaps forgot that he had described this kind of generalization as a masculine fault.) Men's poetic and personal flaws could be summed up in a single word: "Above all, the masculine imagination is essentially theatrical." Among the poets, he continued, "the purest examples of the masculine imagination that I know are Victor Hugo and W. B. Yeats. Who could possibly conceive of either of them as a woman?"

In the summer of 1962 Auden decided that his poem about the kitchen belonged in a sequence of poems about each room in his house, and he wrote the rest during the next two years.† One of his purposes in writing the sequence seems to have been to make amends for the male oversight which had led him to write seven poems in "Horae Canonicae"

---

* Women, Auden added, do not often attempt to write in the genre of fantasy that "is conventionally called Love Poetry. Indeed, when they try, the results can be embarrassingly awful —think of poor Mrs. Browning."

† In a note he attached to the kitchen poem in *About the House*, he wrote that when he included it earlier in *Homage to Clio* he "did not realize that its proper place was in a cycle." He never hesitated to speak of his poems as beings he did not fully understand when he wrote them.

that emphasized the body but said nothing "coolly realistic" about the facts of bodily needs. A house is a frame and an extension of the body, as a city is not. The new sequence included the events of eating and excreting, and where "Horae Canonicae" spoke abstractly about going to sleep, "Thanksgiving for a Habitat" speaks concretely about getting into bed. In "Horae Canonicae," because of our guilt, it was plausible to wonder "if we have a home"; in "Thanksgiving for a Habitat" we are no less guilty, but our guilt is less theatrical, and for better or worse, we have learned to be at home with it.

Having applied Pindaric stanzas to feminine craft in "On Installing an American Kitchen," Auden did so again in 1963 in "Tonight at Seven-Thirty," a poem about the dining room which he dedicated to the writer M.F.K. Fisher, and threaded with allusions to her books about cooking and eating. But as a counterpoint to his praise for the humane, welcoming enclosures of his house, he also acknowledged the colder excluding strengths of its walls, using metaphors from the merciless unempathic world of biology: the second poem in the published sequence was entitled, like the sequence itself, "Thanksgiving for a Habitat." It is dedicated to Geoffrey Gorer, who, as the intimate of Auden's fears of English people in 1955, was especially well-equipped to understand the three things the poem was most thankful for: "Territory, status, / and love, sing all the birds, are what matter."

The sequence, as Auden arranged it in *About the House*, began with the first two of these three and ended—in poems about the dining room shared with guests, the bedroom where Auden slept alone, and the sitting room shared with Kallman—with the third. He hoped to be a sympathetic patron to the inhuman lives in his house and land: "Many are stupid, / and some, maybe, are heartless, but who is not / vulnerable, easy to scare, / and jealous of his privacy?" Yet he had no delusions that his dominion was innocent. He admitted to fear of spiders in earlier poems, and they populated a nightmare in "Plains"; now he confessed elliptically that he feared them because he saw in them an image of his own guilt, that his wish to destroy them was a miniature parallel to the Hitlerian wish to destroy that which one finds most intolerable in oneself:

> Arachnids give me the shudders, but fools
>   who deface their emblem of guilt
>
> are germane to Hitler: the race of spiders
>   shall be allowed their webs.

The sequence keeps its most troubling visions well hidden, and insists on them most in the places where they are most deeply buried. The poem about the cellar, "Down There," presents itself as a calm meditation on the resemblance between cellars and caves, but its vocabulary, flecked with words and images from the first act of *Richard III* ("key-cold," "mew," and Shakespeare's malmsey butt represented by Auden's "barrels, bottles, jars"), threatens the security of home with intimations of usurping violence and civil war.

The concluding poem, "The Common Life," praises the house for its multiple defenses:

> I'm glad the builder gave
> our common-room small windows
> through which no observed outsider can observe us:
> every home should be a fortress,
>
> equipped with all the very latest engines
> for keeping Nature at bay,
> versed in all ancient magic, the arts of quelling
> the Dark Lord and his hungry
>
> animivorous chimeras.

The house Auden bought as a defense against largely imaginary "animivorous"* enemies from outside made possible a victory against the inner foe, the Dark Lord with his chimeras, who had been the real enemy all along.

Auden was now "responsible for a piece of the earth," as he told an interviewer: "dominant / over three acres and a blooming / conurbation of country lives," as he wrote in "Thanksgiving for a Habitat." In the same summers when he wrote his poems about householding, he also wrote about the temptations that come with power over nature. In 1961 he gave himself a vacation in Norway in order to visit Hammerfest, "The northermost township on earth,"† a place to which he had paid "atlas-homage" for more than forty years. His poem about it closed with an

---

* Feeding on living things; apparently one of Auden's rare invented words.
† "Northermost" is the form in Auden's typescript and is attested by the *Oxford English Dictionary*; a copy editor regularized it to "northernmost," which appears in most printed editions.

ethical and ecological point that had not occurred to him in earlier poems about northern industrial wastelands:

> to have disgusted
> Millions of acres of good-natured topsoil
> Is an achievement of a sort, to fail to notice
> How garden plants and farmyard beasts look at us,
> Or refuse to look, to picture them all as dear
> Faithful old retainers, another.

Those achievements "of a sort" were the heartless triumphs of an alienated dominion over the natural world. In 1962, Auden returned to the theme of operative knowledge—as described by Barfield and contemplated in "Friday's Child"—in an essay whose title asked, "What Ought We to Know?" Here he explored the original sense of "knowledge," meaning mutual personal intimacy—as in "Adam knew Eve, his wife" ("because sexual intercourse is a symbol for personal intimacy") or, more simply, "I know him very well." In this sense, knowledge is mutual; the better one knows someone else, the better one comes to know oneself. The modern, emotionally detached meaning offered only an obscene parody of this mutual knowledge: "By the 'truth' we now mean the knowledge that gives power; consequently the more we know about them and the less they know about us, the better." Auden's responsibility for three acres put him, he believed, under the same obligations that scientists, and those who defer to their authority, prefer to ignore.

> We know that most of the universe is composed of things about which we can acquire knowledge but which cannot know us, and that this one-sided relation enables us to manipulate them as we wish, but collectively, we have not yet drawn the obvious moral, namely that if nothing in creation is responsible for our existence then we are responsible for all created things.

This was a belated moral of "Friday's Child," where divine paternal love has withdrawn forever and takes no responsibility for human acts. Auden's essay continued:

> Most individual scientists, certainly all the best ones, have been and still are contemplatives who rejoice in their discoveries, not for the practical value they may have, but because it is a joy and wonder to know that things are as they are. Unfortunately their innocent indifference to practical values has made them the slaves of that faceless fabulously wealthy Leviathan called Science which has

no concern whatever for the right of anything or anyone to exist except its anonymous power that acknowledges no limits, and that has a scarcely disguised contempt for those whom it employs.

The whole issue had urgent practical consequences: "Either we shall commit suicide, by bombs or by exhausting essential natural resources, or we shall change our conception of science." In "After Reading a Child's Guide to Modern Physics," a poem written in 1961, the unspoken answer to the question whether "politicizing Nature / Be altogether wise, / Is something we shall learn."

"This passion of our kind / For the process of finding out" was, in the same poem, an inescapable fact. "But I would rejoice in it more / If I knew more clearly what / We wanted the knowledge for." In 1965, in a commissioned article on the twentieth anniversary of the atomic bomb, Auden wrote as if he knew perfectly well that what we wanted the knowledge for was the Dark Lord's purpose of domination and lust: "Our world will be a safer and healthier place when we can admit that to make an atomic bomb is morally to corrupt a host of innocent neutrons below the age of consent."

He began asking the same ethical questions about art that he was asking about science. Even in his many portrayals of the artist as indifferent, at best, to the suffering of others, he had accepted without question the almost universal assumption that an artist's ethical failures had no harmful effect on the success of his art. "The artist-hero of the nineteenth and early twentieth century," Auden wrote in his note on *Elegy for Young Lovers*, "is a genuine myth because the lack of identity between Goodness and Beauty, between the character of man and the character of his creations, is a permanent aspect of the human condition."

He was unsure he believed this even when he wrote it. He summed up the theme of the opera in two lines by Yeats, the poet he regarded as the most theatrical of all:

> The intellect of man is forced to choose
> Perfection of the life or of the work.

But, he remarked elsewhere, this was untrue: "perfection is possible in neither." A few years later, when he was finishing "Thanksgiving for a Habitat," he stopped paying lip service to the idea that the personal existence of an artist was accidental. Because poetry issued from a personal voice, the merit of a poem was inseparable from the merit of the person who wrote it. Auden understood—against all the assumptions of modern aesthetic thought—that the line between ethics and aesthetics could not be drawn because it did not exist.

He said as much in a "Postscript" to "The Cave of Making," the poem in his house sequence about the study to which he ascended by an outside staircase every morning to do his writing. In quick rhymed half-lines addressed to himself, he admits knowing (as every writer knows) "how much inspiration / your vices brought you." Although, as he tells himself, in church "you sometimes pray / to feel contrite, / it doesn't work," because time and experience have taught him unmistakably that "many a fine / expressive line / would not have existed, / had you resisted." Nevertheless, he concludes, God may reduce you to tears of shame on Judgment Day, "reciting by heart / the poems you would / have written, had / your life been good." The quality of the unwritten poems will be enough to make God's point: He does not underline His rebuke by showing sadness or blame, because "He doesn't need to, / knowing well / what a lover of art / like yourself pays heed to."

In remarks in later years Auden sketched a theory of art that refuted everything he had said earlier about the lack of identity between goodness and beauty. Writers who were monsters of egoism, he suggested, can build elaborate structures of great formal beauty, yet truthfulness and depth—qualities that tend to embarrass modern criticism—require a sympathetic understanding of other persons in their rights and particularities. For a writer who thinks of other persons as behaviorist automata or as servants or impediments to his will, that understanding is impossible. Among the clearest signs that an author takes no interest in the uniqueness of other persons are the muscle-bound symmetries of a book like *Ulysses* or the oceanic dissolutions of a book like *Finnegans Wake*. (Auden said of Joyce: "He asked you to stand in the same relation to his writing as you must to your life.") The signs are less obvious among lyric poets. Auden began remarking to friends that he had met three great lyric poets who were monsters: Yeats, Brecht, and Frost. He had admired and imitated all of them, but was repelled by their cruelty and indifference to vulnerable younger people around them, and in varying degrees he came to see in their poetry the same sterile Promethean egoism that he now condemned in his own earlier work.

"I should like to become, if possible, / a minor atlantic Goethe," Auden
wrote in "The Cave of Making." Dante had provided the model for his
aspirations in the 1930s, when he wrote his uncompleted cantos on the
epic journey from capitalist hell to Communist paradise. Shakespeare
took Dante's place in the 1940s, when Auden appended "The Sea and
the Mirror" to the final scene of *The Tempest.* Goethe had been the
unnamed source of "New Year Letter," but around 1960 Auden began
to make Goethe's life and work an explicit model for his own. (In "Letter
to Lord Byron" Auden had given the three supreme masters the names
Joyce gave them in *Finnegans Wake*: "Daunty, Gouty, Shopkeeper.") Of
Goethe's view of language, Auden wrote in "The Cave of Making" that
while Goethe knew that "Speech can at best . . . bear witness to the
Truth it is not, he wished it were [the truth], as the francophil / gaggle
of pure songsters / are too vain to."* To wish Speech coterminous with
Truth is to wish Speech to be better than it is; the Mallarméan wish to
make Speech independent from Truth or superior to it is to wish Speech
to be more trivial than it is.

Early in 1961 Auden worked with Elizabeth Mayer on their translation
of Goethe's *Italian Journey*, a task they had been discussing for some
years. Auden then wrote a poem, "A Change of Air," in which Goethe's
experiences in Italy are transformed into a parable of Auden's experiences
after he had left Italy forever. Around this time *The Kenyon Review*
planned a series of symposia in which three poets were to comment
on a poem by a fourth, who would then reply with his own commentary
on it. Auden gave the magazine "A Change of Air," and for the only
time in his life committed himself to write for publication about a poem
of his own. He had until now found ways to write in detail about almost
everything private in his life except the process by which his own poetry
came into being. The artist, he said in 1936, "like a secret agent, must
keep hidden / His passion for his shop." When he wrote about composition and revision in "Squares and Oblongs" in 1947, or about literary
development in "Making, Knowing and Judging" in 1956, he said a great
deal about the moral implications of the act of writing but little about
the act itself. And when he described the early drafts of "Prime" in 1950,
he spoke only to a small audience in a lecture hall and never published
his remarks. But now that he could close the door on his private study

* Auden wrote "francophil" on the impersonal biological model of words like "hydrophil"
(water-loving) and "oxyphil" (acid-loving); the overeager copy editor replaced it with
"Francophile."

in Kirchstetten, he seemed willing to report in print what happened inside it.

He wrote for the first time in the name of his craft, instead of in the name of his vocation—about the art of poetry, not the ethics of it. Reviewing Bruno Snell's *The Discovery of Mind* in 1959, he found its technical account of Homeric Greek "of the greatest interest to any twentieth-century poet," and described what he learned from Snell about such matters as the contrast between the use of the first person in Homeric Greek and in English. And for *The Kenyon Review* symposium on "A Change of Air" he provided a list of his trade secrets:

> Whatever else it may or may not be, I want every poem I write to be a hymn in praise of the English language: hence my fascination with certain speech-rhythms which can only occur in an uninflected language rich in monosyllables, my fondness for peculiar words with no equivalents in other tongues, and my deliberate avoidance of that kind of visual imagery which has no basis in verbal experience and can therefore be translated without loss.

In "Squares and Oblongs," he had listed the poet's ideal audience as the beautiful, the powerful, and fellow poets, and the poet's actual audience as the plain, the powerless, and fellow poets. Now he was more revealing but less amusing: "Every poet has his dream reader: mine keeps a lookout for curious prosodic fauna like bacchics and choriambs."*

The poets who wrote about "A Change of Air" in *The Kenyon Review*—George P. Elliott, Karl Shapiro, and Stephen Spender—confessed in varying degrees that they were baffled by it. Auden thanked the first two for their efforts to make sense of it and rebuked the lazy condescension of the third, who had been a close friend for more than thirty years. He then recalled the prehistory of the poem:

> For some time I considered writing a poem specifically about Goethe, but decided against it for two reasons. I had in the past written a number of poems about historical characters and wanted to do something different this time: then, Goethe's actual flight into "elsewhere" was much too dramatic to suit the basic theme of my intended poem, the contrast between a person's inner and outer

---

* "A Change of Air" has two bacchics in the first line ("Corns, heartburn" and "such minor") and a choriamb in a later stanza ("answers, yourself"); the whole poem deviates extravagantly from an underlying iambic pentameter. George Saintsbury wrote in his *Historical Manual of English Prosody* (1910) that the bacchic probably did not occur in English verse; Auden wrote in his *Kenyon Review* essay that one of his "minor pleasures in life is trying to make George Saintsbury turn in his grave."

biography. It is, surely, a general experience that those events in a person's life
which to other people seem decisive and with which biographers are concerned
are never the same as those moments which he himself (or she, herself) knows
to have been the crucial ones: the inner life is undramatic and unmanifestable
in realistic terms.

I set out, therefore, to try to write a poem in which it would be impossible
for a reader to be distracted from its personal relevance to himself by thinking
of Goethe or, even more mistakenly, of me . . .

There is one, only one autobiographical detail in the poem and I couldn't
help smiling at Mr. Elliott's objection to it. Evidently, he has never had the
misfortune to suffer, as I do, from corns . . . If he had . . . he would be only
too familiar with their psychosomatic whims. (For years they tormented my
right foot; then suddenly they transferred their attentions to my left.)

These paragraphs protest strenuously against any easy equation between poem and author, but they also insist that the subject of the poem
is a decisive inner moment invisible to everyone else—"a wordless /
Hiatus in your voluble biography." The costumes, set, and props resemble nothing in Auden's personal history, but the drama is no less
autobiographical for that. Auden's essay about the poem was his first use
of a rhetorical technique that he adopted repeatedly during the next few
years: to leave his secrets hidden in plain sight, and to post signs pointing
in their direction. He used the same technique in the 1963 essay in which
he described his vision of Agape by quoting "from an unpublished account for the authenticity of which I can vouch"—therefore written by
himself.* He revealed other secrets at this time to the one person whom
he could most count on to preserve them for posterity, the American
scholar Monroe K. Spears, who had just finished a book about his poetry.
He told Spears that "A Household" was a work of auto-analysis ("Don't
tell anyone," he warned, ensuring that his remark would be kept for the
archives) and that "There Will Be No Peace" was "one of the most
purely personal poems I have ever written." Two years later he reported
to Spears, "For your private information, I have even written an anonymous piece for the February issue of an S.C.M. [Student Christian Move-
ment] magazine called *Breakdown*"—actually *Breakthrough*—a piece
signed with the same pseudonym, Didymus, that he had used in 1942.

The brisk conversational style and emphatically end-stopped stanzas of
"A Change of Air" seem designed to close off the speculation and discussion that its elusive content invites. The subject is the dissociation of

* A few months later in his introduction to Dag Hammarskjöld's *Markings*, he wrote that we
can never observe anyone else's inner choices, only what they do and how they behave.

a person's private and public aspects, the "you" who is the inner ego and "your name" who is the outer self. And the corns, along with heartburn, sinus headaches, and other minor ailments in the opening line, "Tell of estrangement between your name and you." This was the latest version of Auden's myth of the double man, and introduces the least apocalyptic and theological of his visions of reconciliation.

The poem is persistently cagey on the crucial question of where the change of air is to be found. You won't find it in a dramatic emigration that would let you "trade in an agglutinative tongue / With a stone-age culture" (Auden's commentary points out this could be done in Greenland but not, as the poem seems to imply, in Rimbaud's Abyssinia). "To go Elsewhere is to withdraw from movement." Early drafts of the poem are even more explicit in describing the change as internal and invisible: "Elsewhere cannot be packed for nor requires / The [*illegible*] gesture of a setting-forth. / . . . To withdraw from notice without being noticed." And in notes Auden made to himself he identified *elsewhere* as "life so internal as to be inaccessible to inspection. As like here as possible except that it makes no demands, gives no advice. Ignores you." Auden's published commentary calls the poem a parable; Elsewhere "has a priest, a postmistress, an usher," is a place of "average elsewhereishness." You have invisibly withdrawn there while your name remains as visible as ever. "Your name is as a mirror answers": it is the mirror image of anyone who observes it; they see what they project on you from themselves. "Yourself," during your sojourn into the interior world of Elsewhere, is behavioral, not moral: "How you behave in shops, the tips you give." Elsewhere "sides with neither" your name nor you, "being outside both, / But welcomes both with healing disregard"—because you, by going to it, have chosen not to be affected by it. When you return— "(for you will)"—from Elsewhere to the world that entangles and engages you as before, other people will see no "sudden change in love, ideas, or diet," nothing so visible as a cure. The only thing "Fanatic scholarship" may be able to prove is "That you resigned from some Committee" (or came to the end of a widely publicized professorship). It may also unearth

> A letter from the Grand Duke to his cousin,
> Remarking, among more important gossip,
> That you seem less amusing than you were.

Auden ended his commentary with a paragraph about this final line:

In my experience, wit requires a combination of imagination, moral courage
and unhappiness. All three are essential: an unimaginative or a cowardly or a
happy person is seldom very amusing. The reader of "A Change of Air" who
has had a successful sojourn elsewhere and reintegrated his persona with his
ego need not suppose that he has become duller in mind or more afraid of
life . . . he has only to imagine that he has become happy.

This answered Larkin's question "What's Become of Wystan?" In his
earlier works Auden wrote of being happy in the past—"though one
cannot always / Remember exactly why one has been happy, / There is
no forgetting that one was"—but this was the first time he claimed he
was happy now.

=====

Whatever might be said about him by disappointed reviewers, Auden
knew he was working at the height of his powers from 1961 to 1966—a
period as fertile and inventive as his earlier bumper seasons of 1935–37,
1939–44, and 1949–54. The reintegration that began with his move to
Kirchstetten, and continued with the renewed love poetry of "Dichtung
und Wahrheit," was completed by his withdrawal from the public life of
Oxford in late 1960. His strengths were visible behind the now wrinkled
and very famous mask of his face. (*Time* magazine planned a cover story
about him early in 1963, although, as staff members later reported, it was
dropped when the managing editor objected to honoring a homosexual.
The painter who made the unpublished cover portrait, René Bouché,
seems unconsciously to have modeled his image of Auden on the most
vigorous and potent image available at the time: if one covers the chin
and mouth in the picture, it looks uncannily like an imaginary portrait
of John F. Kennedy at sixty.)

After finishing "A Change of Air" Auden returned to New York and
spent the autumn of 1961 working on *The Dyer's Hand*, an enormous
book of prose compiled partly from his Oxford lectures, partly from essays, reviews, and published and unpublished pensées, some dating back
to his pseudonymous "Lecture Notes" of 1942. He left his Oxford lectures mostly intact but reduced some of the essays to aphorisms and
notes, because, he said, "there is something, in my opinion, lifeless, even
false, about systematic criticism . . . As a reader, I prefer a critic's notebooks to his treatises." In its depth of literary, psychological, and political intelligence—it ranged in subject matter from the theology of

moneylending to the imitation of pregnancy in male obesity—the book surpassed all other critical works by modern poets; as one critic remarked, Eliot made a great display of learning in a few narrow fields, but Auden's eclectic stock of quotations and allusions was a sign of true scholarship. Auden said that the sequence of chapters was deliberate, and the book as a whole is shaped as a quest from the solitary acts of reading and writing; through the loneliness of wishes and guilt; the small-scale societies in Shakespeare; the larger disorders of America; to, finally, the reconciliations performed by comedy and music. (The penultimate chapter, "Translating Opera Libretti," is described as "written in collaboration with Chester Kallman.")

In the next few years Auden enjoyed experimenting widely and copiously in verse forms, and his craft became simultaneously more aristocratic and more democratic. He had loosely imitated classical stanzas since the early 1930s, but he now adapted the patterns used in classical quantitative metres (in which the length of a vowel, not its stress, determines a syllable's metrical weight) as the patterns of his English accentual verse (where the stress of a syllable determines its weight); he copied the patterns of classical metres but substituted stressed and unstressed syllables for long and short vowels. As he told an interviewer: "For years I thought it would be fun" to write a poem in scazons, a so-called limping metre, favored by Catullus, with a trochee or spondee replacing an iamb in the sixth and last foot of an otherwise iambic line; he finally used them in "Down There," the poem about the cellar in "Thanksgiving for a Habitat." He wrote "Up There," the corresponding poem about the attic, in hendecasyllabics, an eleven-syllable line with a pattern of four trochees and iambs followed by an amphibrach. At another extreme, he began to enjoy and to imitate the speech rhythms of William Carlos Williams, whose work he had taken little interest in until he read Williams's late hymn to marriage, "Asphodel, That Greeny Flower," which he thought "one of the most beautiful love poems in the language."*
Adapting Williams's loose rhythms to his own stricter standards, he came up with the form of "Encomium Balnei": alternating lines of thirteen

---

* Auden's occasional meetings with Williams had become progressively more cordial since the time when both were among the poets who spoke at a reading in 1940 and Williams resented Auden's success. In January 1947 Williams invited Auden for a few days of talks with other poets—a symposium from which, Williams hoped, a new American poetry might emerge. Auden seems to have been too embarrassed by Williams's literary naïveté even to reply, but their later meetings were always friendly, and in 1952 Auden offered Williams his house in Ischia for the winter.

and eight syllables split into unpunctuated fragments that look and sound like the most open verse of Williams while conforming to Audenesque rules of number and proportion. In 1963, when he was commissioned to collaborate on the translation of Dag Hammarskjöld's *Markings* (a Swedish-born American professor supplied him with a rough draft which he polished down to the spare prose of the published text), he found the work of translating Hammarskjöld's haiku so difficult and rewarding that he began writing dozens of his own, and intensified the challenge by also writing tanka. He told the English poet and editor James Michie, whose translations of Horace he admired, that in "Thanksgiving for a Habitat" he had consciously tried to write "what I think Horace might write, were he alive today and were English his mother-tongue." And the rhymed epigrams in classical metres that he scattered through his later books were modeled on the classical epigrams of Goethe.

His freedom to experiment required the solitude and security of barriers invincible enough to protect him even from intimacy. "Which of us wants / to be touched inadvertently, even / by his beloved?" he asked in the title poem of "Thanksgiving for a Habitat." In their physiognomy of private life, the twelve poems of the sequence take less interest in the relations between one's intimates and oneself than in the relations between your name and you. The poem about the bedroom, "The Cave of Nakedness," is concerned more with sleep and dreams than with sex. The poem about the study, "The Cave of Making," calls it "an antre" —a cave—"more private than a bedroom even, for neither lovers nor / maids are welcome." This is a place where "silence / is turned into objects," and the historical silence that in "Homage to Clio" was the medium of love for a child or a spouse becomes the quiet of secluded making.* The enclosed bathtub of "Encomium Balnei" takes on the Edenic role that in "Bucolics" was granted to the more impersonal lake: "what Eden is there for the lapsed / but hot water / snug in its caul." The bath, like most of the other rooms, is a stronghold of privacy where even the master's key cannot intrude:

> though our dwellings may still have a master
> who owns the front-door key
> a bathroom

---

* Elsewhere in the sequence, in the postscript to "The Cave of Nakedness," silence regains its earlier role: "Nightmare of the base, / Silence to lovers / Is the welcome third party."

has only an inside lock
                                belongs today to whoever
          is taking a bath
                    among us
          to withdraw from the tribe at will
                                be neither Parent
          Spouse nor Guest
                              is a sacrosanct
          political right

"The Geography of the House," the cheerfully grateful poem about the lavatory ("a rather diffy subject," Auden said before he began), emphasizes the solitude of the morning ritual of the "ur-Act of making, / Private to the artist." This act is the first step in a knightly quest: "Not until our morning / Visit here can we / Leave the dead concerns of / Yesterday behind us, / Face with all our courage / What is now to be."[*] (The title of the poem puzzled American readers who did not recognize the euphemistic British question "May I show you the geography of the house?") Even in his poem about the living room, "The Common Life," Auden took the trouble to note that "a room is too small . . . / if its occupants cannot forget at will / that they are not alone."

Auden called the sequence "a sort of thanksgiving to all of the household gods," but it is also a hymn to the still, small voice of private personal speech, easily overwhelmed by crowds outside and terrors within. "At the Party," written around 1962, provides a brief, terrifying counterpoint. The cocktail party evoked in the poem is the one peacetime event that transforms a home into an impersonal desolation that is no home at all. "Reciprocal mistrust" is the ground bass of the party chatter. Fashionable names exchanged among the guests transmit encrypted "messages of woe." When a voice finally asks to be heard in the first person, it can emerge only as an inhuman, imperceptible din:

> A howl for recognition, shrill with fear,
> Shakes the jam-packed apartment, but each ear
> Is listening to its hearing, so none hear.

More dangerous than the terrors of the din were the tempting comforts of official recognition and public status. "Though I believe it sinful to

---

[*] He dedicated the poem to Isherwood because the hero of Isherwood's new novel, *A Single Man*, Auden thought, spent a remarkable amount of time in the room in question.

be queer," Auden said in a letter to Isherwood around this time, "it has at least saved me from becoming a pillar of the Establishment, and it might not even have done that if I hadn't bolted to America. No power in Heaven or on earth will ever make Chester—God bless him!—respectable."

═══════

One of the temptations of life behind a wall is the temptation to imagine oneself as a potential or actual victim of enemies outside. Auden's moral sanity compelled him to remember his comfort, status, and privilege, and he never forgot that the panic he had felt in 1956 was a dark night of the soul, not a victimization by an oppressor. That episode left him with, among many other things, a clearer understanding of the central moral issue in his own work: the brutal truth of unjust exclusion from the safety of civil peace and the inextricably double truth of the excluded victim's innocence and blood. His understanding became even more acute as he settled into the security and privacy of his house in Austria. In 1961 he insisted that his friends read *Black Like Me*, a book by John Howard Griffin about his experiences traveling through the American South with his skin temporarily darkened by a drug. ("The *Black Like Me* year" was Thekla Clark's shorthand for this period.) Nine years later Auden included excerpts from it in his commonplace book, *A Certain World*, and prefaced them: "In my opinion, the most heroic living white American is Mr. John Howard Griffin," Griffin's heroism being his voluntary acceptance of suffering and humiliations that his neighbor could not avoid but that he himself, until he chose to suffer them, had not felt. Certain theological parallels did not escape Auden's notice.

When he began making organized lecture and reading tours in the early 1960s (he had an earlier one in 1952), the only stipulation Auden made to his agents was that they must not book him in racially segregated colleges or communities, and in 1961 he began to discuss racial injustice in print. In a set of prose pensées on public life, "The Poet and the City," he distinguished "two kinds of political issues, Party issues and Revolutionary issues": the first were those on which all sides agreed on the social goal but differed over the means of achieving it; the second were those "in which different groups within a society hold different views as to what is just . . . Today, there is only one genuine world-wide revolutionary issue, racial equality." A revolutionary issue was experienced by individuals as a question of their inherent worth. "If an African gives his life for the cause of racial equality, his death is meaningful to him." In contrast, the party issues that divided the antagonists in the Cold War had vast and fatal effects, but the issues in themselves had no *personal* meaning for anyone: "What is utterly absurd, is that people should be deprived every day of their liberty and their lives, and the human race may quite possibly destroy itself over what is really a matter of practical policy like asking whether, given its particular historical circumstances, the health of a community is more or less likely to be secured by Private Practice or by Socialized Medicine."*

Party issues were open to debate; the revolutionary issue of race was a matter of absolute right and wrong. Auden, quoting one of G. K. Chesterton's slippery generalizations about Jews, commented:

> The disingenuousness of this argument is revealed by the quiet shift from the term *nation* to the term *race*. It is always permissible to criticize a nation (including Israel), a religion (including Orthodox Judaism), or a culture, because these are the creations of human thought and will: a nation, a religion, a culture, can always reform themselves if they so choose. A man's ethnic heritage, on the other hand, is not in his power to alter. If it were true, and there is no evidence whatsoever to suppose that it is, that certain moral defects or virtues are racially inherited, they could not become the subject for moral judgment by others.

The contrast between party and revolutionary issues reappeared in 1962 in "Whitsunday in Kirchstetten," a poem whose deliberately unemphatic tone pretends to accept simple answers to hard questions:

> about
> catastrophe or how to behave in one
> I know nothing, except what everyone knows—
> if there when Grace dances, I should dance.†

* Auden's views on the racial issues he encountered in the United States are indicated in his letters to E. R. Dodds, quoted above, p. 222. His friend Owen Dodson, a poet and playwright then studying at the Yale School of Drama, reported a characteristic incident in 1939, when Auden, shortly after meeting Dodson, brought him into an all-white hotel dining room in New Haven and acted as if he had not noticed the unignorable disapproval of the staff. In 1970, N. J. Loftis, a young poet Auden met late in life, published under the imprint of the Black Market Press (which used the name to emphasize its authors' skin color) a book of poems, *Exiles and Voyages*, which he dedicated "to my first friend, W. H. Auden."

† The closing phrase, one of the last unironic evocations of dance in Auden's work, refers to the epigraph of the poem, from the apocryphal Acts of John: "Grace dances. I would pipe. Dance ye all."

(Auden revised "I know nothing" to "what do I know" when Kallman pointed out that he had used the same phrase in "The Cave of Nakedness": "about / blended flesh . . . / I know nothing, therefore about certain occult / antipathies perhaps too much." He had become increasingly emphatic about the limits of his certainty.) The congregation at the Whitsunday worship service in the little Austrian Catholic church is ecumenically tolerant to the Anglican Auden—"When Mass is over, / although obedient to Canterbury, / I shall be well gruss-gotted"—but their smiling peacetime acts occur in the shadow of unsmiling divisive ones. Behind the Iron Curtain, "from Loipersbach / to the Bering Sea not a living stockbroker, / and church attendance is frowned upon / like visiting brothels." Yet stockbroking (Auden's perennial example of a profession that diminishes those who practice it) and churchgoing are both party issues, in a different category from the lustful imperial acts that dominate and degrade whole classes of persons or whole regions of nature. The arrogance of his own Anglo-Saxon tribe provides examples: "To most people / I'm the wrong color; it could be the looter's turn / for latrine duty and the flogging block, / my kin who trousered Africa, carried our smell / to germless poles."

The empty northern wastes of "Hammerfest" in 1961 remind him of "how we behave to beings / Who have anything we're after." Typically, the poem asks "but why bring that up now?" only after having done so. "It's heartless to forget about / the underdeveloped countries," says "The Cave of Making" in 1964, in a passage about the subjects of poetry, "but a starving ear is as deaf as a suburban optimist's." Yet the poem, by mentioning them, is only pretending to forget about them. The aggressors Auden is morally obliged to remember in his later poems are ultimately "my kin."

———

Auden and Kallman wrote *The Bassarids*, their second libretto for Hans Werner Henze, in 1963, two years after they had proposed to him an opera based on *The Bacchae*. (The word "bassarid," which puzzled Henze and almost everyone else, is the Greek word for both the men and women who followed Bacchus, unlike Euripides' word "Bacchae," which refers only to women. Auden was surprised to find it missing from the *Oxford English Dictionary*; it was added to the second edition, after his death.) In the same way they rewrote the ending of *The Magic Flute* in 1955 to redress the sexual inequities of the original, so they recast *The Bacchae* to grant both sexes an equal privilege of daemonic murderousness. Auden remarked to friends that *The Bacchae* was *The Magic Flute* without Christianity. The destruction Dionysus inflicts on Pentheus is exactly what the Queen of the Night fails to inflict on Sarastro. And Pentheus' repressed sexuality—in *The Bassarids*, the rhymed rococo dream interlude of "The Judgement of Calliope" displays the giggling prettified tone of his fantasies—brings about the destruction that the mutual sexuality of Tamino and Pamina prevents. Auden and Kallman had translated *The Magic Flute* just before Auden experienced his panic dread of the audience for his Oxford inaugural; afterward, Euripides' darker version of the story seemed more plausible.

The silence on the cross in "Friday's Child" is a silence in which banished pre-Christian gods find freedom to return. A hint of this emerging theme in Auden's work appeared in 1959 in *Elegy for Young Lovers*, where Mittenhofer's murderous triumph is simultaneously a sacrifice to older gods, and the old lady whose visions Mittenhofer plunders for his poems sings (in a lyric written by Kallman in his least comprehensible manner) of the lovers' impending death in the final blizzard: they are, she says, fed "lamb-like" to "the Immortal, high / On their white altar." Kallman explained to Henze that the lovers are " 'sacrificed' to the old gods." Although the old lady's lyric ends, somewhat bafflingly, "Never forget the / Old gods are dead," they are not dead at all: they live on in Mittenhofer's ruthless exploitation and in the storm and avalanche on the inhospitable mountain.

In *Elegy for Young Lovers* Kallman apparently initiated this theme, but Auden developed and sharpened it in *The Bassarids*. The laments and protests of the human characters who survive at the end of the opera include some of his most powerful dramatic verse. Cadmus, in accentual drumbeats, sings his elegy for a habitat—

> Night and again the night.
> The great House has fallen,
> Never to be rebuilt.
> I who raised these walls
> Am brought down to the dust.
> Night and again the night.
> Accursed in my old age,
> Alone, outcast, dishonored.
> Night and again the night.

> Cadmus of Thebes, whose daughter
> Murdered her own child.
> Night and again the night.

—while Tiresias and Pentheus's nurse, Beroe,* grieve in similar dignity, and Autonoe sings in the tripping accents of responsibility evaded:

> I didn't want to do it.
> Agave made me do it.
> She was always the stronger.
> I didn't want to do it.
> Agave made me do it
> And now we both must suffer.
> I didn't want to do it.
> Agave made me do it.

Simultaneously, the Bassarids make their collective claim to have been in another place, like the would-be innocents who melted away from the place of murder in "Nones"—to have been, in the full etymological sense of the word, "ecstatic":

> We were far away on the lonely mountain
> Dancing in innocent joy
> To the pure sound of the flute . . .
> We heard nothing. We saw nothing.
> We took no part in her lawless frenzy,
> We had no share in his bloody death.

After everyone else has sung together, Agave sings alone. Her grief over the child she has murdered is the darkest imaginable variant on Auden's postclassical Clio who nurses and mourns. "The strong Gods are not good": this is an axiom to her, who never heard of a god willing to choose the weakness of a human body. But in her contempt for the strong Gods, she still accepts personal responsibility, and, when the others leave to bury Pentheus, she remains "To receive judgment." Later, just before the final chorus, she warns Dionysus that he, too, can expect to be judged:

---

* An invented character (the librettists also gave a voice to Autonoe, Agave's sister, who is silent in Euripides): opera normally requires at least three female voices and *The Bacchae* has only one.

In the hour of your triumph, I say this,
Say it not only to you
But to Zeus and all on Olympus:
Think of the altarless Fates.
Where is gelded Uranus? Or Chronos,
Once an invincible God?
Rape, torture and kill while you can: one
Tartarus waits for you all.

But this classical anticipation of the Christ who will rout the pagan gods is belied when the chorus kneels in mass adoration for Dionysus and the opera ends. *The Bassarids* and "Thanksgiving for a Habitat" agree that the old gods survive, although not under their old names. They survive in the "latest engines" and the "ancient magic" that every fortress-household still uses to defend itself against the Dark Lord and his chimeras. And whenever his own weapons are taken up, even to be used against him, the Dark Lord triumphs.

CHAPTER SEVENTEEN

This Time Final

Ever since 1948 the annual pattern of Chester Kallman's life had effectively been the same as Auden's: they summered together in Europe and wintered together in New York. But early in 1963 Kallman decided to leave New York permanently and spend his summers in Austria with Auden and his winters in Athens on his own. He told friends he was tired of being arrested by New York police decoys whom he tried to pick up, but he was also responding to Auden's slight but increasing alienation from him by declaring his own independence. Auden, as before, paid for Kallman's food and shelter, maintained their conjugal household during their summers in Austria, and for the remaining ten years of his life found in Kallman's presence his best relief from loneliness. But his allusions to Kallman in prose and verse lost the affectionate, tolerant tone of earlier years and now alternated between cool, analytical anger and clumsy, unconvincing cheer. He continued to shore up the defenses he had begun to build in 1956 against the sufferings that he was now more willing to acknowledge had been inflicted on him by Kallman since 1941.

The sense of isolation in his poems and prose became sharper. He had written earlier about the walls of the city, their cement of blood, and the unjust exile of those forced outside. Now he imagined a more hopeless, isolating loneliness: instead of exile that looked back from outside at the city walls, a pervasive, inescapable alienation, a city without walls that does not protect itself or its citizens against anonymity, compulsion, and chaos. He turned away from communal themes of marriage and the flesh toward the bodiless continuities of language through which the living can remember the dead, and he found more comfort in a companionship remembered from his past than in his broken companionship in the present.

When he wrote in "The Cave of Nakedness," in 1963, about the face he saw in memory as he drifted off to sleep, he emphasized that "unwilling celibates . . . retain the right to choose / our sacred image." This parenthesis immediately followed:

> (That I often start with sundry
> splendors at sundry times greened after,* but always end
>   aware of one, the same one, may be of no importance,
> but I hope it is.)

Auden's friends, and every reader who knew something about his private life, assumed that by "one, the same one," he meant the "sacred image" of Kallman. But the only sacred image to which Auden consistently returned in his later poems was that of the person whose existence had prompted him to write the 1933–37 series of love poems that included "Lay your sleeping head, my love" and, later, "First Things First" in 1957 and "Since" in 1964, where again he used the word "image": "other enchantments / have blazed and faded, / . . . / but round your image / there is no fog." Kallman alone knew what these references meant, and knew also that Auden was drawing away from him, both to past enchantments and to new ones. In May 1963, after spending a few days in London with Adrian Poole, Auden began a series of disguised essays in autobiography; as always, he wrote most revealingly about himself when purporting to write about something else.

The hidden themes of these essays were the visionary experiences he had in 1933 and 1939, about which he had never before written in his prose. (Even the autobiographical essay he wrote in 1955 about his return to the Church had not hinted at these matters.) Introducing Anne Fremantle's anthology *The Protestant Mystics*, and observing that the varied accounts of mystical vision arranged chronologically in the book seemed to divide into four basic types—the Wordsworthian vision of Dame Kind

---

* "To green," in Scottish, means to desire intensely. Auden used the word in a sexual sense, as in "Letter to Lord Byron": "*Post coitum, homo tristis* means / The lover must go carefully with the greens."

and the visions of Eros, Agape, and God—he made no explicit claim to have experienced any of them but signaled obliquely that he believed he had experienced the first, second, and third.

The vision of Dame Kind, "by far the most common," was, he wrote, "the initial cause of all genuine works of art and, I believe, of all genuine scientific inquiry and discovery, for it is the wonder which is, as Plato said, the beginning of every kind of philosophy." The objects of the vision, whether organic or inorganic, "are all non-human, though human artifacts like buildings may be included." Readers familiar with "The Prophets," "Heavy Date," and other well-known poems by Auden could guess that the category of human artifacts might include locomotives and pumping engines.

Despite a Western delusion that it is universal, the vision of Eros is far less common—so rare, in fact, that "one is sometimes tempted to doubt if the experience is ever genuine, even when, or especially when, it seems to have happened to oneself." The third, the vision of Agape, was as unquestionably real as the first, and, because the experience was un-represented in the anthology itself, Auden relied almost exclusively on the "unpublished account for the authenticity of which I can vouch." The account opens by dating the experience to "one fine summer night in June 1933"—a transparent allusion to his poem titled (in the editions then in print) "A Summer Night 1933," and written, according to its first stanza, in "the windless nights of June." The account concludes: "among the various factors which several years later brought me back to the Christian faith in which I had been brought up, the memory of this experience, and asking myself what it could mean was one of the most crucial, though, at the time it occurred, I thought I had done with Christianity for good."

Auden was too alert to self-deception to write about the experiences of Eros and Agape without reminding himself that they could be masks or variations of less generous feelings. The vision of Eros can idealize mere lust. The experience of Agape can be unsettlingly similar to the feelings of violent, murderous crowds: "most of the experiences which are closest to it in mode, involving plurality, equality and mutuality of human persons, are clear cases of diabolic possession, as when thousands cheer hysterically for the Man-God, or cry bloodthirstily for the crucifix-ion of the God-Man. Still, without it, there might be no Church." This made explicit the connection that Auden had lightly sketched in "Horae Canonicae" between the crowd in "Sext" and the mass-bell in "Lauds."

With the vision of God, Auden adopts an entirely different tone. After writing confidently and personally—with greater or lesser degrees of indirection—he now declares his total lack of authority:

No one could be less qualified than I to discuss what the bulk of these selections are concerned with, the direct encounter of a human soul with God. In the first place, because I lead an ordinary sensual life, so that I can scarcely be surprised if I have never seen the God whom no man has seen at any time, a vision which is reserved, the Gospels tell us, for the pure in heart.* In the second place, because I am an Anglican. Of all the Christian Churches, not excluding the Roman Catholic, the Anglican Church has laid the most stress upon the institutional aspect of religion.

He follows these disclaimers with statements of defiant doubt about all the visionaries who claimed to have seen God in person. "The first thing which disturbs me is the number of mystics who have suffered from ill-health and various kinds of psycho-physical disturbances." This, he points out, contrasts with the physical well-being of the disciples in the Gospels, and the complete absence of any indication that Christ himself suffered from psychological disorders. "Then I am a little disturbed by the sometimes startling resemblances between the accounts of their experiences given by mystics and those given by persons suffering from a manic-depressive psychosis." He tries to reason these skeptical analogies away, but insists on warning that "both the ecclesiastical authorities and the mystics themselves have always insisted that mystical experience is not necessary to salvation or in itself a proof of sanctity."

In 1941, in his early burst of enthusiasm for the contemplative saints, he had told Ursula Niebuhr that he allowed a little more place than her politically activist husband, Reinhold Niebuhr, did for the "via negativa," the spiritual way of withdrawal from the world into the silence of the monastery or the desert. Now, in effect making belated amends, he is more coolly analytical: mystics who adopted the via negativa, whether or not rewarded with visions, were perhaps "born to command" but rejected their natural destiny because they were aware that "in their case, their gift for power and domination, if exercised, could only bring disaster to others and themselves." Everything he has to say about the vision of God has an irritable tone found nowhere else in his prose. He acknowledged his "Anglican's prejudices," adding dutifully that he "must

* John 1:18 and Matthew 5:8.

pray that the evidence these writers present will refute them." But his phrasing makes clear that, for him, the evidence did nothing of the kind.

=======

In writing of the vision of Eros, Auden suggested unmistakably that "it seems to have happened to oneself," but said nothing more about his own experience. He returned to the subject of Eros in a commissioned introduction to Shakespeare's sonnets written probably early in 1964; this was the first winter of Kallman's defection. From the first sentence, he left no doubt that he would apply sane common sense to a book of poems that had stimulated "more nonsense . . . than any other literary work in the world," but the essay is one of his most troubled, making the kinds of assertion on one page that he said were impossible on another, and bringing to light the harshest details of his private life while insisting that no writer wants to have any such details made public.

He begins by dismissing the various biographical fantasies that purport to describe this or that external event in Shakespeare's life, then dismisses literary biography wholesale, because it is based on research into external events that inevitably reveal nothing of interest about the meaning of a play or poem. The private life of a man of action like a ruler or a general, he continues, provides suitable material for biography, although in the rare case of a writer with an interesting life, a biography can only be justified "provided that the biographer and his readers realize that such an account throws no light whatever upon the artist's work." No amount of research into the lives of Catullus and Lesbia "can tell us why Catullus wrote the actual poems he did, instead of an indefinite number of similar poems he might have written instead, why, indeed, he wrote any, or why those he did were good." Writers want attentive readers and proofreaders, and can be grateful even for the loving care of explicators who see more in a work than the author imagined, but "Not only would most genuine writers prefer to have no biography written; they would also prefer, were it practically feasible, that their writings were published anonymously."

Yet whenever Auden reviewed a literary biography around this time he managed to justify an exception to his disapproval of the genre itself: "It is not often the case that knowledge of an artist's life sheds any significant light upon his work, but in the case of Pope I think it does." "On principle, I object to biographies of artists . . . However, the story of Wagner's life is absolutely fascinating, and it would be so if he had never written a note." "As a rule, I am opposed to biographies of writers, but in Trollope's case, for a number of reasons I approve." In his introduction to the sonnets, having dismissed literary biography as a category, he waited a decent interval of a dozen pages before sketching his own biography of Shakespeare, an inner biography of internal events discoverable not by archival research but through a sympathetic reading of the poetry. It is no less a biography for that:

> I think that the *primary* experience—complicated as it became later—out of which the sonnets to the friend spring was a mystical one . . .
> Though the primary experience from which they started was, I believe, the Vision of Eros, that is, of course, not all they are about. For the vision to remain undimmed, it is probably necessary that the lover have very little contact with the beloved, however nice a person she (or he) may be . . . The story of the sonnets seems to me to be the story of an agonized struggle by Shakespeare to preserve the glory of the vision he had been granted in a relationship, lasting at least three years, with a person who seemed intent by his actions upon covering the vision with dirt.

The bitterness of this final phrase suggests that Auden had in mind his own struggle to preserve the glory of a vision he had been granted in a relationship, lasting at least two years, with a person whose restless eyes and hands seemed intent on destroying both the love and the vision it induced. This was Auden's first allusion to his crisis with Kallman in July 1941 that did not place the blame entirely on himself.*

Auden's character sketch of Shakespeare's friend has the sharp outlines of a portrait drawn from life: "As outsiders, the impression we get of his friend is one of a young man who was not really very nice, very conscious of his good looks, able to switch on the charm at any moment, but essentially frivolous, cold-hearted, and self-centered, aware, probably, that he had some power over Shakespeare—if he thought about it at all, no doubt he gave it a cynical explanation—but with no conception of

---

* He continued to blame himself, however, when he alluded more explicitly to Kallman. In 1966, when the marriage of his young linguist friend Peter Salus was breaking up, Auden sent this avuncular warning:

> I believe our emotional temperaments are very similar. The Tristan-Isolde myth is more dangerous to us than the myth of Don Giovanni. We have—at least I know I have—to beware in our relations with others of becoming emotional leeches—and in this sphere the one who appears to be *giving* the blood may well be the greater leech of the two. (31 May 1966; Berg Collection)

the intensity of the feelings he had, unwittingly, aroused." We know nothing about the final withdrawal of Shakespeare's vision, Auden adds, but by generalizing from one's own experience one can imagine how Shakespeare felt about it:

> In Shakespeare's case, what happened to his relations with his friend and his mistress, whether they were abruptly broken off in a quarrel, or slowly faded into indifference, is anybody's guess. Did Shakespeare later feel that the anguish at the end was not too great a price to pay for the glory of the initial vision? I hope so and believe so. Anyway, poets are tough and can profit from the most dreadful experiences.

In the spring of 1964, probably a few weeks after writing this essay, Auden wrote a dry poem in haiku stanzas titled "Ascension Day, 1964." He was following his usual practice of adding the year to the title of a poem when he wanted to date a private mood as much as a public event—as in "A Summer Night 1933," "Spain 1937," "Autumn 1940," and others.* The poem lets itself be read as a meditation on the annual ritual that recollects Christ's final appearance on earth and withdrawal to heaven, forty days after the Crucifixion. But the language of the poem insists, without explaining why, that *this* withdrawal, in 1964, has a local and specific finality:

> This Thursday when we must
> Go through the ritual
> Formulae of farewell,
>
> The words, the looks,
> The embraces, knowing
> That this time they are final.

Auden had met Kallman on Easter weekend in 1939 and recalled his vision of Eros in an oratorio composed nominally for Christmas. "Ascension Day, 1964" records the end of the vision, and is also the last of his equations of his vision of Eros with the incarnation of Christ:

* "Whitsunday in Kirchstetten," which appears on the page after "Ascension Day, 1964" in *About the House*, lacks a date in its otherwise similar title because it is concerned more with a recurring ritual event than with a unique private one.

Will as we may to believe
That parting should be
And that a promise

Of future joy can be kept,
Absence remains
The factual loss it is:

Here on out as permanent,
Obvious to all,
As the presence in each

Of a glum Kundry,
Impelled to giggle
At any crucifixion.

Everyone, including Auden himself, has the impulse to giggle at the intensity of love. Auden chooses the temptress from *Parsifal* as his specific figure for the spirit of denial who laughs at the Crucifixion and is doomed to loneliness thereafter, a reminder of the Wagnerian enthusiasm he had learned from Kallman. It was an allusion that Kallman, alone among his readers at the time, would have fully understood.

Auden imagined his own response to the Crucifixion in a preface he contributed, probably the same year, to an anthology of poems about Christ on the cross. "We should do well, I think, to try to picture ourselves," he wrote, "in the light of what we know about ourselves, on that day when, as yet, there is no Easter, no Pentecost, no Church, no creed, and the word Christian has not been invented." In his own case,

the most optimistic image I can form is as follows: I am taking an afternoon stroll with a friend, the two of us engrossed in a philosophical argument. Our path takes us past Golgotha, and suddenly, there above us, is a familiar sight— three crosses and a crowd. With a superior sneer I remark to my friend: "Really, it's disgusting the way the mob enjoy such things. Why can't they kill criminals quickly and painlessly by giving them a draught of hemlock, as they did to Socrates?" Then I shut out the disagreeable picture from my mind, and we resume our fascinating discussion on the nature of the Beautiful.

Kundry's glum exile began in the same superior sensibility.

In 1964, Ascension Day occurred on 8 May, when Auden, after a few solitary days in Kirchstetten, had flown to England to receive an honorary degree from the University of Reading. As in earlier years, a special sense of isolation accompanied public honor. He returned to Kirchstetten soon after, and Kallman arrived from his winter in Athens at around the same time. For the rest of Auden's six months in Kirchstetten, he and Kallman were together only about half the time. They spent much of June and July together, interrupted by Auden's brief visit to the United States to receive another honorary degree, this one from Swarthmore. In August they spent a few days together in Thessalonika, where Kallman attended a wedding in his Greek lover's family; Kallman stayed on for a while before joining Auden again in Austria. In September Auden left Kirchstetten, this time not for New York but for six months in Berlin under the auspices of a visiting artists' program sponsored by a foundation.

Auden's first winter since 1928 in Berlin—now a divided city, with many of its familiar places demolished or replaced—prompted him to new explorations of memory. He had not visited Berlin during his official mission in 1945, but had lectured there a few times in the 1950s, always insulated from daily urban experience by the doors of a hotel or conference center. Settled in the suburban flat where the artists' program had placed him, he bought a notebook and began to keep a journal (just as he had done during his first stay in Berlin) in which he interspersed aphorisms on literature and history with notes about his sexuality. (He also kept a journal in late 1939, but it seems to have been destroyed in a fire in a bookshop where he was storing some manuscripts.) About his preference for mutual oral stimulation, for example, he wrote: "To me the act of fucking, whether heterosexual or homosexual, seems an act of sadistic aggression, to submit to it, masochistic, and neither actively or passively have I ever enjoyed it." About his relations with Kallman—and earlier with Isherwood—he made only one elliptical comment:

> The marriage of true minds.* Between two collaborators, whatever their sex, age, or appearance, there is always an erotic bond. Queers, to whom normal marriage and parenthood are forbidden,† are fools if they do not deliberately look for tasks which require collaboration, and the right person with whom to

---

* Auden had also used Shakespeare's phrase as the title of his review of the correspondence of Richard Strauss and Hugo von Hofmannsthal in *The Times Literary Supplement*, 10 November 1961.

† The moral phrasing is deliberate: they are not *impossible* but *forbidden*, because any attempt to achieve them would require inequality and falsehood.

collaborate—again, the sex does not matter. In my own case, collaboration has brought me greater erotic joy—as distinct from sexual pleasure—than any sexual relation I have had.

The vision of Eros had transformed itself, against all odds, into a marriage that survived the end of the vision. After a few days, Auden stopped using the notebook as a journal, though he continued to use it for drafts of prose and verse. He no longer needed to keep a private record of his inner life, because he had begun to say in public everything he wanted to say.

In November and December 1964, early in his stay in Berlin, he wrote "an immense piece," as he called it, for *The New Yorker* on the autobiographies of Evelyn Waugh and Leonard Woolf. "As It Seemed to Us" was his longest and most explicitly autobiographical prose work. "The piece is turning into a hypertrophied monster," he told a friend, "in which my own life plays a large part—a sort of general picture of the first three decades of this century." He added in another letter, "I found myself getting into the act." He organized the review under various rubrics—"Preliminary Chronicle," "Heredity," "Parents and Home Life," "War," "School," "University," "Money," "Religion," "Events and Acts," "Change"—and in each compared his own experiences with those of his two authors. The effect is one of scattered personal comments interspersed among more thorough accounts of other people's lives, but Auden's remarks about himself amount to a somewhat comprehensive narrative of his childhood and youth. Among many personal details he had not previously mentioned in his prose were some that still could cause him legal and other annoyances. He had been befriended by an older man who had given him books and encouraged his poetry, he recalled, but had to meet him clandestinely, "my housemaster having forbidden me to see him, and not without reason, for he was a practicing homosexual" who had "made advances, which I rejected, not on moral grounds, but because I found him unattractive." Yet having insisted that biographies of artists are of no interest because they throw "no light whatever upon the artist's work," he now said nothing about his own work beyond a few dismissive references to "juvenile verses" and "merely derivative" poems written at Oxford.

During 1965 and 1966 Auden wrote a series of haiku about himself that he gathered under the title "Profile." Their quiet undemonstrative tone conceals a technical and ethical problem he confronted by writing them: that of portraying himself from a perspective outside himself—one can-

not see one's own profile without a carefully arranged set of mirrors—
and at the same time describing matters knowable only from inside; the
poem's third-person voice—"He likes giving presents, / but finds it hard
to forget / what each one cost"—is a transparent mask over the first-
person content.* "Profile" is an example of one of the two kinds of
autobiography Auden had imagined a few years earlier, the kind in which
the decisive Quixote-ego observes the acted-upon Sancho-self and portrays that smaller-than-life figure with a deft balance of self-praise and
self-rebuke. "He thanks God daily / that he was born and bred / a
British pharisee" is a plain statement of gratitude for Auden's native
language and middle-class work ethic, but it is also an ironic reminder
of the Gospel's teaching that it was the publican who was justified by his
self-abasing prayer, not the pharisee by his self-exalting one.

In poems he wrote in 1939 and 1940 Auden had made portraits of
himself when young; now he made double portraits of his late-middle-
aged self looking back on his younger self. He had not thought to use
this technique even in a relatively recent poem like "First Things First,"
in 1956, where a day of perfect silence is remembered from an unspecified
past. Now, in "Since" (begun in December 1964 and finished in January
1965), the present moment is "a mid-December day" when

> I abruptly
> felt under fingers
> thirty years younger the rim
> of a steering wheel,
> on my cheek the parching wind
> of an August noon,
> as passenger beside me
> You as then you were.

"Since" is the mirror image of the self-portrait in "Profile," a report
by the Sancho-self about the Quixote-ego. (And the one follows the
other in the pages of *City Without Walls*, the book in which Auden
gathered the poems he wrote in 1965–68.) Its next two stanzas re-create
an August afternoon in 1934 when "geese fled screaming / as we missed
them by inches," driving eastward, "joyfully certain nightfall / would
occasion joy." After a meal recalled in equally devoted detail—"broiled

---

* The poet G. S. Fraser claimed in a review that he had seen an early version written in the
first person, but Auden's drafts (in a notebook in the Berg Collection) are all in the third
person, as are all known typescripts and published texts.

trout / and a rank cheese"—"Love was made then / and there: so halcyoned, / soon we fell asleep."

Between the event and its anamnesis extend two irreversible histories: a lifetime in which other enchantments have blazed and faded; and the history of an age when "War made ugly / an unaccountable number / of unknown neighbors, / precious as us to themselves." Yet the sacred image of "Since" remains untarnished, like the sacred image of earth, which "can still astonish." The solitude of the present is real, but sacred images command that it be ignored:

> Of what then, should I complain,
> pottering about
> a neat suburban kitchen?
> Solitude? Rubbish!
> It's social enough with real
> faces and landscapes
> for whose friendly countenance
> I at least can learn
> to live with obesity
> and a little fame.

The threatening anonymous outsiders of 1956 have been supplanted by the welcoming faces of a decade later, but the alienating gap remains between *I* and *they*.

"Amor Loci," written six months later, returns to the first of Auden's visions, his adolescent vision of Dame Kind. His pocket diary—one of the annual volumes in which he recorded the composition of most of his poems in later years—refers to this as "the Rookhope poem," a place not named in the poem itself. The abandoned mining country near the village of Rookhope, in the Pennine moors, was the most sacred of Auden's landscapes. When he was twelve, as he wrote in "New Year Letter," "In *Rookhope* I was first aware / Of Self and Not-Self, Death and Dread."* The vision he experienced there, he wrote in "The Prophets," pointed toward an adult vision of Eros that the place itself could not name or provide. Now the place takes on a third meaning, pointing no longer toward itself or an incarnate love but toward something entirely outside the world. To a practical or hedonistic or romantic visitor, it offers nothing:

* See p. 118.

To me, though, much: a vision,
not (as perhaps at
twelve I thought it) of Eden,
still less of a New
Jerusalem, but for one
convinced he will die,*
more comely, more credible
than either day-dream.

This new vision is credible because—as always in the paradox of belief
—it can be endorsed only through a private credo that receives no visible
or practical confirmation. It is comely because it offers an analogy between his own love for the place and the possibility of divine love. And
because he loves a place of desolation, he can imagine his own desolation
being loved, despite the dirt that he himself has smeared over the vision
he was once granted.

How but with some real focus
of desolation
could I, by analogy,
imagine a Love
that, however often smeared,
shrugged at, abandoned
by a frivolous worldling,
does not abandon?

Analogy is not identity. At the beginning of this densely subtle poem
Auden confesses the limits of his vision, its exclusive attention to the
nonhuman subjects of the vision of Dame Kind. He can draw the map
of his sacred place by heart, he begins, "but nameless to me, / faceless

---

* Auden had first written about his sense of impending death in the quatrain "Lost," around
1964:

Lost on a fog-bound spit of sand
In shoes that pinched me, close at hand
I heard the plash of Charon's oar,
Who ferries no one to a happy shore.

As in earlier poems, when left alone with his feet, he was reminded of mortality by his corns
(*Collected Poems*, p. 718).

as heather or grouse, / are those who live there." It is that partial love which needs forgiveness from unconditional love.

———

"Convinced he will die," Auden was now prepared to describe to his readers the shape he perceived in his life history. In 1965 his British publisher asked him to compile a new edition of his *Collected Shorter Poems*,* and during the summer he arranged the book autobiographically, starting in 1927, with the earliest poems he wanted to preserve, and ending in 1957. "In the following year," he wrote in a preface, "I transferred my summer residence from Italy to Austria, so starting a new chapter of my life which is not yet finished." And he explained the autobiographical arrangement autobiographically:

> In 1944 when I first assembled my shorter pieces, I arranged them in the alphabetical order of their first lines. This may have been a silly thing to do, but I had a reason. At the age of thirty-seven I was still too young to have any sure sense of the direction in which I was moving, and I did not wish critics to waste their time, and mislead readers, making guesses about it which would almost certainly turn out to be wrong. Today, nearing sixty, I believe that I know myself and my poetic intentions better and, if anyone wants to look at my writings from an historical perspective, I have no objection.

While he divided the last two "chapters" of the book, 1939–47 and 1948–57, at the publicly visible events of his move first to New York and then to Ischia, he divided the first two, 1927–32 and 1933–38, at the invisible private moment of his vision of Agape—no longer quite so private, now that his introduction to *The Protestant Mystics* had appeared. He identified that visionary moment by opening the second chapter with "A Summer Night," though he now omitted the year from its title.

Auden prepared the book by rewriting many of his best-known poems and abridging or discarding others. When he had revised his work for

---

* The first edition of *Collected Shorter Poems*, published by Faber & Faber in 1950, consisted of the 1945 *Collected Poetry of W. H. Auden* (published by Random House), but without the longer works that Faber had kept in print. The original decision to exclude the longer works was apparently made by T. S. Eliot at Faber; Auden merely accepted the segregation of his longer and shorter works without explicitly favoring or disfavoring it.

earlier editions, he had said nothing about the revisions;* now he devoted most of his foreword to a discussion of the moral and aesthetic
education that led him to make them.

> Some poems which I wrote and, unfortunately, published, I have thrown out
> because they were dishonest, or bad-mannered, or boring.
>
>   A dishonest poem is one which expresses, no matter how well, feelings or
> beliefs which its author never felt or entertained. For example, I once expressed
> a desire for "New styles of architecture"; but I have never liked modern ar-
> chitecture. I prefer *old* styles, and one must be honest even about one's preju-
> dices. Again, and much more shamefully, I once wrote:
>
> > History to the defeated
> > May say alas but cannot help nor pardon.
>
> To say this is to equate goodness with success. It would have been bad enough
> if I had ever held this wicked doctrine, but that I should have stated it simply
> because it sounded to me rhetorically effective is quite inexcusable.

More was at stake than aesthetic prejudice in his dislike for modern
architecture. For a conference organized by the World Council of
Churches the following year, he wrote: "To build a modern church,
flooded with cheerful light like an airport, is an utter falsification of what
we really feel; our hearts are not cheerful nor are our heads clear."

Many of Auden's most famous poems—they had become anthology
warhorses—disappeared from the new collection, among them "Sir, no
man's enemy," "Spain," and "September 1, 1939," with their hollow
anticipations of progress. Auden also wanted to discard "Lay your sleep-

---

* He had retrospectively revised his work twice before, once in 1944 for his first collected
edition, and again early in 1957, when he made a selection commissioned by Penguin Books in
London and published in the United States by the Modern Library. For the 1957 selection he
drafted an introductory note in which he explained that the poems were arranged "more or
less in the chronological order of their writing"—although he still kept his secrets by omitting
the landmark "A Summer Night." His Penguin editor asked for a few words about the changes
because "we are only too likely to be attacked by purists pointing out how and where our
edition differs from the Faber versions." Auden replied: "If any reader happens to notice a
difference between the Penguin text and the original, I imagine he will attribute the change to
me, not to Penguin Books. If, however, you think it worth while adding a sentence in my
preface to the effect that some of the poems have been revised, I have no objection" (*Penguin
Portrait*, ed. Steve Hare, 1995, pp. 220–22). In place of the draft note, the finished book contained a two-sentence note which said only that the poems were in chronological sequence and
that "Some of them I have revised in the interests of euphony or sense or both."

ing head, my love"—that glorification of faithless Eros—but Kallman's furious intervention rescued it. Other poems were scarcely recognizable when he finished with them. Anticipating the kind of reviews he in fact was to receive, he wrote: "I have never, consciously, at any rate, attempted to revise my former thoughts or feelings, only the language in which they were first expressed when, on further consideration, it seemed to me inaccurate, lifeless, prolix or painful to the ear." Poems he now found dishonest he rejected entirely; slovenly ones were corrected.

Most of his revisions were improvements that no one noticed. In the earlier texts of "A Summer Night," for example, through the rash happy cries of a child, "The drowned voices of his parents rise / In unlamenting song." Revision brought more euphony: "The drowned parental voices rise / In unlamenting song." A few changes had the doctrinaire quality of a poet willing to sacrifice sense to a strict set of self-imposed technical rules. Earlier versions of a 1938 sonnet about a dead Chinese soldier read: "Abandoned by his general and his lice, / Under a padded quilt he closed his eyes." The new version corrected the rhyme but sacrificed the plain truth that Auden always demanded when he wrote about the art of poetry: "Abandoned by his general and his lice / Under a padded quilt he turned to ice."

Auden's revisions and preface seem driven by an underlying motive to reclaim his poems as first-person utterances of their author. This personal claim irritated many critics, who imagined that poems, once they were published, became the property of their readers. "The words of a dead man / Are modified in the guts of the living," but the author of those words was unwilling to give up his rights to them while he was alive.

Auden had recently learned how easily a reader could modify the words of a poem to serve purposes its author despised. As early as 1944 he had abandoned the stanza in "September 1, 1939" that ended, "We must love one another or die." This line was more widely quoted and admired than perhaps anything else in his work; E. M. Forster said that because Auden had written it, "he can command me to follow him." Taken by itself, the statement was unexceptionable, and had biblical authority to commend it: "He that loveth not his brother abideth in death" (First Epistle to John 3:14). But Auden knew this was not what he had meant, and knew he had written it in the context of a poem in which he argued that love was not a moral choice but a determined, impersonal drive like hunger, and "Hunger allows no choice / To the citizen or the police." This reduction of love to instinct had seemed hateful to him for more than twenty years, and he was left with the guilty feeling that he had unintentionally deceived readers into praising him for a vaguely inspiring sentiment he had never wanted to express. "Between you and me," he told a critic in 1957, "I loathe that poem."

Then, in 1964, one of his readers put the poem to repugnant use before a large public. The advertising consultant who prepared television spots for Lyndon Johnson's presidential campaign—a campaign that accurately portrayed Johnson's opponent as eager to use nuclear weapons while inaccurately portraying Johnson as a committed peacemaker—produced a thirty-second film in which a young girl counted the petals she was picking from a daisy while a male voice-over counted from ten to zero. When the countdown ended, the image of the girl disappeared and a nuclear explosion filled the screen. Over the expanding mushroom cloud was heard Johnson's voice: "These are the stakes: to make a world in which all of God's children can live, or go into the dark. We must love each other or we must die." The dark, the children, and the night, to-gether with the resonant misquoted line, were all lifted from Auden's poem. Auden's new edition of his poems made clear that if others chose to misuse "September 1, 1939," they would do so without his sanction. When his friend Naomi Mitchison complained in a birthday tribute two years later that he had cut "the most essential verse" of the poem in his 1945 collection, Auden wrote (but did not send) this reply: "Surely, I am the best judge of what is essential. At any rate, I expect personal friends like you, my dear, to respect my judgment on poetry, which is a professional's judgment." Mitchison had written that she no longer read Auden as she used to, but that "he may take another jump into what for me would be memorability." Auden replied, "If by memorability, you mean a poem like *Sept. 1st, 1939*, I pray to God that I shall never be memorable again."* In a postscript he disputed Mitchison's view—and the then common view—of the history of his own career: "P.S. Believe it or not, I have got better. Please *try* 'Thanksgiving for a Habitat.'"

After the election, when Johnson proved the lie of his television spot by sending bomber fleets and ground platoons to Vietnam, Auden began to confront the question whether to make a public response to the war. He was immune to the temptation of self-serving protest gestures and alert to the ambiguities of an issue that was generally treated as a simple matter of villains and victims. This led him at first to take a public stance

---

* In 1971, when as his designated literary executor I asked Auden for instructions about possible republication of "September 1, 1939" after his death, he said only, "I don't want it reprinted during my lifetime."

more sympathetic to the war than anything he privately believed. In the early days of antiwar protest, in 1965, he teased his politically pious friends by describing himself as "the only New York intellectual who supports President Johnson on Vietnam." The following year two British writers circulated among dozens of fellow writers a questionnaire about Vietnam (explicitly modeled on the questionnaire on Spain circulated in 1937 by Nancy Cunard with Auden's name among the twelve signatories). Auden's response, remarkable for its moral and historical intelligence, was studiously self-deprecating:

Why writers should be canvassed for their opinion on controversial political issues, I cannot imagine. Their views have no more authority than those of any reasonably well-educated citizen. Indeed, when read in bulk, the statements made by writers, including the greatest, would seem to indicate that literary talent and political common sense are rarely found together.

When asked about political issues in England, Europe, or the United States, he continued, his answer, "however stupid or prejudiced, is at least based in part upon personal knowledge." But he, like any other writer in the West, knew nothing about Vietnam "except what he can glean from the newspapers and a few hurriedly written books."* His conclusion showed he had not forgotten the Stalinists in Spain:

It goes without saying that war is an atrocious corrupting business, but it is dishonest of those who demand the immediate withdrawal of all American troops to pretend that their motives are purely humanitarian. They believe, rightly or wrongly, that it would be better if the communists won.

My answer to your question is, I suppose, that I believe a negotiated peace, to which the Vietcong will have to be a party, to be possible, but not yet, and that, therefore, American troops, alas, must stay in Vietnam until it is. But it would be absurd to call this answer *mine*. It simply means that I am an American citizen who reads *The New York Times*.

He made essentially the same point in letters to friends, but he came to see that he was overcompensating in public for his private contempt for Johnson's policies. Early in 1967, when told he had been awarded the National Medal for Literature, he wrote to a friend that he "was at first

---

* But, as he pointed out to friends, he was able to make a well-educated guess about the probable failure of the American bombing campaign, based on his work in Germany with the Strategic Bombing Survey in 1945. (Some critics of the war cited the survey's finding that German morale had increased during Allied bombing, but they had no effect on policy.)

worried about the award, because I didn't want to receive it in the White House; on the other hand, I did not want to make a Cal Lowell gesture by a public refusal."* After he learned he could receive the award at the Smithsonian Institution, he wrote an acceptance speech that doubled as a sermon on the political misuse of language. He accepted the award, he said, "in the name of all my fellow-citizens of the Republic of Letters, that holy society which knows no national frontiers, possesses no military hardware, and where the only political duty incumbent on all of us at all times is to love the Word and defend it against its enemies."

The "principal enemies of the True Word are two: the Idle Word and the Black Magician," he continued. But the empty chatter of cocktail parties and journalism was not, finally, a serious enemy:

> More deadly than the Idle Word is the use of words as Black Magic. Like the White Magic of poetry, Black Magic is concerned with enchantment. But while the poet is himself enchanted by the subjects he writes about and only wishes to share his enchantment with others, the Black Magician is perfectly cold. He has no enchantment to share with others, but uses enchantment as a means of securing domination over others and compelling them to do his will.

The Black Magician's technique is to reduce meaningful words to meaningless syllables:

> For millions of people today, words like Communism, Capitalism, Imperialism, Peace, Freedom, Democracy, have ceased to be words the meaning of which can be inquired into and discussed, and have become right or wrong noises to which the response is as involuntary as a knee-reflex. It makes no difference if the magic is being employed simply for the aggrandizement of the magician himself or if, as is more usually the case, he claims to be serving some good cause. Indeed, the better the cause he claims to be serving, the more evil he does.

A year later, when the 1968 presidential campaign was in its early stages, Auden wrote to E. R. Dodds: "Vietnam is ghastly. If [Nelson] Rockefeller is nominated, I shall vote for him; if the choice is between Johnson and Nixon, I don't see how one can vote at all." Before this,

---

* After accepting an invitation to a White House arts festival in 1965, Robert Lowell (nicknamed "Cal" for his Caligula-like temperament) changed his mind, wrote a letter of refusal, and gave it to *The New York Times*, which printed it on the front page. Many of Lowell's allies in the antiwar movement regarded the letter as an act of grandstanding that they were obliged to endorse for the sake of solidarity.

Auden had routinely lectured apolitical friends like Lincoln Kirstein on their civic duty to vote for the least bad among the candidates rather than not vote at all. A few months later, in August 1968, when the Soviet Army marched into Czechoslovakia, a few miles away from Kirchstetten, he wrote "August 1968," a poem that in Auden's finest straightforward and compressed style recognizes the oppressor by his voice:

> The Ogre does what Ogres can,
> Deeds quite impossible for Man.
> But one prize is beyond his reach,
> The Ogre cannot master Speech:
> About a subjugated plain,
> Among its desperate and slain,
> The Ogre stalks with hands on hips,
> While drivel gushes from his lips.

The Ogre's inhuman feats of mastery over persons are precisely what make it impossible for him also to "master Speech." The enemies of the True Word were in power in both Moscow and Washington.

By 1972, Auden had long since given up any pretense of indifference. "I thoroughly sympathize," he wrote in a review, "with those draftees who, instead of registering as CO's publicly burn their draft cards or abscond to Canada." His friend Margaret Gardiner, whom he had repeatedly rebuked for her automatic left-wing responses, sent him a petition denouncing the American delays at the Paris conference held by the combatants in Vietnam. His reply was both prescient and humane:

> I can sign the Appeal without hesitation since I am an American citizen. My complaint about our liberal left is that they are not frank enough about what will happen if and when we go. I have myself no doubt whatever that in a short time the Communists will take over South Vietnam. Disgusting as I find our intervention and unpleasant as I think the Saigon regime, I do not think the North Vietnamese are angels of sweetness and light, who care passionately about saving human lives. We ought in the U.S. to be demanding a relaxation of our Immigration laws and other measures, so that those who want to get out of S. Vietnam can.

Almost all the poems Auden wrote in the mid-1960s looked back from a changed present to a vanished past. In 1962, when he wrote "A Short

Ode to a Philologist" to celebrate J.R.R. Tolkien's retirement, he had said nothing about the effect that Tolkien's lectures had on him in the 1920s and nothing about the difference between the 1920s and the 1960s; but in 1965, when he wrote a "Eulogy" for the retirement of Tolkien's Oxford colleague Nevill Coghill, he built the poem on the effect that Coghill's tutorials had on him in the 1920s and on the difference between then and now. His "Lines for Elizabeth Mayer" on her eightieth birthday in 1964 focused on the two issues that now interested him most: the extinct past and the present of personal speech "Where, in singular, / Name may call to Name, / And Name to Name respond, / Untaunted by numerical haphazard." Later poems like "Epistle to a Godson," "Lines to Dr. Walter Birk," "Doggerel by a Senior Citizen," and "A Toast to William Empson" all build their structures of contrast between present and past on the foundations of personal memory.

For the rest of Auden's life, each summer's crop of poems included at least one that looked back over the whole of a life. The first of these, "River Profile," written in 1966, is the greatest poem of his last years, and one of the greatest and strangest poems of its century. Its rapid, stately, and encyclopedic allegory compresses into twelve Sapphic stanzas the course of a river and the course of a life. It begins with the "bellicose fore-time" of a rainstorm and of the sexual act that initiates a life.* Moving downstream from its mountain source, the river soon grows to "a size to be named and the cause of / dirty in-fighting among rival agencies." As it expands, it "bisects a polyglot metropolis, / ticker-tape, taxi, brothel, foot-lights country, / à la mode always."

In writing these metonymic catalogues, each one identifying one of the river's many landscapes, Auden returned to a technique he had last used in "Spain," and improved on the defects of his earlier attempt. In "Spain" events and objects are strung along an unconvincing partisan thread of historical progress, in "River Profile" along a common personal experience of growth and decline. As the river moves south through "flatter, duller, hotter, cotton-gin country," it retraces the course Auden had sketched in "In Memory of W. B. Yeats," in which a river moves through "ranches of isolation and the busy griefs" to "a way of happening, a mouth." In "River Profile" the river's mouth is a place where something fatal happens, as the river, moving slowly

---

* This is the only trace in Auden's published work of his sense of the procreative act as an act of aggression, as he had described it in his journal in 1964. ("Dame Kind" describes loveless matches but not aggressive ones.)

> through swamps of a delta,
> punting-pole, fowling-piece, oyster-tongs country,
> wearies to its final
>
> act of surrender, effacement, atonement
> in a huge amorphous aggregate no cuddled
> attractive child ever dreams of, non-country . . .

And at this moment, in a series of nouns without a verb, those turbid waters are forgiven and transfigured:

> image of death as
>
> a spherical dew-drop of life. Unlovely
> monsters, our tales believe, can be translated
> too, even as water, the selfless mother
> of all especials.

The vast dank waters of the exhausted river evaporate—then return to earth in a newly formed drop of dew filled with microscopic life. This was a more delicate but also more breathtaking image of resurrection than the one he had placed near the end of "Horae Canonicae," when he imagined his risen body coming "to the picnic / With nothing to hide."

The mood of these retrospective poems gradually changed in the late 1960s. The only birthday poem he ever wrote for himself, "Prologue at Sixty," written in 1967, was triumphant and hopeful, while also looking back gratefully on an eclectically international list of eighteen sacred places from his past. (Of these, four were associated with the sacred image of "First Things First" and "Since," and none specifically with Kallman.) Auden also used the poem to remind himself, as before, that in the world around him, "many are famished, few look good, / and my day"—the first-person possessive accepts responsibility—"turned out torturers / who read *Rilke* in their rest periods." (Nazi concentration-camp officers who supposedly read Rilke were a favorite topic in pompous essays on the dissociations of modern times; but Auden recognized the link between Rilke's grandiloquence and institutionalized murder.) The poem speaks confidently across the generational battle lines of the 1960s and, to the question "Can Sixty make sense to Sixteen-Plus?" answers, "In *Acts* it is written / Taste was no problem at Pentecost"— the same miracle of translation evoked in "Whitsunday in Kirchstetten."

Yet as he began to look toward death, Auden also began to think about language as a means of communicating across other kinds of barriers and alienations. At twenty-five, in 1932, he had described writing as a means of communicating with the future, with those who will live after the writer is gone: "Writing begins from the sense of separateness in time, of 'I'm here today, but I shall be dead tomorrow, and you will be alive in my place, and how can I speak to you.' " Now he thought about it as a way of communicating with the dead, and also as a way of anticipating words spoken from a realm entirely outside that of both the dead and the living. In "The Cave of Making," written in 1964, he tells the departed Louis MacNeice, "we need the companionship / of our good dead"; and again in "The Garrison," five years later, personal speech makes it "possible for the breathing / still to break bread with the dead." The last stanza of "Prologue at Sixty" treats the act of speech as part of a conversation in which the answer may not be heard until the last day of all:

> To speak is human because human to listen,
> beyond hope, for an Eighth Day,
> when the creatured Image shall become the Likeness:
> Giver-of-Life, translate for me
> till I accomplish my corpse at last.*

In the second-century Epistle of Barnabas (quoted by Gregory Dix in *The Shape of the Liturgy*) "the eighth day" is the day after the Sabbath day on which God rested, and "the beginning of another world."

A darker, more elusive tone characterizes the next of his backward- and forward-looking poems, "Forty Years On," written in 1968. Here,

---

* The reconciliation of image and likeness resolves the contradiction Auden had in mind in 1941 when he told Ursula Niebuhr his theology was Augustinian, not Thomist. The two terms come from Genesis 1:26: "And God said, Let us make man in our image, after our likeness." Protestant theologians, following Augustine, interpreted the Fall as leaving humanity in the image of God but no longer in His likeness. Catholics, following Aquinas, argued that an *analogia entis* remained, a likeness between God and man that enabled humanity to recognize natural law. Auden may have returned to this issue after reading about its political implications in Gerhard B. Ladner's *The Idea of Reform: Its Impact on Christian Thought and Action in the Age of the Fathers*, first published in 1959 and reissued in paperback in 1967. Ladner described the progress from image to likeness as the heart of the Christian idea of reform, an idea that, "unlike all absolute or total perfectionist renewal ideas," is "characterized by the belief both in ineradicable terrestial imperfection and in a *relative perfectibility* the extent of which is unforeseeable" (p. 31).

as in "Caliban to the Audience," Auden is most himself when concealed in Shakespearean costume. The aging Autolycus, the voice of the poem, looks back to the world of *The Winter's Tale*, which is simultaneously the world of Auden's century. Like "Prologue at Sixty," the poem ends by welcoming death, but unlike the earlier poem, it imagines no resurrection. Autolycus has dreamed the same dream for three nights, a dream "of a suave afternoon in Fall" when he sees "the mouth of a cave by which (I know in my dream) I am to / make my final exit, / its roof so low it will need an awkward duck to make it." Why should that be shaming, he asks when awake: "When has Autolycus / ever solemned himself?" To dispense with solemnity is to accept one's comic, common humanity, but Autolycus' rhetorical question has another, sadder meaning. Auden's daily readings in the *Oxford English Dictionary* would have reminded him that the verb "to solemn" means *to celebrate a marriage*, which Autolycus has never done.

Around 1965 Auden had begun writing the poems about his sexual life intended "for posthumous publication," and he thought, too, about the proper moment for his career to end. "It is my private belief that artists don't die before they have done the work they can do, are meant to do," he told a visitor in 1966. "Even with Mozart you feel, what *more* could he do?" He made an exception for Keats, but, he said, "I feel it strongly" about everyone else: "They die when they have done what they can. Look at Proust, who kept going until the last page, then died." After saying this he dismissed the idea with a shrug: "Perhaps it is pure superstition." But around the same time he was telling friends that he planned to live to be eighty-four, as if he had a precise intention of finishing his work when he had outlived Goethe by a year.

———

In 1967 Auden delivered under the title *Secondary Worlds* the first series of T. S. Eliot memorial lectures at the University of Kent. As he had done in his *Enchafèd Flood* lectures at Virginia in 1949, he used his public prose to tie up the loose ends of matters that had once concerned him but that he was now mostly finished with. At the lectern he elaborately and persuasively stated the theory of first- and third-person language he had learned partly from Rosenstock-Huessy, partly from Kassner; but his poems, meanwhile, were turning toward different kinds of speech. His verse at the time was composed in idiosyncratic yet impersonal styles that sounded like sets of verbal habits rather than a unique personal voice.

Having achieved the first person in the intimate, conversational mode of "Thanksgiving for a Habitat," he was, restlessly and uncertainly, trying for something new.

This shift away from personal speech followed Kallman's withdrawal from their life together in New York. Auden kept his old friends and made new ones,* but he seemed to have lost much of his genius for talk and intimacy. In the winter of 1965–66, a year after his winter in Berlin, he shared his apartment in New York with a serious, literary young man, Orlan Fox, who had been a friend and occasional lover since the winter of 1959–60. Auden had offered Kallman's old room to Fox the summer before, and wanted the arrangement to succeed, but he had lost the habits of a shared, common life, and Fox moved out early in 1966; he and Auden remained friendly, and through Fox Auden began a late, invigorating friendship with the neurologist Oliver Sacks. Meanwhile, his life in New York grew ever more solitary, with ritual weekly dinners with Lincoln Kirstein and Orlan Fox and little else to break his loneliness. (James and Tania Stern, the friends with whom he had felt most at home in New York, had moved to England in the 1950s.)

Some of the poems he wrote in his new impersonal voices were dry works of ceremonial praise, like his formal tributes to Marianne Moore and Nevill Coghill. Other, far more successful ones, were political poems of a kind he had not written before: public meditations on historical events more remote than "August 1968," written entirely in the third person, with no partisan agenda, and all personal meanings deeply concealed. "Partition," written in 1966, recalls the 1947 partition of India through the eyes of its indifferent architect, Sir Cyril Radcliffe (neither India nor Radcliffe is named in the poem, but both are unmistakable specific referents). "Rois Fainéants," written in 1968, evokes the powerless seventh-century child-kings of France who were ruled by the Mayors of the Palace. Both these poems portray a division between private person and public role. The English civil servant in "Partition" knows nothing about the distant nation he arbitrarily and imperfectly divides, and "quickly forgot / The case, as a good lawyer must" before the (unmentioned) massacres that followed the partition; the child-kings, paraded on feast days by the mayors, dead before they were twenty—"May we

---

* In his dedication to *City Without Walls* he wrote of the music critic Peter Heyworth, whom he had met in Berlin in 1964: "At Twenty we find our friends for ourselves, but it takes Heaven / To find us one when we are Fifty-Seven."

not justly call them political martyrs?"—are reduced to public symbols without personal voices. Earlier, when Auden wrote "On the Circuit" in the spring of 1963, his own lecture tours had been the occasion for amused gratitude: "God bless the U.S.A., / So wide, so friendly, and so rich." But now, as he traveled from one college auditorium to another according to schedules drawn up for him by his agents, he felt like a cross between Sir Cyril Radcliffe, on the one hand and, on the other, the interchangeable "Chloter, Chilperic, / Clovis, Theodoric, Dagobert, Childeric."

His poems of the mid-1940s were essays in anxiety, his poems of the mid-1960s essays in alienation. More than ever, he felt himself divided from both a timeless world of the good and a historical world of evil. A poem inspired by *The Penguin Dictionary of Saints* in 1966, "Insignificant Elephants," discarded his old fantasies about contemplative saints and patrons of vocation (most reported saints' lives are "a deal of bosh"; "there never was . . . a *Barbara* to bless the Artillery"), and instead perceived sanctity as occurring in an inner peace that he could only witness incomprehendingly from without. "A hard life, often a hard death . . . are signs which divulge nothing," but all who met the saints "speak / of a Joy which made their own conveniences / mournfulness and a bad smell."* Around this time, Auden began telling friends that he had met two saints, Charles Williams and Dorothy Day. Real saints live in the world of unemphatic reality; the rest of us live as baffled theatrical outsiders who "add the embarrassing prefix *super-* / to a natural life which nothing prevents us / living except our natures."

He gave a novel twist to a more familiar style of alienation in the vigorous jeremiad of "City Without Walls" in 1967. In its first typescript version this was an uninterrupted complaint against a nightmare civilization, neither worldly nor sacred but vague and chimerical, with fantasies of "flesh debased / by damage, indignities, dirty words" instead of "arcadian lawns where classic shoulders, / baroque bottoms, make *beau gestes*"—and perhaps doomed to even greater vaguenesses:

---

* He wrote later the same year about bad smell as a defensive weapon. In "Metaphor," he told his own nose that although he was free to turn it up or stick it into his neighbor's business or otherwise use it to give offense, it was through his nose that his neighbor "With like insolence may / Make me pay." The title "Metaphor" refers to the series of aggressive metaphors that comprise the poem—turn up one's nose, stick one's nose in someone's business, pay through the nose—as well as to the folklore that links the size of one's nose to the size of another organ of aggression (*Collected Poems*, p. 719).

Quite soon computers may expel from the world
all but the top intelligent few,
the egos they leisure be left to dig
value and virtue from an invisible realm
of hobbies, sex, consumption, vague

tussles with ghosts.

But then, before the poem was published, Auden stepped back from it,
enclosed it in distancing quotation marks to indicate its origin in an inner
voice, and added five stanzas in which a second, sharp inner voice tells
the first, "Shame on you for your *Schadenfreude*," followed by a third
inner voice, which, "bored," tells the first two to go to sleep and feel
better at breakfast. The three-person household of the finished poem is
alienated even from its alienation.

Auden composed straightforward satires on public complacency and
delusion, as in the Aesopian "Moralities" he wrote for music by Hans
Werner Henze at the end of 1967 (Kallman had taken offense at Henze
and refused to collaborate), but whenever he let himself sound complacent in his alienation, he did so to emphasize its moral cost to himself.
"The Horatians," written in the spring of 1968, sounds like a calculatedly
modest work of self-praise, a poem not quite about himself but about
those like himself, "natural bachelors / and political idiots" (with the
Greek sense of *idiotes,* a private apolitical individual), rural clergymen,
curators, writers of short poems. The poem ends in the quietly self-
satisfied *credo* of the Horatians, who have learned from the long-dead
Horace to say of themselves:

> "As makers go,
> Compared with Pindar or any

> of the great foudroyant masters who won't stop to
> amend, we are, for all our polish, of little
>   stature, and, as human lives,
>   compared with authentic martyrs

> like Regulus, of no account. We can only
> do what it seems to us we were made for, look at
>   this world with a happy eye
>   but from a sober perspective."

But the Horatians are horrifyingly wrong, and wrong in a way that is clear to anyone who doubts the absolute virtue of the Pax Romana and its American counterpart. Regulus, ambiguously celebrated by Horace in *Odes* 3.5, was tortured and killed by his Carthaginian captors after he advised Rome to continue its war of aggression; in consequence, as he knew would happen, his army was slaughtered with him: "the captives forfeited his pity, / The young men died." Horace, like all other ancient sources, makes clear that this "authentic martyr" also caused the unwilling martyrdom of those under his command. Most modern sources add that the whole story never happened: it was an imperial big lie devised to justify Rome's murder of Carthaginian prisoners by pointing an accusing finger at the victim. As in Auden's essay on detective stories, a corpse disfigures the vicarage garden, but it is now so carefully obscured that the vicar and villagers fail to notice it.

———

For Auden, the self-congratulatory temptations of loneliness were also the temptations of modern scientific and philosophical thought. Both accepted alienation from the truth as if it were the truth itself—a truth obscured by the apparent but accidental patterns of personal relations and public history. In his earlier arguments with his own philosophical sophistication, Auden had agreed that the truth was ultimately inexpressible and unknowable, but maintained his faith in the reality of persons and promises. Now, in lectures, speeches, and broadcasts in 1966 and 1967, he based his argument more modestly on common experience rather than on faith. In the last of his *Secondary Worlds* lectures, an imposing summing up of all he knew about language, he accepted without regret a world in which "objective knowledge of things-in-themselves is not attainable," but he would not accept the modern equivalents of intellectual errors made in the wake of every unsettling discovery from Copernicus to Darwin to Freud: "The conservatives refused to believe that there could be any truth in them, and the radicals drew theoretical and philosophical conclusions which the discoveries themselves did not warrant." The pragmatic conclusion he drew from twentieth-century discoveries was the culmination of all his earlier thought about nature and history, number and face, body and language:

> We seem to have reached a point where if the word "real" can be used at all,
> then the only world which is "real" for us, as in the world in which all of us,

including scientists, are born, work, love, hate, and die, is the primary phenomenal world as it is and always has been presented to us through our senses, a world in which the sun moves across the sky from east to west, the stars are hung like lamps in the vault of heaven, the measure of magnitude is the human body and objects are either in motion or at rest.

The four lectures were all concerned with the secondary worlds of art, not the primary world offered by the senses,* but he closed them with a utopian hope that secondary worlds might become more integrated with the primary one. If this commonsense view of reality were accepted, he said, artists might become both more modest and more self-assured (unlike the nineteenth-century artists who responded to new discoveries either by trying to imitate science through naturalism or by withdrawing into an egocentric aestheticism), and "may develop both a sense of humor about their vocation and a respect for that most admirable of Roman deities, the god Terminus. No poet will then produce the kind of work which demands that a reader spend his whole life reading it and nothing else." In an echo of Barfield's *Saving the Appearances* he added: "There might even be a return, in a more sophisticated form, to a belief in the phenomenal world as a realm of sacred analogies."

Taking up his own suggestion, he wrote "Ode to Terminus" a few months later, in May 1968. Terminus was the same principle of coherence and particularity he had prayed to in 1932, when he addressed a poem to the twin "Lords of Limit." Terminus, "God of walls, doors, and reticence," giver of "games and grammar and metres," grants form and outline to

our Middle-

Earth, where Sun-Father† to all appearances
moves by day from orient to occident,
and his light is felt as a friendly
presence not a photonic bombardment,

---

* He took the distinction from Tolkien's essay on fairy tales, *Tree and Leaf,* but knew that Tolkien had derived it from Coleridge's distinction in the *Biographia Literaria* between the primary imagination that perceives the world and the secondary one that "dissolves, diffuses, dissipates in order to re-create." Both he and Tolkien silently corrected Coleridge's romantic sense of human perception as the representation of "the act of creation in the infinite I AM."

† A year later, in "Moon Landing," he offered similar tribute to the Moon-Mother: "Unsmudged, thank God, my Moon still queens the Heavens / as She ebbs and fulls, a Presence to glop at . . ." (*Collected Poems,* p. 843).

where all visibles do have a definite
outline they stick to, and are undoubtedly
at rest or in motion, where lovers
recognize each other by their surface,

where to all species except the talkative
have been allotted the niche and diet that
become them. This, whatever micro-
biology may think, is the world we

really live in and that saves our sanity,
who know all too well how the most erudite
mind behaves in the dark without a
surround it is called on to interpret.

As in "The Horatians," Auden pretends to celebrate himself as a priest
of Terminus but ends with a hidden rebuke to his self-praise. The final
lines hope that "In this world our colossal immodesty / has plundered
and poisoned, it is possible / You still might save us," for we have
learned—like the Horatians whose final praise of Regulus was taught
them by their master—

that scientists to be truthful

must remind us to take all they say as a
tall story, that abhorred in the Heav'ns are all
self-proclaimed poets who, to wow an
audience, utter some resonant lie.

The literary world of 1968 was well populated with self-proclaimed poets
who had never sacrificed to Terminus, but the closing phrase of the
poem, with its suggestively familiar rhythm, indicates that Auden had
someone else in mind. The poet who, to Auden's disgust, had uttered
some resonant lie was the one who had proclaimed his hope that he
might—as he said in the closing phrase of another poem—show an affirming flame.

Despite the lucid sanity of his verse and prose, Auden felt during these
years that he had written himself into a corner, that he was becoming
alienated not only from other persons but also from the literary past,
from the companionship he sought with the dead. He became sharply
dissatisfied with his styles and subjects, and was again consciously in
search of something new. "He was feeling a bit glum about his work,"

a younger poet recalled after a visit to him late that summer, "and he spoke for some time about his desire to find a new influence from which to bounce off . . . Feebly plucking a name from the air I suggested Clough. 'Clough? No, I've been through Clough,' he replied, 'I was thinking of the Beatles.' " ("Nothing much ever came of that," wrote the visitor who reported this.)

Against his hopes, Auden's universe had disintegrated into isolated, plural, secondary worlds, all of them alienated from the singular primary world. His plural title *Secondary Worlds* emphasized this new mood, and he made the nature of his alienation clear when he titled the last of the lectures in the book "Words and the Word."

He still sought to hear a personal voice nearer, more immediate, than the distant ones to which he had listened for the past few years which spoke in no person at all, being the voices of artifacts, natural objects, and inhuman lives. His poem in memory of Josef Weinheber in 1965 paid tribute to "one who was graced / to hear the viols playing / on the impaled green." His "Eulogy" for Nevill Coghill, the same year, ended with the wish that through Coghill's dreams "the sound / of lapsing brooks" might assure him that he passes muster. By 1967, after he closed "Prologue at Sixty" by writing that it was "human to listen, / beyond hope, for an Eighth Day," he had grown used to listening beyond hope. What he was listening for was something inaccessible to the "touch, taste, sight" that Ferdinand had praised, something he could not hold or possess.

"Bird-Language," written soon after "Prologue at Sixty," in 1967, has the formulaic triviality that afflicted Auden's work when he had not yet worked out what he wanted to say or how to say it. "Trying to understand the words / Uttered on all sides by birds," the listening poet recognizes fear, rage, bravado, lust, but concludes: "All other notes that birds employ / Sound like synonyms for joy." He was withdrawing from his long conversation with the living; he was not yet ready to join the silence of the dead; and the only voices he heard would neither listen nor respond if he answered.

CHAPTER EIGHTEEN

The Concluding Carnival

C arnival is the realm of laughter, the true belly laughter, as Auden called it, "not to be confused with the superior titter of the intellect." It is a realm that "celebrates the unity of our human race as mortal creatures, who come into this world and depart from it without our consent, who must eat, drink, defecate, belch, and break wind in order to live, and procreate if our species is to survive." This, as Auden imagined it, was a unified community whose noises he could join in making and hearing. When he began thinking about Carnival late in 1968 its anarchic energies suddenly renewed his work.

Auden had recognized the body as an image of community in poems written two decades earlier, when he portrayed the body's crucifixion in "Memorial for the City" and "Horae Canonicae." Now he portrayed the body's laughter, and its ignorance of hierarchy, authority, or distinction. After forty years of praise for the antibureaucratic mistrust that everyone, whether peasant or poet, can experience in solitude, he began to write about an antibureaucratic anarchism that everyone can experience together.

Medieval versions of Carnival "persisted in a few places, like Rome, where Goethe witnessed and described it in February of 1788," Auden wrote late in 1969 or early in 1970. He and Elizabeth Mayer had translated Goethe's report in *Italian Journey* eight years before, but he had then thought that Goethe's account of his second Roman visit, which included the description of the Carnival, was "less interesting than the rest of *Italian Journey.*" Now he derived from it a whole theory of the "absolute equality" of Carnival. "During Carnival," Auden wrote,

all social distinctions are suspended, even that of sex. Young men dress up as girls, young girls as boys. The escape from social personality is symbolized by the wearing of masks. The oddity of the human animal expresses itself through the grotesque—false noses, huge bellies and buttocks, farcical imitations of childbirth and copulation. The protest element in laughter takes the form of mock aggression: people pelt each other with small, harmless objects, draw cardboard daggers, and abuse each other verbally.

As Auden imagined it, Carnival was one of three uniquely human realms; the other two were Work and Prayer. "A satisfactory human life, individually or collectively, is possible only if proper respect is paid to all three worlds." The world of marriage, Auden's metaphor and subject for his first twenty years in America, was not mentioned.

Auden's interest had been directed to Carnival by the guardian angel who, he said, always told him what and whom to read next. In November 1968 he was given a copy of Mikhail Bakhtin's *Rabelais and His World* (published in Russian in 1965 but written in 1940), in a translation by Helene Iswolsky, a fellow member with Auden of the theological discussion group The Third Hour. Six months later, in "Epistle to a Godson," the first poem Auden wrote after receiving Bakhtin's book, he asks himself what might be written to succor the young as they embark on their perilous quests, and answers: "to give a stunning / display of concinnity and elegance / is the least we can do, and its dominant / mood should be that of a Carnival." From Bakhtin Auden derived a context and a name for a more extreme restatement of his earlier idea of art as "a perfect balance between Order and Chaos, Bohemianism and Bourgeois Convention." Instead of mere bourgois order, he now wanted stunning elegance and, instead of mere bohemian chaos, irrepressible laughter.

Through the example of Rabelais, Bakhtin explores the multiple voices of Carnival, all those medieval European "forms of protocol and ritual based on laughter and consecrated by tradition" that "were sharply distinct from the official, ecclesiastical, feudal, and political cult forms and ceremonials."* And in his analysis of Goethe's account of the Roman

* Auden used Bakhtin, but also went out of his way to dispute him. In remarks on Carnival to a Columbia University seminar in January 1970 he said: "On the question of blasphemy, I was

Carnival (the translator used the Auden and Mayer translation) he cited examples that Auden now began to quote in his own work.

In August 1968, Auden had begun writing about poetry as an activity outside the law. Autolycus, in "Forty Years On," prospers in a modern bureaucratic world because he provides goods unavailable on the official market:

> A pedlar still, for obvious reasons
> I no longer cry my wares,
> but in ill-lit alleys coaxingly whisper to likely clients:
> *Anything you cannot buy*
> *In the stores I will supply,*
> *English foot-ware, nylon hose,*
> *Or transistor radios;*
> *Come to me for the Swiss francs*
> *Unobtainable in banks;*
> *For a price I can invent*
> *Any official document.*

Autolycus does not speak in the mass voice of the 1968 rebellions— "today's / audience would boo my ballads: it calls for Songs of Protest, / and wants its bawdry straight / not surreptitious"—but a poet of sixty had more in common with sixteen-plus protesters than Auden's stature allowed him to admit. He already imagined, as they did, that the unregimented powers of the body were defenses against incursion: a "Postscript" to "Thanksgiving to a Habitat" warned potential intruders of his personal space, "I have no gun, but I can spit," and in "Metaphor" he warned himself against the flatulent neighbor who could make him pay through the nose for his intrusions. He grumbled at the excesses of the new counterculture but sympathized with its rebellious spirit of play. "The laughter of carnival is simultaneously a protest and an acceptance." The "buttons and beards and Be-Ins" mentioned in "Prologue at Sixty" were, at least at the start, a genuine folk culture, in opposition to the

---

reading a book by a Russian about Rabelais, who tried to think that the private parodies of religious rites were a protest against religious beliefs. But, of course, this is all nonsense. First of all, if the ecclesiastical authorities had thought so, they soon would have stopped it. The fact is that blasphemy, of course, always implies belief, just as literary parody does, as Lewis Carroll pointed out: you can't parody an author you don't admire. It is no accident that carnival comes just before Lent, which is a time for fasting and prayer" (*Columbia Forum*, Winter 1970, p. 48).

manufactured culture of the mass media.* "The mass media today are what the sword was in the past—a compulsive force," he wrote in 1966, and versified the point in a classical distich around 1969: "Alienation from the Collective is always a duty: / every State is the Beast who is Estrangement itself." (Two years later, he added a prose caveat to this argument: "The hippies, it appears to me, are trying to recover the sense of Carnival which is conspicuously absent in this age, but as long as they reject Work they are unlikely to succeed.") In "Ode to the Medieval Poets," written in 1971, he praised "Chaucer, Langland, Douglas, Dunbar with all your / brother Anons" for a Carnival spirit now lost:

> Long-winded you could be but not vulgar,
>
> bawdy but not grubby, your raucous flytings
> sheer high-spirited fun, whereas our makers,
>   beset by every creature comfort,
>   immune, they believe, to all superstitions,
>
> even at their best are so often morose or
> kinky, petrified by their gorgon egos.

He said in a review around the same time, "Basically I have always thought of myself as a comic poet." The years when he wrote about his poems as acts of sacred awe were long over.

Auden first wrote in detail about Carnival in paragraphs that he acknowledged were a digression from the subject of a review. His thin excuse for bringing in the subject of laughter when writing about Loren Eiseley's *The Unexpected Universe* was his suspicion that Eiseley was a melancholic. He ended his digression with both regret and hope: "Carnival in its traditional forms is not, I think, for Dr. Eiseley any more than it is for me. Neither of us can enjoy crowds and loud noises. But even introverted intellectuals can share the Carnival experience if they are prepared to forget their dignity." Eiseley did exactly that when he came across a fox cub and joined it in tumbling play, as he recalled in a passage that Auden quoted at length.

The spirit of Carnival did not, Auden wrote elsewhere, require the personal speech he had written about for decades. As one of his haiku

---

* "My favorite examples" of buttons with printed mottoes, he told James Stern in 1967, were: "Help Stamp Out Reality," "Save Water: Take Showers Together," "Dracula Sucks," and "Marcel Proust Is a Yenta." This was the same letter in which he mentioned he had not wanted to receive the National Medal for Literature at the White House "because of Vietnam."

said: "In moments of joy / all of us wish we possessed / a tail we could wag." To discover Carnival in late middle age was to recover the wordless uninhibited flesh of the newborn: "Why must Growth rob us / of the infant's heavenly / power to bellow?" The visitor to whom Auden had mentioned the Beatles as a possible poetic model said that nothing much came of that; but when Auden found unity and energy in Carnival's anarchic noises, everything came of it.

In "Circe," written in 1969, Auden was willing to admonish the "not-so-innocents" of the 1960s counterculture only because he had already affirmed his sympathy with them. In the absence of laughter, he warned, Carnival darkens into the feast of the daemonic. Most who enter Circe's garden, where "the rose-bushes / have no thorns," are simplified by her into flowers, "sessile fatalists who don't mind and only / can talk to themselves." Any rebellious protest, even a just and spontaneous one, attracts unjust, calculating leaders, and today, again, Circe awards dominion to "a privileged Few, the elite She / guides to Her secret citadel, the Tower / where a laugh is forbidden and DO HARM AS / THOU WILT is the Law."

Carnival can be converted into an instrument of daemonic power because, as Auden's trinitarian formula of Work, Carnival, and Prayer implies, it participates in the sacred. Not long before, reviewing E. R. Dodds's *Pagan and Christian in an Age of Anxiety* in 1966, Auden had complained that Dodds had said little about "my favorite theologian" of the third century, Irenaeus. As he knew, theologically informed readers would recognize Irenaeus as the first theoretician of the body of Christ. And Irenaeus influenced the allegorical meaning of Auden's formula, in which Work, Carnival, and Prayer corresponded to the creative Father, the incarnate Son, and the gift of tongues that marked the descent of the Spirit.

In 1970 and 1971 Auden worked on a long, often magnificent prose piece, "Work, Carnival and Prayer," which he adapted variously for use as a lecture or sermon, and cannibalized for reviews and other short pieces; he did not live to revise it into a full-scale essay, though it is one of his most comprehensive and authoritative prose works, rich in contemporary detail and historical exegesis. At the same time, he began to put his ideas about Carnival into effect. He wrote explicitly on sexual matters for the first time, and mildly rebuked others for their silence about them. Readers familiar with his insistence that biographical details illuminated nothing in an author's work were surprised to find this complaint in his review of J. R. Ackerley's memoir of "his relations with his family and his sex-life," *My Father and Myself*: "Frank as he is, Mr. Ackerley is never quite explicit about what he *really* preferred to do in bed. The omission is important because all 'abnormal' sex-acts are rites of symbolic magic, and one can only properly understand the actual personal relation if one knows the symbolic role each expects the other to play." (This was a public restatement of a theme in a section on "Buggery" in the journal Auden had kept in Berlin in 1929: "Sex relation an act of sympathetic magic like taking Bovril.") About Ackerley's symbolic role-playing, Auden wrote:

> Trying to read between the lines, I conclude that he did not belong to either of the two commonest classes of homosexuals, neither to the "orals" who play Son-and/or-Mother, nor to the "anals" who play Wife-and/or-Husband. My guess is that at the back of his mind lay a daydream of an innocent Eden where children play "Doctor," so that the acts he really preferred were the most "brotherly," Plain-Sewing and Princeton-First-Year.*

At the same time, he also affirmed the importance of the rules and order that Carnival opposed but Work required. In 1942 he had confided to Stephen Spender his hope of overcoming his "fear of independence" by depriving his poetry "of the support of strict conventional forms." Now he thought differently:

> Blessed be all metrical rules that forbid automatic responses,
>   force us to have second thoughts, free from the fetters of Self.

Strict forms were, literally, a blessing, a means of escape from private personality, as the masks of Carnival were the symbol of "escape from social personality."

Having prompted Auden's most successful writing in his last years, the idea of Carnival also prompted his most disastrous self-defeats. He deliberately jettisoned much of his own public dignity, as he had suggested intellectuals should. In 1970 and 1971 his friends noticed he had begun to talk in any company about peeing in the basin, about farting and nose-

---

* Auden told friends and interviewers that he believed he had used these two capitalized terms for the first time in print, and hoped they would appear in the next edition of the *Oxford English Dictionary*; the editors obliged him. The first means mutual masturbation, the second refers to the practice of rubbing oneself between another's thighs.

picking. His victory over his dignity was a Pyrrhic one, but it was a sign of the depth of his isolation that he felt the need for a victory at all.

=====

Auden's last poems are spoken to—not, as before, spoken *about*—silent objects, persons absent or dead, and the untalkative species. In 1969 he wrote "A New Year Greeting" to the microorganisms on his own body, in 1970 "Talking to Dogs," in 1971 "Talking to Mice" and "Short Ode to the Cuckoo." In a more elaborate return to the manner of "You," composed in an earlier period of alienation, he now, in 1971, wrote "Talking to Myself" to his body, and in 1972 addressed "A Lullaby" to himself as he drifted to sleep. He began to invoke legendary nonpersons, like the proverbial German weather god in "Stark bewölkt" in 1971. He addressed Kallman for the last time in verse in "The Garrison" in 1969, and other acquaintances for the last time in two poems in commemoration of retirements: one, "Lines to Dr. Walter Birk," for his Kirchstetten physician in 1970; the other, "A Toast," for William Empson in 1971, when he also wrote his "Ode to the Medieval Poets." In 1972, after writing his lullaby to himself, and during all of 1973, the last year of his life, he addressed no poems at all to living persons. (The one possible exception was the dedicatory haiku he wrote for his last, unfinished book, *Thank You, Fog*, sometime in 1972 or 1973: "None of us are as young / as we were. So what? / Friendship never ages." It was written to the now middle-aged couple of whom the husband had been, long before, the sacred image of "First Things First" and "Since.") Instead, in 1972, he wrote "A Curse" to the automobile and "Ode to the Diencephalon" to the region of the brain—inaccessible to consciousness—that controls automatic responses.* In 1973 he wrote "Thank You, Fog" to fog itself, not to the three friends (James Stern, Tania Stern, and Sonia Orwell) with whom he had shared a fogbound Christmas in England, and then wrote "No, Plato, No"—another of his disputatious addresses to the philosopher he had imagined arguing with in "Grub First, Then Ethics"

---

* Auden wrote the poem after reading *Man's Presumptuous Brain*, by A.T.W. Simeons (1960), which argues that psychosomatic disease results from the conflict of the conscious cortex and the instinctual diencephalon, a conflict occurring only in human beings and caused by the disharmony between the rapid development of the cortex and the slower development of the diencephalon. This idiosyncratic argument had the same appeal that the theories of Gerald Heard and Eugen Rosenstock-Huessy had had, and provided Auden with a scientific analogue to the doctrine of the Fall of Man.

and in his account of the vision of Eros in his essay on mystics. After this, he wrote "A Thanksgiving" to the shades of the poets whose work had educated him from childhood to old age, and "Address to the Beasts," to the whole animal world.

His conversations with living friends in these last years tended to be repetitious and formulaic. But after years of attention to human speech, he composed in 1969 an ambitious "Natural Linguistics," a poem analyzing the grammar of stones, flowers, fish, birds, and mammals: "though some carnivores, leaving messages written in urine, / use a preterite WAS, none can conceive of a WILL." The poem, Auden told Elizabeth Mayer, was "an attempt to do something in the manner and metre" of Goethe's "Die Metamorphosen der Pflanzen," written in a German imitation of the Greek elegiac distich, with alternating dactylic hexameter and pentameter lines. But Goethe's poem was addressed, as Auden's poems no longer were, to a "beloved."* The poem Auden entitled "Loneliness" in 1971—the most explicit of his variations on this theme—predicted an end to his solitude the following day when "Chester, my chum, will return." Yet the poem addresses in the first person only the figure of Loneliness itself, that "Gate-crashing ghost, aggressive / invisible visitor."

Meanwhile, he began reviewing books translated from Russian, after thirty years when, as a matter of principle, he avoided writing about books translated from languages he could not read. (He had made an exception only for two translations of Dostoevsky in the mid-1950s.) The first of these reviews, on Leontiev's essays, began: "Since I know no Russian . . ." He was, in effect, starting to notice unheard conversations across frontiers of mutual incomprehension:

> The fire mumbles on
> to itself, but allows us
> to overhear it.

"Let difference / remain our bond," he wrote in "Talking to Dogs" in 1970, no longer hoping for an answer. His poem "An Encounter," the same year, took for its subject a conversation that, according to tradition, did occur, but whose words cannot be imagined: after the besieged Pope

---

* Auden explicitly refused to follow Goethe's example and "drag some god-damned sweetheart/ in," as he said in "To Goethe: A Complaint." He added, "They never sound as if they mattered" (*Collected Poems*, p. 718).

Leo spoke privately to the invading Attila in 452, Attila withdrew from the gates of Rome forever. "What can Leo have / actually said? He never told, and the poets / can only imagine / speeches for those who share a common cosmos." The speeches Auden listened for in his final years came from outside the cosmos of his daily reality.

But no conversation was too unimaginable to have occurred. "The Aliens," also written in 1970, opens by pointing to the "prohibitive fracture / empathy cannot transgress" between human beings and insects —"nine-tenths of the living"—and by contrasting that gap with the neighborliness that human beings can share with other beasts and even with plants. Plants respond to the gardener's handling as if to a teacher; beasts seem aware of more than their instincts; and "in our folk-tales, / toads and squirrels can talk, in our epics the great be compared to / lions or foxes or eagles." But insects are utterly different from all these. "They daunt alike the believer's / faith in a fatherly providence and the atheist's dogma of purely / random events." They have no experience of a continuous self: their metamorphoses "must do havoc to any / unitive sense." The poem tactfully does not mention that the same havoc had recently been done to humanity's unitive sense by the skepticism that Auden elsewhere acknowledged as a half-truth too easily confused with the whole.

To explain the existence of insects, "one is tempted to cook up a Gnostic / myth of an earlier Fall, preceding by aeons the Reptiles." In that earlier fall, the Seducer is "not our romantic Satan but a clever cartesian Archon," a voice without a face, a modern technocrat who offers a bewildered crablike Adamic creature a release from anxiety into a world of determined certainty:

> Freedom may manage in Heaven with Incorporeals, but for
> ghosted extended matter the consequence is to be doomed to
> err where an error is mortal. But trust me and live, for I *do* know
> clearly what needs to be done. If I program your ganglia for you,
> you shall inherit the earth.

"Such a myth, we all know, is no answer," the poem disingenuously proceeds, having established a parallel with the political temptations of the present day. What insects "mean to themselves or to God is a meaningless question, / they are to us quite simply what we must never become." And the vocabulary of the poem quietly argues that the temptations of the present are the same as those that in the past were repeatedly confused with promises of salvation.*

Great poets were not exempt from that confusion. A few weeks before Auden began work on the poem, he wrote to a friend: "Have been re-reading *Paradise Lost*. What an unchristian book!" Auden preferred wrestling with un-Christian themes to repeating pious ones, and his poem about the insects is laced with phrases from Milton's. (He said some years earlier about Milton: "I find it much easier to enjoy the poetry of writers whose beliefs I disagree with.") The opening phrase, "Wide though the interrupt be that divides us," adapts "Wide interrupt" (*Paradise Lost*, 3.84, where "interrupt" is an adjective not a noun); Auden's "utterance, joy and collateral love" quotes Milton's "collateral love and dearest amity" (8.426); and the Seducer's speech parodies the dream whispered by the romantic Satan into Eve's ear. A year later, in "A Toast," Auden wrote that in all of William Empson's work he could only fault "your conceit that Milton's / God, obtrusive prolix baroque Olympian, / is our Christian one." He could forgive Empson his "conceit" because Empson was attacking an idea of the Christian God that was as widespread as it was false. "Only modern science," Auden wrote in one of his last book reviews, about the Russian philosopher P. Y. Chaadayev, "could have finally buried that god in whom many people who thought themselves Christians had undoubtedly believed, namely, a Zeus without Zeus's vices. It is only recently that we have learned that we cannot speak of famines, plagues, lightning as 'Acts of God.' "

Auden had long since given up any idea of historical providence, or of a god who intervened in human history to bring about some final justice, but he had not given up the idea that "Acts of God" were in some sense real. In 1972 he wrote "Unpredictable but Providential," a meditation in leisurely hexameters and long sentences on evolutionary biology, and dedicated it to Loren Eiseley. He told E. R. Dodds that he "wanted to see if I could manage a 'Lucretian' poem," but the poem's implications subtly modify the materialism of *De rerum natura*. Overturning Auden's old ideas about nature as the realm of cyclical, involuntary behavior, the poem reimagines it as the realm of freedom, experimentation, and "ir-

---

* An earlier poem on a similar theme, "Bestiaries Are Out," written in 1964, recalled the moral example made in past centuries of ants and bees, an example no longer possible because, now that "Research has demonstrated how / they actually behave, they strike us / As being horribly unlike us." The poem was also an elliptical warning, because "some believe (some even plan / To do it) that from Urban Man, / By advertising plus the aid / Of drugs, an insect might be made" (*Collected Poems*, p. 739).

ritable" relations between self and not-self. The title is the only explicit suggestion that the natural world is affected by Providence even if the historical world is not, and the poem seems to contradict this by referring to the moment when inanimate matter first became animate as "the first / genuine Accident." But "accident" has both its ordinary meaning and the scholastic meaning of a property not essential to the substance it occupies—like the love that Auden had referred to as "an / Accident occurring" in the substance of the double man. The *Oxford English Dictionary*, always consulted by Auden while writing his later poems, observed that the word was applied in scholastic theology "to the material qualities remaining in the sacramental bread and wine after transubstantiation; the essence being alleged to be changed, though the accidents remained the same." Two lines later in the poem, the matter transubstantiated into life is called "some Original Substance," a variation on the scholastic *substantia prima*, the unique singular thing in which accidents inhere, and which, according to the first of the *OED*'s illustrative quotations, identifies "every singular person or proper name."

Thirty years earlier Auden had written that the individual who desires maturity must go on alone; now (using an argument borrowed from Eiseley) he imagined evolution in the same terms:

> As a rule, it was the fittest who perished, the mis-fits,
> forced by failure to emigrate to unsettled niches, who
> altered their structures and prospered.

The poem anthropomorphizes even geological events—the protocontinent "Gondwana / smashed head on into the under-belly of Asia"— and treats them as fortunate "catastrophes" that "only encouraged experiment." Calling attention to its own metaphoric language, the poem insists that its statements are fictions. But so, it says, are statements that claim to be objective and rational:

> Science, like Art, is fun, a playing with truths, and no game
> should ever pretend to slay the heavy-lidded riddle,
> *What is the Good Life?*
>   Common Sense warns me of course to buy
> neither but, when I compare their rival Myths of Being,
> bewigged Descartes looks more *outré* than the painted wizard.

"My private title is *Contra Monod*," Auden told Dodds in his letter about this poem, referring to the molecular biologist Jacques Monod, author of *Chance and Necessity*, a chilly reductionist work of popular science much discussed at the time, which argued that living things were in every respect the product of random events and physical laws. In another poem, "Talking to Myself," Auden treated his own birth as a subject for interpretation by Monod's myth and his own:

> A random event, says Science.
> Random my bottom! A true miracle, say I,
> for who is not certain that he was meant to be?

His answer to Monod is a carnivalesque assertion that he can refute randomness through his first-person statement of disbelief in it, much as Johnson refuted Berkeley. Yet after beginning his credo as a declarative statement, he is careful to end it as nothing more assertive than a rhetorical question.

Most of Auden's affirmations were accompanied by a negating counterpoint. The mirror image of Carnival was the alienation he acknowledged in the act of denying it. "Me alienated? Bosh!" So he wrote near the end of his "Doggerel by a Senior Citizen," a catalogue of the alienating aspects of "Our earth in 1969." The unalienated world was the one remembered from childhood, which still "gives me strength / To hold off chaos at arm's length":

> Reason requires that I approve
> The light-bulb which I cannot love:
> To me more reverence-commanding
> A fish-tail burner on the landing.

The claim he makes in the poem's final lines is that he is not alienated at all, that he merely feels "Most at home with what is Real." But the real world, as he had written repeatedly, is or should be the shared world presented by the senses, and this poem admits that his private reality had separated itself from the shared reality of the present. When, in 1969, he compiled his annotated commonplace book, *A Certain World*, he closed it with a theology of the real:

What the poet has to convey is not "self-expression," but a view of reality common to all, seen from a unique perspective, which it is his duty as well as his pleasure to share with others. To small truths as well as great, St. Augustine's words apply.

"The truth is neither mine nor his nor another's; but belongs to us all whom

Thou callest to partake of it, warning us terribly, not to account it private to ourselves, lest we be deprived of it."

Once again, he was stating in his prose an article of faith while confessing in his poems that he could only partly live up to it. At the same time, he was writing poems that were radically skeptical in their approach to the reality he lived in. Addressing the microorganisms on his skin, in "A New Year Greeting," written in 1969, he wondered about the faith with which they in their world would account for the real world presented to them by their senses:

> If you were religious folk,
> how would your dramas justify
>   unmerited suffering?
>
> By what myths would your priests account
>   for the hurricanes that come
> twice every twenty-four hours,
>   each time I dress or undress,
> when, clinging to keratin rafts,
>   whole cities are swept away
> to perish in space, or the Flood
>   that scalds to death when I bathe?

The poem presents itself as a witty play on the relativity of scale while, under its breath, it calls into question everything that Auden publicly claimed to believe.

Auden recognized and refused the delusive pride that justifies alienation and thereby intensifies it. "A Shock," in 1971, records the shock to his vanity when he was frisked for weapons at the Vienna airport like everyone else. The poem poses as an old fogey's complaint that "Our world rapidly worsens: / nothing now is so horrid / or silly it can't occur." But the opening line—"Housman was perfectly right"—confesses that the same complaint had been voiced by an old man who died thirty-five years earlier, and by old men at all times. The poem protests that the least likely person to bear a weapon is its author,

> upper-middle-class me,
> born in '07 when Strauss
> was beginning *Elektra*,
> gun-shy myopic grandchild
> of Anglican clergymen,

> suspicious of all passion,
> including passionate love,
> day-dreaming of leafy dells
> that shelter carefree shepherds,
> averse to violent weather,
> pained by the predator beasts,
> shocked by boxing and blood-sports . . .

All true. But the idyllic prewar era of 1907 is identified as the moment when Strauss began the most violent and shocking of his operas, his most unsettling portrayal of murder and madness. As for Auden's clergymen grandfathers, he had recently written that one of them "was evidently a sadist," and he had acknowledged in "Prologue at Sixty" that among his more distant Norse ancestry, "Rapacious pirates my people were." He had spent half his career insisting on the Arcadian's guilt, the blood of the victim whom the Arcadian would prefer to forget, the savage dogs and mantraps favored by those who prefer their nature benign. The last lines of the poem point precisely to the egoism that, in those not protected by upper-middle-class comforts and constraints, calls for blood.* The shock of the title occurred, the poem reports,

> when I, I, I, if you please
> at Schwechat Flughafen was
> frisked by a cop for weapons.

In the only trinity worshiped by this poem, all three persons are named *I*.

———

In his poems and essays, Auden's real world continued to overlap with the worlds of his readers, but in his life, it receded irretrievably into the past. In 1969 he began lobbying his Oxford college, Christ Church, for a place to live like the rooms in Cambridge that E. M. Forster had been given by King's College. His terror of the English had evidently abated; he no longer needed distance from England to resist the temptation of public status or the insularity of literary London; in his mirror he saw a

---

* In "Talking to Mice," another poem written in 1971, Auden explained, but did not justify, the mousetraps he was driven to install in order to maintain a civilized household. "We had felt no talent to murder, / it was against our pluck. Why, why then? For *raisons d'État*. As / householders we had behaved exactly as every State does, / when there is something it wants, and a minor one gets in its way."

born-and-bred British pharisee. Thirty years after he had turned away
from the familiar English categories of social class by moving to
America—where his bohemian hygiene, bourgeois timetable, and aristocratic aesthetics combined to refuse any intelligible status—he had begun to reaffirm his membership in the vanished social class of his
childhood. He closed "Marginalia," written in haiku and tanka from 1965
through 1968, with this:

> The class whose vices
> he pilloried was his own,
> now extinct, except
> for lone survivors like him
> who remember its virtues.

And he wrote in "Doggerel by a Senior Citizen" in 1969:

> My family ghosts I fought and routed,
> Their values, though, I never doubted:
> I thought their Protestant Work-Ethic
> Both practical and sympathetic.

These poems treat lightly the survivor's guilt of "The Sea and the Mirror," but their metaphors suggest, against all reason, that the class he
fought is extinct *because* he fought it.

In his first revitalized months in the United States, in 1939, Auden had
written elegies for masters and friends. In the last years of his life he
wrote elegies for himself. The 1967 "Prologue at Sixty" ended with a
single line about his own death: "till I accomplish my corpse at last."
After 1969, his every third thought was of the grave. At the start of his
career, his poems had evoked a doomed country of defunct machinery
and obscure betrayals, and now, at the end, they settled into the doomed
country of his own body, where the obscure betrayer was hidden deep
within himself.

"A New Year Greeting" anticipated the doom of the microorganisms
on his skin as a moment when he, not they, would be judged:

> Then, sooner or later, will dawn
> a day of Apocalypse,
> when my mantle suddenly turns
> too cold, too rancid, for you,
> appetizing to predators

> of a fiercer sort, and I
> am stripped of excuse and nimbus,
> a Past, subject to Judgement.

"Talking to Myself"—the closing poem in his book *Epistle to a Godson*—ended by foreseeing the end of his long relation to his body. It had been years since he had used marriage as a metaphor or theme, but now he wrote:

> Time, we both know, will decay You, and already
> I'm scared of our divorce: I've seen some horrid ones.
> Remember: when *Le bon Dieu* says to You *Leave him!*,
> please, please, for His sake and mine, pay no attention
> to my piteous *Don'ts*, but bugger off quickly.

The last phrase suggests a Carnival refusal of dignity even at the end. But two months later, in "Ode to the Medieval Poets," Auden wrote of "my sad flesh" that, despite its sadness, the carnivalesque poets could still transitively "chuckle."

He now began to set his work in order with a greater urgency than he had felt before. Since 1930 he had published a new collection of short poems once every five years, and had deviated from this schedule by no more than a year.* After 1969, books of his short poems appeared at narrower intervals. *Epistle to a Godson*, with his poems of 1969–71, was published in 1972, only three years after *City Without Walls*. When he died in 1973 he had already prepared the title page, dedication, and perhaps two-thirds of the poems for another book, *Thank You, Fog*. Around 1970 he wanted to gather a new selection of essays under the title *Forewords and Afterwords*, but, as he told friends, he had never bothered to keep copies of his prose or remember what he had written. He appointed his literary executor in 1972—I had recently compiled at his request a tentative table of contents for *Forewords and Afterwords*, a list that he made his own by cutting some essays and adding others—and went out of his way to specify the changes he wanted to make in a future edition of his collected poems. He typed out new versions of poems he had discarded from earlier collections and now wanted to restore, but he

---

* The deviations were *On This Island* in 1936 and *Nones* in 1951, each a year later than the norm, and *City Without Walls* in 1969, a year early. His 1945 *Collected Poetry* included shorter poems of 1940–44 that would otherwise have gone into a separate book.

never mentioned his plans to his agents or publishers, and seemed content to let the edition be a posthumous one.

Night thoughts dominate the poems he wrote in 1972. When he addressed "A Lullaby" to himself, he used the language of finality when writing about sleep: "Let your last thinks all be thanks." (He had used sleep to refer to death in "Old People's Home" in 1970, when he wished for "a speedy / painless dormition" for the aged Elizabeth Mayer, now one of those "assigned to a numbered frequent ward, stowed out of conscience / as unpopular luggage.") "A Lullaby" looked forward to endings, completions, and a state beyond all resentment:

> For many years you envied
> the hirsute, the he-man type.
> No longer: now you fondle
> your almost feminine flesh
> with mettled satisfaction,
> imagining that you are
> sinless and all-sufficient,
> snug in the den of yourself.

The symbolic magic of Auden's sexual life, as he did not quite say in his review of Ackerley's memoir, was the means by which he sought to recover the pre-Oedipal relations of mother and son. Now he no longer needed that magic, for his sleeping self was both "*Madonna* and *Bambino*." Later in 1972, when he contemplated the night stars in "Nocturne," he saw in their motions the visible metaphor of a state of final rest:

> How else shall mannerless minds
> in ignorance imagine
> the Mansion of Gentle Joy
> it is our lot to look for . . . ?

When he had tried to imagine the same mansion a quarter-century earlier, he heard the murmur of underground streams and saw a limestone landscape.

Early in 1972 his wish to return to Oxford was rewarded when Christ Church offered him at low rent a cottage in its grounds, starting in the autumn. When Cecil Day-Lewis died in May, British journalists speculated that Auden, after his return to England, would be the leading candidate to succeed Day-Lewis as poet laureate. The appointment was politically and legally impossible—his departure in 1939 had still not been forgiven, and the laureate was required to be a British subject—but Auden's agent speculated to a reporter that he would be willing to change his citizenship if the post was offered. Auden wrote an indignant letter to *The Times*, saying, "Even if I coveted the post, which I don't, to do such a thing for such a motive, I should regard as contemptible." This did not stop him from speculating on the literary and civic challenges that the laureateship might offer. He told a reporter during a brief visit to London in June: "When the Duke [of Windsor] died, I thought about what I would write if I had been Poet Laureate. It would have been a difficult task; and my sympathy would have gone out to anyone asked to undertake it. But it would have been fun to write, as the Duke was a controversial figure." The laureateship, he continued, would be worth having only if there could be "a very firm understanding that the Poet Laureate could write on controversial issues as well as the traditional ones." As for the pleasures of the job, he would prefer not to write on the investiture of the Prince of Wales, but to write instead a poem of thanksgiving that no disaster had occurred when, a few months before, the Prince's feet got caught in the rigging of his parachute as he made his first jump. The Autolycus of "Forty Years On" found the one public role perfectly suited to his background, skill, and temperament when there was no hope of achieving it.

At the end of the summer of 1972 (a summer in which he had energetically pulled strings to gain money and contacts for Joseph Brodsky, newly exiled from the Soviet Union) Auden returned briefly to New York from Kirchstetten, cleared out the rented apartment he had lived in ever since 1953, and moved back to England. He was at first exhilarated by his return to Oxford in October, but within a few days he was burgled by a laborer whom he had given money a few hours earlier in a quest-hero's gesture of generosity. And within a few weeks he was writing to American friends that Oxford was noisier and more crowded than New York. The dons who had arranged for him to live in Christ Church expected to find him as sociable and receptive as he had been in his years as a professor. Instead, his sometimes hortatory, sometimes carnivalesque attempts at conversation made no friends among the older dons, although some younger ones and undergraduates—especially those interested more in science than in literature—found him approachable and engaging. But he was unhappy, and became miserable; he quickly made arrangements to spend a few weeks teaching and lecturing in New York the following winter, partly in hopes of finding a temporary means of escape.

In the spring of 1973, when he returned to Kirchstetten and began writing poems again, he made a point of insisting that he still wanted to live—a wish that had never been in question before. "This sub-lunar world is such fun," he wrote in "No, Plato, No"; he could imagine nothing he would less like to be "than a disincarnate Spirit, / unable to chew or sip / or make contact with surfaces / or breathe the scents of summer / or comprehend speech and music / and gaze at what lies beyond." But he could imagine that his body, which in "Nones" had restored the order he tried to destroy, had now begun to prefer entropy and disorder instead:

> yes, it well could be that my Flesh
>   is praying for "Him"* to die,
> so setting Her free to become
>   irresponsible Matter.

"What is Death?" he had asked in a haiku a few years earlier. "A Life / disintegrating into / smaller simpler ones."

By now Auden's recollections of the past were taking on an air of finality. He told a friend that he was thinking of writing an autobiographical narrative in verse along the lines of Wordsworth's *Prelude*, but he lived long enough only to write a miniature sketch (which is conceivably all that he ever intended) in the form of the retrospective lyric "A Thanksgiving," a poem that looked back at his poetic masters from the perspective of one who had come full circle. In the opening lines he remembered a childhood when he "felt / that moorlands and woodlands were sacred: / people seemed rather profane." Near the end of the poem, after excursions into love, politics, and religion, "Nature allures me again." The "tutors I need"—he never outgrew the pupil— were now Horace and "*Goethe*, devoted to stones, / who guessed that —he never could prove it— / Newton led Science astray." The poem itself adapts the alternating iambic and amphibrachic trimeters of Goethe's "Gegenwart," but the "presence" that Goethe celebrated in his poem was again that of a beloved to whom all nature pays homage,

---

* The pronoun is the only name the feminine flesh has for the masculine spirit.

while the absences in Auden's poem are those of poets and thinkers, one
of them a Goethe devoted more to stones than to lovers.

In "Address to the Beasts," written a few weeks later, Auden closed a
catalogue of the differences between his own species and all other animal
species by anticipating their joint future:

> Distinct now,
> in the end we shall join you
> (how soon all corpses look alike),
>
> but you exhibit no signs
> of knowing that you are sentenced.
> Now, could that be why
>
> we upstarts are often
> jealous of your innocence,
> but never envious?

Among the many valedictory poems he wrote in this last summer of his
life was one with the ambiguous title "Posthumous Letter to Gilbert
White." He had not called his long earlier poem to Byron a "Posthumous Letter."

===

In his last years Auden found his double theme in the isolating particularity of the human person and the wish to overcome it first in Carnival,
finally in ritual. His name for that particularity was "oddity," a word he
used to mean both uniqueness and strangeness, as in the "Divinity so
odd" in "Friday's Child." (Of the dozen book reviews he wrote in 1973,
three have "odd" in their typescript titles: "An Odd Ball," on Chaadayev; "An Odd Ball in an Odd Country in an Odd Time," on St. John
of the Cross; and "An Odd Fish," a review on Heinrich Heine left unfinished at his death.) The last poem he wrote for publication, "Archaeology," was another attempt to read the unreadable, a speculation on
artifacts whose true meaning can never be known. The spade of the
archaeologist finds evidence

> of life-ways no one
> would dream of leading now,

concerning which he has not much
to say that he can prove:
the lucky man!

The archaeologist, like Goethe in opposition to Newton, guesses at what
he cannot prove. "Guessing is always / more fun than knowing" because
guessing is a first-person act of sympathetic participation, while knowing
something that can be proved is an instrumental act that holds power
over the thing known. We cannot know the invisible feelings of the
dead, and the verb Auden chooses to signify the knowing we cannot
have points to the impulse behind our desire to know: we "cannot *conceit*
/ in what situations they blushed / or shrugged their shoulders." Guessing, like faith, credits the evidence of things not seen, and this poem
professes its faith that the unimaginable dead were no more deceived by
their myths than Auden and his contemporaries are deceived by ours:

When Norsemen heard thunder,
did they seriously believe
Thor was hammering?

No, I'd say: I'd swear
that men have always lounged in myths
as Tall Stories,

that their real earnest
has been to grant excuses
for ritual actions.

The poem has by this point shifted quietly from artifact to myth and
from myth to ritual, from the kind of research that yields the researcher
none of the egoistic satisfactions of proof, to the ritual acts of worship
in which all egoistic demands are silenced by an altogether different kind
of solace:

Only in rites
can we renounce our oddities
and be truly entired

"Entired," as a verb, is one of many instances, among the poems
written during Auden's final summer, of a verbal oddity that signifies a
larger unity. Like "verse" and "home" used as verbs in "A Thanksgiv-

ing," and "worlded" and "adulted" in "Address to the Beasts," it looks
like an arbitrary malformation, an eccentric attempt to add another verb
of action to the language. But, like all these other odd-seeming usages,
"entired" has a long history, which Auden found in the *Oxford English
Dictionary*. His language and meaning return to the theme of shared
worship in "Horae Canonicae" and "Whitsunday in Kirchstetten," but
the common acts of the body are left unmentioned in his evocation of
"ritual actions," and his acts of linguistic anamnesis now had meanings
that were mostly private to himself and to other excavators in the *OED*
—unlike the evocative archaism of his echoes of Old English in earlier
poems. As soon as he uses words for ritual purposes, he reminds himself
that ritual is not enough:

> Not that all rites
> should be equally fonded:
> some are abominable.
>
> There's nothing the Crucified
> would like less
> than butchery to appease Him.

In the same poem in which he withdraws from Clio's realm of history
to the timeless realm of ritual, he remembers the historical act of murder
that ritual is tempted to mythologize and forget.

Auden appended to this poem a "Coda" of three haiku that evoke a
unified continuity, one to which both good and evil rituals could only
point from outside. From the artifacts of archaeology the poem concludes that

> our school text-books lie.
> What they call History
> is nothing to vaunt of,
>
> being made, as it is,
> by the criminal in us:
> goodness is timeless.

In September 1973, during the weeks before he was scheduled to leave
Kirchstetten, Auden worked with Kallman on the last of their dramatic
collaborations, "The Entertainment of the Senses," commissioned by the
composer John Gardner as the text of a modern antimasque to be in-

terpolated in a performance of James Shirley's seventeenth-century masque *Cupid and Death*. Auden and Kallman wrote their text for five apes, each representing one of the senses, each describing with energetic disgust the artificial, intrusive satisfactions offered to the senses in the twentieth century. The ape of Hearing tells his combustion-engine-propelled listeners: "Accelerate, accelerate, / Show your decibel power / At a hundred an hour . . . / Come, girls and boys, / More noise, more noise! / Yell while you can and save / Your silence for the grave." The grave is the last thing named in each of the five speeches, and after the apes are done, the Chamberlain who brought them on stage states the moral of the work: "Be with-it, with-it, with-it till you're dead."

On 28 September 1973, a few days after they finished the antimasque, Auden and Kallman closed up their house in Kirchstetten (Auden had transferred ownership to Kallman a few years earlier to avoid legal complications after his death) and spent the evening in Vienna. Auden expected to fly the next day to England, where he no longer wished to go, and Kallman expected to fly to Greece, where Auden had never wished him to be. Earlier that month Auden had told a friend that he was "beginning to feel my age," that his mind "still seems to function as it should, thank God, but my body gets tired very easily." His Austrian doctor had diagnosed "a weak heart, whatever that means." What it meant was that Auden, having decided to live until he was eighty-four, had at the age of sixty-six used smoke and drink to force his body (as his New York doctor had warned him he was doing) into the condition of an eighty-four-year-old man.

He died in his hotel bed on the same night he arrived in Vienna, and he was buried five days later in Kirchstetten, on the morning when he had planned to arrive in Oxford after a brief stay in London. The last verse he wrote, a day or two before he left Kirchstetten, was a haiku that Kallman, horrified, insisted he destroy:

> He still loves life
> but O O O O how he wishes
> the Good Lord would take him.

The wish he had attributed to his flesh a few months earlier in "No, Plato, No" was now his own. But he could not pray for his own death without simultaneously defying death through the craft that makes a permanently enduring object. The haiku looks as if it is marred by a forbidden eighteenth syllable, but as Auden told Kallman, it conforms to the Latinate rule (which governs most of his syllabic poems) that adjacent vowels are elided and that two syllables joined by adjacent vowels count as one. "O O O O" counts as three syllables, not four—they are scanned as three pairs of adjacent O's, the first two, the middle two, and the last two—and the ancient haiku form is preserved against change.

＝＝

When Auden's papers were sorted after his death, it was found that he had sent off for publication almost all the poems he wrote in his final summer, but had held back one page of verse. This contained a group of five haiku headed "Addenda to *Profile*." He evidently intended them for his future volume of collected poems, where they would appear below the oblique self-portrait he had written in "Profile" seven years earlier. They constituted his final summary version of himself, and they ranged over the same subjects he had named in "Marginalia" when he wrote: "His thoughts pottered / from verses to sex to God / without punctuation."

The order of the five was deliberate; when he inserted a handwritten haiku among the four on the original typescript, he placed it following the first haiku instead of appending it at the end. These first two haiku on the finished page pointed to his acceptance of his weakness and to the persistence of his loyalty, even past all hope of marriage:

> In anxiety dreams,
> at the moment he gives up hope,
> he ejaculates.

> By nature monandrous,
> he finds it hard to desert
> a piece of trade.

The third linked even his wordless noises to the alphabetic signs through which he apprehended the world:

> In a coughing-fit
> he felt he was throwing up
> hard Capital *F*'s.

The rhetorical question he posed in the fourth haiku was a summary form of the Madonna-Bambino themes of his late lullabies to himself:

Why, when passively borne
by train or car, does he feel
less urge to smoke?

He reserved for the fifth and last haiku the theme that had quietly become his greatest concern during his last years, when he wrote less and less about speech, his lifelong subject, and more and more about hearing.

Since his conversion in 1940 he had thought of prayer as a rite of homage, as words of praise spoken in the second person. Around 1970, when he wrote "Work, Carnival and Prayer," he offered a different definition of the third term in his title.

As an antidote to pride, man has been endowed with the capacity for prayer, an activity which is not to be confined to prayer in the narrow religious sense of the word. To pray is to pay attention or, shall we say, to "listen" to someone or something other than oneself. Whenever a man so concentrates his attention—be it on a landscape, or a poem or a geometrical problem or an idol or the True God—that he completely forgets his own ego and desires in listening to what the other has to say to him, he is praying. Choice of attention —to attend to this and ignore that—is to the inner life what the choice of action is to the outer. In both cases a man is responsible for his choice and must accept the consequences.

The special case of petitionary prayer—"of all kinds of prayer, I believe, the least important"—had its value as a means of discovering that one was not listening at all. "When we consciously phrase our desires, we often discover that they are really wishes that two-and-two should make three or five, as when St. Augustine realized that he was praying: 'Lord, make me chaste, but not yet.'"

Be that as it may [he continued], the essential aspect of prayer is not what we say, but what we hear. I don't think it matters terribly whether one calls the Voice that speaks to us the voice of the Holy Spirit, as Christians do, or the Reality Principle, as psychologists do, so long as we do not confuse it with the voice of the Super-Ego, for the Super-Ego, being a social creation, can only tell us something we know already, whereas the voice that speaks to us in prayer always says something new and unexpected, and very possibly unwelcome. The reason why I do not think the label matters very much is because I know the most convinced atheist scientist has prayed at least once in his life, when he heard a voice say: "Thou shalt serve Science."

Two years later, in "Aubade," a spare, grave, and beautiful verse re-statement of the linguistic themes of his own poems and Rosenstock-Huessy's essays, Auden imagined a complex grammar of memory and act, with "many Moods and Tenses, / And prime the Imperative." The closing lines portray time as a city whose motto is "*Listen, Mortals, Lest Ye Die!*"—adapted from a Latin phrase described by Rosenstock-Huessy as "an *a priori* that presupposes a power in man to establish relations with his neighbor that transcend their private interests."

The voices Auden listened to in the years of his final loneliness grew increasingly faint, mysterious, and remote, but they said more than those that shouted into every ear. He wrote in *Epistle to a Godson*:

> It is the unimportant
> who make all the din:
> both God and the Accuser
> speak very softly.

On the subjects that mattered most, the loud familiar language of the present day was likely to confirm one's private interests and prejudices, while the quiet distant languages of the past might perhaps overthrow them. In 1968 Auden had agreed to sit on a committee of the Episcopal Church that was charged with revising the Psalter to make its language more accessible to modern readers. The officials who invited him to serve were not entirely certain he was joking when he said he would do so on condition that the sixteenth-century text prepared by Miles Coverdale be left absolutely unchanged. Writing to J. Chester Johnson, a poet who joined the committee a few years later, Auden said, "All I can do is to try to persuade the scholars not to alter Coverdale unless there is a definite mistranslation." Around 1971, while he continued to serve on the committee, he privately withdrew from attending Episcopal services in revulsion against the modernizations introduced by his church and others in the 1960s. "In my view," he told Johnson,

> the Rite—preaching, of course, is another matter—is the link between the dead and the unborn. This calls for a timeless language which, in practice, means a dead language. My own parish church [St. Mark's in the Bouwerie] has gone so crazy that I have to go to the Russian Orthodox church where, thank God, though I know what is going on, I don't understand a single word.
>   The odd thing about the Liturgical Reform movement is that it is not asked for by the laity—they dislike it—it is a fad of a few crazy priests. If they imagine

that their high-jinks will bring youth into the churches, they are very much mistaken.

In 1973 he made the same argument in print. When the editors of the American edition of *Vogue*, not knowing what they were letting themselves in for, commissioned him to write a column in a series of personal essays headed "On My Mind," he provided his unfashionable thoughts on liturgy. To the obvious objection that the early Christians had not used an ancient language in their worship, he had a considered reply: "The first Christians had no linguistic problems because they expected the Parousia to occur in their lifetime; with us it is different. We are conscious of nearly two thousand years of Christian tradition behind us which it is our duty to transmit to future generations."

In his arguments about prayer and ritual Auden was returning to a matter he had left unsettled in his 1963 essay on the Protestant mystics, when he wrote from personal experience about the visions of Dame Kind, Eros, and Agape but said he knew nothing of the vision of God and expressed doubts about the many reports of it. But in prayer as an act of hearing something that was unwelcome to egoism, and ancient ritual as a means of hearing something that passes understanding, he found the answer to his earlier doubt. The fifth and last haiku of his "Addenda to *Profile*" was his one and only poem about it:

> He has never seen God,
> but, once or twice, he believes
> he has heard Him.

With these words, he gave thanks for the last gift of vision, and his work was done.

Notes and Index

Notes

Quotations from Auden's writings in this book are taken from the original texts, many of which may be found in *The English Auden* (1977) and *Selected Poems* (1979). Some of the texts in his *Collected Poems* (second edition, 1991) closely match the originals, but some are heavily revised, and significant revisions are mentioned in the notes. For work not found in these three volumes I cite readily available clothbound editions if these preserve the original texts. Works by other authors that have been published in various reset editions are usually cited by chapter or section number rather than by any specific edition. I cite texts or translations that were available to Auden; later versions (as in the case of Kierkegaard) sometimes differ substantially.

These abbreviations are used for books by Auden:

ACW *A Certain World* (Viking and Faber editions, 1970)

CP *Collected Poems* (Vintage and Faber second editions, 1991)

CP 1945 *The Collected Poetry of W. H. Auden* (Random House edition, 1945)

DH *The Dyer's Hand* (Random House and Faber editions, 1962, and all reprints)

DM *The Double Man* (Random House edition, 1941)

EA *The English Auden* (Random House and Faber editions, 1978, and all reprints)

FAA *Forewords and Afterwords* (Random House and Faber editions, 1973, and all reprints)

Libretti *Libretti*, by Auden and Chester Kallman (Princeton University Press and Faber editions, 1993)

NYL *New Year Letter* (Faber edition of *DM*, 1941, and all reprints)

PD *The Prolific and the Devourer* (Ecco Press edition, 1993)

Plays *Plays*, by Auden and Christopher Isherwood (Princeton University Press and Faber editions, 1988)

Prose I   *Prose and Travel Books in Prose and Verse*, Volume 1 (Princeton University Press and Faber editions, 1996)
  SP   *Selected Poems* (Vintage and Faber editions, 1979)
  SW   *Secondary Worlds* (reset Faber edition, 1968)

Two volumes in the Auden Studies series, edited by Katherine Bucknell and Nicholas Jenkins (Oxford University Press), are cited by volume number. *Auden Studies 1* is *W. H. Auden: "The Map of All My Youth"* (1990); *Auden Studies 3* is *W. H. Auden: "In Solitude for Company"* (1995). Letters to Stephen Spender and to James and Tania Stern cited in these volumes were edited and annotated by Nicholas Jenkins.

Full bibliographical details of Auden's writings through 1969 may be found in *W. H. Auden: A Bibliography*, by B. C. Bloomfield and Edward Mendelson, second edition (University Press of Virginia, 1972). Supplements to this listing may be found in each volume in the Auden Studies series.

Locations of manuscripts and typescripts, and the present owners of letters no longer in the hands of their recipients or their heirs, are given in parentheses. These abbreviations are used:

  Berg   The Henry W. and Albert A. Berg Collection of English and American Literature, the New York Public Library, Astor, Lenox, and Tilden Foundations
Bodleian Bodleian Library, Oxford
HRHRC The Harry Ransom Humanities Research Center, The University of Texas at Austin

All previously unpublished writings of W. H. Auden quoted in this book are copyright 1999 by the Estate of W. H. Auden, and may not be reproduced without written permission.

Introduction

xiii "conviction (though)": *PD* 9; *EA* 397.
     "passionate love affairs": *PD* 10; *EA* 398.
     "by the involuntary powers": *SP* 51; *EA* 207; *CP* 158.
     "your voluntary love": *EA* 163; *CP* 139.
     "history, that never sleeps": *EA* 157.
     "We live in freedom": *Prose I* 680; *SP* 78; *EA* 262; *CP* 194.
xiv "Abruptly mounting": *EA* 460.
     "For a poet": Letter to James Stern, 1 March 1968 (Berg).
     "plants": *SP* 230; *CP* 640.
     "Unhindered": *CP* 235.

xiv "lacking": *DH* 96.

"new problems": *CP* 717.

xv "Beauty is Truth": Quoted in *DH* 337–38.

"The only end": Quoted in *DH* 338; from Johnson's review of Soame Jenyns's *A Free Enquiry into the Nature and Origin of Evil*. The rest of Johnson's sentence is relevant to Auden's argument: "and how will either of those be put more in our power, by him who tells us, that we are puppets, of which some creature, not much wiser than ourselves, manages the wires!"

"*Ulysses*, Order, and Myth": *The Dial*, November 1923; reprinted in *Selected Prose of T. S. Eliot*, ed. Frank Kermode (1975), pp. 175–78.

xvi "My first religious memories": Untitled contribution to *Modern Canterbury Pilgrims*, ed. James A. Pike (1955), p. 33.

"magical lyrical phrases": "The Rewards of Patience," *Partisan Review*, July–August 1942, p. 337.

"Obscurity is": Letter to Naomi Mitchison, 28 October 1930 (Berg); quoted in *Early Auden*, p. 36.

xvii "There must always": *Prose I* 104; *EA* 341–42.

"The primary function": *Prose I* 470.

"In Defence of Gossip": *Prose I* 425.

xviii "The promise": *SP* 48; *Prose I* 186; revised in *CP* 151.

"The journey": *Prose I* 496; revised in *CP* 174.

"absolutely free America": *Prose I* 685; *EA* 267.

"I get": Letter to A. E. Dodds, [November 1938] (Bodleian); quoted in *Prose I* xxxiv.

xx "Jumbled": *SP* 115; revised in *CP* 269.

"Sing first": *CP* 408; *SP* 133.

"Sylvan meant": *SP* 204; *CP* 558.

"A poem is a rite": *DH* 58.

"Considered": "Squares and Oblongs," in *Language: An Enquiry into Its Meaning and Function*, ed. Ruth Nanda Anshen (1957), p. 174.

xxi "Squares and Oblongs": The other essay with this title appeared in *Poets at Work*, introduction by Charles T. Abbott (1948).

"is evil": *DH* 71.

"an innocent society": *DH* 150.

xxii "The first is technical": *DH* 50–51.

I: Demon or Gift

3 "In Memory of W. B. Yeats": *SP* 80; *EA* 241; revised in *CP* 247.

5 "the expensive": *SP* 80; *CP* 179.

6 *dennoch preisen*: Rilke, *Sonette an Orpheus* (1922), II.23.

7 "Certainly praise": *SP* 71; *Prose I* 673; *CP* 189.

"the first poet": Introduction to *Poets of the English Language* (1950), Vol. 3, p. xv.

8   "As I walked": *SP* 60; *EA* 227; *CP* 133.
    "The bars of love": *EA* 216; *CP* 127.
    "Lords of Limit": *EA* 115; *CP* 63.

9   "O Love": *SP* 25; *EA* 118.
    "The Witnesses": *EA* 126; revised and abridged in *SP* 39 and *CP* 75.
    "a power": *FAA* 69.
    "conviction": *PD* 9; *EA* 397.
    "Friend": MS notebook (Swarthmore College); quoted in *Early Auden*, pp. 241–42.

10 "The vanquished powers": *New Verse*, June–July 1936, p. 8; revised in *EA* 256, *SP* 70, and *CP* 189.
    "noons of dryness": *SP* 51; *EA* 207; *CP* 158.
    "The Novelist": *EA* 238; *CP* 180.
    "The Composer": *EA* 239; *CP* 181.
    "absolutely free America": *Prose I* 685; *EA* 267.
    "owes his influence": "Heretics," *The New Republic*, 1 November 1939, p. 373.

11 "the portion of life": *PD* 8; *EA* 396.
    "Pascal": *EA* 451.
    "In the truest sense": "The Dyer's Hand," *The Nation*, 21 October 1939, p. 444.
    "Matthew Arnold": *EA* 241.

14 "Rimbaud": *EA* 237; *CP* 181.
    "as a man of action": "Heretics," p. 373.
    "Edward Lear": *EA* 239; *CP* 182.
    "intricate and false": *CP* 251.
    "Voltaire at Ferney": *EA* 240; *CP* 250.

15 "a community": "A Great Democrat," *The Nation*, 25 March 1939, p. 353.
    "created": *EA* 392.

16 "You are blind": Charles Hamilton Sorley, *Marlborough and Other Poems* (1916).
    "The Public v. the Late Mr. W. B. Yeats": *EA* 389; title and text emended according to the manuscript (Houghton Library); the date Auden submitted it is taken from his cover letter to F. W. Dupee (Columbia University Library).

17 "A man has": *DH* 82.
    "The Chimeras": *CP* 614.
    "memorable speech": *Prose I* 105.
    "utter lack": "Yeats: Master of Diction," *The Saturday Review of Literature*, 8 June 1940, p. 14.

18 "If he wishes": Letter to George Augustus Auden, [February 1939] (Bodleian); *Bodleian Library Record*, April 1996, p. 327.

20 "All sway": *EA* 157.
    "history, hostile": *Prose I* 242–45.
    "Spain": *SP* 51; slightly revised in *EA* 210.

21 "both are worshippers": *CP* 586.

21 "All poets": "Squares and Oblongs," in *Poets at Work*, p. 179.
22 "was so busy": "Whitman and Arnold," *Common Sense*, April 1939, p. 24.
"a man": W. B. Yeats, "Under Ben Bulben" (1939).
"humility and courage": "The Dyer's Hand," p. 444.
23 "sailed into": *CP* 251.
"Where do They come from?" *EA* 243; revised in *CP* 253.
24 "Self-educated": *CP* 203.
"Enchanted": *SP* 29; *EA* 136; *CP* 117.
26 "The Crisis": Letter to A. E. Dodds, [August 1939] (Bodleian).
27 crooked: For Auden's use of this word, see *Early Auden*, pp. 225–36.
"unity of mankind": *PD* 61.
"You cannot": "Auden Gives Optimistic Faith," *The Daily Tar Heel*, University of North Carolina, 5 April 1939, pp. 1, 4.
28 "the nineteenth-century": *EA* 346; *Prose I* 114.
"The conduct": Sigmund Freud, *The Ego and the Id*, tr. Joan Riviere (1927), Chapter 2.
"We are lived": *CP* 250.
29 "Ode": *As I Walked Out One Evening* (1995).

II: The Vision Enters

31 "Vision of Eros": *FAA* 63.
"a sort of": Letter to Mayer, 26 April 1942 (Berg).
"Hearing of harvests": *SP* 28; *EA* 153; *CP* 119.
"Sermon by an Armament Manufacturer": *EA* 138; *Plays* 182, 575.
32 "A Summer Night": *SP* 29; *EA* 136; revised in *CP* 117.
"The fruit": *EA* 148.
"the first criterion": *EA* 319; *Prose I* 43.
"Dear, though": *SP* 44; *EA* 161; *CP* 137.
"Lay your sleeping head": *SP* 50; *EA* 207; *CP* 157.
"Johnny": *EA* 213; *CP* 142.
"Funeral Blues": *EA* 163; *CP* 141.
33 "Half the literature": *FAA* 63.
"The natural human": "Through the Collarbone of a Hare," *The New Yorker*, 2 May 1953, p. 126.
34 "Heaven and Hell": *EA* 361; *Prose I* 437.
35 "seen compressed": *EA* 33.
"Beauty, midnight": *SP* 51; *EA* 207; *CP* 157.
"I've spent years": Letter to A. E. Dodds, [July 1939] (Bodleian).
"All sexual desire": *FAA* 451.
"Heavy Date": *CP* 259.
36 "the greatest": "Mimesis and Allegory," *English Institute Annual 1940*, p. 5.
"As you know": Christopher Isherwood, *Christopher and His Kind* (1976), chapter 16.

36 "lacked the kind": "Effective Democracy," *Booksellers Quarterly*, May 1939, pp. 7–8.

37 "I suddenly": Letter to A. E. Dodds, [July 1939] (Bodleian).
"I *will*": *SP* 88; *EA* 246.

38 "Never, *never*": Letter to A. E. Dodds, [May 1939] (Bodleian).
"Auden's success": Quoted in Paul Mariani, *William Carlos Williams: A New World Naked* (1981), p. 437.
"The Unknown Citizen": *SP* 85; *CP* 252.
"people are happy": *EA* 372; *Prose I* 477.

39 "The individual": "How Not to Be a Genius," *The New Republic*, 26 April 1939, p. 348.
"I left school": "Poet and Politician," *Common Sense*, January 1940, p. 23.
"these extraordinary scenes": Isherwood, *Christopher and His Kind*, chapter 15.

40 "You cannot give": *PD* 21.
"Whoever you are": *PD* 29.

41 "Over against": "Purely Subjective," *The Chimera*, Summer 1943, pp. 3–22.
"organized common sense": "Auden Gives Optimistic Faith," pp. 1, 4.

42 "made no secret": Junius Irving Scales and Richard Nickson, *Cause at Heart: A Former Communist Remembers* (1987), pp. 65–66.
"bombshell": Unpublished journal of Selden Rodman.
"jolted everybody": Reported (possibly paraphrased) in an unpublished interview with Louis MacNeice by Charles Champlin, 16 February 1963; part of *Time* magazine's research for a projected story about Auden. The list of poems is from Selden Rodman's unpublished journal.

43 "Nothing could have": Letter to A. E. Dodds, [May 1939] (Bodleian).
"anniversary": Letter to Isherwood, 5 April 1944.
"what reason": "Love Letter," *Hika*, Kenyon College, June 1939, p. 9; reprinted in *The Chatto Book of Love Poetry*, ed. John Fuller (1990), p. 274.
"Why this": Letter from Kallman to Auden, 13 May 1939 (Berg).

44 "the published record": Letter to Alan Ansen, 27 August 1947 (Berg).
"Not as that dream Napoleon": *CP* 256.
"The Prophets": *CP* 255.
"Because it is": Letter to Kallman, Christmas Day, 1941 (HRHRC); see p. 182.

45 Keynes: See Robert Skidelsky, *John Maynard Keynes, a Biography, Vol. 2: The Economist as Saviour, 1920–1937* (1992), p. 628.
"Do cease": Letter from Kallman to Auden, 13 May 1939 (Berg).
"I always said": Letter to A. E. Dodds, [May 1939] (Bodleian).

46 "on the arm": *EA* 37; *CP* 45.
"This time": Letter to John B. Auden, [*c.* 10 June 1939].

47 "For some years": Letter to A. E. Dodds, [July 1939] (Bodleian).
"marriage" of Rimbaud: "Heretics," p. 373.
"O but for life": Typescript formerly in the possession of Glenn Horowitz.
"Musée des Beaux Arts": *SP* 79; *EA* 237; *CP* 179.

48 "Kairos and Logos": *CP 1945* 16; revised in *CP* 310.
"look out for": *SP* 106; *CP* 292.
49 "vision of Dame Kind": *FAA* 58.
51 "better far": *EA* 191; *Prose I* 329.
"the young": *EA* 148.
"My area": *EA* 3; *CP* 6.
"the dead howl": *SP* 4; *EA* 26; revised in *CP* 30.
"my character": "Poet and Politician," p. 23.
52 "When I was a child": *CP* 261.
"Calypso": *CP* 266.
"Will it alter": *EA* 231; *CP* 145.
"To Chester": Inscribed copy of *On This Island*, dated 5 September 1939 (HRHRC).
"This is your": *EA* 77; *CP* 69.
"I am very glad": Letter to James Yates, 16 June 1939 (private collection).
"set out to be": Letter to A. E. Dodds, [May 1939] (Bodleian).
53 "I cannot write": "A Literary Transference," *The Southern Review*, Summer 1940, p. 78.
"Under the fronds": The original text appeared in *New Writing*, Autumn 1937, pp. 170–71; revised, with the first line changed to "Wrapped in a yielding air," in *EA* 217 and *CP* 172.
54 "Underneath the leaves": *CP* 257.
56 "a painting I saw": "Phantasy and Reality in Poetry," lecture delivered to the Philadelphia Association for Psychoanalysis, 12 March 1971; typescript (Berg), transcribed with an introduction and notes by Katherine Bucknell in *Auden Studies 3*, pp. 177–96.
"O what is": *SP* 26; *EA* 125; *CP* 120.
" 'Thou shalt love' ": *PD* 43.
57 "true democracy": *CP* 241.
"the artist who": "The Wandering Jew," *The New Republic*, 10 February 1941, pp. 185–86.
"Diaspora": *CP* 300.
58 "In its emphasis": *PD* 64.
59 "Warm are the still": *CP* 267.
"But once in a while": *Libretti* 8.

III: Against the Devourer

62 "needs to be": Postcard to Harold Albaum [Norse], 22 June 1939 (Indiana University Library); Kallman's letters to Albaum at this time are addressed variously to "H. N. Albaum," "Harold Norse-Albaum," and similar forms.
"faith that mankind": *Letters of Katherine Anne Porter* (1990), p. 174.
"The Giants": William Blake, *The Marriage of Heaven and Hell*, plates 16–17.
"The Prolific": *EA* 404; *PD* 23.

63   "the whole of Freud's teaching": *Prose I* 99.
     "Blake's intuition": C. G. Jung, *Psychological Types* (1923), pp. 414–15.
     "condemned to destroy": *CP* 298.
     "I have yet": "A Literary Transference," p. 78.
     "America": Letter to Margaret Gardiner, 19 November 1939 (Berg).
64   "The Farmer": *EA* 402; *PD* 18.
     "When a politician": *CP* 260.
     "Even politicians speak": *CP 1945* 149; revised to "Even orators may speak"
         in *CP* 257.
     "The Enemy": *EA* 399; *PD* 13.
     "a new Marriage": Letter to E. R. Dodds, [May 1939] (Bodleian).
65   "my pensées": Letter to A. E. Dodds, [August 1939] (Bodleian).
     "Few of the artists": *EA* 403; *PD* 20.
     "He who undertakes": *EA* 403; *PD* 21.
     "I have never yet met": *EA* 405; *PD* 24.
     "cultivator, herdsman": *PD* 63.
     "One of the best reasons": *EA* 405; *PD* 24.
66   "Socialism is correct": *PD* 76.
     "It is their tomorrow": *CP* 250.
     "the prime cause": *PD* 62.
67   "forecast": *PD* 40.
     "tradition, community": Letter to E. R. Dodds, 16 January 1940 (Bodleian).
     "Jesus convinces me": *PD* 40.
     "indicated that": *Prose I* 111–12.
     "The unequivocally apocalyptic nature": *PD* 62.
68   "any more than": *PD* 51.
     "Man is aware": "Christian on the Left," *The Nation*, 9 September 1939,
         p. 273; emended on the basis of the manuscript in New York University
         Library.
     "divine laws": *PD* 30.
     "As a society changes": *PD* 38.
     "more and more unique": *PD* 39.
69   "If Jesus was right": *PD* 61–62.
70   "It is, I believe": "Rilke in English," *The New Republic*, 6 September 1939,
         pp. 135–36.
     "Epithalamion": *EA* 453.
71   "Eros, builder": *SP* 95; *CP* 276.
     "I have never written": Letter to Margaret Gardiner, 19 November 1939
         (Berg).
     "intelligence only functions": *PD* 44.
72   "of all the dualists": *PD* 47.
     "the only theological writer": *Modern Canterbury Pilgrims*, ed. Pike, p. 36.
     "born deserted": *EA* 452.
73   "Progress is probable": "Christian on the Left," p. 273.
     "There is a radio": Letter to A. E. Dodds, 28 August 1939 (Bodleian).

73   "The last mad hopes": Typescript of "September 1, 1939" (Berg); the pub-
     lished text is in *SP* 86 and *EA* 245.
74   "Our world is permeated": Jung, *Psychology and Religion* (1938), p. 59.
     in a bar: Harold [Albaum] Norse, in *Memoirs of a Bastard Angel* (1989), in-
     vents a dramatic picture of Auden starting the poem in a gay bar called the
     Dizzy Club on 1 September 1939, but, as Kallman told friends, it was in fact
     written during a visit to Kallman's father in New Jersey.
     "antidote to": *PD* 62.
     "Some politicians": *The Diary of Vaslav Nijinsky* (1937), p. 44.
76   "People have": Unpublished journal of Selden Rodman.
77   "Whichever way": *CP* 224.
     "Again let me": "Poet and Politician," p. 23.
     "the relations between": Course announcement for the Writers' School,
     League of American Writers, Inc., Sixth Term, October 9th to Decem-
     ber 15th 1939, p. 4.
78   "profound disquiet": Letter to Nan Goldin, 8 November 1939 (University of
     California at Berkeley).
     "the extraordinary compulsion": *EA* 158.
     "That last attempt": *EA* 458.
     "Homage to Clio": *SP* 232; *CP* 610.
     "The Shield of Achilles": *SP* 198; *CP* 596.
     "Law Like Love": *SP* 89; *CP* 262.
80   "The Hidden Law": *CP* 264.
     "Hell is neither here": *CP 1945* 51; revised in *CP* 278.
     "The hour-glass whispers": *CP 1945* 118; revised in *CP* 277.
     "For us like any": *CP* 276.
     "Atlantis": *SP* 116; *CP* 315.
83   "pure evil": *PD* 34.
84   "I'm very hopeful": "From the Notebooks of Robert Fitzgerald," *Erato*, Po-
     etry and Farnsworth Rooms, Harvard College Library, Fall–Winter 1986,
     p. 1.
85   "When there are so many": *SP* 91; revised in *CP* 273.
     "interested in the possibilities": "Transcript of a speech by W. H. Auden . . .
     at Swarthmore College on March 9, 1950" [mimeographed text], p. 5.
     "There are some poets": *DH* 22.
86   "seemed so strange": Letter to Marianne Moore, 14 November 1939 (Rosen-
     bach Foundation).
     "the endless": "New Poems," *The New York Times Book Review*, 15 October
     1944, p. 20.
87   "To be forgiven": *PD* 55.
     "Where now": *EA* 165.

IV: Investigating the Crime

89 "quite ordinary": Roy Perrott, "Auden," *Observer*, 28 June 1970, p. 25.
"What was remarkable": Letter to Nevill Coghill, 19 January [?1970] (Berg). An almost identical passage appears in an unsigned "Interview with W. H. Auden," *Concern*, Nyack, N.Y., Winter 1971, p. 12.
"the brutal honesty": [Stephen Spender,] "The Dog Beneath the Gown," *The New Statesman*, 9 June 1956, pp. 656–57.

91 "to extend and qualify it": "Jacob and the Angel," *The New Republic*, 27 December 1939, pp. 292–93.

93 "The reverent fury": *DM* 157; *NYL* 157.

94 "To begin with": *Libretti* 537.
"But let me tell you": *Libretti* 9.
"Young boys": *Libretti* 16.
"I conceive of her": *Libretti* 571.

95 "Here are some": Typescript draft (Berg).
"perfect nullities": *Libretti* 30.

96 "Paul has the brains": *Libretti* 37.
"I must hasten": *Libretti* 45.
"Spain": *SP* 51; slightly revised in *EA* 210.

97 "doing a preparatory course": Letter to A. E. Dodds, 26 November 1939 (Bodleian).
"one whose desire": *DM* 86; *NYL* 90–91.

98 "I have sometimes wondered": Letter to Albaum [Norse], 20 December 1939 (Indiana University Library).
"iconography and portraiture": "The Icon and the Portrait," *The Nation*, 13 January 1940, p. 48.

99 "are conscious": "The Double Focus: Sandburg's Lincoln," *Common Sense*, March 1940, p. 25.
"the powers": *CP* 241.
"Our evil *Daimon*": *CP* 225.
"Consider who": "Open Letter to Knut Hamsun," *Common Sense*, August 1940, pp. 22–23.
"The angel": *SP* 104; *CP* 290.
"Psychotherapy will not": "The Wandering Jew," p. 186.

100 "occasion": Manuscript draft of the first half of "New Year Letter" (Berg).
"In 1931 Pope's ghost": Randall Jarrell, *Kipling, Auden & Co.* (1980), p. 55.

102 "Down to": *CP* 228.
"perfect Being": *CP* 221.
"To what conditions": *CP* 238.
"any skyline": *CP* 223.
"in the civil art": *CP* 242.
"*Das Ewig-Weibliche*": V. S. Yanovksy, "W. H. Auden," *Antaeus*, Autumn 1975, p. 123.

103 "Your poem": Letter to Mayer, 22 February 1940 (Berg).
　　"the voice of Man": *EA* 269; *Prose I* 687.
　　"he's lost": *CP* 214.
　　"The Devil, indeed": *DM* 116; *NYL* 119.
104 "defects": *DH* 115.
　　"unity had come": *CP* 230.
106 "Our minds": *CP* 200.
107 "So though not painstaking": MS notebook with early sketches for "New Year
　　Letter" (Berg); partly also in manuscript draft of the first half of "New Year
　　Letter" (Berg).
　　"The situation": *CP* 205.
108 "to / Prevent": *CP* 209.
　　"Do you know": Charles H. Miller, *Auden: An American Friendship* (1983),
　　pp. 81–82.
　　"For as": *CP* 213.
109 "Faust is saved": "The Wandering Jew," p. 186.
110 "The False Association": *CP* 215.
114 "The one infallible symptom": "The Double Focus: Sandburg's Lincoln,"
　　pp. 25–26.
　　"The either-ors": *CP* 220.
　　"They are our past": *EA* 158.
　　"happens every day": *CP* 221.
　　"I felt": *CP* 220.
115 "They know": *DM* 118; *NYL* 121.
　　"it is not": "Anger," in *The Seven Deadly Sins* (1962), p. 87.
　　"Forgiveness of sin": *DM* 119; *NYL* 122.
116 "Do you care": Letter to E. R. Dodds, [February 1940?] (Bodleian).
　　"The country": MS notebook with early sketches for "New Year Letter"
　　(Berg).
117 "Louder than": MS draft of the second half of "New Year Letter" (HRHRC).
　　"Whatever wickedness": *CP* 224.
121 "In labs": *CP* 239.

V: It Without Image

122 "true democracy": *CP* 241.
124 "Christianity had betrayed": Charles Williams, *The Descent of the Dove* (1939),
　　p. 155.
　　"a certain brother": Ibid., p. 55; the passage is misattributed in some books
　　on Auden to Athanasius, whom Williams quotes on the preceding page.
　　"We are": Ibid., p. 192.
125 "In a publisher's office": *Modern Canterbury Pilgrims*, ed. Pike, p. 41.
　　"the two worlds": *EA* 361; *Prose I* 437.

125 "had an extraordinarily moving note": Letter from Charles Williams to Michal Williams, 12 March 1940, quoted in Humphrey Carpenter, *The Inklings* (1978), p. 188.

"In the Crucifixion": Williams, *The Descent of the Dove*, pp. 174–75.

"was remarkable": Ibid., p. 232.

"*Quando non*": Ibid., p. 39.

"It without image": Ibid., p. 61.

"*O da quod jubes*": Ibid., p. 66.

"this is not": Ibid., p. 62.

126 "without the body": Ibid., p. 138.

"Your life and death": Ibid., p. 46.

"Aloneness is": *CP* 238.

127 "For this quotation": *DM* 153; *NYL* 154.

"The Psychological": *Libretti* 740.

"The Dark Valley": *Libretti* 371.

"has something": *Plays* 437.

128 "I'm delighted": Letter to Monroe K. Spears, 5 May 1963 (Berg).

"Eyes look into the well": *CP* 269; *Libretti* 375.

"Lady, weeping": *CP* 279; *Libretti* 379.

"of folk-song character": Letter to Britten, [April 1939] (Berg); *Libretti* 742.

129 "as an effort": Williams, *The Descent of the Dove*, p. 217.

130 "If, as I am convinced": *Modern Canterbury Pilgrims*, ed. Pike, p. 40.

"knocked the conceit": Recalled by Oliver Sacks; quoted in Humphrey Carpenter, *W. H. Auden: A Biography* (1981), p. 285.

131 "age of disintegration": Walter Lowrie, *Kierkegaard* (1938), p. 445.

"what is most valuable": "A Preface to Kierkegaard," *The New Republic*, 15 May 1944, p. 683.

132 "What you say": Letter to Spender, [?April–May 1940] (Berg); *Auden Studies 1*, p. 72.

"Am reading": Letter to E. R. Dodds, [March 1940] (Bodleian).

"*Verbürgerlichung*": *CP* 232.

"The fundamental error": *The Journals of Søren Kierkegaard*, tr. Alexander Dru (1938), p. 222.

133 "After the individual": Ibid., pp. 82–83.

"We shall never earn": "The Icon and the Portrait," p. 48.

"Among the qualities": "Against Romanticism," *The New Republic*, 5 February 1940, p. 187.

"God is a mathematician": *Libretti* 380.

"Man has a natural dread": Kierkegaard, *Journals*, p. 499.

134 "O season of repetition": *DM* 11; *NYL* 13; *EA* 457.

"It is the sorrow": *SP* 29; *EA* 136; revised in *CP* 120.

135 "The Quest": *CP* 285; the separate sonnets had titles (listed in *CP* 909) in *DM* and *CP 1945*, but not in *NYL* or later collections.

136 "A man cannot": *DM* 84–85; more correctly quoted in *NYL* 88; from Kierkegaard, *Journals*, pp. 413–14.

136 "you would think": Søren Kierkegaard, *Fear and Trembling*, tr. Robert Payne (1939), p. 50.
137 "the universe": Williams, *The Descent of the Dove*, p. 165.
"Song for St. Cecilia's Day": This is the title in Auden's manuscript (Berg); it was published as "Three Songs for St. Cecilia's Day" in 1941, then as "Song for St. Cecilia's Day" in *CP 1945*, and "Anthem for St. Cecilia's Day" in *CP* 280.
138 "dear daughter": The manuscript versions (Kurt Weill Foundation for Music and Berg) are transcribed in Edward Mendelson, "The Making of Auden's *Hymn for St. Cecilia's Day*," in *On Mahler and Britten: Essays in Honour of Donald Mitchell on His Seventieth Birthday*, ed. Philip Reed (1995), pp. 186–92.
139 "One of the most disquieting": " 'What Is Culture?' " *The Nation*, 6 July 1940, p. 18.
"the strength": "Poet in Wartime," *The New Republic*, 8 July 1940, p. 59.
"willing to do anything": Letter to Spender, 13 March 1941 (Berg); *Auden Studies 1*, p. 76.
"only technically": Letter to A. E. Dodds, [June 1940] (Bodleian).
140 "Letters from home": Letter to James Stern, 9 July 1940 (Berg).
"some minor": Letter to John B. Auden, 21 June 1940.
"Open Letter to Knut Hamsun": *Common Sense*, August 1940, pp. 22–23.
141 "His guardian-angel": *CP* 776.
"interdependent whole": "Heretics," p. 373.
"heretical": "The Double Focus: Sandburg's Lincoln," p. 25.
142 "neurosis": R. G. Collingwood, *An Essay on Metaphysics* (1940), p. 46.
"The basic weakness": Letter to Spender, [?April–May 1940] (Berg); *Auden Studies 1*, p. 73.
"the war is": "Romantic or Free?" *Smith Alumnae Quarterly*, August 1940, pp. 353–58.
144 "against a background": Collingwood, *An Essay on Metaphysics*, p. 227.
"as heresies": "Mimesis and Allegory," p. 2.
145 "And write I do": Letter to E. R. Dodds, [?July 1940] (Bodleian).
"The Council": *CP* 302.
146 "Here the Holy Spirit": Williams, *The Descent of the Dove*, p. 187.
"Oh what sign": *DM* 188; slightly different in *NYL* 187; revised in *CP* 284.

VI: Imaginary Saints

148 "began going": *Modern Canterbury Pilgrims*, ed. Pike, p. 41.
"I started going": Letter to Kenneth Lewars, 17 September 1947; quoted in Lewars, "The Quest in Auden's Poems and Plays," M.A. thesis, Columbia University, 1947, p. 104.
"On Sundays": Golo Mann, "A Memoir," in *W. H. Auden: A Tribute*, ed. Stephen Spender (1975), p. 102.

148 "adequate and conscious": "Mimesis and Allegory," p. 19; Auden delivered
this speech on 14 September 1940.

149 "intellectual *avant-garde*": *Prose I* 51.
"Protestant theology": *FAA* 402.

150 "the pernicious influence": *FAA* 396.
"The fundamental Protestant attitude": *DM* 132; *NYL* 134; quoted from Paul
Tillich, *The Interpretation of History* (1936), pp. 134–35.

151 "purely transcendent": Tillich, *The Interpretation of History*, p. 55.
"must end with": Ibid., p. 56.
"The struggle": Ibid., pp. 57–58.
"The abandonment of hope": "Religion and the Intellectuals," *Partisan Review*, February 1950, p. 123.

152 "I owe to Marx": Tillich, *The Interpretation of History*, pp. 62–63.
"I find T[illich]": Letter to Ursula Niebuhr, [Spring 1941] (Library of
Congress).
"and more recently": Letter to Margaret Church, 12 November 1941; quoted
in her "For This Is Orpheus, or, Rilke, Auden and Spender," M.A. thesis,
Columbia University, 1942, p. iii.
"into a land": Tillich, *The Interpretation of History*, pp. 67–68.
"There is a great difference": Quoted in *ACW*, p. 35.
"The substance": Tillich, *The Interpretation of History*, p. 54.

153 "the demonic is": Ibid., p. 93.
"an internal necessity": "Criticism in a Mass Society," in *The Intent of the
Critic*, ed. Donald A. Stauffer (1941), p. 147.
"In Sickness and in Health": *SP* 111; revised in *CP* 317.

154 "believed by virtue": Kierkegaard, *Fear and Trembling*, p. 43.

155 "my words' ": Donne, "Elegy XVI: To His Mistress."
"Time will": *SP* 110; *CP* 314.

156 "The sense of danger": *CP* 313.
"constantly out": Søren Kiekegaard, *Stages on Life's Way*, tr. Walter Lowrie
(1940), p. 402; also quoted in Lowrie's *Kierkegaard*, p. 317.

157 "original sin": "Criticism in a Mass Society," p. 145.
"Our Hunting Fathers": *SP* 33; *EA* 151; *CP* 122.
"A Note on Order": *The Nation*, 1 February 1941, pp. 131–33.
"I think a lot": Letter to Eliot, 17 December 1940 (Faber & Faber).

159 "has long been": "Tract for the Times," *The Nation*, 4 January 1941,
pp. 24–25.

160 "my position": *PD* 87.
"Southern Californian": "Yeats as an Example," *The Hudson Review*, Spring
1948, p. 188.
"As far as writers": "Symposium," *Decision*, January 1941, pp. 44–45.

161 "What has to be done": Letter to Spender, 13–14 March 1941 (Berg); *Auden
Studies I*, pp. 76–77.
"If you are *certain*": Letter to Isherwood, [?early 1941].
"Christmas 1940": *EA* 458.

161 "At the Grave of Henry James": *SP* 119; revised in *CP* 310.
"Kairos and Logos": *CE 1945* 11; revised in *CP* 305.
"We get the Dialectic": MS notebook (Berg).

162 "Comrades, who": *EA* 120 (with the first word revised to "Brothers").

164 "What but the honour": From the version in *Partisan Review*, July–August 1941, p. 268; this was printed after the revised version (quoted a few lines below the quotation) appeared in *Horizon*, June 1941, p. 381.
"How *could* I": Foreword to B. C. Bloomfield, *W. H. Auden: A Bibliography: The Early Years through 1955* (1964), p. viii.

165 "in Jung's terminology": Letter to Spender, 13–14 March 1941 (Berg); *Auden Studies 1*, p. 75.
"beautiful house": Letter to Curtiss, 25 May 1940 (Berg).
"if one likes": Letter to Curtiss, 14 January 1942 (Berg).
"Jumbled in": *SP* 115; revised in *CP* 269.

166 "Atlantis": *SP* 116; revised in *CP* 315.
"neither bowdlerizes": *FAA* 336–38.

167 "be there by himself": Letter to Isherwood, [?early 1941].

168 "Each lover": *CP1945* 35 (titled "Are You There?"); revised in *CP* 312 (titled "Alone").
"concept of Kairos": Tillich, *The Interpretation of History*, p. 57.

170 "Narcissus disbelieves": *CP* 312.
"the Jews have": "The Wandering Jew," pp. 185–86.

171 "That is what Ida is": "All About Ida," *The Saturday Review of Literature*, 22 February 1941, p. 8.
"because I needed": *DH* xi.
"a pleasant excuse": Letter to Angelyn Stevens, [19 September 1942].
"is unpleasant evidence": "Ambiguous Answers," *The New Republic*, 23 June 1941, p. 862.

172 "A real society": "The Masses Defined," *Decision*, May 1941, p. 63.
"In the last few chapters": "Eros and Agape," *The Nation*, 28 June 1941, pp. 757–58.
"one's admiration": "James Joyce and Richard Wagner," *Common Sense*, March 1941, pp. 89–90.

173 "bolt the thor": James Joyce, *Finnegans Wake* (1939), p. 279.
"Hitler is of course": Reinhold Niebuhr, "Mann's Political Essays," *The Nation*, 28 November 1942, p. 584.
"the most lucid": "The Means of Grace," *The New Republic*, 2 June 1941, p. 766.

174 "I think": Postcard to Ursula Niebuhr, 13 May 1941 (Library of Congress).
"the saint must descend": *Libretti* 31.
"frivolity": *Modern Canterbury Pilgrims*, ed. Pike, p. 41.

VII: The Absconded Vision

175 "On account of you": Letter to Kallman, Christmas Day, 1941 (HRHRC); Dorothy J. Farnan, *Auden in Love* (1984), pp. 65–66.

176 "And then": *Modern Canterbury Pilgrims*, ed. Pike, p. 41.
"The Crisis": Letter to Ansen, 27 August 1947 (Berg).
"Though determined": *CP* 270.

177 "boy": Information from Tania Stern; the information in the following paragraph is from Jack Barker.

178 "How like her": Information from Chester Kallman.
"It was a much greater shock": Letter to Spender, 16 January 1942 (Berg); *Auden Studies 1*, p. 81.
"It's a pity": Letter to James Stern, 30 July 1942 (Berg); *Auden Studies 3*, p. 83.

179 "a treaty": "Symposium," *Decision*, January 1941, p. 50.
"to find": Letter to Albaum (Norse), 1 November 1941 (Indiana University Library).
"For the Time Being": *CP* 347.

181 "final vision": *FAA* 65–68.
"The Ballad of Barnaby": *CP* 824.

182 "Because it is": Letter to Kallman, Christmas Day, 1941 (HRHRC); Dorothy J. Farnan, *Auden in Love*, pp. 65–66.

184 "insistence on a nurse": *CP* 364.
"one of the most exciting books": Letter to Spender, 12 April 1942 (Berg); *Auden Studies 1*, p. 83.
"I have read this book": "Augustus to Augustine," *The New Republic*, 25 September 1944, p. 373.
"new deal": Charles Norris Cochrane, *Christianity and Classical Culture* (1940), p. 17.

185 "intermediate beings": Ibid., p. 515.
"Thus, though": Ibid., p. 500.
"fiscal grief": Ibid., p. 202.
"There is one World": *CP* 365.
"there was but one world": Cochrane, p. 238.
"Powers and Times": *CP* 374.
"Victory is not": Cochrane, p. 349.
"Time is not": Ibid., p. 439.
"Ascesis of the senses": *CP* 369.
"rigorous programme": Cochrane, p. 429.
"Her answers": *CP* 369.
"to the assiduous questions": Cochrane, p. 148.

186 "Perhaps you": Letter to George Augustus Auden (transcribed by him), 13 October 1942.
"active love": Ludwig Feuerbach, *The Essence of Christianity*, tr. George Eliot (1841), chapter 26.

187 "Sin fractures": *CP* 364.

"A truth": *EA* 354; *Prose I* 123.

"outrageous novelty": *CP* 351.

188 "crisis of despair": Cochrane, p. 3.

"The wrath of God": *FAA* 176.

"occurred precisely": "The Means of Grace," *The New Republic*, 2 June 1941, p. 765.

189 "and that which hitherto": *CP* 387–88.

190 "*fantastica fornicatio*": Cochrane, p. 418.

"the co-inherence": Ibid., p. 367.

"guardianship": Collingwood, *An Essay on Metaphysics* (1940), p. 198.

192 "It is always silly": "W. H. Auden Speaks of Poetry and Total War," *The Chicago Sun*, 14 March 1942, p. 14; slightly emended.

"our poverty of symbols": "In Praise of the Brothers Grimm," *The New York Times Book Review*, 12 November 1944, pp. 1, 28.

193 "these prudent": Randall Jarrell, "Freud to Paul: The Stages of Auden's Ideology," in *The Third Book of Criticism* (1987), p. 187 (originally in *Partisan Review*, Fall 1945).

194 "I tried": Letter to Theodore Spencer, 29 April 1943 (Harvard University Archives).

"self-development": "The Rewards of Patience," pp. 336–40.

196 "a *Collected Poems*": Letter to Bennett Cerf, 8 January 1942 (Columbia University Library).

197 "The next step": Letter to Spender, 12 April 1942 (Berg); *Auden Studies 1*, pp. 82–83.

"I can only develop": Letter to Spender, 13–14 March 1941 (Berg); *Auden Studies 1*, p. 75.

198 "my mistake": Letter to Spender, 12 April 1942 (Berg); *Auden Studies 1*, p. 82.

"whether his feelings": Letter to Tania Stern, 20 December 1941 (Berg).

"Many Happy Returns": *CP* 320.

"Mundus et Infans": *SP* 123; *CP* 324.

"In War Time": *CP 1945* 3; *EA* 460; in *Nones* (1951) Auden included a lyric from the libretto *The Rake's Progress* that he excluded from later collected editions, apparently because he decided it was not separable from the libretto, not because he thought any less of it.

199 "I have been thinking": Letter to Britten, 31 January 1942 (Berg); Donald Mitchell, *Britten and Auden in the Thirties* (1981), pp. 161–62; *Letters from a Life: The Selected Letters and Diaries of Benjamin Britten, 1913–1976*, ed. Donald Mitchell (1991), Vol. 2, pp. 1015–16.

"didn't mean": Letter to Britten, February 1942 (Berg); *Letters from a Life*, Vol. 2, p. 1016.

200 "the drives of love": *CP* 90.

"The More Loving One": *SP* 237; *CP* 584.

"You can't imagine": Letter to James Stern, 18 June 1942 (Berg); *Auden Studies 3*, p. 80.

200 "I've long cherished": Letter to James Stern, 5 July 1944 (Berg); *Auden Studies 3*, p. 88. To Isherwood he wrote: "One day we have to write a play about Marriage" (23 June 1943).

201 "like everything": *ACW* 248.

"By always presenting": "Some Notes on D. H. Lawrence," *The Nation*, 26 April 1947, pp. 483–84.

"To acknowledge vocation": "Vocation and Society," *Auden Studies 3*, pp. 20–21.

"There are many callings": "Henry James and the Dedicated," *The New York Times Book Review*, 17 December 1944, p. 3.

202 "the poet is": "Squares and Oblongs," in *Poets at Work*, pp. 171–72.

"True Love enjoys": *CP* 787.

"The only antidote": *FAA* 479.

"We look round": *CP* 400.

"important persons": *SP* 168; *CP* 439.

203 "West's Disease": *DH* 238.

"Few and Simple": *CP* 326.

"On the Circuit": *SP* 248; *CP* 729.

204 "hunger for": *CP* 503.

"In youth": *CP* 490.

"Their Lonely Betters": *CP* 583.

VIII: The Murderous Birth

205 "The Sea and the Mirror": *SP* 127; *CP* 401.

"really about": Letter to Ursula Niebuhr, 2 June 1944 (Library of Congress).

"my Ars Poetica": Letter to Theodore Spencer, [?24 March 1944] (Harvard University Archives).

206 "Now it is over": *SP* 173; *CP* 443–44.

207 "Neither the heathen philosophers": *PD* 40.

"I believe because": "Purely Subjective," p. 20.

"Small towns": "Adrian and Francisco's Song," in the version in the posthumous collection of Auden's lighter verse, *As I Walked Out One Evening* (1995).

"Could you find out": Letter to James Stern, 3 November 1942 (Berg); *Auden Studies 3*, p. 86.

submarine duty: *Michigan Daily*, 7 April 1942.

208 "Today I like a weight": *EA* 192.

"ask what doubtful act": *SP* 31; *EA* 137; *CP* 118.

"the conscious acceptance": *SP* 54; revised in 1939 to read "the fact of murder," *EA* 212.

"To you, perhaps": Letter to Albaum [Norse], 20 December 1939 (Indiana University Library).

209 "The terrible thing": Letter to Albaum [Norse], 1 November 1941 (Indiana University Library).

"We should not be sitting": *SP* 155; *CP* 428.

210 "undoubtedly the stupidest": *FAA* 222.

"a first-rate": *FAA* 231.

211 "*le meilleur témoignage*": Baudelaire, "Les Phares."

"I have been certain": MS notebook (Berg).

214 "So at last": *SP* 129; *CP* 404.

215 "And shouldn't you too": *SP* 155; *CP* 428.

"Art may spill over": Quoted in an unpublished essay by Alan Ansen, "Crisis and Festival I: A Study of W. H. Auden's *The Sea and the Mirror*" (1948), p. 26 (Berg).

"The hot": *CP* 331.

"Canzone": *CP* 330.

216 "the satisfaction": *DH* 94.

"Every child": "Lecture Notes," *Commonweal*, 6 November 1942, p. 61; reprinted in John Deedy, *Auden as Didymus* (1993), p. 21.

"The Lesson": *SP* 125; *CP* 326.

218 "in / The germ-cell's": *CP* 366.

"To think his death": *SP* 145; *CP* 419.

219 "Wholly Other Life": *SP* 173; *CP* 444.

"Just a note": Letter to Beata Wachstein [Sauerlander], 6 June 1944.

220 "About / blended flesh": *SP* 274; *CP* 711.

222 "He kissed me awake": *SP* 148; *CP* 422.

"The political outlook": Letter to E. R. Dodds, 1 February 1944 (Bodleian).

"My odds at present": Letter to E. R. Dodds, 14 August 1944 (Bodleian).

223 "without these": *SP* 154; *CP* 427.

"jealous of someone else": Letter to Spender, 12 April 1942 (Berg); *Auden Studies I*, p. 82.

224 "soiled, shabby": *CP* 201–2.

"Art, as the late Professor": "The Poet of the Encirclement," *The New Republic*, 25 October 1943, p. 579.

226 "We can never be certain": *DH* 480.

230 "Your irritation": Letter to Theodore Spencer, [24 March 1942] (Harvard University Archives).

231 "completely stuck": Letter to Isherwood, [March 1944].

"struck oil": Letter to Mayer, 17 October 1943 (Berg).

"Ladies and gentlemen": MS notebook (Berg).

"suddenly got the James idea": Letter to Theodore Spencer, [24 March 1942] (Harvard University Archives).

"since Caliban": Letter to Frederick Bradnum, 16 January 1960 (BBC Written Archives Centre); Bradnum was the producer of a radio version and wanted to drop Caliban's speech as unplayable, but Auden insisted it was essential to the work.

232   "Without exception": "Address on Henry James," *Gazette of the Grolier Club*,
       January 1947, p. 215; the address was delivered on 24 October 1946.
       "The notebooks show": Alan Ansen, *The Table Talk of W. H. Auden* (1990),
       p. 95.
       "Reading Rilke's letters": "Keats in His Letters," *Partisan Review*,
       November–December 1951, p. 704.

235   "a belief": Foreword to *The Flower of Grass*, by Emile Cammaerts (1945),
       p. ix.

239   a diagram: Auden made at least two copies, one an early and less complete
       version, now in Berg (reproduced in *W. H. Auden 1907–1973: An Exhibition
       from the Berg Collection*, by Edward Mendelson [1976], unpaged, and in
       Auden, by Richard Davenport-Hines [1995], facing p. 214); the other, tran-
       scribed in this book, a more polished version, now in Swarthmore College
       Library (reproduced in Kenneth Lewars, "Auden's Swarthmore Chart,"
       Connecticut Review, April 1968, p. 44).

241   "relationship": Letter to Tania Stern, 30 December 1944 (Berg); *Auden Stud-
       ies 3*, p. 92.
       "husband and father": "Henry James and the Dedicated," p. 3.

                          IX: Asking for Neighborhood

242   *The Age of Anxiety*: CP 447.
       "immediately incorporated": Letter to James Stern, 1 March 1968 (Berg).

243   "It is characteristic": Kierkegaard, *Journals*, p. 76.
       "to devise a rhetoric": Letter to Theodore Spencer, [late 1946 or early 1947]
       (Harvard University Archives).

244   "by first-hand observation": Letter to Isherwood, 18 November 1944.
       "everybody is reduced": CP 449.

245   "By brutal bands": CP 518.
       "making my way": Letter to Isherwood, 31 August 1944.
       "fully conscious": CP 451.

246   "The murder": MS notebook (Poetry Library of the State University of New
       York at Buffalo).
       "The Guilty Vicarage": DH 146.
       "A crime": CP 459.
       "Question his crimes": CP 464.
       "familiar": CP 450.

247   "Deep in my dark": CP 470.
       "Bosh": In a copy of *CP 1945* (Robert Franklin).

248   "a state": CP 484.
       "We who are four": CP 355.
       "is the first": CP 485.
       "follows directly": Jung, *Psychological Types*, p. 569.

249 "a recognition": Ibid., p. 611.
"Human beings are": *CP* 518.
"for all gestures": *CP* 535.

250 "to make it easier": Alan Ansen, MS diary (Berg).

251 "really quite straightforward": Alan Ansen, TS diary (Berg); lightly edited.

252 "Lament for a Lawgiver": *Horizon*, March 1948, p. 161.
"great progenitor": Joseph Campbell and Henry Morton Robinson, *A Skeleton Key to Finnegans Wake* (1944), p. 6.

253 "I wake into my existence": "Purely Subjective," p. 3.
"A Healthy Spot": *CP* 328; TS (Berg).
"Temporals pleading": *CP* 535.

254 "desire it": *DH* 323.
"thinking-intuitive": "A Literary Transference," p. 80.
"Where the persona": Jung, *Psychological Types*, p. 594.
"who is now": Letter to Mayer, 17 July 1943 (Berg).

255 "Why have They": *CP* 455.
"Faith for Christianity": "Lecture Notes," *Commonweal*, 4 December 1942, p. 158; Deedy, *Auden as Didymus*, p. 43.

256 "Should I hide away": *CP* 529.
"The fantasy . . . which": *DH* 158.

257 "What it all means": "Lecture Notes," *Commonweal*, 4 December 1942, p. 158; *Auden as Didymus*, p. 43.

258 "Where time": *CP* 535.

259 "I've been increasingly interested": Ansen, *The Table Talk of W. H. Auden*, p. 32.

260 "ever since": Foreword to Eugen Rosenstock-Huessy, *I Am an Impure Thinker* (1970), p. vii.
"gives me the impression": "Thinking What We Are Doing," *The Griffin*, September 1958, p. 4.
"to be a Christian": Eugen Rosenstock-Huessy, *The Christian Future* (1946), p. 123.
"All Souls established": Eugen Rosenstock-Huessy, *Out of Revolution* (1938), p. 507.

261 "vision of": *DH* 42.
"seems to claim": Foreword to Rosenstock-Huessy, *I Am an Impure Thinker*, p. vii.
"sweet-smelling borders": *CP* 504.
"Baroque": Letter to Ursula Niebuhr, 9 August 1946 (Library of Congress).
"the counter-reformation's": TS transcript of Auden's class notes, 1942–43, p. 52 (Swarthmore College Library; Library of Congress).

262 "Under Which Lyre": *CP* 335.

263 "This is the real enemy": Ansen, *The Table Talk of W. H. Auden*, p. 11.
"a bit of Apollo": Ibid., p. 47.
"Nursery Rhyme": *CP* 333.

264   "The Fall of Rome": *SP* 183; *CP* 332. Auden confirmed to W. P. Nicolet that the reindeer were displaced by the approaching invaders (*Explicator*, November 1972).
"Music Is International": *CP* 340.
"In Schrafft's": *CP* 334.
"The Duet": *CP* 342.

265   "Work sticks a bit": Letter to Mayer, 17 July 1947 (Berg).

266   "The weather is lovely": Letter to Rhoda Jaffe, [2 May 1946] (Berg).
"I have pencilled": *CP* 506.
"1922 Robert": Loose pages from MS notebook (Berg).

267   "The Mythical Sex": *Harper's Bazaar*, October 1947, pp. 181–82, 314–16.
"a queer": Letter to Jaffe, 17 June 1947 (Berg).
"Lots and lots of love": Ibid. (Berg).
"I can't tell you": Letter to Jaffe, [11 April 1948] (Berg).
"Careful, careful": Isherwood, *Christopher and His Kind*, chapter 15.
"homosexual chauvinist": Edmund Wilson, *Letters on Literature and Politics 1912–1972* (1977), p. 430 (both quotations).

268   "I've come to the conclusion": Ansen, *The Table Talk of W. H. Auden*, pp. 80, 95.
"I tried writing": Letter to James Stern, 22 October 1954 (Berg).
"A Playboy of the Western World": *Partisan Review*, April 1950, pp. 390–94.
"On and on": *CP* 272 (the title "Serenade" is in earlier editions).

269   "bitter about his age": Kallman, "Portraits and Parables," *Commonweal*, 4 January 1946, pp. 8–9; "The Opera Season," 8 February 1946, p. 431. The private meanings of Kallman's reviews were first noted by Richard Davenport-Hines.
The Rake's Progress: Libretti 47.
"is an imitation": *DH* 470.
"composite personality": Letter to Robert Craft, 10 February 1959 (Sacher Foundation); *Libretti* 575.
"Though the scheme": *Libretti* 574.

271   "repetition palls him": *Libretti* 85.

272   "A work": *Libretti* 93.
"is a manic-depressive": *Libretti* 617.
"It is I": *Libretti* 66.
"represents her genius": *Libretti* 622.
"self-indulgent intermezzo": *Libretti* 81.

273   "I can tell": *Libretti* 80.
"great delight": Letter to Jaffe, 17 May 1949 (Berg).
"When the whole creation": TS (Berg); revised as "Anthem," *CP* 332.

274   "For the new locus": *CP* 534.
"All that was intricate": *CP* 251.

X: The Murmurs of the Body

277 "the missing entry": *SP* 194; *CP* 596.
"simply, publicly, there": *CP* 272.
"Memorial for the City": *SP* 190; *CP* 591.
"done all it can": Interview with Daniel Halpern, *Antaeus*, Spring 1972, p. 145.

278 "the sin of the high-minded": *SP* 114; *CP* 319.
"We are left alone": *SP* 224; *CP* 634; Auden confirmed in conversation in 1971 that the pun was deliberate.
"Under Sirius": *CP* 545.
"my feet": *SP* 29; *EA* 136; *CP* 117.
"the notion": Dom Gregory Dix, *The Shape of the Liturgy* (1945), p. 45.

279 "The Love Feast": *Nones* (1951); revised in *CP* 613.
"A 'high' doctrine": Dix, *The Shape of the Liturgy*, p. 251.
"I am a member": Letter to Kenneth Lewars, 17 September 1947; quoted in Lewars, "The Quest in Auden's Poems and Plays," p. 19.

281 "dangers": Foreword to Rosalie Moore, *The Grasshopper's Man* (1949), p. 9.

282 "The first thing": Introduction to *The Faber Book of Modern American Verse* (1955), pp. 18–19; reprinted without the footnote in *DH* 366.

283 "as a Bishop": Letter to Ursula Niebuhr, 22 August 1947 (Library of Congress).
"Firbank's extraordinary achievement": "Firbank Revisited," *The New York Times Book Review*, 20 November 1949, p. 5.
"Public Statues": *DH* 7.

284 "Oh, Heaven": Slightly misquoted from Firbank, *The Flower Beneath the Foot* (1923), chapter 2.
"*I* think": Letter to Theodore Spencer, [late 1946 or early 1947] (Harvard University Archives).
"Notes on the Comic": *Thought*, Spring 1952; revised in *DH* 372–85, with the final section transferred to the essay "The Prince's Dog."
"making some": "How Can I Tell What I Think Till I See What I Say?" in *New Movements in the Study and Teaching of English*, ed. Nicholas Bagnall (1973), pp. 208–9.
"I keep wishing": Letter to Mayer, 9 May 1945 (Berg).

285 "we asked them": Unpublished interview with Timothy Foote for a projected *Time* cover story on Auden, 1963.
"Washington is going": Letter to Mayer, 4 June 1945 (Berg).
"a *very* high-brow": Letter to Kallman, 24 July 1945.

286 "the body half undressed": *CP* 205.
"The Guilty Vicarage": *DH* 146.
"the bloody corpse": *CP* 577.
"this mutilated flesh": *SP* 225; *CP* 635.

287 "A Walk After Dark": *SP* 188; *CP* 345.

"The small group": Gerald Heard, *Social Substance of Religion* (1931), pp. 213–14.

"the smaller group": *EA* 105.

288 "Poetry and Freedom": *American Letters*, June 1949, pp. 3–12; lecture delivered at the University of Virginia, 27 February 1948.

289 "Italian sunshine": *CP* 539.

"a psychological document": *FAA* 135.

290 "I hadn't realized": Letter to Mayer, 8 May 1948 (Berg).

"Prime": *SP* 216; *CP* 627.

"It is true": "Transcript of a speech by W. H. Auden . . . at Swarthmore College on 9 March 1950" (mimeographed typescript); emended with reference to a recording of the lecture (Swarthmore College Library).

"Not in Baedeker": *CP* 551.

291 "first image of Italy": "Our Italy," *The Griffin*, [April] 1952, p. 1.

"Nature never intended": *DH* 317.

"the growth": *Prose I* 242.

292 "In Praise of Limestone": *SP* 184; revised in *CP* 540.

293 "politics, art": Letter to Mayer, 8 May 1948 (Berg).

294 "It is a major work": Letter to Mayer, [?1946] (Berg).

"an evil book": Letter to Geoffrey Gorer, 17 September 1962 (Sussex University Library).

296 "we too": *SP* 231; *CP* 641.

297 "The Willow-Wren and the Stare": *CP* 574.

298 "the heroic humility": "Mozart and the Middlebrow," *Harper's Bazaar*, March 1946, p. 252.

"Deciding": Letter to Kallman, 13 December 1948 (Berg).

"The Platonic Blow": TS (Lincoln Kirstein Estate); the unauthorized printed versions that appeared some years later are inaccurate.

299 "Since / Nothing": This is the text in *Nones*; revised in *CP* 545.

"Deftly, Admiral": *SP* 187; *CP* 573.

"A Walk After Dark": *SP* 188; *CP* 345.

300 "Pleasure Island": *CP* 343.

"Ischia": *CP* 453.

"Without a cement": *SP* 229; *CP* 639.

"The nature": *DH* 359.

"is humanized": DH 363.

"It has been my experience": MS notebook with a draft of a lecture on T. S. Eliot delivered in Vienna, probably in September 1968 (Berg).

301 "A Household": *CP* 618.

"Port and Nuts with the Eliots": *The New Yorker*, 23 April 1949, pp. 92–97.

"manifests itself": Cochrane, *Christianity and Classical Culture*, p. 490.

303 "The month was April": *EA* 130.

"He sees himself": David Pryce-Jones, "The Rebel Who Got Away," *Daily Telegraph Magazine*, 9 August 1968, p. 20.

305 "Miserable wicked me": *CP* 533.
"Our present": MS draft of "A Walk After Dark" (Berg).

XI: Waiting for a City

306 "In the war years": Maurice Cranston, "Poet's Retreat," *John o'London's Weekly*, 6 February 1948, p. 50.
307 Introduction to *The Portable Greek Reader*: Titled "The Greeks and Us" in *FAA* 3.
308 "In the summer": "Transcript of a speech by W. H. Auden . . . at Swarthmore College on 9 March 1950" (mimeographed typescript); emended with reference to a recording of the lecture (Swarthmore College Library).
"the less exciting figure": *The Enchafèd Flood* (1950), p. 153.
309 "I have heard": *DH* 140.
"Not to know": "Notes on the Comic," *Thought*, Spring 1952, p. 69 (this section omitted when the essay was reprinted in *DH* 371).
310 "Nature, History and Poetry": *Thought*, September 1950, pp. 412–22 (partly reprinted and revised in "The Virgin & The Dynamo" in *DH*).
"Balaam and the Ass": *DH* 107.
311 two charts: Loose pages from MS notebook (Berg).
Hugo de St. Victor: Rosenstock-Huessy, *Out of Revolution*, p. 548.
312 "Where can I get": Letter to Ursula Niebuhr, 16 July 1947 (Library of Congress).
"a possible scheme": Letter to Ursula Niebuhr, [?August 1947] (Library of Congress).
313 "Horae Canonicae": *SP* 216; *CP* 627.
314 "We live": *The Enchafèd Flood*, p. 153.
315 "One Circumlocution": *CP* 626.
"untroubled by sex": Letter to Jaffe, 17 May 1949 (Berg).
"Imago Dei": *CP* 621.
"indescribably inexcusably awful": *SP* 172; *CP* 443.
" 'The Truest Poetry Is the Most Feigning' ": *CP* 619.
316 "At her parties": "Then and Now: 1935–1950," *Mademoiselle*, February 1950, p. 162.
"the Nothing": *CP* 513.
"thrown into being": *CP* 500.
"being-there-ness": Foreword to Cammaerts, *The Flower of Grass*, p. ix.
317 "In the cyclic": Rosenstock-Huessy, *The Christian Future*, pp. 71–72.
318 "is an attempt": *DH* 71; slightly emended from a copy of the original essay corrected by Auden (private collection).
319 "Analogy is not identity": "The Ironic Hero," *The Third Hour*, 1949, p. 50; *Horizon*, August 1949, p. 94.
"The Emperor's": *CP* 574.
"Cattivo Tempo": *CP* 547.

320 "Christendom": Introduction to *Poets of the English Language*, vol. 1, pp. xxv–
     xxvi.
321 "In 1914": Ibid., vol. 5, pp. xxiv–xxv.
322 "Memorial for the City": *SP* 190; *CP* 591.
     "the fair notion": *CP* xxv.
     "To Augustine": Cochrane, *Christianity and Classical Culture*, p. 437.
324 "too easy acceptance": "Religion and the Intellectuals," *Partisan Review*,
     February 1950, p. 123.
     "the vice of pity": "A Note on Graham Greene," *The Wind and the Rain*,
     Summer 1949, p. 54.
325 "combined two purposes": Rosenstock-Huessy, *Out of Revolution*, p. 521.
329 "Under Sirius": *CP* 545.
330 "one of the noblest examples": "A Handbook for All Good Counter-
     Revolutionaries," *The Nation*, 8 April 1950, pp. 327–28.
     "defeat himself": "Fog in the Mediterranean," *The Christian Scholar*, Decem-
     ber 1954, p. 533.

                            XII: The Great Quell

332 "Horae Canonicae": *SP* 216; *CP* 627.
     "series of secular poems": Letter to Ursula Niebuhr, [?August 1947] (Library
     of Congress).
     "My only defense": Letter to E. R. Dodds, 20 January 1945 (Bodleian).
333 "Crane and pickaxe": *SP* 224; *CP* 635.
     "how squalid": *SP* 221; *CP* 632.
     "cement of blood": *SP* 229; *CP* 639.
334 "Delia": *Libretti* 95.
336 "moral courage": "Philosophy with Courage and Imagination," *Quarterly Re-
     view of Literature*, Vol. 4, no. 1 [1948], pp. 99–102.
337 "Hunting Season": *CP* 548.
     "the end": *SP* 231; *CP* 641.
339 "In regard to this poem": "Transcript of a speech by W. H. Auden . . . at
     Swarthmore College on March 9, 1950" (mimeographed typescript);
     emended with reference to a recording of the lecture (Swarthmore College
     Library).
340 "sooner than": *SP* 225; slightly revised in *CP* 635.
345 "The Private Life": The connection between "Nones" and James's story was
     first noted by Richard Davenport-Hines.
     "One of the most horrible": "Hic et Ille," *Encounter*, April 1956, p. 37; prob-
     ably written when Auden was composing a set of *pensées* around 1950.
349 "James Honeyman": *EA* 223; *CP* 162.
     "Fleet Visit": *CP* 549 (with "millions" revised to "billions").
     "The crowd": Søren Kierkegaard, *The Point of View* (1939), p. 115.

350 "a whole": "Nature, History, and Poetry," p. 413; rewritten and abridged in
 DH 63.
 "Not one single": Kierkegaard, *The Point of View*, pp. 114–15.
351 "The crowd collects": "Hic et Ille," p. 39.
 "When the New Testament": *FAA* 43.
 "To all of us: "Our Italy," p. 3.
354 "The psychological difference": *DH* 410.
 "do not have real faces": *DH* 62.
355 "Nobody would call": "On Writing Poetry Today," *The Listener*, 30 June 1955,
 p. 1154.
358 "Precious Five": *CP* 587.
359 "is a good": "Nature, History and Poetry," p. 420; *DH* 69–70.

XIII: Number or Face

360 "The problem": "Notebooks of Somerset Maugham," *The New York Times
 Book Review*, 27 October 1949, p. 1.
361 "a planetary visitor": *Modern Canterbury Pilgrims*, ed. Pike, p. 42.
 "It's such a pity": *EA* 190.
362 "Out of the air": *SP* 198; *CP* 597.
 "Epitaph for the Unknown Soldier": *CP* 570.
363 "Whenever we use": *SW* 108 (slightly corrected on the basis of the first
 edition).
 "Their Lonely Betters": *CP* 583.
364 "and by like": *DH* 47.
 "Song of the Devil": *CP* 782.
365 "Hunting Season": *CP* 548.
366 "the doctrine": Rudolf Kassner, "Concerning Vanity," *The Criterion*, October
 1930, p. 41.
 "half of what": Foreword to Rosenstock-Huessy, *I Am an Impure Thinker*,
 p. viii.
 "The faceless machine": *CP* 452.
 "shock," "*authority*": Denis de Rougemont, "Rudolf Kassner," in *Rudolf
 Kassner zum achtzigsten Geburtstag* (1953), p. 80.
367 "Among all the books": Ibid., p. 58.
 "The Chimeras": *CP* 614.
 "Numbers and Faces": *CP* 623.
368 "About Christ": Quoted in *The Living Thoughts of Kierkegaard*, ed. Auden
 (1952), p. 180.
 "The God-man": Quoted from Kassner's *Die Geburt Christi* (1951) in *DH*
 459; for the German text, see Kassner's *Sämtliche Werke*, vol. 9 (1990),
 pp. 439–40.
 " 'The Truest Poetry Is the Most Feigning' ": *CP* 619.

369   "Footnotes to Dr. Sheldon": *Nones*; reprinted without the title as the fourth
      and fifth "Shorts" in *CP* 570–71.
      "Ode to Gaea": *The Shield of Achilles*, revised in *CP* 553.
370   "with a dictionary": Letter to Mayer, 8 November 1953 (Berg).
      "The Epigoni": *CP* 605.
      "Secondary Epic": *CP* 598.
371   "We Too Had Known Golden Hours": *CP* 621.
      "What I Believe": Published in 1938, reprinted in E. M. Forster, *Two Cheers
      for Democracy* (1951); see *Early Auden*, pp. 329–30.
      "T. S. Eliot": E. M. Forster, *Abinger Harvest* (1936).
      "we may only do this": *DH* 62–63.
      "Nocturne": *CP* 586.
372   "The Moon Like X": *The Third Hour*, 1954, p. 4; another title was "A Face
      in the Moon," *Botteghe Oscure*, no. 8, 1951, p. 222.
      "The Virgin & The Dynamo": *DH* 61; this essay is apparently based on *pensées*
      written in the early 1950s, some of them used in "Nature, History and
      Poetry."
373   "The Christian conception": "The Philosophy of a Lunatic," *The Observer*,
      10 June 1951, p. 7.
      "A well-kempt forest": *SP* 206; *CP* 559.
      "every gorgeous number": *SP* 133; *CP* 408.
374   "that Miss Number": *CP* 614.
      "There was a young poet": Published posthumously in *As I Walked Out One
      Evening*.
      " 'posthumous' poems": Letter to Isherwood, 29 August 1965.
      "Minnelied": *CP* 747.
375   "Glad": *CP* 746.
      "theft": *Prose I* 12.
      "my dove": *SP* 19; *EA* 56; *CP* 57.
      "you, my swan": *EA* 163; *CP* 139.
      "The Shield of Achilles": *SP* 198; *CP* 596.
377   "we tend to deprive": *DH* 62.
      "Bucolics": *SP* 202; *CP* 556.
378   "In Transit": *CP* 539.
379   "the preservation": Foreword to Daniel G. Hoffman, *An Armada of Thirty
      Whales* (1954), [unpaged].
380   "Aloneness": *CP* 238.
      "The Managers": *CP* 603.
381   "baser frankness": *CP* 586.
382   "essentially a spoken": *SW* 114 (slightly corrected on the basis of the first
      edition).
      "for the *anamnesis* of Me": Luke 22:19; Dix, *The Shape of the Liturgy*, pp. 215,
      238, 393, etc.
383   "the Great Society": Rosenstock-Huessy, *The Christian Future*, p. 5.
385   "one of my holy places": Letter to John B. Auden, 9 September 1953.

385 "In each quatrain": Liner notes to *W. H. Auden Reading*, Caedmon TC-1019 (1954).
386 "Innocent Place": "England: Six Unexpected Days," *Vogue*, May 1954, p. 62.
"Ode to Gaea": *The Shield of Achilles*; revised in *CP* 553.
387 "A Permanent Way": *CP* 585.
388 "Guard, Civility": *CP* 572.

XIV: The Altering Storm

389 "muse of the unique": *SP* 234; *CP* 612.
390 "fits": Letter to Spender, 8 May 1956 (Berg).
"From bad lands": *CP* 572.
"I have never": "Holding the Mirror Up to History," *The New Yorker*, 25 September 1954, p. 116.
"Makers of History": *CP* 600.
"Bathtub Thoughts": *CP* 606; the earlier title was used in the pamphlet *The Old Man's Road* (1956).
"Homage to Clio": *SP* 232; *CP* 610.
"The Old Man's Road": *CP* 607.
"The Epigoni": *CP* 605.
"The History of Science": *CP* 608.
391 "essential revolutionary discovery": "The History of an Historian," *The Griffin*, November 1955, pp. 4–10.
"Plato would probably": "Reflections upon Reading Werner Jaeger's *Paideia*," *The Griffin*, March 1958, p. 13.
"The Dyer's Hand": *The Listener*, 16 June 1955, pp. 1063–66.
392 "Life, as I experience it": "At the End of the Quest, Victory," *The New York Times Book Review*, 22 January 1956, p. 5.
394 "Fog in the Mediterranean": *The Christian Scholar*, December 1954, pp. 531–34.
396 "is really": Letter to J.R.R. Tolkien, 14 June 1955.
397 "a succession": *DH* 465.
398 "nothing I wrote": Interview with Daniel Halpern, *Antaeus*, Spring 1972, pp. 138–39; an almost identical remark appears in "Interview with W. H. Auden," *Concern*, Winter 1971, p. 13.
"wicked doctrine": *CP* xxvi.
"Metalogue to *The Magic Flute*": *CP* 578.
399 "I wouldn't call myself": Letter to Gorer, 9 July 1955 (University of Sussex Library).
"Merax & Mullin": *CP* 615.
400 "I am an American citizen": Letter to Enid Starkie, 5 August 1955 (St. Anne's College, Oxford); Joanna Richardson, *Enid Starkie* (1973), pp. 196–97. Auden's second letter is dated 23 August 1955.

401 "Entre nous": Letter to Starkie, 10 February 1956 (St. Anne's College, Oxford); Richardson, *Enid Starkie*, p. 198.

"Now the economic headaches": Letter to Spender, 16 February 1956 (Berg).

402 "the undeserving poor": Auden to Mendelson in conversation, 1971.

"is the one": "The Wish Game," *The New Yorker*, 16 March 1957, p. 132.

"theologically": Yanovsky, "W. H. Auden," p. 119.

"I have been discovering": Letter to Spender, 8 May 1956 (Berg).

"my enemies": Letter to Kallman, 25 June 1956 (Robert A. Wilson).

"Making, Knowing and Judging": *DH* 31–60; originally printed as a pamphlet (1956), with the concluding passage about Thomas Hardy.

405 "Never in my life": Letter to Kallman, 25 June 1956 (Berg).

"some unequivocal blessing": Foreword to Hoffman, *An Armada of Thirty Whales.*

"ever to use": Letter to Robert Graves, 6 March 1961.

406 "That winter": Thekla Clark, *Wystan and Chester* (1995), p. 26.

"There Will Be No Peace": *CP* 617.

"I don't know why": Letter to Monroe K. Spears, 11 May 1963 (Berg).

"theme of paranoia": Reading for the BBC Third Programme, 24 December 1962; transcript in the BBC Written Archives Centre.

407 "Reflections in a Forest": *CP* 669.

408 "A poet": Foreword to Ashbery, *Some Trees*, pp. 11–16.

409 "First Things First": *SP* 236; *CP* 583.

412 "Since": *CP* 777.

"Objects": *CP* 624.

"Words": *CP* 624.

"The Song": *CP* 625.

413 "Limbo Culture": *CP* 616.

XV: Poet of the Encirclement

418 "What I dared": *SP* 255; *CP* 690.

"Good-bye to the Mezzogiorno": *SP* 239; *CP* 642.

"Everything has been observed": "Verga's Place," *The Griffin*, July 1953, p. 4.

419 "to be, simply": *CP* 272.

"Yes, it is a German Age": Letter to Norman Holmes Pearson, 23 March 1943 (Yale University Library).

"*Sie sind*": Mann, "A Memoir," p. 101.

"*Christoph ist falsch*": Information from Stephen Spender, 1994.

"English may be": "The Essence of Dante," *The New York Times Book Review*, 29 June 1947, p. 23.

"slightly unpleasant": *CP* 663.

"rose up excited": *SP* 97; *CP* 280.

"on our side": *SP* 182; *CP* 338.

419 "Dame Kind": *CP* 667.
420 "Lakes": *SP* 208; *CP* 562.
421 "The Sabbath": *CP* 672.
     "Et in Arcadia Ego": *CP* 724.
     "Josef Weinheber": *CP* 756.
     "Walks": *CP* 673.
422 "the poet of the encirclement": *FAA* 351.
     "To give some idea": "K," *Mid-Century*, Fall 1960, p. 7; revised in *DH* 164.
423 "alone in a bed": *CP* 577.
     "Fairground": *CP* 804.
     "Each year brings": *CP* 716.
     "What's Become of Wystan?": *The Spectator*, 15 July 1960, pp. 104–5.
424 "Robert Frost": *DH* 337.
     "The Garrison": *CP* 844.
425 "Friday's Child": *SP* 237; *CP* 675.
     "It is not some": Dietrich Bonhoeffer, *Letters and Papers from Prison*, tr.
       Reginald Fuller (1953), p. 166.
426 "The More Loving One": *SP* 237; *CP* 584.
427 "tolerable": Charles Williams, *The Image of the City* (1958), pp. 133–34.
     "I think he": "The Co-Inherence," *National Review*, 31 January 1959,
       p. 496.
     Patripassianism: Robert Craft, *Stravinsky: Chronicle of a Friendship*, rev. ed.
       (1994), p. 182; John Bridgen, "Auden and Christianity: A Memoir," *W. H.
       Auden Society Newsletter*, 3 (April 1989), p. 4.
428 "as objects": Owen Barfield, *Saving the Appearances* (1957), p. 142.
429 "The History of Truth": *CP* 610.
     "the Event": Barfield, *Saving the Appearances*, p. 171.
     "Between those happenings": *CP* 716.
430 "They had no 'within' ": Barfield, *Saving the Appearances*, p. 63.
431 "A moon profaned": *CP* 719.
     "Whitsunday in Kirchstetten": *CP* 743.
     "Dichtung und Wahrheit": *CP* 647.
432 *Elegy for Young Lovers*: *Libretti* 189.
     "fully and accurately": *FAA* 63.
433 "felt / Unwanted": *SP* 45; *EA* 161; *CP* 138.
     "running away": Clark, *Wystan and Chester*, p. 47.
434 "Genesis of a Libretto": *Libretti* 245.
     "a cross": Letter to James Stern, 22 October 1959 (Berg); *Libretti* 663.
435 "a symbol": Letter to Spender, 20 May 1964 (Berg); *Early Auden*, p. 206.
436 "so much 'serious' poetry": "Reply," *Kenyon Review*, Winter 1964, p. 207.
     "Every writer": Klaus Geitel, "Ein Gedicht kann viele Jahre kosten," *Die Welt*,
       Hamburg, 26 November 1964, p. 7.
437 "Oxford should feel": "The Poet as Professor," *The Observer*, 5 February 1961,
       p. 21.
438 "You": *CP* 722.

438 "Corns, heartburn": *CP* 721.
439 "Reflections in a Forest": *CP* 669.

XVI: The Air Changes

440 "Thanksgiving for a Habitat": *SP* 252; *CP* 688.
"For the first time": Letter to Isherwood, 29 August 1965.
"more private": *SP* 256; *CP* 691.
"The Birth of Architecture": *CP* 687.
441 *Hausgedichte*: Letter to Gorer, 13 September 1963 (Sussex University Library).
"What does the poetry": Introduction to Phyllis McGinley, *Times Three* (1960), pp. x–xiv.
444 "responsible for": Robert Phelps, "A Bird of Passage," *Harper's Bazaar*, March 1963, p. 203.
Hammerfest: *CP* 725.
445 "What Ought We to Know?": Auden's original title, from his agent's correspondence (Curtis Brown archives, Columbia University Library); published as "Do You Know Too Much?" in *Esquire*, December 1962, pp. 163, 269–70.
446 "After Reading a Child's Guide to Modern Physics": *SP* 246; *CP* 740.
"Our world": *Hiroshima Plus 20*, prepared by *The New York Times* (1965), p. 183.
"The artist-hero": *Libretti* 247.
"perfection": *DH* 19.
447 "Postscript": *CP* 695.
"He asked you": Interview with Philip Hodson, *Isis*, Oxford, 8 November 1967, p. 14.
448 "I should like": *SP* 258; *CP* 693.
"Daunty, Gouty, Shopkeeper": *EA* 190; *Prose I* 327.
"A Change of Air": *CP* 721.
"like a secret agent": *CP* 102.
449 "of the greatest": "The Greek Self," *The Griffin*, February 1959, p. 5.
"Whatever else": "Reply," *The Kenyon Review*, Winter 1964, pp. 207–8.
450 "from an unpublished": *FAA* 69.
"Don't tell anyone": Letter to Spears, 11 May 1963 (Berg).
"For your private information": Letter to Spears, 23 March 1965 (Berg).
451 "Elsewhere cannot be packed": Draft version and notes in MS notebook (Berg).
452 "though one": *CP* 645.
"there is something": *DH* xi.
453 "For years": Christopher Burstall, "Portrait Gallery," *Sunday Times Magazine*, London, 21 November 1965, p. 24.
"one of the most beautiful": Advertisement for books by William Carlos Williams, *Encounter*, January 1962, p. 125.

454 "what I think": Letter to James Michie, 28 February 1966 (Edinburgh University Library).

455 "a rather diffy subject": Letter to James Stern, [13 July 1964] (Berg).
"a sort of thanksgiving": Robert Phelps, "A Bird of Passage," p. 203.
"At the Party": CP 738.
"Though I believe": Letter to Isherwood, 9 January 1963.

456 "The Black Like Me year": Clark, Wystan and Chester, p. 60.
"In my opinion": ACW 39.
"The Poet and the City": DH 72.

457 "The disingenuousness": FAA 395–96.
"Whitsunday in Kirchstetten": CP 743.

458 "Hammerfest": CP 725.
"The Cave of Making": SP 256; CP 691.
The Bassarids. Libretti 249.

459 "lamb-like": Libretti 199.
" 'sacrificed' ": Letter from Kallman to Hans Werner Henze, 13 January 1960 (Sacher Foundation); Libretti xxvii.
"Night and again": Libretti 306–9.

XVII: This Time Final

463 "unwilling celibates": SP 274; CP 711.
"Since": CP 777.
Introduction to The Protestant Mystics: FAA 49.

466 Introduction to Shakespeare's sonnets: FAA 88.
"It is not often": FAA 109.
"On principle": FAA 244.

467 "As a rule": FAA 262.

468 "Ascension Day, 1964": CP 742.

469 "We should do well": Preface to The Tree and the Master, ed. Sister Mary Immaculate (1965), pp. xv–xvi.

470 "To me the act": MS notebook, October 1964 (Berg).

471 "As It Seemed to Us": FAA 492.
"an immense piece": Letter to Mayer, 13 January 1965 (Berg).
"The piece": Letter to Kirstein, 2 December 1964.
"I found myself": Letter to Kirstein, 11 December 1964.
"Profile": CP 774.

473 "Amor Loci": CP 779.
"the Rookhope poem": Pocket diary, 1965 (Berg).

475 "In the following year": CP xxvi–xxvii.

476 "To build": "The Worship of God in a Secular Age," The Preacher's Quarterly, March 1969, p. 2; reprinted from a mimeographed leaflet with the same title distributed by the World Council of Churches, Division of Ecumenical Action, in 1966.

477 "The drowned voices": *SP* 32; *EA* 138; revised in *CP* 118.
"Abandoned": *SP* 72; *EA* 258; revised in *CP* 190.
"he can command": E. M. Forster, "The Enchafèd Flood," in *Two Cheers for Democracy* (1951).

478 "Between you and me": Letter to Laurence Lerner, 15 September 1957.
"These are the stakes": The film (commonly titled "Daisy") was made by Tony Schwartz, who chose the excerpt from Johnson's speech without knowing it was paraphrased from Auden (interview, 1996).
"the most essential verse": Naomi Mitchison, "Young Auden," *Shenandoah*, Winter 1967, p. 15.
"Surely, I am": Letter to Mitchison, 1 April 1967 (Berg).

479 "the only New York intellectual": Quoted in *The Daily Telegraph*, 30 August 1965, p. 6.
"Why writers": *Authors Take Sides on Vietnam*, eds. Cecil Woolf and John Bagguley (1967), pp. 59–60.
"was at first worried": Letter to Peter H. Salus, 10 May 1967 (Berg).

480 "in the name": Auden's acceptance speech, distributed by the National Book Committee as a press release, was widely reprinted, e.g., in *The Washington Post*, 3 December 1967, Sect. B, p. 2, and *The New Republic*, 9 December 1967, pp. 25–27.
"Vietnam is ghastly": Letter to E. R. Dodds, 13 March 1968 (Bodleian).

481 "August 1968": *SP* 291; *CP* 804.
"I thoroughly sympathize": "Happy Birthday, Dorothy Day," *The New York Review of Books*, 14 December 1972, p. 3.
"I can sign": Letter to Margaret Gardiner, 22 December 1972 (Berg).
"A Short Ode to a Philologist": *CP* 753.

482 "Eulogy": *CP* 762.
"Lines for Elizabeth Mayer": *CP* 755.
"River Profile": *SP* 282; *CP* 806.

483 "to the picnic": *SP* 231; *CP* 641.
"Prologue at Sixty": *SP* 284; *CP* 828.

484 "Writing begins": *Prose I* 16.
"The Garrison": *CP* 844.
"the eighth day": Dix, *The Shape of the Liturgy*, p. 336.
"Forty Years On": *CP* 783.

485 "for posthumous publication": Letter to Isherwood, 16 April 1965.
"It is my private belief": Polly Platt, "W. H. Auden," *The American Scholar*, Spring 1967, p. 268.

486 "Partition": *CP* 803.
"Rois Fainéants": *CP* 802.

487 "On the Circuit": *SP* 248; *CP* 729.
"Insignificant Elephants": *CP* 807.
"City Without Walls": TS (Berg); *CP* 748.

488 "Moralities": *CP* 816.
"The Horatians": *CP* 771.

489 "the captives": *The Odes of Horace*, translated by James Michie (1966), p. 159;
Auden said this book rendered superfluous his own tentative idea of translating Horace.
"objective knowledge": *SW* 125–26; other versions of this argument appeared
in his broadcast "Nowness and Permanence," *The Listener*, 17 March 1966,
p. 378, and in his acceptance speech for the National Medal for Literature.
490 "Ode to Terminus": *CP* 809.
"Lords of Limit": *EA* 115; *CP* 63.
491 "He was feeling": James Fenton, "Advice to Poets," *New Statesman*, 20 September 1974, p. 381.
492 Josef Weinheber: *CP* 756.
"Eulogy": *CP* 762.
"Bird-Language": *CP* 780.

XVIII: The Concluding Carnival

493 "not to be confused": *FAA* 471.
"less interesting": *FAA* 140.
494 "Epistle to a Godson": *CP* 832.
"a perfect balance": Letter to Britten, 31 January 1942.
"forms of protocol": Mikhail Bakhtin, *Rabelais and His World*, Helene Iswolsky (1968), p. 5. Auden's copy of the book, with a dated inscription by
the author of the preface, is in a private collection.
495 "Forty Years On": *CP* 783.
"I have no gun": *CP* 688.
"Metaphor": *CP* 719.
"buttons and beards": *SP* 287; *CP* 831.
496 "The mass media": "The Worship of God in a Secular Age," p. 6.
"Alienation from the Collective": *CP* 859.
"The hippies": *FAA* 472.
"Ode to the Medieval Poets": *CP* 863.
"Basically": "W. H. Auden on George Orwell," *The Spectator*, 16 January 1971,
p. 87.
"Carnival in its traditional": *FAA* 473.
497 "In moments of joy": *CP* 854.
"Why must": *CP* 855.
"Circe": *CP* 861.
"my favorite theologian": *FAA* 41.
"Work, Carnival and Prayer": TS (Berg).
"his relations": *FAA* 450.
498 "Sex relation": MS journal (Berg).
"Blessed be": *CP* 856.
499 "A New Year Greeting": *SP* 292; *CP* 837.
"Talking to Dogs": *CP* 867.

499   "Talking to Mice": *CP* 868.
      "Short Ode to the Cuckoo": *CP* 862.
      "Talking to Myself": *CP* 870.
      "A Lullaby": *SP* 299; *CP* 875 (retitled "Lullaby").
      "Stark bewölkt": *CP* 846.
      "The Garrison": *CP* 844.
      "Lines to Dr. Walter Birk": *CP* 769.
      "A Toast": *CP* 771.
      "None of us": *CP* 883.
      "A Curse": *CP* 882.
      "Ode to the Diencephalon": *CP* 878.
      "Thank You, Fog": *CP* 886.
      "No, Plato, No": *CP* 888.
      "Grub First, Then Ethics": *SP* 266; *CP* 704.
500   "A Thanksgiving": *SP* 300; *CP* 891.
      "Address to the Beasts": *CP* 889.
      "Natural Linguistics": *CP* 848.
      "an attempt": Letter to Mayer, 24 June 1969 (Berg).
      "Loneliness": *CP* 866.
      "Since I Know": "A Russian Aesthete," *The New Yorker*, 4 April 1970, p. 133.
      "The fire": *CP* 854.
      "An Encounter": *CP* 864.
501   "The Aliens": *CP* 849.
502   "Have been re-reading": Letter to V. S. Yanovsky, 26 April 1970 (Columbia
      University Library).
      "I find it much easier": Ansen, *The Table Talk of W. H. Auden*, p. 53.
      "Only modern science": "W. H. Auden 'On Chaadayev,' " *The Russian Re-
      view*, October 1983, p. 418; originally written for *The New Yorker*, the editors
      of which, after Auden's death, chose not to publish it.
      "Unpredictable but Providential": *CP* 876.
      "wanted to see": Letter to E. R. Dodds, 14 June 1972 (Bodleian).
504   "Doggerel by a Senior Citizen": *CP* 851.
      "What the poet": *ACW* 425.
505   "A Shock": *CP* 865.
506   "was evidently a sadist": *FAA* 498.
507   "The class": *CP* 801.
509   "Old People's Home": *CP* 860.
      "Nocturne": *CP* 879.
510   "Even if I": *The Times*, 31 May 1972, p. 15.
      "When the Duke died": Penny Symon, "Auden 'Cross' at Laureate Ru-
      mours," *The Times*, 22 June 1972, p. 2.
511   "What is Death?": *CP* 856.
512   "Address to the Beasts": *CP* 889.
      "Posthumous Letter to Gilbert White": *CP* 893.
      "An Odd Ball": "W. H. Auden 'On Chaadayev,' " p. 418.

512 "An Odd Ball in an Odd Country in an Odd Time": *The New York Review of Books*, 1 November 1973, p. 8.

"An Odd Fish": TS (Berg).

"Archaeology": *SP* 302; *CP* 894.

514 "The Entertainment of the Senses": *Libretti* 359.

515 "beginning to feel": Letter to Kirstein, 2 September 1973.

"He still loves life": Reported to Mendelson by Kallman.

516 "Addenda to *Profile*": *CP* 776.

"His thoughts pottered": *CP* 797.

518 "Aubade": *CP* 881.

"an *a priori*": Eugen Rosenstock-Huessy, *Speech and Reality* (1970), p. 24.

"It is the unimportant": *CP* 853.

"All I can do": Letter to J. Chester Johnson, 28 January 1971.

"In my view": Letter to Johnson, 6 July 1971.

519 "On My Mind": *Vogue*, October 1973, p. 189.

Index

Dates of birth and death are provided for Auden's family and acquaintances.

About the House, 440, 442*n*, 443
"Abruptly mounting," 198; quoted, xiv
Ackerley, J. R., 497–98, 509
Adams, Henry, 372
"Addenda to 'Profile,'" 516–17, 519
"Address to the Beasts," 500, 512, 514
"Aesthetic Point of View, The," 392*n*
"After Reading a Child's Guide to Modern Physics," 446
Agape, vision of, 9, 24, 31–33, 44, 91, 114, 248, 450, 463–64, 475, 519
Age of Anxiety, The, 204, 229*n*, 242–70, 264*n*, 273–74, 284, 286–88, 291, 296, 299, 303, 305, 314–16, 366, 401
"Air Port," 378–79, 385
Albaum, Harold (Harold Norse, 1916–), 98, 179, 208–9
"Alfred," 127
"Aliens, The," 501–2
"Alone," 167–70, 361*n*
"Amor Loci," 473–75
"And the age ended," quoted, 10, 23
Andersen, Hans Christian, 183, 265*n*
Anderson, Hedli, 32, 52
Another Time, 12, 42*n*, 55, 82
Ansen, Alan (1922–), 250, 251, 259, 263, 264*n*, 268, 269, 279*n*, 293*n*, 307, 316
"Anthem," 273*n*
"Anthem for St. Cecilia's Day," 137–39, 163, 199, 220, 327, 419
Aphrodite, 87–88, 138, 252, 263, 348, 395, 419
"Archaeology," 512–13
"Are You There?" 167–70, 361*n*
Arendt, Hannah, 260*n*
Arnold, Matthew, 11–12, 21–22, 25
artist-hero, myth of, 1–12, 70–71, 314–15, 434–46
"As I Walked Out One Evening," 8, 297
"As It Seemed to Us," 471
"Ascension Day, 1964," 468–69

Ascent of F6, The, xvii, 9, 41, 141, 178, 221*n*, 247, 267, 327, 435–36
Ashbery, John, 282, 408–10, 431
"At the Grave of Henry James," 161, 163–66, 170
"At the Party," 455
Atlantic, The, 26, 100
"Atlantis," 80–81, 166–67, 177
"Aubade," 518
Auden, Constance Rosalie Bicknell (1869–1941, mother), xvi, 178
Auden, George Augustus (1872–1957, father), xvi, 23*n*, 53, 186, 201, 261, 290
Auden, John Bicknell (1903–91, brother), 46, 48, 221
Auden, Wystan Hugh (1907–73). Chronology: family background, xvi; begins writing poetry (1922), xvi, 211, 266; early career, xvi–xvii; Spain (1937), xvii, 20, 91; China (1938), xviii; visits New York (1938), xviii; emigrates to America (1939), xviii; New York (1939–41), 1, 36–37, 42–43, 89–90, 139–40, 148–49, 167, 177; New Orleans, Taos, California (1939), 46, 62, 72–73; Olivet College (1941), 178–79; Rhode Island (1941), 177–79; University of Michigan (1941–42), 179, 197, 207; Swarthmore College (1942–45), 155*n*, 207–8, 259; Germany (1945), 242–43, 259, 284–86, 325, 378*n*; New York (1945–72), 210, 259, 269, 273, 281–83, 300, 314, 378, 418, 462; Bennington College (1946), 266; Ischia (1947–58), xviii, 277, 289–91, 299, 315, 402, 406, 417; Oxford (1956–60), 401–02, 405, 417, 437; Kirchstetten (1958–73), 417–18, 432–33, 440, 470, 511, 515; Berlin (1964–65), 470–71; Oxford (1972–73), xix, 506, 509–11. Works: listed, ix–x; *see also individual titles and first lines*
"August for the people," quoted, xiii

"August 1968," 481, 486
Augustine, Saint, 62, 101, 125, 137, 174, 190, 214, 303, 322, 356n, 393, 484n, 504, 517
Aurelius, Marcus, 186, 192n
"Autumn 1940," 82, 146–47, 468
Ayer, A. J., 145n

Bach, Johann Sebastian, 180, 274
Bakhtin, Mikhail, 494–95
"Balaam and the Ass," 310
"Ballad of Barnaby, The," 181–82
"Barbed Wire," 325–26
Barfield, Owen, 428–30, 445, 490
Barker, Jack (1915–95), 177–78, 198, 273, 435
Barnes, Bishop Ernest William, xvi, 411
Barth, Karl, 149, 151, 236, 324, 419
Barzun, Jacques, 280
Bassarids, The, 458–61
"Bathtub Thoughts," 390
Baudelaire, Charles, 104–5, 132, 210–11
Beatles, the, 492, 497
Beckett, Samuel, 337, 394
Belloc, Hilaire, 42, 150
Bergson, Henri, 20, 142–43, 171, 183
Berlin, Isaiah, 383–84, 390
Bessie, Alvah, Auden's review of, 39–40, 77
Betjeman, John (1906–84), 243, 290
"Between those happenings," 429–30
"Bird-Language," 492
"Birth of Architecture, The," 440–41
Blake, William, 24, 41, 45, 49n, 54, 62–63, 64–65, 71, 104–5, 107, 167n
Bogan, Louise, 194–96
Bogardus, Edgar, 282
Bonhoeffer, Dietrich, xix, 425–27
Bowra, Maurice, 400
Brecht, Bertolt, 438, 441n, 447
Brenan, Gerald, 358
Britten, Benjamin (1913–76), 10, 32, 59, 93–94, 101, 137, 148, 179, 199
Brodsky, Joseph, 510
Brontë, Charlotte, 180–81
"Brothers, who when the sirens," 142
Browning, Elizabeth Barrett, 442n
Browning, Robert, 256, 423
Buber, Martin, 189n, 365n
"Bucolics," 334, 336, 377–78, 381–87, 454. See also "Islands," "Lakes," "Mountains," "Plains," "Streams," "Winds," "Woods"
Burgess, Guy, 334n
Burns, Robert, xvii, 59n
Byron, George Gordon, Lord, xviii, 13n, 136n, 240

"C. 500 A.D.," 390
"Caliban to the Audience." See "Sea and the Mirror, The"
"Calypso," 52
Campbell, Joseph, 252, 258
Camus, Albert, 330–31, 394

Canetti, Elias, 350n
cantos, untitled poem in, 103, 332, 448
"Canzone," 215–17, 219
Carroll, Lewis, 137, 240, 248n, 384n, 442
"Cattivo Tempo," 319
Cavafy, C. P., 166
"Cave of Making, The," 447–48, 454, 458, 484; quoted, 440
"Cave of Nakedness, The," 220, 454, 458, 463
Cecil, Lord David, 400
Cerf, Bennett, 196, 262n
Certain World, A, 456, 504
Chaadayev, P. Y., 502
"Change of Air, A," 438–39, 448–52
Chesterton, G. K., 110, 457
Chicago Sun, The, 192, 196n
"Chimeras, The," 17, 367
Christianity, 56, 58, 61, 66–70, 110, 123–27, 129–63, 170–74, 180–83, 189–90, 213, 244, 255–59, 273–74, 278–80, 285, 308–9, 324, 368, 373, 381, 394n, 425–31, 459, 464, 484n, 502, 517–19; Anglicanism, Episcopalianism, and Anglo-Catholicism, xvi, xviii, 148, 174, 176, 241, 279–80, 396n, 465–66, 518–19; Catholicism, xix, 142, 144, 174, 484n; Russian Orthodoxy, xix, 518
Christianity and the Social Revolution, Auden's essay in, 67
"Christmas 1940," 161–63, 306
"Circe," 497
City Without Walls, 472, 486n, 508
"City Without Walls," 487–88
Clark, Thekla, 267n, 406, 433, 456
Claudel, Paul, 15, 42n
Clough, Arthur Hugh, 492
Cochrane, Charles Norris, 184–91, 260, 301, 322, 356n, 397n
Coghill, Nevill (1899–1980), 89–90, 400, 482, 486, 492
Coldstream, William (1908–87), 266n
Collected Poetry of W. H. Auden, The, 189n, 196–97, 307, 334, 475n, 508n
Collected Shorter Poems 1927–1957, ix, 315, 335, 378, 475
Collected Shorter Poems 1930–1944, 475n
Collett, Anthony, 293n
Collingwood, R. G., 141–42, 144–45, 184, 190, 224
"Common Life, The," 444, 455
Common Sense (ed. Selden Rodman and Alfred Bingham), 42
Commonweal, The, 213
Communism and Communists, 19, 41–42, 65, 69, 78n, 103, 111–12, 120, 159, 171, 187, 193
"Compline," 296, 313, 335, 337, 341, 345, 346, 355–56, 363; quoted, xiv
"Comrades, who when the sirens," 162
Conant, James Bryant, 263

Connolly, Cyril (1903–74), 39
Crashaw, Richard, 45
"Crisis," 23–28, 31, 40, 45, 47, 86
Criterion, The (ed. Eliot), 366
Crossman, Richard, 20
"Curse, A," 373n, 499
Curtiss, Mina, 165

daemon and daemonic forces, xiii, 9–30, 87,
    91–92, 94–95, 99, 106, 152–53, 221n, 397n,
    406–7, 413
"Dame Kind," 338, 419–20, 432, 482n
Dame Kind, vision of, 49, 463–64, 474, 519
Dante, 26, 31, 33, 45, 50–51, 60, 107, 126–27,
    134, 167, 181, 215, 220, 332, 357, 414n, 448
"Dark Valley, The," 127–29, 133
"Dark Years, The," 146–47, 468
Darwin, Charles, 92, 111, 171, 489
Davis, George, 148
Day, Dorothy (1897–1980), 401–2
Day-Lewis, Cecil (1904–72), 400, 509
de la Mare, Walter, 53n, 91–92
"Dear, though the night is gone," 32
Decision (ed. Klaus Mann), 160, 166
"Deftly, Admiral," 299
"Delia," 334, 352n, 358, 398n
"Diaspora," 57–58, 126n
"Dichtung und Wahrheit," 431–33, 436,
    452
Dickey, William, 282
Dickinson, Emily, 195
Didymus (pseudonym), 213, 450
Dix, Dom Gregory, 278–79, 382, 484
"Do Be Careful" ("Upon this line between
    adventure"), 361n
Dodds, A. E. (d. 1973), 26, 35, 37–38, 43,
    46–47, 52, 57, 73, 77, 97
Dodds, E. R. (1893–1979), 26n, 67, 116, 132,
    140, 145, 185n, 222, 332, 400, 457n, 480,
    497, 502–3
Dodson, Owen, 457n
Dog Beneath the Skin, The, xvii, 31, 112n, 327,
    400
"Doggerel by a Senior Citizen," 482, 504,
    507
Don Quixote (Cervantes), 135, 240, 314, 319,
    328, 339n, 383n, 472
Donne, John, 153, 155
Doone, Rupert, 282
Dostoevsky, Fyodor, 16n, 68, 240, 500
Double Man, The, 100, 124, 134, 145n, 148,
    150, 221
"Down There," 444, 453
Drucker, Peter F., 151
Dryden, John, 7, 94, 137–38
"Duet, The," 178n, 264, 316
Dyer's Hand, The, 11, 368, 404, 452
"Dyer's Hand, The" (broadcasts), 11, 391–
    92, 408; quoted, 355
"Dyer's Hand, The" (review), 11

"Each lover has some theory," 167–70, 361n
"Each year brings new problems," 423
"Edward Lear," 14
Eiseley, Loren, 496–97
Elegy for Young Lovers, 392, 432, 433–36,
    446, 459
Eliot, T. S. (1888–1965), xv, 45, 101, 138, 146,
    150, 158–59, 165, 213, 224, 268n, 286, 301–
    2, 343, 371, 381, 422, 475n
Empson, William, 316, 319, 482, 499, 502
Enchafèd Flood, The, 314–17, 383n, 484
"Encomium Balnei," 453–54
Encounter, 268
"Encounter, An," 500–1
"Entertainment of the Senses, The," 514–15
"Epigoni, The," 370, 390, 431
"Epilogue" ("Certainly our city"), 55, 87
"Epilogue" ("Returning each morning"),
    146–47, 468
Epistle to a Godson, 273n, 508, 518
"Epistle to a Godson," 482, 494, 508
"Epitaph for the Unknown Soldier," 362
"Epitaph on a Tyrant," 23n
"Epithalamion," 70–71
Eros, vision of, 31–34, 44–53, 463–64, 466–
    68, 519
Esders, Christa, 417
"Et in Arcadia Ego," 421
"Eulogy," 482, 492
"Every eye must weep alone," 84n
"Eyes look into the well," 128, 156n

"Fairground," 423
"Fall of Rome, The," 264
Fascism and Nazism, xvii, xix, 36–37, 78, 89,
    91–93, 120, 130, 139–40, 257, 285, 361–62,
    421, 430
Feuerbach, Ludwig, 186
"Few and Simple," 203–4, 244
Fifteen Poets, 13n
Firbank, Ronald, 283–84, 353, 370
"First Things First," 409–12, 420, 428, 463,
    472, 483, 499
Fisher, M.F.K., 443
Fitzgerald, Robert, 84
"Fleet Visit," 349
"Fog in the Mediterranean," 394; quoted,
    330–31
"Footnotes to Dr. Sheldon," 367n, 369
For the Time Being (book), 182
"For the Time Being," 82, 179–99, 202,
    207, 211–14, 218, 221, 243, 246, 255, 315,
    356n, 357, 373, 468
"For us like any other fugitive," 80–82
Forester, C. S., 192n
Forewords and Afterwords, 508
Forster, E. M., 100n, 189n, 371, 477, 506
Fortunatus, Venantius, 329–30, 334–35, 414n
"Forty Years On," 484–85, 495, 510
Fox, Orlan (c. 1939–87), 486

Fremantle, Anne, 463
Freud, Sigmund, xv, 19, 28, 85–88, 92, 131, 158, 391, 489
"Friday's Child," 425–30, 445, 459, 512
"From bad lands," 390
"From scars where kestrels hover," 81
Frost, Robert, 364, 378, 424, 447
"Funeral Blues," 32

Gardiner, Margaret, 267n, 481
Gardner, John, 514
"Garrison, The," 424–25, 484, 499
"Genesis of a Libretto," 434
"Geography of the House, The," 455
George, Stefan, 434
German language, 119, 419, 436
Gilbert, Stuart, 311, 313
"Glad," 375
God, vision of, 463–66, 519
Goethe, J. W. von, 41, 71, 72, 101–2, 104–6, 170, 289–90, 393, 432, 448–49, 454, 485, 493–95, 500, 511–13
"Good-bye to the Mezzogiorno," 336, 418–19
Gorer, Geoffrey, 350n, 399, 443
Graves, Robert, 437–38
Greenberg, Clement, 339n
Greenberg, Noah, 282
Greene, Graham, 324–5, 381
Grierson, John, 179n
Griffin, John Howard, 456
Grimm, Jacob and Wilhelm, 48, 183, 192, 265n
Groddeck, Georg, 28, 82, 152, 419
"Grub First, Then Ethics," 441, 443, 499
"Guard, Civility," 388
"Guilty Vicarage, The," 246, 256–57, 286, 314

Hammarskjöld, Dag, 450n, 454
"Hammerfest," 444–45, 458
Hamsun, Knut, 140
Hardy, Thomas, xvi, 53, 63, 378, 404
Harper's Bazaar, 148, 267
Hart, Lawrence, 281
"He still loves life," 515–16
"Healthy Spot, A," 253
Heard, Gerald (1889–1971), 261, 287–88, 320, 499n
"Hearing of harvests," 31
"Heavy Date," 35, 56, 58–59, 64, 464; quoted, 52
Hegel, G.W.F., 19, 92, 317, 330, 391
Heidegger, Martin, 316–17, 323, 326, 340–41, 419
"Hell is neither here nor there," 80, 83–84
Henze, Hans Werner (1926–   ), 392, 433–34, 458–59, 488
Herbert, George, 169
"Heretics," 141

"Herman Melville," 14, 23; quoted, 274
Heyworth, Peter, 486n
"Hic et Ille," 339n
"Hidden Law, The," 80
history, 19–20, 61, 361–62, 389–99; purposive and determined, 8, 41, 66, 96–97, 169, 190, 195, 208, 287, 306–9, 330
"History of Science, The," 390
"History of Truth, The," 429
Hitler, Adolf, 26–27, 36, 40, 41, 73, 74, 99, 173
Hoffman, Daniel, 282, 379–81, 405
Hoffmann, E.T.A., 167n
Hofmannsthal, Hugo von, 392, 470n
Hölderlin, Friedrich, 34n, 71, 317n, 370
Hollander, John, 282
Homage to Clio, 420, 423–24, 429, 431–32, 442n
"Homage to Clio," 78, 389, 390, 393–99, 414, 441
Homer, 104, 323, 375–76
homosexuality, 181, 220–21, 227n, 254, 265–67, 283, 374, 455–56, 470, 497–98
Hopkins, Gerard Manley, 45, 338
Horace, 454, 488–89, 511
"Horae Canonicae," 221, 279, 308–9, 311–14, 320, 322, 326, 332–59, 377–78, 385, 442–43, 464, 483, 493, 514. See also "Compline," "Laud," "Nones," "Prime," "Sext," "Terce," "Vespers"
Horan, Robert, 281
"Horatians, The," 488–89, 491
"Household, A," 301–5, 307, 450
Housman, A. E., 195, 505
Hugo, Victor, 442
"Hunting Season," 365
Huxley, Aldous, 97
"Hymn to St. Cecilia," 137–39, 163, 199, 220, 327, 419

"I Am Not a Camera," 324n
I Believe, Auden's essay in, 38–39, 49n
"I Shall Be Enchanted" ("Enter with him"), 361n
"Icon and the Portrait, The," 98–99, 133
"In Defence of Gossip," xvii
"In Memoriam L.K.A.," 386n
"In Memory of Ernst Toller," 28–29, 85, 110, 396; quoted, 82
"In Memory of Sigmund Freud," 85–88, 89
"In Memory of W. B. Yeats," 1–13, 16–17, 22, 30, 42, 70, 85, 156n, 422, 482; quoted, 477
"In Praise of Limestone," 290–96, 298, 301, 307, 317–18, 335, 414
"In Schrafft's," 264, 316
"In Sickness and in Health," 153–57
"In Time of War," 7, 54n, 103, 122, 208, 305, 307, 317; quoted, xiii, 156n, 332, 477
"In Transit," 378–79, 385

"In War Time," 198; quoted, xiv
"Insignificant Elephants," 348n, 487
Irenaeus, 497
"Ischia," 299, 300
Isherwood, Christopher (1904–86), xvii,
    xviii, 10, 12, 34, 39, 42–43, 97, 116, 160–
    61, 167, 178, 189n, 201, 229n, 231, 244, 245,
    266, 267, 323, 419, 436, 455–56. See also
    Ascent of F6, The; Dog Beneath the Skin,
    The; On the Frontier
"Islands," 384

"Jacob and the Angel," 91–93, 95, 123
Jaffe, Rhoda (1924–65), 198n, 265–69, 272–
    73, 290, 433
James, Henry, 121, 161, 163–65, 168, 201, 226,
    230–32, 243, 254, 272, 291, 345
"James Honeyman," 349
Jarrell, Randall, 100, 193
Jenkins, Nicholas, 90n
Jesus, 42, 53, 55, 56, 61, 66–69, 146, 186, 207,
    252n, 255, 308, 327n, 354, 368, 382, 469
Jews and Judaism, 35–36, 37n, 52, 57, 149–
    50, 165, 170–71, 173, 191, 222, 244, 251, 254,
    256–59, 265, 398, 457
"Johnny," 32
Johnson, J. Chester, 518–19
Johnson, Lyndon, 478–80
Johnson, Samuel, xv
Johnson, Wendell Stacy (1927–90), 252n,
    385n
Jones, Ernest, 391
Jonson, Ben, 7
"Josef Weinheber," 421, 430, 492
"Journey to Iceland," 436; quoted, xviii
Joyce, James, xv, 172–73, 189n, 252, 258, 311,
    313, 447–48
Julian of Norwich, 277, 320
"Jumbled in the common box," 165–66,
    178; quoted, xx, xxi
Jung, C. G., 63, 75, 92, 94, 95n, 126, 165,
    247–48, 254, 277, 300, 307

Kafka, Franz, 57, 121, 170–71, 422–23
"Kairos and Logos," 48, 161, 168–70, 295n,
    306, 309
Kallman, Chester (1921–75), 31–36, 42–44,
    59, 62, 80, 90, 98, 148, 153, 155, 165, 166,
    175–79, 184, 197–98, 202–4, 207, 209, 215,
    226, 241, 265–66, 269–70, 273, 282, 298–
    99, 334, 341, 357, 378, 392, 398–99, 412,
    432–35, 443, 453, 456, 458–59, 462–63,
    466–70, 477, 486, 488, 499, 500, 514–15;
    Auden's Christmas 1941 letter to, 44, 57,
    175–76, 181, 182–83, 193
Kallman, Edward (Chester's father), 148, 352n
Kassner, Rudolf, 366–68, 370–71, 374n, 413,
    485
Keats, John, 232, 485
Kenyon Review, 448

Ker, W. P., 261, 403n
Keynes, John Maynard, 45
Kierkegaard, Søren, 41, 129–41, 149, 152–54,
    159, 162, 163, 176, 187, 188, 196, 243, 247,
    259, 263, 274, 277, 291–92, 316, 349, 350–
    51, 361, 368
Kinsey, Alfred, 268, 374
Kipling, Rudyard, 15, 42, 85, 223, 422, 424–
    25
Kirstein, Lincoln (1907–96), 165, 281, 352n,
    412n, 481, 486
Knight, G. Wilson, 400–1
Köhler, Wolfgang (1887–1967), 152, 207,
    236n, 253n, 345n, 419

Ladner, Gerard B., 484n
"Lady, weeping at the crossroads," 128–29
"Lakes," 378, 383–84, 386, 420–21
Langland, William, 332
Lao Tsu: Tao Te Ching, 238
Larkin, Philip, 423–24, 452
Laski, Harold, 362n
"Lauds," 311, 334, 357–58
"Law Like Love," 78–80, 167
Lawrence, T. E., 9, 23
Lawrence, D. H., 10–11, 27, 56, 62, 141, 149,
    173, 201
"Lay your sleeping head," 10, 27, 32, 476–
    77; quoted, xiii, 35; subject of, 32, 266,
    397n, 411–12, 463, 483, 499
Layard, John (1891–1975), 95n
League of American Writers, 42, 69n, 77–78
Lear, Edward, 14, 255
"Lecture Notes," 213, 216, 239, 253, 255, 257,
    450, 452
Lenin, Vladimir Ilyich, 9, 20
Leontiev, K. N., 500
"Lesson, The," 216–17
"Let History Be My Judge" ("We made all
    possible preparations"), 361n
"Letter to Lord Byron," 51, 200, 208, 211n,
    307, 361, 448, 463; quoted, 448
"Letter to R.H.S. Crossman, Esq.," 291;
    quoted, 20
Letters from Iceland, 69n, 122, 291
Lichtenberg, G. C., 152
"Like a Vocation," 44–48, 361n
"Limbo Culture," 413–14
"Lines for Elizabeth Mayer," 482
"Lines to Dr. Walter Birk," 482
Loftis, N. J., 457n
London Mercury, 12
"Loneliness," 500
"Look, stranger," 343
"Lost," 474n
"Love Feast, The," 279, 373–74
"Love Letter," 43–44, 57n, 71
Lowell, Robert, 480
Lucretius, 502
Luhan, Mabel Dodge, 62

"Lullaby," 10, 27, 32, 476–77; quoted, xiii, 35; subject of, 32, 266, 397*n*, 411–12, 463, 483, 499
"Lullaby, A," 509
Lynch, William F., S.J., 310

McGinley, Phyllis, 441–42
Maclean, Donald, 334*n*
MacNeice, Louis (1907–63), 42, 484
Mademoiselle, 316
Magic Flute, The, 298, 334, 398–99, 458–59
"Make this night loveable," 203*n*, 423
"Make Up Your Mind" ("Between attention and attention"), 361*n*
"Makers of History," 390, 397
"Making, Knowing and Judging," 53*n*, 364, 402–5, 407, 448; quoted, 261
Mallarmé, Stéphane, 169, 190, 448
Man of La Mancha (rejected lyrics for), 364
"Managers, The," 380
Mandelbaum, Maurice and Gwen, 155*n*
Mann, Elisabeth, 70
Mann, Erika (1905–69), 70
Mann, Golo, 148, 419
Mann, Klaus, 160
"Many Happy Returns," 198–99, 238
"Marginalia," 507
marriage, 27, 46–47, 56, 60, 62, 102, 153–55, 200–2, 240, 241, 272–73, 484, 494, 516
Marvell, Andrew, 395
Marx, Karl, xv, 19, 27, 41–42, 63, 66, 69, 111–13, 131, 152, 158, 186–87, 202, 330, 391, 394*n*
"Matthew Arnold," 11–12, 21–22
Matthiessen, F. O., 165
Mayer, Elizabeth (1884–1970), 101–3, 105, 106, 114, 125–26, 178, 219, 227*n*, 231, 254, 265, 284, 289–90, 292, 294, 320*n*, 448, 493, 509
"Maze, The," 129*n*, 145*n*
Medley, Robert (1905–94), 211*n*, 266, 282, 290
Melville, Herman, 14
"Memorial for the City," 277, 286–87, 320–28, 335, 345, 493
Mendelson, Edward, 508
Mephistopheles. *See* Satan
"Merax & Mullin," 319*n*, 399
Merwin, W. S., 282
"Metalogue to *The Magic FLute*," 398–99
"Metaphor," 487*n*, 495
metre and prosody, 85–86, 100, 102, 215, 243, 263, 298, 338, 340, 385–86, 441, 449, 453–54, 500
Michie, James, 454
Mid-Century Book Society, 280
Milton, John, 7, 340, 502; "Lycidas": 4, 7–8, 13, 264
"Minnelied," 374–75
"Miss Gee," 23

Mitchison, Naomi (1897–   ), 478
"Model, The," 239*n*
Monod, Jacques, 503–4
Montaigne, Michel de, 124
"Moon Landing," 490*n*
"Moon Like X, The," 371–72
Moore, Marianne (1887–1972), 86, 280*n*, 441, 486
Moore, Rosalie, 281
Moraes, Dom, 405*n*
"Moralities," 488
"More Loving One, The," 200, 426
"Mountains," 352, 383, 387
Mozart, Wolfgang Amadeus, 71, 398, 484
"Mundus et Infans," 198–200, 441
Murray, Joan, 281
"Musée des Beaux Arts," 5, 47–48, 208, 343
"Music Ho!" 319
"Music Is International," 264
myth, xv, xix xxii, 59, 98–99, 195–96, 267, 372, 379–80, 408–13, 446, 513
"Mythical Sex, The," 267

Nation, The, 157–58
National Review, 427*n*
"Natural Linguistics," 500
"Nature, History and Poetry," 310–11, 318, 350, 359
New Republic, The, 1, 42*n*, 70, 74, 75, 91, 173, 184
New Statesman, The, 116, 244
"New Year Greeting, A," 499, 505, 507–8
New Year Letter. *See Double Man, The*
"New Year Letter," xiv, 77, 82, 99–129, 133, 134, 138, 158, 170–71, 307, 332, 359, 448, 473; quoted, xiv, 177, 286, 380
New York Pro Musica, 282, 353
New York Times, The, 283, 401–2, 479
New Yorker, The, 194, 263
Newman, Geoffrey, 266*n*
Newton, Caroline (1893–1975), 178, 435
Nicolson, Harold, 400–1
Niebuhr, Reinhold (1892–1971), 149–50, 159, 160, 173–74, 179*n*, 188–89, 200, 236, 260, 261, 425
Niebuhr, Ursula (1907–87), 173–74, 205, 261, 283, 312, 329, 396*n*, 465, 484*n*
Nietzsche, Friedrich, 19, 56
Nijinsky, Vaslav, 74
"1929," quoted, 35
"No, Plato, No," 499, 511, 515
"No Time" ("Clocks cannot tell our time of day"), 82
"Nobody Understands Me" ("Just as his dream foretold"), 361*n*
"Nocturne" ("Appearing unannounced"), 371–72
"Nocturne" ("Do squamous and squiggling"), 509
Nones, 302, 334, 370

"Nones," 278, 334, 337, 340, 342–47, 349, 350*n*, 353, 355, 356
Norse, Harold. *See* Albaum, Harold
"Not as that dream Napoleon," 44–48, 361*n*
"Not in Baedeker," 290–91, 293
"Note on Order, A," 157–58
"Notes on the Comic," 284, 310
"Novelist, The," 10
"Numbers and Faces," 367–68, 374
"Nursery Rhyme," 263

"O Love the interest itself," 9, 55
"O what is that sound," 56
"Objects," 412–13
"Odd Ball, An," 512
"Odd Ball in an Odd Country in an Odd Time, An," 512
"Odd Fish, An," 512
"Ode" (to the George Washington Hotel), 29
"Ode to Gaea," 369–70, 386–87, 398
"Ode to Terminus," 490–91
"Ode to the Diencephalon," 499
"Ode to the Medieval Poets," 496, 499, 508
O'Hara, Frank, 282*n*
"Old Man's Road, The," 391, 402
"Old People's Home," 509
"On Installing an American Kitchen in Lower Austria," 441, 443, 499
"On the Circuit," 203, 440, 487
On the Frontier, xvii, 122
On This Island, 52, 82, 371*n*, 508*n*
"One Circumlocution," 315–19, 342, 412–13
"Open Letter to Knut Hamsun," 140
Orators, The, 9, 207, 247, 304, 322, 431
"Orpheus," 13
Ortega y Gasset, José, 172
Otto, Rudolf, 236
"Our Hunting Fathers," 157
Owen, Wilfred, 192*n*
Oxford, professorship of poetry at, 389–90, 399–405, 424, 437, 451
Oxford Book of Light Verse, The, 26*n*, 134
Oxford English Dictionary, 424, 444*n*, 458–59, 484, 498*n*, 503, 514

Paid on Both Sides, 51, 178, 209, 267, 397
Panofsky, Erwin, 352*n*
Partisan Review, 16, 78*n*, 151, 165, 324
"Partition," 486–87
"Pascal," 11, 72–73
Pascal, Blaise, 11, 62, 64, 72–73
Paul Bunyan, 36, 59, 93–97, 120, 174
Pears, Peter, 101, 148, 199
Pearson, Norman Holmes, 307, 320*n*
Pennine moors, 116, 473
"Permanent Way, A," 387–88
Petzold, Hedwig, 417
"Plains," 384–85, 443

Plato, xvii, 33–34, 101, 328, 391, 441, 499
"Platonic Blow, The," 298, 325
Play of Daniel, The, 282
"Please Make Yourself at Home," 44–48, 361*n*
"Pleasure Island," 300
Poems (1930), 55
"Poet and the City, The," 456–57
"Poetry and Freedom," 28–29, 312, 321
Poets of the English Language, 307, 320–22, 330
Poet's Tongue, The, 307
Poole, Adrian (1934–   ), 433, 463
Pope, Alexander, 100–1, 466
"Port and Nuts with the Eliots," 301–2
Portable Greek Reader, The, 307
Porter, Katherine Anne, 62
"Posthumous Letter to Gilbert White," 512
Pound, Ezra, 104, 150, 262*n*
Powell, Anthony, 116
Praed, Winthrop Mackworth, 29, 369–70
"Precious Five," 358–59
"Prime," 290, 308, 311, 333–34, 338–40, 344, 346, 347, 448
"Profile," 471–72. *See also* "Addenda to 'Profile' "
Prolific and the Devourer, The, 9, 11, 40, 49*n*, 53, 56–57, 62–70, 72, 74, 79, 81*n*, 82–83, 87, 115, 131, 143, 151, 160, 207
"Prologue" ("O Love, the interest itself"), 9, 55
"Prologue" ("O season of repetition"), 134–35, 188*n*; quoted, 78
"Prologue at Sixty," 483–85, 492, 495, 506, 507
"Prophets, The," 44, 49–53, 325, 464
"Prospero to Ariel." *See* "Sea and the Mirror, The"
Protestant Mystics, The, introduction to, 450, 463–66, 475, 519
Proust, Marcel, 173, 485
"Public v. the Late Mr. W. B. Yeats, The," 16–21, 65, 196*n*
Purcell, Henry, 94, 137
"Purely Subjective," 40–41, 253, 310, 348; quoted, 207

"Quest, The," 48, 99, 135–39, 217*n*

Raby, F.J.E., 329, 370*n*
Rake's Progress, The, 269–73, 392, 434
Ransom, Michael. *See Ascent of F6, The*
Readers' Subscription, The (book club), 280
"Reflections in a Forest," 407, 439
"Refugee Blues," 37*n*
"Religion and the Intellectuals" (symposium), 324
revisions, textual, 1, 12, 47, 55, 73–76, 84, 133, 145*n*, 150, 164, 167*n*, 180, 211–14, 273, 305, 317, 335*n*, 341, 458, 476–78, 487–88

Rich, Adrienne, 282
"Riddle, The," 64
Rilke, Rainer Maria, 6, 42, 70, 86, 139, 192, 232, 284n, 366, 419, 483
"Rimbaud," 14, 23, 408, 430, 451
Rimbaud, Arthur, 14, 42, 46, 107, 142, 431
"River Profile," 482–83
Rodman, Selden (1909–   ), 42, 76
"Rois Fainéants," 486–87
Rookhope, 51, 118, 170, 473–74
Rosenstock-Huessy, Eugen, 260–61, 287–88, 309, 311–12, 317, 320, 324n, 325, 338, 365–66, 383, 394n, 485, 499n, 518
Rossini, Gioacchino, 369–70
Rougemont, Denis de, 154, 172, 174, 280, 320, 366
Rousseau, Jean-Jacques, 41, 104

"Sabbath, The," 421, 430
Sacks, Oliver, 486
Saintsbury, George, 449n
Salus, Peter, 467n
Sandburg, Carl, 99, 114, 141
Sartre, Jean-Paul, 316
Satan, Mephistopheles, xxii, 67–68, 103–14, 176–77, 179, 270–72, 364–65, 381, 501
"Schoolchildren," quoted, 8
"Sea and the Mirror, The," xiv, 182, 202–3, 205–6, 246, 253, 273, 278, 296, 298, 305, 307, 314, 315, 321, 327, 337, 355, 361, 369, 370, 386, 393, 412, 427, 435, 448, 485, 507
"Secondary Epic," 370
Secondary Worlds, 485, 489, 492
"September 1, 1939," 73–80, 82, 88, 103, 117, 147, 160, 343, 371, 476–78; quoted, 21
"Serenade," 268, 419
"Sermon by an Armament Manufacturer," 31
"Sext," 335, 338, 346, 355
Shakespeare, William, 11, 33, 60, 162n, 205, 210, 222, 223, 230, 239, 244, 310, 315, 337, 340, 384, 430, 444, 448, 466–68, 470n, 485
Shaw, George Bernard, 20, 171
Sheldon, W. H., 367n
Shield of Achilles, The, 401
"Shield of Achilles, The," 78, 362, 373, 375–77, 420
Shirley, James, 515
"Shock, A," 505–6
"Short Ode to a Philologist," 481–82
"Short Ode to the Cuckoo," 499
"Shut Your Eyes and Open Your Mouth" ("Sentries against inner and outer"), 361n
"Since," 412, 463, 472–73, 483, 499
Sitwell, Edith, 382n
Smith, Sidney, 172
Snell, Bruno, 449
"Some say that Love's a little boy," quoted, 52

"Song, The," 412–13
"Song for St. Cecilia's Day," 137–39, 163, 199, 220, 327, 419
"Song of the Devil," 364–65
"Sonnets from China," 7, 54n, 103, 122, 208, 305, 307, 317; quoted, xiii, 156n, 332, 477
Sorley, Charles Hamilton: "To Germany," 16
"Spain" ("Spain 1937"), 13, 73, 96–97, 162, 190–91, 196, 208, 295, 307, 332, 338, 468, 476, 482
Spanish Civil War, xvii, 20, 27, 36, 91, 113, 125, 176, 208, 227n, 479
Sparrow, John, 400
Spears, Monroe K., 128, 424n, 450
Spencer, Theodore (1902–49), 194, 197, 205, 230, 233n, 243, 246, 263–64, 284, 341
Spender, Stephen (1909–95), 89, 132, 140, 142, 160–61, 164–65, 197–98, 201, 212, 223, 268n, 303, 334n, 401, 402, 412n, 419, 434–35, 449
Spengler, Oswald, 294
Spenser, Edmund, 155
"Spring in Wartime," 134–35, 188n; quoted, 78
"Squares and Oblongs" (1947), xxi, 21, 336n, 448–49
"Stark bewölkt," 499
Starkie, Enid, 399–401
Steig, William, 98
Stein, Gertrude, 171
Stern, James (1904–93), xiv, 62, 97, 140, 178, 200, 207, 268, 285, 300, 434, 436, 486, 496n, 499
Stern, Tania Kurella (1904–95), 97, 178n, 198, 300, 436, 486, 499
Stevens, Albert and Angelyn, 199–200
Stevens, Wallace, 169, 295n
"Stop all the clocks," 32
Strategic Bombing Survey, 285, 479n
Strauss, Richard, 392, 470n
Stravinsky, Igor (1822–1971), 269–70, 334, 434
"Streams," 385–86, 420
"Summer Night, A" ("A Summer Night 1933), 31–32, 49, 208, 221, 248, 278, 321, 464, 468, 475, 477
Swinburne, Algernon, 85
"Symposium" (on "A Change of Air"), 448–52; quoted, 436

"Talking to Dogs," 499, 500
"Talking to Mice," 499, 506n
"Talking to Myself," 499, 504, 508
Tchelitchew, Pavel, 352n
Tennyson, Alfred Lord, 18, 210–11
"Terce," 313, 314, 337, 340, 346, 347–48, 352
Thank You, Fog, 499, 508
"Thank You, Fog," 499
"Thanksgiving, A," 500, 511, 513–14